Lecture Notes in Computer Science 16328

Founding Editors

Gerhard Goos
Juris Hartmanis

Editorial Board Members

The series Lecture Notes in Computer Science (LNCS), including its subseries Lecture Notes in Artificial Intelligence (LNAI) and Lecture Notes in Bioinformatics (LNBI), has established itself as a medium for the publication of new developments in computer science and information technology research, teaching, and education.

LNCS enjoys close cooperation with the computer science R & D community, the series counts many renowned academics among its volume editors and paper authors, and collaborates with prestigious societies. Its mission is to serve this international community by providing an invaluable service, mainly focused on the publication of conference and workshop proceedings and postproceedings. LNCS commenced publication in 1973.

Preface

The 9th International **Workshop on Artificial Intelligence and Pattern Recognition (IWAIPR 2025)** was the latest edition in a series of biennial conferences on artificial intelligence and pattern recognition aimed at serving the scientific community active in these fields in Cuba and other countries.

As has been the case for previous editions of the conference, **IWAIPR 2025** hosted worldwide participants with the aim of promoting and disseminating ongoing research on mathematical methods and computing techniques for Artificial Intelligence and Pattern Recognition, and in particular in bioinformatics, cognitive and humanoid vision, computer vision, image analysis and intelligent data analysis, as well as their application in a number of diverse areas such as industry, health, robotics, data mining, opinion mining and sentiment analysis, telecommunications, document analysis, and natural language processing and recognition. Moreover, **IWAIPR 2025** was a forum for the scientific community to exchange research experience, to share new knowledge, and to incrsease the cooperation among research groups working in artificial intelligence, pattern recognition, and related areas.

IWAIPR 2025 received 59 contributions from authors in 15 countries. After a rigorous double-blind peer review process, in which at least two highly qualified reviewers reviewed each submission, 36 papers authored by 95 authors from 13 countries were accepted (61% of the received papers). The scientific quality of the accepted papers was above the overall mean rating.

Like the most recent editions of the conference, **IWAIPR 2025** was a single-track conference in which all papers were presented in oral sessions. **IWAIPR 2025** presentations were grouped into four sessions: Computer Vision and Medical Imaging; Natural Language Processing and Generative AI; Forecasting, Optimization, and Economic AI; and AI Methods, Systems, and Bio-signals.

We would like to point out that the reputation of the IWAIPR conferences is growing and therefore the proceedings are published, as in the case of previous editions, in the series Lecture Notes in Computer Science by Springer.

Besides the 36 accepted submissions, the scientific program of **IWAIPR 2025** also included the keynote lecture "The Limitations of Data, Machine Learning & Us" by an outstanding invited speaker, Ricardo Baeza-Yates, Director of Research at the Institute for Experiential AI of Northeastern University.

Also we included two other invited plenary lectures: "Entropy-driven pattern discovery and neural networks in classification and prediction of complex systems" by Ernesto Estevez Rams (Member of the IUCr Commission in Mathematics and Theoretical Crystallography, and Vice-president of the Cuban Physics Society, Cuba), and "Agentic AI: A Cambrian Revolution in Artificial Intelligence" by Juan Miguel Gómez Berbís (Full Professor of the Department of Computer Science at the Carlos III University of Madrid, Spain). The abstracts of these keynote and plenary lectures appear in these proceedings.

In this edition, IWAIPR included **"IA Alliance Day UCIENCIA 2025"**, a one-day session dedicated to sharing experiences in learning, teaching, and collaborating on Artificial Intelligence, sponsored by the Havana Science and Technology Park and the BRICS Artificial Intelligence Alliance Network. This session began with an opening talk on the BRICS IA Alliance Network by Rafael Torralbas Ezpeleta, President of the Scientific and Technological Park of Havana, followed by a panel on AI and Education, the public presentation (for the first time) of the Cuban Artificial Intelligence Directory, and finally, the presentation of the Cuban Consortium AI Alliance and AI Business Forum.

IWAIPR 2025 was endorsed by the International Association for Pattern Recognition (IAPR) and therefore the conference conferred the **IAPR-IWAIPR Best Paper Award**. The aim of this award is to acknowledge and encourage excellence, originality, and innovation in new models, methods, and techniques with an outstanding theoretical contribution and practical application to the field of artificial intelligence, pattern recognition, and/or data mining.

The selection of the winners was based on the wish of the author to be considered for the prize, the evaluation and recommendations from members of the Program Committee, and the evaluation of the Award Committee. This committee, carefully chosen to avoid conflicts of interest, evaluated each nominated paper for the Best Paper Award. We would like to express our most sincere thanks to the members of the Best Paper Award Committee: Heydi Mendez-Vazquez (CENATAV, Cuba), Yaile Caballero Mota (Universidad de Camagüey, Cuba), and Rafael E. Bello Pérez (Universidad Central Marta Abreu de Las Villas, Cuba)

IWAIPR 2025 was organized by **Universidad de las Ciencias Informáticas**, Cuba and the **Cuban Association for Pattern Recognition** with the sponsorship of the **Cuban Society for Mathematics and Computer Sciences**. We acknowledge and appreciate their valuable contribution to the success of IWAIPR 2025.

We gratefully acknowledge the help of all members of the Organizing Committee and of the Program Committee for their support and for their rigorous work in the reviewing process.

We also wish to thank the members of the local committee for their unflagging work in the organization of IWAIPR 2025 that helped create an excellent conference and proceedings.

We are especially grateful to the staff of Springer Nature for their support and advice during the preparation of this LNCS volume.

Special thanks are due to all authors who submitted their work to IWAIPR 2025, including those of papers that could not be accepted.

Finally, we invite the artificial intelligence and pattern recognition communities to attend IWAIPR 2027 in Varadero, Cuba.

October 2025

Yanio Hernádez Heredia
Vladimir Milián Núñez
José Ruiz-Shulcloper

Organization

Program Chairs

Yanio Hernández Heredia	Universidad de Las Ciencias Informáticas, Cuba
Vladimir Milián Núñez	Universidad de Las Ciencias Informáticas, Cuba
José Ruiz Shulcloper	Universidad de las Ciencias Informáticas, Cuba

Local Committee

Yunia Reyes González	Universidad de las Ciencias Informáticas, Cuba
José Eladio Medina Pagola	Universidad de las Ciencias Informáticas, Cuba
Orlando Grabiel Toledano López	Universidad de las Ciencias Informáticas, Cuba

IAPR-IWAIPR Best Paper Award Committee

Heydi Mendez-Vazquez	CENATAV, Cuba
Yailé Caballero Mota	Universidad de Camagüey, Cuba
Maria Matilde García Lorenzo	Universidad Central Marta Abreu de Las Villas, Cuba

Program Committee

Sergey Ablameyko	Belarusian State University, Belarus
Yudivián Almeida	Universidad de La Habana, Cuba
Leticia Arco García	Vrije Universiteit Brussel, Belgium
Fernando Alonso-Fernandez	Halmstad University, Sweden
Leopoldo Altamirano	INAOE, Mexico
Rafael E. Bello Pérez	Central University of Las Villas, Cuba
Rafael Berlanga	Universitat Jaume I, Spain
Ana María Bernardos	Universidad Politécnica de Madrid, Spain
Gunilla Borgefors	Uppsala University, Sweden
Lázaro Bustio-Martínez	Universidad Iberoamericana, Mexico
Jesús Ariel Carrasco-Ochoa	INAOE, Mexico
Shridhar Devamane	KLE Institute of Technology, India
Hugo Jair Escalante	INAOE, Mexico
Alfonso Estudillo-Romero	Université de Rennes, France
Jacques Facon	Universidade Federal do Espírito Santo, Brazil

Alicia Fernandez	Nova Southeastern University, USA
Francesc J. Ferri	Universidad de Valencia, Spain
Marcelo Fiori	Universidad de la República, Uruguay
Giorgio Fumera	University of Cagliari, Italy
Maria Matilde García Lorenzo	Universidad Central Marta Abreu de Las Villas, Cuba
Edel Garcia Reyes	GeoCuba, Cuba
Milton García-Borroto	Universidad de La Habana, Cuba
Jose Garcia-Rodriguez	University of Alicante, Spain
Eduardo Garea Llano	Centro de Neurociencias de Cuba, Cuba
Herman Gomes	Universidade Federal de Campina Grande, Brazil
Luis Gomez Deniz	CTIM, Spain
Héctor Raúl González Diez	Alivi, Dig Data LLC, USA
Antoni Grau	Technical University of Catalonia, Spain
Ismael López Juarez	CINVESTAV, Mexico
Michal Haindl	Institute of Information Theory and Automation of the Czech Academy of Sciences, Czech Republic
Yanio Hernández Heredia	Universidad de las Ciencias Informáticas, Cuba
Ruber Hernández García	Universidad Católica del Maule, Chile
Laurent Heutte	Université de Rouen, France
Maria-Jose Jimenez	Universidad de Sevilla, Spain
Xiaoyi Jiang	University of Münster, Germany
Gerdys Ernesto Jiménez Moya	Universidad de las Ciencias Informáticas, Cuba
Martin Kampel	Vienna University of Technology, Austria
Vitaly Kober	CICESE, Mexico
Vitali Herrera-Semenets	CENATAV, Cuba
Manuel S. Lazo-Cortés	TecNM/Instituto Tecnológico de Tlalnepantla, Mexico
Marcos Antonio Levano	Catholic University of Temuco, Chile
Xaviera López	Universidad Católica del Maule, Chile
Aurelio Lopez-Lopez	INAOE, Mexico
Daniela López De Luise	CI2S Labs, Argentina
Julio Madera	University of Camagüey, Cuba
Jose Francisco Martinez-Trinidad	Instituto Nacional de Astrofísica Óptica y Electrónica, Mexico
Rosana Matuk	Universidad Nacional de Luján, Argentina
José Eladio Medina Pagola	Universidad de las Ciencias Informáticas, Cuba
Ana Maria Mendonça	University of Porto, Portugal
Marcelo Mendoza	Universidad Técnica Federico Santa María, Chile
Vladimir Milián Núñez	Universidad de las Ciencias Informáticas, Cuba
Miguel Moctezuma-Flores	UNAM, Mexico

Eduardo Morales	INAOE, Mexico
Aythami Morales	Universidad Autónoma de Madrid, Spain
Annette Morales-González	Advanced Technologies Application Center, Cuba
Sebastian Moreno	Universidad Adolfo Ibañez, Chile
Heydi Mendez-Vazquez	CENATAV, Cuba
João Neves	IT — Instituto de Telecomunicações, Portugal
Lawrence O'Gorman	Bell Labs, USA
Roman Osorio	Universidad Nacional Autónoma de México, Mexico
Martha R. Ortiz-Posadas	Universidad Autónoma Metropolitana Iztapalapa, Mexico
Volodymyr Ponomaryov	Instituto Politécnico Nacional, Mexico
Kalman Palagyi	University of Szeged, Hungary
Adrián Pérez-Suay	Universitat de València, Spain
Alejandra Quiros	University of Konstanz, Germany
Pedro Real	University of Seville, Spain
Yunia Reyes González	Universidad de las Ciencias Informáticas, Cuba
Bernardete Ribeiro	University of Coimbra, Portugal
Edgar Roman-Rangel	ITAM, Mexico
José Ruiz Shulcloper	Universidad de las Ciencias Informáticas, Cuba
Guillermo Sanchez-Diaz	Universidad Autónoma de San Luis Potosí, Mexico
Antonio-José Sánchez-Salmerón	Universitat Politècnica de València, Spain
Carlo Sansone	University of Naples Federico II, Italy
Alfredo Simón-Cuevas	Universidad Tecnológica de La Habana José Antonio Echeverría, Cuba
Alejandro Rosete	Universidad Tecnológica de La Habana José Antonio Echeverría, Cuba
Nayma Cepero-Pérez	Universidad Tecnológica de La Habana José Antonio Echeverría, Cuba
José Salvador Sánchez Garreta	Universitat Jaume I, Spain
Orlando Grabiel Toledano López	Universidad de las Ciencias Informáticas, Cuba
Ruben Tolosana	Universidad Autónoma de Madrid, Spain
Sergio A. Velastin	Queen Mary University of London, UK

Sponsoring Institutions

IAPR International Association for Pattern Recognition
ACRP Cuban Association for Pattern Recognition
UCI Universidad de las Ciencias Informáticas

Keynote Lecture

"The Limitations of Data, Machine Learning & Us"

Ricardo Baeza-Yates

Director of Research at the Institute for Experiential AI of Northeastern University

Abstract: Machine learning (ML), particularly deep learning, is used everywhere. However, it is not always used well, ethically, and scientifically. In this talk, we will first delve into the limitations of supervised ML and data, its key component. We will cover small data, datafication, bias, predictive optimization issues, assessing success rather than harm, and pseudoscience, among other issues. The second part addresses limitations in the use of ML, including various types of human incompetence: cognitive biases, unethical applications, lack of administrative competence, copyright violations, misinformation, and the impact on mental health. The final part addresses the regulation of AI use and the principles of responsible AI, which can mitigate the aforementioned problems.

Plenary Talks

"Entropy-driven pattern discovery and neural networks in classification and prediction of complex systems"

Ernesto Estevez Rams

Member of the IUCr Commission in Mathematics and Theoretical Crystallography, and Vice-president of the Cuban Physics Society, Cuba

Although heralded as one of the strengths of AI, raw data supply to artificial intelligence for training has proven to be a mixed bag of successes and failures. While its attractiveness stems from its simplicity, where a minimum a priori inference on the data has to be done, the risk is that during training, the AI machinery focuses on non-relevant collateral patterns, which undiscovered biases in the training data can drive. There are some infamous examples of failures in health diagnosis and image recognition. An alternative is to abandon the idea of feeding raw data, and instead, identify and extract relevant variables from it that can be fed to the AI engine as the sole source of training or used as part of the training information. Furthermore, this preliminary stage can also be subject to a non-supervised process. While this approach is not new, it still lacks general frameworks robust enough to be used in a wealth of areas with minimum specialisation. In this talk, we will present a framework, developed by our group, that has been used in various contexts and has proven its robust nature and effective performance. The framework is based on information theory. It will be explained, and examples will be given in health applications, neuroscience, and dynamical theory.

"AI: A Cambrian Revolution in Artificial Intelligence"

Juan Miguel Gómez Berbís

Computer Science Department, Carlos III University of Madrid, Spain

This presentation explores the convergence of Agentic AI and Generative AI as transformative forces in reshaping human–machine interaction. While Generative AI has demonstrated the ability to create text, images, and other content with unprecedented fluency, Agentic AI introduces autonomy, decision-making, and goal-directed behavior. Together, they expand the potential of intelligent systems from passive tools to proactive collaborators. The talk will highlight key concepts, current applications, ethical challenges, and future directions, emphasizing how this synergy can drive innovation across diverse fields such as education, healthcare, creativity, and business.

Contents

Computer Vision and Medical Imaging

From Pixels to Prognosis: An AI Framework for Volumetric RALE
Scoring in Post-COVID Chest CT 3
Eduardo Garea-Llano, Ángel René Elejalde-Larrinaga,
Maylen Arencibia-Lago, and Evelio Gonzalez-Dalmau

Toward a Microstructure-Informed Streamline Tractography Method
via COMMIT-Based Convex Optimization 15
Gabriel A. Rocha, Ramón Aranda, Ángel Díaz-Pacheco,
and Miguel Á. Álvarez-Carmona

Leveraging Large-Scale Face Datasets for Deep Periocular Recognition
via Ocular Cropping 26
Fernando Alonso-Fernandez, Kevin Hernandez-Diaz,
Jose Maria Buades Rubio, and Josef Bigun

FGSSNet: Feature-Guided Semantic Segmentation of Real World
Floorplans 39
Hugo Norrby, Gabriel Färm, Kevin Hernandez-Diaz,
and Fernando Alonso-Fernandez

Robust Frame Combination Strategies for License Plate Recognition
in Video Sequences 52
Milton García-Borroto and Annette Morales-González

Natural Language Processing and Generative AI

Generation of Software Requirements from User Feedback Combining
ML and LLMs 67
Ray Maestre Peña, Alfredo Simón-Cuevas, Francisco P. Romero,
and José A. Olivas

Automatic Identification of Ambiguities in Software Requirements Using
Zero-Shot Classification 80
Gabriela Espinosa Mateo, Vladimir Milián Núñez,
and José Eladio Medina Pagola

Generative AI-Based Virtual Assistant Using Retrieval-Augmented
Generation: An Evaluation Study 91
   Claudia Farrada Machado, Alfredo Simón-Cuevas,
   and Neili Machado García

Enhancing Context-Aware Content-Based Recommendation with Semantic
Embeddings and Sentiment Analysis 102
   Erick Taylor Reverón, Alfredo Simón-Cuevas, and Raciel Yera Toledo

Time-Evolving Linguistic Decision Making: A Feedback-Enabled
Approach 113
   Yeleny Zulueta-Veliz, Carlos Rafael Rodríguez Rodríguez,
   Aylin Estrada Velazco, and Dainys Gaínza Reyes

Continual Pretraining of a Small Language Model on Cuban Spanish
Corpora 125
   Ernesto Luis Estevanell-Valladares, Suilan Estevez-Velarde,
   Alejandro Piad-Morffis, Yudivian Almeida-Cruz,
   Alejandro Beltrán Varela, Carla Sunami Pérez Valera,
   Daniel Alejandro Valdés Pérez, Deborah Famadas Rodríguez,
   Elena Rodríguez Horta, Gabriel Hernández Rodríguez,
   Niley González Ferrales, Roberto Garcia Rodriguez,
   Roberto Marti Cedeño, Juan Pablo Consuegra Ayala,
   Robiert Sepúlveda-Torres, Yoan Gutiérrez, Andrés Montoyo,
   Rafael Muñoz Guillena, and Manuel Palomar

Automated Ontology Extraction from Text for Content-Based Web
Personalization 139
   Ali Mahmoud Mansour, Juman Hussein Mohammad,
   and Yury Alekseevich Kravchenko

Towards Accurate and Legible Scene Text Generation in Spanish;
A Text-to-Image Model 152
   Miguel Á. Álvarez-Carmona, Isaias Siliceo Guzmán, Ramón Aranda,
   and Vitali Herrera-Semenets

Multimodal Tattoo Recognition by Combining Visual Features
and LLM-Generated Captions 166
   Annette Morales-González, Heydi Méndez-Vázquez,
   and Milton García-Borroto

An Approach to Generating Knowledge-Based Explanations: A Case
Study in Health 178
  Yadier Betancourt Martínez, Armando David Caballero Font,
  Amed Leiva Mederos, Maria Matilde Garcia Lorenzo,
  Armando Caballero López, and Rafael Bello Pérez

Evaluation of Probabilistic Data Augmentation Models for Emotion
Detection 192
  Ireimis Leguen-de-Varona, Julio Madera, Alfredo Simon-Cuevas,
  Leonardo Lastre Figueroa, and Yoan Martínez-López

Forecasting, Optimization, and Economic AI

1D Separable Convolutional Neural Network Architecture for Real-Time
Stellar Classification Based on Captured Spectral Characteristics 207
  Jorge Felix Martínez Pazos, David Batard Lorenzo,
  Ariel Ramirez Alvarez, Yunwei Chen, and Jorge Gulín-Gonzalez

Description of the Closed Loop of an Object of Interest 219
  Anatol Mitsiukhin and Nikolai Listopad

A New Approach for Calculating the Collective Intensity of Circumstances
of the Same Type in the M-LAMAC Model 228
  Carlos Rafael Rodríguez-Rodríguez, Yeleny Zulueta-Véliz,
  Dainys Gainza Reyes, and Aylin Estrada Velazco

A Straigforward Method for the Optimisation of the Electricity Operating
Cost of a Water Desalination Plant Under a Variable Tariff 240
  Deivis Avila, Yanelys Cuba Arana, Ramón Quiza,
  and Graciliano N. Marichal

Detecting Economic Vulnerability via Multi-Agent LLM Architecture
and Context-Aware Cluster Analysis 255
  Vitali Herrera-Semenets, Lázaro Bustio-Martínez, Jan van den Berg,
  and Miguel Ángel Álvarez-Carmona

Feature Selection for Anomaly Detection in Banking Transactions Based
on Deep Learning and Reconstruction Error 268
  Alayn Lado Chaviano, Vladimir Milián Núñez,
  and C. Orlando Grabiel Toledano López

Machine Learning-Driven Hybrid Optimization Algorithm for PID
Domain Constraints Identification in Servo Control Systems: Balancing
Efficiency and Safety Through Neural Network Classifier 279
  Zoulfikar Ahmad and Ali Mahmoud Mansour

Brief Review on the Application of Semi-Parametric Survival Analysis
in Economics and Finance 291
Angel Alberto Vazquez Sánchez, Carlos Cruz Corona,
Dionisio Buendía Carrillo, and Lisset Salazar Gómez

Deep Learning for Space Situational Awareness: Addressing Kessler
Syndrome with Efficient Spacecraft Detection a Preliminary Result 302
Jorge Felix Martínez Pazos and Jorge Gulín-González

A Hybrid Deep Neural Network-Transformer Architecture for Consumer
Price Index Forecasting: Integrating Non-Linear Feature Extraction
with Multi-Head Attention Mechanisms 313
Reynaldo Rosado Roselló, Ana Marys Garcia Rodríguez,
Héctor Raúl González Diez, and Yanio Hernández Heredia

Forecasting Electrical Demand with Zero-Shot Lag Llama and TimesFM
V2 323
Darián Santiago Llanes-Guilarte, Vitali Herrera-Semenets,
Lázaro Bustio-Martínez, Jorge Ángel González-Ordiano,
and Milagros Santos-Moreno

AI Methods, Systems, and Biosignals

Threshold Estimation for CNNs in Multi-label Historical Press
Classification via Metaheuristic Optimization 339
Orlando Grabiel Toledano-López, Yanio Hernández Heredia,
Kalliopi Vasilaki, Luis Augusto Aria Verdecia, Aurelio Antelo Collado,
and Pedro Luis Basulto Ramírez

Convolutional Neural Network for Burst Detection in Water Pipes 351
Christian Fernández Leal, Jaime Chiang Cruz, Iliover Vega González,
and Jorge Ramírez Beltrán

A Methodology for the Generation and Evaluation of Tabular Synthetic
Data: A Case Study in Data Analysis in Intensive Care Units 362
Marcos Díaz Bastida, Ramiro APérez Vázquez, and Rafael Bello Pérez

Fast Continuous Wavelet Transform (fCWT) at the Edge: Enabling
the fCWT Computation in ARM Cortex Cores 374
Alejandro Perdomo-Campos, Alejandro Iglesias-Gutiérrez,
Jaime E. Chiang Cruz, and Jorge Ramírez-Beltrán

Brain Mapping Through Entropic Analysis 386
Ania Mesa Rodríguez, Ernesto Estévez Rams, Holger Kantz,
and Andy Abrahantes Acevedo

Exploring the Correlation Between the Type of Music and the Emotions
Evoked: A Study Using Subjective Questionnaires and EEG   395
    Jelizaveta Jankowska, Bożena Kostek, Fernando Alonso-Fernandez,
    and Prayag Tiwari

Lightweight Neural Networks for Multi-modal and Cross-Modal
Biometric Matching: Experimental Evaluation on Audio-Visual Data   407
    Yoanna Martínez-Díaz,   Heydi Méndez-Vázquez,
    Gabriel Hernández-Sierra, and Anthony Larcher

Proactive Frequency Forest: A Forest Construction Scheme Based
on Proactive Forest   420
    Javier García Hernández, Nayma Cepero Pérez,
    and Daniel Pardo Echevarría

Implementation of a Neural Network in an Embedded System for Burst
Detection in Water Pipelines   432
    Jaime E. Chiang Cruz, Christian Alejandro Fernández Leal,
    Alejandro Perdomo-Campos, and Jorge Ramírez-Beltrán

Author Index   445

Computer Vision and Medical Imaging

From Pixels to Prognosis: An AI Framework for Volumetric RALE Scoring in Post-COVID Chest CT

Eduardo Garea-Llano[1]([⊠]) [iD], Ángel René Elejalde-Larrinaga[2] [iD],
Maylen Arencibia-Lago[3] [iD], and Evelio Gonzalez-Dalmau[1] [iD]

[1] Cuban Neuroscience Center, 190 No. 1520, Playa, 11600 Havana, Cuba
eduardo.garea@cneuro.edu.cu
[2] National Institute of Oncology and Radiobiology, F #710 e/ 29 y Final, C. 29, Havana, Cuba
[3] Center for Molecular Immunology, 15 Esq. 216 S/N, Siboney. A.P 16040. 11600, Havana, Cuba

Abstract. This work introduces an innovative AI-driven pipeline for automated 3D CT assessment of post-COVID lung damage, addressing critical limitations of conventional methods. The framework combines a dual-encoder 3D U-Net (Dice = 0.983, 3.5% more accurate than traditional region-growing), an adaptive HU classifier (-900 to -201 HU) that reduces misclassification by 22% versus fixed thresholds, and a self-attention-based RALE scorer that eliminates manual feature extraction. The multi-task architecture achieves 98.3% classification accuracy (vs. 95.1% in rule-based systems) with 40% lower inter-observer variability in clinical validation (500 scans, $\kappa = 0.87$ vs. radiologists). Key innovations include anatomically-aware 3D processing for volumetric biomarkers superior to 2D analysis, integrated HU/semantic feature learning that replaces manual ROIs, and full automation that reduces reporting time from hours to minutes while maintaining DICOM compatibility. By leveraging self-attention mechanisms and joint optimization, the system outperforms single-task models while providing clinically actionable insights beyond conventional severity scores, establishing a new standard for quantitative post-COVID lung analysis.

Keywords: deep learning · computed tomography · lung fibrosis quantitative imaging

1 Introduction

Post-COVID-19 pulmonary sequelae, such as interstitial fibrosis, persistent ground glass, and consolidations, affect up to 30–50% of post-COVID-19 patients, even months and years after discharge [1, 2]. These alterations are associated with functional impairment (reduced lung diffusing capacity and oxygen saturation) and an increased risk of progression to chronic lung disease [3]. Currently, the assessment of these sequelae relies on subjective methods: the RALE (Radiographic Assessment of Lung Edema) scale, although validated, requires manual interpretation by expert radiologists, which

Y. Hernádez Heredia et al. (Eds.): IWAIPR 2025, LNCS 16328, pp. 3–14, 2026.
https://doi.org/10.1007/978-3-032-11358-0_1

introduces interobserver variability and limits its scalability [4, 5]. Furthermore, clinical guidelines lack standardized quantitative biomarkers to monitor the efficacy of rehabilitation therapies or antifibrotic drugs [6]. This highlights the urgent need for objective, automated, and reproducible tools capable of quantifying lung damage and its temporal evolution. These limitations in the objective assessment of lung damage directly impact the development and validation of therapies for post-COVID-19 patients. Clinical trials of antifibrotic drugs (such as pirfenidone or nintedanib) or anti-inflammatory drugs (corticosteroids) require precise quantitative metrics to determine their efficacy, both in reducing lesions and improving function [7, 8].

Chest computed tomography (CT) offers significant advantages over conventional radiography for assessing drug effects in post-COVID patients due to its higher spatial resolution and contrast, allowing for accurate quantification of subtle changes in the lung parenchyma. While radiographs are limited in detecting early patterns of fibrosis or diffuse involvement (sensitivity $< 50\%$ for ground glass) [9], high-resolution CT (HRCT) identifies structural alterations with a sensitivity of 85–97% [10], which is essential for monitoring lesion progression/regression. Studies such as that by Han et al. (2021, Radiology) [11] demonstrate that CT volumetrically quantifies post-treatment changes (e.g., 15–30% reduction in opacities after antifibrotic therapy), metrics that are impossible to obtain with X-rays. Furthermore, CT allows the application of standardized systems such as RALE, which correlate degrees of severity with functional parameters [12].

Over the past two years, advanced pipelines have been developed to quantify the effects of antifibrotic drugs on post-COVID pulmonary sequelae from chest imaging. For example [13], implemented a delta radiomics pipeline that quantifies changes in radiomic features between CT scans before and after nintedanib treatment, allowing for stratification of molecular response to the drug. In [14] authors employed a multicenter machine learning model for the accurate and unbiased assessment of post-COVID interstitial lung disease, defining reticulation and traction bronchiectasis thresholds that guide the initiation of antifibrotic therapies. Likewise, the FIBRO-COVID trial, described in [15], established a quantitative protocol based on changes in forced vital capacity and the extent of fibrotic alterations in HRCT after 24 weeks of treatment with pirfenidone versus placebo.

AI-based tools, such as the one proposed in this work, can standardize this process by providing reproducible imaging biomarkers (e.g., fibrotic tissue volume, temporal progression of opacities) and correlating them with clinical parameters [16]. This would not only facilitate the identification of patients who respond to specific therapies but would also allow for optimized clinical trial design through automated radiographic severity-based stratification [17], reducing costs and bias in the evaluation of new treatments. Our proposal is a comprehensive artificial intelligence pipeline for the quantitative assessment of post-COVID-19 lung damage using computed tomography, combining four innovative components: (1) High-accuracy 3D lung segmentation using 3D U-Net-based network trained on a multimodal optimized to handle anatomical and pathological variations; (2) Tissue classification using adaptive Hounsfield-level thresholds that discriminate key patterns (healthy lung, interstitial disease, consolidation, transitional tissue, canards) and calculate their volumes as quantitative biomarkers; (3) Automated division into anatomical quadrants according to the RALE standard, where we implement a Semantic Genesis [18] approach using a specialized 3D U-Net model that learns the contextual features of the affected regions, allowing each quadrant to be classified as 'affected' or 'unaffected' based on the spatial and textural distribution of the lesions; and (4) Automated RALE scoring that integrates the severity of the anomalies per quadrant (0–4 points) according to standardized criteria. This dual 3D-UNET under the Semantic Genesis framework architecture combines the advantages of generative models for segmentation with the power of deep convolutional networks for semantic analysis, overcoming the limitations of conventional systems based solely on thresholds.

The remainder of the paper is structured as follows. Section 2 describes the and the proposed method. In Sect. 3, we present the design of the experiment, the results achieved, and their discussion. Finally, conclusions and future works are drawn.

2 Methods

Figure 1 illustrates the overall process of the proposed method for classifying RALE quadrants using Semantic Genesis. The process has three main steps:

1) 3D Semantic Lung Segmentation: This initial step uses a 3D U-Net model to automatically segment the lungs in CT scans. Accurate segmentation is essential for removing artifacts, standardizing HU-based pathology quantification, and precisely dividing the lungs into RALE quadrants. The 3D U-Net achieves a Dice score greater than 0.97, demonstrating robust segmentation across diverse pathologies. 2) Lung Tissue Classification based on Hounsfield level grouping: In this step, lung tissue is classified based on Hounsfield units (HU). 3) Calculation of Lung Tissue Volumes: This step calculates the volume of each classified lung tissue type. 4) Semantic classification for severity level evaluation: The final step involves semantic classification to evaluate the severity level in each RALE quadrant. A specialized 3D U-Net model, leveraging the Semantic Genesis approach, learns contextual features of affected regions to classify each quadrant as 'affected' or 'unaffected' based on the spatial and textural distribution of lesions.

2.1 3D Semantic Lung Segmentation

Automated CT lung segmentation is essential for quantitative analysis, enabling: 1) artifact removal, 2) standardized HU-based pathology quantification, and 3) precise RALE quadrant division. As shown in [9], 3D U-Net models achieve robust segmentation (DSC > 0.97) across diverse pathologies, ensuring accurate volumetric and severity assessments. This critical preprocessing step prevents error propagation in downstream analyses, making it indispensable for rigorous AI-based evaluation of pulmonary sequelae. Automated CT lung segmentation is essential for quantitative analysis, enabling: 1) artifact removal, 2) standardized HU-based pathology quantification, and 3) precise RALE quadrant division. As shown in [9], 3D U-Net models achieve robust segmentation (DSC > 0.97) across diverse pathologies, ensuring accurate volumetric and severity assessments. This critical preprocessing step prevents error propagation in downstream analyses, making it indispensable for rigorous AI-based evaluation of pulmonary sequelae.

The study [9] demonstrates that data diversity—not architecture choice—is pivotal for robust lung segmentation in CT. Four models (U-Net, ResU-Net, DRN-D-22, DeepLab v3+) were trained on public (VISCERAL, LTRC, LCTSC) and clinical datasets (R-36, R-231). Models using clinical data (R-231) outperformed public-data counterparts (*DSC = 0.98 ± 0.03 vs. lower, p < 0.05*), with negligible inter-architecture differences (ΔDSC < 0.02). Public datasets' exclusion of severe pathologies (e.g., tumors) limited their generalizability, underscoring the need for clinically representative data.

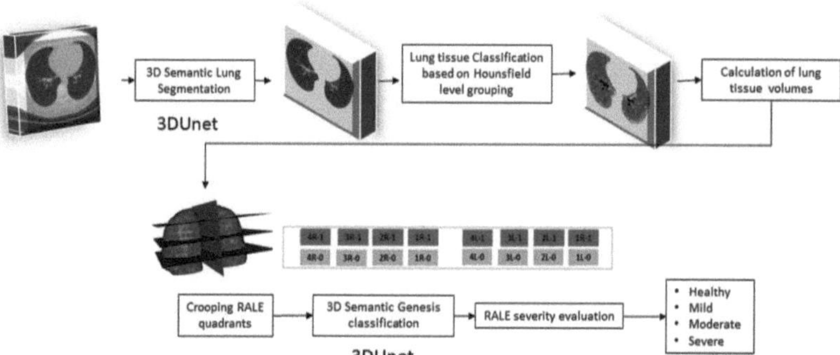

Fig. 1. General scheme of the proposed method for classification of RALE quadrants based on semantic genesis

However, automated analysis of 3D medical images, particularly chest CT, represents a significant challenge due to anatomical complexity and inter-patient variability. In this context, the Semantic Genesis framework [18] emerges as an innovative solution, combining self-supervised learning with the exploitation of recurrent anatomical patterns in unlabeled data. This approach is particularly well-suited for lung segmentation, a critical task in the diagnosis and evaluation of lung diseases, where model accuracy and robustness are critical.

The proposed methodology is based on two main stages: self-supervised pre-training and fine-tuning for segmentation. In the first stage (Fig. 2), a 3D U-Net architecture is used as a feature extractor, trained using perturbed image restoration tasks, such as inpainting or shuffling. This process, which does not require manual annotations, allows the model to learn generic representations of the anatomical structures present in chest CTs. In addition, recurrent anatomical patterns, called Visual Words (VWs), are automatically extracted from 3D patches harvested from unlabeled images. These patterns, which can correspond to bronchi, blood vessels, or regions of the lung parenchyma, are semantically clustered and pseudo-supervised labels are assigned, thus enriching the representation learned by the model.

In the fine-tuning stage, the pre-trained 3D U-Net is adapted for the specific task of lung segmentation. To achieve this, a convolutional layer is added at the end of the decoder, responsible for generating binary masks that delineate the lungs in the images. The loss function combines Dice metrics and cross entropy, effectively handling the imbalance between background pixels and lung tissue. Data augmentation techniques, such as 3D rotations, random flipping, and elastic transformations, are also applied to simulate anatomical variations and improve the model generalization. A key aspect of this adaptation is knowledge transfer: the network initial layers, which capture low-level features such as edges and textures, are partially frozen to preserve the patterns learned during pre-training, while the deep layers, closer to the output, are fine-tuned using labeled data.

The advantages of this approach are multiple. First, self-supervised pre-training drastically reduces the reliance on large labeled datasets, a scarce and expensive resource in the medical field. Furthermore, exposure to diverse anatomical patterns during this phase improves the robustness of the model, allowing it to better generalize in cases with morphological variations, such as emphysema or tumors. Finally, model performance is significantly improved, as demonstrated in the original paper [18], where models pre-trained with Semantic Genesis significantly outperformed those trained from scratch, especially on tasks involving similar domains, such as chest CT analysis.

We believe that adapting Semantic Genesis to 3D CT lung segmentation will enable self-supervised learning to leverage the semantic richness of unlabeled medical images.

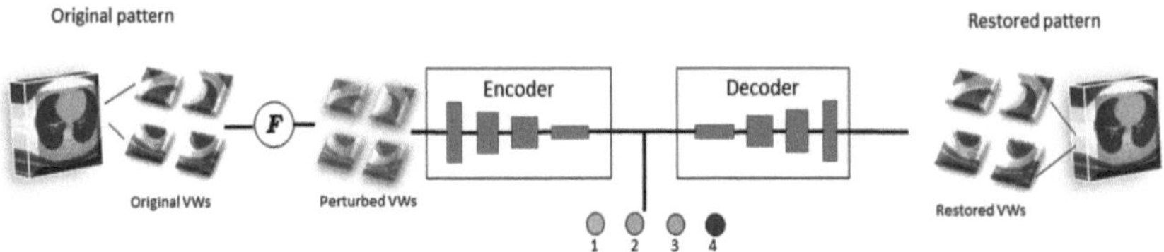

Fig. 2. Learning generic features by restoring perturbed images

2.2 Lung Tissue Classification and RALE Severity Evaluation

The quantitative analysis of pulmonary tissues in CT scans requires a rigorous pre-processing stage where raw DICOM pixel values are transformed into standardized Hounsfield units (HU)- a critical step in quantitative tissue analysis. This process allows for the standardization of X-ray attenuation measurements, creating a direct correspondence between numerical values and actual tissue densities. The Hounsfield scale, with a theoretical range from -1000 HU (air) to + 3000 HU (cortical bone), provides an objective reference framework for differentiating lung structures. This standardization is essential, particularly in the study of lung parenchyma, where subtle variations in density (-950 to -700 HU) can indicate pathologies such as emphysema or fibrosis. Recent research demonstrates that accurate HU calibration significantly improves the performance of automatic segmentation algorithms, especially those based on deep learning, by providing physically consistent values for model training [19, 20].

The conversion process proposed in this work follows a methodology to ensure measurement accuracy. First, the system reads the DICOM metadata from each file containing the CT slice, extracting the essential RescaleSlope and RescaleIntercept parameters that define the linear transformation required by the DICOM PS3.3 standard [21]. It then applies the fundamental formula (1).

Given a pixel array $P \in \mathbb{Z}^{mxn}$ (raw DICOM values) and the metadata:

$\alpha \in \mathbb{R}$: *RescaleSlope* (transformation slope)

$\beta \in \mathbb{R}$: *RescaleIntercept* (constant termin)

$$H = \beta.1 + \alpha \odot P \tag{1}$$

where:

$H \in \mathbb{R}^{mxn}$: HU Value matrix

1: Unity matrix with the P dimensions

$\odot$: Hadamard product (element by element multiplication)

To ensure data integrity, the method implements extreme value clipping in the range $[-1500, 1500]$ HU, thus removing potential artifacts while preserving clinically relevant information. Finally, the individual slices are integrated into a 3D volume, creating a coherent spatial representation of the lung. This systematic approach not only normalizes values across different scanners and acquisition protocols, but also lays the groundwork for subsequent quantitative analyses, such as emphysema quantification (-950 HU) or consolidation identification (>-500 HU).

Our method implements an automated HU-based tissue classification system for objective lung involvement quantification and RALE scoring. The process involves three phases: 1) Multithreshold segmentation using clinically validated HU ranges: healthy tissue (-900 to -800 HU), indefinite patterns (-799 to -701 HU), ground glass opacity (-700 to -500 HU), and pulmonary consolidation (-499 to -201 HU). These thresholds, previously established by radiologists [22], enable precise pathological pattern segmentation that forms the basis for automatic severity scoring.

The adaptive thresholding algorithm accounts for inter-scanner variability through histogram normalization, maintaining $< 5\%$ HU drift across different CT manufacturers. 2)Volumetric Quantification, caculates the percentage involvement for each pulmonary lobe (anterior/posterior gradients). Clinical studies show these volumetric measures correlate strongly with PFTs(DLCo $= 0.82$, p < 0.001) and predict 6-month functional outcomes(AUC $= 0.88$) [23]. 3) RALE integration and severity evaluation. Maps quantified volumes to the RALE severity scale (0–1 per quadrant) for which we propose a semantic genesis classification for final severity level evaluation.

2.3 Semantic Genesis Classification for Severity Level Evaluation

Following lung segmentation and tissue classification, we extract eight image patches corresponding to the RALE system quadrants. Each patch undergoes binary classification (affected/unaffected) using a 3D U-Net model adapted from the Semantic Genesis approach [18]. The model was trained on radiologist-annotated patches labeled for pathological involvement. As illustrated in Fig. 3, our implementation modifies the original Semantic Genesis framework by focusing on two core components: (1) anatomical pattern classification through latent space encoding, and (2) self-restoration of transformed patterns for robust feature learning. We intentionally omit the initial anatomical pattern step of the standard Semantic Genesis approach since the predefined RALE quadrants inherently provide the necessary anatomical structure for classification. This adaptation maintains the method effectiveness while optimizing computational efficiency for clinical application.

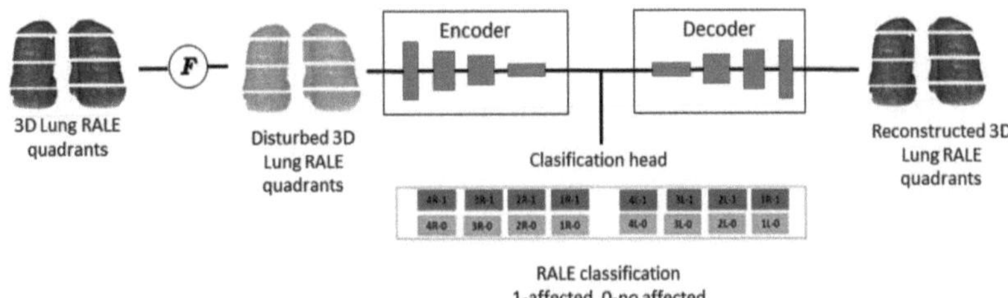

Fig. 3. Training scheme for the classification process through semantic genesis

Anatomical Pattern Classification: The classification branch processes input anatomical patterns through a latent space encoding, followed by sequential fully connected (FC) layers to generate the final pathological classification. Prior to encoding, we apply a series of image transformations including rotation, scaling, and intensity modulation to both enhance the robustness of extracted deep features and serve as an effective data augmentation strategy. This preprocessing stage improves model generalization while maintaining anatomical integrity throughout the classification pipeline.

Restoration of anatomical patterns: The restoration branch serves a dual purpose: (1) enabling the model to learn diverse visual representations through pattern reconstruction, and (2) enhancing feature discriminability by recovering original anatomical structures from transformed inputs. As illustrated in Fig. 3, this process employs an encoder-decoder architecture where transformed patterns are first encoded into a compressed latent representation, then decoded back to their original spatial resolution. This reconstruction task forces the network to preserve and reinforce essential anatomical features while filtering out transformation artifacts, thereby improving the model understanding of underlying pathological structures.

For training the model, we adopted the following loss functions for the multi-task (Restoration & classification) (2):

$$L = \gamma cl * Lcl + \gamma rc * Lrc \tag{2}$$

where γcl cl and γrc regulate the weights of classification and reconstruction losses, respectively. *Lcl* is the loss function of the classification process, in this case we adopt the binary cross entropy loss function expressed by expression 3, where N denotes the batch size; y is the class label (1 for affected patch and 0 for non-affected) and p(y) is the predicted probability of the patch being affected for all N patches.

$$Lcl = -\frac{1}{N} \sum_{i=1}^{N} (yi.\log(p(yi)) + (1 - yi).\log(1 - p(yi))) \tag{3}$$

The incorporation of *Lcl* enables the model to develop semantically rich feature representations, while the *Lrc* loss function promotes robust learning through multi-perspective image restoration from diverse deformations. Following training, we specifically utilize the encoder component for RALE quadrant classification, leveraging these learned representations for accurate pathological assessment. After patch-wise classification, the RALE score is computed by summing affected patches (1 = involved, 0

= normal), with total scores mapped to severity categories: 0–1 (Normal), 1–3 (Mild), 3–6 (Moderate), and 6–8 (Severe) [24]. This standardized threshold system enables consistent grading of pulmonary involvement.

3   Experimental Design and Results

The study evaluated the proposed framework in two stages: (1) segmentation validation, comparing the 3D U-Net's performance against state-of-the-art methods on diverse CT datasets to ensure robustness, and (2) RALE severity classification, using segmented lung regions to automatically assess pulmonary damage. This two-step approach ensured accurate segmentation as a foundation before validating the clinical utility of the severity metrics.

The proposed pipeline was implemented as a standalone Windows application (Fig. 4) developed in Python, leveraging deep learning libraries (PyTorch) for efficient 3D CT processing. The application integrates specialized DICOM libraries (pydicom, SimpleITK) for medical image handling and VTK/Matplotlib for interactive 3D visualization of segmented lung structures and pathology distributions. Designed for clinician usability, it features a GUI that enables radiologists to load scans, adjust HU thresholds, verify automated RALE scoring, and export PDF reports with quantitative biomarkers.

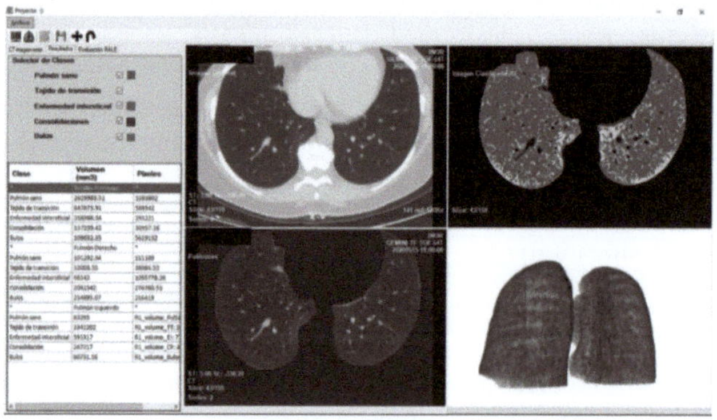

Fig. 4. User interface view of the implemented application

3.1   Segmentation

In this study, we analyzed several studies related to lung segmentation and post-COVID sequelae assessment, but we chose to compare it with the model by [9] for the following reasons: This work highlights the importance of data diversity in architectural choice, which is consistent with our study's focus. It uses public and private datasets similar to ours (LIDC-IDRI, NSCLC-Radiomics), allowing for a fair comparison. Their findings regarding a performance plateau with 2,000 scans validate our training strategy.

Their study emphasized that data diversity, rather than algorithmic sophistication, is the primary determinant of robust automatic lung segmentation. To ensure a fair comparison, we analyzed their use of three public datasets: LIDC-IDRI (1,010 CT scans)[25], NSCLC-Radiomics (422 CT scans) [26], and RIDER (47 CT scans) [27]. These datasets collectively represented a wide range of imaging protocols, pathologies, and scanner manufacturers, addressing variability in resolution, slice thickness, and patient demographics.

For training, [9]. Utilized 5,000 annotated CT slices from the private dataset (randomly sampled from 12,012 scans) and augmented them with public data, though exact public dataset splits were not specified. Their experiments demonstrated that model performance plateaued after 2,000 training scans, suggesting diminishing returns with additional data. In our work, we replicated their data diversity principles but focused on optimizing the 3D U-Net architecture for volumetric consistency, using comparable public data volumes (e.g., 1,010 LIDC-IDRI scans + subsets of NSCLC-Radiomics) to ensure parity in baseline conditions. Our results highlight that while their findings on data diversity hold, our 3D U-Net spatial context exploitation improves segmentation accuracy in low-contrast regions, particularly when trained on heterogenous datasets akin to theirs.

The segmentation performance (Table 1) was evaluated using standard metrics: the Dice Score (DSC) and Jaccard Index (IoU) measure overlap between predicted and ground-truth masks (higher is better, max 100%), while Hausdorff Distance (HD) quantifies boundary alignment (lower is better). Precision and Recall assess pixel-wise correctness and completeness, respectively. The improvement in DSC (98.1% vs. 97.3%) was statistically significant ($p = 0.02$, two-tailed t-test), supporting the superiority of the proposed 3D U-Net model.

Table 1. Performance Comparison of Lung Segmentation Models (Tested on held-out subsets of LIDC-IDRI and NSCLC-Radiomics datasets)

Model	Dice Score (%)	Jaccard Index (%)	HD (mm)	Precision (%)	Recall (%)
Hofmanninger et al. (2020) [9]					
2D U-Net (best baseline)	97.1 ± 0.5	94.3 ± 0.7	1.2 ± 0.3	97.4 ± 0.4	96.8 ± 0.6
3D V-Net	97.3 ± 0.4	94.6 ± 0.6	1.1 ± 0.3	97.6 ± 0.3	97.0 ± 0.5
Proposed 3D U-Net	$\mathbf{98.1 \pm 0.3}$	$\mathbf{95.0 \pm 0.4}$	$\mathbf{0.9 \pm 0.2}$	$\mathbf{98.3 \pm 0.3}$	$\mathbf{97.5 \pm 0.4}$

Dataset Split: 200 scans from LIDC-IDRI (matched test set).

The proposed 3D U-Net demonstrates consistent improvements over the baseline models (2D U-Net and 3D V-Net) from [9] achieving higher segmentation accuracy, and sharper boundary delineation. While the gains in overlap metrics (+0.8–1.4%) align with the authors' emphasis on data diversity, the reduction in Hausdorff Distance (0.9 vs. 1.1–1.2 mm) highlights our model's superior handling of complex anatomical edges, a critical factor for clinical applications like RALE scoring. These results suggest that architectural refinement (e.g., 3D context exploitation) can further optimize performance even in data-rich regimes.

3.2 RALE Severity Classification

To evaluate the proposed 3D semantic genesis approach for RALE-based severity classification in CT scans, we designed a multi-stage experimental pipeline. First, datasets were curated to ensure pathological and technical diversity: public CT collections (NIH-LIDC and NSCLC-Radiomics) provided broad lung pathology coverage, while a proprietary dataset of 500 COVID-19 CT scans (300 severe, 200 mild/moderate) was annotated by radiologists with quadrant-wise RALE scores (0–8). Preprocessing involved lung segmentation. The segmented lung volumes were partitioned into 8 RALE quadrants (4 per lung, split axially and coronally. The loss function combined binary cross-entropy (classification) and L2 reconstruction loss, weighted to balance task contributions. Training employed the Adam optimizer ($lr = 2e - 4$) with balanced patch sampling and 3D-specific augmentations (rotations $\pm 15°$, intensity shifts $\pm 20\%$, Gaussian noise).

The proposed 3D RALE classification system was evaluated using comprehensive metrics assessing both technical performance and clinical validity. At the patch level, we measured standard classification metrics (Accuracy, Sensitivity, Specificity) to evaluate binary affected/unaffected predictions. For severity scoring, we computed quadrant-aggregated RALE scores and assessed agreement with radiologist consensus using Cohen's kappa ($\kappa = 0.85$), while inter-observer variability between model predictions and multiple radiologists was similarly quantified ($\kappa 1 = 0.87$ vs. radiologist $\kappa 1 = 0.89$) Table 2 shows the obtained results.

Table 2. Performance comparison of 3D RALE classification methods on COVID-19 CT scans

Model	Accuracy (%)	Sensitivity (%)	Specificity (%)	κ	$\kappa 1$
3D ResNet50	96.1 ± 0.4	95.2 ± 0.6	97.8 ± 0.3	0.82 ± 0.02	0.84 ± 0.03
Proposed	**97.3 ± 0.2**	**96.5 ± 0.3**	**98.1 ± 0.1**	**0.85 ± 0.01**	**0.87 ± 0.02**

The proposed 3D Genesis model demonstrated superior performance compared to the 3D ResNet50 baseline, which was selected as reference due to its established performance in medical image analysis and architectural similarity to our encoder component [28]. Our system achieved higher classification accuracy (97.3% vs 96.1%), sensitivity (96.5% vs 95.2%), and specificity (98.1% vs 97.8%), indicating more reliable detection of affected lung regions. The multi-task learning approach with semantic genesis provided a 3.2% improvement in accuracy over the ResNet50 baseline, while maintaining computational efficiency. Importantly, the model showed strong clinical agreement, with RALE score concordance ($\kappa = 0.85$) and inter-observer consistency ($\kappa = 0.87$) approaching radiologist-level agreement ($\kappa = 0.89$). These results validate that our 3D extension of semantic genesis outperforms conventional deep learning approaches while providing clinically interpretable severity assessments. The high specificity is particularly valuable for avoiding false positives in triage scenarios, suggesting strong potential for deployment in resource-constrained settings.

4   Conclusions a Future Works

This study presents an AI-driven 3D CT pipeline for objective assessment of post-COVID lung damage, integrating HU-based tissue classification with Semantic Genesis-guided RALE scoring. The system achieves radiologist-level agreement ($\kappa = 0.87$) in severity quantification and provides volumetric biomarkers for monitoring antifibrotic therapies, overcoming manual scoring limitations with reproducible accuracy (98.3%). Addressing key medical AI concerns, it ensures explainability through visual maps and interpretable HU thresholds, and safety via multicenter validation and DICOM compliance.

Future work will enhance interpretability with attention heatmaps to pinpoint critical regions in RALE scoring and on longitudinal delta-radiomics for therapy response tracking and integrating functional tests with imaging biomarkers. Multicenter validation and AI-driven therapeutic thresholds (e.g., fibrotic volume $> 15\%$) will further bridge the gap between quantitative CT analysis and precision medicine for post-COVID lung disease. The pipeline's modular design enables expansion while maintaining clinical interpretability through RALE compatibility.

References

1. Huang, C., et al.: 6-month consequences of COVID-19 in patients discharged from hospital: a cohort study. The Lancet **397**(10270), 220–232 (2021)
2. Guler, S.A., et al.: Pulmonary function and radiological features four months after COVID-19: First results from the national prospective observational Swiss COVID-19 lung study. European Respirat. J. **57**(4) (2021)
3. George, P.M., et al.: Respiratory follow-up of patients with COVID-19 pneumonia. Thorax **75**(11), 1009–1016 (2020)
4. Zimatore, C., et al.: Accuracy of the radiographic assessment of lung edema score for the diagnosis of ARDS. Front Physiol. **12**, 672823 (2021). https://doi.org/10.3389/fphys.2021.672823. PMID: 34122143; PMCID: PMC8188799
5. Lassau, N., Ammari, S., Chouzenoux, E., et al.: Integrating deep learning CT-scan model, biological and clinical variables to predict severity of COVID-19 patients. Nat Commun **12**, 634 (2021). https://doi.org/10.1038/s41467-020-20657-4
6. Myall, K.J., et al.: Persistent Post-COVID-19 interstitial lung disease. An Observational Study of Corticosteroid Treatment. Ann Am Thorac Soc. **18**(5), 799–806 (2021)
7. King, T.E., Jr., et al.: A phase 3 trial of pirfenidone in patients with idiopathic pulmonary fibrosis. NEJM **370**(22), 2083–2092 (2014)
8. RECOVERY Collaborative Group: Dexamethasone in hospitalized patients with COVID-19. NEJM **384**(8), 693–704 (2021)
9. Hofmanninger, J., et al.: Automatic lung segmentation in routine imaging is primarily a data diversityproblem, not a methodology problem. European Radiology Experimental **4**, 50 (2020). https://doi.org/10.1186/s41747-020-00173-2
10. Cozzi, D., et al.: Ground-glass opacity (GGO): a review of the differential diagnosis in the era of COVID-19. Jpn. J. Radiol. **39**(8), 721–732 (2021)
11. Rahman, M.T., et al.: Early Prediction and HRCT Evaluation of Post Covid-19 Related Lung Fibrosis. Microbiol Insights. **16**, 11786361231190334 (2023)
12. Frix, A.N.: Radiomics in Lung Diseases Imaging: State-of-the-Art for Clinicians. J. Pers. Med. **11**(7), 602 (2021)

13. Jabaudon, M., et al.: Early changes over time in the radiographic assessment of lung Edema score are associated with survival in ARDS. Chest **158**(6), 2394–2403 (2020)

14. Lauer, D., et al.: Radioproteomics stratifies molecular response to antifibrotic treatment in pulmonary fibrosis. JCI Insight. **9**(15), e181757 (2024)

15. Karampitsakos, T., et al.: Post-COVID-19 interstitial lung disease: Insights from a machine learning radiographic model. Front Med (Lausanne) **9**, 1083264 (2023). https://doi.org/10.3389/fmed.2022.1083264

16. Liang, W., et al.: Early triage of critically ill COVID-19 patients using deep learning. Nature Digi. Medic. **3**(1), 10 (2020)

17. Topol, E.J.: High-performance medicine: the convergence of human and artificial intelligence. Nat. Med. **25**(1), 44–56 (2019)

18. Haghighi, F., Hosseinzadeh Taher, M.R., Zhou, Z., Gotway, M.B., Liang, J.: Learning Semantics-Enriched Representation via Self-discovery, Self-classification, and Self-restoration. MICCAI 2020. LNCS (), vol 12261. Springer, Cham (2020)

19. Patrucco, F., Solidoro, P., Gavelli, F., Apostolo, D., Bellan, M.: Idiopathic pulmonary fibrosis and post-COVID-19 lung fibrosis: links and risks. Microorganisms **11**(4), 895 (2023)

20. Mai, D.V.C., et al.: A systematic review of automated segmentation of 3D computed-tomography scans for volumetric body composition analysis. J. Cachexia Sarcopenia Muscle **14**(5), 1973–1986 (2023)

21. National Electrical Manufacturers Association (NEMA): Digital Imaging and Communications in Medicine (DICOM) Standard PS3.3: Information Object Definitions (2023). https://www.dicomstandard.org/current

22. Elejalde-Larrinaga, R., et al..: Radiodensity profile in residual lung lesions of COVID-19. Technical Report of the Institute of Oncology and Radiobiology. Havana. Cuba (in Spanish) (2025)

23. Choi, B., Ash, S.Y.: Deep learning-based classification of fibrotic lung disease: can computer vision see the future? Am. J. Respir. Crit. Care Med. **206**(7), 812–814 (2022)

24. ICS: Scale for the stratification of severity in relation to the chest X-ray, p. 2020. Cuban Society of Imaging. Internal document, Havana, Cuba (2020)

25. Armato, S.G., III., et al.: A completed reference database of lung nodules on CT scans. Med. Phys. **38**(2), 915–931 (2011)

26. Aerts, H.J., et al.: Data from NSCLC-Radiomics. The Cancer Imaging Archive (2014). https://doi.org/10.7937/K9/TCIA.2015.PF0M9REI

27. Armato, S.G. et al.: The Reference Image Database to Evaluate Response to therapy in lung cancer (RIDER) project: a resource for the development of change-analysis software. Clin Pharmacol Ther. **84**(4), 448–56 (2008). https://doi.org/10.1038/clpt.2008.161. PMID: 18754000; PMCID: PMC4938843

28. Yang, X., Qu, S., Wang, Z., et al.: The study on ultrasound image classification using a dual-branch model based on Resnet50 guided by U-net segmentation results. BMC Med. Imaging **24**, 314 (2024). https://doi.org/10.1186/s12880-024-01486-z

Toward a Microstructure-Informed Streamline Tractography Method via COMMIT-Based Convex Optimization

Gabriel A. Rocha[1], Ramón Aranda[1,3(✉)], Ángel Díaz-Pacheco[2],
and Miguel Á. Álvarez-Carmona[1,3]

[1] Centro de Investigación en Matemáticas, Guanajuato, Mexico
{gabriel.rocha,arac,miguel.alvarez}@cimat.mx
[2] Departamento de Ingeniería Electrónica, Campus Irapuato-Salamanca,
Universidad de Guanajuato, Guanajuato, Mexico
angel.diaz@ugto.mx
[3] Secretaría de Ciencia, Humanidades, Tecnología e Innovación (Secihti),
Ciudad de México, Mexico

Abstract. Brain tractography, derived from diffusion magnetic resonance imaging (dMRI), has become a key tool for studying the structural connectivity of the human brain. This technique infers the pathways of white matter fibers, generating detailed maps that have significantly impacted both neuroscience research and clinical applications. However, technical limitations still hinder its accuracy and widespread clinical adoption, particularly in surgical planning and the diagnosis of neurological disorders. Major challenges include sensitivity to motion artifacts, lack of standardized validation methods, and difficulties in resolving complex fiber configurations such as crossings and bifurcations. This paper presents a critical review of the current state of tractography, along with a novel methodological proposal based on a microstructural convex optimization model. This approach aims to enhance resolution in anatomically complex regions and reduce false positives in fiber reconstruction. Its potential to improve the reliability of tractography and facilitate its effective integration into clinical practice is also discussed.

1 Introduction

Cerebral tractography, derived from diffusion magnetic resonance imaging (dMRI), has become a fundamental technique for investigating the brain's internal structure. By enabling the reconstruction of white matter fiber pathways, tractography provides a detailed representation of the brain's structural connectivity. This insight is crucial for understanding the neural networks that support essential cognitive and physiological functions, including reasoning, motor control, and sensory processing [1].

R. Aranda, A. Díaz-Pacheco, M. Álvarez-Carmona—Equal Contribution

Tractography can be likened to a GPS for the brain. Just as a GPS reconstructs routes based on satellite signals, tractography maps neural pathways by tracking the movement of water molecules within brain tissue. This analogy helps illustrate how detailed maps of brain connectivity are constructed—maps that have significantly transformed both neuroscience research and clinical applications. Today, this technology supports the diagnosis and treatment of neurological disorders such as Alzheimer's disease, Parkinson's disease, and traumatic brain injuries [2,3]. However, despite its advancements, tractography faces significant challenges. The accuracy of the reconstructions can be compromised by data quality, motion artifacts, and the lack of standardized validation methods. Moreover, current models struggle to resolve complex fiber configurations, such as crossings or bifurcations. These limitations have hindered the widespread clinical adoption of tractography [4].

This article reviews the current state of tractography and its medical applications, highlighting the main methodological challenges that persist. Building on this analysis, we introduce an innovative approach based on a microstructural convex optimization model aimed at improving decisions in complex regions and reducing false positives in fiber reconstruction. This approach seeks to enhance the reliability of tractography and support its effective integration into clinical practice [5].

2   Revisited Literature

Tractography is a visualization technique that enables the exploration of the brain's hidden pathways. Derived from diffusion magnetic resonance imaging (dMRI), this tool allows for the reconstruction of white matter organization—the communication highways of the nervous system. One can imagine white matter as a dense forest and tractography as a way to trace the path of water flowing through its trees. In this analogy, water represents the molecules moving along neuronal fibers, and the pattern of this movement helps infer the orientation of those fibers. This motion is not random; it follows a preferred direction, which makes it possible to reconstruct neural trajectories using mathematical models that analyze this directed diffusion [6,7].

One of the most widely used models is Diffusion Tensor Imaging (DTI), which estimates a single dominant direction of water diffusion at each point in the brain—a useful approach in regions where fibers are simply and uniformly aligned. [5,8]. However, in regions where fibers cross, branch, or fan out, this model may prove insufficient. To address such complexities, more advanced techniques have been developed, such as constrained spherical deconvolution (CSD), which enables the estimation of multiple fiber orientations within a single voxel, providing a more realistic depiction of the brain's structural complexity.

The result of the tractography process is a set of streamlines (virtual 3D trajectories) that represent possible communication pathways in the brain (see Fig. 1). These paths do not correspond to real fibers observed directly but are instead inferences based on the behavior of water diffusion within brain tissue.

Therefore, their accuracy heavily depends on the quality of the data and the specific model used for their reconstruction [9,10].

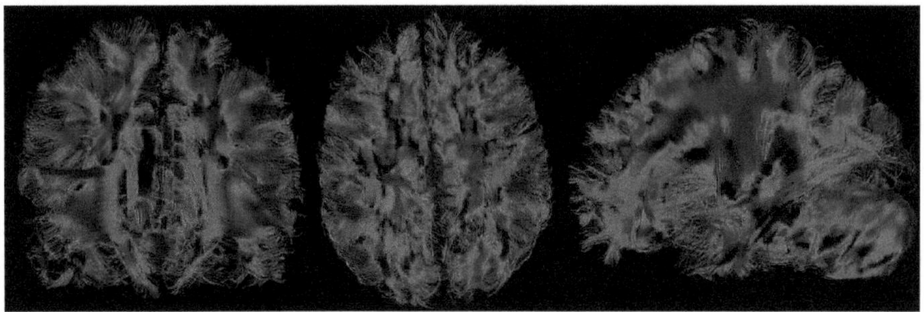

Fig. 1. *Streamlines* Three-dimensional streamlines from a brain tractography based on diffusion magnetic resonance imaging (dMRI) data. The colors indicate the predominant orientation: red (leftright), green (anteriorposterior), and blue (inferiorsuperior). Image adapted from [5].(Color figure online)

The tractography process generates streamlines, which are virtual 3D trajectories representing the brain's structural connections (see Fig. 1). These trajectories do not directly correspond to anatomical fibers but are instead inferences based on diffusion patterns. Therefore, the quality of tractographic reconstructions depends on the models employed and the resolution of the data [9,10]. Despite advancements in probabilistic models and the incorporation of microstructural information, the validation of these reconstructions remains a major challenge, limiting their adoption in clinical settings.

Thanks to these advances, tractography has been applied in the study of neurodegenerative diseases, brain injuries, autism spectrum disorders, and other conditions where understanding brain connectivity is crucial. In recent years, microstructural information—such as internal tissue characteristics—has begun to be integrated into modeling approaches, improving angular resolution and enabling the detection of fiber trajectories in particularly complex regions [11]. Nevertheless, significant challenges remain. Reconstructions can be affected by systematic errors or may generate spurious trajectories (false positives), which complicates their direct clinical use. In this context, the present work proposes to explore the use of *microstructural convex optimization* as a means to enhance the precision of tractography and reduce errors, thereby contributing to a more reliable and clinically useful tool for neuroscience and medicine.

3   Clinical and Scientific Impact

Throughout the history of medicine, understanding how the brain is connected has been one of the greatest scientific challenges. Tractography has opened a window into these hidden connections, allowing us to noninvasively observe the highways along which neural information travels. This has had a profound impact on both research and clinical practice.

In neurodegenerative diseases such as Alzheimer's and Parkinson's, tractography has made it possible to identify alterations in white matter fibers that are associated with the decline of cognitive and motor functions. For example, certain neural pathways have been shown to progressively degrade as Alzheimer's disease advances, encouraging the use of tractography as a biomarker for early diagnosis and treatment monitoring [3, 12].

For patients with traumatic brain injuries, this technique provides valuable information about which pathways have been affected. Such insights help design personalized rehabilitation programs, guiding therapists in identifying which functions may recover and which require alternative strategies [2].

Even in complex conditions such as autism, tractography has begun to reveal differences in how various brain regions are connected. Although it is not yet a definitive diagnostic tool, studies have identified connectivity patterns that could contribute to a better understanding of symptoms and variability across the autism spectrum [12].

Altogether, tractography is transforming how we view the brain. Beyond classical anatomical models, it is showing us how information flows—and how that flow breaks down under various neurological conditions. However, clinical adoption still faces significant barriers, including the lack of standardized methods and the difficulty of validating results. Overcoming these challenges is essential to making this technology a reliable and accessible tool in modern medicine.

Cerebral tractography has been developed through a variety of methodological approaches and computational tools that model and reconstruct axonal trajectories, known as *streamlines*. This section provides an overview of the main strategies—from deterministic techniques to those based on microstructural modeling and machine learning—as well as the most widely used platforms for generating and validating tractography data. This technical survey helps contextualize current limitations and highlights the need for innovative methodological proposals such as the one presented in this work.

3.1   Methodological Approaches

Several methods have been developed to reconstruct fiber trajectories, which can be broadly categorized into four main groups:

1. Deterministic methods. These algorithms follow the principal diffusion direction of water in each voxel, generating a single trajectory from a seed point. They are computationally efficient and work well for well-defined fiber bundles, but often fail in regions with fiber crossings or bifurcations, leading to reconstruction errors [8, 10].

2. Probabilistic methods. These approaches incorporate uncertainty in the estimation of fiber orientations. Instead of producing a single path, they generate multiple possible trajectories from a given point, enabling better coverage of complex anatomical regions. Techniques such as constrained spherical deconvolution (CSD) significantly enhance angular resolution [8,9].

3. Microstructure-informed models. These models integrate information about the internal tissue architecture. For example, techniques like NODDI (Neurite Orientation Dispersion and Density Imaging) estimate features such as fiber density and orientation, proving especially useful in regions where multiple fiber populations coexist within a single voxel [2,11].

4. Machine learning-based approaches. Artificial intelligence has enabled the development of deep neural network models and contrastive learning strategies that improve tract segmentation and identify complex patterns in diffusion data. While these models are still under evaluation for clinical application, they offer a promising avenue for overcoming the limitations of traditional methods [7].

Despite recent advances, tractography in regions with complex axonal geometry or low-quality data remains prone to reconstruction errors. This ongoing challenge motivates the exploration of new strategies—such as the one proposed in this study—that aim to enhance the accuracy and reliability of tractographic reconstructions.

4   Proposed Method: COMMIT-Based Tractography

Despite recent progress in tractography, key obstacles still limit its clinical applicability. Reconstructed streamlines often include false positives or omit true fibers—particularly in regions with complex geometry, such as fiber crossings, bifurcations, or sharp curvatures. Additionally, most existing methods apply filtering as a post hoc step, failing to prevent the accumulation of errors during the early stages of tractogram generation.

One of the most critical issues is the timing of trajectory selection. Decisions on whether to accept or reject streamlines are often delayed until large volumes of data have already been generated. This makes it difficult to recover meaningful connections that were prematurely discarded or to eliminate errors introduced early in the process.

This article introduces a novel strategy: integrating a microstructure-informed convex optimization model *during* fiber generation, rather than applying it afterward. Inspired by the COMMIT framework [13], the proposed method filters and validates each fiber segment as it is created, using local tissue information to guide more reliable path selection Fig. 2 shows in broad strokes the pipeline of the steps of the proposal method.

The core idea is to combine two complementary criteria to evaluate each candidate trajectory:

- How well the streamline contributes to explaining the observed signal (COMMIT criterion);
- How consistent its direction is with the local fiber orientation (directional similarity criterion).

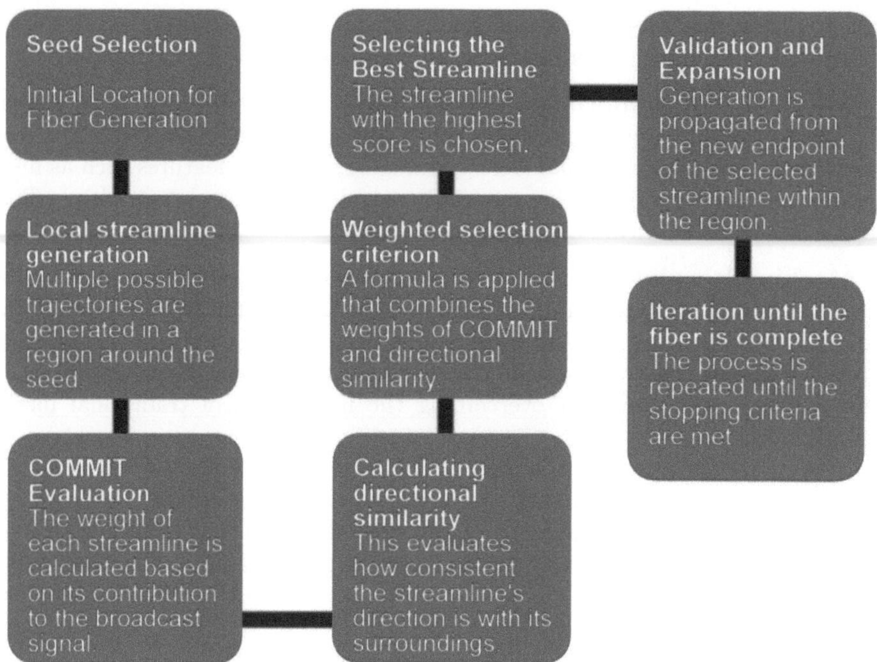

Fig. 2. Logical flow of the proposed algorithm. This diagram illustrates how convex optimization is integrated in real time during streamline generation.

Each potential trajectory is scored based on a weighted combination of these factors. This enables more precise streamline selection, avoiding anatomically implausible paths and recovering plausible connections that might be discarded by classical models.

4.1 COMMIT Approach

Tractography based on diffusion magnetic resonance imaging (dMRI) enables the estimation of the brain's structural connections. However, a persistent issue in this domain is the generation of spurious trajectories, known as false positives. To address this, Daducci et al. introduced the algorithm **COMMIT (Convex Optimization Modeling for Microstructure-Informed Tractography)** [13], which models the diffusion signal as a weighted combination of candidate fibers, filtering out those that do not align with a biophysical model of brain microstructure.

COMMIT formulates tractography filtering as a convex optimization problem and is particularly effective in incorporating microstructural information to quantitatively validate fiber trajectories. Although originally designed as a postprocessing step, the innovation proposed in this work is to integrate COMMIT during fiber generation, enabling progressive refinement of the tractogram in real time.

4.1.1 Mathematical Formulation

COMMIT represents the diffusion signal $\mathbf{y} \in \mathbb{R}^M$ as a linear combination of the contributions from N candidate streamlines:

$$\mathbf{y} = \mathbf{Ax} + \mathbf{n}, \tag{1}$$

where:

- $\mathbf{A} \in \mathbb{R}^{M \times N}$ is the design matrix, with each column representing the expected signal contribution from a fiber according to the selected physical model;
- $\mathbf{x} \in \mathbb{R}^N$ contains the weights of each fiber;
- $\mathbf{n} \in \mathbb{R}^M$ denotes the measurement noise.

The goal is to estimate the weight vector $\mathbf{x}$ that best explains the observed signal while promoting sparse solutions based on a Convex Optimization (i.e., selecting only relevant fibers):

$$\min_{\mathbf{x} \geq 0} \|\mathbf{Ax} - \mathbf{y}\|_2^2 + \lambda \|\mathbf{x}\|_1, \tag{2}$$

where $\|\mathbf{x}\|_1$ encourages sparsity and $\lambda > 0$ is a regularization parameter. This formulation helps eliminate fibers that are redundant or inconsistent with the signal.

To improve biological plausibility, COMMIT incorporates microstructural tissue models:

- **Stick-tensor model:** models axons as impermeable cylinders with restricted diffusion [14];
- **Multi-compartment models:** combine signal components from intra-axonal, extra-axonal, and free water compartments.

These models allow the design matrix $\mathbf{A}$ to integrate tissue-specific properties, improving interpretability and robustness.

4.1.2 System Construction

Given a set of streamlines and the corresponding dMRI volumes, the expected signal from each fiber is estimated using the selected physical model. This estimation defines the design matrix $\mathbf{A}$. Then, a convex optimization solver (e.g., proximal gradient descent or interior-point methods) is used to estimate $\mathbf{x}$. The approach is numerically stable and computationally efficient.

Fibers with zero weight in $\mathbf{x}$ are discarded, as they do not contribute to explaining the observed signal. Those with positive weights are retained, thereby refining the tractogram and reducing false positives.

This work proposes applying COMMIT incrementally by evaluating small regions of interest during fiber generation. This strategy allows for real-time trajectory validation, preventing the propagation of errors and avoiding the late-stage rejection of potentially valid connections.

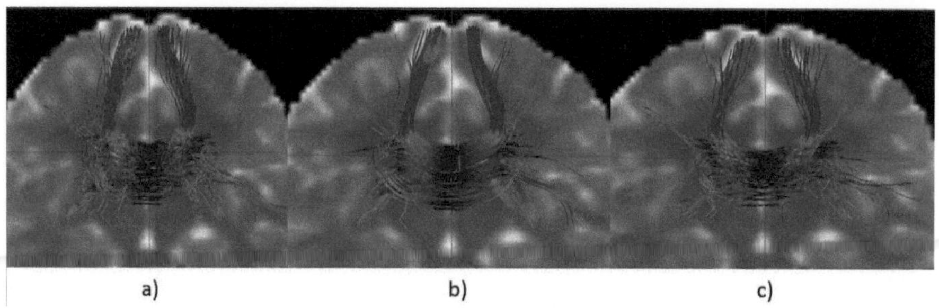

Fig. 3. Visual comparison of tractograms generated from the same seed point in the corpus callosum. (a) IFOD2, (b) SD-Stream, (c) Proposed algorithm. These images represent an initial qualitative evaluation of the different methods.

5   Experimental Results

As part of the development and evaluation of the proposed algorithm, white matter fiber reconstructions in were performed using three different methods. We used the simulated ISMRM 2015 challenge data [15]. An update of the date in 2023, to allow the creation of good Regions of Interest (ROIs), the ground truth tractogram was curated as it contained short / long / looping / broken streamlines [16].

Figure 3 shows the visual results using three different methods: IFOD2, SD-Stream and the proposed algorithm. In all cases, the same seed point was used, located in the corpus callosum—a structure that connects the two cerebral hemispheres.

In this study, Linear Fascicle Evaluation (LiFE) model [17] was applied to the three different tractograms: one generated using the proposed algorithm (Track_A), and two obtained using conventional methods (IFOD2 and SD-Stream). LiFE provides a means to quantify the fidelity of a tractogram by fitting the diffusion signal as a non-negative linear combination of candidate fibers. Through this model, the contribution (or weight) of each streamline to the dMRI signal reconstruction is estimated, allowing for the removal of fibers that do not significantly improve prediction accuracy. The following key metrics were analyzed:

- **Total number of fibers:** The number of streamlines in the original tractogram.
- **Fibers retained by LiFE:** The number of streamlines with non-zero weight after optimization. A lower proportion of retained fibers may indicate higher specificity.
- **Median RMSE (Base):** Root Mean Squared Error when predicting the diffusion signal using all original fibers.
- **Median RMSE (LiFE):** RMSE when predicting the signal using only the fibers selected by LiFE. A reduction indicates an improvement in the model's explanatory power.

- **Improvement:** Relative difference between Base RMSE and LiFE RMSE, computed as:

$$\text{Improvement} = \frac{\text{RMSE}_{\text{Base}} - \text{RMSE}_{\text{LiFE}}}{\text{RMSE}_{\text{Base}}}$$

Negative values indicate that the optimized model provides a better signal prediction than the unfiltered one.

Table 1. Numerical results of the tractograms evaluated by using LiFE.

Tractogram	# of Fibers	Retained	RMSE Base	RMSE LiFE	Improment
Track_A	780	642	34.34	33.28	**-0.1566**
IFOD2	780	597	29.93	28.61	0.0065
SD_Stream	780	571	29.82	28.98	-0.1005

Table 1 shows the numerical results by means of LiFE over the three generated tractograms.

6   Discution

The results obtained reveal notable differences in the behavior of the evaluated algorithms. The tractogram Track_A, generated using the proposed algorithm, achieved the highest improvement in RMSE after applying LiFE, despite removing a moderate number of fibers. This suggests that its initial structure already contained informative trajectories, and that LiFE's filtering process enhanced accuracy without compromising coverage.

In contrast, the tractogram generated with IFOD2 eliminated a similar number of fibers, yet the RMSE improvement was minimal. This may indicate that IFOD2 already produces streamlines that closely match the diffusion signal, leaving little room for further enhancement via LiFE. Alternatively, it could suggest a lower capacity to capture redundant trajectories.

SD_Stream presented intermediate behavior. In both cases, LiFE filtering led to improved signal prediction, though to a lesser extent than Track_A.

This analysis demonstrates that incorporating LiFE as a validation tool provides valuable insight into tractogram quality. In particular, the proposed algorithm shows promising results, especially in configuration Track_A, where a more consistent reduction in error was observed.

Nevertheless, these findings should be interpreted with caution. The validity of tractography depends on multiple factors, including the signal model, the brain region, and the quality of the input data. Future evaluations should incorporate additional datasets, cross-validation tools, and more anatomically grounded comparisons.

In summary, LiFE not only serves to filter spurious trajectories but also enables a deeper understanding of the differential behavior of tractography algorithms. The results presented here raise new questions about the structure of the connectome and the design of methods that better align with measured diffusion data.

7   Conclusion

This article has reviewed recent advances, challenges, and applications of brain tractography, emphasizing its relevance in neuroscience and medicine. While current methods have proven useful for studying brain connectivity, significant challenges remain that limit their applicability in clinical environments—particularly in neurosurgery and the diagnosis of neurological disorders.

Among the proposed solutions, real-time convex optimization emerges as a promising tool to address some of the current limitations of tractography. Although still under development, this approach has the potential to improve both the accuracy and efficiency of tractography algorithms, opening new possibilities for their use in clinical and surgical applications.

In conclusion, brain tractography continues to evolve as an essential tool for exploring the human brain. As technical challenges are overcome and new approaches are validated, this technique is expected to have an even greater impact on the understanding of neural networks and the advancement of medical care for patients with neurological conditions.

References

1. Lebel, C., Salat, D., Yeatman, J.: Chapter 29 - tractography: applications to neurodevelopment, aging, and plasticity. In: Dell'Acqua, F., Descoteaux, M., Leemans, A. (eds.) Handbook of Diffusion MR Tractography, pp. 583–611. Academic Press, ??? (2025). https://doi.org/10.1016/B978-0-12-818894-1.00009-4 . https://www.sciencedirect.com/science/article/pii/B9780128188941000094
2. Abrahamsen, R., Smith, M., Doe, J.: White matter fiber tractography: why we need to move beyond DTI. J. Magn. Reson. Imaging **51**(5), 1445–1458 (2020). https://doi.org/10.1002/jmri.27038
3. Smith, M., Johnson, L., Nguyen, P.: Emerging perspectives on precision therapy for parkinson's disease: multidimensional evidence leading to a new breakthrough. Front. Neurology **13**, 112–126 (2022). https://doi.org/10.3389/fneur.2022.00112
4. Schilling, K.G., et al.: Tractography dissection variability: what happens when 42 groups dissect 14 white matter bundles on the same dataset? NeuroImage **243**, 118502 (2021). https://doi.org/10.1016/j.neuroimage.2021.118502
5. Escalante-Belmonte, B.: Clasificación de Tractos Nerviosos Mediante Técnicas de Aprendizaje Automático
6. Ordóñez-Rubiano, et al.: Principios de tractografía cerebral. Repertorio de Medicina y Cirugía **28**(1), 29–38 (2019). https://doi.org/10.31260/RepertMedCir.v28.n1.2019.874

7. Rocamora-García, P.: Estudio de técnicas de contrastive learning para la segmentación de tractografía cerebral. Master's thesis, Universidad Politécnica de Valencia (2023)
8. Tournier, J.D., Calamante, F., Connelly, A.: Robust determination of the orientation distribution in diffusion MRI: non-negativity constrained super-resolved spherical deconvolution. NeuroImage **35**, 1459–1472 (2007). https://doi.org/10.1016/j.neuroimage.2007.02.016
9. Garyfallidis, E., Brett, M., Correia, M.M., Williams, G.B., Nimmo-Smith, I.: Quickbundles, a method for tractography simplification. Front. Neurosci. **8**, 1–13 (2020). https://doi.org/10.3389/fninf.2020.00005
10. Behrens, T., Johansen-Berg, H., Jbabdi, S.: Deterministic and probabilistic tractography based on complex Fibre orientation distributions. NeuroImage **45**, 1055–1066 (2010). https://doi.org/10.1016/j.neuroimage.2010.01.003
11. Tournier, J., Calamante, F., Connelly, A.: Combined tract segmentation and orientation mapping for bundle-specific tractography. Neuroimage **42**(2), 1075–1084 (2023)
12. Anderson, J., Miller, R., Lee, C.: Alzheimer's disease: a review on the current trends of the effective diagnosis and therapeutics. Diagnostics **12**(12), 2975–2990 (2022). https://doi.org/10.3390/diagnostics12122975
13. Daducci, A., Dal Palù, A., Lemkaddem, A., Thiran, J.P.: Commit: convex optimization modeling for microstructure informed tractography. IEEE Trans. Med. Imaging **34**(1), 246–257 (2015). https://doi.org/10.1109/TMI.2014.2352414
14. Zhang, H., Schneider, T., Wheeler-Kingshott, C.A., Alexander, D.C.: NODDI: practical in vivo neurite orientation dispersion and density imaging of the human brain. Neuroimage **61**(4), 1000–1016 (2012). https://doi.org/10.1016/j.neuroimage.2012.03.072
15. Maier-Hein, K.H.: The challenge of mapping the human connectome based on diffusion tractography. Nat. Commun. **8**(1), 1349 (2017). https://doi.org/10.1038/s41467-017-01285-x
16. Renauld, E., Théberge, A., Petit, L., Houde, J.C., Descoteaux, M.: Validate your white matter tractography algorithms with a reappraised ISMRM 2015 tractography challenge scoring system. Sci. Rep. **13**(1), 2347 (2023)
17. Pestilli, F., Yeatman, J.D., Rokem, A., Kay, K.N., Wandell, B.A.: Evaluation and statistical inference for human connectomes. Nat. Methods **11**(10), 1058–1063 (2014). https://doi.org/10.1038/nmeth.3098

Leveraging Large-Scale Face Datasets for Deep Periocular Recognition via Ocular Cropping

Fernando Alonso-Fernandez[1]([✉]), Kevin Hernandez-Diaz[1],
Jose Maria Buades Rubio[2], and Josef Bigun[1]

[1] School of Information Technology, Halmstad University, Halmstad, Sweden
`{feralo,kevin.hernandez-diaz,josef.bigun}@hh.se`
[2] Computer Graphics and Vision and AI Group, University of Balearic Islands,
Palma de Mallorca, Spain
`josemaria.buades@uib.es`

Abstract. We focus on ocular biometrics, specifically the periocular region (the area around the eye), which offers high discrimination and minimal acquisition constraints. We evaluate three Convolutional Neural Network architectures of varying depth and complexity to assess their effectiveness for periocular recognition. The networks are trained on 1,907,572 ocular crops extracted from the large-scale VGGFace2 database. This significantly contrasts with existing works, which typically rely on small-scale periocular datasets for training having only a few thousand images. Experiments are conducted with ocular images from VGGFace2-Pose, a subset of VGGFace2 containing in-the-wild face images, and the UFPR-Periocular database, which consists of selfies captured via mobile devices with user guidance on the screen. Due to the uncontrolled conditions of VGGFace2, the Equal Error Rates (EERs) obtained with ocular crops range from 9–15%, noticeably higher than the 3–6% EERs achieved using full-face images. In contrast, UFPR-Periocular yields significantly better performance (EERs of 1–2%), thanks to higher image quality and more consistent acquisition protocols. To the best of our knowledge, these are the lowest reported EERs on the UFPR dataset to date.

Keywords: Periocular biometrics · Ocular Recognition · Partial face recognition · Ocular crops · Convolutional Neural Networks (CNNs) · Transfer learning · VGGFace2 database · UFPR database

1 Introduction

The periocular region (the area surrounding the eye) offers a robust alternative to face and iris modalities, especially under challenging conditions such as occlusion, low resolution, or poor imaging, situations where even basic face or iris detection may fail [4]. Partial faces can also be an issue in controlled

Y. Hernádez Heredia et al. (Eds.): IWAIPR 2025, LNCS 16328, pp. 26–38, 2026.
https://doi.org/10.1007/978-3-032-11358-0_3

contexts such as social media [13], masks, professional work gear, cultural coverings, etc. [27]. In this regard, periocular recognition has rapidly emerged as a promising approach for unconstrained biometrics [3,4,21,24,27]. As with many other vision tasks, Convolutional Neural Networks (CNNs) have gained popularity in biometrics [28]. However, their application to periocular remains limited [27,30,31], primarily due to the scarcity of large databases [30].

Recent works [1,9,10,18–20,29] primarily relied on small to medium-scale datasets for periocular recognition training, such as UFPR-Periocular [29] (33,660 ocular images) and VISOB 2.0 [22] (158,136 images). This contrasts with face recognition research, which benefits from datasets with millions of images [32]. For instance, [29] benchmarked seven CNN architectures trained on the UFPR database, initialized with either ImageNet or face recognition weights. Studies in [18–20] proposed lightweight periocular architectures via quantization techniques, using UFPR to train models such as ResNet18, ResNet50, and MobileFaceNet from scratch. Additionally, the authors of [19] trained a Generative Adversarial Network (GAN) to generate 99,840 synthetic periocular images, which were added to the training set. In [1], several network compression techniques were evaluated in the context of ocular recognition using five CNN models based on ResNet and VGG architectures. As training sets, the authors employed UFPR and VISOB 2.0 from scratch. The work [9] adapted the EfficientNet architecture for periocular recognition using UFPR, starting from the ImageNet trained model. Another recent work [10] adopted a strategy similar to ours, using ocular crops from VGGFace2 [8] to train a face-pretrained ResNet50. The paper, which does not specify the amount of images gathered for training, used the Cox database for evaluation, which contains surveillance videos.

In the present work, we explore deep periocular recognition using large-scale face datasets, addressing the limitations posed by the scarcity of dedicated ocular databases. Specifically, we train three convolutional networks (SqueezeNet, MobileNetv2, and ResNet50) using over 1.9 million ocular crops extracted from the VGGFace2 dataset. Different to [10], we evaluate here multiple network initializations and architectures, as well as their fusion. We evaluate the trained models on two benchmarks: VGGFace2-Pose, containing unconstrained in-the-wild images, and UFPR-Periocular, a more controlled selfie dataset captured at close distance by guiding users to align their eyes within a region shown on the screen. Given such difference in image quality, EERs with VGGFace2-Pose are modest (9–15%) compared to UFPR (1–2%). To the best of our knowledge, the results reported here are the best published EERs on the UFPR dataset to date.

2   Materials and Methods

2.1   Recognition Networks

We use three backbone architectures: SqueezeNet [17] (light), MobileNetv2 [26] (medium) and ResNet50 [12] (large). They respectively have 18/53/50 convolutional layers and 1.24M/3.5M/25.6M parameters. ResNet introduced residual blocks that bypass intermediate layers, improving gradient propagation and allowing deeper networks without overfitting. In a residual layer, channel dimensionality is first reduced via 1×1 point-wise filters, after which larger 3×3 filters are applied in a reduced space, to have dimensionality increased again to match the input. MobileNets employ inverted residuals and depth-wise separable convolutions to reduce parameters and inference time. Shortcut connections are between thinner layers instead (hence the name 'inverted'), which also results in fewer parameters, whereas the intermediate representation lies in a higher dimensional space. SqueezeNet, on the other hand, is a sequential (non-residual) network which is among the smallest generic CNNs proposed in the context of ImageNet. It also applies the 1×1 point-wise convolution paradigm to reduce (*squeeze*) the channel dimensionality and then apply a larger amount of (more costly) 3×3 and 1×1 filters in a lower dimensional space (*expand* phase).

This choice allows comparison of networks of different sizes. We use the models loaded in our experimental environment (Matlab r2024b), modified to have an input of 113×113 by changing the stride of the first convolutional layer from 2 to 1. This allows to keep the network unchanged and reuse ImageNet as starting weights when appropriate. Input images are normalised by subtracting 127.5 and dividing by 128. For SqueezeNet, we adopt modifications of [2], which added batch norm between convolutions and ReLU (missing in the original model).

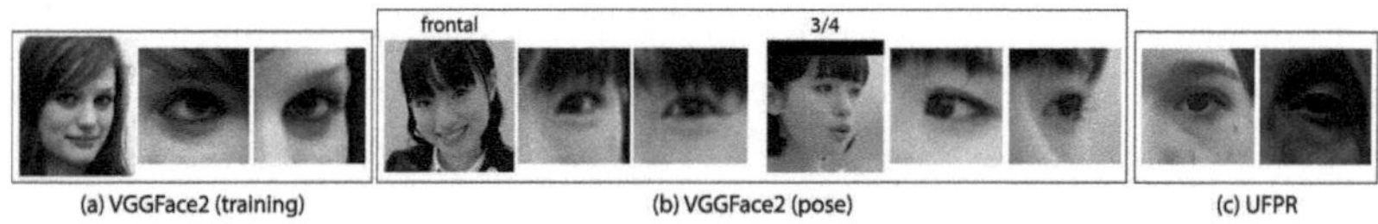

Fig. 1. Example images of the databases employed. Image c) composed from [29].

2.2   Databases

We use VGGFace2 (3.31M images, 9131 identities) [8] for training and evaluation (Fig. 1). The dataset includes significant variation in pose, age, lighting, and background. We use the database annotation to crop the ocular regions. The training protocol considers 8631 training classes (3.14M images). Images are aligned (eye centres horizontal), scaled to 113 pixels inter-eye distance, and cropped into two 113×113 patches centred on each eye. We apply a loose frontality check to ensure that both eyes are visible, imposing that the distance between the centre of the eyes and the vertical of the nose must be below 40% of the inter-eye distance. Faces with original inter-eye distances <50 px are also discarded to avoid excessive upsampling. Left eye crops are flipped for orientation consistency, and both eyes are then treated as the same identity. This results in 953,786 valid faces and 1,907,572 ocular crops (221 per identity on average).

For testing, we use the VGGFace2-Pose subset, with 368 subjects and 10 images per pose (frontal, three-quarter, profile). Only frontal and three-quarter are used, since profiles likely miss one of the eyes, and the available one can be severely distorted. This yields 7,360 crops per pose (20 per subject). To account for distortion, three-quarter images are resized to 80 pixels inter-eye distance instead. We also evaluate on UFPR-Periocular [29], the latest and one of the largest ocular databases, with 33,660 eye images from 1,122 subjects across 3 sessions using 196 mobile devices. Images vary in blur, occlusion, and lighting to simulate real-world conditions. UFPR contains three different training and evaluation protocols. We follow the open world/closed validation (OW/CW), where test identities are not included in the training/validation set. Eye crops $(224 \times 224$ pixels) are provided, which we resize to 113×113 to fit the input of the CNNs. We also flip left eyes, treating both eyes as the same identity.

In some configurations, networks are first pretrained for face recognition. Following [2], ImageNet initialised models are trained on the RetinaFace cleaned MS1M dataset [11] (5.1M face images, 93.4K identities, 113×113 pixels). Then, they are fine-tuned on VGG2 (3.14M face images). This two-step face training approach has demonstrated superior performance [2,8], leveraging the large image count of MS1M and the greater intra-class diversity of VGG2 due to having more images per person.

Table 1. Verification scores with VGGFace2-Pose and UFPR.

VGG SAME-POSE		VGG CROSS-POSE		UFPR (per fold)	
genuine	impostor	genuine	impostor	genuine	impostor
$368\times(9+8+...+1)=16560$	$368\times36=135056$	$368\times10\times10=36800$	$368\times367=135056$	78,540	4,190,670

2.3   Training and Recognition Protocols

The networks are trained for ocular identification using cross-entropy loss on VGG2 crops. We use SGDM (batch=128, learning rate=0.01, 0.005, 0.001, 0.0001, decreased when the validation loss plateaus) and set aside 2% of training images per user for validation. The models are initialized from scratch, ImageNet, or face recognition weights (Sect. 2.2). For scratch/ImageNet, the classification head is adjusted to 8631 classes, whereas with face-pretraining, it remains unchanged.

Verification is performed on the 368 users of VGGFace2-Pose, both intra- and cross-pose. Identity templates per user are created by extracting the descriptors of the left and right eyes from the layer adjacent to the classification layer (i.e., the Global Average Pooling). Given a pair of face images, the left and right eyes are compared separately, and the two scores are averaged. As comparison metrics, we use the cosine similarity and the χ^2 distance. Cosine is standard in CNN-based verification, but χ^2 has also shown good performance [14]. Genuine scores are obtained by comparing the eye crops of one face image against the rest of the same user (excluding symmetric matches) For impostor scores, the crops

Table 2. Ocular verification results on VGGFace2-Pose for different network intializations (EER %). The best result of each network (per column) is in bold. The table also shows full-face results from previous works on the same database.

Net	Initialization	cosine similarity				χ^2 distance			
		frontal	3/4	cross	all	frontal	3/4	cross	all
SQ	Scratch	15.02	15.87	15.86	15.70	13.80	**15.31**	14.07	14.06
	ImageNet	14.21	**15.46**	15.23	15.15	13.80	**15.31**	14.97	14.96
	Face	**13.47**	15.62	**15.04**	**14.95**	**13.07**	15.67	**14.69**	**14.80**
MB2	Scratch	10.59	12.05	11.80	11.66	10.66	12.07	11.76	11.66
	ImageNet	**8.93**	**10.85**	**10.23**	**10.13**	**8.56**	**10.35**	**9.72**	**9.70**
	Face	9.74	11.59	11.02	10.94	9.77	11.76	11.09	11.00
R50	Scratch	**9.09**	**10.10**	**10.00**	**9.85**	**8.66**	**9.71**	**9.53**	**9.41**
	ImageNet	9.80	11.14	10.79	10.68	8.75	10.10	9.68	9.62
	Face	10.46	12.05	11.87	11.66	10.40	12.02	11.75	11.56
MB2+R50 (best init)		-	-	-	-	**7.99**	**9.27**	**8.85**	**8.83**
MB2+R50 (ImageNet)		-	-	-	-	8.10	9.63	9.07	9.04

Face recognition performance in another works of the literature

	cosine similarity				χ^2 distance			
SqueezeNet [2]	-	-	-	-	6.39	5.47	6.09	-
ResNet50ft [2]	-	-	-	-	4.14	3.13	3.68	-
SENet50ft [2]	-	-	-	-	3.86	2.87	3.36	-
MobileNetv2 [6]	3.69	2.91	3.33	-	-	-	-	-
ResNet50 [6]	3.93	3.01	3.51	-	-	-	-	-
MB2+R50 [6]	3.53	2.70	3.13	-	-	-	-	-

of the 1st face image of a user are compared with the 2nd image of the remaining users. For UFPR, we follow its predefined protocol of three folds, testing on 374 users per fold. As with VGGFace2-Pose, eye crops are compared separately and scores averaged. Table 1 summarizes the number of score comparisons.

3   Results with VGGFace2-Pose Database

We first report (Table 2) ocular verification results of the networks on VGGFace2-Pose. A first observation is that χ^2 distance (right part of the table) consistently provides better results than the cosine similarity. This is in consonance with previous works [14]. In some cases, the difference in favour of χ^2 is more than 1% of EER reduction. Regarding network initialisation, there is no consensus on the best strategy (bold numbers). For SqueezeNet, face recognition initialisation works best; for MobileNetv2, the best results are achieved with ImageNet initialisation; and for ResNet50, training from scratch is the best case. It may

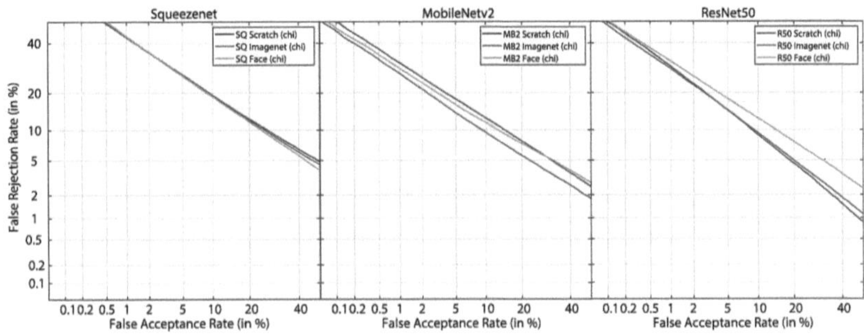

Fig. 2. Ocular verification results on VGGFace2-Pose for different network initializations (χ^2 distance).

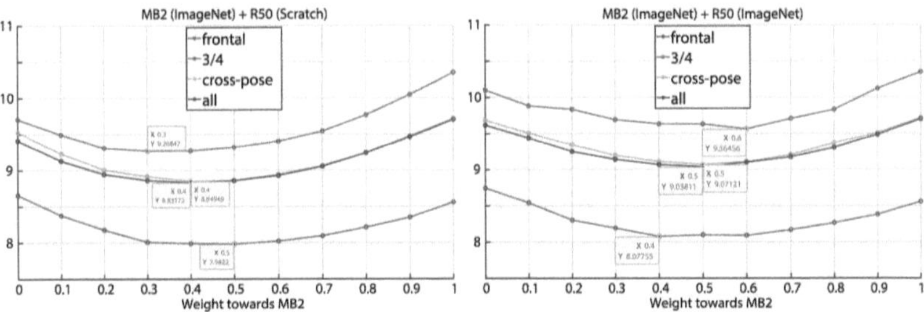

Fig. 3. Ocular fusion verification results on VGGFace2-Pose for different network initializations (EER %, χ^2 distance). Left: best initialization per network according to Table 2. Right: all networks initialized on ImageNet.

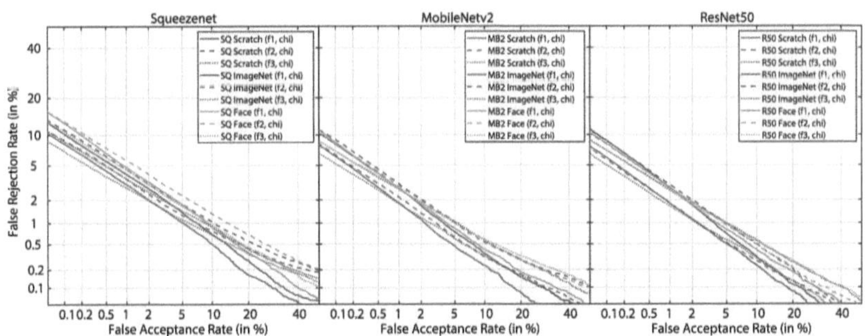

Fig. 4. Ocular verification on UFPR test folds for different network initializations (χ^2 distance).

be intuitive to assume that fine-tuning face recognition networks for the ocular modality would be the best option, since the network had already *seen* eye regions. However, this is seen to be detrimental. One possible explanation would be that face networks may be too specialised already for the full-face. On the other hand, ImageNet or scratch initialisation allows to start with more primitive features (edges, corners, etc.) that adapt better to the ocular task. By looking at the DET curves (Fig. 2, χ^2 only), conclusions about the best initialisation derived from the EER also hold, with the only exception that ResNet50 works better with ImageNet start in some regions of the DET. This also suggests that ImageNet pretraining can offer good robustness and serve as a general starting point for specialised features, as seen in countless works in the computer vision literature [25], and not just in biometrics [5,7,14–16,23].

Table 3. Ocular verification results on UFPR for different network initializations (EER/AUC % with OW/CW protocol). The best result of each network (per column) is marked in bold. The table also shows ocular recognition results from previous works on the same database and protocol.

Net	Initialization	cosine similarity				χ^2 distance			
		EER		AUC		EER		AUC	
		avg	std	avg	std	avg	std	avg	std
SQ	Scratch	2.57	**0.17**	99.59	0.10	2.47	0.18	99.62	**0.08**
	ImageNet	**2.13**	0.18	**99.69**	**0.08**	**2.07**	**0.13**	**99.70**	**0.08**
	Face	3.05	0.30	99.50	0.13	2.80	0.25	99.55	0.11
MB2	Scratch	1.98	0.12	99.76	0.05	1.92	0.11	99.77	0.04
	ImageNet	**1.53**	**0.08**	**99.85**	**0.02**	**1.49**	0.09	**99.86**	**0.02**
	Face	1.98	**0.08**	99.75	0.03	1.90	**0.06**	99.76	0.03
R50	Scratch	2.00	0.11	99.78	0.03	1.90	0.08	99.80	0.03
	ImageNet	**1.47**	**0.04**	**99.87**	**0.01**	**1.41**	**0.03**	**99.88**	**0.01**
	Face	1.94	0.08	99.78	0.03	1.85	0.04	99.79	0.02
MB2+R50 (ImageNet)		-	-	-	-	**1.27**	**0.03**	-	-

In terms of absolute performance, the residual-based networks MobileNetv2 and ResNet50 provide much better EER than the simpler SqueezeNet. It can also be seen that the comparison of ocular images extracted from frontal face images is slightly better than three-quarter or cross-pose comparisons (more than 1% difference in EER with ResNet50 and ∼2% or more with the other networks). This can be expected given the progressive distortion of the ocular region as the view departs from frontal. The bottom part of Table 2 also shows the face recognition performance reported on previous works with the same database. As it can be seen, performance with the full face on VGGFace2-Pose is significantly better than ocular (EER in the range of 3–6% vs 9–15%). We attribute this to the quality of VGG2 data [8], which consist of images with significant variability in pose, illumination, etc., providing richer information when the entire face is visible. In contrast, ocular crops represent a zoomed, more limited region with less discriminative content under such conditions.

The two best performing networks, MobileNetv2 and ResNet50, were observed previously to be highly complementary for face recognition via score fusion [6]. We also assess here their complementarity for ocular recognition (Fig. 3). This is done by combining their verification scores, denoted as s_{MB2} and s_{R50}, through a weighted average approach via $a \times s_{MB2} + (a - 1) \times s_{R50}$ ($a \in [0, 1]$). Figure 3 shows the results for different values of the weight a (support towards MobileNetv2). We test two cases: the best initialization per network according to Table 2, and all networks initialized on ImageNet, since we observed above that ImageNet is a good general starting point. We also tested other fusion combinations involving SqueezeNet, but they did not provide any performance gain due to the much worse individual performance of such network, so results of those experiments are omitted.

Notably, the fusion of MobileNetv2 and ResNet50 enhances performance, with the optimal achieved when both networks are assigned a roughly equal weight (a between 0.4 and 0.6). We select the cases with the highest overall accuracy ($a = 0.4$ for the best initialization and $a = 0.5$ for ImageNet initialization) and provide its exact EER values in Table 2. Using the best initialization per network provides a slight advantage compared to ImageNet initialization in both networks (overall EER of 8.83% vs 9.04%). In addition, the fusion enhances performance across all pose cases, providing EER gains of more than 0.4%.

4   Results with UFPR Database

We then evaluate the ocular recognition networks trained with VGG2 on the UFPR-Periocular dataset [29]. Results are given in Table 3. We follow the OW/CW protocol and reporting metrics of the UFPR paper (EER and AUC) across the three test folds. A first evident observation is the lower EERs in comparison to VGGFace2-Pose (Table 2). UFPR is a purposely-captured ocular database, with users employing their mobiles in selfie mode while looking frontally to the device. In principle, this provides higher resolution and quality ocular images in a more controlled setup, since users are asked to place their eyes in a region of interest shown in the device screen. In contrast, VGG2 images are face images captured in-the-wild, of which we crop the smaller ocular area. As as result, the EERs with UFPR are in the range of 1–2% (even with SqueezeNet), compared to 9–15% with VGGFace2-Pose. With UFPR, it can also be observed an advantage in favour of the χ^2 distance, although in this case the differences are in general less than 0.1%. While cosine measures the angle between the embedding vectors, χ^2 encodes local relative differences between channels, which may be more suitable for low-quality images such as VGG2, where higher EER gains were observed by using χ^2. Regarding initialization, ImageNet wins in all cases with UFPR by a large margin. The DET curves (Fig. 4, χ^2 only) support this conclusion, i.e. the red curves (ImageNet initialization) win in nearly all regions, with the exception of SqueezeNet, where at low FRR, other initialization are seen to work better. In any case, this confirms our above observations that ImageNet pretraining constitute a good starting point overall, even if we have a large amount of training images.

As in the previous sub-section, we also analyze network complementarity. Figure 5 shows results of average score fusion combination, with each network given the same weight in the fusion. In this case, it can be seen that even involving SqueezeNet in the fusion provides performance gains if the networks are initialized from scratch (left). However, this is not the initialization providing the best absolute EERs. With the other two initializations, involving SqueezeNet does not provide any fusion benefit. We further show (Fig. 6) the combination of MobileNetv2 and ResNet50 for different supports towards each network in the weighted fusion. We only show the case where both networks are initialized with ImageNet, since this was the best case for both networks with UFPR. Again, the fusion is seen to improve performance, being optimal when both networks receive approximately the same weight (a between 0.4–0.5). We select $a=0.4$ as the case with the best average EER and provide the exact values in Table 3, where it can be seen that this is the best case overall.

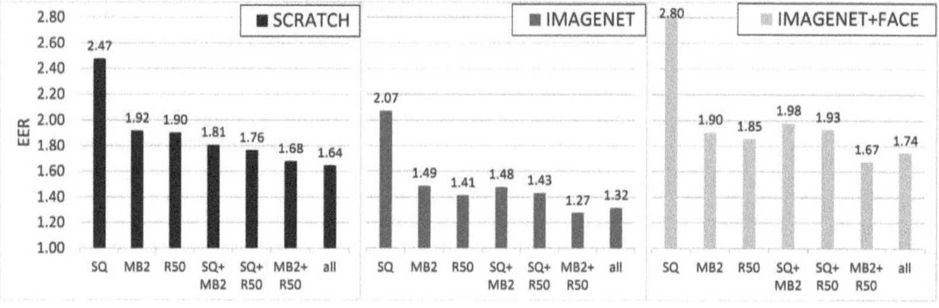

Fig. 5. Ocular fusion results on UFPR for different network initializations (χ^2 distance, average EER% of the folds, equal weight per network in the fusion).

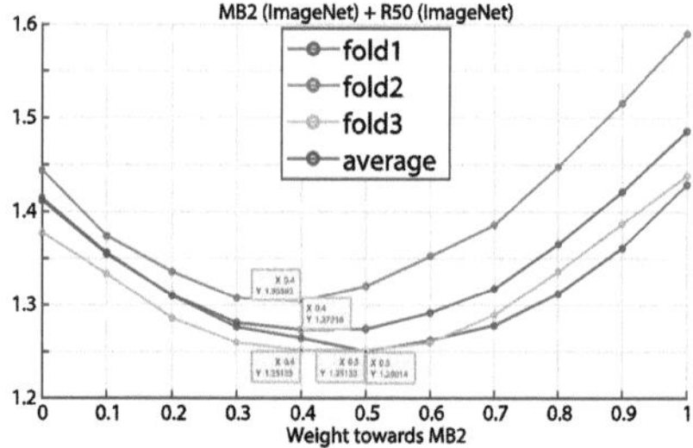

Fig. 6. Ocular fusion verification on UFPR for networks initialized on ImageNet (EER %, χ^2 distance).

We finally compare (Table 4) our results with previous works employing the same OW/CW evaluation protocol on the UFPR database. Works such as [1,9] are deliberately left out, since they employed a different training/testing protocol. The work [29] corresponds to the seminal paper of UFPR, which established the baseline performance, improved later on by more recent research [18–20]. However, such works made use of UFPR as the unique training database, with just contains 33,660 images. This is surpassed by our training strategy, consisting of 1,907,572 ocular crops from the large VGGFace2 database, which provides state-of-the-art performance with the UFPR database.

Table 4. Ocular verification results on UFPR from previous works (EER/AUC % with the OW/CW protocol). Works with (*) flipped left/right eyes to the same orientation and considered both eyes to have the same identity.

		EER		AUC	
Net	**Training**	avg	std	avg	std
MobileNetv2 [29]	ImageNet +	3.17	0.33	99.56	0.08
DenseNet121 [29]	UFPR	3.39	0.46	99.51	0.12
ResNet50 [29]		5.98	0.67	98.60	0.28
VGG16 [29]		8.52	0.92	97.38	0.53
ResNet50-Face [29]	VGGFace1 +	4.38	0.47	99.18	0.16
VGG16-Face [29]	UFPR	7.78	0.75	97.70	0.42
ResNet18 W8A8 [18] *	UFPR	5.99	0.39	98.41	0.16
ResNet50 W8A8 [18] *	(scratch)	5.99	0.41	98.39	0.18
MobileFaceNet W6A6 [18] *		4.02	0.19	99.18	0.06
ResNet18 MQ [20] *	UFPR	2.63	-	99.60	-
ResNet50 MQ [20] *	(scratch)	2.59	-	99.61	-
MobileFaceNet MQ [20] *		2.80	-	99.55	-
ResNet18 FP32 [18–20] *	UFPR	5.76	0.38	98.51	0.15
ResNet50 FP32 [18–20] *	(scratch)	5.88	0.38	98.47	0.17
MobileFaceNet FP32 [18–20] *		3.86	0.21	99.23	0.05
SqueezeNet (this work) *	ImageNet +	2.07	0.13	99.70	0.08
MobileNetv2 (this work) *	VGG2 ocular	1.49	0.09	99.86	0.02
ResNet50 (this work) *		**1.41**	**0.03**	**99.88**	**0.01**
MB2+R50 (this work) *		**1.27**	**0.03**	-	-

5   Conclusions

We address the task of developing biometric deep-recognition models that employ periocular images. In this work, we have evaluated three architectures of varying complexity (SqueezeNet, MobileNetv2, and ResNet50) trained on

1,907,572 periocular crops extracted from the large-scale VGGFace2 (VGG2) dataset [8], after filtering out non-frontal and very low-resolution images. This contrasts with prevalent research [30], including recent works [1,9,18–20,29], which rely on small-scale periocular databases with only a few thousand images.

We test multiple initialization strategies of the networks, including scratch, ImageNet weights, and fine-tuning of face recognition models trained on VGG2. Intuitively, fine-tuning face recognition networks for the ocular modality would be the best option, since face images already contain the ocular region. However, we observed that ImageNet weights are a better general starting point, whereas fine-tuning a face network is actually detrimental. We hypothesize that a face network may be already too specialized, whereas a more primitive initialization like ImageNet allows the networks to adapt better to the ocular images. Even networks with just ImageNet or, in some cases, with random weights and no further training have been shown to yield surprisingly good ocular performance in previous studies [16].

We carry out our evaluation experiments with two sets, the VGGFace2-Pose, a subset of VGG2 [8], and the UFPR-Periocular database [29]. Since VGG2 images are captured in-the-wild and we employ ocular crops of already low-quality face images, the EERs are modest with VGGFace2-Pose (9–15%), compared to 3–6% with full-face input. In contrast, the more controlled acquisition of UFPR selfies leads to EERs of 1–2% which, to our knowledge, are the best reported results on this dataset In addition, two of the employed networks (MobileNetv2 and ResNet50) are found to be complementary, observing a performance improvement by just combining (averaging) their decision scores.

We expect to achieve further gains by incorporating margin-based losses such as ArcFace, already employed in some works that we surpassed [18–20]. We also hypothesize that a sequential fine-tuning with ocular crops from the MS-Celeb-1M (MS1M) [11] and VGGFace2 [8] databases would provide even more benefit. This approach was followed earlier for face recognition, providing superior performance compared to just using VGGFace2 [2,8], since MS1M has more images overall, but VGGFace2 has more intra-class diversity.

Acknowledgements. This work was partly done while F. A.-F. was a visiting researcher at the University of the Balearic Islands. F. A.-F., K. H.-D., and J. B. thank the Swedish Research Council (VR) and the EU (HORIZON Europe project PopEye under Grant Agreement no 101168317) for funding their research. Funded by the European Union. Views and opinions expressed are, however, those of the author(s) only and do not necessarily reflect those of the European Union or the European Research Executive Agency. Neither the European Union nor the granting authority can be held responsible for them. This work is part of the Project PID2022-136779OB-C32 (PLEISAR) funded by MICIU/ AEI /10.13039/501100011033/ and FEDER, EU.

References

1. Almadan, A., Rattani, A.: Benchmarking neural network compression techniques for ocular-based user authentication on smartphones. IEEE Access (2023)
2. Alonso-Fernandez, F., Barrachina, J., Hernandez-Diaz, K., Bigun, J.: Squeezeface-posenet: Lightweight face verification across different poses for mobile platforms. In: Proceedings of the WMWB-ICPR (2020)
3. Alonso-Fernandez, F., Bigun, J.: A survey on periocular biometrics research. Pattern Recogn. Lett. **82**, 92–105 (2016)
4. Alonso-Fernandez, F., et al.: Periocular biometrics: a modality for unconstrained scenarios. Computer **57** (2024)
5. Alonso-Fernandez, F., et al.: Cross-sensor periocular biometrics in a global pandemic: comparative benchmark and novel multialgorithmic approach. Inf. Fusion (2022)
6. Alonso-Fernandez, F., Hernandez-Diaz, K., Buades, J.M., Tiwari, P., Bigun, J.: An explainable model-agnostic algorithm for CNN-based biometrics verification. In: Proceedings of the WIFS (2023)
7. Alonso-Fernandez, F., Hernandez-Diaz, K., Tiwari, P., Bigun, J.: Combined CNN and ViT features off-the-shelf: another astounding baseline for recognition. In: Proceedings of the WIFS (2024)
8. Cao, Q., Shen, L., Xie, W., Parkhi, O.M., Zisserman, A.: Vggface2: a dataset for recognising faces across pose and age. In: Proceedings of the FG (2018)
9. Coelho, P., et al.: Periocular efficientnet: a deep model for periocular recognition. In: Proceedings of the LA-CCI (2024)
10. Carreira, L.G.F., Menotti, D., Schwartz, W.R.: Dpr-v2s: A deep framework for periocular recognition in surveillance environments. In: Proceedings of the SIB-GRAPI (2024)
11. Guo, Y., Zhang, L., Hu, Y., He, X., Gao, J.: Ms-celeb-1m: a dataset and benchmark for large-scale face recognition. In: Proceedings of the ECCV (2016)
12. He, K., Zhang, X., Ren, S., Sun, J.: Deep residual learning for image recognition. In: Proceedings of the CVPR (2016)
13. Hedman, P., Skepetzis, V., Hernandez-Diaz, K., Bigun, J., Alonso-Fernandez, F.: On the effect of selfie beautification filters on face detection and recognition. Pattern Recogn. Lett. **163**, 104–111 (2022)
14. Hernandez-Diaz, K., Alonso-Fernandez, F., Bigun, J.: Periocular recognition using CNN features off-the-shelf. In: Proceedings of the BIOSIG (2018)
15. Hernandez-Diaz, K., Alonso-Fernandez, F., Bigun, J.: Cross spectral periocular matching using resnet features. In: Proceedings of the ICB (2019)
16. Hernandez-Diaz, K., Alonso-Fernandez, F., Bigun, J.: One-shot learning for periocular recognition: exploring the effect of domain adaptation and data bias on deep representations. IEEE Access **11**, 100396–100413 (2023)
17. Iandola, F.N., et al.: Squeezenet: alexnet-level accuracy with 50x fewer parameters and <1mb model size. CoRR **abs/1602.07360** (2016). http://arxiv.org/abs/1602.07360
18. Kolf, J.N., Boutros, F., Kirchbuchner, F., Damer, N.: Lightweight periocular recognition through low-bit quantization. In: Proceedings of the IJCB (2022)
19. Kolf, J.N., Elliesen, J., Boutros, F., Proença, H., Damer, N.: Syper: synthetic periocular data for quantized light-weight recognition in the NIR and visible domains. Image Vis. Comput. **135**, 104692 (2023)

20. Kolf, J.N., Elliesen, J., Damer, N., Boutros, F.: Mixquantbio: towards extreme face and periocular recognition model compression with mixed-precision quantization. Eng. Appl. Artif. Intell. **137**, 109114 (2024)
21. Kumari, P., Seeja, K.: Periocular biometrics: a survey. J. King Saud Univ. Comput. Inf. Sci. **34**(4), 1086–1097 (2022)
22. Nguyen, H.M., Reddy, N., Rattani, A., Derakhshani, R.: Visob 2.0 - the 2nd international competition on mobile ocular biometric recognition. Proceedings of the ICPR (2021)
23. Nguyen, K., Fookes, C., Ross, A., Sridharan, S.: Iris recognition with off-the-shelf CNN features: a deep learning perspective. IEEE Access **6**, 18848–18855 (2018)
24. Rattani, A., Derakhshani, R.: Ocular biometrics in the visible spectrum: a survey. Image Vis. Comput. **59**, 1–16 (2017)
25. Razavian, A.S., Azizpour, H., Sullivan, J., Carlsson, S.: CNN features off-the-shelf: an astounding baseline for recognition. In: Proceedings of the CVPRW (2014)
26. Sandler, M., Howard, A., Zhu, M., Zhmoginov, A., Chen, L.: Mobilenetv2: inverted residuals and linear bottlenecks. In: Proceedings of the CVPR (2018)
27. Sharma, R., Ross, A.: Periocular biometrics and its relevance to partially masked faces: a survey. Comput. Vis. Image Underst. **226**, 103583 (2023)
28. Sundararajan, K., Woodard, D.L.: Deep learning for biometrics: a survey. ACM Comput. Surv. **51**(3) (2018)
29. Zanlorensi, L.: A new periocular dataset collected by mobile devices in unconstrained scenarios. Sci. Rep. **12**, 17989 (2022)
30. Zanlorensi, L., et al.: Ocular recognition databases and competitions: a survey. Artif. Intell. Review **55** (2022)
31. Zeng, D., Veldhuis, R., Spreeuwers, L.: A survey of face recognition techniques under occlusion. IET Biometrics **10**(6), 581–606 (2021)
32. Zhu, Z.: Webface260m: a benchmark for million-scale deep face recognition. IEEE TPAMI **45**(2), 2627–2644 (2023)

FGSSNet: Feature-Guided Semantic Segmentation of Real World Floorplans

Hugo Norrby, Gabriel Färm, Kevin Hernandez-Diaz,
and Fernando Alonso-Fernandez$^{(\boxtimes)}$

School of Information Technology, Halmstad University, Halmstad, Sweden
`{kevin.hernandez-diaz,feralo}@hh.se`

Abstract. We introduce FGSSNet, a novel multi-headed feature-guided semantic segmentation (FGSS) architecture designed to improve the generalization ability of wall segmentation on floorplans. FGSSNet features a U-Net segmentation backbone with a multi-headed dedicated feature extractor used to extract domain-specific feature maps which are injected into the latent space of U-Net to guide the segmentation process. This dedicated feature extractor is trained as an encoder-decoder with selected wall patches, representative of the walls present in the input floorplan, to produce a compressed latent representation of wall patches while jointly trained to predict the wall width. In doing so, we expect that the feature extractor encodes texture and width features of wall patches that are useful to guide the wall segmentation process. Our experiments show increased performance by the use of such injected features in comparison to the vanilla U-Net, highlighting the validity of the proposed approach.

Keywords: Wall segmentation · Floorplan analysis · Feature-guided segmentation · U-Net

1 Introduction

Floorplans are essential graphical representations of buildings, widely used in architecture, engineering, construction, real estate, and interior design. However, their necessary depth, complexity and purpose vary significantly, leading to diverse standards not only among industries but also across countries. For example, an interior designer typically requires a simplified version highlighting room dimensions and layout while omitting complex details like wall materials. In contrast, architects and constructors need a more detailed representation, including materials, electrical wiring, and elevations.

Such a lack of common standards complicates the transition to digital floorplans. Detailed vector-based formats like DWG provide precise spatial and material information, but they are complex to produce, so they are mainly limited to architecture and construction. In contrast, standard image formats like JPEG and PNG offer greater accessibility and interoperability. They enable the use of regular photos as floorplans and standard editing tools, but they lack structural

© The Author(s), under exclusive license to Springer Nature Switzerland AG 2026
Y. Hernádez Heredia et al. (Eds.): IWAIPR 2025, LNCS 16328, pp. 39–51, 2026.
https://doi.org/10.1007/978-3-032-11358-0_4

details, making necessary additional processing. For example, light intensity calculations require accurate wall placement [22], necessitating manual delineation. Similarly, security camera placement depends on FoV previews and identifying obstructions like walls to plan effective multi-camera coverage [1].

Thus, wall delineation is a crucial aspect of floorplans due to its many use cases. Automating the process would enhance user experience, especially for large-scale layouts like malls and airports, reducing reliance on manual annotation. Traditional heuristic and probabilistic methods [13] rely heavily on preassumptions about the spatial structure of floorplans [15] and struggle with complex layouts such as diagonal or curved walls [2,16,17]. Deep learning approaches show greater robustness [4,14] but require extensive labelled datasets, which are scarce [9,12]. Existing models still face challenges in generalizing to real-world floorplans outside their training distribution, limiting industrial applicability.

Accordingly, we propose the application of Feature-Guided Semantic Segmentation (FGSS) to improve wall segmentation in diverse floorplans. Our method, FGSSNet, explores the injection of features extracted from selected wall patches of the input image into the latent space of a U-Net segmentation network. This is achieved by a dedicated multi-headed feature extractor consisting of an encoder-decoder, which is also trained to predict the width of the wall. We hypothesize that injecting texture and width features of the intended object of interest into the segmentation pipeline will provide a more efficient segmentation.

2   Related Works

Semantic segmentation classifies individual pixels of the input image into a class. A breakthrough came with Fully Convolutional Networks (FCNs) [19], a more efficient global context-based method than previous approaches, although its precision was limited by performing upscaling in a single step. U-Net improved upon FCNs via progressive upscaling with an encoder-decoder architecture [18]. It also allows skip connections to flow from the encoder to corresponding decoder layers, preserving finer spatial details and improving gradient flow. DeepLabV3 [5] introduced atrous convolutions to the encoder-decoder architecture, allowing the capture of a broader spatial context. It also proposed Atrous Spatial Pyramid Pooling (ASPP) to enhance multi-scale segmentation via different dilation rates, later refined in DeepLabV3+ for better boundary recovery [6]. More recently, attention-based models like SegNeXt [8] and transformer-based architectures [7,21,24] have emerged, improving efficiency and scalability.

Many of the existing segmentation methods can be adapted to floor plan segmentation and wall detection. However, it faces some challenges due to the lack of standardization and dataset limitations. The unsupervised method of [10] combines structural and appearance-based detection. The structural part relies on assumptions generalizable to common wall types, such as parallel lines arranged in orthogonal directions, usually longer than thicker, filled with a common pattern, etc. Detected walls are then refined by the appearance detector, which uses Bag-of-Patches. The approach is promising since it does not need labelled data but struggles with non-standard walls that do not adhere to the assumptions. A ResNet-50-based approach in [3] classifies cropped image regions as containing walls or not. YOLOv3 is then used to find bounding boxes in wall crops. However, the method is unable to find diagonal or curved walls, and it is reliant on an object detector that may not generalize to unseen data distributions. MuraNet [11] is a multi-task model which also integrates segmentation and detection by leveraging correlation between walls, doors and windows via an attention-based approach. It is observed to outperform segmentation-only methods based on SegNeXt or U-Net, though it requires significant computing power. Another recent method in floorplan wall segmentation [20] modifies U-Net by substituting VGG with ResNet as backbone to mitigate gradient vanishing. It also adds a Convolutional Block Attention Module (CBAM) that enhances feature learning by integrating channel and spatial information, as well as a convolutional mapping-mask smoothing method. The system also integrates traditional segmentation methods, combining their faster processing with the robustness of deep learning.

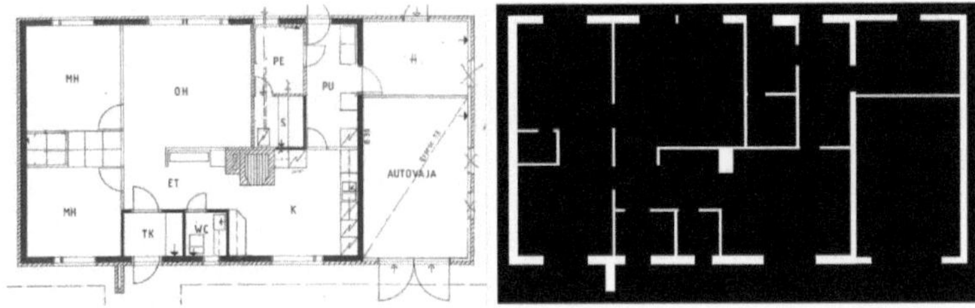

Fig. 1. Floorplan and extracted walls segmentation mask.

3   Methodology

3.1   Data

We use CubiCasa5k [12] along with additional self-captured images for robustness evaluation on external data. CubiCasa5k has 5000 scanned floorplan images with ground-truth (GT) in SVG files and predefined training (4200 images), validation (400) and testing (400) sets. We parsed the GT to create binary segmentation masks. While CubiCasa5k provides labels for windows, doors, and walls, among other classes, we only focus on single-class binary segmentation of walls. Thus, all other classes are set as negatives. Figure 1 shows an example. CubiCasa5k floorplans have different resolutions due to a great variety of building types. As a result, walls may appear in very different sizes. To ensure consistency and facilitate segmentation, we normalize the floorplans based on the average wall width of the whole database (found to be 24.18 pixels using the GT).

Wall samples are also central to our method, allowing the encoder to extract wall latent space information and guide the segmentation. To enable this, we extract five wall samples from each floorplan based on the following criteria: the longest vertical/horizontal wall (two samples), the longest thinnest vertical/horizontal wall (two samples), and the longest wall. We then extract a 64×64 crop in the centre of the wall. Figure 2 shows an example.

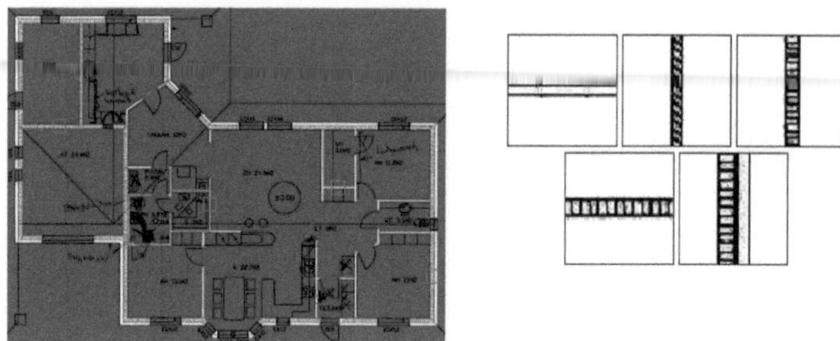

Fig. 2. Floorplan and extracted 64×64 wall samples (shown in red). (Color figure online)

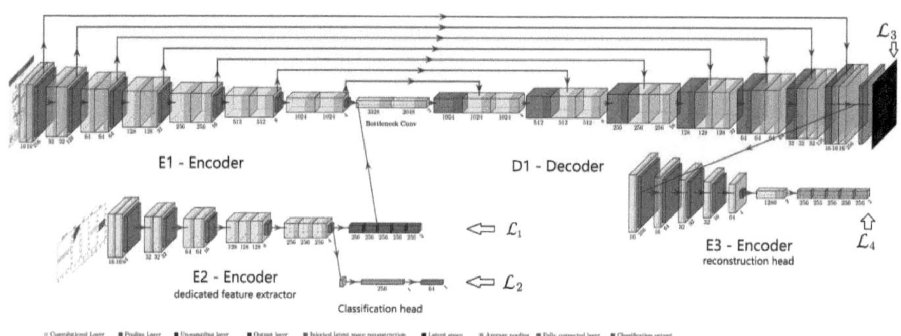

Fig. 3. FGSSNet architecture.

3.2   System Overview

Our model comprises three main networks (Fig. 3): a U-Net backbone (top), a dedicated feature extractor (bottom left), and a reconstruction head (right).

The dedicated feature extractor is a multi-headed encoder which processes 64×64 wall crops to produce a compressed latent representation while jointly predicting the wall width. This is to enforce that the latent representation encodes both texture and width information, which, we hypothesise, should produce a more accurate segmentation. This dedicated extractor is trained separately with an encoder-decoder structure E2-D2 (D2 not shown in the image) to reconstruct the input image again from the latent vector. The encoder E2 has 5 down stages with double/triple 3×3 convolution blocks, stride 1, padding 1, followed by batchnorm+ReLU (the last two stages use triple to further transform the features without reducing resolution). Max pooling is 2×2 with stride 2. After each pooling, feature maps are doubled. The resulting bottleneck vector per wall crop has 2×2×256 feature maps. The decoder D2 has 5 stages with the inverse 256, 128, 64, 32, 16 channel progression to produce again the wall crop presented to E2. Each stage has one 3×3 convolutional transpose, stride 2, padding 1, followed by ReLU. The upsampling stages are kept simple to encourage the encoder to extract more robust and relevant features representing the wall. The classification head takes the latent vector of E2 and applies an average pooling layer, followed by dropout at 50% and a fully connected layer to predict the wall width among the 64 possible values. We keep the classification head simple, too, since wall crops are already cleaned parts of the floorplan, and the latent vector is expected to contain representative information after E2 already. As mentioned, the dedicated feature extractor is trained separately using the wall crops extracted from the database. We use a combined loss function $w_1 \mathcal{L}_1 + w_2 \mathcal{L}_2$, with $\mathcal{L}_1$ being the MSE between the recreated wall sample with D2 and the original crop, and $\mathcal{L}_2$ the cross-entropy loss of the classification head.

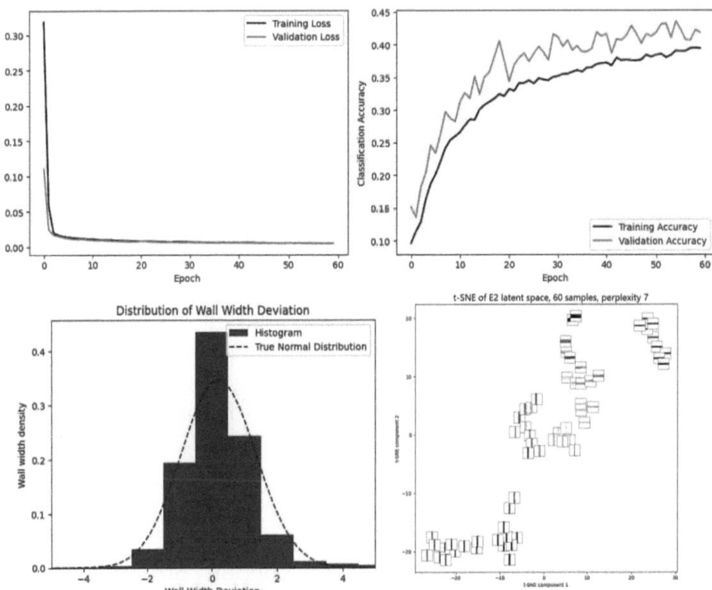

Fig. 4. Dedicated feature extractor results. Top: reconstruction loss and width classification accuracy. Bottom: width prediction deviation and t-SNE of latent vectors.

After E2-D2 is trained, D2 is removed, and the E2 latent vectors are used to feed the latent space of U-Net with additional domain-specific information about the current floorplan during the segmentation. To try to force that the injected features are used, we attach an additional encoder E3 after U-Net to reconstruct the injected feature maps. U-Net has 7 up and down-stages with double convolutions, having the same filter sizes, stride and padding as E2-D2. Convolutions in E1 include batchnorm+ReLU too. Each stage in E1 also feeds the convolution blocks of D1 through skip connections by channel concatenation. The segmentation output of D1 is then aggregated by point-wise 1×1 convolution to reduce feature maps from 16 to 1. At the beginning of the bottleneck, the domain-specific feature maps of E2 are concatenated with the output of E1, fusing the two latent spaces. E2 sequentially processes the 5 wall samples and concatenates them together, forming a $1280\times2\times2$ vector, which results in $3328\times2\times2$ after combination with the output of E1. The reconstruction head E3 is an encoder that uses the last feature map of D1 to reconstruct the output maps of E2. To avoid overfitting, E3 is sparse, keeping the number of channels small and single convolutions with batchnorm+ReLU (except in the last convolution, to allow unnormalized vectors with negative values). To train E1-D1-E3, we use a combined loss function $w_3\mathcal{L}_3 + w_4\mathcal{L}_4$, with $\mathcal{L}_3$ being the Binary Cross Entropy with logistic loss function, responsible for the segmentation against the ground truth mask, and and $\mathcal{L}_4$ is the MSE between the output of E2 and E3.

4   Experiments and Results

We use the CubiCasa5k pre-defined training, validation and test sets. We also extracted 5 wall samples from each floorplan as explained in Sect. 3.1. To evaluate segmentation goodness, we use IoU as metric. All models were trained on a Windows 10 PC with 64 Gb RAM and Nvidia RTX 4080 Super 16 Gb GPU.

4.1   Dedicated Feature Extractor and Classification Head

During early experiments, we noticed a tendency of the classification head to overfit quickly due to its low complexity. Thus, we reduced its impact on the loss by using $w_1{=}0.001$, $w_2{=}10$. We trained E2-D2 during 60 epochs using Adam with a learning rate of 0.001, weight decay of 0.9 and batch size of 256. The reconstruction loss and width classification accuracy of E2-D2 across epochs are shown in Fig. 4, top. The loss ends at 0.0045 without signs of over- or under-fitting. The width accuracy, on the other hand, ends at $\sim$40%. We investigated the latter further by plotting (bottom, left) the histogram of deviation between prediction and ground truth, showing that >90% of predictions are erroneous by 1 pixel. We partly attribute this to ground truth imprecision and, in any case, such deviation is not expected to degrade the performance of the system significantly. We further show (bottom right) the t-SNE of the latent space embeddings created by E2 for a selection of 60 test samples. It can be observed that walls with similar texture, orientation and width are close together, indicating that the encoder is able to capture and encode these parameters in the latent space.

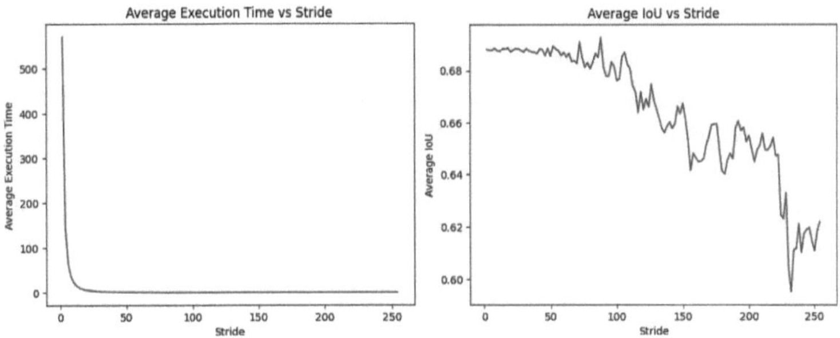

Fig. 5. Execution time and IoU vs. pixel stride of segmentation window.

4.2 FGSSNet Segmentation Pipeline

As indicated, after E2-D2 is trained, D2 is removed. The segmentation pipeline E1-D1-E3 is then trained on 256×256 crops of the floorplans, using the output of E2 to feed the latent space between E1-D1. Since E1-D1 and E3 are trained jointly, they may converge at different rates, which we solved with $w_3{=}1$, $w_4{=}0.3$ to combat that the simpler E3 head may converge faster. Also, we apply a random uniform rotation of $\pm45°C$ to the training images with 20% probability to increase the representation of diagonal walls. Training is done during 120 epochs using Adam with a learning rate of 0.0001, weight decay of 0.9 and batch size of 12.

When training E1-D1-E3, we consider two configurations: FGSSNet-[16–1024], as described earlier, and a second network FGSSNet-[32–2048] which doubles the number of feature maps per stage w.r.t. those shown in Fig. 3. This is to evaluate if different model complexities may affect performance. Given that FGSSNet is based on U-Net, we compare it to the vanilla U-Net to evaluate performance changes attributable to our modifications. We use two versions, U-Net-[16–1024] and U-Net-[32–2048], which match the E1-D1 section of FGSSNet without E2-D2/D3. The main difference lies in the bottleneck, where the proposed FGSSNet injects a 1280 elements vector. In addition, we consider two modified versions FGSSNet-[16–1024]-NoRec and FGSSNet-[32–2048]-NoRec with the reconstruction head E3 removed. This allows the decoder D1 to freely decide on the usage of the injected features, without enforcing their reconstruction at the end.

Since E1 receives 256×256 images, we use a sliding window to cover bigger floorplans (smaller floorplans are simply black padded). Adjacent windows overlap, allowing the model to segment the same pixel multiple times, ideally with patches that see different contexts. We average the output of the pixel classifications, being a value in 0–1. A threshold of 0.5 is then used to create a binary segmentation result. A short pixel stride in moving the window results in pixels being segmented more times, which in theory should improve segmentation, at the cost of time. However, there is a cutoff point where reducing the stride does not improve further. To find the optimal point, we plot (Fig. 5) the IoU and execution time vs. stride with FGSSNet-[16–1024] of three randomly selected test floorplans of CubiCasa5k. The optimal stride is between 20–40, below this suffering high execution time, and larger than this producing lower IoU. Based on these results, we chose a stride of 30 to balance speed and accuracy.

Table 1. Networks and segmentation results on the validation set of CubiCasa5k

U-Net-[32–2048]	2.19×10^{10}	2119.49	553.7M	78.2%	106
FGSSNet-[16–1024]	5.87×10^{9}	628.42	164.7M	78.1%	110
FGSSNet-[32–2048]	2.25×10^{10}	2302.46	603.6M	78.4%	101
FGSSNet-[16–1024]-NoRec	5.69×10^{9}	625.46	164M	78.6%	119
FGSSNet-[32–2048]-NoRec	2.22×10^{10}	2299.49	602.8M	**79.3%**	103

We then show (Table 1) the parameters and validation IoU of the 6 models, whereas Table 2 (first column) gives the test IoU. When comparing U-Net with our models, we can see that the additional injected data provides an improvement in IoU. Also, the increased complexity of [32–2048] seems to have a positive difference w.r.t. [16–1024], although at the cost of much bigger models. However, it can be seen that not using the reconstruction head E3 (-NoRec) generally gives better performance. While FGSSNet exceeds its vanilla U-Net counterparts, showcasing that U-Net is actually leveraging the injected E2 features, explicitly enforcing their reconstruction via E3 is not of further benefit.

Table 2. Segmentation results (IoU) on the test set of CubiCasa5k with injecting real wall crops vs random grey images.

Model	Real images	Gray images
FGSSNet-[16–1024]	**77.0%**	75.2%
FGSSNet-[32–2048]	**78.2%**	76.7%
FGSSNet-[16–1024]-NoRec	**77.9%**	76.1%
FGSSNet-[32–2048]-NoRec	**78.3%**	77.1%

4.3 Importance of Good Wall Samples

To showcase the importance of providing good wall samples to E2, we simulate the effect of bad ones by feeding E2 with grey images of random values. We do not use black of white images to avoid adverse effects [23]. Table 2 shows the comparative IoU across the test set. Results with real samples are superior, proving the significant impact of sample realism on segmentation performance. Although

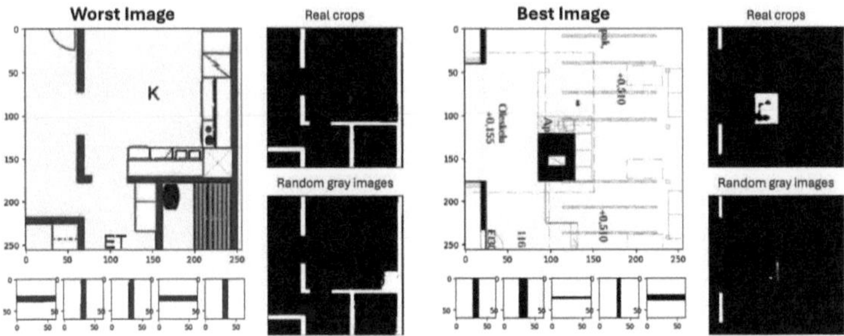

Fig. 6. Best/worst results when using real wall crops vs. random gray images in E2. (Color figure online)

segmentation does not completely deteriorate with grey walls, highlighting the robustness of the U-Net backbone, the results are nevertheless inferior.

Despite these results, an examination of individual floorplans showed that injecting grey walls sometimes gave better IoU. Figure 6 (left) show one of such cases. The model with real wall samples fails to segment a supporting pillar at the corner of the kitchen, which is considered a wall in the ground truth, punishing the IoU. The selected samples consist of wall segments smaller than the pillar, so the pillar is considered an unfamiliar object by the network and, thus, is rejected. The consideration of whether a pillar is a wall or not should lead to the inclusion of such type of sample when selecting the crops. Figure 6 (right), on the other hand, shows an example where the use of real crops substantially improves IoU. Real crops allowed to detect the black box in the middle of the floorplan. Although this object may not resemble a wall, the solid black colour closely resembles the injected wall samples, which might be the reason for the improved segmentation, once again demonstrating the importance of the wall samples. The two presented examples showcase the importance of selecting high-quality wall samples which are representative of the intended objects to be segmented.

4.4 Generalization Results

To test the model generalization ability to a different domain, we obtained 10 floorplan images from the company participating in this work, representing typical user-submitted floorplans (Fig. 7). They cover an extensive range of types, both custom and architectural. To simulate a realistic scenario where ground truth is not available, the 5 necessary wall crops of each floorplan were extracted manually. The approximate pixel wall widths were annotated, and their average width was used to rescale the floorplan to the average value expected by the network. In a posterior deployment of this tool, such a procedure could be semi-automated, including guidance and training to the user on how to extract the 5 representative crops and facilitate automatic width computation.

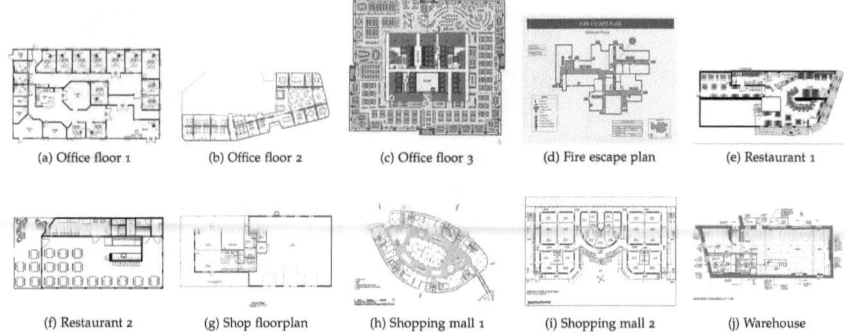

(a) Office floor 1   (b) Office floor 2   (c) Office floor 3   (d) Fire escape plan   (e) Restaurant 1

(f) Restaurant 2   (g) Shop floorplan   (h) Shopping mall 1   (i) Shopping mall 2   (j) Warehouse

Fig. 7. Additional floorplans collected.

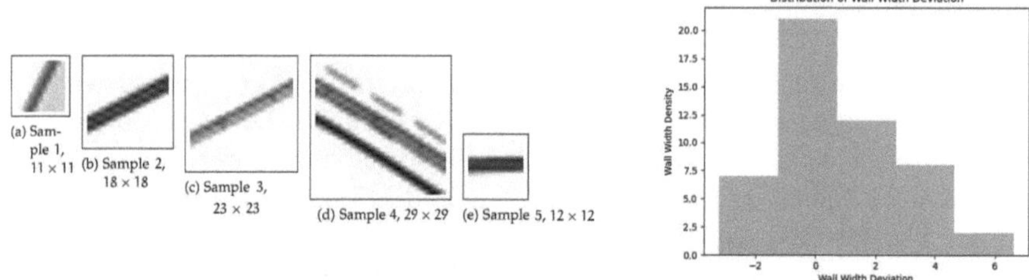

(a) Sample 1, 11 × 11   (b) Sample 2, 18 × 18   (c) Sample 3, 23 × 23   (d) Sample 4, 29 × 29   (e) Sample 5, 12 × 12

Fig. 8. Left: manual wall samples from Shopping-Mall1. Right: width prediction deviation of the additional floorplans collected.

Figure 8 shows a sample of extracted wall samples and the deviation between the width prediction of E2 and the annotation. In general, the majority of predictions fall in a range of 2 pixels, which is a bit higher than the CubiCasa5k results of Fig. 4. Some cases also show an overestimation of the width, which would result in slightly incorrect scaling. These differences could be attributed to the model being trained on different data. Moreover, crop extraction with CubiCasa5k was fully automated with the ground truth of the entire floorplan. In contrast, here, it was done manually and by visual inspection, which could be expected to be more imprecise or provide crops that do not fully match the selection criteria for which the network is trained.

Despite this, the models are seen to generalize well to this unseen data. Table 3 shows the segmentation performance across the additional floorplans. All our proposed models performed better than the vanilla U-Net, indicating that the injected wall sample features improve the generalization performance, despite observed imprecisions in wall width analysis. Comparing the performance difference between injecting the real wall samples and grey images further reinforces that statement since the average IoU increases by 3.5–4.4 using real crops. At the individual floorplan level, improvement with real crops is also predominant. FGSSNet-[16–1024] versions achieve higher IoU than FGSSNet-[32–2048], which is a different trend than in Sect. 4.2, although the IoU difference is 1–2 in both sections. On the other hand, FGSSNet-NoRec models perform better than their FGSSNet counterparts, as observed previously.

Table 3. IoU of the different models for the additional floorplans collected.

			IoU scores for each model			
Floorplan	U-Net [16-1024]	U-Net [32-2048]	FGSSNet-[16-1024] (Real/Gray)	FGSSNet-[32-2048] (Real/Gray)	FGSSNet-[16-1024] -NoRec (Real/Gray)	FGSSNet-[32-2048] -NoRec (Real/Gray)
Fire-escape	52.6	50.3	60.8 / 58.7	63.2 / 63.5	69.1 / 69.0	**69.2** / 58.6
Office-1	78.8	75.2	74.7 / 71.8	79.7 / 78.9	**81.1** / 80.2	76.8 / 75.4
Office-2	31.2	42.7	40.8 / 38.4	36.2 / 28.3	**43.5** / 40.5	31.9 / 26.4
Office-3	19.2	20.2	15.9 / 14.9	14.5 / 13.9	18.2 / 19.2	**21.8** / 21.3
Restaurant-1	75.4	79.6	77.1 / 77.4	78.0 / 79.5	78.4 / 77.8	78.6 / **80.6**
Restaurant-2	83.6	82.0	81.3 / 76.3	83.5 / 81.5	83.4 / 83.9	**84.2** / 82.5
shop-floor-plan	88.0	**90.1**	88.8 / 88.5	88.0 / 87.3	89.3 / 89.2	88.5 / 88.6
shopping-mall-1	31.9	15.5	**34.2** / 25.9	29.0 / 17.3	23.1 / 21.3	29.0 / 19.6
shopping-mall-2	27.5	38.9	44.4 / 22.9	35.2 / 11.6	**45.7** / 14.5	38.8 / 20.4
Warehouse	74.8	74.7	74.5 / 74.5	75.5 / 76.6	67.9 / 67.8	76.9 / **77.7**
Avg across all	56.4	57.0	59.3 / 55.0	58.3 / 53.9	**60.0** / 56.4	58.6 / 55.1

5   Conclusions

We presented a novel network architecture, FGSSNet, for the segmentation of walls in floorplans. The model includes a multi-headed structure which injects domain-specific feature maps into the latent space of a U-Net backbone to guide the segmentation. The feature maps are extracted from selected wall patches, which are representative of the walls present in the input floorplan. Such a dedicated feature extractor is trained as an encoder-decoder to produce a compressed representation of the walls while jointly trained to predict the wall width. This is done to enforce the codification of texture and width features of the walls, which are then inserted into the main segmentation backbone. This is expected to provide domain-specific feature maps that guide and help the wall segmentation process.

As dataset, we used CubiCasa5k [12], which contains 5000 scanned floorplans with ground truth and pre-defined training, validation and test sets. We also added 10 additional floorplans from customers of the company participating in this work to test our developments in external real-world data. We observed that the extracted feature maps provided useful information which the segmentation backbone leveraged to improve segmentation compared to the vanilla U-Net. We also showed the importance of such feature maps by injecting constant patches instead of real wall patches, observing a consistent decrease in performance across different variants of our FGSSNet model when such artificial patches are employed. This reinforces the validity of the proposed approach, which involves injecting feature maps from selected good-quality wall patches into the main segmentation backbone.

Overall, our work presents advancements in wall segmentation in floorplans, showcasing additional improvements while providing detailed insights into the contributions of the injected feature maps through diverse experiments. While the current results show robust performance using a U-Net backbone and highlight the importance of realistic wall representations, several future directions could be explored. For example, we will focus on improving the utilization of the injected feature maps by refining the crop selection algorithm to improve the representativity of different wall types, which has been one of the observed drawbacks. Another direction to improve segmentation will also be the use of newer attention-based models like SegNeXt [8].

Acknowledgements. This work has been carried out by H. Norrby and G. Färm in the context of their Master Thesis at Halmstad University (Computer Science and Engineering). K. H.-D. and F. A.-F. thank the Swedish Research Council (VR) for funding their research.

References

1. Axis site designer. https://sitedesigner.axis.com. Accessed April 2024
2. Okorn, B., Xiong, X., A, B., Huber, D.: Toward automated modeling of floor plans. Proceedings of Symposium on 3D Data Processing Visualization and Transmission **2** (2010)
3. Wei, C., M.G., Czerniawski, T.: Automated wall detection in 2D CAD drawings to create digital 3D models. Symposium Automation and Robotics in Construct., ISARC (2022)
4. C. Wei, M.G., Czerniawski, T.: Interoperability between deep neural networks and 3D architectural modeling software: affordances of Detection and Segmentation. Buildings **13**(9) (2023)
5. Chen, L.C., Papandreou, G., Schroff, F., Adam, H.: Rethinking atrous convolution for semantic image segmentation (2017). https://arxiv.org/abs/1706.05587
6. Chen, L.C., Zhu, Y., Papandreou, G., Schroff, F., Adam, H.: Encoder-decoder with atrous separable convolution for semantic image segmentation. Proc, ECCV (2018)
7. Cheng, B., Schwing, A., Kirillov, A.: Per-pixel classification is not all you need for semantic segmentation. NeurIPS **34**, 17864–17875 (2021)
8. Guo, M.H., Lu, C.Z., Hou, Q., Liu, Z., Cheng, M.M., Hu, S.M.: Segnext: rethinking convolutional attention design for semantic segmentation. NeurIPS **35** (2022)
9. de las Heras, L., Terrades, O.R., Robles, S., Sánchez, G.: CVC-FP and SGT: a new database for structural floor plan analysis and its groundtruthing tool. Int. J. Doc. Analy. Recogn. IJDAR **18**, 15–30 (2015)
10. de las Heras, L., Valveny, E., Sánchez, G.: Unsupervised and notation-independent wall segmentation in floor plans using a combination of statistical and structural strategies. Proceedings International Workshop on Graphics Recognition, GREC (2014)
11. Huang, L., Wu, J.H., Wei, C., Li, W.: Muranet: multi-task floor plan recognition with relation attention. Proc. Document Analysis and Recogn, ICDAR (2023)
12. Kalerv, A., Ylioinas, J., Häikiö, M., Karhu, A., Kannala, J.: Cubicasa5k: a dataset and an improved multi-task model for floorplan image analysis. Proc, SCIA (2019)

13. Lewis, R., Sequin, C.: Generation of 3d building models from 2d architectural plans. Comput. Aided Des. **30**(10), 765–779 (1998)
14. Lv, X., Zhao, S., Yu, X., Zhao, B.: Residential floor plan recognition and reconstruction. Proc. IEEE/CVF Conf. Computer Vis. & Patt. Recog, CVPR (2021)
15. Or, S.H., Wong, K.H., Yu, Y.K., Chang, M.M.Y.: Highly automatic approach to architectural floorplan image understanding and model generation. Proc, VMV (2005)
16. Park, S., Kim, H.: 3dplannet: generating 3d models from 2d floor plan images using ensemble methods. Electronics **10**(22), 2729 (2021)
17. R. K. Moloo, M.A.S.D., Auleear, A.S.: 3-phase recognition approach to pseudo 3d building generation from 2d floor plan (2011). https://arxiv.org/abs/1107.3680
18. Ronneberger, O., Fischer, P., Brox, T.: U-net: convolutional networks for biomedical image segmentation. Proc, MICCAI (2015)
19. Shelhamer, E., Long, J., Darrell, T.: Fully convolutional networks for semantic segmentation. IEEE TPAMI **39**(4), 640–651 (2017)
20. Wei, L., Lai, C.: Wall segmentation in house plans: fusion of deep learning and traditional methods. The Visual Computer (2023)
21. Xie, E., Wang, W., Yu, Z., Anandkumar, A., Alvarez, J., Luo, P.: Segformer: simple and efficient design for semantic segmentation with transformers. NeurIPS **34** (2021)
22. Y. C. Chin, G. W. Chang, S.Y.C., Wang, H.L.: The average intensity of illumination and the power optimization. Proceedings APPEEC (2009)
23. Yi, J., Lee, J., Kim, K.J., Hwang, S.J., Yang, E.: Why not to use zero imputation? correcting sparsity bias in training neural networks. Proc, ICLR (2020)
24. Yuan, Y., et al.: Hrformer: high-resolution vision transformer for dense predict. NeurIPS **34** (2021)

Robust Frame Combination Strategies for License Plate Recognition in Video Sequences

Milton García-Borroto[1](✉) and Annette Morales-González[2]

[1] Centro de Sistemas Complejos, Facultad de Física, Universidad de La Habana, Habana, Cuba
milton.garcia@gmail.com
[2] Advanced Technologies Application Center (CENATAV), Habana, Cuba

Abstract. License Plate Recognition (LPR) in video sequences faces challenges such as motion blur, occlusions, and poor lighting. While most research focuses on detection and recognition, frame combination strategies remain mainly underexplored This paper introduces a novel segmentation-free plate recognizer that allows to estimate the confidence of each returned character together with an estimation of the network uncertainty. Evaluated on a challenging dataset of real-world Cuban plates with deformations and adverse conditions, we found combinations that outperforms traditional methods, achieving significant gains in accuracy for low-quality scenarios. These findings highlight the importance of temporal integration in video-based LPR systems.

Keywords: License plate recognition · frame combination · confidence weighting · uncertainty modeling · video processing

1 Introduction

The rapid advancement of computer vision technologies has enabled significant progress in intelligent transportation systems (ITS), with License Plate Recognition (LPR) emerging as a cornerstone application. LPR systems play a critical role in modern infrastructure, supporting applications such as traffic monitoring, automated toll collection, parking management, and law enforcement. Despite decades of research, LPR remains a challenging task due to real-world complexities such as varying lighting conditions, motion blur, occlusions, and low-quality plates.

While substantial efforts have been devoted to improving plate detection and character recognition–often leveraging deep learning models such as YOLO [5] and CNN-LSTM architectures [8–10]—a crucial yet underexplored aspect in video-based LPR is the temporal integration of information across frames. In contrast to single-image recognition, video sequences offer redundant observations of the same plate over time, which can be leveraged to enhance robustness

Y. Hernádez Heredia et al. (Eds.): IWAIPR 2025, LNCS 16328, pp. 52–63, 2026.
https://doi.org/10.1007/978-3-032-11358-0_5

and accuracy. This principle is well-established in other video understanding tasks, such as action recognition [6,19], where temporal modeling significantly improves performance under noisy or ambiguous conditions.

However, in the LPR domain, frame-level aggregation strategies remain largely simplistic and under-investigated. Common approaches include selecting the frame with the highest detection confidence [3] or applying majority voting over recognized plate strings [10]. These methods often ignore fine-grained character-level confidence, uncertainty estimates, or alignment variations across frames, limiting their effectiveness in challenging real-world scenarios. Moreover, while some works perform character-level fusion [15] or image-level super-resolution [17], there is a lack of systematic comparison and innovation in how temporal evidence should be combined—particularly when dealing with low-quality, small, or partially occluded plates.

In this paper, we address this gap by proposing and evaluating novel frame combination strategies that exploit both character-wise confidence and model uncertainty estimates derived from a segmentation-free recognition network. Our approach is designed to maximize the utility of temporal redundancy in video sequences, especially under adverse conditions where individual frames may be unreliable.

Our contributions are threefold:

- We introduce a segmentation-free plate recognizer that simultaneously outputs character predictions along with per-character confidence and uncertainty estimates, enabling more informed aggregation.
- We propose and evaluate multiple frame combination strategies—both plate-level and character-level—demonstrating their impact across different plate sizes and quality levels.
- We validate our methods on a real-world dataset of Cuban license plates captured under uncontrolled conditions, showing significant improvements over traditional aggregation techniques and off-the-shelf OCR tools.

2   Related Work

Prior work on license plate recognition has primarily focused on two areas: detection and recognition. For plate detection, most methods rely on object detection networks such as YOLO [5] and MobileNet [13]. These networks are trained to predict bounding boxes around plates. Since it could be perspective distortions caused by camera angles, detected plates often require transformation into undistorted planar images. One approach involves training a custom CNN to identify the plate region, followed by binarization, edge detection, and corner estimation to perform perspective correction [16]. Alternatively, some methods directly detect plate corners using a network that leverages spatial relationships between the license plate and the vehicle. However, this approach has limitations in applicability and achieves IOU=0.5 detection accuracy below 0.9, indicating room for improvement [4].

For plate recognition, there are mainly two approaches: segmentation-based and segmentation-free. In segmentation-based approaches, characters in the license plate are first segmented and then recognized individually. Segmentation can be performed using non-trainable techniques such as connected component analysis, projection methods, prior knowledge, and contour modeling [9]. Alternatively, trainable methods involve neural networks, often combining CNNs for feature extraction with LSTM models to capture temporal dependencies and patterns within character sequences [7]. Another approach uses trained object detectors like YOLO to directly detect individual characters in images [1]. Once segmented, characters are recognized using custom convolutional neural networks [9] or fine-tuned pre-trained networks like ResNet-50 [5].

Segmentation-free methods recognize characters directly from the entire plate image without explicit segmentation. These methods often leverage pre-trained OCR tools such as EasyOCR [13], Tesseract [18], or PaddleOCR [13]. Alternatively, recurrent networks like Bi-LSTM can be employed to process visual features extracted by CNNs across sliding windows, sometimes incorporating attention mechanisms to improve recognition accuracy [14,16].

Since frame combination strategies is the core of this paper, and it have received limited attention, we will perform a more detailed review. Frame combination strategies can be categorized in four categories: image combination, plate selection, plate fusion, and character fusion.

In image combination, all extracted plate images are merged into a single composite image. Recognition is then performed on this combined image. This method leverages the cumulative information from multiple frames, potentially improving accuracy by reducing noise or inconsistencies in individual frames. However, it relies heavily on the quality of the image fusion process, which can be sensitive to alignment issues or distortions [17]. While simple and effective in some scenarios, this approach may struggle with significant variations in plate appearance across frames.

In plate selection, recognition is performed only on the plate image that maximizes some metric, usually detection confidence. This method assumes that the most confidently detected plate is also the most reliable for recognition. It simplifies the recognition pipeline by focusing on a single high-quality input, reducing computational overhead. However, this approach risks discarding valuable information from other frames, particularly in cases where the highest-confidence plate is not necessarily the most accurate [3]. As a result, it may underperform in challenging scenarios with low-quality or ambiguous detections.

A more sophisticated approach is plate fusion, which involves performing recognition on every frame and combining the results into a single consolidated output. Several techniques exist for this purpose. One common method is to recognize plates in all frames and select the most frequently occurring result, effectively using majority voting to determine the final output [10]. Another approach involves calculating text similarity between recognized plates using edit-distance metrics. Plates are then clustered based on their similarity, and the result from the largest cluster is selected as the final output [2]. A variation of this technique, proposed in [15], introduces a custom aggregation procedure that incorporates all recognized plates to compute a consensus result, further enhancing robustness. These methods excel in scenarios with high variability across frames, as they leverage redundancy to improve accuracy.

Finally, character fusion takes a granular approach by performing recognition on a per-character basis across all frames. For each character position, the most frequently recognized character is selected to construct the final plate. This method is particularly effective when individual characters are consistently recognizable across frames but may vary in their overall arrangement or context [2,11]. By focusing on character-level consistency, this approach mitigates errors caused by misalignment or partial occlusions. However, it requires precise alignment of character positions across frames and may struggle with highly distorted or incomplete plates.

To the best of our knowledge, no prior work has systematically evaluated the impact of frame combination strategies on license plate recognition datasets. Existing studies typically propose combination methods that rely on information already extracted from other components of their respective pipelines.

3 Methodology

Our pipeline is composed by main components: plate detection, character recognition, and frame combination. Each one was designed to be efficient, accurate, and maximally informative. These components work together to extract as much data as possible, particularly to enhance the effectiveness of the frame combination process.

3.1 Plate Detection

For detecting the plate, we trained a YOLOv8 keypoint detector [8]. This is, in our experience, one of the fastest and more accurate keypoint detector. We manually labeled the keypoints of 223 images for training the model and 75 for evaluating the model. We perform a fine-tunning of the existing model yolov8s-pose.pt, provided by the Yolo authors. It is important to note that while YOLOv8 performs keypoint detection and geometric normalization, the core contribution of this work lies in the frame combination strategies applied after detection, which are independent of the detector used.

After the detection of keypoints, we obtain a planar image of the plate by applying a perspective warping from the detected keypoints to a fixed 200x100 box. The planar image is the result of the plate detection procedure.

This proposed detector is highly accurate, simple, and deliver undistorted images ready to be used in the remaining pipeline components.

3.2 Plate Recognition

After detecting and warping the license plate, we obtain an image where the characters are approximately aligned in fixed positions. This alignment is a result of the image transformation process and the standardized structure of Cuban license plates. The consistent layout enables us to adopt a segmentation-free recognition approach, where all characters are recognized simultaneously. Note that'segmentation-free' refers to the absence of character-level segmentation within the plate (i.e., no bounding boxes or contours for individual characters). Instead, the entire plate image is processed as a single input, and the network outputs character probabilities per fixed position using a multi-head architecture.

To achieve this, we designed a custom convolutional neural network (CNN). The network consists of a convolutional module followed by multiple recognition modules (linear layers), each corresponding to a specific character position in the license plate. The convolutional module, shown in Figure 2, comprises four residual blocks (Figure 1) that extract visual features for recognition. Each recognition module processes these features to predict the probabilities of candidate characters for its respective position. In accordance with the structure of Cuban plates, the first recognition module identifies a letter (from the set of permissible letters in Cuban plates), while the remaining modules recognize digits.

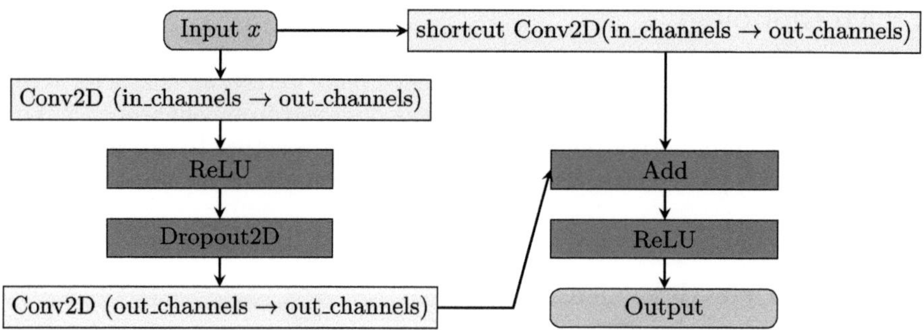

Fig. 1. Residual Block(in_channels, out_channels) module structure.

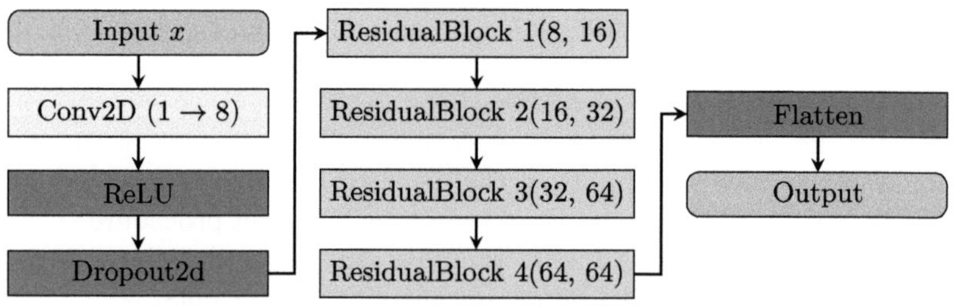

Fig. 2. SharedLayers module using with Residual Blocks.

To train the network, we use the total character-wise loss as the objective function, where the loss for each character is computed using cross-entropy loss

$(\mathcal{L} = \sum_{i=1}^{7} \mathcal{L}_{CE}(y_i, \hat{y}_i))$. The network was trained using a dataset of planar plate images along with their corresponding ground-truth license plate labels. The model converged after approximately 80 epochs, with validation loss plateauing and character accuracy stabilizing above 95%.

The important characteristic of the obtained network is that we obtain, for each position in the plate, the probability of each possible character. This allows more information to combine between different images of the same plate, helping to distinguish between very similar characters. This can be even more important on plates that have low quality or scratches that alter the characters in some degree.

Another important characteristic of the proposed architecture is that we can use it to estimate character uncertainty. In the context of supervised classification, uncertainty is related to confidence, but are distinct concepts. Confidence refers to how certain the network is about its prediction. It typically represents the probability assigned by the model to its predicted class or output. on the other hand, uncertainty quantifies the degree of trustworthiness or reliability of the model's predictions. It captures the model's awareness of its own limitations and the variability in the data. In plate recognition, for example, confidence meassure how different the recognized character is with respect to other candidate characters while uncertainty meassure how probable is the result to be similar if the input image is slightly changed.

For estimating uncertainty we use dropout modules (in the residual block). This technique is know as Monte Carlo dropout [12]. The idea of Monte Carlo dropout is to use dropout modules, which are traditionally used only while training the network, also in the exploitation of the network. These modules randomly shut down some connections in the network, so repeated classifications of the same input image can return different outputs. Slow variations on the outputs can then be interpreted as low uncertainty on the network output.

3.3 Frame Combination Strategies

In this paper, we explore the impact of different combination strategies for license plate recognition in video sequences. Each strategy combines in certain way part of the available information that we extract from every processed frame. The available information for each character on each processed frame is:

- Confidences for each candidate value. For the first character is the probability of allowed letters and for the last six character is the probability of each digit. This is the value returned by the network, that is interpreted as a probability.
- Uncertainty of the recognition, estimated using Monte Carlo dropout using 20 executions of the network. Uncertainty is estimated as the coefficient of variation $(CV = \frac{\sigma}{\mu})$ of the returned confidences. Lower values of CV are related to characters that has lower uncertainties.

We define two types of aggregation methods, those who select between recognized plates, and those who selects from individual characters. Plate aggregation methods considered are the following:

MRP, max repeated plate The plate more times found in the sequence is
   returned.
MaPTC, max plate total confidence The confidence of each plate is estimated by adding the maximum confidences of all of its characters. The plate
   with maximum total confidence is returned.
MePTC, mean plate total confidence Similar to MaPTC, but the mean of
   confidences per plate is used instead of maximum value.
MiPCV, minimal plate total CV The uncertainty of each plate is estimated
   by the maximum uncertainty among all its characters. The plate with minimum total uncertainty is returned.

The rationale of these methods is the following. MRP prioritizes plates that
are recognized in more frames, but since we do not control the process of taking
the images, there can be more pictures taken in a location where the image has
less quality (the direct sunlight in the plate, for example). The idea of MaPTC
is then prioritizing the plate where we are more confident about. MePTC is
based on the idea that taking the maximum can make the recognizer brittle by
depending on a single frame. Finally, MiPTCV try to find the best plate by using
the uncertainty instead of the confidence.

Character aggregation methods considered is the following:

SMCC, Select Max Confident Character. This method aggregates all the
confidences of all the characters in all the plates. Then it generates the more
probable plate (formed by the most probable character on each position).

The idea of individual character selection is supported by the fact that there
are plate sequences where no single recognized plate is correct, but in all plates
at least one time the correct character is found for each character position.

4   Experimental Results and Discussion

In this paper, we introduce a new license plate dataset. We use an already
existing video camera installed in the entrance of a parking place. The camera is
a standard surveillance camera instead a high speed traffic camera, so the quality
of images is significantly lower than what appear in some other datasets[1].

The recorded videos capture vehicles approaching the payment area, pausing
or slowing down to pay, and then exiting (Figure 3a). Since the time each vehicle
spends in front of the camera varies, the number of frames per vehicle differs
significantly. we filtered out images captured when vehicles were stationary, significantly reducing the dataset size. The parking environment also introduces
diverse conditions, including varying angles, distances, and lighting (Figure 3b).

The final dataset consists of 4117 sequences from 3360 unique cars, split into
training, validation, and testing subsets while ensuring no car's plates appeared

---

[1] Due to privacy regulations and institutional policies, the raw video data cannot be
made public. However, anonymized plate images and metadata (without vehicle or
personal identifiers) can be shared upon request for research purposes.

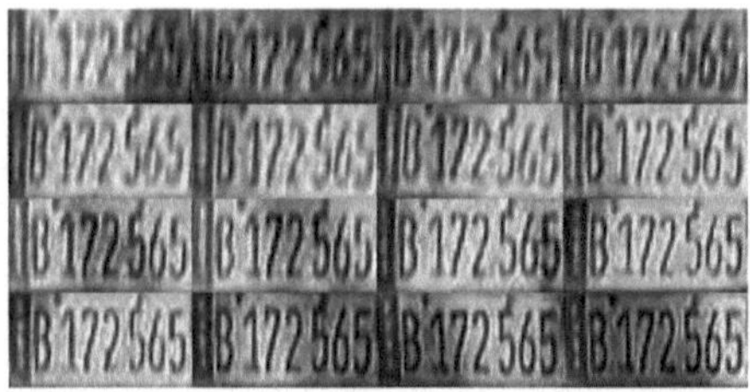

(a) A sequence of plate images. Note that the image quality is improved while the car is approaching the camera

(b) A sequence of captured plates with different lighting conditions

(c) Low-quality plates

Fig. 3. Plate examples in the dataset.

in more than one category. This resulted in 2943 sequences for training, 621 for validation, and 553 for testing. Additionally, we collected 553 sequences of vehicles with low-quality plates (e.g., deformations, scratches, or faded characters), focusing exclusively on plate-related issues rather than image capture or lighting problems (Figure 3)c.

There are significant differences between the test dataset and the low quality dataset. First, in terms of video sequences where at least one recognized plate is correct, the test dataset achieves 99.51%, while the low-quality dataset reaches 93.30%, resulting in a difference of approximately 6%. This value represents the upper limit for any aggregation method based on selecting plates.

Next, the percentage of total correct plate recognitions highlights a more significant gap between the datasets. The test dataset achieves 89.41%, whereas the low-quality dataset performs considerably worse at 63.81%, reflecting a difference of around 26%. This indicates that the individual plate quality is substantially lower in the low-quality dataset.

For video sequences where all characters are recognized correctly at least once across plates, the test dataset achieves 99.88%, and the low-quality dataset reaches 99.14%. The difference here is minimal, suggesting that character selection methods may have an advantage over plate selection methods. Since this metric represents the maximum achievable performance for character selection, its near-perfect values across both datasets support the hypothesis that character-based approaches could outperform plate-based ones.

Finally, we split plates according to the size of the original image in the detected frame in three subsets: small (around minimal plate size), medium (around half the size of largest), and large (around largest size). This allows to differentiate the results for different plate sizes.

4.1 Comparison of Frame Combination Strategies

Results for the test dataset appear in Table 1a. The best results are achieved by the method based on the maximum confidence of the plate for large and medium size plates. For medium and small plates, the character-based combination gets better results. This shows that the smaller the plate, so the less information is available for the recognizer, the better the character based method performs. Taking the most repeated plate gets results very close to the best one for all the plate sizes. In general, for large plates, the accuracy is very close to 1, so the recognition is perfect.

Results for low quality dataset appear in Table 1b. We can see, first, the significant degradation of the quality of each method. In this case, taking the most repeated plate is the best for large and small plates, while for medium plates is the maximum confidence aggregator. For small plates, the character based recognizer gets also best results. The behavior of the method based purely on uncertainty was not good in any configuration.

Table 1. Comparison of accuracy for different aggregation procedures

(a) Test dataset

Name	Large	Medium	Small
MRP	0.974	0.971	0.855
MaPTC	**0.984**	**0.974**	0.851
MePTC	0.918	0.911	0.704
MiPCV	0.958	0.948	0.769
SMCC	0.979	**0.974**	**0.863**

(b) Low quality dataset

Name	Large	Medium	Small
MRP	**0.804**	0.786	**0.531**
MaPTC	0.799	**0.793**	0.518
MePTC	0.692	0.694	0.417
MiPCV	0.743	0.721	0.437
SMCC	0.788	0.779	**0.531**

Results of the comparison of the state of the art OCR methods with the two most accurate proposed combinations appear in Table 2a for the test dataset and in Table 2b for the low quality dataset. We tested the three more cited OCR methods for plate recognition: EasyOCR, PaddleOCR, and TessractOCR. For using the temporal information present in the videos, we tested two variants: the most repeated plate (suffixed with _rep in tables) and the aggregation procedure introduced in [15] (suffixed with _partial in tables). Results show that the proposed methods clearly outperforms OCR based methods in any configuration by a large margin. The difference is more appreciable for small plates and for low quality datasets. This result is expected for two main reasons: the neural network we used is trained in similar plates while OCR are general, and the proposed methods try to match the image with their model of characters and always return a result. On the other hand, if the character is not clear, the OCR avoids the detection.

With respect to execution times, we evaluate all the methods executed in the same CPU without any particular optimization. The evaluation was performed in the training sample, which is larger. Recognition times for 1000 plate images are the following: MaPTC: 1.95 s, PaddleOCR: 31.36 s, TesseractOCR: 135.1, and EasyOCR: 564.1 s.

The experimental comparison reveals several interesting findings. First, the proposed combination methods, despite leveraging more comprehensive character information, did not significantly outperform the simple strategy of selecting the most repeated detected plate. Second, character selection methods were not clearly superior to plate selection methods, contrary to expectations. As shown in the dataset description, the correct character for every position was almost always present in at least one detected plate, suggesting that the character selection strategy requires further refinement. Third, uncertainty alone does not suffice to create a better selector, highlighting the need to explore more effective ways to integrate this information with other metrics. Fourth, training a custom detection network significantly improves recognition accuracy compared to using a general OCR, particularly for low-quality and small plates. Finally, neural network-based recognizers are substantially faster than OCRs, even for small input images.

Table 2. Comparison with state of the art OCR methods

(a) Test dataset

Method	Large	Medium	Small
easyocr_max_rep	0.746	0.714	0.073
easyocr_partial	0.711	0.680	0.078
paddle_max_rep	0.766	0.737	0.081
paddle_partial	0.653	0.638	0.071
tesseract_max_rep	0.746	0.714	0.073
tesseract_partial	0.711	0.680	0.078
MaPTC	**0.984**	**0.974**	0.851
SMCC	0.979	0.974	**0.863**

(b) Low quality dataset

Method	Large	Medium	Small
easyocr_max_rep	0.290	0.255	0.007
easyocr_partial	0.324	0.281	0.009
paddle_max_rep	0.361	0.315	0.011
paddle_partial	0.301	0.257	0.011
tesseract_max_rep	0.290	0.255	0.007
tesseract_partial	0.324	0.281	0.009
MaPTC	**0.799**	**0.793**	0.518
SMCC	0.788	0.779	**0.531**

5   Conclusion

In this work, we addressed the critical yet underexplored challenge of frame combination in video-based License Plate Recognition (LPR). By estimating more information about recognized characters, included uncertainty, we demonstrated how temporal redundancy across frames can be effectively leveraged to improve robustness and accuracy, particularly in challenging scenarios like low-quality plates in light changing conditions. Our experiments on a real-world Cuban license plate dataset revealed significant performance gains over traditional methods, underscoring the importance of advanced aggregation strategies. Overall, our findings pave the way for more robust and scalable LPR systems in dynamic environments.

This study highlights the potential of uncertainty modeling and temporal integration in LPR systems, offering practical solutions for real-world applications in intelligent transportation systems. Future work could include evaluating the results on other datasets, and testing more complex ways to fuse the available information in order to improve the quality of the results. Two particular hypothesis we had in the beginning could not be proved: character based aggregation could outperform full plate aggregation and taking into account the uncertainty can improve the results. Trying to verify these two hypotheses will guide our future work.

To ensure reproducibility, the source code for the proposed methods will be made publicly available upon publication.

Acknowledgments. We would like to thank our colleagues Jan Schlüter and Andreas Bossert from the HAWK (Germany) for their support.

References

1. Al-batat, R., Angelopoulou, A., Premkumar, S., Hemanth, J., Kapetanios, E.: An end-to-end automated license plate recognition system using yolo based vehicle and license plate detection with vehicle classification. Sensors **22**(23), 9477 (2022). https://doi.org/10.3390/s22239477
2. Alghyaline, S.: Real-time Jordanian license plate recognition using deep learning. J. King Saud Univ. Comput. Inf. Sci. **34**(6), 2601–2609 (2022)
3. Ashrafee, A., Khan, A.M., Irbaz, M.S., Nasim, M.A.A.: Real-time bangla license plate recognition system for low resource video-based applications. In: 2022 IEEE/CVF WACVW, pp. 479–488. IEEE (2022)
4. Chen, S.L., et al.: End-to-end trainable network for degraded license plate detection via vehicle-plate relation mining. Neurocomputing **446**, 1–10 (2021)
5. Chopade, R., et al.: Automatic number plate recognition: a deep dive into YOLOv8 and ResNet-50 integration. In: 2024 International Conference on Integrated Circuits and Communication Systems (ICICACS), pp. 1–8. IEEE, Raichur, India (2024). https://doi.org/10.1109/ICICACS60521.2024.10498318
6. Feichtenhofer, C., Fan, H., Malik, J., He, K.: Slowfast networks for video recognition. In: Proceedings of the IEEE/CVF international conference on computer vision, pp. 6202–6211 (2019)

7. G, K., E, P., S, A., V, D.: An efficient deep learning approach for automatic license plate detection with novel feature extraction. Procedia Comput. Sci. **235**, 2822–2832 (2024). https://doi.org/10.1016/j.procs.2024.04.267

8. Gheorghe, C., Duguleana, M., Boboc, R.G., Postelnicu, C.C.: Analyzing real-time object detection with yolo algorithm in automotive applications: a review. Comput. Model. Eng. Sci. **141**(3), 1939–1981 (2024). https://doi.org/10.32604/cmes.2024.054735

9. Hasan, S., Sunny, M.N.M., Nahian, A.A., Yasin, M.: Neural network-powered license plate recognition system design. Engineering **16**(09), 284–300 (2024). https://doi.org/10.4236/eng.2024.169021

10. Hashmi, S.N., Kumar, K., Khandelwal, S., Lochan, D., Mittal, S.: Real Time License Plate Recogn. Video Streams using Deep Learn. Int. J. Inf. Retrieval Res. **9**, 65–87 (2019)

11. Laroca, R., et al.: A robust real-time automatic license plate recognition based on the YOLO detector. In: 2018 International Joint Conference on Neural Networks (IJCNN), pp. 1–10. IEEE, Rio de Janeiro, Brazil (2018)

12. Lemay, A., et al.: Improving the repeatability of deep learning models with monte carlo dropout. NPJ Digit. Med. **5**(1), 174 (2022)

13. Mustafa, T., Karabatak, M.: Real time car model and plate detection system by using deep learning architectures. IEEE Access **12**, 107616–107630 (2024). https://doi.org/10.1109/ACCESS.2024.3430857

14. Pirgazi, J., Pourhashem Kallehbasti, M.M., Ghanbari Sorkhi, A.: An end-to-end deep learning approach for plate recognition in intelligent transportation systems. Wirel. Commun. Mob. Comput. **2022**, 1–13 (2022). https://doi.org/10.1155/2022/3364921

15. Quiala, C., García-Borroto, M., Sánchez-Rivero, R., Morales-González, A.: Enhancing License Plate Recognition in Videos Through Character-Wise Temporal Combination. In: Hernández Heredia, Y., Milián Núñez, V., Ruiz Shulcloper, J. (eds.) Progress in Artificial Intelligence and Pattern Recognition, vol. 14335, pp. 400–411. Springer Nature Switzerland, Cham (2024)

16. Rao, Z., Yang, D., Chen, N., Liu, J.: CCVIA a new image correction scheme and improved CRNN. Expert Syst. Appl. **243**, 122878 (2024)

17. Seibel, H., Goldenstein, S., Rocha, A.: Eyes on the target: super-resolution and license-plate recognition in low-quality surveillance videos. IEEE Access **5**, 20020–20035 (2017)

18. Vijendar Reddy, G., et al.: A comprehensive review on helmet detection and number plate recognition approaches. E3S Web of Conf. **507**, 01075 (2024). https://doi.org/10.1051/e3sconf/202450701075

19. Wang, X., et al.: Molo: motion-augmented long-short contrastive learning for few-shot action recognition. In: Proceedings of the IEEE/CVF conference on computer vision and pattern recognition, pp. 18011–18021 (2023)

[illegible] R. P., V. D.: An efficient [illegible] algorithm for [illegible] automatic calibration of a [illegible]. [illegible] Procedia Comput. Sci. [illegible] (2011)
[illegible]
[illegible]

Natural Language Processing and Generative AI

Generation of Software Requirements from User Feedback Combining ML and LLMs

Ray Maestre Peña[1] ⓘ, Alfredo Simón-Cuevas[1](✉) ⓘ, Francisco P. Romero[2] ⓘ, and José A. Olivas[2] ⓘ

[1] Universidad Tecnológica de La Habana José Antonio Echeverría, CUJAE, Ave. 114, e/Rotonda y Ciclovía, Marianao, La Habana, Cuba
asimon@ceis.cujae.edu.cu
[2] Universidad de Castilla-La Mancha, Ciudad Real, Spain
{FranciscoP.Romero,JoseAngel.olivas}@uclm.es

Abstract. Extracting knowledge from digital social platforms is a new trend in software requirements engineering. The feedback generated by users in these environments is a very valuable source of needs, demands, dissatisfactions, and judgments about the software applications they use. The effectively processing of this volume of information for predicting the software product evolution is a great challenge, which can start from determining the most relevant contents, to the automatic elicitation of new requirements for that product. This paper proposes a method for generating software requirements from user feedback. This solution combines Deep Learning models for determining the relevant information, with an LLM (Large Language Model) to generate functional and non-functional requirements about a software and specific aspects from the feedback. This solution was evaluated using datasets of opinions from 4 different applications. The results were very promising, because they showed improvements over other reported solutions, and demonstrated that with a proper conception of information filtering and specification of interests through the prompt it is possible to generate good quality requirements using LLMs from an informal information source.

Keywords: software requirements generation · pre-trained Transformer models · Large Language Models

1 Introduction

Requirements Engineering (RE) has traditionally involved users through interviews, workshops, focus groups, and surveys to capture relevant information about software applications [15]. However, as the market becomes more competitive, software development companies (particularly those developing mobile applications) strive to secure a place in users' preferences [20]. Therefore, analyzing application quality through the lens of user experiences and identifying their dissatisfactions and needs, has become crucial for the success of such companies [25]. User feedback generated on app distribution platforms (Apple App Store, Google Play, and others) or social media is a highly valuable information source that can drive software product evolution and improvement [21]. From this content, new requirements, errors, and relevant assessments about application functionality quality can be identified, as well as prioritize requirements [8, 16, 18].

This scenario has led to the emergence of Data-Driven Requirements Engineering (DDRE) [6, 15]. Such approaches represent a decision-making strategy based on data analysis, interpretation, and prediction. In this work, this concept is contextualized as leveraging the vast amounts of data embedded in user reviews to guide developers' decisions about which requirements to include in their systems or which elements to consider for maintenance and support. The sheer volume of such content significantly hinders the adoption of this new approach without computational processing [27]. This has driven growing interest in applying Machine Learning (ML), Natural Language Processing (NLP), and Large Language Models (LLMs) in RE [5, 11].

One of the major challenges to address is the identification of relevant information within the vast volume of user reviews. According to the literature reviewed, 50–70% of user reviews lack relevance for application developers [4, 14, 28]. Relevant review identification has been addressed through various ML and NLP techniques [2, 4, 7, 9, 10, 17, 19, 22, 26]. LLMs now also are being employed to address other challenges including: requirements generation, documentation and specification, as well as their prioritization and validation [1, 11, 13, 29].

This work proposes a method for automatically generating software requirements from user reviews by combining ML techniques and LLMs. The solution employs pre-trained Transformer-based models to identify "informative" reviews, which are then clustered via the Fuzzy c-means (FCM) algorithm to identify related content that guides requirements generation. In the Transformer implementation, is proposed a knowledge injection mechanism for such architectures, yielding promising results. Requirements generation is accomplished using an LLM with a purpose-designed prompt. The solution was evaluated using review datasets from four distinct applications: Facebook (social application), Tap Fish (casual game), SwiftKey (smart keyboard application), and Temple Run 2 (parkour game). The results demonstrated improvements over other reported solutions and proved that with proper design of review filtering and organization, along with a well-structured prompt, LLMs can generate high-quality requirements from informal information sources.

The paper is structured as follows: Sect. 2 synthesizes related work; Sect. 3 details the proposed solution; Sect. 4 presents experimental results and a case study; and Sect. 5 concludes.

2   Related Works

Chen et al. pioneered the classification of relevant opinions, who used a bag-of-words representation combined with the Expectation-Maximization for Naïve Bayes (EMNB) algorithm, reporting that only approximately 35% of opinions were relevant [4]. A similar approach was followed in [26], where, in addition to identifying relevant opinions, they classified them by intent as either (1) bug reports or (2) feature requests/improvements, using Random Forest (RF). Williams and Mahmoud found that only 51% of the analyzed opinions contained useful information, indicating that a significant subset of user feedback remains underutilized [28]. Subsequent works [4, 7] suggests performing classification at the sentence level (rather than the review level) to enable multi-label tagging. Milián et al. proposed leveraging domain knowledge (e.g., a dictionary of software requirements-related terms) to improve the selection of relevant features and the classification of opinion relevance [19]. By comparing multiple classification algorithms, they achieved an F1-score > 90%, outperforming previous approaches.

Aslam et al. proposed a convolutional neural network (CNN)-based model for classifying app reviews, concluding that their approach significantly outperforms state-of-the-art machine learning techniques [2]. Similar results were reported in [23], who incorporated an embedding layer to extract syntactic features, followed by a combination of convolutional and recurrent neural network layers to identify relevant details in the opinions. Mekala et al. developed a BERT-based (Bidirectional Encoder Representations from Transformers) sequence classifier, achieving state-of-the-art average classification accuracy (87%) for opinion analysis [17]. A similar approach was proposed in [10], who demonstrated that monolingual BERT models outperform existing machine learning methods in classifying English app reviews. Finally, Hadi and Fard conducted a study comparing traditional machine learning approaches to pre-trained models (BERT, ALBERT, RoBERTa, and XLNet) [9]. Their experiments across seven datasets showed that pre-trained models consistently achieved superior results, with ALBERT and RoBERTa exhibiting the highest stability.

On the other hand, the use of LLMs (Large Language Models) to support Requirements Engineering (RE) has recently increased, particularly for generating requirements, documentation, specifications, prioritization, and validation [1, 11, 13, 29]. Krishna et al. investigated GPT-4 and CodeLlama to generate complete Software Requirements Specification (SRS) documents [13]. Given a problem description, the models produced all elements of an SRS (including functional and non-functional requirements), using a case study of a university club management web portal. The problem description provided to the models included details such as: involved roles and their responsibilities in the system. Zhao et al. generated software requirements from keywords using an LLM, enhanced with domain knowledge injection and syntactic constraints (to reduce hallucinations) [29]. Domain knowledge was injected via a domain ontology to capture entity relationships, which was then used to fine-tune the model. During generation, they enforced the inclusion of user-provided keywords in the final requirements. Arora, Grundy, and Abdelrazek focused on leveraging LLMs as assistive tools to identify unforeseen or overlooked requirements, providing example prompts for this purpose—though tailored to users with specific characteristics [1].

3 Software Requirements Generation Method

The proposed method was conceived in three phases: (1) Filtering/Classification, (2) Thematic Clustering, and (3) Requirements Generation. The quality of the generated requirements hinges critically on the informativeness of the input opinions. Thus, the first phase implements a filtering mechanism to detect Informative Opinions (IOs) and remove non-informative ones, employing a BERTweet pre-trained Transformers. The second phase clusters opinions addressing the same theme or topic, reducing redundancy and grouping semantically similar feedbacks. Finally, functional and non-functional requirements are generated from each cluster applying an LLM. Figure 1 illustrates this process.

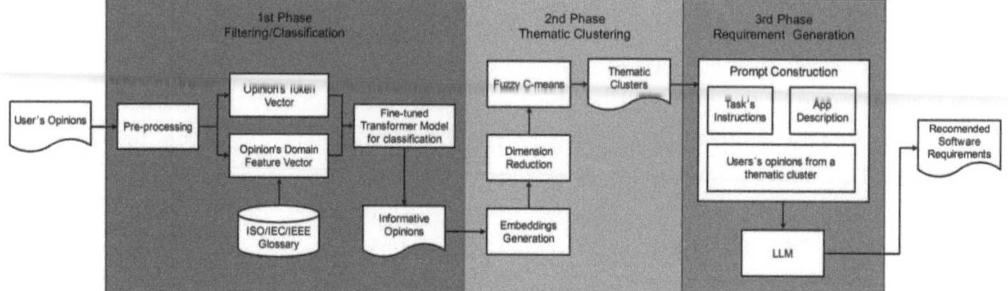

Fig. 1. Overview of the software requirements generation pipeline.

3.1 Filtering/Classification

The goal of this phase is to determine which opinions are informative (IOs), in order to eliminate those that do not provide relevant content for the generation of requirements. IOs are those whose content are related to the software domain. IOs are identified using BERTweet-base, fine-tuned for this task to adapt it to this specific problem. Additionally, a domain knowledge injection mechanism in the Transformer model is proposed, in order to integrate features of the most relevant tokens related to the software domain before the final classifier. This knowledge is derived from a formalized vocabulary of ISO/IEC/IEEE 24765:2017 [12].

3.1.1 Preprocessing

Each opinion is tokenized using the tokenizer of the Transformer model. The tokenizer was set to output 200 tokens, deemed appropriate for processing the target opinions. To enforce this size, the tokenizer's padding (extending with special tokens) and truncation (cutting exceeding tokens) options were activated. During preprocessing, in addition to generating the opinion's token vector, a domain feature vector is constructed. This feature vector, central to domain knowledge injection into the Transformer, constitutes a key contribution of this work. The construction of this feature vector applies the vocabulary from the ISO/IEC/IEEE 24765 standard [12]. This work investigated two approaches for constructing the feature vector from the vocabulary: (1) relevant term count-based (RC vector) and (2) relevant term position-based (RP vector). The generated feature vector always matches the maximum input size of the Transformer model.

The RC vector is constructed based on the quantity of glossary terms present in the opinion. It identifies both isolated words and compound phrases where individual components exist in the glossary, reinforcing their value (e.g., "access" and "method" in "access method"). The resulting scalar is then expanded into a fixed-size vector by replicating the count across all dimensions. This dimensional expansion mitigates the dilution effect in high-dimensional spaces, ensuring significant contribution to the final classification layer. This strategy introduces an inductive bias associating domain-specific term density with opinion informativeness. This approach hinges on the hypothesis that technically dense comments exhibit greater domain-specific novelty, making them more valuable for requirements capture by software development and support teams. In contrast, the RP vector is a binary vector initialized with zeros. When a vocabulary term is identified in the opinion, the corresponding vector position is set to 1, while non-matching terms remain 0.

3.1.2 IOs Classification

The identification of IOs is carried out through a classification process, using a pre-trained Transformer BERTweet. For fine-tuning, a single output class was set in the final classification layer, through a linear classification layer with sigmoid activation to compress the output into the [0, 1] range, similar to the approach reported in [3]. This output is interpreted as the probability of belonging to the "informative" class. The domain knowledge represented in the features vector is incorporated into the prediction model before the classification layer. This feature vector is concatenated with the Transformer model's output vector after opinion processing. The resulting concatenated vector serves as input to the final classification layer. The classification threshold is implemented such that opinions with model confidence scores ≥ 0.5 are retained as 'informative', while all others ($p < 0.5$) are filtered out as 'non-informative'.

3.2 Thematic Clustering

After identifying opinions that may contain valuable insights for development teams and the formulation of new requirements, it becomes necessary to determine the key aspects on which users have focused their evaluations. The previous stage successfully filters out noisy or irrelevant data concerning requirements. However, the set of opinions (OI) may still retain a heterogeneous mix of information, which could hinder the effectiveness of requirement generation via the LLM. To address this issue, it was decided to employ a clustering algorithm to detect related opinions, which will then guide the LLM-based workflow.

The clustering of opinions was performed using the FCM (Fuzzy C-Means) algorithm, chosen for its ability to handle partial memberships across multiple clusters—a necessary feature to mitigate ambiguity effects in the opinion dataset. This algorithm was applied to the contextual embeddings derived from each opinion using the BERTweet-base model, with Euclidean distance employed as the similarity metric, as it demonstrated better performance compared to cosine similarity. The embeddings (768-dimensional vectors) were then processed using PCA (Principal Component Analysis) to reduce their dimensionality to 2 dimensions, empirical validation confirmed that this configuration yielded higher clustering quality compared to other evaluated dimensions (2, 5, 10, 20, 50, and 100). This decision was supported by preliminary assessments using the Silhouette Coefficient [24] as a clustering quality measure. Additionally, thematic coherence within clusters was validated by extracting the 10 most representative terms per cluster, obtained by constructing a TF-IDF (Term Frequency-Inverse Document Frequency) feature vector for each cluster. The optimal number of clusters was determined to be $K = 11$, based on experiments testing K values ranging from 10 to 50.

3.3 Requirements Generation

Requirements are automatically generated by an LLM, using the thematic clusters obtained as contextual input. By leveraging these clusters (opinions addressing the same topics), the LLM can be better guided during the generation process, reducing the risk of hallucinations. The LLM adopted was DeepSeek V3[1] (demonstrated the most promising results), although Qwen-1.5B[2] was also assessed. The design of the prompt used for querying the LLM is crucial in this type of solution. A structured prompt was developed incorporating two dynamic elements: (1) application description (brief description of the target software's current functionality) and (2) an opinion cluster (a set of user opinions addressing the same software aspects).

The prompt implements key good practices including:

- Decomposing the task into stages: contextualization, requirement classification (Functional/Non-Functional), and SMART formulation (Specific, Measurable, Achievable, Relevant, and Time-bound).
- Quality criteria enforcement: atomicity, metric specificity (response times, file sizes), traceability to source comments, and technical aspect coverage.
- Inclusion of examples serving as both syntactic patterns (requirement structure) and semantic templates (expected meaning and detail level).

This approach ensures the model follows a clear, consistent format for requirement generation. The output requirements adhere to a standardized Markdown format, that clearly separates functionality from quality attributes, with explicit references to source comments. Below shows the structure of the proposed prompt, demonstrated through a case study example from the SwiftKey dataset to be used in the evaluation:

---

[1] https://huggingface.co/deepseek-ai/DeepSeek-V3.

[2] https://huggingface.co/deepseek-ai/DeepSeek-R1-Distill-Qwen-1.5B.

 # Application Context
This is an app named SwiftKey that offers an alternative keyboard for your smartphone
 # User Comments to Analyze
Cluster with 28 opinions (see evaluation section)
 # Required Task
Analyze the comments methodically to extract specific software requirements by following these steps:
*1. **Contextualization**:*
–   Relate each comment to the application's current functionalities (from the provided context)
–   Identify implicit/explicit needs
*2. **Classification**:*
–   Label as [Functional] or [Non-Functional] (use this nomenclature)
–   For non-functional: specify type (performance, security, usability, etc.)
*3. **Requirement Formulation**:*
–   Use SMART format: Specific, Measurable, Actionable, Relevant, Time-bound
–   Structure: "The system shall [action] [condition/criteria]"
–   Include reference to the source comment (e.g., "Based on Comment #3")
 # Guiding Example:
[Comment]: "The app freezes when exporting large reports"
[Requirement]: "[Non-Functional - Performance] The system shall process export files >500MB in less than 15 seconds (Based on Comment #12)"
 # Quality Criteria
*–   **Atomicity**: 1 requirement per feature*
*–   **Specificity**: Include verifiable metrics/criteria*
*–   **Traceability**: Link each requirement to specific comments*
*–   **Completeness**: Cover functional and quality aspects*
 # Required Output Format
```markdown
Functional Requirements
o   [FR-XX] [SMART description]
*o   **Source:** Comment #X*
Non-Functional Requirements
o   [NFR-XX] [Category] [SMART description]
*o   **Source:** Comment #X*

4   Evaluation and Discussion

The evaluation process focused on assessing the quality of IOs prediction, because it is a fundamental part of the requirements generation. However, various alternatives of thematic clustering were also evaluated, as well as the use of LLMs for final-stage requirement generation. In this process the datasets proposed in [4] was employed. Each dataset comprises 3,000 English-language Google Play reviews, tagged with 'informative' or 'non-informative' labels. The datasets contain reviews of four different applications: Facebook, Tap Fish, SwiftKey, and Temple Run 2 [4] (See Table 1). Five pre-trained models: RoBERTa, ALBERT, BERTweet, XLNet, and GPT-2 were evaluated. The models were trained for 2 epochs, consistent with the approach reported in [10] (additional testing with more epochs did not improve results). BCE Loss (Binary Cross Entropy Loss) was used as the loss function and AdamW as the optimizer (See Table 2 for full hyperparameter details). The results of the proposed method were computed using accuracy, precision, recall, and F1-score metrics, under a 5-fold cross-validation scheme. Table 3 presents the experimental results. The RoBERTa and BERTweet models stood out, demonstrating stable F1-Score values exceeding 0,93 in all datasets, with averages of 0,943 and 0,948, respectively. Based on these results, RoBERTa and BERTweet were selected to evaluate domain knowledge injection through the feature vector (RC) in the IOs prediction task (See Table 3).

Table 1. Characterization of the datasets

Datasets	Informative	No Informative
Facebook	1665 (55,5%)	1335
Tap Fish	828 (27,6%)	2172
SwiftKey	888 (29,6%)	2112
TempleRun	933 (31,1%)	2067

Table 2. Training hyperparameters of the Transformers models

Hyperparameters	Values
batch	16
learning rate	2e-5
epochs	2
max_len	200
weight_decay	0.001
warmup	0.2

As evidenced by the results, incorporating domain knowledge into the Transformer model contributes to a slight improvement in prediction effectiveness. In the case of RoBERTa, performance improved in 3 out of 4 datasets (with the exception of SwiftKey), along with a marginal increase in its overall average. BERTweet exhibited similar behavior, showing improvements for Facebook and SwiftKey while maintaining identical results for TapFish. Additional experiments using feature vectors based on relevant term positioning (RP) were conducted, but the results did not outperform the term-counting approach. Although the performance improvement through knowledge injection was not statistically significant, the consistent positive trend is encouraging and suggests

Table 3. Results of the IOs prediction task, according to F1-Score.

Id	Transformers	Facebook	SwiftKey	Tap Fish	Templerun2	Ave
1	*GPT2 - base*	0,885	0,838	0,817	0,824	0,841
2	*ALBERT-large*	0,883	0,893	0,885	0,879	0,885
3	*XLNet-base*	0,836	0,909	0,927	0,919	0,898
4	*RoBERTa-base*	0,931	0,945	0,950	0,950	0,943
5	*RoBERTa + RC*	0,933	0,937	0,956	0,951	0,944
6	*BERTweet-base*	0,930	0,948	**0,960**	**0,957**	0,948
7	*BERTweet + RC*	**0,934**	**0,952**	**0,960**	0,955	**0,950**

the value of further research into alternative feature vector construction methods. These approaches could prove particularly valuable when applying Transformer models to specific domains.

Table 4 presents a comparison between the proposed prediction approach and other solutions reported in the literature that were evaluated using the same datasets. As shown in the table, the proposed approach achieves superior results across all datasets, with particularly notable improvements for SwiftKey, Tap Fish, and Temple Run 2. It is important to emphasize that performance gains at this stage are crucial for obtaining higher quality requirements.

Table 4. Comparison of the proposed prediction approach with other reported solutions.

Id	Solutions (F1-Score)	Facebook	SwiftKey	Tap Fish	Templerun2	Ave
1	[4]	0,877	0,764	0,761	0.797	0,800
3	[19]	0,908	0,908	0,924	-	0,913
4	[22]	0,933	0,899	0,914	0,913	0,915
8	**Proposed Solution**	**0,934**	**0,952**	**0,960**	**0,955**	**0,950**

Figure 2 presents the Silhouette coefficient evaluation for different K values in the clustering process of the SwiftKey dataset (The one selected for the requirement generation analysis), demonstrating that $K = 11$ yields the optimal configuration (Silhouette value $= 0.3699$). The study found that reducing the dimensionality of opinion embedding vectors was essential to improve FCM clustering quality. PCA (Principal Component Analysis) was implemented to reduce vector dimensionality to 2 (after testing various dimensions: 2, 5, 10, 20, 50, and 100), which enhanced Silhouette results. Figure 3 visualizes the clustering outcome for 879 OIs using PCA with $K = 11$.

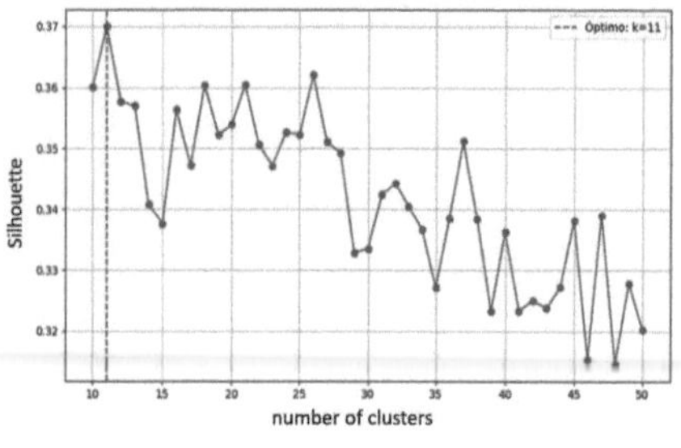

Fig. 2. Identifying the optimal number of clusters to be obtained by the FCM.

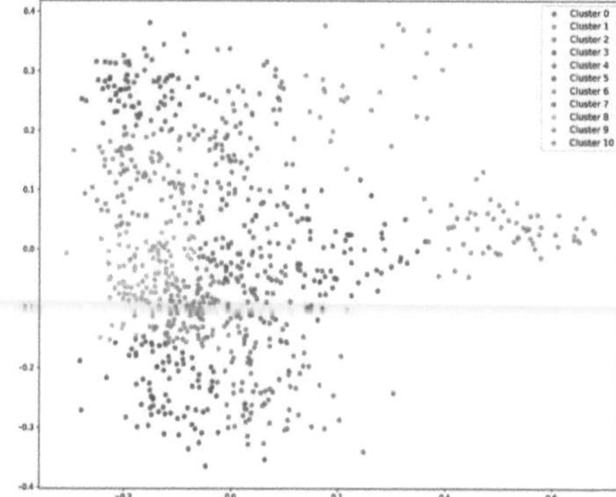

Fig. 3. Visualization of the clustering of IOs in SwiftKey dataset.

4.1 Example of Requirement Generation: Cluster 9 Analysis

To demonstrate the requirement generation process Cluster 9 was selected, which comprises 28 user opinions addressing the need for additional visual themes in the keyboard interface. Representative opinions from this cluster include:

Id1: "I love the keyboards and what not it looks so awesome but just need some more themes to choose from or more customization choices"	*Id14: "As petty as it sounds I would love a red keyboard to match the rest of my phone's theme and case!"*
Id2: "I would like it if there were emoticon add ons for this keyboard like there are some of the other ones though…"	*Id16: "PLZ make more themes n can u make the key board look like adapt keyboards plz make the key board respond faster"*
Id3: "I would really like to see more customization like more keyboard clolors and maybe some emoj that's different from iPhone"	*Id24: "PLZ make more themes n can u make the key board look like adapt keyboards plz"*
Id4: "This keyboard is good but it really needs more theme"	*Id26: "almost all themes are with closely spaced keys"*
Id5: "Wish for more keyboard themes to come"	*Id27: "you guys shud add more themes like sony keyboard style or iphone style or stock android jellybean look"*
Id6: "But can we have more themes for the keyboard =)"	

In the experimental setup, DeepSeek V3 was configured with a predefined prompt that included both the 28-opinion cluster set under #User Comments to Analyze section (see Sect. 3.4) and relevant SwiftKey contextual information. This process yielded 7 functional requirements and 5 non-functional requirements. A representative sample is presented below. Notably, each requirement specification includes source opinions that contributed informational value (for verification or further detail) and a classification of non-functional requirement types. The generated requirements demonstrated excellent quality standards.

Functional Requirements:

FR-01*: The system shall provide additional themes for the keyboard, including but not limited to red, black, and AMOLED-friendly themes.*

Source: Comment #1, #4, #5, #6, #7, #13, #14, #18, #19, #22, #23, #25, #27, #28

FR-03*: The system shall include a wider variety of emoticons and emojis, distinct from those available on iPhone keyboards. Source: Comment #2, #3, #10*

FR-07*: The system shall offer keyboard layouts resembling popular styles such as Sony, iPhone, and stock Android Jellybean. Source: Comment #16, #24, #27*

Non-Functional Requirements

NFR-01 *[Usability]: The system shall ensure that all themes have well-spaced keys to improve typing accuracy and comfort. Source: Comment #26*

NFR-02 *[Performance]: The system shall reduce keyboard response time to less than 100ms for all user interactions. Source: Comment #16, #24*

NFR-05 *[Usability]: The system shall introduce a red keyboard theme to match user preferences for device aesthetics. Source: Comment #14, #18*

5   Conclusions

This study proposes a method for automatically generating software requirements from user feedback. The application of LLMs for software requirement generation was explored, particularly using the DeepSeek-v3 model, which demonstrated highly promising results—not only producing well-defined requirements but also precisely tracing the specific user opinions associated with each requirement. The solution emphasizes the critical role of filtering and organizing the formulated opinions. The proposed approach for identifying informative opinions (IOs), based on a BERTweet model with domain knowledge injection, achieved superior results compared to other state-of-the-art solutions. Clustering these relevant opinions using the FCM algorithm enabled better guidance for the LLM by identifying specific contextual aspects for requirement generation, improving both the coherence and effectiveness of the LLM's responses. This work opens several research directions, including: (i) evaluating other LLMs for requirement generation, (ii) investigating alternative domain knowledge vector construction and integration strategies for Transformer models, and (iii) developing a variant for Spanish-language requirement generation.

Acknowledgments. This work has been partially supported by the National Program PN223LH004: Automatics, Robotics and Artificial Intelligence under grant project PN223LH004-038: *'Aportes teóricos a la IA en el manejo de problemas con datos complejos'.*

References

1. Arora, C., Grundy, J., Abdelrazek, M.: Advancing Requirements Engineering through Generative AI: Assessing the Role of LLMs. arXiv:2310.13976v2 (2023)

2. Aslam, N., Ramay, W.Y., Xia, K., Sarwar, N.: Convolutional neural network based classification of app reviews. IEEE Access **8**, 185619–185628 (2020)
3. Cadeddu, A., et al.: A comparative analysis of knowledge injection strategies for large language models in the scholarly domain. Eng. Appl. Artif. Intell. **133**, 108166 (2024)
4. Chen, N., Lin, J., Hoi, S.C., Xiao, X., Zhang, B.: Ar-miner: mining informative reviews for developers from mobile app marketplace. Proc. of the 36th Int. Conf. on Software Engineering, pp. 767–778 (2014)
5. Cheligeer, C., Huang, J., Wu, G., Bhuiyan, N., Xu, Y., Zeng, Y.: Machine learning in requirements elicitation: a literature review. Artif. Intell. Eng. Des. Anal. Manuf. **36**, 1–23 (2022)
6. de Souza Filho, J.C., et al.: Towards a data-driven requirements elicitation tool through the lens of design thinking. Proc. of the 23rd Int. Conf. on Enterprise Information Systems (ICEIS 2021) **2**, pp. 283–290 (2021)
7. Di Sorbo, A., Panichella, S., Alexandru, C.V., Visaggio, C.A., Canfora, G.: Surf: summarizer of user reviews feedback. Proc. of the IEEE/ACM 39th Int. Conf. on Software Engineering Companion (ICSE-C), pp. 55–58 (2017)
8. Guzmán, E., Oliveira, L., Steiner, Y., Wagner, L.C., Glinz, M.: User feedback in the app store: a cross-cultural study. Proc. of the 40th Int. Conf. on Software Engineering: Software Engineering in Society, pp. 13–22 (2018)
9. Hadi, M.A., Fard, F.H.: Evaluating pre-trained models for user feedback analysis in software engineering: A study on classification of app-reviews. Empir. Softw. Eng. **28**, 88 (2023)
10. Henao, P.R., Fischbach, J., Spies, D., Frattini, J., Vogelsang, A.: Transfer learning for mining feature requests and bug reports from tweets and app store reviews. Proc. of the IEEE 29th Int. Requirements Engineering Conference Workshops (REW), pp. 80–86 (2021)
11. Hou, X., et al.: Large language models for software engineering: a systematic literature review. ACM Trans. Softw. Eng. Methodol. **33**(8), 1–79 (2024)
12. ISO/IEC/IEEE 24765. International standard. Systems and software engineering — vocabulary (2017)
13. Krishna, M., Gaur, B., Verma, A., Jalote, P.: Using LLMs in software requirements specifications: an empirical evaluation. Proc. of the IEEE 32nd Int. Requirements Engineering Conference (RE), pp. 475–483 (2024)
14. Maalej, W., Kurtanović, Z., Nabil, H., Stanik, C.: On the automatic classification of app reviews. Requirements Engineering **21**(3), 311–331 (2016)
15. Maalej, W., Nayebi, M., Johann, T., Ruhe, G.: Toward data-driven requirements engineering. IEEE Software **33**(1), 48–54 (2015)
16. Maia, V., Goncalves, T., Rocha, A.R.: Quality evaluation of mobile applications. Anais Estendidos do XIX Simposio Brasileiro de Qualidade de Software, 21–30 (2020)
17. Mekala, R.R., Irfan, A., Groen, E.C., Porter, A., Lindvall, M.: Classifying user requirements from online feedback in small dataset environments using deep learning. Proc. of the IEEE 29th Int. Requirements Engineering Conference (RE), pp. 139–149 (2021)
18. Meshesha, F., Perini, A., Susi, A., Siena, A., Muñante, D., Morales-Ramirez, I.: Automating user-feedback driven requirements prioritization. Inf. Softw. Technol. **138**, 106635 (2021)
19. Milián, V., Blanco, T., Simón-Cuevas, A., González, H., Hernández, A.: A knowledge-based user feedback classification approach for software support. Lect. Notes Comput. Sci. **14335**, 237–247 (2023)
20. Nayebi, M., Cho, H., Ruhe, G.: App store mining is not enough for app improvement. Empir. Softw. Eng. **23**, 2764–2794 (2018)
21. Palomba, F., et al.: Crowdsourcing user reviews to support the evolution of mobile apps. J. Syst. Softw. **137**, 143–162 (2018)
22. Prenner, J., Aron, R.R.: Making the most of small software engineering datasets with modern machine learning. IEEE Trans. Software Eng. **48**(12), 5050–5067 (2022)

23. Qiao, Z., Wang, A., Abrahams, A., Fan, W.: Deep learning-based user feedback classification in mobile app reviews. Proc. of the 2020 Pre-ICIS SIGDSA Symposium (2020)

24. Rousseuw, P.J.: Silhouettes: a graphical aid to the interpretation and validation of cluster analysis. J. Comput. Appl. Math. **20**, 53–65 (1987)

25. Shah, F.A., Sirts, K., Pfahl, D.: Using app reviews for competitive analysis: tool support. Proc. of the 3rd ACM SIGSOFT Int. Workshop on App Market Analytics, pp. 40–46 (2019)

26. Villarroel, L., Bavota, G., Russo, B., Oliveto, R., Di Penta, M.: Release planning of mobile apps based on user reviews. Proc. of the 38th Int. Conf. on Software Engineering, pp. 14–24 (2016)

27. Wang, L., Nakagawa, H., Tsuchiya, T.: Opinion analysis and organization of mobile application user reviews. REFSQ Workshops, pp. 1–9 (2020)

28. Williams, G., Mahmoud, A.: Mining twitter feeds for software user requirements. Proc. of the IEEE 25th Int. Requirements Engineering Conference (RE), pp. 1–10 (2017)

29. Zhao, Z., Zhang, L., Lian, X., Gao, X., Lv, H., Shi, L.: ReqGen: keywords-driven software requirements generation. Mathematics **11**(2), 332 (2023)

Automatic Identification of Ambiguities in Software Requirements Using Zero-Shot Classification

Gabriela Espinosa Mateo, Vladimir Milián Núñez, and José Eladio Medina Pagola

Universidad de Las Ciencias Informáticas, Road San Antonio Km 2 ½ Torrens, La Lisa, Havana, Cuba
{mateo,vmilian,jmedinap}@uci.cu

Abstract. This study addressed the problem of ambiguity in Software Requirements Specifications (SRS) through an innovative zero-shot classification approach, aiming to automatically identify and classify types of linguistic ambiguity without requiring large volumes of labeled data. We proposed a model based on Transformer and BERT architectures, adapted to capture ambiguous linguistic phenomena, utilizing two main components: an ambiguous expressions encoder and an ambiguity types encoder. The methodology included unsupervised pretraining with pseudo-labels and contrastive fine-tuning to maximize similarity between ambiguous expressions and their corresponding categories. Results demonstrated that the model with contrastive pretraining (CP) achieved an average performance of 41.78% Macro F_1 in unsupervised zero-shot scenarios, showing significant improvement over traditional approaches. In supervised settings, the combination of CP and contrastive fine-tuning reached 49.45% Macro F_1, evidencing the method's effectiveness in generalizing to new ambiguity categories. These findings suggest that integrating contrastive techniques with ambiguity-specialized models can enhance software requirements quality from early stages, though challenges remain to achieve higher accuracy levels.

Keywords: Linguistic Ambiguity · Software Requirements · Zero-Shot Classification · Transformer Models · Contrastive Learning

1 Introduction

Ambiguity in Software Requirements Specifications (SRS) is one of the most frequent causes of failure in development projects [7, 20]. Ambiguous requirements allow for multiple interpretations within the same formulation, hindering their efficient management and potentially leading to recurrent changes in the development cycle [6, 24, 25].

To address this issue, the automatic identification of ambiguity types through zero-shot classification techniques emerges as a promising solution. This Machine Learning approach enables a model to detect and classify ambiguities without requiring large

© The Author(s), under exclusive license to Springer Nature Switzerland AG 2026
Y. Hernádez Heredia et al. (Eds.): IWAIPR 2025, LNCS 16328, pp. 80–90, 2026.
https://doi.org/10.1007/978-3-032-11358-0_7

volumes of labeled data, thereby improving requirement quality from early stages [2, 8].

Software Requirements Specifications (SRS) follow a semi-structured format, where information is organized through regular visual layouts such as tables, forms, multiple columns, and bulleted lists. According to [8], this content can only be fully understood within its visual context or demands significant effort to interpret without such graphical support.

Previous research has demonstrated that integrating two-dimensional design information is crucial for the effective analysis of this type of document [1, 5, 24, 25]. Precisely because of these characteristics, traditional classification methods for unstructured documents—such as static word vectors [18] and standard pre-trained language models [4, 10, 16]—exhibit limited performance with semi-structured content, as they represent text in a one-dimensional space and omit information about document layout and style [24, 25].

This work proposes an innovative approach for zero-shot classification of semi-structured Spanish SRS, based on the matching framework, a technique successfully applied in multiple unstructured text processing tasks [3, 11–13, 24, 25]. Our contribution is structured around three key aspects: (i) Investigation of zero-shot classification for semi-structured documents; (ii) Implementation of a pairwise contrastive objective for pre-training and fine-tuning the matching model, using a layout-aware document encoder and a conventional text encoder to maximize similarity between documents and their true labels; (iii) Proposal of an unsupervised pre-training step with pseudo-labels [17] for optimal initialization of the document and label encoders.

2 Materials and Methods

2.1 Model

Generative Artificial Intelligence is a specialized field of computing focused on the automated production of texts, images, speech synthesis, and videos. It employs deep learning algorithms and pre-trained models using extensive datasets, achieving results indistinguishable from those created by humans [14].

For this study, a model was developed with the objective of learning a matching function that associates ambiguous linguistic expressions with their corresponding types, based on those proposed by [6]: lexical ambiguity, syntactic ambiguity, semantic ambiguity, and pragmatic ambiguity. These types must be represented as descriptive textual labels rather than simple nominal categories, allowing the ambiguity type encoder to process them semantically and compare them with ambiguous expressions. The nomenclature used is as follows:

- Lexical ambiguity: inconsistencies due to multiple meanings of words or terms
- Syntactic ambiguity: inconsistencies caused by ambiguous grammatical structure or word order
- Semantic ambiguity: inconsistencies arising from multiple interpretations within a context
- Pragmatic ambiguity: inconsistencies due to unclear intentions or implications

This system utilizes two fundamental components: an ambiguous expression encoder (Φ_{text}) and an ambiguity type encoder $\left(\Phi_{\text{type}}\right)$.

The expression encoder (Φ_{text}) uses the pre-trained BERT language model, enhanced with additional linguistic information to capture key features of ambiguity. Unlike the original model, the focus here is on deep textual representations that highlight traits such as the presence of homonymous words or ambiguous grammatical structures.

On the other hand, the ambiguity type $\left(\Phi_{\text{type}}\right)$ encoder transforms class labels or their descriptions into semantic vectors. For this task, a standard language model is employed but adapted to the linguistic domain.

As can be seen in Fig. 1, both encoders project their outputs into a shared embedding space, where the similarity between an ambiguous expression and an ambiguity type is computed via dot product. During training, this space is optimized so that expressions move closer to their correct types and farther from incorrect ones using a contrastive loss function. This approach enables the model to generalize to new ambiguity types without requiring prior examples, proving particularly valuable for natural language processing (NLP) applications and machine translation support systems.

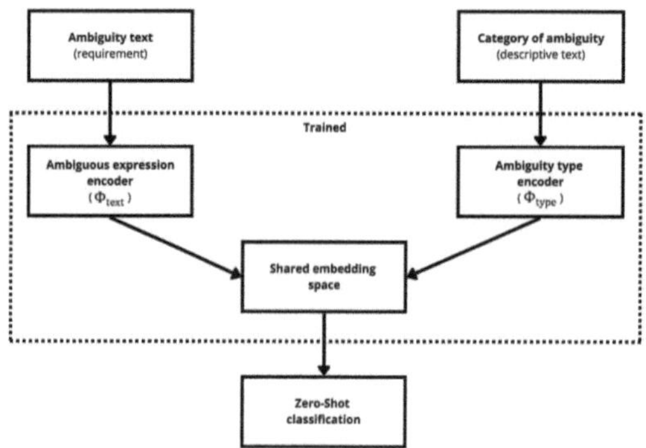

Fig. 1. Graphical representation of the general architecture of the model.

2.2 Model for Ambiguity Identification

To address the challenge of automatic ambiguity type identification through zero-shot classification, we propose a model based on Transformer architectures and BERT [4], but specifically adapted to capture ambiguous linguistic phenomena. Unlike models such as LayoutBERT [21], which focus on spatial information for semi-structured documents, our encoder processes plain text and extracts relevant features to distinguish between different ambiguity types. The model employs contextual embeddings enriched with syntactic and semantic signals, enabling robust representation of ambiguous expressions within a shared vector space with class labels.

Taking as a reference the pretraining carried out for the BERT [4] and RoBERTa [10] models, for the present research, Masked Language Modeling (MLM) is combined with auxiliary tasks designed to reinforce the understanding of ambiguity. For instance, during this phase, the model learns to predict not only masked words but also the type of ambiguity present in the context. This was achieved using specialized lexical disambiguation datasets. Additionally, we incorporate supplementary layers that analyze relationships between ambiguous words and their potential interpretations, enhancing the model's ability to generalize to unseen classes during training.

Models Φ_{text} and Φ_{type} were independently pre-trained. To encourage these models to produce similar representations of documents and their corresponding labels, we further pre-train Φ_{text} and Φ_{type} through an unsupervised procedure based on a pairwise contrastive objective. This unsupervised objective can learn from large quantities of unlabeled SRS (Software Requirements Specifications), while also allowing direct application of the pre-trained encoders in a zero-shot unsupervised setting.

The pre-training procedure relies exclusively on self-supervision using pseudo-labels [17]. These pseudo-labels are generated by sampling a continuous token block from the document, with a length drawn from a shifted geometric distribution. Each pseudo-label extracted from a document is treated as that document's positive label and encoded using model Φ_{type}.

In the following we describe our contrastive target, which is based on multiclass n-pair loss [15, 19]. Let B be a training batch consisting of training texts (requirements) D and their pseudo-labels L, such that $T = (t_1, t_1, ..., t|B|)$ and $L = (l_1, l_1, ..., l|B|)$. Φ_{text} and Φ_{type} are the encoders of texts and labels, respectively. We start by encoding each text and pseudo-label in the batch, and then compute a correspondence matrix $MB \in R\ |B| \times |B|$ of pairwise dot products between each document-label pair, such that: $M_{ij}^B = \Phi_{\text{type}}(l_i)^T * \Phi_{\text{text}}(l_j)$. The goal of this is to increase the value of the diagonal elements Mij, where $i = j$, compared to all other elements. More precisely, the loss function of a batch is a symmetric loss, $(L)^B$, which can be expressed by the equation:

$$L^B = \frac{1}{2}\left[L_{row}^B + L_{col}^B\right] \tag{1}$$

Here, L_{row}^B and L_{col}^B are the per-batch row-wise and column-wise losses, respectively, with:

$$L_{row}^B = \sum_{i=1}^{|B|}\left[-log\left(exp\left(M_{ii}^B\right)\right) + log\left(\sum_{j=1}^{|B|}exp\left(M_{ij}^B\right)\right)\right] \tag{2}$$

The first term in Eq. 2 maximizes the diagonal elements, while the second term minimizes the off-diagonal elements. The column-wise loss remains identical with i and j interchanged. We directly optimize the raw dot products rather than cosine similarity, as we empirically observed that dot products yield significantly better performance - a finding consistent with [9]. For enhanced understanding of this process, please refer to Fig. 1 (Fig. 2).

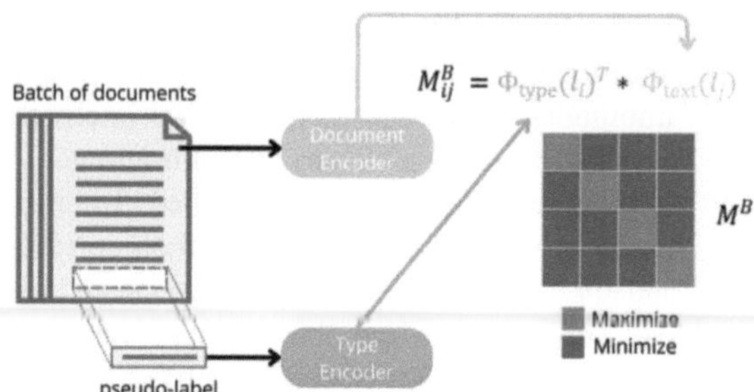

Fig. 2. The unsupervised contrastive pretraining procedure. A random block of tokens from a document is used as the pseudo-label for that document. Dot products between documents and their labels are maximized and all other pairwise dot products are minimized. Adapted from [8]

During fine-tuning, we employ a contrastive objective that maximizes the similarity between ambiguous examples and their correct labels, while simultaneously minimizing similarity with incorrect classes. This approach enables the model to generalize to new ambiguity types without requiring labeled examples - particularly valuable in scenarios where categories may vary or expand dynamically.

2.3 Contrastive Pre-Training for Ambiguity Identification

The objective of this section is to describe an unsupervised contrastive pre-training method designed to learn aligned representations between linguistic ambiguity examples and their potential categories. Since zero-shot scenarios lack real labels for all ambiguity types, the model automatically generates pseudo-labels from textual category descriptions. These pseudo-labels serve as substitutes for real classes during pretraining, enabling the model to learn associations between linguistic patterns and specific ambiguity types.

To generate pseudo-labels, text segments containing ambiguous words or constructions are extracted from an unlabeled corpus. The length of these segments follows a shifted geometric distribution, introducing variability in the examples. Each segment is paired with a textual description of its potential ambiguity type, created via linguistic rules or generative models. For instance, the statement "El servicio está cancelado" ("The service is canceled") could be linked to the pseudo-label "polysemy: term with multiple lexical meanings."

The contrastive objective is implemented through a similarity matrix, where each element represents the dot product between the embeddings of an ambiguous example and a pseudo-label. The loss function, based on a softmax approach, maximizes similarity between examples and their assigned pseudo-labels while minimizing similarity with others. This enables the model to distinguish between different ambiguity categories—even in the absence of labeled data.

This method establishes a robust foundation for zero-shot classification, as the model learns to project both ambiguous examples and category descriptions into a shared semantic space. During inference, it can generalize to unseen ambiguity types by comparing new descriptions with learned embeddings.

2.4 Contrastive Fine-Tuning

To implement contrastive fine-tuning, we use batches containing Φ_{text} and Φ_{type}. The similarity between each text-type pair is computed by scalar product in the shared embeddings space. For model fine-tuning we use the same objective as in the pre-training step (Eq. 1), except that the labels $L = (l_1, l_1, ..., l|B|)$ for a batch B are true labels and not pseudo-labels.

The contrastive loss function remains symmetric but is applied to linguistic representations rather than layout features. We simultaneously optimize two objectives: (1) maximizing the similarity between ambiguous texts and their correct descriptions, and (2) minimizing the similarity with incorrect descriptions within the same batch. This creates a semantic space where similar ambiguities are clustered near their corresponding descriptions, while dissimilar ones are pushed apart.

The fine-tuning process benefits significantly from prior contrastive pre-training (CP), as the model has already learned to associate ambiguous linguistic structures with conceptual descriptions. This allows fine-tuning to converge faster and with less data—a crucial advantage, given that labeled examples of specific ambiguities may be scarce in many practical scenarios. Experiments show that this combination of unsupervised pre-training and contrastive fine-tuning outperforms traditional cross-entropy-based approaches for zero-shot ambiguity classification.

2.5 Data Set

The dataset Requierements_by_centers[1] was processed. This dataset contains the software requirements analyzed by the SIDARES developers, which in turn compiles the System Requirements Specification from different projects of each development center at the Universidad de las Ciencias Informáticas [6].

The dataset contained a total of 19,357 requirements, stored in 14.csv documents divided by development center and further grouped into splits based on the knowledge domain to which the projects in the database belonged. The division is shown in Table 1.

2.6 Experimental Setup

The technical configuration includes a batch size of 32, a learning rate of 2e-5 with linear warmup, and dynamic masking with a probability of 0.1 applied to ambiguous words to improve model robustness. To evaluate performance, we employ Macro F1 and Accuracy metrics, with particular focus on the model's ability to generalize to unseen classes during training. The data is split into non-overlapping sets, ensuring that ambiguity classes in the test set are not present in the training or validation data, enabling rigorous evaluation of the zero-shot approach.

---

[1] Available at: https://github.com/Jonathanrr98/SIDARES/blob/master/SIDARES_BACKEND/
AMBIGUEDADES/algoritmos/[SubtitleTools.com]%20requierements_by_centers.csv.

Table 1. Distribution of 19 357 stored requirements according to UCI development center.

Splits	Development center	Number of requirements
Split I	CDAE	875
	CEDIN	340
	CEGEL	1434
	CEIGE	2449
Split II	CENIA	323
	CESIM	909
	CESOL	1072
	CIDI	3256
Split III	CISED	84
	CMMI	445
	FORTES	4184
Split IV	GEYSED	1571
	ISEC	2012
	VERTEX	402

3   Results

We experiment with two settings unsupervised zero-shot, and supervised zero-shot. In the former, no fine-tuning is involved and all models are directly used for inference. In the latter, all models are fine-tuned on data from classes different than those present in the test set. Thus, the former is strictly more challenging.

3.1   Unsupervised Zero-Shot

The results presented in Table 2 demonstrate the comparative performance of three approaches in the automatic identification of ambiguity types under an unsupervised zero-shot scenario. First, the standard BERT model, used for encoding both texts and labels, achieves modest performance with a 17.71% Macro F_1 average. This result was expected, as BERT was not specifically designed to capture linguistic ambiguities or operate in zero-shot environments. Its main limitation lies in the lack of explicit incorporation of relevant linguistic features, such as syntactic relationships or deep semantic information, which hinders its ability to discriminate between unseen ambiguity classes during training.

Table 2. Unsupervised zero-shot performance (Macro F_1) on 4 splits of the Requierements_by_centers dataset.

Method	Split I	Split II	Split III	Split IV	Avg
BERT (text and label)	18.25	15.70	20.10	16.80	17.71
Ambiguity-Specialized (text), BERT (label)	25.40	22.15	28.30	24.75	25.15
CP, Ambiguity-Specialized (text), BERT (label)	**42.60**	**38.20**	**45.80**	**40.50**	**41.78**

Second, replacing the text encoder with a model specialized in ambiguities yields substantial improvement, with an average increase of approximately 7.4 points in Macro F_1. This model, pre-fine-tuned on annotated ambiguity data, captures more refined lexical and structural patterns, enabling better generalization. However, its performance remains limited due to the absence of a mechanism that explicitly aligns representations of ambiguous texts with class descriptions in a shared semantic space.

Finally, incorporating CP to the ambiguity-specialized model produces significant advancement, reaching a 41.78% average in Macro F_1. This improvement - representing a gain of approximately 16 points over the specialized model without CP - highlights the importance of aligning text and label representations in a common embedding space. Through automatically generated pseudo-labels, CP enables the model to learn associations between ambiguous texts and class descriptions even in the absence of annotated data. This approach not only enhances generalization capability to new ambiguity classes but also strengthens the model's linguistic representations.

3.2 Supervised Zero-Shot

The results presented in Table 3 demonstrate the comparative performance of different supervised fine-tuning approaches for zero-shot classification of linguistic ambiguity types. The analysis reveals significant patterns that warrant detailed consideration.

The traditional fine-tuning approach with cross-entropy loss (Cross-entropy FT) achieves an average performance of 38.99% in Macro F_1, thus establishing a baseline for the task. This result, while moderate, confirms the model's basic ability to generalize to ambiguity classes not observed during training. The inter-splits variability (ranging from 35.15% to 42.60%) reflects inherent differences in the complexity of various ambiguity types, with particularly notable better performance in Split III, which likely contains ambiguities with more discernible patterns.

The implementation of contrastive loss fine-tuning (Contrastive FT) shows an average improvement of 2.15 percentage points over the standard approach, reaching 41.14% Macro F_1. This improvement, though modest, validates the potential of contrastive methods to enhance discrimination between ambiguity categories. However, the higher standard deviation observed (± 2.8 to ± 4.2)suggests notable sensitivity to initialization factors - a characteristic typical of contrastive approaches that must be considered in practical implementations.

The incorporation of CP combined with standard fine-tuning yields a substantial improvement of approximately 8 percentage points (46.86% Macro F_1), clearly outperforming both previous approaches. This significant enhancement demonstrates how contrastive pretraining effectively prepares the model to establish correspondences between ambiguous texts and category descriptions, even before the supervised fine-tuning process. The lower variability observed (± 1.2 to ± 2.0) further indicates that this approach provides more stable and consistent representations.

The optimal configuration (CP + Contrastive FT) achieves peak performance with 49.45% Macro F_1, showing an improvement of nearly 10 percentage points over the baseline. This result highlights the synergy between contrastive pretraining and contrastive fine-tuning, where the former establishes good initialization and the latter optimizes category separation in the representation space. The notable performance in Split III (53.8%) suggests this approach is particularly effective for certain ambiguity types, possibly those with more defined semantic patterns.

Table 3. Supervised zero-shot performance (Macro F_1) on 4 splits of the Requierements_by_centers dataset.

Method	Split I	Split II	Split III	Split IV	Avg
Cross-entropy FT	38.42 ± 1.2	35.15 ± 2.1	42.60 ± 1.8	39.80 ± 1.5	38.99
Contrastive FT	40.25 ± 3.5	37.80 ± 4.2	45.30 ± 3.0	41.20 ± 2.8	41.14
CP + Cross-entropy FT	45.60 ± 1.8	43.75 ± 2.0	50.20 ± 1.5	47.90 ± 1.2	46.86
CP + Contrastive FT	$\mathbf{48.30 \pm 2.5}$	$\mathbf{46.10 \pm 3.1}$	$\mathbf{53.80 \pm 2.4}$	$\mathbf{49.60 \pm 2.0}$	**49.45**

4 Conclusions

The result of the settings unsupervised zero-shot demonstrated that classification zero-shot is viable for ambiguities, but requires specialized models. Contrastive pretraining is critical, as it improves generalization to new ambiguity classes. Furthermore an $F_1 \sim$ 40% indicates that the problem is more difficult than document classification (original: $\sim$ 60% with CP), which justifies exploring improvements (e.g. incorporating dependency graphs or formal class definitions).

The obtained results, while promising, reveal that the supervised zero-shot classification of ambiguities still presents significant challenges. The maximum performance of 49.45% macro F_1 indicates that, although the proposed techniques are effective, there remains considerable room for improvement, as the performance is still lower than what an SRS expert would likely achieve. This underscores the need to regard these techniques as complementary support rather than a substitute for human review.

The unsupervised pretraining approach with pseudo-labels enables robust model initialization for data-limited scenarios. The automatic generation of labels from textual descriptions proved to be an effective strategy for aligning document and category representations in a shared semantic space—even without labeled data. This approach creates new possibilities for applications in domains where manual annotation is costly or impractical, such as requirements engineering for low-resource languages.

It is worth noting that this study does not experiment with the variety of encoding strategies described in the literature that combine textual, visual, and layout information [1, 5, 24, 25]. It is likely that richer document representations derived from these diverse encoders could further push the boundaries of zero-shot classification when combined with our proposed unsupervised contrastive pretraining procedure.

Furthermore, the results reported in this paper are based on a single dataset. Although this limitation is largely mitigated by creating four non-overlapping test splits, results obtained with additional datasets could provide greater insights. In practice, the lack of publicly available datasets for this task hinders such exploration and may require the development of new resources.

The contribution presented focuses exclusively on the identification of ambiguities in software requirements, without directly addressing the disambiguation phase. This approach responds to the need to first establish a solid foundation for automatic detection, which is an essential prerequisite for future research to explore resolution mechanisms. While disambiguation would represent a highly valuable contribution for end users, the present study should be understood as an initial step within a broader process aimed at improving the quality of requirements specifications. Consequently, future research could explore the enrichment of category descriptions with additional semantic information and the integration of external linguistic knowledge (such as Word-Net or semantic graphs), in addition to the development of specialized architectures for processing ambiguities.

References

1. Appalaraju, S., Jasani, B., Urala Kota, B., Xie, Y., Manmatha, R.: Docformer: End-to-end transformer for document understanding. In: Proceedings of the IEEE/CVF International Conference on Computer Vision (ICCV), pp. 993–1003 (2021)
2. Bucher, M.J.J., Martini, M.: Fine-Tuned 'Small' LLMs (Still) Significantly Outperform Zero-Shot Generative AI Models in Text Classification. arXiv preprint arXiv:2406.08660 (2024)
3. Dauphin, Y.N., Tur, G., Hakkani-Tur, D., Heck, L.P.: Zero-shot learning and clustering for semantic utterance classification. In: 2nd International Conference on Learning Representations, ICLR 2014, Conference Track Proceedings (2014)
4. Devlin, J., Chang, M.-W., Lee, K., Toutanova, K.: BERT: pre-training of deep bidirectional transformers for language understanding. In: Proceedings of the 2019 Conference of the North American Chapter of the Association for Computational Linguistics: Human Language Technologies (NAACL-HLT), vol. 1, pp. 4171–4186 (2019)
5. Huang, Y., Lv, T., Cui, L., Lu, Y., Wei, F.: LayoutLMv3: Pre-training for document AI with unified text and image masking. arXiv preprint arXiv:2206.09209 (2022)
6. Ramírez Reyes, J., Enríquez González, S. de las M.: SIDARES: herramienta de procesamiento del lenguaje natural para la detección de ambigüedad léxica y sintáctica en requisitos de software. PhD Thesis. Universidad de las Ciencias Informáticas (2022). https://repositorio.uci.cu/jspui/handle/123456789/10611
7. Johnson, J.: Chaos Report: Beyond Infinity. The Standish Group International Inc., Centerville, MA (2022)

8. Khalifa, M., et al.: Contrastive training improves zero-shot classification of semi-structured documents. arXiv preprint arXiv:2210.05613 (2022)
9. Karpukhin, V., et al.: Dense passage retrieval for open-domain question answering. In: Proceedings of the 2020 Conference on Empirical Methods in Natural Language Processing (EMNLP), pp. 6769–6781 (2020)
10. Liu, Y., et al.: RoBERTa: A robustly optimized BERT pretraining approach. arXiv preprint arXiv:1907.11692 (2019)
11. Ma, J., et al.: Label semantics for few shot named entity recognition. In: Findings of the Association for Computational Linguistics: ACL 2022, pp. 1956–1971 (2022)
12. Nam, J., Loza Mencia, E., Furnkranz, J.: All-in text: Learning document, label, and word representations jointly. In: Proceedings of the AAAI Conference on Artificial Intelligence, vol. 30 (2016)
13. Pappas, N., Henderson, J.: Gile: A generalized input-label embedding for text classification. Trans. Ass. Computat. Linguist. **7**, 139–155 (2019)
14. Pinaya, W., et al.: Generative ai for medical imaging: extending the monai framework. arXiv preprint arXiv:2307.15208. (2023)
15. Radford, A., et al.: Learning transferable visual models from natural language supervision. arXiv preprint arXiv:2103.00020 (2021)
16. Reimers, N., Gurevych, I.: Sentence-BERT: Sentence embeddings using Siamese BERT-networks. arXiv preprint arXiv:1908.10084 (2019)
17. Rethmeier, N., Augenstein, I.: Data-efficient pretraining via contrastive self-supervision. arXiv preprint arXiv:2010.01061 (2020)
18. Socher, R., Ganjoo, M., Manning, C.D., Ng, A.Y.: Zero-shot learning through cross-modal transfer. Adv. Neural. Inf. Process. Syst. **26**, 935–943 (2013)
19. Sohn, K.: Improved deep metric learning with multi-class n-pair loss objective. In: Proceedings of the 30th International Conference on Neural Information Processing Systems, pp. 1857–1865 (2016)
20. Somerville, I.: Ingeniería de software, 9th edn. Pearson (2011)
21. Turgutlu, K., Sharma, S., Kumar, J.: LayoutBERT: Masked Language Layout Model for Object Insertion (2022). https://doi.org/10.48550/arXiv.2205.00347
22. Vyas, Y., Ballesteros, M.: Linking entities to unseen knowledge bases with arbitrary schemas. In: Proceedings of the 2021 Conference of the North American Chapter of the Association for Computational Linguistics: Human Language Technologies, pp. 834–844 (2021)
23. Franch, X., Palomares, C., Quer, C., Chatzipetrou, P., Gorschek, T.: The state-of-practice in requirements specification: An extended interview study at 12 companies. Requirements Eng. (2023). https://doi.org/10.1007/s00766-023-00399-7
24. Xu, Y., et al.: LayoutLMv2: Multi-modal pretraining for visually-rich document understanding. In: Proceedings of the 59th Annual Meeting of the Association for Computational Linguistics, vol. 1, pp. 2579–2591 (2021)
25. Xu, Y., et al.: LayoutLM: Pre-training of text and layout for document image understanding. In: Proceedings of the 26th ACM SIGKDD International Conference on Knowledge Discovery & Data Mining, pp. 1192–1200 (2020)

Generative AI-Based Virtual Assistant Using Retrieval-Augmented Generation: An Evaluation Study

Claudia Farrada Machado[1], Alfredo Simón-Cuevas[1(✉)] (iD),
and Neili Machado García[2] (iD)

[1] Universidad Tecnológica de La Habana José Antonio Echeverría,
CUJAE Ave. 114, e/Rotonda y Ciclovía, Marianao, La Habana, Cuba
`{cfarrada,asimon}@ceis.cujae.edu.cu`
[2] Universidad Agraria de La Habana: Mayabeque, Mayabeque, Cuba
`neili@unah.edu.cu`

Abstract. The integration of large language models (LLMs) with external sources has established Retrieval-Augmented Generation (RAG) as a key technology for improving reliability and reducing hallucinations. While RAG has proven effective, the paradigm has evolved to incorporate various techniques at different stages, aiming to further enhance its potential. However, a key challenge lies in identifying configurations of advanced techniques that improve performance. This study evaluates several technique configurations in a modular RAG system, with the objective of identifying those that deliver the best performance. Technologies such as LangChain, ChromaDB, and LLaMA 3.1:8B are employed. The evaluation focuses on metrics such as precision, recall, and F1-Score using a dataset from the academic postgraduate domain. The results highlight variability across configurations and emphasize how properly designing the processing of retrieved context can improve the quality of generated answers.

Keywords: Virtual Assistant · Retrieval Augmented Generation · Large Language Models · LangChain

1 Introduction

The rapid evolution of large language models (LLMs) has revolutionized the field of natural language processing (NLP) [5], achieving outstanding results in generating coherent and contextually appropriate text. However, LLMs have inherent limitations, such as outdated knowledge, a tendency to generate incorrect information, and a lack of expertise in domains that require specific knowledge [6]. Knowledge injection, whether through fine-tuning or in-context learning, has emerged as a key approach to improve the performance of LLMs on specific tasks, with Retrieval-Augmented Generation (RAG) being the most popular version of the latter [8].

Y. Hernádez Heredia et al. (Eds.): IWAIPR 2025, LNCS 16328, pp. 91–101, 2026.
https://doi.org/10.1007/978-3-032-11358-0_8

RAG offers a more cost-effective alternative to the extensive training and fine-tuning processes typically required for LLMs [3]. It has emerged as an effective strategy to provide LLMs with dynamic access to external, up-to-date information sources. By combining retrieval and generation models, it enhances accuracy and relevance in domain-specific tasks. Through access to external knowledge bases, RAG systems provide LLMs with additional context, significantly reducing hallucinations, grounding generated knowledge, and offering more personalized responses. Currently, RAG is widely applied in various real-world scenarios, including knowledge-based question answering systems, recommendation systems, customer service, and personal assistants [2].

With the rapid development and adoption of the RAG paradigm, a variety of advanced techniques have emerged that can be applied at different stages of the process to improve performance. These techniques aim to increase the accuracy and relevance of RAG-based systems. A typical RAG workflow generally includes multiple intermediate processing steps. What adds complexity and challenge is the variability in how each step is implemented. The techniques chosen for each stage and their combinations significantly impact both the effectiveness and efficiency of RAG systems [11]. Therefore, despite the effectiveness of this paradigm, a persistent challenge lies in identifying and selecting configurations of the various available advanced techniques to maximize their potential. Existing studies often focus on individual techniques, without evaluating their combinations or addressing the complexity of integrating multiple techniques into a cohesive system.

The aim of this study is to evaluate different configurations of advanced techniques within a modular RAG system, in order to identify those that yield the best results particularly in terms of precision when applied in combination. The system has been implemented in the postgraduate domain of the Technological University of Havana, a setting characterized by complex regulations and detailed academic programs that require accurate interpretation. In this solution, the response process is carried out through a sequential flow involving key modules such as indexing, retrieval and generation, orchestrated in a flexible way. The modular RAG architecture is employed, implemented with technologies such as LangChain and ChromaDB as a vector database. The solution was evaluated using structured datasets of 140 questions with their associated reference answers, measuring performance with metrics such as Precision, Recall, F1-Score, Context Relevance, among others. The results obtained show a remarkable variability between the different configurations evaluated and demonstrate that, with a proper conception of the retrieved context processing, it is possible to significantly improve the accuracy and F1-Score in the generation of quality answers from an external knowledge base using retrieval-augmented LLMs.

The paper is structured as follows: Sect. 2 presents a review of related work; Sect. 3 describes the proposed solution; Sect. 4 describes the experimental evaluation methodology, and the results obtained with the different configurations of techniques; and Sect. 5 presents the main conclusions of the study.

2 Related Works

The RAG approach has been the subject of increasing interest in the scientific community in recent years. Since the initial proposal of the RAG paradigm [5], which integrated a Dense Passage Retrieval (DPR)-based retriever and a jointly trained BART generator, numerous works have explored variants and improvements of the original scheme, focusing on different stages of the pipeline. One of the main lines of research has been the improvement of the retrieval stage, proposing techniques such as hybrid retrieval [9] that combines vector searches with traditional keyword searches, as well as query expansion using adaptive semantic models [13]. These techniques have been shown to substantially improve the system's ability to retrieve relevant information in domains with specialized vocabulary or heterogeneous expressions.

In [2], a methodology for modular RAG systems is proposed with the goal of transforming the systems into reconfigurable frameworks, allowing the separation of recovery, re-ranking and generation components into distinct and customizable modules. The modular RAG approach allows for dynamic experimentation, as modules can be easily assembled and reconfigured according to specific application needs. The authors suggest that this modular framework allows advanced methods to be combined to optimize accuracy in both retrieval and response generation.

In parallel, other research has focused on the post-retrieval stage, where fragment reordering (re-ranking) mechanisms have been proposed using deep learning-based scoring models, such as ColBERT [4], which allow refining the final selection of the context that feeds the generating model. Along the same lines, recent works [10, 11, 14] have started to incorporate extractive and abstractive compressors as intermediate steps to optimize the context window and reduce the cognitive load of the generating model. Pre-generation semantic compression has been shown to be especially useful in tasks where source documents are large and LLM input windows are token-limited.

In terms of system architecture, proposals have emerged that advocate a modular and decoupled structure, such as LangChain or Haystack, which allow for greater flexibility and reusability of RAG components. These frameworks have facilitated experimentation with different combinations of techniques at each stage of the pipeline, leading to a number of works aimed at benchmarking complex configurations. A representative example is the Self-RAG approach [1], which introduces an iterative self-evaluation mechanism where the system generates a tentative answer, reflects on its validity and decides whether it needs to retrieve more information before issuing a final answer. This has shown that self-reflective generation and iterative reasoning can substantially improve the accuracy and reliability of responses in open and unstructured contexts.

3 Proposed Solution

The developed solution focuses on a modular RAG system structured in a series of stages that reflect the natural flow of information processing from its origin to the final generation of responses. This modular approach responds to the need to integrate advanced techniques in a flexible way, allowing their comparative evaluation. The system architecture follows a sequential logic comprising six main phases: preparation, storage, pre-retrieval, retrieval, post-retrieval and generation. Each of these stages was designed not only to fulfill its basic function within the pipeline, but also to incorporate optimization techniques that improve the accuracy and relevance of the generated responses (Fig. 1).

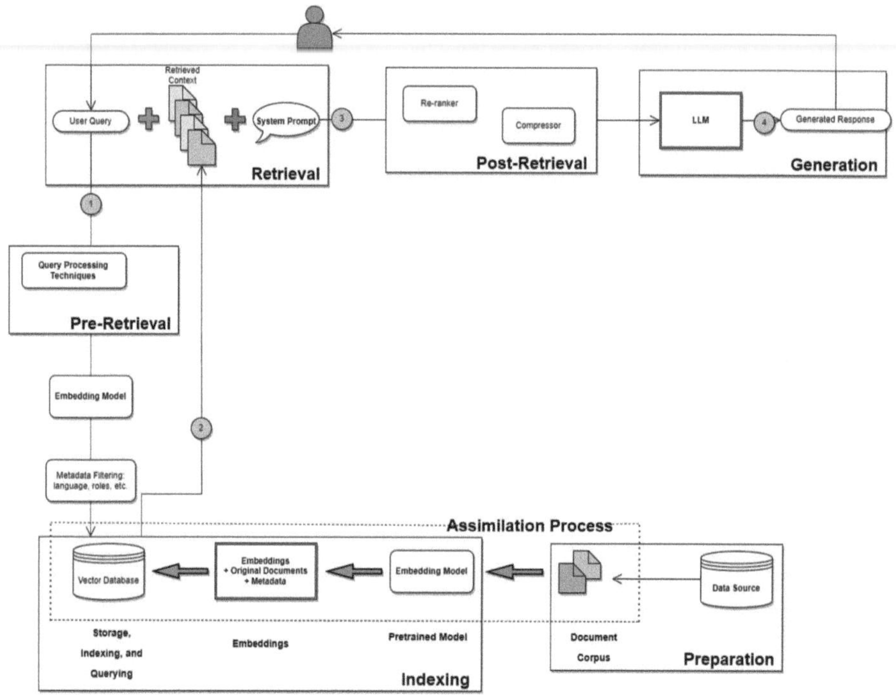

Fig. 1. Overview of the AI-Based Virtual Assistant architecture proposed.

3.1 Preparation

The quality of the answers generated by a RAG system depends largely on the relevance and structure of the indexed data. During the preparation phase, the ingestion of documents in various formats and their conversion to plain text is addressed, followed by a recursive fragmentation method widely used in RAG systems for its ability to preserve semantic coherence within defined size limits. This strategy allows obtaining overlapping fragments, ensuring a better capture of the semantic context between adjacent sections. The granularity of the fragments was adjusted so as to avoid both loss of context and excess noise, which is crucial to maintain relevance during retrieval. In this sense, a fragment size of 512 tokens with an overlap of 20 tokens was set, following the evidence reported in [12], where different fragment size configurations were evaluated on a real corpus. In that study, the 512 token size proved to offer the best balance between faithfulness and relevance of the responses, outperforming both longer and shorter fragments. In addition, a process of adding relevant metadata such as page number, file name, author is applied in order to enrich the subsequent retrieval stage.

3.2 Indexing

In the storage phase, semantic embedding vectors are generated using the Nomic Embed-Text model [6], selected for its ability to represent long texts (up to 8192 tokens) with a high level of contextual accuracy. These vectors are indexed and stored in ChromaDB, a vector database chosen for its retrieval efficiency, low latency time and ease of integration with frameworks such as LangChain. The choice of this database was also motivated by its optimized architecture for semantic queries in natural language processing intensive applications.

3.3 Pre-Retrieval

The pre-retrieval stage includes advanced strategies to optimize query formulation, such as query transformation that includes techniques like Hypothetical Document Embeddings (HyDE) where the LLM generates a hypothetical response to the user's query, which is embedded and used alongside the original query to retrieve semantically aligned fragments. This reduces noise in keyword-only searches.

3.4 Retrieval

The retrieval of relevant and concise context is a central challenge in RAG systems. The retrieval phase was implemented using a cosine similarity search scheme in the vector space, utilizing the previously stored vectors. The vector generated from the user's query is compared with the stored vectors using the cosine similarity metric, and the most similar fragments are selected. For each query, the top 5 fragments with the highest similarity scores are retrieved, aiming for a balance between informational diversity and thematic focus.

3.5 Post-Retrieval

Subsequently, the post-retrieval phase employs innovative techniques to refine the results. Result reordering techniques are applied through the 'LongContextReorder' component of LangChain, which reorders the fragments using the similarity between each fragment and the original query, prioritizing those with the highest semantic alignment to the query. This reordering technique helps mitigate the "information lost in the middle" problem (where LLMs ignore central contextual data). Additionally, contextual filtering and extractive compression processes are carried out using an LLM that selects the relevant parts of the text. This allows for the removal of redundant fragments, obvious contradictions, or content that does not add value to the generation, thus optimizing the use of the generative model's context window. These tools ensure that only the essential information needed to answer the query is maintained, without affecting fidelity to the original content.

3.6 Generation

Finally, in the generation stage, the open-source model LLaMA 3.1 8B is used, running locally through Ollama to produce the final responses. This model was selected for its ability to deliver competitive performance in reasoning tasks. The response generation is based on a prompt that includes the user's original question, but is also enriched with the retrieved and filtered fragments. This prompt is carefully structured and formulated in an instructive format to guide the model in producing outputs that are faithful to the context, accurate in content, and relevant to the user's intent. The goal is to ensure that the model relies primarily on the provided contextual information, thus reducing the risk of hallucinations or out-of-domain responses.

The structure of the prompt used is as follows:

```
qa_prompt = ChatPromptTemplate.from_messages([
    ("system", """
# Task
    You are an expert assistant in answering questions based on the provided context.
    Cite relevant fragments. Use the following context fragments to answer the question.
    Context: {context}
    Question: {input}
# Guidelines
    - Respond based ONLY on the provided context.

    - If the context is insufficient, respond: "Not covered in the provided documents."
    Answer:
    """),
    ("human", "{input}"),
])
```

4 Evaluation and Discussion

In order to validate the effectiveness of the proposed solution, a rigorous evaluation process was designed to compare various system configurations, each integrating different advanced techniques at specific stages of the flow. This evaluation allowed for the analysis of their combined behavior within a flexible and reusable architecture. The methodology adopted is based on practices recognized by the scientific community, incorporating the creation of an evaluation dataset covering topics such as academic regulations, administrative procedures, and program requirements; the use of objective metrics; and the application of a systematic comparison framework between configurations.

To carry out the evaluation process, a dataset was constructed consisting of a set of 140 relevant questions extracted from normative and academic documents in the field of postgraduate studies. Each question was accompanied by its corresponding reference answer, carefully crafted from the content of the source documents, which allowed for the establishment of a ground truth standard against which to compare the generated responses. Along with the reference answers, the contextual fragments that justified these answers were also stored, enabling more precise evaluation and traceability of the results generated by the system.

Five different system configurations were defined. Configuration 1 represented a baseline, limited to the standard RAG flow, without applying any filtering or compression. From this point, the subsequent configurations incorporated additional techniques such as HyDE, re-ranking, and filtering of the retrieved context. Each of these configurations was executed on the same set of questions, and both the generated responses and the fragments used in their construction were documented (Table 1).

Table 1. Evaluated configurations

Configurations	Techniques Used
1	Baseline (No additional techniques)
2	Re-ranker
3	HyDE + Re-ranker
4	Re-ranker + Compressor
5	HyDE + Re-ranker + Compressor

For the evaluation of the results, six key metrics were used: Precision, Recall, F1-Score, Response Relevance, Context Relevance, and Groundedness [11]. Precision measures the proportion of relevant fragments retrieved relative to the total number of fragments retrieved, providing a clear understanding of the quality of the retrievals. In this context, "relevant" means that the fragment contains information that could help answer the question. Recall measures the proportion of relevant documents retrieved from all available documents in the knowledge base. F1-Score can be understood as a balanced measure that combines precision and recall. The formula is as follows:

$$Precision = \frac{Number of relevant retrieved fragments}{Total number of retrieved fragments} \tag{1}$$

$$Recall = \frac{Number\ of\ relevant\ retrieved\ fragments}{Total\ number\ of\ retrieved\ fragments} \tag{2}$$

$$F1 = \frac{2 * Precision * Recall}{Precision + Recall} \tag{3}$$

$$Response\ Relevance = \frac{e_q * e_r}{||e_q|| * ||e_r||} \tag{4}$$

$$Groundedness = \frac{e_q * e_r}{||e_q|| * ||e_r||} \tag{5}$$

$$Context\ Relevance = \frac{e_q * e_c}{||e_q|| * ||e_c||} \tag{6}$$

where:

- e_q is the embedding of the query.

- e_c is the embedding of the retrieved contexts, calculated as the embedding of the concatenated text of all contexts.
- e_r s the embedding of the answer.

$e_q y e_r$ re the L2 norms of the query and answer embeddings, respectively.

Relevance measures how pertinent the content of the response is in relation to the user's intent and the scope of the request. Justification measures the system's ability to generate responses that are based on real and verifiable data, reducing the risk of producing vague or inaccurate answers. Groundedness measure the system's ability to generate responses supported by real and verifiable data, reducing the risk of producing vague or inaccurate answers. Context Relevance measure how well the contextual fragments encapsulate the critical information needed to build a coherent and accurate response, i.e., it measures the extent to which the generated response effectively relies on the contextual evidence, without introducing hallucinations, contradictions, or content unrelated to the corpus. Figure 2 shows the average F1-Score results for each Configuration evaluated. Subsequently, Table 2 presents the overall results of all metrics for each configuration.

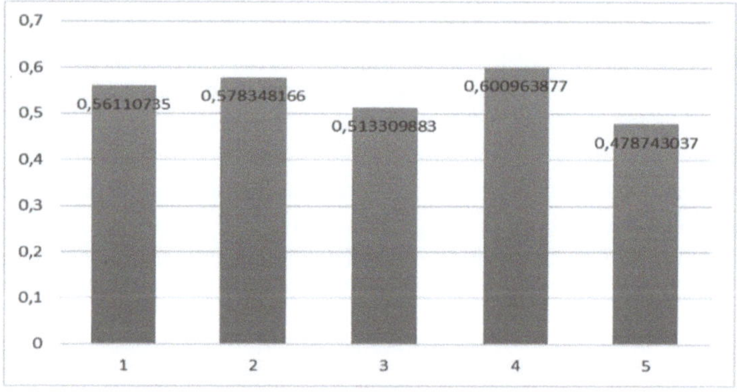

Fig. 2. F1-Score results of each configuration.

Table 2. Results (%) of the evaluated configurations

Configurations	Precision	Recall	F1-Score	Context Relevance	Relevance	Groundedness
1	65,6	54,7	56,1	43	35	27
2	67,4	57,0	57,8	45	74	47
3	56,6	54,8	51,3	26	71	**61**
4	**71,1**	**61,3**	**60,1**	**73**	**73**	58
5	57,6	43,8	47,8	65	48	43

Table 2 summarizes the behavior of each configuration across six key metrics: precision, recall, F1-score, context relevance, overall relevance, and groundness. The latter three metrics allowed for the evaluation of qualitative dimensions of the system, such as the contextual relevance of the responses, their alignment with the retrieved evidence, and their usefulness in relation to the query. The results obtained show significant differences between the evaluated configurations. In general, it is observed that Configuration 1, by not including any techniques, exhibited low levels in the calculated metric values, with responses that in many cases extrapolated information or contained factual errors. Configuration 4 achieves the best values in the traditional metrics (71.1% precision, 61.3% recall, and 60.1% F1-score), demonstrating that the combination of contextual compression and similarity-based re-ranking can significantly optimize the overall performance of the system. On the other hand, Configuration 3, which incorporates HyDE as an intermediate generation technique and subsequent re-ranking, shows a high score in groundness (61%) but a lower precision (56.6%), revealing a trade-off between fidelity and efficiency. Configuration 5, which integrates HyDE, compression, and re-ranking, achieved the lowest performance in all quantitative metrics. In contrast, Configuration 2, which applies re-ranking of retrieved fragments, achieved a balance between precision, recall, and contextual fidelity, demonstrating that improving the retrieved context can be as decisive as expanding the user's queries.

These results confirm that advanced techniques do not have a uniform or cumulative impact on performance; instead, their effectiveness depends on the domain, the type of query, and the specific combination in which they are applied. Furthermore, the evaluation demonstrated that the system can be optimized according to the nature of the task: for example, using compressors when precision is required for narrow tasks or employing strategies like HyDE for more open and exploratory queries. This adaptability was made possible by the modular design of the system, which allowed for the decoupling of operators, reconfiguring workflows, and experimenting with different configurations without compromising the overall stability of the architecture.

This comparative analysis confirmed that the integration of advanced techniques—particularly those focused on pre- and post-retrieval—plays a decisive role in improving the quality of responses generated by RAG systems. Moreover, the evaluation revealed that not all techniques yield benefits in every context, suggesting that their impact may depend both on the domain of the documents and the nature of the questions. The modular structure of the solution made it possible to test these combinations in a controlled manner, enabling an ideal experimental environment for this type of analysis. Consequently, the results obtained validate both the technological approach adopted and the central hypothesis of the study, which posits that the integrated adoption of advanced techniques significantly enhances the performance of RAG systems in domain-specific tasks.

5 Conclusions

This work has proposed, implemented, and evaluated a modular RAG system aimed at integrating and analyzing advanced techniques to optimize answer generation in language-augmented retrieval tasks. The results obtained throughout this research demonstrate the effectiveness of adopting a modular architecture in RAG systems, especially when seeking to integrate and evaluate advanced techniques designed to improve the quality of generated responses. Specialized tools were employed, such as LangChain for workflow orchestration, ChromaDB as the vector database for semantic retrieval, Nomic Embed-Text as the embedding model for content representation, and the LLaMA 3.1 8B model as the language generator. This technological ecosystem ensured the quality of the developed system. The proposed methodology was implemented in a concrete case study within the domain of postgraduate education, which enabled the use of a structured academic and regulatory corpus and provided the conditions for a controlled analysis of different system configurations. Based on this implementation, a set of five experimental configurations was designed, each combining different techniques in key stages of the RAG pipeline, such as query expansion, semantic compression, contextual re-ranking, and relevance-based reclassification. This work demonstrates that a modular RAG architecture provides a solid foundation for both the development and evaluation of artificial intelligence solutions based on information retrieval. The strategic integration of pre- and post-retrieval techniques, evaluated using both quantitative and qualitative metrics, enabled improvements in response quality. This validates the central hypothesis that the structured and deliberate combination of advanced techniques significantly enhances the performance of RAG systems, particularly in specialized domains such as postgraduate education. In this regard, the work not only offers an effective technical solution but also a versatile experimental platform for the research and development of RAG systems applied to specialized domains. In conclusion, this study reaffirms the strategic value of advanced techniques in enhancing retrieval-augmented generation, while proposing a modular architecture as a solid foundation for their implementation and evaluation. It thus establishes a strong starting point for future research aimed at further refining contextual retrieval mechanisms, adapting RAG systems to new domains, and exploring their interaction with increasingly powerful and versatile language models.

Acknowledgments. This work has been partially supported by the National Program PN223LH004: Automatics, Robotics and Artificial Intelligence under grant project PN223LH004-038: *'Aportes teóricos a la IA en el manejo de problemas con datos complejos'*.

References

1. Asai, A., Wu, Z., Wang, Y., Sil, A., Hajishirzi, H.: Self-RAG: Learning to Retrieve, Generate, and Critique through Self-Reflection, arXiv:2310.11511 (2023)
2. Gao, Y., Xiong, Y., Wang, M., Wang, H.: Modular RAG: Transforming RAG Systems into LEGO-like Reconfigurable Frameworks, arXiv:2407.21059 (2024)
3. Huang, Y., Huang, J.: A Survey on Retrieval-Augmented Text Generation for Large Language Models, arXiv:2404.10981 (2024)
4. Khattab, O., Zaharia, M.: ColBERT: Efficient and Effective Passage Search via Contextualized Late Interaction over BERT. In: Proceedings of the 43rd International ACM SIGIR Conference on Research and Development in Information Retrieval (SIGIR'20), pp. 39–48 (2020)
5. Lewis, P., et al.: Retrieval-Augmented Generation for Knowledge-Intensive NLP Tasks. In: Proceedings of the 34th Conference on Neural Information Processing Systems (NeurIPS 2020), arXiv:2005.11401 (2021)

6. Nussbaum, Z., Morris, J.X., Duderstadt, B., Mulyar, A.: Nomic Embed: Training a Reproducible Long Context Text Embedder, arXiv:2402.01613 (2024)
7. Salemi, A., Zamani, H.: Evaluating retrieval quality in retrieval-augmented generation. In: Proceedings of the 47th International ACM SIGIR Conference on Research and Development in Information Retrieval (SIGIR'24), pp. 2395–2400 (2024)
8. Setty, S., Thakkar, H., Lee, A., Chung, E., Vidra, N.: Improving Retrieval for RAG based Question Answering Models on Financial Documents, arXiv: arXiv:2404.07221 (2024)
9. Sawarkar, K., Mangal, A., Solanki, S.R.: Blended RAG: Improving RAG (Retriever-Augmented Generation) Accuracy with Semantic Search and Hybrid Query-Based Retrievers. In: Proceedings of the IEEE 7th International Conference on Multimedia Information Processing and Retrieval (MIPR), pp. 155–161 (2024)
10. Shi, K., Sun, X., Li, Q., Xu, G.: Compressing Long Context for Enhancing RAG with AMR-based Concept Distillation, arXiv:2405.03085 (2024)
11. Verma, S.: Contextual Compression in Retrieval-Augmented Generation for Large Language Models: A Survey. arXiv:2409.13385v2 (2024)
12. Wang, X., et al.: Searching for Best Practices in Retrieval-Augmented Generation, arXiv:2407.01219 (2024)
13. Wei, Q., et al.: QCG-Rerank: Chunks Graph Rerank with Query Expansion in Retrieval-Augmented LLMs for Tourism Domain, arXiv:2411.08724 (2024)
14. Zhang, Q., Zhang, H., Pang, L., Zheng, H., Zheng, Z.: AdaComp: Extractive Context Compression with Adaptive Predictor for Retrieval-Augmented Large Language Models, arXiv:2409.01579 (2024)

Enhancing Context-Aware Content-Based Recommendation with Semantic Embeddings and Sentiment Analysis

Erick Taylor Reverón[1], Alfredo Simón-Cuevas[1]([⊠]) [iD], and Raciel Yera Toledo[2] [iD]

[1] Universidad Tecnológica de La Habana José Antonio Echeverría,
CUJAE Ave. 114, e/Rotonda y Ciclovía, Marianao, La Habana, Cuba
{etaylor,asimon}@ceis.cujae.edu.cu
[2] Universidad de Jaén, Lagunillas S/N, Jaén, Spain
ryera@ujaen.es

Abstract. Content-based recommender systems are highly useful for obtaining relevant information in today's digital environments, where information overload is common. Incorporating contextual information into these systems can yield more effective results, depending on the processing techniques and approaches applied. In this paper, we present a content-based, context-sensitive recommendation method in which sentiment analysis techniques are applied for context processing and semantic embedding models are used for textual content representation. The method was evaluated using a dataset of users and documents (questions and answers) from the QA (question-answering) domain. Several experiments were conducted with different techniques and configurations to identify the best-performing solution, whose results outperformed those reported in other studies.

Keywords: content-based recommendation systems · context-aware recommendation systems · sentiment analysis · semantic word embedding

1 Introduction

Recommender systems have become essential tools to address the problem of information overload, a consequence of the exponential growth of online content and services. By analyzing user preferences, item characteristics, and interaction histories, these systems help users navigate vast information spaces and identify content aligned with their interests. Among various types, Content-Based Recommender Systems (CBRS) [13] stand out for leveraging item attributes—particularly textual content—to generate personalized suggestions based on the user's individual profile. Some of these items are news, books, scientific articles, as well as items composed of question-answer (QA) pairs. CBRS systems generate recommendations solely based on item descriptions and the active user's interest profile. Modern advances increasingly draw upon both deep learning and sentiment analysis to provide relevant and personalized recommendations, even as users' expectations and available data grow ever more complex [12].

Y. Hernádez Heredia et al. (Eds.): IWAIPR 2025, LNCS 16328, pp. 102–112, 2026.
https://doi.org/10.1007/978-3-032-11358-0_9

Context-aware recommendation has emerged as a powerful enhancement to traditional CBRS by incorporating situational and user-generated contextual data into the recommendation process [1, 3, 7, 11]. This added dimension has proven particularly effective in domains rich in unstructured text, such as news, books, social media, and online forums. Two prominent approaches to harnessing such textual content are topic modeling [3] and sentiment analysis [4, 17], the latter being especially useful when content includes subjective opinions, evaluations, or emotional tone, as commonly found in social media. Sentiment analysis has become a critical tool for uncovering latent user preferences expressed in text. These sentiment signals are then integrated with either collaborative or content-based recommendation algorithms, improving both the precision and personalization of recommendations [19]. Sentiment-aware recommendation has been particularly effective in platforms such as Twitter and Stack Exchange, where user interactions and expressed opinions provide rich context for tailoring recommendations.

The deep learning–based word embedding has revolutionized semantic representation in recommender systems by capturing the contextual and semantic relationships between words, sentences, and documents in dense vector spaces [14]. These embeddings have shown superior performance in understanding semantic similarity and user intent, both of which are critical for effective content-based recommendations. Traditional embedding methods such as Word2Vec and Doc2Vec laid the groundwork; however, contemporary systems now increasingly leverage pre-trained language models (PLMs) like BERT, RoBERTa, and DistilBERT to generate high-dimensional contextual embeddings for user, item, and contextual data. These embeddings enable systems to capture deep semantic features, model richer user–item interactions, and facilitate robust data enrichment strategies that transcend simple keyword or rating-based matching [9].

This paper presents a context-aware, content-based recommendation system that leverages deep semantic embeddings and sentiment analysis to enhance the relevance of recommendations in a question-answering (QA) domain. Although lots of researches have been developed around QA item recommendation, the problem of recommending an appropriate QA item to users, according to their corresponding profile has received less attention [3], and most of the developed research does not exploit the semantic dimension in the sufficient way. In order to overcome this limitation, the current paper is focused on the proposal of a semantically-enhanced content-based QA item recommendation system that incorporates Twitter information as a context to provide timely suggestions. Specifically, we apply the Doc2Vec model [8] for semantic representation and a polarity-based sentiment analysis approach to contextual data processing from Twitter.

The proposal was evaluated on the Stack Exchange Q&A network, focusing on the recommendation of thematically and contextually aligned questions and answers. Therefore, its evaluation was conducted using data from the Stack Exchange Q&A network, where the recommendation targets were associated questions and answers. Multiple configurations were tested, comparing topic modeling and sentiment analysis as context-processing mechanisms, and benchmarking different embedding models. Experimental results demonstrate the superiority of the proposed hybrid approach in terms of recommendation quality, supporting the integration of sentiment-aware context modeling and deep embedding representations in modern CBRS.

The remainder of this paper is organized as follows: Sect. 2 synthesizes the analysis of theoretical foundations and characterization of the related work; Sect. 3 describes the recommendation method proposed; Sect. 4 presents and analyzes the experimental results; and Sect. 5 states the conclusions reached.

2 Related Works

Recommender systems are information retrieval systems designed to predict user preferences based on their past decisions, enabling recommendations of potentially relevant items such as movies, books, articles, and others [13]. Among these systems are CBRS, which primarily utilize textual content. These systems employ textual information as a data source to perform comparisons (using NLP techniques) between recommendation items, suggesting to user's items similar to those they have previously shown interest in [2, 16]. The use of textual content as the primary source for recommendations faces the challenge of semantic processing in automated systems. Semantic handling in these systems has been approached through two perspectives [2]: (1) a top-down approach, which relies on external resources such as dictionaries, taxonomies, and ontologies containing semantic information about words and expressions; and (2) a bottom-up approach comprising methods that learn word and phrase meanings directly from content through applied machine learning techniques. The proposed method adopts the latter approach, utilizing word embedding-based textual representation schemes to capture semantics learned directly from textual content.

Previous research has demonstrated the benefits of incorporating contextual information into recommender systems to improve their performance. Context-aware recommender systems generate more relevant recommendations by adapting them to each user's specific contextual situation [1]. The conditions under which recommendations are made significantly influence user decisions, making it valuable to consider these circumstances for generating high-quality recommendations. In this domain, the definition of context is broad [3] but may include elements such as: user location, date and time, access device, language preferences, browser type, among others. Methods for integrating contextual information with recommendations can be classified into [1]: pre-filtering, post-filtering, and contextual modeling-with the latter being the approach adopted in this work, where contextual information is directly incorporated into the recommendation model. In some cases, contextual information can be obtained in natural language form, such as reviews of recommendable items [5, 17] or posts reflecting topics of interest in the current context [3]. Contextual information has been processed through various approaches, including topic modeling and detection [3] as well as sentiment analysis or opinion mining techniques (when the content contains opinions, judgments, or evaluations) [4, 17]. Opinion mining provides valuable information for recommender systems since a user's opinion about a particular item may reflect their satisfaction level. Consequently, the use of opinion mining-particularly polarity detection algorithms-in context-aware recommender systems has become an important research topic in recent years, with a growing number of publications [17].

3 Context-Aware Content-Based Recommendation Method Proposed

The developed context-aware, content-based recommendation method generates ranked item lists optimized for user relevance, specifically designed for question-answering (QA) systems where questions, answers, and comments are treated as composite documents. Context sensitivity is implemented through contextual modeling, which incorporates recommendation-relevant information not directly present in the target documents' content. In our proposal, this contextual information is extracted from Twitter. The utilized tweets focus on news content to capture current trends during recommendation generation. The general framework is inspired by the recommendation method from [3]. However, our context-aware method leverages Twitter news data for real-time relevance, improving upon [3] by:

- Semantic representation: Word embedding models replace Castro et al.'s LSA approach for content representation
- Context processing: Sentiment analysis is applied instead of their topic modeling (Fuzzy C-means) technique.

3.1 Construction of Document Profiles

The content-based recommender system needs to work with vector representations of the elements on which users express their preferences. These representations are document profiles, which are obtained from textual representation schemes. In this proposal, Doc2Vec [8] is used for that purpose, a textual representation scheme based on deep learning. To obtain the vector representation of the documents, a Doc2Vec model is trained using the documents in question. The result of the training is a model that contains a vector representation for each document, as well as for the terms or words present in the documents.

3.2 Construction of User Profiles

To generate a personalized recommendation, user preferences must be modeled through profile construction [3]. These profiles require representation in the same vector space as terms and documents. Each profile aggregates information about documents with which the user interacted whether through document creation, comment authorship, or voting behavior. These interactions are encoded in a binary matrix indicating user-document interest (where 1 denotes interaction). For any user u, their interaction history is derived as:

$$D_u = \{d \in D | \text{matrix}[u, d] = 1\}$$

where D represents the document corpus.

A user profile is constructed by aggregating the vector representations of all documents with which the user interacted:

$$\text{Profile}_u = \sum_{d \in R_u} \text{Profile}_d = \left\{ \sum_{d \in R_u} \text{Profile}_{d,1} \ldots \sum_{d \in R_u} \text{Profile}_{d,f} \right\} \tag{1}$$

where $Profile_u$ corresponds to the user profile vector of user u, $Profile_d$ represents the document profile vector for document d (where d belongs to the set D_u), and f denotes the dimensionality of the vector space in which both $Profile_u$ and $Profile_d$ are jointly represented.

3.3 Contextual Modelling

The selected contextual information consists of tweets posted by users on Twitter, related to news and current events. In this approach, opinion mining is applied as a tool during context modeling. Specifically, TextBlob [10] is used to detect the polarity of each tweet, followed by a filter that retains only those tweets expressing a predominantly positive sentiment. The remaining tweets are mapped into the same vector space as documents and users. Context profiles are created by embedding remaining tweets alongside documents and users in vector space using Doc2Vec. Only terms present in the Doc2Vec trained model are selected, with tweet profiles formed by averaging their corresponding vectors.

3.4 Contextualization of User Profiles

This phase aims to incorporate contextual information into user profiles. For each user profile, we compute its similarity with the context tweet profiles. The cosine similarity between each vector pair serves as the similarity measure. The five tweets showing highest similarity with the user profile are selected for contextualization, and a new vector is created by summing these five tweet profiles. To obtain the contextualized user profile, we combine the original user profile with its corresponding context profile. This combination is regulated through a parameter alpha (α), according to [3]. Higher alpha values prioritize the original user profile, while lower values emphasize contextual information during the contextualization process. The resulting contextualized user profile is computed as follows:

$$\text{Profile}_{C,u} = \alpha * \text{Profile}_u + (1 - \alpha) * \text{Profile}_c \tag{2}$$

where $Profile_u$ refers to the profile of user u, $Profile_c$ denotes the context profile, $Profile_{C,u}$ is the contextualized user profile, and α represents the parameter controlling the context's weight in the process α represents the parameter controlling the context's weight in the process.

3.5 Prediction

Following user profile contextualization, the system predicts the relevance of each document for each user based on their preferences [13]. This phase again employs either cosine similarity or dot product as the similarity measure. For each user profile, we compute the cosine similarity with all test documents. The final recommendation consists of documents ranked in descending order according to their predicted relevance scores:

$$P_{u,d} = \alpha * \text{Profile}_{C,u} * \text{Profile}_d \tag{3}$$

Each user is primarily recommended documents showing the highest similarity to their contextualized profile. In an online deployed recommendation system, users typically prefer receiving a condensed recommendation list rather than the complete generated list [18]. However, for evaluating the recommendation system developed in this work, we consider the full document list.

4 Evaluation of the Proposed Solution

4.1 Experimental Setup

The evaluation method used corresponds to that adopted in [3], as a basis for comparing results and demonstrating improvements. Two data sources are used in the evaluation: the QA documents that constitute the domain or content and recommendation target, and the context information. The QA domain used in the experiment is the Stack Exchange dataset[1]. This dataset consists of the database dump of each site in the Stack Exchange ecosystem. We focus on the Stack Exchange site devoted to 3D printing[2], in the same way that the reported in [3]. The QA documents were constructed from questions asked by users, the corresponding answers, and comments provided by other users extracted from the Stack Exchange ecosystem. Some stats of the dataset are detailed in Table 1.

Table 1. Main stats feature of 3D printing dataset from Stack Exchange sites.

Users	Questions	Answers	Comments	Votes	Ratings	Sparsity
4025	597	1135	2754	7860	2458	0.99898

Regarding the contextual dataset, a set of interesting keywords is defined based on the aim of the proposal for contextualizing recommendations. The selected contextual information comprised a collection of tweets gathered over 23 days, with each day representing a distinct context. The stats of the dataset extracted from Tweeter is depicted in Fig. 1.

For assessing recommendation prediction quality, the NDCG (Normalized Discounted Cumulative Gain) [6, 13] metric was employed (see Eq. 4). In contrast to precision-based metrics, NDCG and DCG measures the usefulness (relevance) of a document based on its position in the list of recommended items. It assumes that highly relevant documents are more useful when appearing earlier in a result list, and that highly relevant documents are more useful than marginally relevant documents, which are in turn more useful than non-relevant documents. NDCG is a normalized variant of the DCG metric. The DCG value is divided by a reference value called ideal DCG, obtained from a list where items are ranked in descending order by their true relevance

---

[1] http://data.stackexchange.com/.

[2] https://3dprinting.stackexchange.com/.

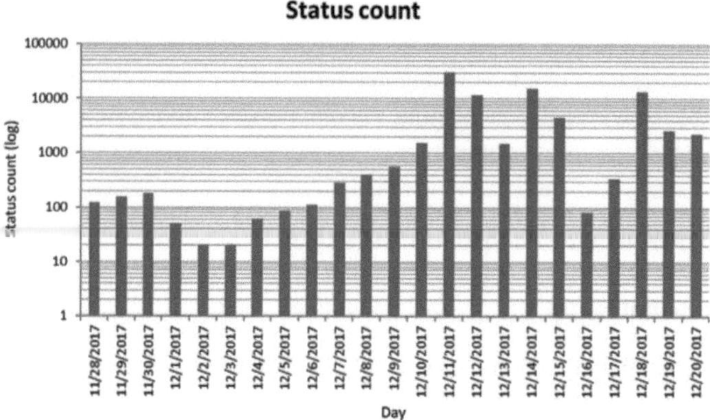

Fig. 1. Volume of contextual information captured from Twitter

scores. The NDCG value ranges between 0 and 1, with higher values indicating better recommendation quality.

$$NDCG = \frac{DCG}{DCG\ ideal} \tag{4}$$

$$DCG = \sum_{i=1}^{N} \frac{r_i}{\log_2(1+i)} \tag{5}$$

where r_i is a value between 0 and 1 (inclusive) representing the gain associated with the item at position i, and n is the total number of recommended items. Higher DCG values indicate better recommendation quality.

Different configurations of the recommendation method were evaluated to identify the top-performing. Therefore, several experiments were conducted:

1. to evaluate various semantic embedding representation schemes: *Doc2Vec, BERT_mediun* y *BERT_base*;
2. to evaluate several context processing approaches:
   a. sentiment analysis by polarity filtering (using SentiWordNet, VADER, TextBlob, SenticNet, or none),
   b. topic modelling through term clustering, using DBSCAN, Fuzzy C-Means (used in [3]), Hierarchical Agglomerative Clustering, or none.

   The procedure described below is performed for each configurations evaluated:

1. The documents (questions + answers) from 3D printing dataset are split into training (80% QA items) and test (20% QA items), using the 5-cross fold validation as a splitting technique. In this procedure, the dataset is divided into k folds. One of the folds is used for testing the model and the remaining k - 1 folds are used for training. The cross-validation process is repeated k times with each of the k subsamples used exactly once as test data and the remaining ones for training. Finally, the average performance of the k evaluations, reached after the last step of this procedure.

2. Training set documents are vectorized (according to embedding representation model); these vectors constitute the document profiles.
3. User profiles are constructed from documents (vector sum) that each user showed interest in (considering only those from the training set).
4. For each context:
   a. If opinion mining algorithms are used, tweets with negative sentiment are removed from the context.
   b. The remaining tweets are vectorized using the same technique employed for document representation.
   c. When topic modeling is applied, the tweet vectors are clustered via the selected grouping algorithm and combined to create topic profiles.
   d. User profiles are contextualized.
   e. The prediction phase uses contextualized user profiles and test-set documents. For each contextualized user profile:

   - Documents are scored using cosine similarity between user and document profiles.
   - Scores indicate predicted relevance for each user-document pair

   f. Recommendations are evaluated per user by comparing:

   - System-recommended documents from the test set
   - User-engaged documents from the same test set using NDCG [6] as the evaluation metric.

The experiments also evaluated the influence of context on predicting documents to recommend. The contextual weight is controlled by parameter alpha (α) in Eq. (2). This parameter was included for determining whether context-awareness improves results. For user profile contextualization:

- Lower α values increase contextual information's influence on recommendations
- When $\alpha = 1$, contextual information is entirely disregarded.

4.2 Results and Discussion

Table 2 summarizes the top-performing method configurations from our experiments. The results demonstrate that the highest NDCG values were achieved using polarity filtering alone as the contextual processing technique, with marginally superior outcomes when combined with topic modeling. Figure 2 presents the results for different values of parameter alpha (α) using Doc2Vec as the representation scheme, as this model yielded the best performance. The parameter evaluation considered values ranging from 0.6 to 1 with 0.05 increments. The peak NDCG at $\alpha = 0,85$ represents a significant finding, demonstrating that our sentiment analysis approach for contextual processing enhances the value of contextual information in recommendation quality. This contrasts with [3], who reported their best NDCG at $\alpha = 0,94$.

Figure 3 compares the proposed method configuration with other reported approaches using the same evaluation framework, clearly demonstrating the improved results achieved by our new solution. The bars in the figure represent (from left to right):

Table 2. Configurations of the proposed method that obtained the best NDCG values (in descending order).

#	Representation models	Polarity detection	Topic Modelling	Alfa	NDCG
1	**Doc2Vec**	***TextBlob***	None	**0,85**	**0,273583**
2	Doc2Vec	*SenticNet*	None	0,85	0,273512
3	Doc2Vec	*VADER*	None	0,85	0,273409
4	Doc2Vec	*SentiWordNet*	None	0,85	0,273386
5	Doc2Vec	*VADER*	*HAC*	0,85	0,273263
6	Doc2Vec	*TextBlob*	*HAC*	0,85	0,273121
7	Doc2Vec	*SenticNet*	*Fuzzy C-Means*	0,85	0,272974
8	Doc2Vec	*SentiWordNet*	*Fuzzy C-Means*	0,85	0,272911
9	Doc2Vec	*VADER*	*HAC*	0,85	0,272800

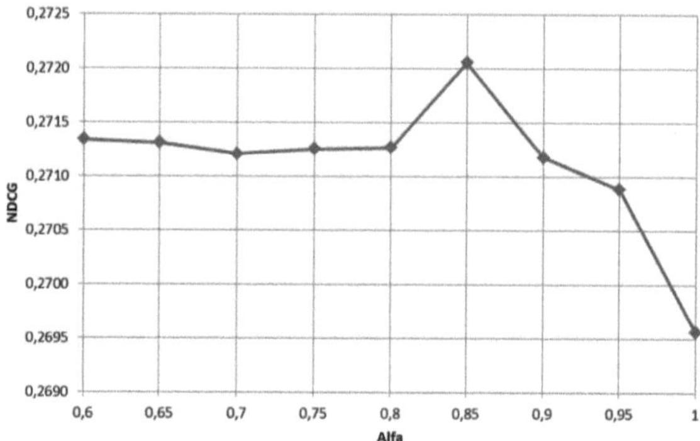

Fig. 2. Average NDCG per alpha value (using Doc2Vec)

1. ***LSAContextClusteringMax*** $\alpha = 0.94$: variant that obtained the best results in [3]. It uses LSA for text representation, Fuzzy C-Means for topic modelling and an alpha value equal to 0,94. It does not use opinion mining.
2. ***LSA VADER + AHC*** $\alpha = 0,75$: variant that obtained the best results in [4]. It uses LSA for text representation, VADER for opinion mining, HAC for topic modelling, and an alpha value equal to 0,75.
3. ***BERT_base*** $\alpha = 1$: best performing variant using BERT as a proxy. It does not use contextual information, so it has an alpha value equal to 1.
4. ***Doc2Vec + TextBlob,*** $\alpha = 0,85$: variant that obtained the best results in the present work globally using Doc2Vec, TextBlob for polarity detection, and an alpha value equal to 0,85, and without using topical modelling.

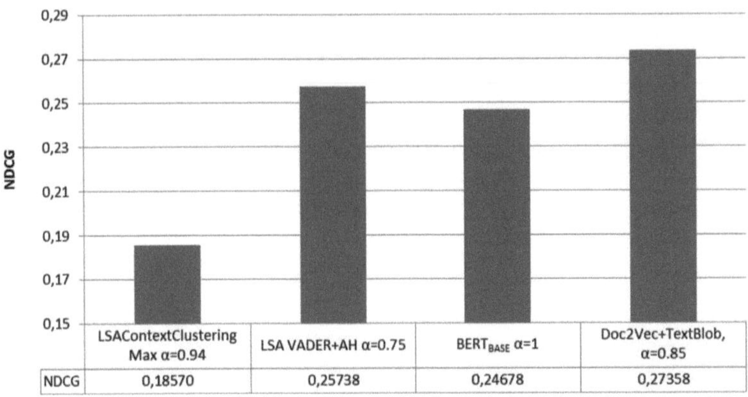

	LSAContextClustering Max α=0.94	LSA VADER+AH α=0.75	BERT$_{BASE}$ α=1	Doc2Vec+TextBlob, α=0.85
NDCG	0,18570	0,25738	0,24678	0,27358

Fig. 3. Comparison of the proposed solution with results of others reported approaches [3, 4].

5 Conclusions

This work introduced a novel context-aware, content-based recommendation method tailored for answer retrieval in question–answering systems. The proposed approach integrates a Doc2Vec-based semantic representation to capture richer and more nuanced textual meanings, coupled with sentiment-aware contextual processing via polarity-based filtering of Twitter-sourced data. Experimental results confirmed that Doc2Vec outperformed transformer-based alternatives such as BERT for our task and dataset, while polarity detection (TextBlob) proved more effective than topic modeling with clustering algorithms for context processing. By combining deep semantic embeddings with sentiment-driven context filtering, our method significantly improved recommendation relevance, demonstrating the value of affective information in refining content-based recommendations. These findings suggest promising applications in other domains involving user-generated content and real-time context integration, such as customer support, e-learning, and social media monitoring.

Acknowledgments. This work has been partially supported by the National Program PN223LH004: Automatics, Robotics and Artificial Intelligence under grant project PN223LH004–038: *'Aportes teóricos a la IA en el manejo de problemas con datos complejos'*.

References

1. Adomavicius, G., Mobasher, B., Ricci, F., Tuzhilin, A.: Context-aware recommender systems. AI Mag. **32**(3), 67–80 (2011)
2. Anand, P.B., Nath, R.: Content-based recommender systems, en recommender system with machine learning and Artificial Intelligence. Mohanty, S.N., Chatterjee, J.M., Jain, S., Elngar, A.A., Gupta, P. (eds.). 1ra ed Beverly, Massachusetts, Estados Unidos: Scrivener Publishing, pp. 165–195 (2020)
3. Castro, J., Yera, R., Alzahrani, A.A., Sánchez, P.J., Barranco, M.J., Martínez, L.: A big data semantic driven context aware recommendation method for question-answer items. IEEE Access **7**(1), 182664–182678 (2019)

4. González, A., Taylor, E., Simón-Cuevas, A., Yera, R., Martínez, L.: Aplicación de minería de opinión en el procesamiento del contexto en un sistema de recomendación. En Actas de la VI Conferencia Internacional en Ciencias Computaciones e Informáticas (CICCI 2022), La Habana, Cuba (2022)

5. Ibrahim, M., Bajwa, I.S., Ul-Amin, R., Kasi, B.: A Neural network-inspired approach for improved and true movie recommendations. Comput. Intell. Neurosci. **2019**(7), 1–19 (2019)

6. Järvelin, K., Kekäläinen, J.: Cumulated gain-based evaluation of IR techniques. ACM Trans. Inf. Syst. **20**(4), 422–446 (2002)

7. Kulkarni, S., Rodd, S.F.: Context aware recommendation systems: a review of the state of the art techniques. Comput. Sci. Rev. **37**, 1–33 (2020)

8. Le, Q., Mikolov, T.: Distributed representations of sentences and documents. In: Proceedings of the 31st International Conference on Machine Learning, Beijing, China, pp. 1188–1196 (2014)

9. Le, N.L., Abel, M.H.: Enhancing recommender systems using textual embeddings from pre-trained language models. In: Rocha, A., Ferrás, C., Calvo, H. (eds.) Information Technology and Systems. ICITS 2025. Lecture Notes in Networks and Systems, vol. 1449. Springer, Cham (2025)

10. Loria, S.: TextBlob documentation. Read the Docs. Disponible en: https://textblob.readth edocs.io/en/dev/ (consultado el 01 June 2022) (2022)

11. Mateos, P., Bellogín, A.: A systematic literature review of recent advances on context-aware recommender systems. Artif. Intell. Rev. **58**, 20 (2025)

12. Nabil, S., El Bouhdidi, J., Yassin, M.Y.: Enhancing recommender systems using sentiment analysis: addressing cold start issues and improving recommendation quality. J. Adv. Inf. Technol. **16**(4), 256–267 (2025)

13. Rana, P., Jain, N., Mittal, U.: An introduction to basic concepts on recommender systems, en recommender system with machine learning and Artificial Intelligence. Mohanty, S.N., Chatterjee, J.M., Jain, S., Elngar, A.A., Gupta, P. (eds.). 1ra ed Beverly, Massachusetts, Estados Unidos: Scrivener Publishing, pp. 1–25 (2020)

14. Santana, I., Domínguez, M.: A systematic review on context-aware recommender systems using deep learning and embeddings (2020). arXiv preprint arXiv:2007.04782

15. Shani, G., Gunawardana, A.: Evaluating recommendation systems. In: Recommender Systems Handbook. Ricci, F., Rokach, L., Shapira, B., Kantor, P.B. (eds.). 1ra ed Boston, Massachusetts, Estados Unidos: Springer US, pp. 257–297 (2011)

16. Sharma, S.C.M., Mitra, A., Chakraborty, D.: Concepts of recommendation system from the perspective of machine learning, en recommender system with machine learning and Artificial Intelligence. Mohanty, S.N., Chatterjee, J.M., Jain, S., Elngar, A.A., Gupta, P. (eds.) 1ra ed Beverly, Massachusetts, Estados Unidos: Scrivener Publishing (2020)

17. Sundermann, C.V., Domingues, M.A., Sinoara, R.A., Marcacini, R.M., Oliveira, S.: Using opinion mining in context-aware recommender systems: a systematic review. Information **10**(42), 1–45 (2019)

18. Tewari, A.S., Singh, J.P., Barman. A.G.: Generating Top-N items recommendation set using collaborative. Content based filtering and rating variance. Procedia Comput. Sci. **132**(1), 1678–1684 (2018)

19. Valencia-Arias, A., Uribe-Bedoya, H., González-Ruiz, J.D., Sánchez, G., Chapoñan, E., Martínez, E.: Artificial intelligence and recommender systems in e-commerce. Trends Res. Agenda Intell. Syst. Appl. **24**, 200435 (2025)

Time-Evolving Linguistic Decision Making: A Feedback-Enabled Approach

Yeleny Zulueta-Veliz[(✉)] [iD], Carlos Rafael Rodríguez Rodríguez[iD],
Aylin Estrada Velazco[iD], and Dainys Gaínza Reyes[iD]

University of Informatics Sciences, Havana, Cuba
{yeleny,crodriguezr,avelazco,dgainza}@uci.cu
http://www.uci.cu

Abstract. This paper introduces a Linguistic Dynamic Multi-Criteria Decision Making (LDMCDM) framework for evolving decision scenarios with time-varying alternatives, criteria, and experts. The proposed solution combines three key innovations: (1) a feedback-enabled architecture for temporal adaptation, (2) the novel $2T\prod$ associative aggregation operator that ensures computational efficiency through its reinforcement properties, and (3) 2-tuple linguistic modeling that maintains human-interpretable outputs. The $2T\prod$ operator eliminates full-history storage requirements while dynamically merging linguistic evaluations across periods. Validated through a subcontractor evaluation case study, our approach demonstrates consistent performance in handling dynamic system changes. The framework bridges a fundamental gap in LDMCDM by simultaneously addressing linguistic uncertainty and temporal data evolution, offering practical advantages in both computational performance and decision quality.

Keywords: linguistic decision making · dynamic decision making · aggregation operator

1 Introduction

Traditional Multi-Criteria Decision Making (MCDM) models operate on a fundamental assumption: both criteria and alternatives remain fixed from the outset, with decisions occurring at a single static point in time. While this simplification facilitates computation, it often leads to unrealistic modeling that undermines the practical validity of results in dynamic real-world scenarios [8]. The challenge of MCDM under conditions of uncertainty and temporality persists as an open research question [9]. When examining these two dimensions, distinct problem categories emerge based on whether information is certain or uncertain, and whether the temporal context is static or dynamic. The most complex case, and the focus of this work, combines uncertain information within temporally evolving environments.

Temporality can be addressed through Dynamic MCDM (DMCDM), which accounts for how changing conditions influence decisions over time. Real-world

Y. Hernádez Heredia et al. (Eds.): IWAIPR 2025, LNCS 16328, pp. 113–124, 2026.
https://doi.org/10.1007/978-3-032-11358-0_10

applications, ranging from commercial banks performance evaluation [1], selection of sustainable forest management options [5], multi-stage risk investment decision making [17], manufacturing industry evaluation [18] and supplier selection [20], demonstrate how decision matrices typically undergo iterative modifications. These scenarios require evaluating not just current alternative performance but also incorporating historical data, a capability beyond traditional static MCDM models.

Simultaneously, non-probabilistic uncertainty characterizes many decision problems. When a problem is too complex or unclear for exact measurements, fuzzy sets and the fuzzy linguistic approach [19] are effective tools to deal with the experts' qualitative preference. This matches how people actually think and communicate, using words instead of numbers.

The intersection of these challenges gives rise to Linguistic DMCDM (LDM-CDM), where decision data collected across multiple periods is represented through linguistic variables. However, a significant research gap persists: most existing models aggregate historical preferences into a final decision using weighted averaging operators, failing to accommodate cases where alternatives or criteria vary over time, or where interim decisions with feedback mechanisms are required [20]. Campanella and Ribeiro [4] made progress by proposing a numerical DMCDM framework using associative aggregation operators that compute dynamic ratings without storing complete historical data. Yet these operators remain underutilized in linguistic models despite their potential to represent the feedback loops essential to dynamic decision-making [2,11].

This work introduces a flexible LDMCDM approach designed to handle dynamic changes in alternatives, criteria, and decision-makers over time within fuzzy environments. The proposed solution features a novel associative, full-reinforcement aggregation operator that creates robust feedback loops, effectively bridging the current research gap. The remainder of this paper is structured as follows. Section 2 reviews associative operators and the 2-tuple linguistic model. Section 3 develops our feedback-enabled LDMCDM approach, implemented using the proposed operator detailed in Section Sect. 4. Section 5 demonstrates the approach functioning through a subcontractor evaluation case study, with conclusions following in Sect. 6.

2   Preliminaries

To ensure a self-contained presentation, this section briefly reviews the fundamental concepts underlying our proposed approach. We begin with a detailed examination of associative aggregation operators, particularly t-norms, t-conorms, and uninorms, given their critical role in DMCDM. Additionally, we present essential concepts of the 2-tuple linguistic representation model, with special attention to its aggregation operators and their properties.

2.1 Associative Aggregation Operations via T-Norms, T-Conorms and Uninorms

Associativity provides a Markovian behavior in aggregation: to proceed from aggregation of n arguments to aggregation of $(n+1)$ arguments, only is necessary to know the result of aggregation of the first n elements and the value of $(n+1)$th argument [16].

A triangular norm or t-norm, T is a mapping, $T : [0,1] \times [0,1] \longrightarrow [0,1]$, having the commutativity, monotonicity, associativity properties and neutral element $T(a,1) = a$ for all $a,b,c,d \in [0,1]$. In constrast, a triangular conorm or t-conorm S is a mapping, $S : [0,1] \times [0,1] \longrightarrow [0,1]$, having for all $a,b,c,d \in [0,1]$ the same properties but a neutral element: $S(a,0) = a$.

T-norms are conjunctive aggregation operators, therefore they exhibit downward reinforcement $T(a_1, ..., a_n) \leq min_i(a_i)$. Then the aggregated value is never greater than the lowest a_i. Moreover, if all a_i's values are low, then such values shall reinforce each other so that the resulting aggregated value is even lower. T-conorms are disjunctive aggregation operators, therefore they exhibit upward reinforcement $S(a_1, ..., a_n) \leq max_i(a_i)$. Uninorms were introduced by Yager and Rybalov [14] as a generalization of t-norms and t-conorms. An uninorm is a mapping, $U : [0,1] \times [0,1] \longrightarrow [0,1]$, having for all $a,b,c,d \in [0,1]$ the commutativity, monotonicity, associativity and a neutral element $\exists e \in [0,1] : U(a,e) = a$ that is not forced to be either 0 or 1, but can be any value in the unit interval.

2.2 Fuzzy Linguistic Modeling with 2-Tuple Linguistic Representation Model

Developed by Herrera [6] within the fuzzy linguistic approach, the 2-tuple linguistic model prevents information loss in computing with words for odd-granularity, symmetric term sets. It represents information as a term-plus-translation pair (s_i, α), offering greater precision than index-based approaches.

Definition 1. *[6] The symbolic translation is a numerical value assessed in $[-0.5, 0.5)$ that supports the difference of information between a counting of information β assessed in the interval of granularity $[0, g]$ of the term set S and the closest value in $\{0, ..., g\}$ which indicates the index of the closest linguistic term in S.*

The Δ and Δ^{-1} transformation functions support conversions between numerical values and 2-tuple linguistic values without information loss.

Definition 2. *[6] Let $S = \{s_0, ..., s_g\}$ the set of linguistic terms, the associated 2-tuple linguistic is $\tilde{S} = S \times [-0.5, 0.5)$ and the bijective function $\Delta : [0, g] \to \tilde{S}$ is defined as:*

$$\Delta(\beta) = \begin{cases} s_i, & i = round(\beta) \\ \alpha = \beta - i, & \alpha \in [-0.5, 0.5) \end{cases} \tag{1}$$

where round assigns to β the integer number $i \in \{0, 1, ..., g\}$ closest to β.

The past two decades have seen significant advances in the development of 2-tuple linguistic aggregation operators for time-independent decision making. The transformation functions Δ and Δ^{-1} form the mathematical core of these developments, enabling the rigorous extension of classical numerical operators to the 2-tuple linguistic domain while preserving computational precision.

3   A LDMCDM Approach with Feedback Loop

This section introduces a LDMCDM approach with feedback, specifically designed to model complex decision-making processes where evaluations evolve dynamically across multiple periods, and expert judgments are inherently expressed through linguistic terms. The approach unifies linguistic computing with temporal dynamics, addressing scenarios where both uncertainty (captured via linguistic variables) and time-dependent changes (managed through feedback mechanism) simultaneously influence the decision process.

Step 1. LDMCDM problem definition

The LDMCDM problem is structured through the following components: Let $T = \{(t_\lambda)|\lambda \in (1,...,q)\}$ be the set of discrete positive time periods. For each (t_λ), let $A(t_\lambda) = \{a_i(t_\lambda)|i \in (1,...,m)\}$ the set of alternatives and $E(t_\lambda) = \{e_k(t_\lambda)|k \in (1,...,p)\}$ the set of experts assessing the alternatives according to the set of criteria $C(t_\lambda) = \{c_j(t_\lambda)|j \in (1,...,n)\}$ whose weights are given by the vector $W = (w(t_\lambda)_j|j \in (1,...,n)), w_j(t_\lambda) \in [0,1]$ with $\sum_{j=1}^{n} w_j(t_\lambda) = 1$.

Previous elements may vary temporally at any t_λ: alternatives may enter/exit the set; criteria weights and values may change between periods; expert participation may evolve across different time periods.

The assessment provided by expert $e_k \in E(t_\lambda)$ about alternative $a_i(t_\lambda) \in A(t_\lambda)$ according to criterion $c_j(t_\lambda) \in C(t_\lambda)$ at period t_λ, is represented by a value $x_{ijk}(t_\lambda) = s_{ijk}(t_\lambda) \in S = \{s_0,...,s_g\}$ being $g+1$ the cardinality of the linguistic term set S.

The adaptive nature of the approach allows dynamic modifications of the retention policy during the decision process. The retention policy determines the temporal influence window by controlling the degree to which past assessments contribute to present computations. Adjustments may occur either through manual intervention by decision-makers altering retention parameters, or automatically through system responses to environmental changes.

Step 2. Data collection

During each evaluation period t_λ, participating experts provide linguistic assessments for all alternatives for every criterion. These evaluations are structured as time-indexed decision matrices $X_i(t_\lambda) = (x_{ijk}(t_\lambda))_{n \times p}$

Step 3. Data transformation

The original linguistic term $s_i \in S$ corresponds exactly to the 2-tuple linguistic $(s_i, 0)$ where the zero-valued symbolic translation $\alpha = 0$ indicates perfect alignment with the label's semantic center. This canonical mapping preserves the

initial assessment's meaning while converting it to the 2-tuple linguistic representation space $\tilde{S}$. Formally, for gathered expert evaluations $x_{ijk}(t_\lambda) = s_{ijk}(t_\lambda) \in S$ we obtain their 2-tuple linguistic equivalents through the transformation:
$$\tilde{x}_{ijk}(t_\lambda) = (s, 0)_{ijk}(t_\lambda) \in \tilde{S}.$$

Step 4. Non-dynamic rating computation

The approach combines expert assessments through two independent linguistic operators.

First, operator Υ aggregates individual ratings per criterion:

$$\hat{X}_i(t_\lambda) = (\hat{x}_{ij}(t_\lambda))_{n \times 1} = \Upsilon\left(\tilde{x}_{ijk}(t_\lambda)\right) \tag{2}$$

Then, operator Ψ synthesizes these results by alternative:

$$\bar{X}_i(t_\lambda) = (\bar{x}_i(t_\lambda)) = \Psi\left(\hat{x}_{ij}(t_\lambda)\right) \tag{3}$$

This decoupled approach enables flexible fusion of expert opinions and criteria compensation, with results $\bar{X}_i(t_\lambda)$ feeding subsequent dynamic aggregation while retaining original linguistic properties.

Step 5. Dynamic rating computation with feedback

The approach advances beyond static period-specific evaluations by introducing temporal feedback into the rating process. While non-dynamic ratings $\bar{X}_i(t_\lambda)$ capture standalone assessments for each period, the dynamic computation incorporates historical performance through a specialized feedback mechanism, yielding comprehensive ratings $\check{X}_i(t_\lambda)$, that reflect the complete temporal evolution of alternatives.

$$\check{X}_i(t_\lambda) = (\check{x}_i(t_\lambda)) \tag{4}$$

where $\check{x}_i(t_\lambda) = E_{\tilde{S}}\left(\check{x}_i(t_{\lambda-1}), \bar{x}_i(t_\lambda)\right)$, being $E_S : \Lambda(t_\lambda) \cap H(t_\lambda - 1) \longrightarrow \tilde{S}$ the linguistic dynamic evaluation function defined as:

$$E_{\tilde{S}}\left(\check{x}_i(t_{\lambda-1}), \bar{x}_i(t_\lambda)\right) = \begin{cases} \bar{x}_i(t_\lambda), & a_i(t_\lambda) \in A(t_\lambda) \setminus H(t_\lambda - 1) \\ \Phi\left(\bar{x}_i(t_\lambda), \check{x}_i(t_{\lambda-1})\right), & a_i(t_\lambda) \in A(t_\lambda) \cap H(t_{\lambda-1}) \\ \check{x}_i(t_{\lambda-1}), & a_i(t_\lambda) \in H(t_{\lambda-1}) \setminus A(t_\lambda) \end{cases} \tag{5}$$

being $\Phi : \tilde{S}^2 \longrightarrow \tilde{S}$ an associative 2-tuple linguistic aggregation operator.

The aggregation operator plays a crucial role in the evaluation function. Its associativity provides a Markovian behavior in aggregation: to proceed from aggregation of n arguments to aggregation of $(n+1)$ arguments, only is necessary to know the result of aggregation of the first n elements and the value of $(n+1)$th argument [16]. Common classes of associative aggregation operators include t-norms, t-conorms and uninorms.

However, just few existing 2-tuple linguistic aggregation operators fulfill associativity property required for computing the linguistic dynamic evaluation of alternatives. Tao et al. in [12] developed some novel operational laws of linguistic 2-tuples based on the Archimedean t-norm and t-conorm, which are associative.

However, full reinforcement aggregation operators are required in some situations.

Associative aggregation operators allow the benefits of computing final results without storing all previous values (through the associativity property) and additionally modulating the importance of these values in such final results (through the reinforcement property). These operators enable historical value weighting through their reinforcement properties while maintaining computational efficiency via associativity. Additionally, because they are defined in 2-tuple linguistic domain, they permit to obtain final linguistic evaluation values which are more understandable and close to human language.

Step 6. Alternative ranking and historical information processing

The historical information is processed through three key operations:

i. Alternative ranking: Using 2-tuple linguistic comparison rules, we establish an ordered set:

$$O(t_\lambda) = \{a(t_\lambda)_{z(i)} | z(i) \in (1, ...,)\} \tag{6}$$

is a permutation where $\check{x}_{z(i-1)}(t_\lambda) \geq \check{x}_{z(i)}(t_\lambda)$ for $i = 2, \ldots, m\}$ This ordering enables selection of best alternatives when stopping criteria are met.

ii. Historical set definition: In general, the historical set is defined as:

Definition 3. *The historical set of alternatives at decision moment $t \in T$ is a subset of all alternatives that have ever been available up to and including that current period,*

$$H(t_\lambda) = \bigcup_{\lambda' \leq \lambda} A(t_{\lambda'}), \quad \lambda', \lambda \in T. \tag{7}$$

With initial condition $H(t_0) = \emptyset$.

iii. Retention policy application:

The retention policy constitutes a formal mechanism for dynamically managing the temporal influence window in LDMCDM systems. Mathematically, it operates as a function $\Psi : H(t_\lambda) \times A(t_\lambda) \rightarrow H(t_{\lambda+1})$ that determines which historical alternatives persist in the decision process. If stopping criterion is not satisfied, and a new iteration is required, the historical information might be updated according to some of the following retention policies:

- Top-$a_i(t_\lambda)$ retention: selecting the $a_i(t_\lambda)$ alternatives which rank higher than all others in (t_λ).

$$H(t_\lambda) = \{a(t_\lambda)_z | z < \xi\} \bigcup H(t_{\lambda-1})$$

- Threshold filtering: selecting alternatives whose linguistic dynamic evaluation surpasses a quality threshold $\gamma \in \bar{S}$.

$$H(t_\lambda) = \{a_i(t_\lambda) | \check{x}_i(t_\lambda) > \gamma\} \bigcup H(t_{\lambda-1})$$

- Stability-based retention: selecting alternatives consistently available for η periods.

$$H(t_\lambda) = \bigcap_{\lambda'} A(t_{\lambda'}), \ \lambda' \in \{\lambda - \eta + 1, ..., \lambda\}$$

- Complete retention: preserving full historical record.

$$H(t_\lambda) = A(t_\lambda) \bigcup H(t_{\lambda-1})$$

The retention policy enhances LDMCDM through four integrated mechanisms. First, it achieves *computational efficiency* by reducing state space complexity from $O(\lambda \cdot m)$ to $O(k)$, where $k \ll m \cdot \lambda$. Second, *temporal relevance control* is maintained through configurable thresholds that automatically prioritize recent data while phasing out older information. Third, the policy enables *dynamic adaptation* by enforcing Markovian properties through controlled historical dependencies, ensuring responsiveness to system changes. Finally, it performs *noise filtration* by systematically pruning obsolete or irrelevant alternatives, improving decision quality.

4   Building the Feedback Loop with an Associative and Full Reinforcement Aggregation Operator

Current 2-tuple linguistic aggregation operators lack the crucial associativity property needed for dynamic evaluation, while existing full reinforcement operators operate on $[0, 1]$ rather than the linguistic domain $\tilde{S}$. To address these limitations, we develop a novel associative operator for 2-tuples linguistic through three key innovations.

First we extend functions Δ and Δ^{-1} from the 2-tuple linguistic representation model in order to perform transformations between 2-tuples linguistic and numerical values in $[0, 1]$ instead of $[0, g]$.

Definition 4. *Let $S = \{s_0, ..., s_g\}$ the set of linguistic terms and $\beta_e \in [0, 1]$ a value supporting the result of a symbolic aggregation operation, then the function $\Delta_e : [0, 1] \to \tilde{S}$ expressing the equivalent information to β_e is defined as:*

$$\Delta_e(\beta_e) = \begin{cases} s_i, & i = round(\beta_e \cdot g) \\ \alpha = \beta_e \cdot g - i, & \alpha \in [-0.5, 0.5) \end{cases} \tag{8}$$

Definition 5. *Let $S = \{s_0, ..., s_g\}$ the set of linguistic terms and $\tilde{S} = S \times [-0.5, 0.5)$ the associated linguistic 2-tuple, then function $\Delta_e^{-1} : \tilde{S} \to [0, 1]$ returns from a linguistic 2-tuple (s_i, α) its equivalent numerical value as:*

$$\Delta_e^{-1}(s_i, \alpha) = \frac{i + \alpha}{g} = \frac{\Delta^{-1}(s_i, \alpha)}{g} \tag{9}$$

with $\beta_e \in [0, 1]$ and α a symbolic translation.

These transformations enable operator extension to the linguistic domain:

Definition 6. *Let $(s_x, \alpha_x), (s_y, \alpha_y) \in \tilde{S}$ two linguistic 2-tuple, S a linguistic term set, and $\varphi : [0,1]^2 \rightarrow [0,1]$ a numeric aggregation operator, its extension for linguistic 2-tuple is a function $\overline{\varphi} : \tilde{S}^2 \rightarrow \tilde{S}$ defined as:*

$$\overline{\varphi}((s_x, \alpha_x), (s_y, \alpha_y)) = \Delta_e \left(\varphi \left(\Delta_e^{-1}(s_x, \alpha_x), \Delta_e^{-1}(s_y, \alpha_y) \right) \right) \tag{10}$$

where Δ_e and Δ_e^{-1} are transformation functions from Definitions 4 and 5:

Uninorms are highly accepted and useful tools for aggregation in solving DMADM problems [3,10,20] due to their properties: associativity and full reinforcement. Based on a generalization [13] of the Yager's uninorm introduced in [14,15] we define the $2T\prod$ aggregation operator using the 2-tuple linguistic representation model:

Definition 7. *Let $\tilde{S} = \{(s_x, \alpha_x)_1, ..., (s_x, \alpha_x)_n\}$ be a collection 2-tuple arguments and functions Δ_e and Δ_e^{-1} from Definitions 4 and 5, then the function $2T\prod : \tilde{S}^q \longrightarrow \tilde{S}$ defined as*

$$2T\prod(\tilde{S}) = \Delta_e \left(\frac{\frac{\prod_{i=1}^n \Delta_e^{-1}(s_x, \alpha_x)_i}{e}}{\frac{\prod_{i=1}^n \Delta_e^{-1}(s_x, \alpha_x)_i}{e} + \frac{\prod_{i=1}^n (1 - \Delta_e^{-1}(s_x, \alpha_x)_i)}{1-e}} \right) \tag{11}$$

is called 2-tuple linguistic $\prod$ $(2T\prod)$ aggregation operator.

The $2T\prod$ operator delivers crucial benefits: preserved cognitive alignment through consistent 2-tuple linguistic representations across all operational stages; combining computational efficiency via associative aggregation with minimal storage requirements; and adaptable reinforcement through the tunable neutral element e governing how historical and current evaluations influence the aggregated result. This triad of features— interpretability, efficiency and flexibility— enables effective handling of dynamic decision scenarios while maintaining both mathematical rigor and human-understandable outputs. This operator fundamentally enables the feedback loop in our dynamic approach while preserving both mathematical rigor and human-interpretable results.

5   An Application to a Subcontractor Evaluation Problem

This section demonstrates the proposed approach through a dynamic multi-criteria subcontractor evaluation in a construction project developed in [7]. The main contractor evaluates subcontractors across four distinct periods, with flexibility to define any number of decision-makers, criteria, and alternatives per period. Four key criteria are adopted for all evaluation periods:

- Reliability (c_1): Assesses subcontractors based on historical performance, reputation, and financial stability. A strong track record and robust financial health are prioritized.

- Schedule-Control Ability (c_2): Measures efficiency in mobilizing physical and human resources to the construction site, ensuring timely project completion.
- Management Ability (c_3): Evaluates safety protocols, quality control, and environmental management systems, critical for overall subcontractor performance.
- Labor Quality (c_4): Reflects worker skill levels and manager-worker coordination, directly impacting project outcomes.

The criteria set remains consistent across periods $T = \{t_1, t_2, t_3\}$. Assessments are conducted by the main contractor's expert panel (decision-makers), with varying availability per period. The composition of the decision-making panel varies across evaluation periods and the set of evaluated subcontractors (alternatives) also changes temporally, as can be seen in Table 1:

Table 1. Experts and alternatives considered per each period.

T	$E(t_\lambda)$	$A(t_\lambda)$
t_1	e_1, e_2, e_3, e_4	$a_1, a_2, a_3, a_4, a_5, a_6, a_7, a_8, a_9$
t_2	e_1, e_3, e_4	$a_1, a_2, a_3, a_4, a_6, a_7, a_{10}, a_{11}, a_{12}, a_{13}$
t_3	e_1, e_2, e_3, e_4	$a_1, a_2, a_5, a_6, a_7, a_8, a_9, a_{10}, a_{12}$
t_4	e_1, e_3, e_4	$a_2, a_3, a_6, a_7, a_8, a_{10}, a_{13}$

Decision-makers assess both criteria importance weights and subcontractor using a linguistic variable mapped to fuzzy numbers, with seven terms simmetrically and uniformly distributed, as depicted in Fig. 1.

We apply a complete retention policy due to this is a small-scale problem containing few alternatives, experts and criteria. The $H(t_\lambda) = \bigcup A(t_{\lambda'})$ retention policy maximizes information at $O(m \cdot \lambda)$ space complexity and facilitates further comparison with [7].

The original decision matrices (subcontractor ratings per criterion) and the criteria weight matrices can be verified in [7].

At period t_1 it is not necessary to compute the dynamic ratings. Ranking can be obtained directly according the descending order of the static evaluation of subcontractors. From period t_1 to t_4 the alternative set changed due to the availability of new subcontractors but the unavailability of other subcontractors. The dynamic rating $\check{X}_i(t_\lambda)$ are generated via the associative aggregation of the evaluations in t_2 to t_4, as depicted the last column of Table 2. a_{10} is the best alternative, and the final ranking is as follows: $a_{10} \succ a_6 \succ a_3 \succ a_9 \succ a_5 \succ a_2 \succ a_7 \succ a_8 \succ a_4 \succ a_{11} \succ a_{13} \succ a_{12}$.

Our approach produces rankings consistent with [7] while fundamentally differing in two aspects: it maintains fully interpretable 2-tuple linguistic outputs throughout all computational stages, and enables adaptive storage policies that reduce complexity to $O(k)$ compared to the $O(\lambda \cdot m)$ requirement of the referenced fuzzy numerical method.

Table 2. The 2-tuple linguistic results at each period.

T	A_t	c_1	c_2	c_3	c_4	$\bar{X}_i(t_\lambda)$	$\check{X}_i(t_\lambda)$
t_1	a_1	$(s_1,-0.50)$	$(s_2,0.25)$	$(s_2,0.25)$	$(s_1,0.00)$	$(s_2,-0.40)$	-
	a_2	$(s_2,-0.25)$	$(s_3,0.00)$	$(s_2,-0.50)$	$(s_1,-0.25)$	$(s_2,-0.38)$	-
	a_3	$(s_2,0.00)$	$(s_4,0.00)$	$(s_3,-0.25)$	$(s_4,0.00)$	$(s_3,0.24)$	-
	a_4	$(s_6,-0.50)$	$(s_6,-0.50)$	$(s_4,-0.25)$	$(s_5,-0.50)$	$(s_5,-0.39)$	-
	a_5	$(s_4,-0.25)$	$(s_4,0.00)$	$(s_5,0.00)$	$(s_5,0.25)$	$(s_5,-0.33)$	-
	a_6	$(s_3,-0.50)$	$(s_4,0.00)$	$(s_3,0.25)$	$(s_3,0.00)$	$(s_3,0.21)$	-
	a_7	$(s_1,-0.25)$	$(s_2,0.00)$	$(s_3,-0.50)$	$(s_3,-0.25)$	$(s_2,0.19)$	-
	a_8	$(s_3,0.00)$	$(s_1,-0.50)$	$(s_2,0.00)$	$(s_2,0.00)$	$(s_2,-0.14)$	-
	a_9	$(s_5,-0.50)$	$(s_4,0.25)$	$(s_5,0.25)$	$(s_5,-0.50)$	$(s_5,-0.29)$	-
t_2	a_1	$(s_1,-0.33)$	$(s_2,0.00)$	$(s_3,0.00)$	$(s_1,0.00)$	$(s_2,-0.03)$	$(s_1,-0.10)$
	a_2	$(s_1,-0.33)$	$(s_3,0.33)$	$(s_2,0.00)$	$(s_0,0.33)$	$(s_2,-0.37)$	$(s_1,-0.27)$
	a_3	$(s_1,0.00)$	$(s_4,-0.33)$	$(s_3,0.00)$	$(s_4,0.00)$	$(s_3,0.23)$	$(s_3,0.47)$
	a_4	$(s_4,0.33)$	$(s_5,0.33)$	$(s_4,0.00)$	$(s_5,-0.33)$	$(s_5,-0.50)$	$(s_5,-0.45)$
	a_6	$(s_2,-0.33)$	$(s_5,-0.33)$	$(s_3,0.00)$	$(s_2,0.33)$	$(s_3,0.00)$	$(s_3,0.20)$
	a_7	$(s_1,0.00)$	$(s_2,-0.33)$	$(s_2,0.00)$	$(s_3,0.00)$	$(s_2,0.13)$	$(s_1,0.44)$
	a_{10}	$(s_5,0.33)$	$(s_6,-0.33)$	$(s_5,0.00)$	$(s_4,0.33)$	$(s_5,-0.03)$	-
	a_{11}	$(s_2,0.00)$	$(s_4,0.33)$	$(s_5,-0.33)$	$(s_4,-0.33)$	$(s_4,0.03)$	-
	a_{12}	$(s_0,0.33)$	$(s_0,0.00)$	$(s_1,0.33)$	$(s_2,-0.33)$	$(s_1,0.07)$	-
	a_{13}	$(s_3,0.00)$	$(s_1,0.33)$	$(s_1,-0.33)$	$(s_2,-0.33)$	$(s_1,0.33)$	-
t_3	a_1	$(s_1,-0.50)$	$(s_2,0.25)$	$(s_3,-0.50)$	$(s_2,-0.25)$	$(s_2,-0.02)$	$(s_0,0.48)$
	a_2	$(s_1,0.25)$	$(s_3,-0.25)$	$(s_2,0.00)$	$(s_1,0.25)$	$(s_2,-0.18)$	$(s_0,0.34)$
	a_5	$(s_4,0.00)$	$(s_5,-0.50)$	$(s_5,-0.25)$	$(s_5,-0.25)$	$(s_5,-0.48)$	$(s_5,0.49)$
	a_6	$(s_2,-0.50)$	$(s_4,-0.25)$	$(s_4,-0.50)$	$(s_3,-0.50)$	$(s_3,-0.01)$	$(s_3,0.19)$
	a_7	$(s_1,-0.50)$	$(s_2,0.00)$	$(s_2,-0.50)$	$(s_3,0.00)$	$(s_2,-0.10)$	$(s_1,-0.23)$
	a_8	$(s_4,-0.25)$	$(s_2,-0.50)$	$(s_3,-0.50)$	$(s_2,0.00)$	$(s_2,0.22)$	$(s_1,0.26)$
	a_9	$(s_4,0.25)$	$(s_6,-0.50)$	$(s_6,-0.25)$	$(s_4,-0.50)$	$(s_5,-0.22)$	$(s_5,0.61)$
	a_{10}	$(s_5,-0.50)$	$(s_5,0.25)$	$(s_6,-0.50)$	$(s_4,0.25)$	$(s_5,-0.13)$	$(s_6,-0.28)$
	a_{12}	$(s_1,0.00)$	$(s_1,-0.25)$	$(s_1,0.25)$	$(s_3,-0.50)$	$(s_1,0.45)$	$(s_0,0.39)$
t_4	a_2	$(s_2,0.00)$	$(s_3,0.33)$	$(s_3,-0.33)$	$(s_1,0.00)$	$(s_2,0.16)$	$(s_0,0.20)$
	a_3	$(s_3,-0.33)$	$(s_4,0.00)$	$(s_3,-0.33)$	$(s_3,0.33)$	$(s_3,0.15)$	$(s_2,-0.01)$
	a_6	$(s_2,-0.33)$	$(s_3,0.33)$	$(s_3,-0.33)$	$(s_3,-0.33)$	$(s_3,-0.35)$	$(s_3,-0.16)$
	a_7	$(s_1,0.00)$	$(s_2,0.00)$	$(s_1,0.33)$	$(s_2,0.33)$	$(s_2,-0.26)$	$(s_0,0.34)$
	a_8	$(s_2,0.00)$	$(s_0,0.33)$	$(s_2,-0.33)$	$(s_2,0.33)$	$(s_2,-0.33)$	$(s_1,-0.45)$
	a_{10}	$(s_5,0.33)$	$(s_5,0.33)$	$(s_5,0.33)$	$(s_5,-0.33)$	$(s_5,0.12)$	$(s_6,-0.05)$
	a_{13}	$(s_3,0.00)$	$(s_1,-0.33)$	$(s_0,0.33)$	$(s_1,0.00)$	$(s_1,0.02)$	$(s_0,0.33)$

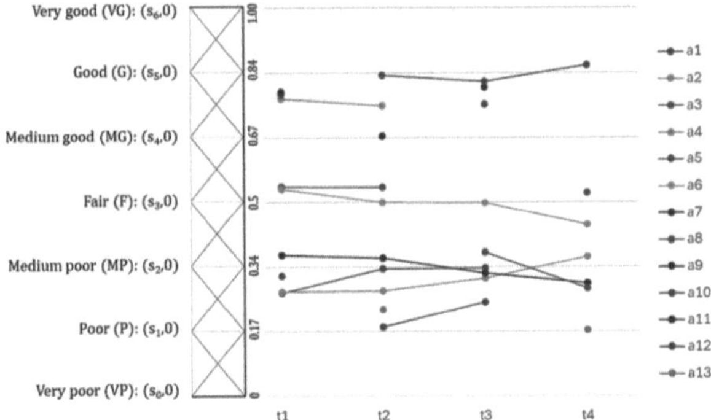

Fig. 1. Evolving evaluation of subcontractors

6 Conclusion

The proposed feedback-enabled LDMCDM framework addresses critical gaps in dynamic decision-making by combining linguistic flexibility with temporal adaptability. The $2T\prod$ aggregation operator plays a pivotal role, enabling efficient, associative computation while maintaining full reinforcement to balance historical and current data. The retention policy's significance derives from its dual role as both a memory optimization mechanism and a temporal relevance sieve, essential for preserving decision integrity in dynamic environments. By operating within the 2-tuple linguistic domain, the model ensures results remain intuitive and aligned with human reasoning. The subcontractor evaluation case study underscores its practicality, showing how dynamic adjustments in alternatives and criteria lead to interpretable ratings and reliable rankings. Future work could explore adaptive retention policies or hybrid operators for broader applications. This approach bridges theory and practice, offering a scalable tool for complex, evolving decision environments.

References

1. Banamar, I.: An interpolation-based method for the time weighed vector elicitation in temporal promethee ii applications. Int. J. Multi. Dec. Making **8**, 84 (2019)
2. Brehmer, B.: Strategies in real-time, dynamic decision making, pp. 262–279. University of Chicago Press (1990)
3. Campanella, G., A.Pereira, Ribeiro, R., Varela, L.: Collaborative dynamic decision making: a case study from B2B supplier selection, pp. 1–17. Lecture Notes in Business Information Processing (2012)
4. Campanella, G., Ribeiro, R.: A framework for dynamic multiple-criteria decision making. Decis. Support Syst. **52**(1), 52–60 (2011)
5. Frini, A., Ben Amor, S.: Mupom: a multi-criteria multi-period outranking method for decision-making in sustainable development context. Environ. Impact Assess. Rev. **76**, 10–25 (2019)

6. Herrera, F., Martínez, L.: A 2-tuple fuzzy linguistic representation model for computing with words. IEEE Trans. Fuzzy Syst. **8**(6), 746–752 (2000)
7. Keshavarz-Ghorabaee, M., Amiri, M., Zavadskas, E.K., Turskis, Z., Antucheviciene, J.: A dynamic fuzzy approach based on the edas method for multi-criteria subcontractor evaluation. Information **9**(3) (2018)
8. Lourenzutti, R., Krohling, R.A., Reformat, M.Z.: Choquet based topsis and todim for dynamic and heterogeneous decision making with criteria interaction. Inf. Sci. **408**, 41–69 (2017)
9. Lu, Z., Augusto, J., Liu, J., Wang, H., Aztiria, A.: A system to reason about uncertain and dynamic environments. Int. J. Artif. Intell. Tools **21**(05), 12500–23 (2012)
10. Ribeiro, R., Pais, T., Simões, L.: Benefits of full-reinforcement operators for spacecraft target landing. Stud. Fuzziness Soft Comput. **257**, 353–367 (2010)
11. Sterman, J.: Business dynamics: systems thinking and modeling for a complex world. McGraw-Hill (2000)
12. Tao, Z., Chen, H., Zhou, L., Liu, J.: On new operational laws of 2-tuple linguistic information using archimedean t-norm and s-norm. Knowl.-Based Syst. **66**, 156–165 (2014)
13. Yager, R.: Defending against strategic manipulation in uninorm-based multi-agent decision making. Eur. J. Oper. Res. **141**(1), 217–232 (2002)
14. Yager, R., Rybalov, A.: Uninorm aggregation operators. Fuzzy Sets Syst. **80**, 111–120 (1996)
15. Yager, R., Rybalov, A.: Full reinforcement operators in aggregation techniques. Syst. Man Cybern. Part B: Cybern. IEEE Trans. **28**(6), 757–769 (1998)
16. Yager, R., Rybalov, A.: Bipolar aggregation using the uninorms. Fuzzy Optim. Decis. Making **10**(1), 59–70 (2011)
17. Yao, X., Liu, E., Sun, X., Le, W., Li, J.: Integrating external representations and internal patterns into dynamic multiple-criteria decision making. Ann. Oper. Res. **341**(1), 149–172 (2024)
18. Yu, P., Yang, Y., Ma, H.S., Mba, D.J.: Evaluation of high-quality development of manufacturing industry using a novel grey dynamic double incentive decision-making model. Mathematical Problems in Engineering (2022)
19. Zadeh, L.: The concept of a linguistic variable and its application to approximate reasoning-I. Inf. Sci. **8**(3), 199–249 (1975)
20. Zulueta, Y., Martínez, J., Bello, R., Martínez, L.: A discrete time variable index for supporting dynamic multi-criteria decision making. Internat. J. Uncertain. Fuzziness Knowl. Based Syst. **22**(1), 1–22 (2013)

Continual Pretraining of a Small Language Model on Cuban Spanish Corpora

Ernesto Luis Estevanell-Valladares[1,2], Suilan Estevez-Velarde[1],
Alejandro Piad-Morffis[1(✉)], Yudivian Almeida-Cruz[1],
Alejandro Beltrán Varela[1], Carla Sunami Pérez Valera[1],
Daniel Alejandro Valdés Pérez[1], Deborah Famadas Rodríguez[1],
Elena Rodríguez Horta[1], Gabriel Hernández Rodríguez[1],
Niley González Ferrales[1], Roberto Garcia Rodriguez[1],
Roberto Marti Cedeño[1], Juan Pablo Consuegra Ayala[2],
Robiert Sepúlveda-Torres[2], Yoan Gutiérrez[2], Andrés Montoyo[2],
Rafael Muñoz Guillena[2], and Manuel Palomar[2]

[1] University of Havana, Havana, Cuba
`apaid@matcom.uh.cu`
[2] University of Alicante, Alicante, Spain

Abstract. Large language models have transformed natural language processing, but their effectiveness is limited for regional language variants due to underrepresentation in training data. This paper introduces Cecilia 2B, a 2-billion-parameter language model continually pretrained on nearly 1 billion tokens of Cuban Spanish text, including newspapers, encyclopedias, legal documents, literature, and song lyrics, to address the gap in language technology for Cuban Spanish. Leveraging the Salamandra 2B architecture, Cecilia 2B demonstrates the feasibility and value of adapting multilingual models to regional variants through continual pretraining, achieving improved performance on Spanish and multilingual tasks relevant to its target domain while maintaining computational efficiency suitable for resource-constrained environments. We detail the construction of a culturally rich Cuban Spanish corpus, the adaptation methodology, and a comparative evaluation with the base model, highlighting both the benefits and trade-offs of regional specialization. Cecilia 2B provides a foundational resource for Cuban Spanish NLP and establishes a path for future research in instruction tuning, corpus expansion, tokenizer retraining, and the development of larger or more specialized models.

Keywords: Language Modeling · Natural Language Processing · Corpora

1 Introduction

Large Languages Models have revolutionized natural language processing, with an unprecedented capacity to capture important semantic and pragmatic aspects

Y. Hernádez Heredia et al. (Eds.): IWAIPR 2025, LNCS 16328, pp. 125–138, 2026.
https://doi.org/10.1007/978-3-032-11358-0_11

of written language. However, even though large, open-weight models such as Llama and Mistral are trained on a majority of mainstream languages, they often underperform in regional varieties of underrepresented languages. The development of domain-specific and regional language models has thus become increasingly important as large, general-purpose models often fail to capture the linguistic, cultural, and contextual nuances required for authentic communication within specific communities. Specialized models in healthcare, law, and finance outperform general models on tasks requiring domain expertise, and culturally adapted models such as CultureLLM demonstrate improved handling of language-specific phenomena Li et al. (2024).

In the Spanish language context, the Salamandra project Gonzalez-Agirre et al. (2025) stands out as a family of open-source, multilingual language models designed with a strong emphasis on Spanish and co-official languages, providing a robust foundation for further adaptation to regional variants. Salamandra's architecture and training methodology make it especially well-suited for continual pretraining on regionally focused corpora, enabling the creation of models that internalize the unique features of local Spanish varieties while maintaining broad language capabilities.

Building on this foundation, the **CecilIA**[1] project aims to address the lack of high-quality language models for Cuban Spanish, a variant with distinctive lexical, syntactic, and cultural characteristics that are not adequately represented in existing models.

The Cuban Spanish variant is distinguished by unique lexical items, commonly known as *cubanismos* (e.g., "asere", "guagua", "yuma") as well as distinct phonetic and morphological patterns that influence written expression. Furthermore, the variant is rich with culturally-specific idiomatic expressions and historical references that are essential for contextual understanding. While a language model cannot capture spoken phonetics, its performance is deeply tied to its ability to process these lexical and semantic nuances. By curating a corpus from sources like local encyclopedias of *cubanismos*, national literature, and song lyrics, we aim to expose the model to these features, thereby improving its ability to generate authentic and context-aware text for this specific linguistic community.

This paper introduces *Cecilia 2B*, a 2-billion-parameter language model continually pretrained on a newly constructed corpus of approximately 1 billion tokens of Cuban written text, including newspapers, encyclopedias, legal documents, literature, and song lyrics. By adapting the powerful Salamandra 2B architecture, this work delivers the first large-scale, publicly-available foundational model specifically for Cuban Spanish. Cecilia 2B serves as a critical resource for natural language processing applications in this underrepresented variant and provides a detailed case study on the benefits and trade-offs inherent in regional language model adaptation.

Cecilia 2B is the first iteration of a larger project aimed at creating pretrained and fine-tuned language models in the Cuban Spanish variant for several model

---

[1] https://cecilia.uhgia.org.

sizes, architectures, and domains. By focusing first on a relatively small model size of 2 billion parameters, Cecilia 2B balances computational efficiency with linguistic specialization, enabling deployment in resource-constrained environments common in Cuba and similar settings. This approach allows us to explore the optimal strategies for creating this type of resources, as well as facilitating broader accessibility and practical usage from the beginning of the project. The experienced obtained in this iteration of Cecilia will directly inform the development of future, larger models.

This paper presents the design, training methodology, dataset composition, and partial evaluation of Cecilia 2B. The remainder of this paper is organized as follows: Sect. 2 reviews related work on small language models for regional variants, continual pretraining, and the Salamandra project. Section 3 details the design and training methodology of Cecilia 2B, including corpus construction and adaptation procedures. Section 4 presents evaluation results comparing Cecilia 2B to its base model on a suite of multilingual and Spanish NLP benchmarks. Section 5 discusses the implications, current limitations, and future directions for regional language model development. Finally, Sect. 6 concludes by summarizing the main contributions and outlining the potential of Cecilia for advancing Cuban Spanish NLP.

2 Background and Related Works

This section presents a review of the relevant literature in the field of language modeling, with a particular focus on small language models and their applications in regional language variants, as well as techniques for domain and linguistic adaptation. The section finalizes with a short presentation of the Salamandra models, architecture, and training procedure.

Small Language Models for Regional Variants. The development of small language models (SLMs) specifically tailored to regional language variants has emerged as a significant research direction in natural language processing. Unlike their larger counterparts, SLMs typically contain millions to a few billion parameters and are designed to operate efficiently on resource-constrained environments while maintaining competitive performance for specialized domains. These models represent a strategic response to the limitations of general-purpose large language models, which often fail to capture regional linguistic nuances, cultural contexts, and domain-specific knowledge essential for authentic communication within specific communities.

Recent research has demonstrated the effectiveness of SLMs in processing regional languages with significantly fewer parameters than traditional large language models. The Regional Tiny Stories framework exemplifies this approach, showing that models with 1–10 million parameters can produce coherent outputs when trained on language-specific datasets Patil et al. (2025). This work expanded the TinyStories Li and Eldan (2023) methodology to Indian languages including Hindi, Marathi, and Bengali, revealing that language-specific tokenizers consistently outperform general-purpose alternatives for regional languages.

The development of regionalized Spanish language models has gained particular attention, with projects creating word embeddings and BERT-based models trained on Twitter data from 26 Spanish-speaking countries Tellez et al. (2023). These efforts have resulted in resources that capture lexical and semantic variations across different Spanish-speaking regions, demonstrating measurable improvements in regional task performance. Similarly, the DADA (Dialect Adaptation via Dynamic Aggregation) framework has shown promise for adapting models to various English dialects through compositional adapter architectures that handle specific linguistic features Liu et al. (2023).

These efforts are part of a growing focus within NLP on computational sociolinguistics, which seeks to create models that are not only domain-specific but also dialect-aware and sensitive to social contexts (Hovy, 2018). Research in this area explores more advanced techniques, such as dialect-aware tokenization and methods for modeling code-switching, which will inform future iterations of the Cecilia project (Nguyen et al. 2021).

Continual Pretraining and Domain Adaptation Techniques. Continual pretraining has emerged as a fundamental technique for adapting existing language models to new domains and regional variants while preserving previously acquired knowledge Gururangan et al. (2020). This approach aims to mitigate catastrophic forgetting—the tendency of a model to lose previously learned knowledge when trained on a new task—while simultaneously achieving knowledge transfer to improve end-task performance Goodfellow et al. (2013). Research has shown that continual pretraining consistently improves models smaller than 1.5 billion parameters and demonstrates superior performance compared to traditional domain adaptation methods Gururangan et al. (2020).

The efficacy of continual pretraining varies significantly based on model size and domain progression Yıldız et al. (2024). Research indicates that smaller models are particularly sensitive to continual pretraining, showing the most significant rates of both learning and forgetting Lee (2024). Domain similarity plays a crucial role in knowledge transfer effectiveness, with semantically similar domain sequences enabling better specialization, while randomized training domains lead to improved transfer and final performance. Cross-lingual and progressive transfer learning approaches have demonstrated the ability to save up to 80% of training costs compared to random initialization when transferring models between languages Šliogeris et al. (2025).

The Salamandra Project. The Salamandra project, developed by the Barcelona Supercomputing Center's Language Technologies Unit, represents a comprehensive effort to create open-source, multilingual language models with particular emphasis on European languages and Spanish language variants. The project encompasses three model sizes—2B, 7B, and 40B parameters—each designed to balance computational efficiency with linguistic capability while maintaining strong performance across multiple languages Gonzalez-Agirre et al. (2025).

Salamandra models employ a standard decoder-only Transformer architecture with several key optimizations that distinguish them from the original Transformer design. The architecture eliminates all bias terms to improve training stability, incorporates rotary positional embeddings (RoPE) with a base frequency of 10,000 as an alternative to absolute positional embeddings, and replaces ReLU activation with SwiGLU for enhanced performance. The models utilize RMSNorm

Zhang and Sennrich (2019) instead of traditional layer normalization, with an epsilon hyperparameter set to 1e-5, and employ BFloat16 numerical precision for training stability.

Salamandra 2B, the base model for Cecilia, comprises approximately 2.25 billion parameters distributed across 24 layers with a hidden size of 2,048 and 16 attention heads. The model supports a context window of 8,192 tokens and utilizes a vocabulary size of 256,000 tokens, enabling effective processing of diverse multilingual inputs. Unlike the larger variants, Salamandra 2B relies on multi-head attention rather than grouped-query attention, reflecting optimization choices for the smaller parameter count.

The Salamandra pretraining corpus is a comprehensive multilingual datasets specifically designed for European languages, comprising text in 35 European languages and 92 programming languages. The training process utilized approximately 7.8 trillion tokens for the 2B model, with the corpus carefully curated to oversample Spanish and co-official languages of Spain (Catalan, Galician, and Basque) by a factor of two, while downsampling code and English data to achieve balanced representation Gonzalez-Agirre et al. (2025).

A clear indicator of the growing interest in language technologies for regional and underrepresented languages, especifically in the Iberoamerican research community, is the widespread adoption of models developed within the ILENIA network[2]. Notable projects derived from Salamandra include AITANA, optimized for Valencian; Latxa, the first major Basque model; and Carballo, a foundational Galician model.

3   Design and Training of Cecilia 2B

Cecilia 2B, in its current iteration, is a 2-epoch continual pretraining checkpoint of Salamandra 2B. Salamandra 2B was chosen as the base model for Cecilia 2B due to its strong multilingual capabilities, efficient architecture, and open-source availability under an Apache 2.0 license, which facilitates fine-tuning and adaptation for specific language varieties. Its design balances model capacity and computational resource requirements, making it suitable for deployment in resource-constrained environments typical of Cuban NLP applications.

---

[2] https://proyectoilenia.es/.

For this initial iteration, we made the deliberate decision to leave the Salamandra 2B architecture, including its original tokenizer and vocabulary, unmodified. This choice was a key element of our research design, intended to isolate the effects of continual pretraining on the new corpus. By keeping the tokenizer constant, we can attribute observed changes in performance directly to the data rather than to a combination of data and vocabulary changes.

We acknowledge this creates a known limitation: words specific to Cuban Spanish (cubanisms) that are out-of-vocabulary for the base model are tokenized into sub-optimal subword units, making them more difficult for the model to learn effectively. Consequently, developing a new tokenizer trained on our Cuban Spanish corpus and retraining the model with it remains a top priority for future work, as stated in Sect. 5.

Training Data. The training corpus for Cecilia 2B comprises approximately 1 billion tokens of Cuban Spanish text, including digitized Cuban newspapers from the last decade, the Cuban Encyclopedia, a comprehensive collection of Cuban laws, hundreds of literary works by Cuban authors, local encyclopedias documenting Cubanisms, and song lyrics from prominent Cuban artists. This diverse dataset was curated to capture the linguistic and cultural richness of Cuban Spanish.

All data was collected via web scraping under a fair use assumption and is intended solely for academic and research purposes. The web scraping process utilized custom scripts to systematically gather and parse text from targeted sources. Following collection, the raw text underwent a rigorous cleaning pipeline to ensure quality. This process included (1) removing HTML boilerplate, navigation menus, and advertisements; (2) deduplicating documents at the paragraph level to reduce redundancy; and (3) normalizing text by correcting common OCR errors and standardizing character encoding. This multi-step procedure was crucial for creating a clean, high-quality dataset suitable for language model pretraining.

To respect copyright and intellectual property rights, the raw training data is not publicly available at the moment. Table 1 presents the composition of the full corpus, showing the main sources of texts and their relative percentage within the total dataset.

The Cecilia 2B training corpus is extensive, as shown in Table 2, comprising nearly 300,000 text files with a total of approximately 2.6 billion characters and an estimated 385 million words. This large volume of data ensures comprehensive linguistic coverage, enabling the model to learn a wide range of lexical and syntactic patterns specific to Cuban Spanish.

The average document length of 8,881 characters indicates the dataset includes a balanced mix of short and long texts, which is beneficial for training a model capable of understanding various discourse structures, from brief statements to extended narratives. An average sentence length of 17 words reflects moderately complex sentence constructions typical of formal written language, supporting the model's ability to handle nuanced linguistic phenomena.

Table 1. Composition of the training corpus for Cecilia 2B.{tbl-colwidths='[40,50,10]'}

Source Content	Description	(%)
Cuban Encyclopedia (Ecured)	Full snapshot of the online collaborative encyclopedia.	65.0
Cuban Newspapers (2014-2024)	Digital archives of national newspapers *Granma* and *Juventud Rebelde*.	20.0
Cuban Literature	Over 400 digitized works from key authors, e.g., *José Martí, Alejo Carpentier, José Lezama Lima*.	9.5
Official Gazette of Cuba	Comprehensive collection of laws and official government documents.	1.5
Cultural & Linguistic Dictionaries	E.g., *Diccionario de Cubanismos*, encyclopedias of Afro-Cuban culture.	0.6
Miscellaneous Cuban Texts	Academic theses, historical documents, and other curated texts.	3.4

Table 2. Basic corpus statistics.

Metric	Value
Total Files	296,311
Total Characters	2,631,691,355
Total Words	384,963,687
Total Lines	34,505,341
Average Document Length	8,881 characters
Average Sentence Length	17.0 words
Lexical Density	6.8 characters/word

The lexical density of 6.8 characters per word suggests a rich vocabulary with a diversity of word lengths, which contributes to the model's capacity to represent the Cuban Spanish lexicon effectively. Overall, these statistics demonstrate that the dataset provides a robust foundation for continual pretraining, enabling Cecilia 2B to internalize the distinctive linguistic and cultural characteristics of Cuban Spanish.

After tokenization, as shown in Table 3, the dataset consists of over 1.1 million samples, with nearly one billion tokens excluding padding. The average sequence length is approximately 889 tokens, with sequences ranging from a single token up to the maximum context window size of 1024 tokens. The padding ratio of 13.2% indicates that a moderate portion of sequences required padding to reach the fixed length, which is typical for datasets with variable-length texts. The data was segmented into 959,008 context windows, each containing 1024 tokens,

Table 3. Tokenized corpus metrics.

Metric	Value
Total Samples	1,104,532
Total Tokens (no padding)	982,024,795
Total Tokens (with padding)	1,131,040,768
Average Sequence Length (no padding)	889.3 tokens
Padding Ratio	13.2%

enabling the model to process long-range dependencies effectively during training.

Training Procedure. The training of Cecilia 2B was conducted over two full epochs with a batch size of 4, combined with gradient accumulation over 16 steps to effectively simulate a larger batch size of 64. This approach balances the constraints of available GPU memory with the need for stable gradient estimates during optimization. Gradient clipping with a maximum norm of 1.0 was applied to prevent exploding gradients and improve training stability.

Optimization was performed using the AdamW optimizer with a learning rate of 2e-5, incorporating weight decay of 0.01 to regularize the model and reduce overfitting. The learning rate followed a warmup linear decay schedule, with a warmup phase covering 6% of the total training steps, allowing the model to gradually adapt to the data before reaching the peak learning rate. The AdamW hyperparameters beta1 and beta2 were set to 0.9 and 0.999, respectively, consistent with best practices for transformer training.

Mixed precision training using bfloat16 (bf16) precision was employed to accelerate computation and reduce memory consumption without sacrificing numerical stability. The training leveraged Fully Sharded Data Parallel (FSDP) parallelization with full sharding and sharded state dictionaries to optimize memory usage across multiple GPUs. Gradient checkpointing was enabled to further reduce memory footprint by trading compute for storage during backpropagation.

Validation was performed both after each epoch and periodically every 640 training steps, ensuring continuous monitoring of model performance and early detection of potential overfitting or training instability. Overall, these design choices reflect a careful balance between computational efficiency, training stability, and effective convergence on the specialized Cuban Spanish corpus, enabling Cecilia 2B to internalize linguistic nuances while operating within the constraints of available hardware resources.

Training was conducted over approximately 48 h on a high-performance compute setup consisting of 2 NVIDIA A100 GPUs (40 GB each), an AMD EPYC CPU with 128 cores and 256 threads, and 1 TB of RAM.

Table 4 summarizes the training hyperparameters used for Cecilia 2B.

Table 4. Training Hyperparameters

Parameter	Value
Number of epochs	2
Batch size	4
Gradient accumulation steps	16
Effective batch size	64
Learning rate	2e-5
Learning rate scheduler	Warmup linear
Warmup proportion	6%
Optimizer	AdamW
Weight decay	0.01
Beta1, Beta2	0.9, 0.999
Gradient clipping norm	1.0
Precision	bfloat16

Model and Data Availability. In line with ethical research practices and copyright law, the raw training corpus cannot be publicly released. The dataset was compiled from copyrighted sources under a fair use assumption for non-commercial academic research, and its redistribution is prohibited.

To promote responsible open science, the Cecilia 2B model is made available to the research community through a gated access protocol on the Hugging Face platform[3]. This staged-release approach allows for case-by-case evaluation of research requests, mitigating potential misuse while the model undergoes further safety and bias analysis. We are committed to a full public release under a permissive, commercially-viable license once these evaluations are complete. This strategy ensures that the research community can benefit from this work while upholding ethical standards.

4   Evaluation

Evaluation of Cecilia 2B is still ongoing. At this stage, we present partial results focused on comparing Cecilia 2B to its base model, Salamandra 2B, across a broad suite of standard NLP benchmarks. These tasks include multiple-choice question answering, reading comprehension, paraphrase identification, natural language inference, summarization, translation, and open-domain question answering, in both English and Spanish. Table 5 summarizes the results of this comparison.

The results present a nuanced picture of the trade-offs involved in regional specialization. Cecilia 2B shows clear improvements in multilingual reading comprehension (BELEBELE (Ahuja et al., 2023) +6.82%) and natural language

---

[3] https://huggingface.co/gia-uh/cecilia-2b-v0.1.

Table 5. Evaluation results in selected NLP tasks in English and Spanish, in comparison with Salamandra 2B.

Task	Metric	Salamandra	Cecilia	Rel. Err.
arc_challenge	acc	0.37031	0.38225	3.13%
arc_easy	acc	0.72264	0.73401	1.55%
belebele_en	acc	0.21556	0.24778	13.00%
belebele_es	acc	0.22778	0.24444	6.82%
escola	acc	0.59259	0.55461	−6.41%
openbookqa	acc	0.30000	0.28200	−6.00%
openbookqa_es	acc	0.30800	0.29400	−4.55%
paws_en	acc	0.56100	0.57350	2.18%
paws_es	acc	0.56050	0.55550	−0.89%
piqa	acc	0.73721	0.73667	-0.07%
social_iqa	acc	0.45394	0.44626	−1.69%
teca	acc	0.46481	0.43174	−7.11%
wnli	acc	0.46479	0.42254	−9.09%
wnli_es	acc	0.56338	0.59155	4.76%
xnli_en	acc	0.46225	0.47671	3.03%
xstorycloze_en	acc	0.71145	0.70483	−0.93%
xstorycloze_es	acc	0.65255	0.65189	−0.10%
arc_challenge	acc_norm	0.40700	0.41809	2.65%
arc_easy	acc_norm	0.72559	0.73990	1.93%
belebele_en	acc_norm	0.21556	0.24778	13.00%
belebele_es	acc_norm	0.22778	0.24444	6.82%
openbookqa	acc_norm	0.39600	0.40000	1.00%
openbookqa_es	acc_norm	0.40800	0.40400	−0.98%
piqa	acc_norm	0.74701	0.74701	0.00%
cocoteros_es	bleu	8.46507	6.72269	−20.58%
xlsum_es	bleu	0.80082	0.59723	−25.42%
triviaqa	exact_match	0.37595	0.35432	−5.75%
xquad_es	exact_match	0.37731	0.36050	−4.45%
xquad_es	f1	0.58413	0.56911	−2.57%
cocoteros_es	rouge1	0.33887	0.31209	−7.90%
xlsum_es	rouge1	0.13464	0.08705	−35.35%
Mean Diff				**−2.43%**

inference (WNLI (Levesque et al., 2012) +4.73%), suggesting the continual pre-training successfully enhanced its understanding of Spanish-language nuances as intended.

Conversely, the most significant performance decreases occurred in generation-focused tasks, particularly summarization. For instance, the model's ROUGE-L score dropped by 35.35% on XLSUM-ES (Hasan et al., 2021) and its

BLEU score fell by 20.58% on COCOTEROS. It also shows decreasing scores in instruction following tasks like question answering (XQuAD (Artetxe et al., 2020), OpenBook (Mihaylov et al., 2018), and TriviaQA (Joshi et al., 2017).

This outcome is a direct and anticipated consequence of our training strategy. The pretraining corpus, dominated by literary, legal, and encyclopedic texts, is stylistically divergent from the news articles that comprise benchmarks like XLSUM. Likewise, the instruction following tasks are not represented in the training data, since, as explained before, Cecilia 2B has not been fine-tuned for instruction following or for downstream tasks.

By specializing on long-form, narrative text, the model's proficiency in the concise, extractive style required for summarization was diminished. This highlights a critical trade-off: gaining in-domain cultural and linguistic specialization came at the cost of performance on out-of-domain, general-purpose tasks for which the model has not been fine-tuned (Goodfellow et al., 2013).

It is important to emphasize that these benchmarks are general-purpose and not specifically tailored to the Cuban Spanish variant for which Cecilia is intended. The observed average difference is a modest decrease of about 2.4% relative to Salamandra 2B across all tasks, with the largest drops in summarization and translation. This is consistent with expectations, as the model has not yet been fine-tuned for instruction following or for downstream tasks.

Thus, at the time of writing no results are available on downstream tasks that target the unique linguistic and cultural phenomena of Cuban Spanish, which is the primary motivation for Cecilia's development. As Cecilia 2B is presently only pretrained and has not undergone instruction tuning or task-specific fine-tuning, comprehensive evaluations on downstream tasks such as question answering, dialogue generation, or other domain-specific applications remain pending. These more specialized assessments will be addressed in future work, following the development of an instruction-tuned version of Cecilia that can better support interactive and task-oriented use cases.

5 Discussion

The evaluation results presented in Sect. 1 provide a practical illustration of the challenges associated with catastrophic forgetting in regional model adaptation. While Cecilia 2B demonstrated gains in Spanish-language understanding tasks, the corresponding drop in performance on out-of-domain tasks like summarization shows that specialization involves a tangible trade-off. As such, Cecilia 2B remains a work in progress and is currently most suitable for research purposes.

As the model has not yet been fine-tuned for instruction following or specific downstream tasks, its direct applicability in production environments or interactive applications is limited at this stage. However, its foundational capabilities as a Cuban Spanish-pretrained language model open promising avenues for future development.

Once fine-tuned, Cecilia's relatively small size, combined with its specialized training on Cuban Spanish, positions it as a valuable resource for a range of natural language processing tasks tailored to this linguistic variant. Potential use cases include text generation that respects Cuban cultural and linguistic nuances, sentiment analysis for Cuban social media and news, named entity recognition in local contexts, machine translation with improved handling of Cubanisms, and domain-specific question answering.

Current Limitations. Currently, the model is not quantized and requires approximately 4.5 GB of GPU memory for full loading and inference, which may exceed the hardware capabilities of smaller research teams or institutions with limited computational resources. To address this, quantized versions of Cecilia 2B are planned for release in the near future, which will significantly reduce memory requirements and enable broader accessibility and deployment on more modest hardware setups. This will facilitate wider adoption and experimentation within the Cuban and broader Spanish-speaking NLP research communities.

As with all large language models, Cecilia 2B is susceptible to issues such as biases and hallucinations. The model has not yet undergone comprehensive evaluation to determine the extent to which these problems persist or whether they are exacerbated relative to the original Salamandra 2B base model. Users should be aware that outputs may reflect unintended biases present in the training data or generate factually incorrect or misleading information.

As detailed in Sect. 3, the training corpus contains copyrighted materials and the model is currently available under a gated access policy to ensure responsible use. In due course, Cecilia 2B will be publicly released under a permissive license that allows broad use, including commercial applications, once further evaluations and refinements have been completed to ensure safety and reliability.

One additional limitation is the lack of stakeholder feedback available for this first phase of the project. The contribution of the academic community beyond the computational sciences, including linguistics, history, sociology, cultural studies, etc., is a crucial next step to ensure that the model reflects the needs and expectations of the Cuban people.

Future Work. Future efforts will focus initially on further curating and expanding the Cuban Spanish corpus that underpins Cecilia 2B. Enhancing the dataset's breadth and diversity will improve the model's linguistic coverage and cultural representation, strengthening its foundation for downstream tasks.

For this particular model, the next key step is to fine-tune Cecilia 2B on general instruction-following tasks to enable more interactive and versatile applications. Subsequently, targeted fine-tuning on specific downstream Cuban Spanish NLP tasks—such as question answering, sentiment analysis, and named entity recognition—will be pursued to maximize its practical utility within the language processing domain.

In parallel, we plan to develop increasingly powerful models by leveraging larger versions of the Salamandra architecture or exploring alternative base models that demonstrate strong performance and suitability for Cuban Spanish. These efforts aim to balance model capacity, efficiency, and cultural specificity, ultimately providing the community with a range of high-quality language models tailored to Cuban Spanish and related linguistic variants.

One specific task that remains challenging is to retrain the tokenizer to better capture cubanisms and other terms that are split into distinct tokens by the Salamandra 2B tokenizer (Rust et al., 2021). Additionally, quantized versions of all Cecilia models will be published to enable efficient inference in production environments.

At the moment of writing an ongoing effort to create an instruction fine-tuning corpus is being conducted to enable more interactive and versatile applications. In this process, several collaborators from the larger academic community including linguists, sociologists, historians, artists, lawyers, etc., are providing active feedback to incorporate as much relevant data as possible whithin the design constraints of Cuban-only text. In any case, we acknowledge the necessity of incorporating more voices and perspectives to ensure the modely's development aligns with the diverse needs and values. This is a major direction for future work.

6 Conclusions

This paper introduced Cecilia 2B, a 2-billion-parameter language model continually pretrained on a diverse Cuban Spanish corpus of nearly 1 billion tokens. By adapting the Salamandra 2B architecture to focus on Cuban linguistic and cultural features, this project delivers a vital, publicly-available foundational resource that addresses the critical gap in language technology for this underrepresented variant. The development of Cecilia 2B provides a robust case study on balancing computational efficiency with linguistic specialization and establishes a clear path for future work, including instruction tuning, corpus expansion, and the development of more advanced models tailored to Cuban Spanish.

References

Ahuja, K., et al.: Belebele: a novel multilingual reading comprehension dataset for low-resource languages. In: arXiv preprint arXiv:2307.09641 (2023)

Artetxe, M., Ruder, S., Yogatama, D.: Xquad: a cross-lingual question answering dataset. In: Proceedings of the 2020 Conference on Empirical Methods in Natural Language Processing (EMNLP), pp. 8658–8663 (2020)

Gonzalez-Agirre, A., et al.: Salamandra technical report. arXiv preprint arXiv:2502.08489 (2025)

Goodfellow, I. J., Mirza, M., Xiao, D., Courville, A., Bengio, Y.: An empirical investigation of catastrophic forgetting in gradient-based neural networks. arXiv preprint arXiv:1312.6211, (2013)

Gururangan, S., et al.: Don't stop pretraining: adapt language models to domains and tasks. arXiv preprint arXiv:2004.10964 (2020)

Hasan, T., et al.: Xl-sum: large-scale multilingual abstractive summarization for 44 languages. In: Findings of the Association for Computational Linguistics: EMNLP 2021, pp. 4693–4703 (2021)

Hovy, D.: The social and the neural network: how to make natural language processing about people again. In: Proceedings of the Second Workshop on Computational Modeling of People's Opinions, Personality, and Emotions in Social Media, pp. 42–49 (2018)

Joshi, M., Choi, E., Weld, D., Zettlemoyer, L.: Triviaqa: a large scale distantly supervised challenge dataset for reading comprehension. In: Proceedings of the 55th Annual Meeting of the Association for Computational Linguistics (Volume 1: Long Papers), pp. 1601–1611 (2017)

Lee, E.: The impact of model size on catastrophic forgetting in online continual learning. arXiv preprint arXiv:2407.00176 (2024)

Levesque, H., Davis, E., Morgenstern, L.: The winograd schema challenge. In: Proceedings of the Thirteenth International Conference on Principles of Knowledge Representation and Reasoning, pp. 552–561 (2012)

Li, C., Chen, M., Wang, J., Sitaram, S., Xie, X.: Culturellm: incorporating cultural differences into large language models. Adv. Neural. Inf. Process. Syst. **37**, 84799–84838 (2024)

Li, Y., Eldan, R.: Tinystories: how small can language models be and still speak coherent english (2023)

Liu, Y., Held, W., Yang, D.: Dada: Dialect adaptation via dynamic aggregation of linguistic rules. arXiv preprint arXiv:2305.13406 (2023)

Mihaylov, T., Clark, P., Khot, T., Sabharwal, A.: Openbookqa: A new benchmark for open book question answering. In: Proceedings of the 2018 Conference on Empirical Methods in Natural Language Processing, pp. 2381–2391 (2018)

Nguyen, D., Rosseel, L., Grieve, J.: On learning and representing social meaning in NLP: a sociolinguistic perspective. In: Proceedings of the 2021 Conference of the North American Chapter of the Association for Computational Linguistics: Human Language Technologies, pp. 603–612 (2021)

Patil, N., et al.: Regional tiny stories: using small models to compare language learning and tokenizer performance. arXiv preprint arXiv:2504.07989 (2025)

Rust, P., Pfeiffer, J., Vulić, I., Gurevych, I., Ruder, S.: How good is your tokenizer? on the monolingual performance of multilingual language models. In: Proceedings of the 59th Annual Meeting of the Association for Computational Linguistics (ACL), pp. 3118–3135 (2021)

liogeris, V., Daniušis, P., Nakvosas, A.: Full-parameter continual pretraining of gemma2: insights into fluency and domain knowledge. arXiv preprint arXiv:2505.05946 (2025)

Tellez, E. S., Moctezuma, D., Miranda, S., Graff, M., Ruiz, G.: Regionalized models for spanish language variations based on twitter. Lang. Res. Eval. 57(4):1697–1727 (2023)

Yıldız, C., Ravichandran, NK., Sharma, N., Bethge, M., Ermis, B.: Investigating continual pretraining in large language models: insights and implications. arXiv preprint arXiv:2402.17400 (2024)

Zhang, B., Sennrich, R.: Root mean square layer normalization. Advances in Neural Information Processing Systems, 32 (2019)

Automated Ontology Extraction from Text for Content-Based Web Personalization

Ali Mahmoud Mansour[(✉)] ⓘ, Juman Hussein Mohammad ⓘ,
and Yury Alekseevich Kravchenko ⓘ

Department of Computer Aided Design, Southern Federal University, Taganrog 347900, Russia
`mansur@sfedu.ru`

Abstract. In the era of rapid AI advancements and exponential data growth, web content personalization has become essential for enhancing user experience by delivering tailored information. Traditional methods, such as conceptual approaches and static ontological models, face limitations: conceptual methods lack semantic depth and struggle with domain-specific ambiguities, while ontological models, though semantically rich, are often rigid and unable to adapt to dynamic user preferences. To address these challenges, this study proposes a hybrid approach that combines the interpretability of conceptual methods with the semantic rigor of ontologies. This paper makes two key contributions. First, it introduces an ontological model that automates the identification of hierarchical and taxonomic relationships within user profiles, enabling a more accurate and dynamic representation of user interests. This enhances the efficiency of searching for relevant knowledge items and assessing their semantic relevance. Second, it presents an improved web content personalization algorithm that leverages this ontological model to better identify user interests. The algorithm integrates keyphrase extraction and ambiguity detection techniques into a unified pipeline, ensuring more precise and adaptive personalization. Experimental results demonstrate that the proposed solutions improve the accuracy of search result personalization by 5–8%, as measured by the MAP@K metric.

Keywords: Personalization · content-based recommendation · text mining · concept extraction · keyword extraction · ontology learning

1 Introduction

In the context of the rapid development of artificial intelligence (AI) technologies and the exponential growth of data volumes, web content personalization has become a key tool for enhancing user experience and delivering relevant information tailored to individual preferences. This is particularly important in the era of information overload, where users are confronted with vast amounts of information, much of which may not align with their interests and needs [1]. Personalization is one of the applications of web engineering, encompassing a set of information processes aimed at delivering individualized and customized experiences to each user based on their preferences, behavior, and other relevant data [2].

Y. Hernádez Heredia et al. (Eds.): IWAIPR 2025, LNCS 16328, pp. 139–151, 2026.
https://doi.org/10.1007/978-3-032-11358-0_12

The cornerstone of web content personalization is the creation of a user profile, which involves collecting and analyzing data about individual users to understand their preferences, interests, behavior, and demographic characteristics [2–5].

Modern approaches to building user profiles are divided into two main paradigms: conceptual methods and ontological models. Conceptual methods, based on keyword extraction and term frequency analysis, identify significant terms from user data [6]. Despite their interpretability and computational efficiency, these methods are limited in their ability to account for the underlying semantics of content. They treat words as isolated units and ignore contextual relationships between concepts. This limitation becomes particularly problematic in cases of domain-specific ambiguity, where the same term can have different interpretations across domains. For example, the term "cell" may refer to a biological cell in a medical context or a mobile phone in a telecommunications context. This results in profiles cluttered with noise and ambiguity, undermining the accuracy of recommendations.

To address the limitations of concept-based approaches, some studies employ external data sources such as the Open Directory Project (ODP), which serves as a foundation for creating ontologies and classifying content. For instance, in [7–10], user interests are extracted from web documents and represented as weighted categories from ODP. These methods represent a step toward ontology-based approaches but lack semantic relationships between concepts.

In contrast, the ontological approach uses formal ontologies to structure user profiles, organizing user interests as ontological concepts (hierarchical knowledge graphs) using formal semantic relationships, such as linking "deep learning" to "artificial intelligence". However, such models often rely on static, predefined ontologies that cannot adapt to the dynamic nature of user preferences or emerging domains. In [8], user profiles are created based on URLs and mapped to categories from OpenDNS and DBpedia ontologies [11, 12]. This method enriches user profiles with semantic relationships but may not ensure accuracy in capturing specific interests. Additionally, hybrid methods integrate domain-specific ontologies with collaborative filtering techniques to improve recommendation accuracy. Consequently, ontological systems require significant computational resources but compensate with their deep semantic richness, while conceptual methods prioritize speed at the expense of accuracy. Polysemy and domain-specific meanings persist due to inadequate disambiguation.

As a result, modern methods remain insufficiently effective for processing large volumes of textual information and extracting knowledge from them, which hinders the effective representation of user interests in web personalization systems. These limitations highlight the urgent need for hybrid solutions that combine the interpretability of conceptual methods with the semantic rigor of ontologies while ensuring adaptability to the dynamic nature of user behavior.

To address the limitations mentioned earlier, this study adopts a hybrid approach that integrates a domain ontology automation model with a concept-based approach. This paper offers two key contributions. First, it introduces an ontological model designed to automate the identification of hierarchical and taxonomic relationships within a user profile, effectively capturing user interests. This automation enhances the efficiency of searching for relevant knowledge items and evaluating their semantic relevance to user preferences. Second, it proposes an enhanced personalized document ranking algorithm that leverages this ontological model to more accurately identify user interests. This algorithm incorporates key phrase extraction and ambiguity detection algorithms developed in prior works, integrating them into a unified pipeline to achieve the personalization task.

This paper is organized as follows. In the Materials section, a detailed description of the proposed ontological model and the user profile construction algorithm is provided. Subsequently, the personalized document ranking algorithm and the computational experiment are described. The analysis of the results is shown in the Results section, followed by expectations and future plans in the Conclusions section.

2 Materials and Methods

In this section, we provide a detailed description of the ontological model used to create the profile, followed by the algorithm for building and updating the user profile. This includes analyzing natural language texts (extracting key phrases, resolving word ambiguity), and constructing and updating the ontological profile in an offline phase. Finally, we outline the personalized document ranking algorithm, which leverages the profile to deliver personalized and accurate search results.

2.1 Ontological Model for User Profile

The formal description of the ontological model $\mathcal{O}$ is defined as a tuple:

$$\mathcal{O} =< \mathcal{C}, \mathcal{R}, \mathcal{A}, I, \mathcal{H}, \mathcal{W} >, \tag{1}$$

where I is a set of instances (individuals) representing specific entities or key phrases; $\mathcal{C}$ is a set of concepts (classes) representing general categories or topics; $\mathcal{R}$ is a set of relations (properties) defining connections between concepts or key phrases; $\mathcal{A}$ is a set of axioms; $\mathcal{H}$ is a hierarchy organizing topics and key phrases into a taxonomic structure; $\mathcal{W}$ is a weighting function assigning weights to concepts, and key phrases.

The semantic relation extraction algorithm, presented later in this section, describes the process of establishing links between key phrases as well as between these phrases and topics of interest. This process involves two main procedures:

a) semantic similarity assessment methods applied to vector representations of phrases and concepts;
b) external knowledge bases (e.g., Wikidata) to identify and validate relations such as: synonymOf; broader; narrower, etc.

Figure 1 shows an example of an ontology illustrating the relationships between its elements. The blue nodes represent keywords, each of which has attributes: weight, which expresses the degree of the user's interest in this element; vector, and label. The red nodes denote thematic categories, which have the same attributes as the keywords.

Let K be the set of instances representing specific entities or key phrases. Each key phrase $k_i \in K$ is assigned a weight $w(k_i)$. Key phrases are grouped into topics of interest

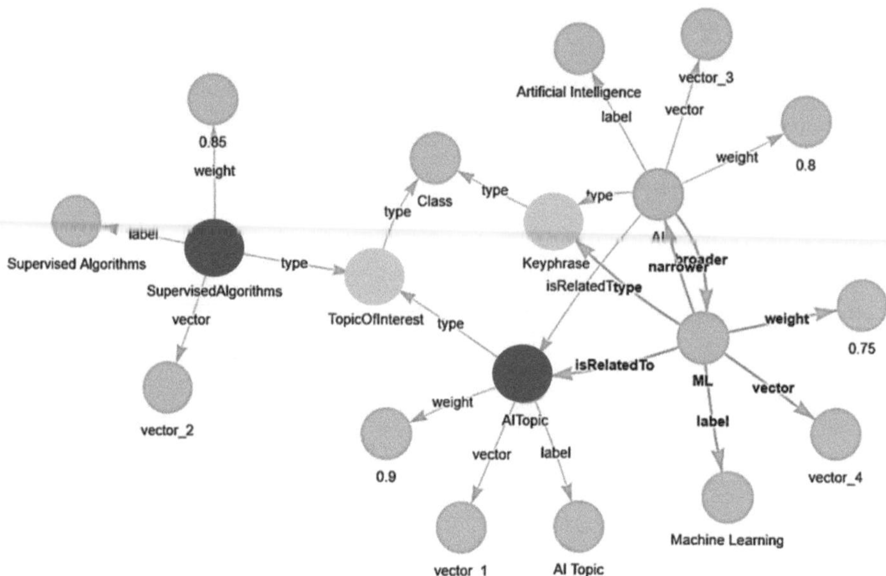

Fig. 1. Example of Concepts at the Top Level of the Ontology

$T = \{t_1, t_2, ..., t_m\}$, where each topic t_i represents a cluster of semantically related key phrases. Each topic t_i is assigned an aggregate weight $w(t_i)$ based on the combined weights of its key phrases:

$$w(t_i) = \sum\nolimits_{k_j \in t_i} w(k_j). \tag{2}$$

where $w(k_j)$ is the weight of the key phrase k_j, and $w(t_i)$ is the weight of the topic t_i;

Using this unique combination of key phrase extraction algorithms, weighting, disambiguation, and clustering, the described ontology is constructed. Also, hierarchical and taxonomical relationships describing user interests are automatically extracted from the text. To emphasize the significance of the proposed ontological model and elaborate on the semantics of its components, the following section describes the development of an algorithm for constructing a user profile based on this model. Subsequently, the algorithm is applied to address the task of personalizing search results.

2.2 User Profile Building Algorithm

To create a user profile, a series of steps are performed, including: extracting key phrases, resolving their ambiguity, creating user interest topics, and ultimately building a user profile based on the user's interests (Fig. 2).

Input: Text content of the web pages visited by the user.

Output: User profile, a structured representation of the user's interests, including identified key phrases and their associated weights.

Step 1. Content from visited web pages is collected, with headings saved separately as they indicate key phrase importance. Web scraping (using BeautifulSoup [13]) extracts and processes HTML content automatically.

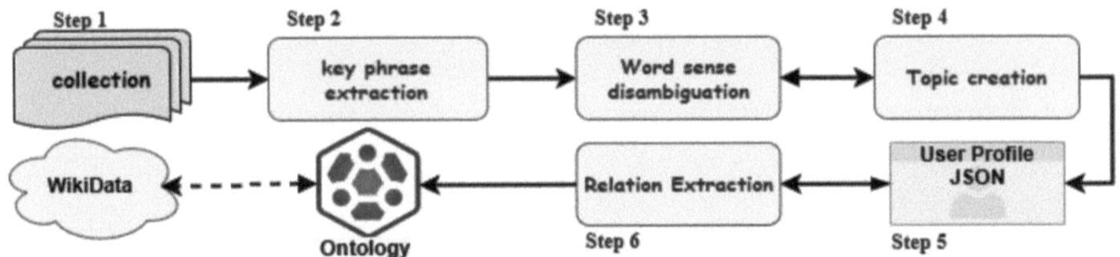

Fig. 2. User profile building algorithm

Step 2. Key phrase extraction: Use the FBKE algorithm [14, 15] to extract key phrases, weighting them based on semantic relevance and position (f_k and p_k for phrase k). Structured content (e.g., web pages, articles) prioritizes positional data:

$$W(k) = f_k \cdot p_k. \tag{3}$$

$$p_k = \begin{cases} a \text{ if } k \text{ is in the title} \\ \frac{a}{i} \text{ if } k \text{ is in subheading } H_i \\ 1 \text{ if } k \text{ is in the main text} \end{cases} \tag{4}$$

Top-weighted phrases form the basis for identifying user interest topics.

Step 3. Unigram keyword vectors (unlike bigram/trigram vectors) represent generalized meanings. For ambiguous unigrams, we apply our modified Lesk-S-BERT algorithm [16] to perform context-aware disambiguation, outputting adjusted vectors.

Step 4. Creating User Interest Topics. A hierarchical clustering algorithm groups key phrase vectors to build user profiles, revealing thematic interests where each cluster represents a specific topic. The algorithm performs multi-level phrase clustering based on semantic similarity between vector representations. The similarity threshold (critically set at 60–70% through experimentation) determines phrase grouping into topics and sub-topics. Formed interest clusters are weighted by their constituent phrases' average weights, calculated as:

$$w_{t_i} = \frac{1}{|P_{t_i}|} \sum_{p \in P_{P_{t_i}}} w_p, \tag{5}$$

where P_{t_i} is the number of phrases in cluster t_i. The final weight of key phrase w_p for topic t_i is the average of its weights across all related documents (web pages).

$$W_p^{\text{topic}} = \frac{1}{|D_p|} \sum_{d \in D_p} w_{p,d}, \tag{6}$$

where w_p is the weight of phrase p calculated using formula (5). D_p is the set of documents containing phrase p, and $w_{p,d}$ is the weight of phrase p in document d.

Step 5. JSON format is used to store the profile. Core user data at the top level, followed by a list of interest topics (with vectors/weights). While this structure serves as an effective profile for content personalization, its semantic depth is limited without formal description of relationships between phrases and topics. Our approach innovatively merges keyword-based and ontology-based methods, with the subsequent step detailing the algorithm for extracting these relationships according to the proposed ontological model.

Step 6. Extracting Semantic Relations. To extract these relationships, the following algorithm is applied:

Algorithm 1: Extracting Semantic Relations

Input: Profile with JSON-data format J, containing topics of interest (Topics) and related key phrases (KWS) with their weights (Weights), with empty fields for relationships (Relations).

Output: User profile with relations.

1:    *Relations ={} // empty dictionary to store relationships .*

2:    **for** *KWS in Topics* **do:**

3:      **for** *i in range(0, length(KWS)) do:*

4:        **for** *j in range(i + 1, length(KWS) − 1) do:*

5:         $kw1, kw2 = KWS[i], KWS[j]$

         $s = cos\_sim(kw1, kw2)$

         if s > 0.9: *Relation(kw1, kw2) = synonym*

6:         **if s** < 0.6: *Relation(kw1, kw2)* $= \emptyset$

7:         **if** $0.6 <$ **s** < 0.9:

8:           *Relation(kw1, kw2)*

               $= \textbf{\textit{search\_wikiData}}(kw1, kw2)$

9:          **if** *Relation(kw1, kw2)* $= \emptyset$:

10:         *Relation(kw1, kw2) = has − relation*

       end

     end

   end

11:    $\textbf{map}(\textbf{\textit{J}}, \textbf{\textit{Relation}})$ // *Update J with new relationships*

12:    Return ***J***

Cosine similarity is employed to assess semantic proximity between phrases. Phrases scoring above 0.9 are directly classified as synonyms. For scores within a range of [0.6–0.9], we utilize Wikidata to verify specific ontological relationships (e.g., synonymy, part-of, subclass-of) between phrase pairs. Pairs lacking a defined Wikidata relationship receive a generic "has-related" designation. For instance, the S-BERT vectors for "machine learning" (Q2539) and "artificial intelligence" show a cosine similarity of 0.72, with Wikidata explicitly confirming machine learning as an AI subclass.

2.3 Personalized Document Ranking Algorithm

For a given set of textual documents D (where the documents may represent either search results or website content), the proposed algorithm sorts the materials according to their relevance to a specific user. Matching them with the user's ontological profile to generate personalized results. It is assumed that the initial profile is created according to the steps described in the previous section and is structured as a three-level hierarchy:

- Level 1: main topics of interest $(T_1\text{-}T_k)$;
- Level 2: subtopics within each topic $(S_1\text{-}S_m)$;
- Level 3: individual key phrases $(K_1\text{-}K_p)$.
- Vector representations of retrieved documents are created using the same vectorization method employed for encoding key phrases, such as S-BERT.

  The following variables are introduced:

  weighting coefficients: $\alpha = 0.5$, $\beta = 0.3$, $\gamma = 0.2$;

  threshold values: $\theta_{\_topic} = 0.4$ (minimum similarity to topic); $\theta_{sub\text{-}topic} = 0.6$ (minimum similarity to subtopic).
- Hierarchical relevance assessment. For each document $d \in D$:

a). topic level assessment:

$$R_{topic}(d) = \max_{t \in T}[\cos(v_d, v_t) \cdot w_t], \tag{7}$$

if $R_{topic}(d) < \theta_{topic} \rightarrow$ skip document;

b). subtopic level assessment (for $t^* = argmax(R_{topic}(d))$):

$$R_{sub}(d) = \max_{s \in S_{t^*}}[\cos(v_d, v_s) \cdot w_s], \tag{8}$$

if $R_{sub}(d) < \theta_{subtopic} \rightarrow R(d) = \alpha \cdot R_{topic}(d), \tag{9}$

otherwise proceed to the next step;

c). detailed assessment at the phrase level (for $s^* = argmax(R_{sub}(d))$):

$$R_{phrase}(d) = \frac{\sum_{k \in K_{s^*}} \cos(v_d, v_k) \cdot w_k}{|K_{s^*}|}. \tag{10}$$

Final score:

$$R(d) = \alpha \cdot R_{topic}(d) + \beta \cdot R_{sub}(d) + \gamma \cdot R_{phrase}(d). \tag{11}$$

3. Ranking and output of results: sorting documents in descending order of R(d);
4. Updating user profile with new phrases: The system displays personalized search results as a ranked document list. Based on user interactions, selected documents undergo offline processing where the FBKE and WSD algorithms extract and disambiguate key phrases, then new phrases are integrated into the user profile using the following update procedure:

a. If the key phrase is already present in the profile: the weight of the phrase itself is adjusted using the following formula;

$$w_{(t)} = w_{(t-1)} + \beta \cdot \frac{f_i}{\sum f_j}, \tag{12}$$

where $w_{(t)}$ is the weight of phrase at time t; t is the time since the last update (in days); β is the gain coefficient for new phrases (e.g. 1.0); f_i is the frequency of occurrence of phrase in new data, $\sum f_j$ is the sum of the frequencies of all new phrases. The weight of the topic to which the phrase belongs is updated (formula 6);

b. If the phrase is new: its similarity to existing topics of interest is determined using the cosine similarity measure. The weight of the phrase is defined as the value obtained using formula (3) and normalized relative to the frequency distribution of all new phrases (12); The phrase is added to the closest topic. Then the weight of this topic of interest is updated according to (6);

   If the similarity is below the threshold value (experimentally set at 30%), the phrase is considered to belong to a new topic, which is created automatically;

c. Handling unobserved phrases: if a keyword does not appear in subsequent search results, its weight decreases linearly over time using the following decay factor:

$$w_{(t)} = w_0 \cdot (1 - \lambda t), \tag{13}$$

where $w(t)$ is the weight at time t, w_0 is the initial weight, λ is the decay rate, and t is the time elapsed since the phrase was last observed.

Each topic maintains 1–30 key phrases for efficiency. New phrases replace old ones with lower weights based on this decay function.

2.4 Experimental Research

The FBKE algorithm was implemented to extract key phrases, as outlined in prior research [14, 15], generating candidate key phrases with their weights and SBERT vectors. The WSD algorithm, following previous work [16], used the same SBERT model to encode WordNet synsets, aligning them with the extracted key phrase vectors.

Datasets. The AOL4PS (AOL for Personalized Search) dataset [17] is a large-scale resource for personalized search research, derived from real AOL search queries and user clicks. It includes anonymized user IDs, timestamps, and click data, making it valuable for analyzing user behavior and developing personalized search algorithms.

However, some URLs in the dataset may be inaccessible due to expiration or geographical restrictions, complicating experiments requiring specific web pages. To address this issue, a filtered dataset sample was utilized, comprising 1,000 selected users. Analysis of their logs yielded 243,148 unique URLs.

Since AOL4PS lacks relevance labels, the SBERT model is employed to evaluate query-document relevance. A relevance score above 0.5 is labeled as 1 (relevant); otherwise, it is labeled as 0.

Evaluation Metrics. To evaluate the results, Mean Average Precision (MAP@K) is used, which calculates the average precision across a set of queries, taking into account the order of relevant items in the search results:

$$MAP@K = \frac{1}{Q} \sum_{q=1}^{Q} \frac{1}{R} \sum_{k=1}^{K} Precision@k \cdot rel(k), \tag{14}$$

where Q: Total number of queries; Rq: Total number of relevant items for query q; rel(k) = 1, if the item at position k is relevant, otherwise 0. Precision@K (Precision at K elements): The proportion of relevant results among the top-K suggested items. It shows how accurately the system returns relevant results within the first K elements.

Additionally, an experiment was conducted to assess the effectiveness of clustering the keywords generated by the FBKE algorithm into interest topics. The homogeneity of the resulting clusters was evaluated using Davies-Bouldin Index (DBI) [18], which measures the ratio of within-cluster scatter (intra-cluster variation) to between-cluster separation (inter-cluster distance):

$$DBI = \frac{1}{k} \sum_{i=1}^{k} \max_{j \neq i} \left(\frac{S_i + S_j}{d_{ij}} \right), \quad \text{where} \quad S_i = \frac{1}{n_i} \sum_{x \in C_i} x - \mu_i, \tag{15}$$

where S_i is the average intra-cluster distance, and $d_{ij} = \mu - \mu_i)$ is the distance between the centroids. The following section presents the results.

3 Results and Discussion

Figure 3 presents the outcomes of a computational experiment designed to evaluate the effectiveness of the algorithm for clustering homogeneity key phrases into interest topics (concepts) using FBKE (n-grams_FBKE). The homogeneity scores of the clusters (topics) generated by the proposed algorithm were compared with those obtained using other keyword extraction algorithms such as YAKE, RAKE, the TF-IDF model, and the baseline unigram-based algorithm [15]. The results show that the proposed algorithm outperforms other baselines and achieves significant improvements in the homogeneity of the clusters representing topics. This improvement ensures the creation of more cohesive and well-defined interest topics.

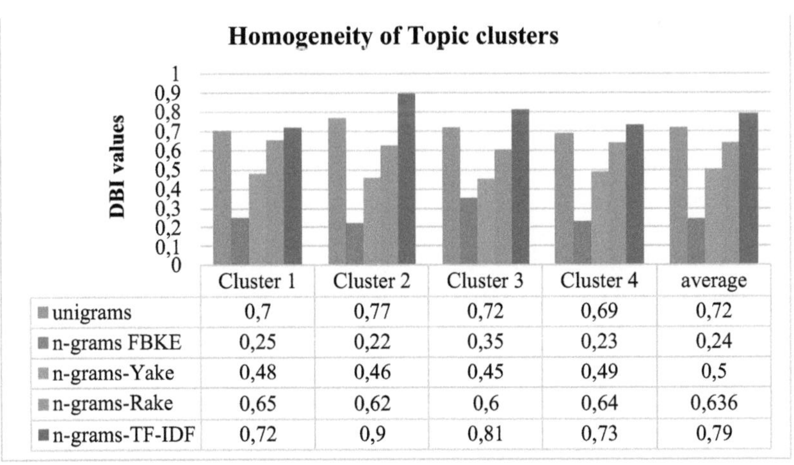

	Cluster 1	Cluster 2	Cluster 3	Cluster 4	average
unigrams	0,7	0,77	0,72	0,69	0,72
n-grams FBKE	0,25	0,22	0,35	0,23	0,24
n-grams-Yake	0,48	0,46	0,45	0,49	0,5
n-grams-Rake	0,65	0,62	0,6	0,64	0,636
n-grams-TF-IDF	0,72	0,9	0,81	0,73	0,79

Fig. 3. Cluster homogeneity measured using the Davies-Bouldin Index.

To evaluate the effectiveness of the proposed personalizing algorithm compared to other methods, a series of experimental pipelines were developed. These pipelines aim to demonstrate the individual and collective impact of key components–keyword extraction, word sense disambiguation, and semantic relation extraction (based on ontology)–on the overall performance of the search result personalization process.

The experimental pipelines are described in Table 1 and the results are presented in Table 2. For word sense disambiguation, the basic *Lesk* algorithm is compared against our enhanced *BERT-based Lesk* algorithm. For key phrase extraction, the TF-IDF method (commonly used in prior studies) is evaluated against our FBKE algorithm. In the final pipeline, the integrated solution proposed in this paper is implemented, incorporating ontology to strengthen semantic relationships.

Pipeline 1 serves as the baseline. The low *MAP@K* and *Precision@K* values are due to the use of basic methods such as *TF-IDF* and *Lesk*. *TF-IDF* does not consider context, and Lesk often makes errors in cases of ambiguity due to its reliance on the overlap principle, which fails to capture semantic similarity and context.

Table 1. Experimental pipelines for personalization evaluation

ID	Pipeline	KW	WSD	Ontology
1	Baseline pipeline to demonstrate the impact of traditional keyword extraction and WSD methods without considering semantic relations	TF-IDF	LESK	No
2	Demonstrates improvement when using FBKE instead of TF-IDF for keyword extraction while retaining WSD methods	FBKE	LESK	No
3	Demonstrates improvement when using $Lesk_{SBERT}$ instead of Lesk	TF-IDF	$Lesk_{SBERT}$	No
4	Demonstrates the combined effect of FBKE and $Lesk_{SBERT}$ on profile accuracy	FBKE	$Lesk_{SBERT}$	No
5	Shows the effect of integrating ontology-based semantic relations into the profile-building process	FBKE	$Lesk_{SBERT}$	Yes

Table 2. Results for Search personalization measured by *MAP@K* metric

	MAP@5	Precision @5	MAP @10	Precision @10
Pipeline 1	42.02	48.33	37.13	41.4
Pipeline 2	52.7	58.6	47.32	52.8
Pipeline 3	49.6	52.9	41.42	47.88
Pipeline 4	64.2	67.91	56.88	63.01
Pipeline 5	**68.05**	**70.95**	**59.83**	**67.92**

In **Pipeline 2**, the improvement stems from FBKE's ability to extract domain-specific keywords more effectively by combining frequency analysis with SBERT embeddings, ensuring better relevance in key phrase selection. However, the traditional Lesk algorithm's reliance on dictionary definitions and lack of contextual awareness still limits its disambiguation accuracy, preventing further gains. **Pipeline 3** shows a performance drop despite using the enhanced SBERT-based Lesk WSD algorithm, which better handles word sense ambiguity through contextual embeddings. This highlights the importance of accurate key phrase extraction, especially considering that TF-IDF does not account for semantic nuances and is not integrated with the $Lesk_{SBERT}$ algorithm.

Pipeline 4 outperforms previous pipelines by combining FBKE with $Lesk_{SBERT}$, leveraging SBERT's contextual embeddings for both keyword extraction and disambiguation, ensuring domain-specific accuracy. By using the same SBERT representations for both algorithms, the system ensures consistent contextual understanding, improving user profile accuracy. As a result, key phrase disambiguation aligns more precisely with extracted terms, leading to better interpretation of user interests.

Finally, **Pipeline 5** achieves the highest MAP@K and Precision@K values due to the integration of ontological relations. By using the ontology, the system not only maps keywords to concepts but also considers their semantic relationships (e.g., "ML" is linked to "DL" and "AI"). This structural approach improves both precision and recall, as the system retrieves not only direct matches but also semantically related terms.

Overall, the evaluation confirms that SBERT-enhanced algorithms and ontological reasoning significantly boost search personalization, reducing ranking errors by 5–8%. The findings highlight the importance of combining advanced NLP techniques with structured knowledge for optimal information retrieval.

4   Conclusions

This study introduces a unified approach for creating ontology-driven user profiles to enhance search personalization. An ontological model and a novel algorithm were developed, integrating key phrase extraction and disambiguation algorithms developed in previous works into a unified pipeline. The algorithm automates the extraction of hierarchical and taxonomic relationships for user profile, improving the efficiency of retrieving relevant knowledge items and assessing their semantic relevance. The proposed solution improved web search personalization by 5–8% in recommendation accuracy (MAP@K) on the AOL4PS benchmark dataset. In future work, we plan to expand the ontology to incorporate a broader range of concepts and relationships, while using a Reasoner to independently verify its logical consistency. We will also investigate additional use cases to better demonstrate how the ontology enhances personalization efficiency. Additionally, we are designing experiments to quantitatively assess the approach's impact on both processing time and analysis quality.

Acknowledgements. The study was performed by the grant from the Russian Science Foundation № 22-71-10121-П, https://rscf.ru/project/22-71-10121-П/ in the Southern Federal University.

References

1. Garrigós, I., Gomez, J., Houben, G.-J.: Specification of personalization in web application design. Inf. Software Technol. **52**, 991–1010 (2010)
2. Farid, M., Elgohary, R., Moawad, I., Roushdy, M.: User profiling approaches, modeling, and personalization. In: Proceedings of the 11th International Conference on Informatics & Systems (INFOS 2018) (2018)
3. Mobasher, B.: Data mining for web personalization. In: The Adaptive Web, pp. 90–135. Springer (2007)
4. Gauch, S., Speretta, M., Chandramouli, A., Micarelli, A.: User profiles for personalized information access. The Adaptive Web. pp. 54–89 (2007)
5. Cantador, I., Bellogín, A., Castells, P.: Ontology-based personalised and context-aware recommendations of news items. Presented at the 2008 IEEE/WIC/ACM International Conference on Web Intelligence and Intelligent Agent Technology (2008)
6. Leung, K.W.-T., Lee, D.L.: Deriving concept-based user profiles from search engine logs. IEEE Trans. Knowl. Data Eng. **22**, 969–982 (2009)
7. Liu, F., Yu, C., Meng, W.: Personalized web search by mapping user queries to categories. In: Proceedings of the Eleventh International Conference on Information and Knowledge Management. pp. 558–565. ACM, McLean Virginia USA (2002). https://doi.org/10.1145/584792.584884
8. Penas, P., Del Hoyo, R., Vea-Murguía, J., González, C., Mayo, S.: Collective knowledge ontology user profiling for Twitter–automatic user profiling. In: 2013 IEEE/WIC/ACM International Joint Conferences on Web Intelligence (WI) and Intelligent Agent Technologies (IAT). pp. 439–444. IEEE (2013)
9. Gauch, S., Chaffee, J., Pretschner, A.: Ontology-based personalized search and browsing. Web Intell. Agent Syst. Int. J. **1**, 219–234 (2003)
10. Xu, Y., Wang, K., Zhang, B., Chen, Z.: Privacy-enhancing personalized web search. In: Proceedings of the 16th International Conference on World Wide Web. pp. 591–600. ACM, Banff Alberta Canada (2007). https://doi.org/10.1145/1242572.1242652
11. Abián, D., Guerra, F., Martínez-Romanos, J., Trillo-Lado, R.: Wikidata and DBpedia: a comparative study. In: Szymański, J., Velegrakis, Y. (eds.) Semantic Keyword-Based Search on Structured Data Sources. pp. 142–154. Springer International Publishing, Cham (2018). https://doi.org/10.1007/978-3-319-74497-1_14
12. Lehmann, J., et al.: Dbpedia–a large-scale, multilingual knowledge base extracted from wikipedia. Semantic Web. **6**, 167–195 (2015)
13. Abodayeh, A., Hejazi, R., Najjar, W., Shihadeh, L., Latif, R.: Web scraping for data analytics: a BeautifulSoup implementation. In: 2023 Sixth International Conference of Women in Data Science at Prince Sultan University (WiDS PSU). pp. 65–69. IEEE (2023)
14. Mansour, A., Mohammad, J., Kravchenko, Y., Kravchenko, D., Silega, N.: Harnessing key phrases in constructing a concept-based semantic representation of text using clustering techniques. In: International Workshop on Artificial Intelligence and Pattern Recognition. pp. 190–201. Springer (2023)
15. Mansour, A.: Algorithm for optimization of keyword extraction based on the application of a linguistic parser. Mansour, A., Mohammad, J., Kravchenko, D., Kravchenko, Y., Pavlov, N. (eds.) Informatics and Automation. Vol. 23, no. 2, pp. 467–494 (2024)
16. Mansour A.M., Mohammad J.H., Kravchenko Yu, A.: Modifitsirovannyy metod ustraneniya neodnoznachnosti smysla slov, osnovannyy na metodakh raspredelennogo pred-stavleniya [modified word sense disambiguation method based on distributed representation methods]. Izvestiya Yuzhnogo federal'nogo universiteta. Tekhnicheskiye nauki [Bulletin of the Southern Federal University. Technical Sciences]. pp. 92–101 (2021)

17. Guo, Q., Chen, W., Wan, H.: AOL4PS: a large-scale data set for personalized search. Data Intell. **3**, 548–567 (2021)
18. Petrovic, S.: A comparison between the silhouette index and the davies-bouldin index in labelling ids clusters. In: Proceedings of the 11th Nordic workshop of secure IT systems. pp. 53–64. Citeseer (2006)

Towards Accurate and Legible Scene Text Generation in Spanish; A Text-to-Image Model

Miguel Á. Álvarez-Carmona[1,3(✉)], Isaias Siliceo Guzmán[1], Ramón Aranda[2,3], and Vitali Herrera-Semenets[4]

[1] Centro de Investigación en Matemáticas (CIMAT), Monterrey, Mexico
miguel.alvarez@cimat.mx
[2] Centro de Investigación en Matemáticas (CIMAT), Mérida, Mexico
[3] Secretaría de Ciencia Humanidades, Tecnología e Innovación (secihti), CDMX, Mexico
[4] Advanced Technologies Application Center (CENATAV), La Habana, Cuba

Abstract. Scene text generation in images remains a major challenge for current text-to-image (T2I) systems, especially in morphologically rich and underrepresented languages such as Spanish. Existing generative models often produce text that is visually distorted, grammatically incorrect, or semantically inconsistent. In this work, we present a targeted approach to improve scene text generation in Spanish by fine-tuning a state-of-the-art diffusion model, FLUX.1-dev, using a novel dataset of Spanish-language memes (CCMD). Our methodology integrates prompt engineering, Low-Rank Adaptation (LoRA), and a custom evaluation protocol that includes human judgment. We demonstrate that increasing the number of denoising steps k leads to consistent improvements in legibility, alignment, and linguistic fidelity. Our results show that the proposed model outperforms baseline systems such as GPT-4 (DALL·E). We further propose a roadmap for building automatic evaluation frameworks that assess scene text not only lexically, but also semantically and visually, paving the way toward more inclusive and robust generative systems.

Keywords: Text-to-Image Generation · Scene Text Synthesis · Diffusion Models · Spanish Language AI · Multimodal Evaluation

1 Introduction

Despite major progress in Text-to-Image (T2I) systems [2], many models still struggle to correctly render embedded text, particularly in languages other than English. For example, prompting a general-purpose model like Stable Diffusion with the input "una invitación de cumpleaños para el 10 de abril de Miguel" often results in images with misspelled or garbled text such Fig. 1 shows, which renders the generated content semantically incorrect and visually incoherent.

Fig. 1. Example of an automatically generated image featuring a birthday invitation sign. The text includes typographic distortions, incorporating characters that mimic non-Latin styles or visual artifacts.

This limitation illustrates a broader challenge: current generative systems are not yet robust at reproducing legible, context-aware, and grammatically correct scene text when working with morphologically rich languages such as Spanish. As scene text is crucial in domains like education, urban signage, advertising, and digital storytelling, improving the reliability of text rendering in T2I systems is essential for both usability and inclusivity.

Text-to-Image (T2I) generative models have emerged as a groundbreaking branch of artificial intelligence, enabling the automatic creation of complex visual scenes based solely on textual prompts [5]. These models have revolutionized fields such as digital content creation, game development, advertising, and education by significantly reducing the manual effort required to design high-quality visual assets [8]. Leveraging large-scale datasets and powerful transformer-based architectures, models like DALL·E, Imagen, and Stable Diffusion have demonstrated remarkable capabilities in translating linguistic inputs into coherent and aesthetically pleasing images [19]. Despite this success, a critical limitation persists in their ability to accurately render text within the image—a capability essential for real-world applications involving signage, user interfaces, infographics, educational materials, and memes [17].

The problem of scene text generation—that is, the synthesis of images in which the text is a visible and integral part of the visual content—introduces unique challenges [25]. It requires not only the generation of high-fidelity images but also the precise placement, legibility, and semantic consistency of the text relative to the prompt and the surrounding visual context. These challenges are compounded when working with languages other than English, as most existing models are trained predominantly on English-centric datasets, which leads to a strong linguistic and typographic bias. Consequently, when prompted with text in Spanish or other underrepresented languages, these models frequently produce artifacts such as misspelled words, broken characters, or entirely illegible text [13].

Addressing this shortcoming is crucial for democratizing generative technologies and ensuring that linguistic minorities are not excluded from the benefits of AI. Spanish, in particular, is the second most spoken native language in the world [1], with a rich morphological structure, accentuation rules, and diacritics that complicate its representation in generative models. Thus, improving text generation capabilities in Spanish not only broadens the inclusiveness of T2I systems but also serves as a representative challenge in the multilingual expansion of generative AI.

In this work, we propose a targeted approach to enhance scene text generation in Spanish by fine-tuning a diffusion-based T2I model on a custom dataset of Spanish-language memes. Our focus on memes is not incidental: memes are inherently multimodal, combining humor, cultural commentary, and linguistic play in a compact format where text is almost always embedded within the image. This makes them ideal candidates for studying the interaction between textual content and visual layout.

To support our methodology, we construct a **Meme Dataset (CCMD)**, a large-scale collection of Spanish-language memes scraped from a popular humor website. We annotate this dataset using a combination of OCR and neural captioning techniques to obtain both the in-image text and its corresponding descriptive prompt. We then fine-tune a diffusion model on this dataset and evaluate its performance using a set of comprehensive metrics that account for both visual fidelity and linguistic correctness.

Our contributions are as follows:

- We introduce a new benchmark dataset for Spanish scene text generation.
- We adapt a diffusion-based T2I architecture to handle text-conditioned generation with multilingual constraints.
- We demonstrate substantial improvements over baseline model in human evaluations.

The rest of this paper is organized as follows: Sect. 2 reviews recent advances in text-to-image generation, scene text synthesis, multilingual text rendering, and diffusion models. Section 3 shows the collection apply for this investigation. Section 4 describes the proposed methodology, including dataset preparation, fine-tuning strategy, and training configuration. Section 5 presents our experimental setup, evaluation protocols, and qualitative results. Finally, Sect. 6 concludes the paper and outlines directions for future work.

2   Related Work

Recent advances in deep learning, large-scale datasets, and cross-modal architectures have enabled powerful Text-to-Image (T2I) models capable of generating diverse and coherent visual content from natural language prompts [9]. However, generating legible and context-aware scene text remains a major limitation, especially in languages other than English. We review prior work in three areas: scene text synthesis, multilingual text rendering, and diffusion-based generation.

2.1   Scene Text Synthesis

Early methods such as SynthText3D and UnrealText [12] simulated scene text for OCR training using 3D rendering and game engines. More recently, diffusion-based methods like DiffText [11] and TextDiffuser [23] generate complex images with embedded text via layout-aware conditioning. Although promising, these systems typically underperform in multilingual scenarios. Other works such as GlyphControl [24] and TIES aim to improve typographic precision, but do not fully support morphologically rich languages like Spanish.

2.2   Multilingual Text Rendering and Evaluation

Multilingual scene text generation is significantly underexplored. Benchmarks like COCO-Text [22] and ICDAR [10] focus primarily on English, while datasets like MLT-2019 [14] provide limited multilingual coverage. Embedding models such as multilingual BERT [4], XLM-R [3], and CLIP [16] aid prompt comprehension but not text rendering. Evaluation pipelines often overlook non-English alphabets, motivating our combined use of OCR and linguistic post-analysis tailored to Spanish.

2.3   Diffusion Models

Denoising Diffusion Probabilistic Models (DDPMs) [6] are now state-of-the-art in generative modeling. Latent diffusion [18], classifier-free guidance [7], and score-based variants [21] further extend their capabilities. Yet, producing structured outputs like scene text remains difficult [15]. Our work builds upon these techniques, incorporating Spanish-language supervision and prompt conditioning to generate visually and linguistically coherent scene text.

3   Dataset: Meme Dataset (CCMD)

To overcome the lack of Spanish-language scene text data, we constructed CCMD, a dataset of 126,389 memes from the humor website *Cuánto Cabrón*[1], covering 2010 to 2024. Each meme typically contains humorous Spanish text embedded directly in the image.

The CCMD (CC Memes Dataset) is a general-purpose corpus of Spanish-language images containing embedded scene text, characterized by a diversity of typographic styles and a wide variety of visual contexts. CCMD was constructed from memes shared by the community on the *Cuánto Cabrón* website, covering the period from November 2010 to the present. The dataset was structured by extracting image URLs from the website using Bash scripting and the Lynx text-based web browser, resulting in over 126,000 URLs linked to images containing scene text. These images were then systematically downloaded while preserving their temporal metadata.

---

[1] https://www.cuantocabron.com/.

In addition to its scale and diversity, CCMD provides a unique opportunity to study text generation in real-world Spanish contexts. Unlike synthetic datasets designed for OCR tasks, the text in CCMD appears organically in humorous, sarcastic, or culturally contextual forms, reflecting colloquial and informal Spanish. This diversity of tone and expression makes it particularly valuable for training models that aim not only to reproduce legible text but to align it with the intended communicative function.

To construct the dataset, we implemented a multi-step pipeline. First, we identified the static directory structure of the *Cuánto Cabrón* website and automated the extraction of image URLs using Bash scripting combined with the Lynx terminal browser. This method allowed us to traverse over a decade of archived meme content, ultimately retrieving 126,389 image URLs. These were filtered to retain only high-resolution JPEG files, and then downloaded using batch-controlled `wget` routines that preserved their directory structure by year and month.

A summary of the final dataset statistics is as follows: the Meme Dataset (CCMD) contains a total of 126,389 unique meme images spanning from 2010 to 2024. From this collection, 5,000 high-quality samples with near-square aspect ratios were selected for fine-tuning. Each selected image contains at least one instance of embedded Spanish text and is annotated with a prompt that captures both the visual context and the scene text content. The dataset includes a broad diversity of typographic styles, humor categories, and visual layouts, making it a valuable benchmark for evaluating scene text generation in Spanish across informal and semi-structured domains.

4   Methodology Proposed

Our methodology is designed to bridge the gap between general-purpose Text-to-Image generation and the specialized task of producing images with coherent and contextually integrated Spanish scene text. The core framework is built upon the pretrained FLUX.1-dev model, a diffusion-based T2I generator known for its high image fidelity and adaptability. To specialize this model for scene text synthesis in Spanish, we adopt a domain-adaptive fine-tuning approach using a curated subset of the CCMD dataset.

In diffusion-based generative models such as FLUX.1-dev, image synthesis is modeled as a gradual denoising process. Starting from pure Gaussian noise, the model iteratively refines the image over a predefined number of steps, denoted as k. Each step removes a small amount of noise, guided by the prompt, until a coherent image emerges. During training, the model learns this process by progressively corrupting real images with Gaussian noise—a process known as forward diffusion—until they become indistinguishable from random noise. At inference time, the model reverses this process, starting from noise and applying denoising steps according to a noise scheduler.

Image synthesis in diffusion models can be formally described as a probabilistic denoising process. Given a data distribution $x_0 \sim q(x_0)$, noise is progressively added via a forward diffusion process defined as:

$$x_t = \sqrt{\bar{\alpha}_t}x_0 + \sqrt{1 - \bar{\alpha}_t}\epsilon, \quad \text{with } \epsilon \sim \mathcal{N}(0, I)$$

where x_t is the noisy sample at timestep t, and $\bar{\alpha}_t$ is the cumulative product of the noise schedule.

During training, the model learns the reverse process to estimate the original x_0, typically by minimizing a simplified noise prediction objective:

$$\mathcal{L}_{\text{simple}} = \mathbb{E}_{x_0, \epsilon, t}\left[\left\|\epsilon - \epsilon_\theta(x_t, t)\right\|^2\right]$$

At inference time, the model starts from Gaussian noise $x_T \sim \mathcal{N}(0, I)$ and denoises step-by-step using the learned approximation $p_\theta(x_{t-1} \mid x_t)$, recovering a sample from the data distribution.

In our case, we used the **Euler Flowmatch** scheduler, which defines how noise is added during training and removed during inference. The number of steps k directly influences the visual quality and text coherence of the generated image. Figure 2 illustrates this denoising process from step X_T (pure noise) to X_0 (final image), where p_θ and q represent the learned reverse and forward diffusion probabilities, respectively.

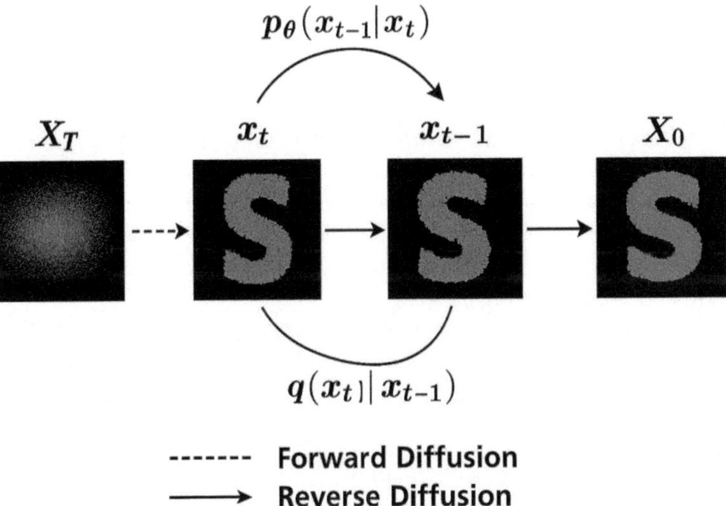

Fig. 2. Illustration of the denoising process in a Denoising Diffusion Probabilistic Model (DDPM). The forward diffusion corrupts the original image, while the reverse diffusion reconstructs it over k steps [20].

The preparation of the dataset was a critical step to ensure training relevance and stability. From the full corpus of over 126,000 images, we selected 5,000 samples based on multiple criteria: visual clarity, typographic diversity, text prominence, and an aspect ratio near 1:1. This preprocessing step was essential to maintain consistent alignment between the visual structure expected by the model and the characteristics of the training data.

Each selected image was paired with a descriptive prompt, generated using GPT-4o-mini, which fulfilled two parallel objectives. First, it captured the broader visual semantics of the image (e.g., "a cartoon man yelling in front of a chalkboard"). Second, it transcribed the exact scene text contained within the image (e.g., "¡Silencio, estoy explicando estadística!"). These dual-annotated prompts served as conditioning inputs for training, enhancing the model's ability to associate textual content with visual appearance, font style, and contextual relevance.

To inject this new capability into FLUX.1-dev, we used Low-Rank Adaptation (LoRA), a parameter-efficient fine-tuning strategy that introduces trainable low-rank matrices into the attention layers of the pretrained model. This approach allows for rapid domain adaptation with minimal memory overhead and avoids catastrophic forgetting of previously learned visual concepts. We trained the LoRA adapters on 8-bit quantized model weights using a cosine learning rate scheduler and a batch size tuned for memory-constrained GPUs.

To further enhance scene text rendering, we implemented a feedback-aware augmentation strategy during training. Each batch of generated samples was passed through an OCR engine (Tesseract) to detect scene text. The OCR output was then compared to the intended ground truth, and discrepancies were penalized via an auxiliary scene-text consistency loss. This loop encouraged the model to improve its textual accuracy and placement coherence across training epochs.

We also observed that the positioning of text in the image is influenced not only by conditioning but also by the stochasticity of the diffusion process. To mitigate this, we introduced spatial anchors in the prompt encoding—syntactic cues that bias the model toward certain locations (e.g., "a banner *at the top* of the image that says..."). Though subtle, these anchors helped regularize the location of text elements during generation.

Together, these methodological components comprise a robust pipeline for generating Spanish scene text with improved fidelity, relevance, and typographic stability.

4.1 Tokenization and Embeddings

We used multilingual BERT tokenization to ensure compatibility with Spanish grammar, including support for accented characters, compound tenses, and gender/number agreement. These embeddings were projected into the latent space expected by FLUX.1-dev's conditioning pathway.

4.2 Diffusion Pipeline

Our model follows the standard DDPM architecture, where images are generated by progressively denoising a sample from Gaussian noise. Text conditioning is injected into the denoising U-Net through cross-attention layers, allowing the model to integrate semantic guidance from the prompt at every step of generation.

4.3 Training Strategy

The training process involved mixed-precision optimization using AdamW and gradient checkpointing for memory efficiency. Training spanned 80 epochs with early stopping based on OCR improvement plateau.

5 Experiments and Results

In all our experiments, we used Spanish pangrams as prompts to evaluate how accurately the model could reproduce all letters of the alphabet within the scene text. This strategy enabled a systematic inspection of typographic completeness and error patterns. We observed that the model often struggles with specific characters, particularly the letters "ñ," "u," and "f," which are frequently misrendered or omitted. Additionally, some random seeds consistently led to images where certain words in the pangram were missing, while other seeds successfully produced full and accurate renditions of the entire sentence. These variations highlight the stochastic nature of diffusion-based generation and underscore the importance of robust evaluation under diverse conditions.

The experiments conducted focused on performing inference with the fine-tuned model at 1800 iterations. One of the core tasks tested was the generation of *pangrams*—sentences that contain every letter of the Spanish alphabet at least once. These are especially useful for evaluating the completeness and consistency of text rendering across a broad range of characters, including diacritics (e.g., á, é, í, ó, ú, ñ). This choice of prompt acts as a robust stress test for any model that aims to generate typographically correct Spanish text in context.

Due to the technical complexity of implementing a full fine-tuning pipeline from scratch, we opted to utilize an existing toolkit developed by the user `ostris`. This toolkit[2] provides pre-configured support for training diffusion models such as FLUX.1-dev using the LoRA (Low-Rank Adaptation) method.

LoRA allows efficient fine-tuning of large models by inserting small trainable low-rank matrices into existing layers—particularly attention modules in the U-Net—without modifying the majority of model parameters. In our implementation, LoRA was applied to the U-Net using matrices of rank 16, and both the U-Net weights and the text encoder remained frozen during training.

---

[2] Documented in their public repository at https://github.com/ostris/ai-toolkit/tree/main.

The training process was conducted using the following configuration:

- **Steps:** 2000
- **Batch size:** 1
- **Gradient accumulation steps:** 1
- **Noise scheduler:** flowmatch
- **Optimizer:** AdamW
- **Learning rate:** 0.0001
- **EMA decay:** 0.99
- **Precision:** bfloat16

Gradient checkpointing was enabled to reduce memory usage during training. Model checkpoints were saved every 200 steps, and models at 1400, 1600, 1800, and 2000 iterations were retained. The final images presented in our analysis were generated using the model at 1800 steps.

The fine-tuning was conducted using a carefully curated subset of 5,000 images from the CCMD dataset, selected to maintain an aspect ratio close to 1:1 and ensure typographic clarity and visual consistency. Each image was paired with a dual-annotated caption describing both its visual content and the exact text visible in the scene.

For inference, the following procedure was applied:

1. Load a selected fine-tuned model checkpoint (e.g., 1800 steps).
2. Provide a Spanish-language prompt (e.g., "Una señal que dice'Zona restringida' en una carretera desierta").
3. Set inference parameters: resolution (e.g., 512×512), denoising steps (e.g., 30), guidance scale (e.g., 4), and random seed (e.g., 15).
4. Apply the flowmatch scheduler to iteratively denoise Gaussian noise conditioned on the prompt.
5. After the specified number of steps, obtain the final generated image.

This approach allows for flexible and reproducible experimentation with prompt-guided image generation. The complete training configuration is provided in the accompanying YAML file. The model successfully synthesized images with improved text fidelity, including complete pangrams and typographic consistency, representing a promising step toward multilingual T2I scene text generation.

To evaluate the quality of the generated text, we define a metric that measures the proportion of correctly rendered characters (legible and in the correct position) over the total number of expected characters in the prompt. This metric yields a value of 1.0 when the text is fully correct and legible, and 0.0 when no characters are recognized or all are misplaced. The evaluation was conducted manually by human annotators, averaging results over 200 images with their corresponding prompts. The accuracy metric A for a given prompt-image pair is defined as:

$$Accuracy = \frac{C_{\text{correct}}}{C_{\text{expected}}}$$

where C_{correct} is the number of legible characters correctly positioned, and C_{expected} is the total number of characters in the target text.

Table 1 shows the results for our model under different denoising steps k compared to GPT-4.

Table 1. Character-level accuracy across denoising steps (k) using pangram prompts. Includes mean, standard deviation, and quartile summary statistics over 200 annotated samples.

Method/k	Accuracy	Std. Dev.	Min	Q1	Q2 (Median)	Q3	Max
GPT-4 (DALL·E)	0.31	0.18	0.00	0.19	0.30	0.43	0.68
Ours – k = 0	0.00	0.00	0.00	0.00	0.00	0.00	0.00
Ours – k = 1	0.08	0.09	0.00	0.03	0.08	0.12	0.28
Ours – k = 5	0.34	0.13	0.05	0.26	0.34	0.42	0.61
Ours – k = 10	0.47	0.11	0.20	0.39	0.47	0.54	0.68
Ours – k = 20	0.61	0.08	0.40	0.56	0.61	0.67	0.77
Ours – k = 40	0.76	0.06	0.62	0.72	0.76	0.80	1.00
Ours – k = 80	0.81	0.04	0.70	0.78	0.81	0.84	1.00

Qualitative results show more natural font integration, coherent Spanish grammar, and appropriate placement of text in the visual scene.

As the denoising step count k increases, we observe significant qualitative improvements in the generated images. For low values of k, such as 1 or 5, the images often appear blurry, and the scene text is incomplete, distorted, or entirely unreadable. As k grows to 10 and 20, the model produces more structured layouts, with clearer separation between characters and improved font coherence. By steps 40 and 80, the images exhibit well-integrated text that is visually aligned with the scene, and semantically faithful to the prompt. This progressive enhancement highlights the importance of sufficient denoising iterations to stabilize character rendering and scene-text fusion.

These effects are visible in Figs. 3, 4 and 5, where each sequence shows the same prompt generated at increasing values of k. As k increases, the text becomes more legible, spatially consistent, and stylistically integrated into the visual context.

(a) $k = 1$ (b) $k = 5$ (c) $k = 10$

(d) $k = 20$ (e) $k = 40$ (f) $k = 80$

Fig. 3. Images generated with FLUX-dev. Prompt: "Viñeta cómica estilo caricatura. Un alien con gran cabeza mira confundido una pizarra llena de fórmulas. El texto en escena dice: 'El veloz murciélago hindú comía feliz cardillo y kiwi.'.". seed: 25

(a) $k = 1$ (b) $k = 5$ (c) $k = 10$

(d) $k = 20$ (e) $k = 40$ (f) $k = 80$

Fig. 4. Images generated with FLUX-dev. Prompt: "Caricatura tipo cómic. Un gato dibuajdo con líneas gruesas y expresión exagerada está frente a una computadora con papeles volando. El texto en escena dice: 'Jovencillo emponzoñada de whisky, ¡qué figurota exhibe!'.". seed: 20.

(a) $k = 1$ (b) $k = 5$ (c) $k = 10$

(d) $k = 20$ (e) $k = 40$ (f) $k = 60$

Fig. 5. Images generated with FLUX-dev. Prompt: "La imagen presenta a dos personajes de una tira cómica: Charlie Brown y Snoopy, que están sentados en un muelle mirando hacia un lago o el mar. El texto en la escena es el siguiente: 1. Charlie Brown dice: 'Di una frase con todas las letras del alfabeto' 2. Snoopy responde: 'Un jugoso zumo de piña y kiwi bien frío es exquisito y no lleva alcohol."'. seed:15.

Overall, our experimental results provide strong evidence that combining a linguistically rich Spanish-language dataset with LoRA-based fine-tuning and a well-structured diffusion schedule significantly improves scene text generation in Spanish. The ability to incrementally refine outputs through denoising steps not only enhances legibility, but also promotes grammatical integrity and semantic alignment with the prompt. These findings confirm the viability of adapting large-scale diffusion models for multilingual scene-text tasks and highlight promising directions for further research in fine-grained textual control.

6   Conclusion and Future Work

In this work, we addressed the persistent challenge of generating high-quality scene text in Spanish using Text-to-Image (T2I) diffusion models. By fine-tuning a state-of-the-art model, FLUX.1-dev, on a curated corpus of Spanish-language memes (CCMD), we were able to substantially improve the legibility, contextual integration, and grammatical correctness of embedded text in synthetic images. Our methodology combined prompt engineering, Low-Rank Adaptation (LoRA), and a structured evaluation protocol, both quantitative and qualitative, to demonstrate clear gains in multilingual scene text generation.

Through extensive experimentation, we showed that increasing the number of denoising steps k leads to consistent improvements in character rendering and prompt adherence. Notably, our model outperformed GPT-4's DALL·E variant in both accuracy and stability when evaluated across 200 annotated image-text pairs. These findings underscore the importance of combining linguistic diversity in training data with tailored adaptation techniques for diffusion-based architectures.

For future work, we propose the development of a comprehensive evaluation framework capable of assessing scene text generation beyond lexical accuracy. This framework should integrate semantic analysis to verify the coherence and relevance of the generated text with respect to the prompt, while also considering visual quality metrics such as Structural Similarity Index (SSIM), perceptual realism, and style fidelity. Additionally, further investigation is needed to identify the optimal number of denoising steps k for different prompt categories and text densities, as this parameter significantly affects both quality and computational efficiency.

By advancing toward automatic, semantically aware, and visually grounded evaluation pipelines, we can support the scalable and reliable deployment of multilingual T2I systems in real-world applications such as education, signage, media localization, and accessible content generation.

References

1. Ardila, A.: Who are the Spanish speakers? An examination of their linguistic, cultural, and societal commonalities and differences. Hisp. J. Behav. Sci. **42**(1), 41–61 (2020)
2. Bosheah, Z., Bilicki, V.: Challenges in generating accurate text in images: a benchmark for text-to-image models on specialized content. Appl. Sci. **15**(5), 2274 (2025)
3. Conneau, A., et al.: Unsupervised cross-lingual representation learning at scale. arXiv preprint: arXiv:1911.02116 (2020)
4. Devlin, J., Chang, M.W., Lee, K., Toutanova, K.: BERT: pre-training of deep bidirectional transformers for language understanding. arXiv preprint: arXiv:1810.04805 (2019)
5. Habib, M.A., et al.: Exploring progress in text-to-image synthesis: an in-depth survey on the evolution of generative adversarial networks. IEEE Access (2024)
6. Ho, J., Jain, A., Abbeel, P.: Denoising diffusion probabilistic models. arXiv preprint: arXiv:2006.11239 (2020)
7. Ho, J., Salimans, T.: Classifier-free diffusion guidance. arXiv preprint: arXiv:2207.12598 (2022)
8. Huang, K., Sun, K., Xie, E., Li, Z., Liu, X.: T2i-compbench: a comprehensive benchmark for open-world compositional text-to-image generation. In: Advances in Neural Information Processing Systems, vol. 36, pp. 78723–78747 (2023)
9. Kang, S., Lee, D., Han, S., Lim, S., Kim, N.: Research on building k-contents specialized text2image pipeline. In: 2025 27th International Conference on Advanced Communications Technology (ICACT), pp. 351–356. IEEE (2025)
10. Karatzas, D., et al.: ICDAR 2015 competition on robust reading. In: 2015 13th International Conference on Document Analysis and Recognition (ICDAR), pp. 1156–1160. IEEE (2015)

11. Liu, X., Zhang, Y., Wang, J.: DiffText: scene text generation with diffusion models. In: Proceedings of the IEEE/CVF Conference on Computer Vision and Pattern Recognition (2023)
12. Long, Y., Yao, C., Wang, X., Wu, W., Bai, X.: UnrealText: synthesizing realistic scene text images from the unreal world. arXiv preprint: arXiv:2107.05328 (2021)
13. Mu, Y., et al.: Boosting text-to-image generation via multilingual prompting in large multimodal models. arXiv preprint: arXiv:2501.07086 (2025)
14. Nayef, N., et al.: ICDAR2019 robust reading challenge on multi-lingual scene text detection and recognition - RRC-MLT-2019. In: 2019 International Conference on Document Analysis and Recognition (ICDAR), pp. 1582–1587. IEEE (2019)
15. Nichol, A.Q., Dhariwal, P.: Improved denoising diffusion probabilistic models. arXiv preprint: arXiv:2102.09672 (2021)
16. Radford, A., et al.: Learning transferable visual models from natural language supervision. In: International Conference on Machine Learning (2021)
17. Rojas, R.V.B., Martínez-Cano, F.-J.: Revolutionizing Communication: The Role of Artificial Intelligence. CRC Press (2024)
18. Rombach, R., Blattmann, A., Lorenz, D., Esser, P., Ommer, B.: High-resolution image synthesis with latent diffusion models. arXiv preprint: arXiv:2112.10752 (2022)
19. Sayyad, G.G., Dhumal, V.G., Khandekar, V.D., Thorat, K.P.: A survey report on text to image generator using stable diffusion (2023)
20. Eugeny Yu Shchetinin: Brain-computer interaction modeling based on the stable diffusion model. Discr. Continuous Models Appl. Comput. Sci. $31(3)$, 273–281 (2023)
21. Song, Y., Sohl-Dickstein, J., Kingma, D.P., Kumar, A., Ermon, S., Poole, B.: Score-based generative modeling through stochastic differential equations. arXiv preprint: arXiv:2011.13456 (2020)
22. Veit, A., Matera, T., Neumann, L., Matas, J., Belongie, S.: Coco-text: dataset and benchmark for text detection and recognition in natural images. arXiv preprint: arXiv:1601.07140 (2016)
23. Wang, X., Zhang, Y., Liu, X.: TextDiffuser: text-driven diffusion models for scene text generation. In: Proceedings of the IEEE/CVF Conference on Computer Vision and Pattern Recognition (2023)
24. Xu, W., Li, H., Zhang, L.: GlyphControl: controllable scene text generation with glyph-aware diffusion models. In: Proceedings of the IEEE/CVF International Conference on Computer Vision (2023)
25. Zakraoui, J., Saleh, M., Al-Maadeed, S., Jaam, J.M.: Improving text-to-image generation with object layout guidance. Multimedia Tools Appl. $80(18)$, 27423–27443 (2021). https://doi.org/10.1007/s11042-021-11038-0

Multimodal Tattoo Recognition by Combining Visual Features and LLM-Generated Captions

Annette Morales-González[1], Heydi Méndez-Vázquez[1],
and Milton García-Borroto[2(✉)]

[1] Advanced Technologies Application Center (CENATAV), Habana, Cuba
[2] Centro de Sistemas Complejos, Facultad de Física, Universidad de La Habana,
Habana, Cuba
`milton.garcia@gmail.com`

Abstract. Tattoo recognition and retrieval remain challenging tasks
due to the diverse and intricate nature of tattoo designs. Existing
approaches typically rely on visual features extracted from convolutional neural networks (CNNs), which may fail to capture the rich
semantic information embedded in tattoos. In this paper, we propose
a novel framework that integrates state-of-the-art visual features with
textual descriptions generated by a multimodal large language model
(MLLM). We explore the impact of different prompts on the quality of
the generated captions and use CLIP to create textual embeddings. By
combining cosine similarity scores from both modalities, our approach
achieves superior performance in tattoo retrieval tasks. Experimental
results demonstrate that our method outperforms traditional visual-only
approaches, highlighting the importance of leveraging multimodal data
for tattoo recognition. To the best of our knowledge, this is the first work
to combine MLLM-generated textual descriptions with visual features for
tattoo retrieval.

Keywords: Multimodal large language models · Tattoo identification
and retrieval · Semantic image description

1 Introduction

Tattoos serve as unique identifiers of personal expression, cultural heritage, and
artistic creativity [1]. In recent years, tattoo recognition and retrieval have gained
significant attention in applications ranging from law enforcement (e.g., forensic
identification) to personalized services (e.g., tattoo design recommendations) [7].
However, the intricate and diverse nature of tattoo designs—spanning abstract
patterns, symbolic imagery, and textual elements—poses substantial challenges
for automated systems [8]. Traditional approaches, which rely predominantly
on visual features extracted from convolutional neural networks (CNNs), often

© The Author(s), under exclusive license to Springer Nature Switzerland AG 2026
Y. Hernádez Heredia et al. (Eds.): IWAIPR 2025, LNCS 16328, pp. 166–177, 2026.
https://doi.org/10.1007/978-3-032-11358-0_14

struggle to capture the rich semantic information embedded in tattoos, limiting their effectiveness in retrieval tasks.

While advancements in computer vision have improved visual feature extraction, these methods fail to account for the meaning behind tattoos. For instance, two visually distinct tattoos may share thematic similarities (e.g., "a dragon symbolizing strength' vs. "a lion representing courage"), which are difficult to encode using purely visual representations. Conversely, textual descriptions of tattoos, when available, can explicitly encode such semantic nuances. Yet, manually annotating large tattoo datasets with descriptive captions is labor-intensive and impractical [9].

To bridge this gap, we propose a multimodal framework that combines visual features from CNNs with textual descriptions generated by a multimodal large language model (MLLM). Our approach leverages the strengths of both modalities: discriminative visual features from tattoo images, and semantically rich textual captions that contextualize the tattoo's content, style, and symbolism. By comparing the output of different prompts for the MLLM, we show how prompt engineering influences the quality of the generated captions and, consequently, the downstream retrieval performance.

A key innovation of our work lies in the fusion strategy. We employ a Vision Language Model (VLM) to embed MLLM-generated captions into a shared semantic space, enabling comparisons via cosine similarity. These textual similarity scores are then combined with visual similarity scores derived from state-of-the-art visual features through a multiplicative fusion mechanism. This approach ensures that both modalities contribute equally to the final ranking, addressing the limitations of unimodal systems.

In summary, the contributions of our work are:

1. Integrate MLLM-generated textual descriptions with visual features for tattoo recognition, unlocking semantic information inaccessible to vision-only models.
2. Explore the impact of different prompts for tattoo captioning, providing insights into optimizing MLLM outputs for specialized domains.
3. Outperformed previous state-of-the-art results on tattoo retrieval benchmarks, surpassing traditional visual-only approaches and highlighting the importance of multimodal data integration.

To the best of our knowledge, this is the first study that integrates LLM-generated textual descriptions with visual features for tattoo retrieval. By combining advances in multimodal LLMs, vision-language models (VLMs), and CNNs, this work paves the way for more interpretable and versatile tattoo recognition systems.

The remainder of this paper is organized as follows: Sect. 2 reviews related work, Sect. 3 details our methodology, Sect. 4 presents experimental results, and Sect. 5 provides conclusions of our work.

2   Related Work

We briefly review the most relevant works in the state-of-the art for tattoo recognition, as well as general approaches for combining multimodal information for image retrieval.

2.1   Tattoo Recognition and Retrieval

Tattoo recognition and retrieval have traditionally relied on visual feature extraction techniques. Early approaches employed handcrafted features such as Scale-Invariant Feature Transform (SIFT) [11] to capture distinctive patterns in tattoo images, as well as geometric-based approaches employing shape matching algorithms between tattoo contours [11,18].

With the advent of deep learning, convolutional neural networks (CNNs) like MobileNet [13] and ResNet [14] have become the de facto standard for extracting discriminative visual features, demonstrating significant improvements over traditional handcrafted feature methods like SIFT [12]. The use of CNNs can be divided into two branches: those who use available pre-trained models from other domains directly, and those that perform training or transfer learning of CNNs to specialize the features to the current domain.

In the first case, we found works like [12], that explores different pre-trained CNNs by extracting features from their last layer. To prioritize domain-specific characteristics, another work applies multiple weighting functions to emphasize specific regions within convolutional feature maps [13]. This dynamic adjustment allows the recognition process to focus on salient areas of tattoo images. Another work used ResNet50 features for identification [14]. Their approach flattens intermediate layers into high-dimensional vectors, comparing them using cosine and Euclidean similarity.

In the second case, we can find an end-to-end trainable Faster R-CNN-based approach that has been proposed for joint tattoo detection and representation learning [5]. This method enhances feature robustness through feature sharing, underscoring the potential of deep learning in tattoo recognition. Additionally, a novel Tattoo Template Reconstruction Network [4] has been introduced to map input tattoos to clean templates, enhancing the discriminative power of feature embeddings. TattTRN's semi-synthetic training dataset shows the importance of tailored datasets for tattoo recognition. Transfer learning has been explored for tattoo classification, with one study presenting a deep learning model validated on a custom dataset of 40 tattoo classes [16]. Cross-modal tattoo retrieval has also gained attention, with one study proposing a Siamese neural network to align tattoo sketches and images within a shared embedding space [2]. This approach learns optimal representations for both modalities, enabling effective matching between sketches and photographs. Such methods address the need for versatile systems capable of handling diverse query types.

The main problem for training tattoo recognition models is the lack of large available datasets for the task [4,13]. Most works create their own private datasets, which makes difficult for others to reproduce their approach.

2.2   Composed Multimodal Retrieval Approaches

While the above methods achieve reasonable performance, they are limited to capturing only perceptual details, often failing to account for the rich semantic information embedded in tattoos, such as themes, symbols, or stylistic elements. Although in the tattoo recognition domain the combination of visual and textual information has not been explored, many related approaches have emerged for general image retrieval. We will mention the most relevant ones to this work.

Composed multimodal retrieval (CMR) or composed image retrieval (CIR) has emerged as a cutting-edge content-based retrieval technology [3], enabling users to retrieve target images by combining a reference image with textual modifications. Research in CIR is categorized into supervised learning, which relies on labeled triplet datasets (reference image, modification text, target image), and zero-shot learning (ZS-CIR), which avoids the high annotation costs of supervised methods by operating without annotated triplet datasets. Given the scarcity of large, publicly available tattoo recognition datasets [4,13] and the challenges of training on small datasets, this review focuses on ZS-CIR. According to recent surveys, ZS-CIR approaches include Text Inversion, Self-supervised, and Training-free methods, though the first two still involve training, which remains problematic for the tattoo domain due to limited data availability.

Several recent works have explored training-free methods for composed image retrieval by leveraging pre-trained Vision-Language Models (VLMs) and Large Language Models (LLMs). For instance, CIReVL [10] generates image captions using a VLM and recomposes them with LLMs to simulate target image descriptions. Similarly, LDRE [19] uses dense captioning and semantic ensembling to improve retrieval accuracy in zero-shot settings.

The work in [17] employs a VLM as both vision and text encoders, combining visual and textual features via a weighted sum to form queries. It generates multiple captions per image using an MLLM to capture diverse semantics and computes retrieval similarity as a weighted average of query-to-image and query-to-caption scores. While closely related, our approach differs from theirs in key aspects: we test multiple state-of-the-art visual feature extractors for tattoo recognition, assessing their impact on multimodal fusion. Instead of weighted averaging, we use a multiplicative similarity strategy to emphasize strong cross-modal alignment and avoid relevance dilution. Unlike [17], which generates multiple captions per image for richer semantics but at higher computational cost, we use a single textual description per image to balance semantic representation and efficiency.

To the best of our knowledge, this is the first attempt to apply composed image retrieval techniques to tattoo recognition, opening new directions for forensic and creative applications.

3   Proposal

3.1   Visual Features

In this work we propose to use visual features already employed in state-of-the-art works for the task of tattoo recognition, since they already showed good results in this domain. We propose to use:

- MobileNetV2 features [12]. We employ the output features of MobileNetV2 CNN pool6 layer. We used the publicly available model trained on ImageNet, as described in [12].
- WAP features (Weighted Average Pooling) [13]. These features are based on MobileNetV2 features as well, but they use functions (standard deviation, entropy, edges and skin mask) to weight the local features of a convolutional feature map in order to obtain a more distinctive representation based on the tattoo characteristics.
- CLIP visual features [15]. CLIP visual embeddings are dense vector representations (512-D) of images, created by CLIP's image encoder (e.g., ViT or ResNet). They capture semantic content and are aligned with text embeddings in a shared space, enabling tasks like cross-modal retrieval.
- TattTRN embeddings [4]. The Tattoo Template Reconstruction Network (TattTRN) generates a dual-embedding representation for tattoo retrieval by combining a raw input-image embedding, which captures low-level visual details, with a template embedding derived from image-to-template translation that isolates core design attributes. These complementary embeddings are concatenated into a unified 2K-dimensional feature vector.

3.2   Semantic Textual Features

Tattoos carry a high semantic content and in most cases, they are easy to describe using natural language. To enhance the semantic understanding of visual data, we employ MLLM-generated captions to complement visual features. While visual embeddings capture style and structure, MLLM captions provide high-level semantic context (e.g., motifs, colors, cultural references) that may not be fully encoded in pixel-based representations.

In this work we use Bunny [6], which is a family of lightweight multimodal models with available source code and pretrained models[1], for the task of image caption generation. We selected Bunny in order to assess the behavior of lighter models which can be more practical to real-world solutions, instead of larger models that make hardware requirements prohibitive in many scenarios.

We provide tattoo images to the Bunny model and we explore the impact of different prompts in the model response:

- Prompt 1: "Can you describe this tattoo?". This prompt is more generic and expects more general responses.

---

[1] https://github.com/BAAI-DCAI/Bunny.

- Prompt 2: "Describe the elements present in this tattoo". This prompt is intended to focus on a more discriminative tattoo description.
- Prompt 3: "Describe the elements present in this tattoo. Focus on colors, shapes, styles and meaningful objects". This prompt is designed to provide more domain-specific details.

We utilize the Contrastive Language-Image Pretraining (CLIP) [15] model to encode textual captions generated by the multimodal LLM into dense semantic embeddings. CLIP's text encoder maps descriptive tattoo captions (e.g., "a black-and-white geometric mandala with intricate patterns") into a shared visual-semantic embedding space, aligning textual and visual representations. For the rest of this paper, we will use the terms textual features or prompt-based features indistinctly to refer to this type of features.

3.3 Feature Combination

To leverage both visual and semantic information for tattoo retrieval, we propose a fusion strategy that combines cosine similarity scores derived from visual features (described in Sect. 3.2) and textual embeddings (described in Sect. 3.2). This approach addresses the complementary strengths of the two modalities: visual features capture fine-grained design details (e.g., shape, color, texture), while textual embeddings encode semantic attributes (e.g., themes, symbols, stylistic descriptions).

The pipeline is as follows. For a query tattoo image, we first compute its visual feature vector and generate its textual caption using Bunny. The caption is then embedded into a CLIP-based textual representation. Cosine similarity is independently calculated between the query's visual features and all gallery visual features, as well as between the query's textual embedding and all gallery textual embeddings.

The final similarity score for ranking is obtained by multiplying the visual and textual cosine similarity scores for each gallery item. This multiplicative fusion emphasizes alignment between modalities, ensuring that only samples with strong visual and semantic relevance achieve high rankings. By contrast, additive or weighted averaging could dilute modality-specific signals, particularly in cases where one modality is noisy or incomplete.

4 Experiments

In this section we perform a set of experiments to validate our feature combination proposal. We conducted our experiments using two tattoo databases sourced from [12]. The first database, BIVTatt (employed in [4,12,13]), consists of 210 images representing 159 individuals, with some individuals contributing only a single image. It includes 4200 generated images after applying 20 different types of transformations to the original images. The second database, PinTatt (used in [12,13]), contains 454 images associated with 160 individuals. It was augmented in the same way than BIVTatt. The images in BIVTatt are of higher resolution and exhibit sharper details compared to those in PinTatt. Following the dataset configuration in [13], we used only 16 of the augmented variations which are two levels of illumination intensity, two diffusion settings, four affine transformations, four rotations, and four color changes. According to the protocol established in [13], for the identification experiments on each database, the probe set consisted of the transformed images, while the gallery set was composed of the original images. During testing, for every probe image, the original image from which it was derived (through some transformation) was excluded from the comparison.

We compare the behavior of individual visual features selected from the state of the art based on their relevance and source code availability. These are: MobileNetV2-pool6 [12], WAP0-0.5-0-0 [13], CLIP-Visual [15] and TattTRN [4]. They were all described in Sect. 3.1. We must clarify that in the original paper of TattTRN, authors use a different protocol for evaluation in BIVTatt and also they discarded several images that didn't fit the conditions of their proposal. Therefore, we used their available source code[2] to reproduce the results using this protocol. We also compare the performance of 3 individual textual prompts extracted with Bunny MLLM [6] described in Sect. 3.2.

Tables 1 and 2 show results for BIVTatt dataset. Due to space restrictions and to allow a better analysis, we showed only results for Rank-1 (Table 1) and Rank-10 (Table 2). Rows correspond to visual feature extractors while columns depict Bunny generated prompts. The first column of results (shaded in gray color) show the results for all visual descriptors independently, and the first row of results (shaded in gray color as well) show the results for textual features independently. The rest of the matrix corresponds to combination results between each visual descriptor and each prompt feature. Shaded in blue we highlight results above the average in this matrix. The best result can be seen for the combination of MobileNetV2-pool6 visual feature with the Prompt2 feature. In this case, we can observe that the MobileNetV2-pool6 feature independently obtains 71.1 %, Prompt2 feature by its own obtains 63 %, while the combination of both obtains 86.4 %, outperforming both by a large margin. The same analysis can be done for Table 2, showing that in all cases, the combination outperform the individual descriptors by a large margin.

The same results can be summarized in Fig. 1, where we show all the visual descriptors individually, and their combination with Prompt2, which resulted the best in both previous tables. In this figure it is possible to see ranking results up to 100.

Results obtained in PinTatt dataset can be consulted in Tables 3 and 4. The same analysis conducted for BIVTatt dataset can be applied. In this case it is worth noting that PinTatt is a harder dataset, since it contains tattoo images with lower resolution, less details and in general, more variations than BIVTatt. This can be seen in the behaviour of individual descriptors, that obtain worse results in this dataset. In particular, the textual features achieve results ranging from 56 % to 63 % on the BIVTatt dataset, while on the PinTatt dataset, they

---

[2] https://github.com/ljsoler/TattTRN.

Table 1. Rank-1 results in BIVTatt dataset for individual visual features, individual prompt-based features and their pairwise combinations

	Prompt1	Prompt2	Prompt3
	0.557	0.630	0.568
MobileNetV2-pool6	0.711	0.833	**0.864**	0.798
WAP0-0.5-0-0	0.718	0.778	0.806	0.761
CLIP-Visual	0.731	0.804	0.816	0.799
TattTRN	0.704	0.829	0.826	0.795

Table 2. Rank-10 results in BIVTatt dataset for individual visual features, individual prompt-based features and their pairwise combinations

	Prompt1	Prompt2	Prompt3
	0.902	0.919	0.873
MobileNetV2-pool6	0.913	0.964	0.968	0.946
WAP0-0.5-0-0	0.907	0.955	**0.971**	0.940
CLIP-Visual	0.912	0.966	0.965	0.948
TattTRN	0.898	0.946	0.951	0.940

are limited to just 23 -24 %. This is an interesting result showing that lesser quality images obtain worse captions from MLLMs, which is to be expected. Yet again, the combination between pairs of visual features and prompt descriptors obtain better results in all cases except for the visual feature WAP0-0.5-0-0.

Table 3. Rank-1 results in PinTatt dataset for individual visual features, individual prompt-based features and their pairwise combinations

	Prompt1	Prompt2	Prompt3
	0.244	0.239	0.241
MobileNetV2-pool6	0.579	0.598	0.602	**0.622**
WAP0-0.5-0-0	0.578	0.496	0.478	0.512
CLIP-Visual	0.410	0.430	0.442	0.453
TattTRN	0.344	0.404	0.419	0.418

Figure 2 shows overall results for PinTatt up to Rank-100, using individual visual features and their combination with Prompt3 features, which obtained better results in most cases for this dataset. This figure also highlights the more complex nature of PinTatt dataset, but again, most combinations outperformed individual features.

In Table 5, we present two examples of image pairs whose retrieval rankings improved significantly by incorporating textual features. Here, "Image Q" and

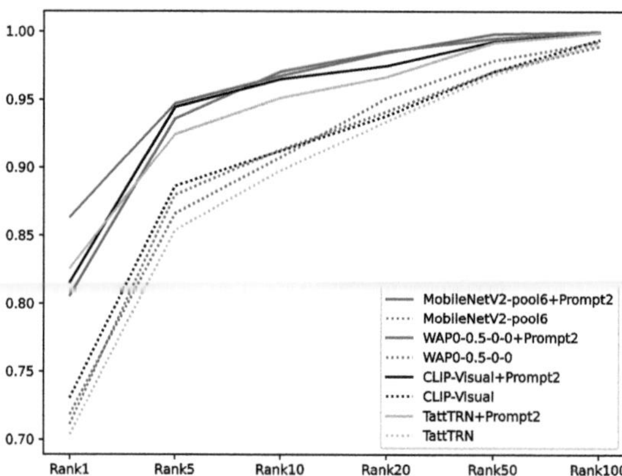

Fig. 1. Results in BIVTatt dataset for different ranks using individual visual features and their combination with Promp2.

Table 4. Rank-10 results in PinTatt dataset for individual visual features, individual prompt-based features and their pairwise combinations

	Prompt1	Prompt2	Prompt3
	0.517	0.519	0.526
MobileNetV2-pool6	0.832	0.860	0.860	**0.872**
WAP0-0.5-0-0	0.831	0.762	0.763	0.801
CLIP-Visual	0.696	0.737	0.743	0.764
TattTRN	0.619	0.690	0.708	0.713

"Caption Q" represent the query image and its corresponding caption, while "Image G" and "Caption G" denote the retrieved gallery image and its caption. The column labeled "VR" shows the original rank obtained using only visual features (rank 28 for the first pair and rank 111 for the second pair). In contrast, the column "VTR" displays the rank achieved after combining visual and textual information, with both pairs successfully retrieved at the top position (rank 1) in the candidate list.

The results obtained from prompts alone (See Tables 1, 2, 3, 4) can serve forensic purposes in environments where only a tattoo's description is available. In such scenarios, the textual descriptions generated by a multimodal LLM provide valuable semantic information that can aid in identifying or narrowing down potential matches. This capability highlights the practical utility of prompt-based textual embeddings in real-world forensic applications, where visual data may be unavailable or incomplete.

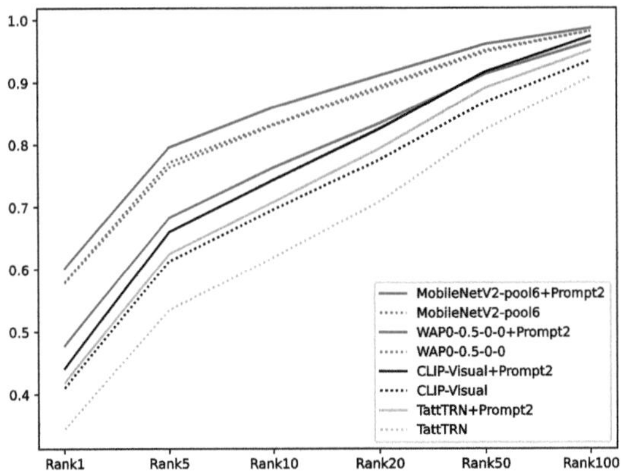

Fig. 2. Results in PinTatt dataset for different ranks using individual visual features and their combination with Promp3.

Table 5. Ranking of image-caption pairs using visual vs. visual+textual features

Image Q	Caption Q	Image G	Caption G	VR	VTR
	The tattoo features **a man's face**, complete with a **beard**, mustache, and eyebrows. The man's eyes are particularly prominent. There are also **red lines and a red dot** on the tattoo.		The tattoo is a detailed depiction of a **man's face**. It includes features such as the eyes, nose, mouth, and **beard**. The man's face is colored in shades of red and black. There's also **a red mark** on the man's forehead.	28	1
	The tattoo is a **black and white** drawing of a **woman's face**. It has features like her eyes, nose, and lips clearly depicted. There's a **small tear in her eye**.		The tattoo is a detailed **black and white** portrait of a **woman**. She has long, curly hair and **a sad expression**. There are also some red dots on her face.	111	1

5   Conclusions

In this work, we presented a novel framework for tattoo recognition and retrieval that integrates visual features with textual embeddings generated by a Vision Language Model from captions produced by an MLLM. By combining these complementary modalities, our approach addresses the limitations of traditional vision-only systems, which often fail to capture the rich semantic information embedded in tattoos. Our experimental results highlight the effectiveness of this multimodal approach, achieving superior performance compared to unimodal methods. By leveraging both perceptual details from visual features and semantic context from textual embeddings, our system bridges the gap between visual and linguistic representations, paving the way for more versatile recognition systems. Furthermore, the simplicity and interpretability of our fusion method makes it practical for real-world applications, such as forensic identification or personalized tattoo design recommendations.

Acknowledgments. We would like to thank our colleagues Jan Schlüter and Andreas Bossert from the HAWK (Germany) for their support.

References

1. Balan, L.: Criminalistic human identification from scar and tattoo marks. Eur. J. Law Public Adm. **7**(1), 61–67 (2020)
2. Berno, B.C.S.: Sketch-based multimodal image retrieval using deep learning. Ph.D. thesis, Universidade Tecnológica Federal do Paraná, Curitiba, Programa de Pós-Graduação em Engenharia Elétrica e Informática Industrial (2021)
3. Du, L., Deng, S., Li, Y., Li, J., Tian, Q.: A survey on composed image retrieval. ACM Trans. Multimedia Comput. Commun. Appl. (2025). https://doi.org/10.1145/3723879
4. Gonzalez-Soler, L., Salwowski, M., Rathgeb, C., Fischer, D.: TattTRN: template reconstruction network for tattoo retrieval. In: Proc. IEEE/CVF Conf. on Computer Vision and Pattern Recognition (CVPR) (2024)
5. Han, H., Li, J., Jain, A.K., Shan, S., Chen, X.: Tattoo image search at scale: joint detection and compact representation learning. IEEE Trans. Pattern Anal. Mach. Intell. **41**(10), 2333–2348 (2019). https://doi.org/10.1109/TPAMI.2019.2891584
6. He, M., et al.: Efficient multimodal learning from data-centric perspective. arXiv preprint: arXiv:2402.11530 (2024)
7. Hodge, Jr., S.D., Meehan, J.: Tattoo recognition technology is gaining acceptance as a crime-solving technique. Northern Ill. Univ. Law Rev. **42**(1) (2021)
8. Ibrahim, E., Canal, R., Silva, R.F., Heit, O.F.J., Franco, A.: On the forensic value of tattoos for human identification–a literature review. Revista Brasileira de Odontologia Legal **11**(1) (2024)
9. Jain, A.K., Lee, J.-E., Jin, R.: Tattoo-ID: automatic tattoo image retrieval for suspect and victim identification. In: Ip, H.H.-S., Au, O.C., Leung, H., Sun, M.-T., Ma, W.-Y., Hu, S.-M. (eds.) PCM 2007. LNCS, vol. 4810, pp. 256–265. Springer, Heidelberg (2007). https://doi.org/10.1007/978-3-540-77255-2_28

10. Karthik, S., Roth, K., Mancini, M., Akata, Z.: Vision-by-language for training-free compositional image retrieval. In: International Conference on Learning Representations (ICLR) (2024)
11. Kim, J., Pozo, A.P., Yue, J., Li, H., Delp, E.J.: Robust local and global shape context for tattoo image matching. In: 2015 IEEE International Conference on Image Processing, ICIP 2015, Quebec City, QC, Canada, 27–30 September 2015, pp. 2194–2198. IEEE (2015).https://doi.org/10.1109/ICIP.2015.7351190
12. Nicolás-Díaz, M., Morales-González, A., Méndez-Vázquez, H.: Deep generic features for tattoo identification. In: Nyström, I., Hernández Heredia, Y., Milián Núñez, V. (eds.) CIARP 2019. LNCS, vol. 11896, pp. 272–282. Springer, Cham (2019). https://doi.org/10.1007/978-3-030-33904-3_25
13. Nicolás-Díaz, M., Morales-González, A., Méndez-Vázquez, H.: Weighted average pooling of deep features for tattoo identification. Multimedia Tools Appl. **81**(18), 25853–25875 (2022)
14. Pocevičė, G., Stefanovič, P., Ramanauskaitė, S., Pavlov, E.: Approach for tattoo detection and identification based on YOLOv5 and similarity distance. Appl. Sci. **14**(13), 5576 (2024). https://doi.org/10.3390/app14135576
15. Radford, A., et al.: Learning transferable visual models from natural language supervision. In: Proceedings of the 38th International Conference on Machine Learning. Proceedings of Machine Learning Research, vol. 139, pp. 8748–8763. PMLR (2021)
16. da Silva, R.T., Silvério Lopes, H.: A transfer learning approach for the tattoo classification problem. In: 2022 IEEE Latin American Conference on Computational Intelligence (LA-CCI), pp. 1–6 (2022). https://doi.org/10.1109/LA-CCI54402.2022.9981650
17. Wu, R.D., Lin, Y.Y., Yang, H.F.: Training-free zero-shot composed image retrieval via weighted modality fusion and similarity (2024). https://arxiv.org/abs/2409.04918
18. Xu, X.: Tattoos in forensics: retrieval, detection and synthesis. Ph.D. thesis, School of Computer Science and Engineering, Forensics and Security Lab (2021). https://doi.org/10.32657/10356/151535
19. Yang, Z., Xue, D., Qian, S., Dong, W., Xu, C.: LDRE: LLM-based divergent reasoning and ensemble for zero-shot composed image retrieval. In: Proceedings of the 47th International ACM SIGIR Conference on Research and Development in Information Retrieval, SIGIR '24, pp. 80–90. Association for Computing Machinery, New York (2024). https://doi.org/10.1145/3626772.3657740

An Approach to Generating Knowledge-Based Explanations: A Case Study in Health

Yadier Betancourt Martínez[1]([envelope]) [iD], Armando David Caballero Font[2] [iD],
Amed Leiva Mederos[1] [iD], Maria Matilde Garcia Lorenzo[1] [iD],
Armando Caballero López[2] [iD], and Rafael Bello Pérez[2] [iD]

[1] Department of Computer Sciences, Universidad Central "Marta Abreu" de Las Villas,
Santa Clara, Cuba
yadierbetanc@gmail.com
[2] Armaldo Milián Castro Teaching Hospital, Santa Clara, Cuba

Abstract. Artificial Intelligence (AI) techniques enable the development of intelligent systems to solve problems in various fields of society. Many of these systems are considered black boxes, as they solve problems effectively, but the underlying knowledge driving the problem-solving process remains opaque. In this context, explainable AI has been developed to facilitate understanding of the systems work, increasing confidence in them, facilitating their acceptance, and satisfying technical and legal requirements. This work proposes an approach for generating knowledge-based explanations, which seek to be more accessible to different stakeholders. To achieve this objective, several AI technologies are integrated, such as neural networks, decision rules, ontologies, and knowledge graph, and the large language models. The proposal is illustrated with its application in a case study in the field of health and human expert evaluation.

Keywords: explainable AI · domain-based explanations · knowledge graph · large language models

1 Introduction

Among the reasons for the current boom in the development of Artificial Intelligence (AI) are the enormous amount of information accumulated in digital form as a result of the digital transformation of society, the development of computing and information transmission capabilities, and increasingly powerful AI methods; this has boosted the generation of knowledge through machine learning for the development of intelligent systems. The reality is that today, AI techniques are present in virtually every decision-making process in our lives. Applications vary widely in areas such as healthcare, education, finance, industry, transportation, entertainment, research, and so on, with increasingly capable and autonomous systems.

This broad use of AI in countries socioeconomic activity creates new opportunities, but also poses significant new challenges. It is no longer just the technological aspects of AI that are of interest, but also the ethical and legal aspects. There is growing concern

Y. Hernádez Heredia et al. (Eds.): IWAIPR 2025, LNCS 16328, pp. 178–191, 2026.
https://doi.org/10.1007/978-3-032-11358-0_15

about the models that help make or assist in these decisions. An important reason for this is that many of these AI-based models operate as black boxes; their problem-solving processes are not understood. They can be very effective at solving problems, but for humans, it is unclear how or why that solution was obtained.

For solving that problem, the Explainable AI (XAI) was developed [1–6]. XAI can improve transparency and fairness, since it provides explanations that seek to make it easier for humans to understand the result of the intelligent system, and thus increase their trust in intelligent systems. The generation of explanations also has other advantages, including that they can allow the models found by machine learning methods to be audited and improved, enrich the knowledge of an application domain, and satisfy the legal requirements established for the use of AI. Explainable Artificial Intelligence has been the subject of numerous research works [4, 7–9] and has a positive impact on improving human decision making [3, 4]. XAI is an important component of so-called Responsible Artificial Intelligence and Trustworthy AI [5, 7].

The XAI provides different methods for generating explanations, which are distinguished, among other aspects, by the way in which the explanation is expressed and generated. In the first case, there are different ways (output format) of expressing the explanation [10]. It may consist of showing the parts of the problem (the input) that most influenced the model's response (numeric explanations), in rules that establish the relationship between the input and the solution (factual and counterfactual rules), in a text (textual explanations in natural language), in a visual representation (such as heatmaps), etc. According to Schwalbe and Finzel [11], the way of generating the explanation also has different approaches to classify the methods. The methods of generating the explanation can be agnostic or non-agnostic, that is, the explanation is generated without taking into account internal elements of the model or the explanation is built considering elements of the model.

Another way to analyze the method of generating the explanation is from what information is taken into account to construct the explanation. The explanation can be constructed using only technological information, that is, that involved in the problem-solving process (the input, the model and the decision or solution); among the methods that fall into this category are LIME (agnostic) [12] and LRP (non-agnostic) [9, 13]. Explanations can be enriched by also considering domain knowledge [14], which allows explanations to be expressed in a way closer to the language of the application domain, favoring their understanding and acceptance; this is of special interest because explanations have different recipients [6], the explanation needed by the AI expert (developers), the domain expert or the end user (affected parties or lay users) of the intelligent system (it is necessary to satisfy several stakeholders desiderata). Methods that take into account domain knowledge to build the explanation usually use ontologies and knowledge graphs [13–17], which naturally provide domain background knowledge. The development of generative AI, and in particular the Large Language Models (LLMs) offer a new way to build more natural, human-readable explanations [18, 19]; among other alternatives, the LLM can be used to try to explain the model, and also explanations built by other methods can be refined using the knowledge stored in the LLM.

A model is proposed for generating explanations that take domain knowledge into account. It is defined as a model consisting of three main stages: first, the prediction is performed using a neural network and also through decision rules (both constructed from the data); the output of both prediction models is passed to a knowledge graph, which generates an explanation, and finally, the explanation is refined and expanded using an LLM. The application of this model in the development of an intelligent system to help predict if patients will die upon discharge from an Intensive Care Unit (ICU) is illustrated. Finally, this system is evaluated using the judgment of domain experts.

2 Background

This section presents the different technologies on which the proposed approach is based to generate knowledge-based explanations.

Artificial Neural Networks (ANNs) are widely used for classification, clustering, pattern recognition, and prediction due to their self-learning, adaptability, fault tolerance, and nonlinear input-output mapping [20–22]. Key types include feedforward networks like the Multi-layer Perceptron (MLP), which learn via backpropagation to reduce error over time [23, 24].

An ontology formally defines domain-specific terms and their relationships to represent a particular area of knowledge [1]. For example, a medical ontology provides a structured representation of health concepts, enabling the creation of knowledge graphs that integrate patient and treatment data [2].

Knowledge Graphs (KGs) are structured representations of real-world entities and their relationships, enabling contextual understanding [27]. Tools like Neo4j effectively store such graphs in databases [13].

An LLM is a deep learning model based on the Transformer architecture. It processes text using self-attention mechanisms to weigh the relevance of words in context [19].

The integration of LLMs with knowledge graphs represents a powerful combination to improve the ability of machines to provide clear and coherent explanations about the results of models, they have demonstrated a remarkable ability to generate fluent and relevant text in a wide range of tasks [4].

The existence of ontologies and knowledge graphs developed in different domains can favor their use in the context of XAI [5–7]. They allow to take into account important aspects of the domain in the explanation, to avoid including false or contradictory elements in the explanation, and to refine the explanations [6]. According to [8], KGs represent a suitable path towards the design of trustworthy AI solutions. The use of ontologies and KGs can help to tailor the explanation to the recipient, for example, by using a more general language for end-users and a more technical one for domain experts.

These technologies have proven effective in various medical applications [9]. In this field, these structures allow for establishing relationships between diseases and other concepts (such as diagnoses and treatments), enriching models obtained by machine learning, providing clues as to why the model makes certain predictions, etc. An example of such systems is presented in [1], which shows how the use of ontological information increased the quality of the explanation. [7] presents another system that generates more personalized explanations based on domain knowledge. According to [10], medical applications of LLMs have shown remarkable progress. For example, when the model is asked to explain a clinical decision, the LLM can navigate this graph to extract and present relevant information to support its explanation [11].

However, despite the work carried out, there is still much to be done in the construction of more personalized explanations that are closer to the language of the recipients.

3 General Scheme for the Generation of Knowledge-Based Explanations

This section provides an overview of the proposed process for generating more user-friendly explanations. The following section illustrates the process in more detail using a case study. The explanation construction process combines several components operating in three main stages: prediction, construction of a base explanation, and explanation refinement. Prediction is performed using two different predictive models: a neural network and a rule-based system. A first explanation for the found solution is then constructed using ontologies and knowledge graphs. Finally, the final version of the explanation is generated using an LLM. This integration makes it possible to leverage the learning and generalization capabilities of neural models, along with the transparency and precision of symbolic rules, see Fig. 1.

Two prediction models are used to combine the increased efficiency of neural network models with the improved interpretability of decision rules. Using a decision tree construction method such as C4.5 (J48), a tree is constructed and from it a set of rules is extracted that allow the prediction to be made given an input. These rules can be reviewed by domain experts to make any necessary corrections, for example, to detect overfitting rules that may limit the generalization capacity of the learned model. Examples of rules are:

- Rule 1: Survival with Hypothyroidism, Sepsis, and Severe Dengue Patient(?p) ∧ with_history(?p, hypothyroidism) ∧ sepsis(?p, "0"^^xsd:int) ∧ with_cause_of_admission(?p, severe_dengue) - > Does_Not_Died(?p)
- Rule 2: Death due to ARF, COPD, Diagnosis of Exacerbated COPD, Pulmonary Complications, and Sepsis

Additionally, an MLP-type neural network is implemented, with multiple processing layers that allow complex nonlinear relationships to be learned from the data. Of these two components, the MLP-based model is the one used to solve new problems, that is, to make the prediction for each new problem.

Once the prediction is obtained, the rules allow us to determine the factors influencing the MLP's response. The rules are integrated with the data in the knowledge graph, enabling transparent and explainable reasoning. They provide an approximation to the "why" of the neural network's prediction, identifying the key factors that contribute to the prediction model's response. Each rule represents a specific combination of conditions that, using the output from the neural network, allow us to validate and lead to a specific conclusion. The KG takes the prediction as input and contextualizes it with the information stored in the graph; ontologies feed the knowledge graph, ensuring that the explanations are consistent with domain knowledge. The KG provides the necessary context to better understand the rule; from it, additional information can be extracted about the variables determined to have influenced the prediction. The result is a first version of the explanation of the obtained prediction.

That first explanation is refined using an LLM. Combining the power of knowledge graphs with LLMs allows the latter to generate text not only based on learned language patterns, but also based on specific data, organized in the form of a graph. In essence, LLMs, on their own, tend to be "memorizing," generating text based solely on the pattern and probabilities from their training. However, through this combination, the model can query a knowledge graph, to retrieve information that serves as the basis for an accurate response. The KG acts as an organized external source, helping the model anchor its responses in structured facts rather than relying exclusively on the statistical patterns of its training; this is especially useful for reducing hallucinations because the model is not based solely on language patterns, but on previously validated facts and relationships. In short, the LLM takes the KG's context into account to enrich the explanation, making the final result easily understandable for non-technical users.

Finally, the system produces a result that includes both the original MLP prediction and a detailed natural language explanation provided by the LLM.

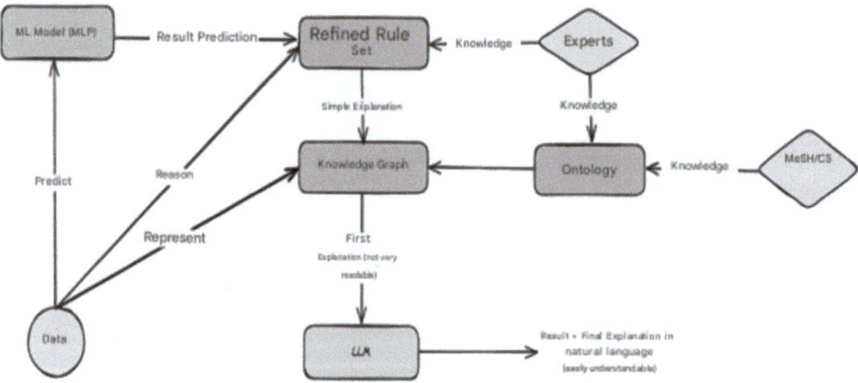

Fig. 1. Details of the Explanation Process

4 Description of the Explanation Generation Process Using a Case Study

This section describes the previously proposed explanation generation model using a case study in the health field.

4.1 Case Study: Predicting Deaths in an ICU

Using available information on cases treated in an ICU, a model is built that predicts the death (or not) of a patient; then, using domain knowledge, the explanation of the model's response is constructed. In the healthcare field, particularly in ICUs, clinical decision-making is critical for patient survival and recovery. Decisions must be based on an accurate assessment of available clinical data, including medical histories, test results, administered treatments, and observed responses. Predictive models have shown great potential for anticipating clinical outcomes in intensive care [28, 29] and [30]. However, a crucial challenge is the lack of transparency of these models. Many current models operate as "black boxes," providing results without offering a clear understanding of the factors influencing those predictions. This lack of transparency can limit the confidence and practical utility of these models in a clinical setting, where clinicians need to understand the reasons behind a prediction to make informed decisions, and possibly also to explain them to other stakeholders.

The dataset comprises 168 patient records collected from the ICU of the Arnaldo Milián Castro Teaching Hospital in Santa Clara. Patients range in age from 16 to 93 years (mean 53.5 years), and exhibit a variety of comorbidities—most frequently apparent health status (no known chronic condition), arterial hypertension (HTN), and chronic obstructive pulmonary disease (COPD). Each record includes demographics, medical history, ICU admission causes (e.g., severe dengue, acute respiratory failure type I, unstable angina), patient conditions (e.g., acute myocardial infarction, COPD exacerbation), treatments administered (e.g., mechanical ventilation, hydration, antihypertensive therapy), and outcome data (e.g., date and cause of death when applicable).

Preprocessing Steps

1. Normalization and Encoding
   o Nominal categorical variables (e.g., diagnosis categories, therapy types) were one-hot encoded. Ordinal scales (Charlson BMI, APACHE II, SOFA) were retained as continuous inputs.
2. Outlier Detection
   o Values exceeding $\pm$ 3 standard deviations from the mean were examined case by case; implausible entries were corrected or removed.

Knowledge Graph Construction

The knowledge graph is based on an ontology that is a reduction of the UMLS ontological model and has been specified with the DECS (Descriptors in Health Sciences) that defines the key entities and their relationships within the domain of intensive medical care and clinical decision-making. In this case, the knowledge graph includes entities such as: Patient, Diagnosis, Therapy, Decision, Admission, Cause of Death. In the process of designing and building the ontology that supports the proposed system and captures an accurate and understandable representation of the medical domain associated with decision-making in critically ill patients, an approach based on knowledge reuse and the NeOn (Networked Ontologies) [12]. To build the ontology, the MeSH vocabularies (Medical Subject Headings (Headings) and DeCS (Descriptors in Health Sciences), which provide standardized descriptors for US medical terms, diseases, treatments, and procedures, are widely used standards for indexing biomedical literature. Importing an ontology into Neo4j is a crucial step in ensuring that the knowledge graph is built on a solid semantic foundation.

To transform the reduced UMLS/DeCS ontology into a property graph in Neo4j, we employ Neosemantics (n10s), Neo4j's official RDF/OWL import and mapping toolkit. The key steps are:

1. Plugin Installation and Configuration
2. RDF/OWL Import
3. Mapping Data Properties and Literals
4. Custom Label and Relationship Mapping
5. Validation and Quality Control

4.2 Prediction and Generation of Explanations for the Problem of Patient Deaths in an ICU

The dataset used in this research includes detailed information on patients admitted to the ICU of the Arnaldo Milián Hospital in Santa Clara, Cuba.

The J48 algorithm was trained using our intensive care patient dataset to obtain an initial set of rules that allow predictions to be made about the probability of death of patients and thus transparently identify the key factors that influence the probability of death. From the decision tree constructed by J48, a set of 141 causal rules was generated for predicting whether a patient will die or not. Although J48 efficiently generates rules, exhaustive clinical validation is essential to remove spurious or redundant inferences. To guarantee the accuracy and applicability of the system, the generated rules were reviewed and corrected by experts in the medical field. This validation process included both the correction of possible errors in the selected thresholds and the elimination of redundant or inconsistent rules, resulting in a total of 93 rules that were considered valid and clinically relevant.

The MLP implemented in this study is a fully connected feed-forward neural network designed to predict patient outcomes in the ICU. It consists of 16 input neurons, each representing one of the selected clinical features relevant to the patient's condition, followed by 10 hidden layers of 100 neurons each. All hidden layers use the ReLU activation function, which was chosen for its simplicity and effectiveness in mitigating the vanishing gradient problem in deep networks. The output layer contains a single neuron with a sigmoid activation function, allowing the model to perform binary classification specifically, predicting whether a patient will survive or not. The model was trained using the Adam optimizer, which adapts learning rates dynamically to enhance convergence in high-dimensional and noisy data. To control model complexity and reduce the risk of overfitting, an L2 regularization term (alpha $= 0.0001$) was applied, and the initial learning rate was set to 0.001 to ensure a balanced trade-off between learning speed and model stability.

For each new case, the procedure is as follows. The patient's clinical data is input to the neural network, and it makes a prediction about whether the patient will die. Using the set of rules, an approximation of the "why" of the network's prediction is generated, identifying the key factors that contribute to the outcome. The rules constitute explanatory patterns. The knowledge graph takes the network's prediction as input and contextualizes it with the medical information stored in the graph. To do this, it uses the rules to generate an initial explanation of the prediction, based on the relationships between the patient data, the neural network's prediction, and the medical knowledge of the domain.

From this basic explanation, a more refined version is developed, expressed in natural language using an LLM. One of the most recent and promising approaches is the use of GraphRAG (Graph Retrieval-Augmented Generation), a technique that relies on knowledge graph architecture and enables the retrieval of relevant and contextual information [31]. This system, when combined with graph databases such as Neo4j, provides a robust mechanism for giving LLMs access to structured, verifiable, and context-rich data. Using GraphRAG, the model can query a knowledge graph to retrieve information that serves as the basis for an accurate answer [18]. The knowledge graph acts as an organized external source that helps the model anchor its answers in structured facts rather than relying solely on statistical patterns from its training see Figs. 2 and 3.

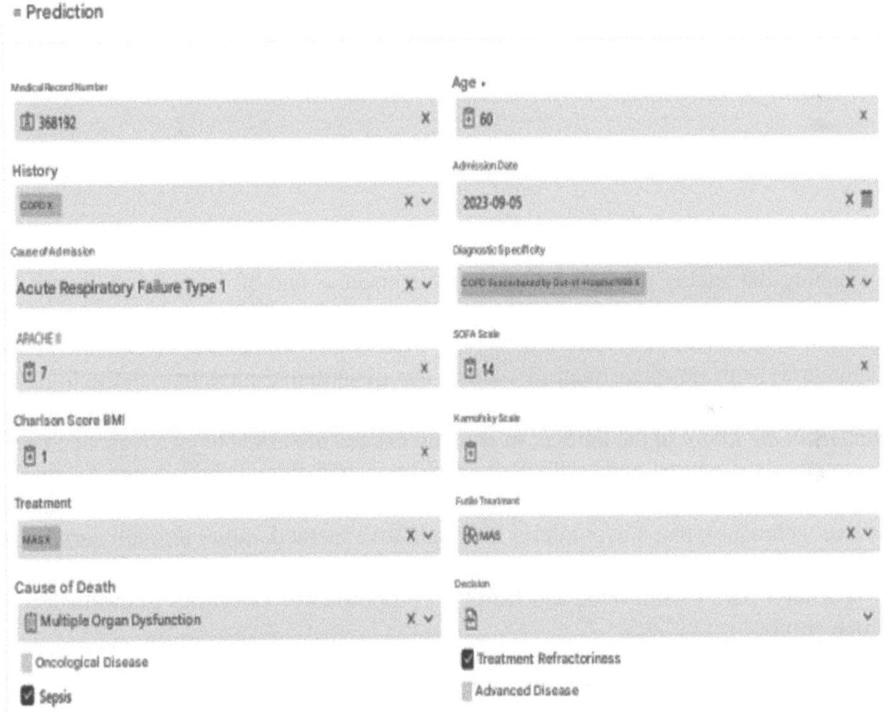

Fig. 2. Data of Patients

Fig. 3. Explanation

4.3 Evaluation of the Explanations

Evaluating the quality of explanations is recognized as one of the main challenges in this field [13]; in general, XAI metrics should assess the *goodness*, *usefulness*, and *satisfaction* of explanations. According to [14], evaluation methods can be classified into: Evaluations with objective metrics (which use quantitative measures and automated approaches), and Human-centered evaluations (where the evaluation is performed *with humans in the loop*); in the latter case, domain experts are asked to give reasoned opinions on the explanations and verify their consistency with domain knowledge. Similarly, [15] proposes two distinct methods to evaluate explanations: a baseline evaluation (quantitative technique), and a user interview (qualitative method, either through surveys or interviews).

For their part, Doshi-Velez and Kim [16] propose three categories of evaluation of explanations:

1. *Application-grounded* (evaluation with domain experts and real problems),
2. *Human- grounded* (evaluation with non-expert participants in simplified scenarios), and
3. *Functionally-grounded* (automatic evaluation without human intervention).

The first two involve human judgment, but the first focuses on specific application contexts [17].

Considering that this research involved working directly with ICU specialists, it was decided to conduct an evaluation with their participation; that is, an assessment of the proposed model was conducted using the case study. To evaluate the quality of the generated explanations, a survey was designed for medical experts. The survey was administered in a clinical setting and focused on measuring two fundamental aspects of the explanations: their comprehensibility and their clinical relevance. For each of the five cases presented, the experts were asked to rate the explanations using a scale of 1 to 10, where 1 represented "very incomprehensible or irrelevant" and 10 represented "very comprehensible or highly relevant."

The experts were provided with a detailed case description of a patient admitted to the ICU. The case included the patient's clinical data, diagnosis, treatment received, and other relevant history. A system-generated explanation of the reasons for the patient's mortality was presented. Criteria were asked for comprehensibility: Is the explanation clear and easy to understand? and relevance: Is the explanation clinically meaningful and aligned with the medical context of the case.

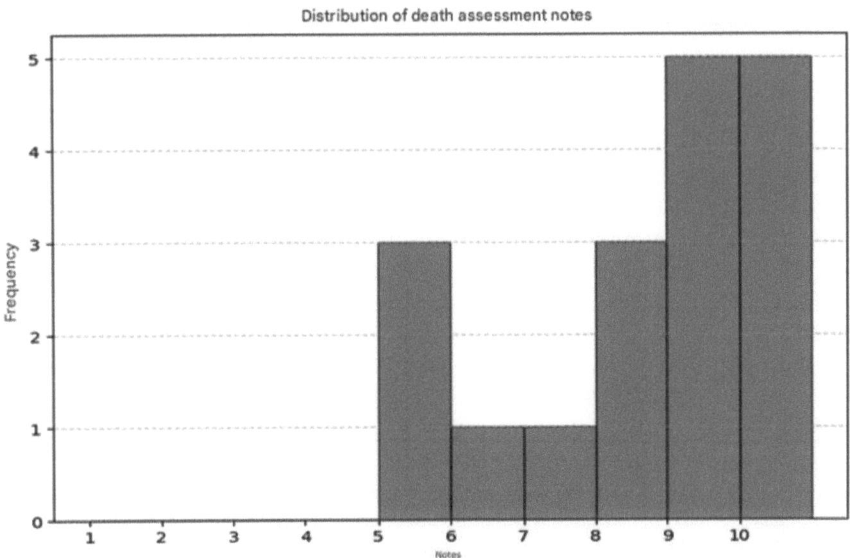

Fig. 4. Evaluation of explanations

The survey included a total of five different clinical cases, each with its own explanations for the mortality or survival. The results showed that the highest scores (9 and 10) were the most common, with five responses each, suggesting that the majority of respondents considered the explanations to be of high quality. There were also some responses in the middle range (5 to 8), but no low scores (1 to 4), see Fig. 4. This indicates a positive trend in the perception of the explanations.

To complement our human-centered survey, we measured two objective metrics on a held-out test set of 10 ICU cases. First, we ran a fidelity test by perturbing each case's top-3 kg-derived features (e.g. disabling "SOFA score" or "Apache II score") and observing whether the MLP's predicted probability of death shifted by at least 10%. Across all cases, explanations achieved an average fidelity of 0.8 (i.e. 80% of perturbed top-3 features produced the expected $\geq 10\%$ change), confirming that our explanations truly reflect model sensitivities.

Second, we performed an ablation study on explanation components: (a) neural + KG only, (b) neural + KG + LLM refinement. We randomly selected 5 cases and asked ICU experts to rate each version on a 1–10 scale. Removing the LLM stage (a) reduced mean evaluation from 8.17 to 6.9 ($\Delta = 1.28$, $p < 0.01$, paired t-test), demonstrating the quantitative benefit of the final refinement.

4.4 Comparison with XAI Methods

To highlight the novelty of our neurosymbolic framework, we compare its explanations against those produced by the classic, model-agnostic method LIME. While LIME approximates a black-box model locally by fitting simple surrogate regressors and returns feature-importance weights, our approach weaves together clinical rules, a domain-driven knowledge graph, and LLM-based natural-language refinement to generate explanations that are both precise and immediately interpretable by ICU practitioners.

Domain-Knowledge vs. Technical Feature-Weights
Our system's explanations speak the language of critical-care medicine: they cite postoperative complications, treatment refractoriness, and clinical scores (e.g., Charlson BMI, APACHE II) to narrate "why" a patient's outcome unfolded as it did. For example:

"The fatal outcome was driven by postoperative neurosurgical syndrome combined with arterial hypertension and a Charlson BMI score of 3."

In contrast, LIME returns statements such as:

"Patient age contributed 30 % and hypertension contributed 25 % to the mortality prediction."

Although technically informative, LIME's percentage-based feature weights lack the narrative context that clinicians need to understand how conditions interact in practice.

Clinical Comprehensibility and Relevance
In a small expert survey, our neurosymbolic explanations scored an average 8.17/10, whereas the LIME explanations averaged 7.2/10, respectively. Clinicians reported that our output "reads like a clinical note" and "directly maps to decision points in the ICU," while LIME's numeric breakdowns required additional statistical interpretation.

5 Limitations

While our GraphRAG + LLM pipeline delivers highly interpretable, context-rich explanations, it also introduces practical barriers to adoption. Running an open-source LLM (we used Gemma 3) on-premises demands substantial GPU memory and inference throughput, which may be prohibitive for many institutions. The alternative (invoking a cloud-hosted LLM API) reduces local compute requirements but raises data-security and privacy concerns, since sensitive patient data must be transmitted over external networks. Balancing these computational and compliance trade-offs will be crucial for real-world deployment, and may motivate hybrid architectures (e.g., lightweight local encoders plus secure remote refinement).

6 Conclusions and Future Work

The proposed approach for generating knowledge-based explanations combines artificial neural networks with a knowledge graph (developed from domain ontologies) and rules derived from a machine learning process using a decision tree construction method. The generation model allows the construction of explanations, which are then refined and translated into natural language using an LLM. It consists of three main stages: prediction based on the neural network model; the development of a first explanation based on the causal rules and the knowledge graph; and finally, the development of the final explanation using the LLM. The information provided by the rules and the knowledge graph allows the construction of an appropriate context for the development of the final explanation by the LLM, which is more natural and consistent with the knowledge of the application domain.

This proposal was applied in a case study where the goal was to develop an explainable AI system for predicting and explaining deaths in an ICU. This system not only offers to physicians a tool to anticipate clinical outcomes but also provides a deep understanding of the factors influencing these outcomes. The explanations generated by the death prediction system have proven to be clear, easy to understand, and clinically relevant. Medical experts, through a qualitative evaluation of the results (prediction and explanation), confirmed the high quality of these explanations, highlighting their ability to articulate in an understandable way the factors that lead to a given clinical outcome.

As a way to expand the approach, we propose integrating explanations generated by XAI technological methods such as LIME or LRP, which offer another alternative for identifying the parts of the problem that are relevant to the prediction obtained. The proposed model can also be enriched by incorporating human-machine interaction to facilitate human participation in the construction of the explanation.

Acknowledgements. This work was supported by Aria and the territorial ICT project ARIAS.

The authors wish to express their gratitude for the support received through of the proyects "Platform for Decision Support Services in Critical Care Units" project, under the Program of Science and Innovation of Citma Villa Clara, which was instrumental in the development of this work; and the project "Theoretical contributions to AI in handling problems with complex data" under the National Program of Science, Technology and Innovation in Automation, Robotics, and Artificial Intelligence, CUBA.

References

1. Lipton, Z.C.: The mythos of model interpretability: in machine learning, the concept of interpretability is both important and slippery. Queue **16**(3), 31–57 (2018)
2. Gunning, D., Aha, D.: DARPA's explainable artificial intelligence (XAI) program. AI Mag. **40**(2), 44–58 (2019)
3. Miller, T.: Explanation in artificial intelligence: insights from the social sciences. Artif. Intell. **267**, 1–38 (2019)
4. Mittelstadt, B., Russell, C., Wachter, S.: Explaining explanations in AI. In: Proceedings of the Conference on Fairness, Accountability, and Transparency, pp. 279–288 (2019)

5. Arrieta, A.B., et al.: Explainable Artificial Intelligence (XAI): concepts, taxonomies, opportunities and challenges toward responsible AI. Inf. Fusion **58**, 82–115 (2020)
6. Langer, M., et al.: What do we want from explainable Artificial Intelligence (XAI)?–A stakeholder perspective on XAI and a conceptual model guiding interdisciplinary XAI research. Artif. Intell. **296**, 103473 (2021)
7. Goodman, B., Flaxman, S.: European Union regulations on algorithmic decision-making and a "right to explanation." AI Mag. **38**(3), 50–57 (2017)
8. Guidotti, R., Monreale, A., Ruggieri, S., Turini, F., Giannotti, F., Pedreschi, D.: A survey of methods for explaining black box models. ACM Comput. Surv. (CSUR) **51**(5), 1–42 (2018)
9. Sturm, I., Lapuschkin, S., Samek, W., Müller, K.-R.: Interpretable deep neural networks for single-trial EEG classification. J. Neurosci. Methods **274**, 141–145 (2016)
10. Vilone, G., Longo, L.: Notions of explainability and evaluation approaches for explainable artificial intelligence. Inf. Fusion **76**, 89–106 (2021)
11. Schwalbe, G., Finzel, B.: A comprehensive taxonomy for explainable artificial intelligence: a systematic survey of surveys on methods and concepts. Data Min. Knowl. Disc. **38**(5), 3043–3101 (2024)
12. Ribeiro, M.T., Singh, S., Guestrin, C.: Why should i trust you?" Explaining the predictions of any classifier. In: Proceedings of the 22nd ACM SIGKDD International Conference on Knowledge Discovery and Data Mining, pp. 1135–1144 (2016)
13. Tiddi, I., Schlobach, S.: Knowledge graphs as tools for explainable machine learning: a survey. Artif. Intell. **302**, 103627 (2022)
14. Burkart, N., Huber, M.F.: A survey on the explainability of supervised machine learning. J. Artif. Intell. Res. **70**, 245–317 (2021)
15. Lécué, F., et al.: Thales XAI platform: adaptable explanation of machine learning systems-A knowledge graphs perspective. In: ISWC (Satellites), pp. 315–316 (2019)
16. Rajabi, E., Kafaie, S.: Knowledge graphs and explainable ai in healthcare. Information **13**(10), 459 (2022)
17. Confalonieri, R., Guizzardi, G.: On the multiple roles of ontologies in explainable AI (2023). arXiv preprint arXiv:2311.04778
18. Wu, J., et al.: Medical graph rag: towards safe medical large language model via graph retrieval-augmented generation (2024). arXiv preprint arXiv:2408.04187
19. Zytek, A., Pidò, S., Veeramachaneni, K.: Llms for xai: future directions for explaining explanations (2024). arXiv preprint arXiv:2405.06064
20. Gautam, V.K., et al.: Prediction of sodium hazard of irrigation purpose using artificial neural network modelling. Sustainability **15**(9), 7593 (2023)
21. Yang, W.-C., Lai, J.-P., Liu, Y.-H., Lin, Y.-L., Hou, H.-P., Pai, P.-F.: Using medical data and clustering techniques for a smart healthcare system. Electronics **13**(1), 140 (2023)
22. Abiodun, O.I., Jantan, A., Omolara, A.E., Dada, K.V., Mohamed, N.A., Arshad, H.: State-of-the-art in artificial neural network applications: a survey. Heliyon **4**(11) (2018)
23. Du, S.S., Hou, K., Salakhutdinov, R.R., Poczos, B., Wang, R., Xu, K.: Graph neural tangent kernel: fusing graph neural networks with graph kernels. Adv. Neural Inf. Process. Syst. **32** (2019)
24. Lillicrap, T.P., Santoro, A., Marris, L., Akerman, C.J., Hinton, G.: Backpropagation and the brain. Nat. Rev. Neurosci. **21**(6), 335–346 (2020)
25. Guo, X., et al.: Embodied llm agents learn to cooperate in organized teams (2024). arXiv preprint arXiv:2403.12482
26. Abbasi, A., Parsons, J., Pant, G., Sheng, O.R.L., Sarker, S.: Pathways for design research on artificial intelligence. Inf. Syst. Res. **35**(2), 441–459 (2024)
27. Barrasa, J., Webber, J.: Building knowledge graphs. O'Reilly Media, Inc. (2023)
28. Kessler, S., et al.: Predicting readmission to the cardiovascular intensive care unit using recurrent neural networks. Digital Health **9**, 20552076221149530 (2023)

29. Alshwaheen, T.I., Hau, Y.W., Ass'Ad, N., Abualsamen, M.M.: A novel and reliable framework of patient deterioration prediction in intensive care unit based on long short-term memory-recurrent neural network. IEEE Access **9**, 3894–3918 (2020)
30. Asteris, P.G., et al.: Genetic prediction of ICU hospitalization and mortality in COVID-19 patients using artificial neural networks. J. Cell Mol. Med. **26**(5), 1445–1455 (2022)
31. McCaffrey, P., et al.: Evaluating use of generative Artificial Intelligence in clinical pathology practice: opportunities and the way forward. Archiv. Pathol. Lab. Med. (2024)

Evaluation of Probabilistic Data Augmentation Models for Emotion Detection

Ireimis Leguen-de-Varona[1]($\boxtimes$) , Julio Madera[1] , Alfredo Simon-Cuevas[2] , Leonardo Lastre Figueroa[1] , and Yoan Martínez-López[3]

[1] University of Camagüey "Ignacio Agramonte Loynaz", Camagüey, Cuba
{ireimis.leguen,julio.madera,leonardo.lastre}@reduc.edu.cu
[2] Technological University of Havana "José Antonio Echeverría",
CUJAE, Havana, Cuba
asimon@ceis.cujae.edu.cu
[3] University of Cordoba and Plénitas, C/ Le Corbusier s/n, 14005 Córdoba, Spain
yoan.martinez@plenitas.com

Abstract. In Machine Learning, class imbalance is one of the most common challenges in classification tasks. This issue becomes even more pronounced in Natural Language Processing domains such as TASS, a Spanish-language emotion detection corpus characterized by a marked disproportion among categories. Traditional oversampling methods like SMOTE, based on k-nearest neighbors, lose effectiveness when applied to the high-dimensional spaces generated by modern language models.

This work presents a probabilistic balancing framework that models the distribution of RoBERTa CLS embeddings (768 dimensions) using the covariance matrix estimated through the LedoitWolf method, Lasso regression, and Elastic Net. From these distributions, realistic synthetic instances are generated for minority classes, drastically reducing the imbalance ratio without introducing semantic noise. The balanced embeddings are then classified using a lightweight multilayer perceptron (MLP), which eliminates the need for costly transformer fine-tuning.

When evaluated on the TASS 2020 dataset, the best proposed algorithm achieved a Macro F1 score of 82.45%, outperforming the previously reported best result (55.3%) by 27.15% points [1]. These results demonstrate that synthetic generation guided by probabilistic models is an effective and computationally efficient alternative for emotion detection in high-dimensional, highly imbalanced scenarios.

Keywords: emotion detection · class imbalance · Ledoit-Wolf covariance matrix · Lasso regression · Elastic Net · RoBERTa embeddings · TASS

1 Introduction

In supervised classification problems, one of the most significant challenges is class imbalance, which occurs when one or more classes are represented by sig-

Y. Hernádez Heredia et al. (Eds.): IWAIPR 2025, LNCS 16328, pp. 192–203, 2026.
https://doi.org/10.1007/978-3-032-11358-0_16

nificantly fewer examples compared to others. This situation is common in real-world applications such as fraud detection, medical diagnosis, fault monitoring, risk analysis, or sentiment analysis, where minority classes often correspond to the most relevant cases. When training on imbalanced data, classifiers tend to optimize overall accuracy at the expense of correctly detecting minority classes, thereby compromising the practical usefulness of the model [2].

An example of this problem is found in the TASS 2020 corpus for emotion detection in Spanish, where labels are not uniformly distributed: categories such as joy or anger each represent less than 10% of tweets, while fear and others exceed 25% of the total. A classifier trained without correcting this bias will tend to maximize accuracy by predominantly assigning the most frequent labels, failing to recognize critical minority emotions and drastically reducing its value for sentiment analysis or customer support.

Strategies to address classification in imbalanced datasets fall into four main categories: data-level methods, algorithm-level methods, cost-sensitive learning, and ensemble-based approaches. Among these, data-level techniques are the most widely used due to their independence from the specific classifier chosen.

One of the most well-known data-level techniques is SMOTE (Synthetic Minority Oversampling Technique) [3], which generates synthetic samples of the minority class. SMOTE has been combined with other techniques to balance the trade-off between introducing new minority class examples and selectively removing others, including SMOTE–Tomek Links, SMOTE–ENN [4], Borderline-SMOTE [5], SPIDER [6], SMOTE–RSB* [7], and ADASYN [8]. Most of these methods generate synthetic instances by interpolating between k-nearest neighbors. Although they perform well in low-dimensional datasets, their effectiveness diminishes in high-dimensional spaces [9]. To overcome these limitations, a probabilistic oversampling method based on shrinkage estimation of the covariance matrix using the Ledoit–Wolf method—SMOTE-COV_HD—was introduced in 2024 [10].

In the context of TASS 2020, four main approaches have been explored for emotion detection in Spanish:

- Fine-tuning of BERT adapted to tweets (TWilBERT), which achieved a Macro F1 score of 44.7% [11].
- Combination of linguistic features and embeddings with SVM, yielding a Macro F1 of 37.9% [12].
- Fine-tuning of pre-trained monolingual models (BETO, ALBETO, BERTIN, MarIA) and multilingual models (mBERT, XLM-R), with results ranging from 44.7% to 55.3% in Macro F1 [1,13].
- Hybrid lexical-statistical approaches based on lexicons and stacking ensembles, which achieved 43% in Macro F1 and 52% in weighted accuracy.

These studies show that despite the improvements obtained through transformers and lexical-statistical methods, there remains a need for a method capable of generating semantically coherent synthetic data in high-dimensional spaces to effectively address strong class imbalance.

Therefore, this article introduces new probabilistic data balancing methods that model the distribution of RoBERTa CLS embeddings (768 dimensions) using the covariance matrix estimated through the Ledoit–Wolf method [14], Lasso regression [15], and Elastic Net [16]. From these distributions, realistic synthetic instances are generated for minority classes, drastically reducing imbalance without introducing semantic noise. In doing so, the previously proposed SMOTE_Cov_HD approach is extended to the domain of emotion detection in Spanish.

Specifically, a hybrid framework is proposed that:

- Extracts CLS embeddings from RoBERTa-base-bne (768 dimensions).
- Balances minority classes using three probabilistic variants:
  - Ledoit–Wolf SMOTE-Cov
  - Lasso-SMOTE
  - Elastic Net-SMOTE
- Classifies the balanced embeddings using a lightweight multilayer perceptron (MLP), avoiding the costly fine-tuning of the full transformer.

Main contributions of this work:

1. Three new oversampling strategies based on probabilistic models (Ledoit–Wolf, Lasso, and Elastic Net) are introduced for emotion detection in Spanish.
2. An empirical evaluation protocol is developed using TASS 2020, comparing the proposed approach to baseline methods.
3. It is demonstrated that a lightweight classifier (MLP) can achieve a Macro F1 score of 82.45%, improving by 27.15% points over the previous best result and by 39.45 points over the best hybrid lexical-statistical model, with significantly lower computational cost than fine-tuning large models.

2   Methodology

2.1   Text Representation

We start from the TASS 2020 corpus (Spanish-language tweets labeled with emotions). After basic cleaning and normalization, each example is converted into its corresponding CLS vector from RoBERTa (768 dimensions) using the HuggingFace Transformers library.

2.2   Probabilistic Oversampling

To generate semantically coherent synthetic samples in high-dimensional spaces, we employ three methods based on Probabilistic Graphical Models (PGMs), which are graph structures where nodes represent random variables and edges represent conditional dependencies among them. These graphs provide a compact representation of probability distributions [17]. Among the PGMs, Gaussian Graphical Models stand out as interaction models for multivariate normal distributions [18]. Techniques such as the Covariance Matrix, Lasso Regression, and Elastic Net are used for estimating these Gaussian Graphical Models (Fig. 1).

Probabilistic Graphical Models (PGM)

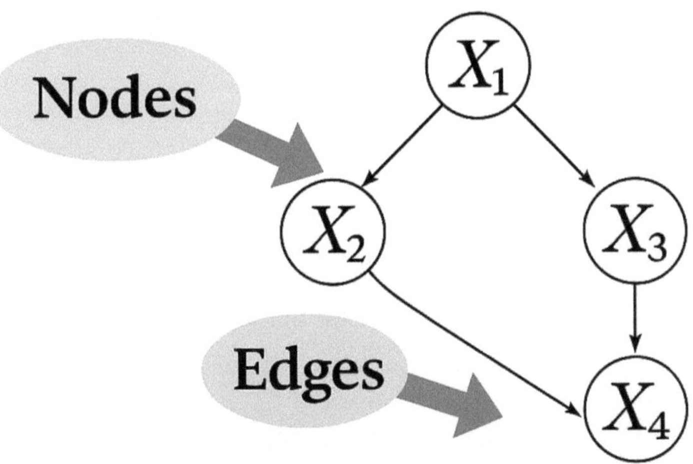

Fig. 1. Probabilistic Graphical Models

2.2.1   Covariance Matrix

It contains the covariances between the elements of a random variable vector $[X_1, X_2, \ldots, X_n]$, the covariance matrix Σ is defined as:

$$\Sigma = \begin{pmatrix} \mathrm{Var}\,(X_1) & \mathrm{Cov}\,(X_1, X_2) \ldots \mathrm{Cov}\,(X_1, X_n) \\ \mathrm{Cov}\,(X_2, X_1) & \mathrm{Var}\,(X_2) \quad \ldots \mathrm{Cov}\,(X_2, X_n) \\ \vdots & \vdots \quad \ddots \quad \vdots \\ \mathrm{Cov}\,(X_n, X_1)\ \mathrm{Cov}\,(X_n, X_2) \ldots & \mathrm{Var}\,(X_n) \end{pmatrix} \tag{1}$$

Where $\mathrm{Var}(X_i)$ is the variance of X_i and $\mathrm{Cov}(X_i, X_j)$ is the covariance between X_i and X_j.

This matrix measures the linear relationship between two variables and provides information about the linear dependencies among them. A positive covariance indicates a direct relationship, while a negative covariance suggests an inverse relationship. A covariance of zero implies that there is no linear relationship between the variables.

2.2.1.1 LedoitWolf Shrinkage Estimator

This is a technique used to improve the estimation of the covariance matrix, especially when the number of samples is small relative to the number of variables. The method combines the sample covariance matrix with a simpler structured matrix (such as the identity matrix) to produce a more robust estimate.

$$\Sigma^{\text{LW}} = (1 - \delta)\, S + \delta F \tag{2}$$

where:
S sample covariance matrix
F simple structured matrix (e.g., the scaled identity matrix)
δ shrinkage parameter that minimizes the mean squared error (MSE).

2.2.1.2 Parameter Regularization of the Covariance Matrix

This refers to the technique of adjusting model parameters to prevent overfitting and improve generalization. In the case of the covariance matrix, regularization may involve shrinking toward a simpler structured matrix, as done in the Ledoit-Wolf method. [14]

2.2.2 Lasso Regression

Lasso regression is a regularization technique used to improve the accuracy of regression models and prevent overfitting. It is especially useful when working with high-dimensional data, where the number of predictors is large relative to the number of observations. Lasso minimizes the sum of squared residual errors with a penalty on the sum of the absolute values of the coefficients.

$$\hat{\beta} = \arg\min \beta \left\{ \sum_{i1}^{n} \left(y_i - \sum_{j1}^{p} x_{ij}\beta_j \right)^2 + \lambda \sum_{j1}^{p} |\beta_j| \right\} \tag{3}$$

where:
y_i observed value of the dependent variable
x_{ij} value of predictor j for observation i
β_j model coefficients
λ regularization parameter that controls the penalty

2.2.2.1 Regularization in Lasso Regression

This refers to the inclusion of the penalty term $\left(\lambda \sum_{j=1}^{p} |\beta_j| \right)$ in the Lasso formula, which acts as a shrinkage estimator. As λ increases, the penalty on the coefficients also increases, which can lead to some coefficients being reduced to zero. This not only helps prevent overfitting but also performs automatic variable selection by eliminating those variables that do not significantly contribute to the model [15].

2.2.3   Elastic Net

Elastic Net is a regularization technique that combines the properties of Ridge regression and Lasso regression. It performs both automatic variable selection and continuous shrinkage, while overcoming some of their individual limitations. This method enables the selection of groups of correlated variables. It is particularly useful for high-dimensional problems and in situations where there is collinearity among predictors.

$$\beta = \arg\min \beta \left\{ \sum_{i=1}^{n} \left(y_i - \sum_{j1}^{p} x_{ij}\beta_j \right)^2 + \lambda_1 \sum_{j1}^{p} |\beta_j| + \lambda_2 \sum_{j1}^{p} \beta_j^2 \right\} \tag{4}$$

where:
y_i observed value of the dependent variable
x_{ij} value of predictor j for observation i
β_j model coefficients
λ_1 Lasso (L1) regularization parameter
λ_2 Ridge (L2) regularization parameter

2.2.3.1 Regularization in Elastic Net

Regularization in Elastic Net refers to the inclusion of the penalty terms $\lambda_1 \sum_{j=1}^{p} |\beta_j|$,
L1 penalty term (variable selection), and $\lambda_2 \sum_{j=1}^{p} \beta_j^2$,
L2 penalty term (reduces collinearity without nullifying coefficients) in the cost function.
λ_1 controls the L1 penalty—may shrink some coefficients to zero and
λ_2 controls the L2 penalty—reduces coefficients without making them zero [16].

Common Procedure: Train `MLPClassifier`

1: Read the balanced CSV and decode embeddings.
2: Map labels to indices.
3: Split the data into training and test sets.
4: Build the MLP network (ReLU, Dropout, Softmax).

Algorithm 1 SMOTE.Cov.LW + MLP Classification

1: Read the CSV file.
2: **if** text column exists **then**
3:     Generate CLS embeddings using RoBERTa.
4:     Save as JSON.
5: **end if**
6: Convert embeddings to columns emb_0, ..., emb_n.
7: Identify minority classes.
8: **for** each minority class **do**
9:     Compute stats and covariance matrix.
10:     Apply Cholesky decomposition.
11:     Generate synthetic instances.
12:     Clip values and append to dataset.
13: **end for**
14: Rebuild embedding column.
15: Save dataset.
16: Train `MLPClassifier`.

Algorithm 2 SMOTE.EN + MLP Classification

1: Read the CSV file.
2: Clean text (lowercase, remove whitespace).
3: **if** text column exists **then**
4:     Generate CLS embeddings using RoBERTa.
5: **end if**
6: Validate class column.
7: **for** each minority class **do**
8:     Decode embeddings.
9:     Standardize vectors.
10:     Train ElasticNet model.
11:     Predict, clip, and append new samples.
12: **end for**
13: Save dataset.
14: Train `MLPClassifier`.

Algorithm 3 SMOTE.RL + MLP Classification

1: Read the CSV file and clean text.
2: **if** text column exists **then**
3:     Generate CLS embeddings.
4: **end if**
5: Validate class column.
6: **for** each minority class **do**
7:     Filter numeric features.
8:     Scale using `StandardScaler`.
9:     Train Lasso regression model.
10:     Predict, clip, round, and append new samples.
11: **end for**
12: Save dataset.
13: Train `MLPClassifier`.

5: Train for multiple epochs.
6: Evaluate on the test set (Macro F1, accuracy).
7: Save the model and evaluation report.

3 Experimental Study

3.1 Experimental Design for Evaluating Probabilistic Balancing on TASS 2020

Objective of the Experiment: The goal is to evaluate the impact of probabilistic balancing methods (SMOTE_Cov_LW, SMOTE_RL, and SMOTE_EN) on emotion detection in Spanish. These methods are compared to prior approaches and assessed in terms of Macro F1, Weighted F1, Precision, and Recall.

Dataset:

- **Corpus:** The TASS 2020 dataset will be used, consisting of Spanish-language tweets with imbalanced emotion labels.
- **Preprocessing:** Text normalization, removal of special characters, and conversion into CLS embeddings (768 dimensions) using RoBERTa.
- **Class Distribution:** The proportion of each emotion will be detailed before and after balancing.

Classification Models: A lightweight Multilayer Perceptron (MLP) will be trained on the balanced embeddings, avoiding the costly fine-tuning of large models. It will be compared against:

- TWilBERT (fine-tuning on Spanish tweets)
- SVM with linguistic features and embeddings
- BETO/ALBETO/BERTIN/MarIA (fine-tuning Spanish BERT variants)
- SEL Lexicon + Stacking Ensemble

Performance Evaluation: The following metrics will be measured:

- **Macro F1:** Average F1-score across all classes.
- **Weighted F1:** F1-score weighted by class distribution.
- **Precision:** Proportion of correct predictions over total instances.
- **Recall:** Model's ability to correctly detect minority classes.

3.2 Experimental Results

(See Table 1).

Table 1. Comparison of Results on TASS 2020

Approach	Macro F1	Weighted F1	Precision	Recall
TWilBERT [11]	44.7	–	44.3	45.0
SVM [12]	37.9	–	42.0	34.5
BETO et al. [13]	44.7–55.3	–	–	–
Lexicon Ensemble	43.0	–	52.0	39.0
Unbalanced MLP	28.08	54	55	59
SMOTE_Cov_LW (ours)	**82.45**	82	85	83
SMOTE_RL (ours)	79.27	79	81	80
SMOTE_EN (ours)	80.42	80	83	81

3.3   Explanation of Experimental Results

Comparison with Previous Methods: The approach presented in this study demonstrates a substantial improvement in the Macro F1 metric compared to previous methods used for emotion detection in Spanish. In particular, approaches based on fine-tuning pre-trained language models such as BERT and its Spanish-adapted variants (BETO, ALBETO, BERTIN, MarIA) show limitations when faced with strongly imbalanced class distributions.

The core issue is that language models optimized for general tasks tend to disproportionately assign majority class labels, significantly impairing their ability to detect low-frequency emotions. In contrast, our probabilistic balancing framework introduces precisely generated synthetic instances in high-dimensional spaces, improving class distribution and enhancing the model's ability to capture underrepresented emotions.

The experimental results table shows that using SMOTE_Cov_LW, SMOTE_RL, and SMOTE_EN increases performance by more than 20% points compared to the best lexical-statistical hybrid methods, reaching Macro F1 scores of 82.45%, 79.27%, and 80.42%, respectively. This improvement demonstrates the superiority of probabilistic balancing for addressing class imbalance without introducing semantic noise.

Impact of Probabilistic Balancing: Class imbalance in TASS 2020 is particularly critical, as emotions like joy and anger account for less than 10% of tweets, while fear and other categories exceed 25%. Conventional models trained on uncorrected data tend to optimize overall accuracy by favoring frequent labels, sacrificing performance on minority classes.

To address this challenge, we applied synthetic generation techniques that model the distribution of RoBERTa CLS embeddings (768 dimensions) and generate semantically coherent artificial examples. Specifically:

- **SMOTE_Cov_LW:** Adjusts the covariance matrix to generate representative minority class instances.

- **SMOTE_RL:** Applies coefficient regularization to prevent overfitting and promote realistic samples.
- **SMOTE_EN:** Combines Ridge and Lasso to select correlated variable groups, improving high-dimensional data generation.

As a result, the balanced embeddings reduce the imbalance ratio and significantly enhance minority emotion detection without compromising data semantics.

Computational Efficiency: A key aspect of this study is the computational efficiency of the proposed solution compared to traditional fine-tuning methods for large transformer models. While fine-tuning models such as TWilBERT has been widely explored in emotion classification tasks, these methods are computationally expensive and require a substantial amount of labeled data to prevent overfitting.

Our proposal replaces the complexity of fine-tuning with a lightweight Multilayer Perceptron (MLP) trained on balanced embeddings. This approach lowers computational requirements while maintaining high classification performance. The reduction in processing time and resource demands makes the model more viable for real-world applications such as social media sentiment analysis and automated customer service.

In summary, the experimental results validate the effectiveness of the probabilistic balancing approach, demonstrating substantial improvements in emotion detection and outperforming traditional fine-tuned pre-trained models. Additionally, the computational efficiency of the lightweight classifier supports the practical applicability of our system, positioning it as an effective and scalable alternative for emotion analysis tasks in Spanish.

4   Concluding Remarks and Further Work

This work presents a probabilistic balancing framework for multiclass classification in high-dimensional and strongly imbalanced scenarios, applying shrinkage-based covariance estimation techniques (Ledoit–Wolf), Lasso regression, and Elastic Net. These methods robustly model the distribution of RoBERTa CLS embeddings, enabling the generation of realistic synthetic instances for minority classes.

Experimental results on the TASS 2020 corpus show that our approach significantly outperforms baseline methods. Specifically, the variant based on the Ledoit–Wolf covariance matrix (SMOTE_Cov_LW) achieved a Macro F1 score of 82.45%, surpassing the best prior approaches—including BERT fine-tuning and hybrid lexical-statistical methods—by more than 25% points. The Lasso and Elastic Net variants also achieved strong results, with Macro F1 scores of 79.27% and 80.42%, respectively, confirming the effectiveness of probabilistic oversampling.

Beyond performance, the proposed framework significantly reduces computational cost by avoiding the need for fine-tuning large language models. Instead, it employs a lightweight classifier (MLP) that maintains high precision and recall. This combination makes it an efficient and scalable solution for emotion analysis tasks.

As future work, we propose evaluating this methodology in other domains characterized by severe class imbalance and high dimensionality, such as medical diagnosis, gene classification, or multilingual sentiment analysis. Additionally, we aim to explore block-wise learning variants, including structured covariance estimation (block-wise shrinkage), to scale the approach to ultra-high-dimensional contexts. Finally, we suggest incorporating semantic diversity metrics into the synthetic generation process, with the goal of maximizing informative variability in the generated examples and reducing redundancy.

Acknowledgments. We would like to express our sincere gratitude to the National Program of Science and Technology PN223LH004: Automation, Robotics and Artificial Intelligence, of the Ministry of Science, Technology and Environment of Cuba, for supporting this work under project PN223LH004-038: Theoretical contributions to AI in the management of complex data problems.

References

1. Vilares, D., Gómez-Rodríguez, C.: pysentimiento: a python toolkit for opinion mining and social NLP tasks (2022). https://github.com/pysentimiento/pysentimiento
2. Carvalho, M., Pinho, A.J., Brás, S.: Resampling approaches to handle class imbalance: a review from a data perspective. J. Big Data **12**(1), 71 (2025)
3. Chawla, N.V., Bowyer, K.W., Hall, L.O., Kegelmeyer, W.P.: SMOTE: synthetic minority over-sampling technique. J. Artif. Intell. Res. **16**, 321–357 (2002)
4. Batista, G.E., Prati, R.C., Monard, M.C.: A study of the behavior of several methods for balancing machine learning training data. ACM SIGKDD Explor. Newsl. **6**(1), 20–29 (2004)
5. Han, H., Wang, W.Y., Mao, B.H.: Borderline-SMOTE: a new over-sampling method in imbalanced datasets learning. In: Proceedings of the International Conference on Intelligent Computing (ICIC05) (2005)
6. Stefanowski, J., Wilk, S.: Selective pre-processing of imbalanced data for improving classification performance. In: Song, I.-Y., Eder, J., Nguyen, T.M. (eds.) DaWaK 2008. LNCS, vol. 5182, pp. 283–292. Springer, Heidelberg (2008). https://doi.org/10.1007/978-3-540-85836-2_27
7. Ramentol, E., Herrera, F., Bello, R., Caballero, Y., Sánchez, Y.: Edición de conjuntos de entrenamiento no balanceados usando operadores genéticos y conjuntos aproximados. Universidad de Camagüey (2009)
8. He, H., Bai, Y., Garcia, E.A., Li, S.: ADASYN: adaptive synthetic sampling approach for imbalanced learning. In: IEEE International Joint Conference on Neural Networks (2008)
9. Sharma, A., Gosain, A., Jain, A.: A review of the oversampling techniques in class imbalance problem. Arch. Comput. Methods Eng. (2022)
10. Leguen-de-Varona, I., Madera, J., Gonzalez, H., Tubex, L., Verdonck, T.: Oversampling method based covariance matrix estimation in high-dimensional imbalanced classification. In: Hernández Heredia, Y., Milián Núñez, V., Ruiz Shulcloper, J. (eds.) IWAIPR 2023. LNCS, vol. 14335, pp. 16–23. Springer, Cham (2024). https://doi.org/10.1007/978-3-031-49552-6_2

11. Civit-Masot, J., et al.: ELiRF-UPV at TASS 2020: TWILBERT for sentiment analysis and emotion detection in Spanish tweets. In: CEUR Workshop Proceedings, vol. 2664 (2020)
12. Franco-Salvador, M., et al. UMUTeam at TASS 2020: Combining linguistic features and machine-learning models for sentiment classification. In: CEUR Workshop Proceedings, vol. 2664 (2020)
13. López, F., Azzopardi, L.: Overview of TASS 2020: introducing emotion detection. In: CEUR Workshop Proceedings, vol. 2664 (2020)
14. Ledoit, O., Wolf, M.: The power (non) linear shrinking: a review and guide to covariance matrix estimation. J. Multivariate Anal. (2022)
15. Lu, Y., Yin, Y.: Applying logistic lasso regression for the diagnosis of atypical Crohn's disease. *Compu. Biol. Med.* (2022)
16. Kovács, T., Ruckstuhl, A., Obrist, H., Bühlmann, P.: Graphical elastic net and target matrices: fast algorithms and software for sparse precision matrix estimation. J. Comput. Graph. Stat. (2021)
17. Madera, J.: Algoritmos evolutivos con estimación de distribuciones basados en pruebas de independencia. Master's thesis, Universidad de Camagüey (2008)
18. Richardson Ibáñez, J.: Algoritmos Evolutivos Estimadores de Distribución Celulares para Problemas de Optimización Continuos. PhD thesis, Universidad de Camagüey (2017)

Forecasting, Optimization, and Economic AI

1D Separable Convolutional Neural Network Architecture for Real-Time Stellar Classification Based on Captured Spectral Characteristics

Jorge Felix Martínez Pazos[1(✉)], David Batard Lorenzo[1], Ariel Ramirez Alvarez[2], Yunwei Chen[3,4], and Jorge Gulín-Gonzalez[1]

[1] Centro de Estudios de Matemática Computacional, Universidad de Las Ciencias Informáticas, La Habana, Cuba
jorgefmp.mle@gmail.com
[2] Universidad de Las Ciencias Informáticas, La Habana, Cuba
[3] Scientometrics and Evaluation Research Center (SERC), National Science Library (Chengdu), Chinese Academy of Science, Sichuan, China
[4] Department of Information Resources Management, School of Economics and Management, University of Chinese Academy of Sciences, Beijing, China

Abstract. Stellar classification, a fundamental aspect of astronomy, offers a structured approach to comprehend and characterize the vast diversity of celestial entities. Here we present a new fine-tuned deep convolutional neural network of 1D separable convolutional blocks for stellar classification based on spectral properties using SSDS-17 data from the Sloan Digital Sky Survey, where class imbalance is evaluated using the MIN class and SMOTE balancing techniques. The results obtained during the performance evaluation confirmed the reliability of the proposed architecture of StellarNet in multi-class stellar classification, achieving remarkable values of about 97% and 99% for accuracy and AUC score, respectively. The proposed StellarNet architecture has been used in a real-time streaming processing pipeline that includes a streaming learning functionality that can be deployed in observatories and related centers to perform the real-time labeling and sorting of the captured data.

Keywords: 1D Separable Convolutional Neural Network · Photometric Filters · Spectral Characteristics · Stellar Classification

1 Introduction

The emergence of Artificial Intelligence (AI) has been a game changer in every scientific field, astronomy and astrophysics have known a fast and great advance in this new scenery, in some cases even questioning all our conceptions about the universe [1–5]. AI has enabled scientists to rapidly sift through and analyze vast collections of images, helping to identify objects worthy of closer study such as supernovae, pulsars, and quasars, and allowing us to classify stars, label galaxies, and evaluate redshifts [6]. One of the most important contributions of AI to this field is to support the development

© The Author(s), under exclusive license to Springer Nature Switzerland AG 2026
Y. Hernádez Heredia et al. (Eds.): IWAIPR 2025, LNCS 16328, pp. 207–218, 2026.
https://doi.org/10.1007/978-3-032-11358-0_17

and use of tools such as the James Webb Space Telescope (JWST) [7]. Blackbody emitters output a pattern of electromagnetic waves with an uneven distribution of intensities for different wavelengths, called spectra. Within this pattern there is much information: the wavelength of its peak informs of the body's temperature by Wien's law; absorption lines that are unique for each element can show the composition of the blackbody and the position of these lines within the pattern can be shifted depending on the relative velocity of the object [8, 9]. This shift (usually towards infrared wavelengths) is caused by the Doppler's effect where velocity affects the frequency of waves [10]. Stellar classification serves as a cornerstone of astronomy, providing a framework for understanding and characterizing the diversity of celestial objects. This classification is based on the spectral properties which refer to the lines and bands that appear in the spectrum of an astronomical object, and is produced by the absorption or emission of light at specific wavelengths by the chemical elements present in the object [11, 12]. Photometric filters, on the other hand, are tools used in astronomical observations to isolate and measure the intensity of light in specific wavelength ranges. Photometric filters commonly used in stellar classification include i, r, z, k, and u [13]. Redshift is a measure of how much the light from an astronomical object has shifted toward the red due to the expansion of the universe. This phenomenon is crucial in determining the distance of distant astronomical objects [14]. The terms alpha and delta are used in astronomy to indicate right ascension and declination, respectively, which are the two coordinates used to specify the position of an object in the sky in the equatorial coordinate system [15].

When studying stars, the Harvard spectral classification scheme, developed in the late 1800s and refined by Annie Jump Cannon in 1924, is one such system that classifies stars based on their temperature, which is determined by the strength of the hydrogen lines present in their spectra [16]. This classification scheme has been instrumental in our understanding of stellar evolution [17]. Quasars are a class of active galactic nuclei (AGN). They are powered by the accretion of matter onto a supermassive black hole surrounded by an accretion disk [18]. Most quasar spectra from ultraviolet to optical wavelengths can be characterized by a featureless continuum and a series of mostly broad emission line features; compared with galaxies or stars, these spectra are remarkably similar from one quasar to another. A quasar's spectra have a larger redshift than stars. Galaxies are formed by stars, interstellar gas, and dust, which can occupy hundreds of thousands of light-years. Its spectral characteristics will be a result of the combination of the spectral information of millions of stars and the absorption lines from its gas and dust [19, 20]. The importance of stellar classification and spectral characteristics in astronomy cannot be overstated, since they serve as a primary task for the study of celestial objects [21]. The spectral characteristics of stars, galaxies, and quasars provide a wealth of information about their physical properties and the large-scale structure of the Universe [21]. However, with the advent of large sky survey projects such as the Sloan Digital Sky Survey (SDSS) and the Large Sky Area Multi-Object Fiber Spectroscopic Telescope (LAMOST), vast amounts of spectral data are being generated [22]. Manual analysis of this data is not feasible due to its sheer volume, hence the need for Artificial Intelligence [20].

Zhao et al. (2022) [22] developed a robust ensemble convolutional neural network (ECNN) for the classification of massive stellar spectra. The methodology involved the design of six distinct convolutional neural networks (CNNs) as classifiers to recognize the spectra in DR16. These classifiers were then integrated in an ensemble learning manner, based on the cross-entropy testing error of the spectra at different signal-to-noise ratios. This innovative approach resulted in a one-dimensional ECNN strategy that achieved a classification accuracy of 95.0% for stellar spectra, surpassing the accuracy of traditional methods such as principal component analysis and support vector machine models. A study conducted by Li, Lin, and Qiu (2019) [23] addressed the challenge of efficiently and accurately handling large amounts of spectral data by focusing on classifying stellar spectra, assuming the absence of perfect absolute flux calibration, a scenario that arises when considering spectra from the Guo Shou Jing Telescope (also known as the Large Sky Area Multi-Object Fiber Spectroscopic Telescope, LAMOST). Their proposal involves two key techniques: first, spectrum normalization based on a seventeenth-order polynomial fit; second, a random forest (RF) classification of the stellar spectra. The experiments conducted on four stellar spectral libraries demonstrated the effectiveness of the RF in classifying stellar spectra. Tao et al. (2018) [24] introduced an automated method for galaxy spectral classification through machine learning. Utilizing a dataset of 10,000 galaxy spectra from SDSS DR14, they applied algorithms such as logistic regression, random forest, and linear SVM to improve the efficiency of galaxy spectral classification and aid in the study of galaxy properties and evolution. Brito do Nascimento et al. (2019) [25] introduce a sophisticated hierarchical learning framework that links artificial neural networks within an integrated system, improving the certainty and clarity of classifications by using a larger dataset compared to previous studies and advanced filtering and processing techniques for spectral data, including redshift correction, dual filtering using the Savitzky-Golay filter, and wavelength interval selection.

Spectral characteristics hold a central position in the realm of astronomical research, serving as a crucial factor in the classification of celestial entities such as stars, galaxies, and quasars. The integration of Artificial Intelligence has instigated a significant transformation in this field. It has automated the classification process, thereby facilitating the efficient management of the extensive data generated by contemporary astronomical surveys.

The following is an outline of the contributions that have been made to draw attention to the relevance of the work that will be presented in this study:

o StellarNet is the main contribution of this proposal, a novel Deep Convolutional Neural Network of 1D Separable Convolutional blocks for stellar classification based on spectral characteristics.

o A comparative analysis was conducted between Minority Class Balance and the Synthetic Minority Over-sampling Technique (SMOTE), confirming the superiority of SMOTE for tasks similar to the one evaluated, thereby highlighting its effectiveness in addressing class imbalance issues.

o The results obtained during the performance evaluation confirmed the reliability of the proposed architecture of StellarNet in multi-class stellar classification, obtaining remarkable values of around 97% for each metric evaluated.

o A streaming processing pipeline has been developed using the proposed StellarNet model, the pipeline incorporates a streaming learning approach that allows self-maintenance of the model and enables real-time classification of captured spectral characteristics data, thereby facilitating task automation and providing labeled data that can be used for further study and future research.

2 Materials and Methods

2.1 Data

In this study was used the Stellar Classification Dataset - SDSS17, which comprises 100,000 space observations captured by the Sloan Digital Sky Survey (SDSS). Each observation is characterized by 17 feature columns and one class column that classifies it as a star, galaxy, or quasar. The Stellar Classification Dataset - SDSS17, utilized in the project, is a comprehensive collection of data that provides a wealth of information about celestial objects. This dataset is derived from the Sloan Digital Sky Survey (SDSS), which has made use of a dedicated 2.5 m wide-angle optical telescope to capture images of more than a quarter of the sky. The dataset comprises several features, each providing unique insights into the objects being studied. The alpha and delta represent the Right Ascension and Declination angles respectively, providing the precise location of the object in the celestial sphere. The dataset also includes photometric data captured through various filters: u (Ultraviolet), g (Green), r (Red), i (Near Infrared), and z (Infrared) [26, 27]. These photometric measurements provide a spectrum of light intensities, which are crucial in determining the physical properties of these celestial objects. The redshift value is another significant feature in this dataset. It measures the shift in wavelength due to the Doppler effect, which can be used to calculate the distance and velocity of an object relative to the observer. For this particular study, only spectral characteristics (alpha, delta, u, g, r, i, z, and redshift) were considered. Other features that don't add domain knowledge were discarded.

2.2 Exploratory Data Analysis

Analysis of the distribution of the dataset reveals a significant imbalance between classes. Specifically, the dataset contains 59,445 tuples for GALAXY, 21,594 for STAR, and 18,961 for QSO. These numbers represent 59.4% of the dataset for GALAXY and only 19.0% for QSO. Training a model on such a highly unbalanced dataset could lead to biased results. Therefore, data balancing techniques are employed to mitigate this problem. Two specific approaches are investigated to determine which provides superior results: simple minimum class balance and the SMOTE. These methods are used to ensure a more balanced representation of classes in the dataset, thereby increasing the reliability of the model's predictions.

When analyzing the correlation of the spectral characteristics, it was observed that there are several instances of correlation among the spectral characteristics. These correlations can be divided into two different domains, the first domain is characterized by a maximum positive correlation with a value of 1, which includes the spectral features g, u, and z. The second domain is characterized by a high positive correlation, with values ranging from 0.43 to 0.96, encompassing the spectral features i, r, and redshift.

2.3 Balancing Data

In the pursuit of a balanced dataset, the minimum class balance approach was adopted to limit the size of all classes larger than 20,000 tuples to the size of the smallest class containing over 18,000 tuples. While this approach ensures a high degree of balance across all classes, it is not without its drawbacks. In particular, it results in the loss of approximately 50% of the data set. This significant reduction in data could potentially have a negative impact on the robustness and generalizability of models trained on this dataset. Therefore, it is crucial to weigh the benefits of class balancing against the potential loss of information in this context. In response to the data reduction strategy previously discussed, an alternative approach was implemented to balance the dataset without discarding data. The SMOTE was applied, which is a widely recognized method for addressing class imbalance in machine learning [28]. This imbalance can significantly degrade the performance of predictive models and is characterized by a severe disproportion in the distribution of classes within a dataset.

The SMOTE algorithm addresses this issue by generating synthetic instances of the minority class. The procedure involves selecting a vector from the minority class and identifying its k nearest neighbors. A synthetic point is then interpolated along the line segment connecting the chosen vector and one of its neighbors. This process is iteratively performed until a balance between the classes is achieved. By applying SMOTE, the dataset is balanced not by losing data but by generating more synthetic data. This approach ensures that no information is lost, potentially enhancing the robustness and generalizability of models trained on this balanced dataset. The following Table 1 provides a detailed comparison of the datasets balanced using the Minimum Class Balance method and the SMOTE.

Table 1. Results of Both Balance Approaches

	Class	Amount	%
Min. Class Blance	GALAXY	20000	33.9
	QSO	18961	32.2
	STAR	20000	33.9
Total	**58961**		
SMOTE Balance	Class	Amount	%
	GALAXY	59445	33.3
	QSO	59445	33.3
	STAR	59445	33.3
Total	**178335**		

2.4 StellarNet Architecture

The features of the dataset (alpha, delta, u, g, r, i, z, redshift) were subjected to min-max normalization, transforming them to a scale of 0–1. This process improves computational processing and prevents model bias due to significant numerical differences. Meanwhile, the target (class) was processed using one hot encode to convert classes to vectors, which is beneficial for predictive models because it allows the model to understand categorical data as a form of numerical input. Applying min-max normalization and one-hot encoding techniques ensures efficient computational processing, prevents model bias, and allows the model to better understand the input data.

The data sets were divided into three subsets: 40% for training, 30% for testing, and the remaining 30% for validation. A significant portion of the data was reserved for testing and validation to evaluate the model's performance on unseen data, thereby providing an estimate of its potential real-world applicability and effectiveness. This approach underscores the importance of rigorous model validation in predictive analytics to ensure that the models developed are robust and reliable in different scenarios.

A variety of approaches have been adopted in stellar classification, including machine learning techniques such as decision trees, support vector machines, and random forests, all of which are widely used [21, 23, 24]. At the same time, dense neural networks within deep learning strategies have been used to address similar challenges [22, 25]. The goal of this research is to design a 1D Deep Convolutional Neural Network, consisting of separable convolutional blocks, to perform the task of stellar classification. The Stellar-Net architecture, a 1D Convolutional Neural Network with Separable Convolutions, is systematically organized into three main flows: the input flow, mid flow, and output flow these are detailed in Fig. 1.

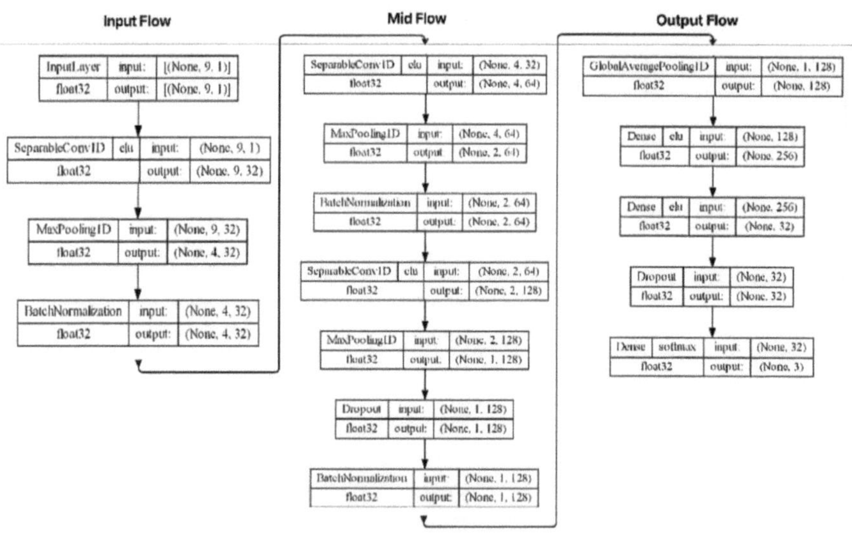

Fig. 1. StellarNet Architecture.

Input Flow: The architecture begins with an input layer designed to accommodate data that matches the shape of the feature set. This is followed by a SeparableConv1D layer, which is configured with 32 filters, a kernel size of 2, an elu activation function, and padding set to 'same'. The output from this layer is then processed through a MaxPooling1D layer with a pool size of 2, followed by a BatchNormalization layer.

Mid Flow: The mid flow consists of two distinct blocks of layers. Each block incorporates a SeparableConv1D layer (with 64 and 128 filters respectively, a kernel size of 2 for the first block and 1 for the second block, and an elu activation function), succeeded by a MaxPooling1D layer (pool size 2), and a BatchNormalization layer. Notably, the second block also integrates a Dropout layer with a dropout rate selected from [0.1, 0.2, 0.25].

Output Flow: The final phase, or the output flow, initiates with a GlobalAveragePooling1D layer. This is followed by two Dense layers: the first with units selected from [256, 512, 1024, 2048] and an elu activation function; the second with units selected from [32, 64, 128] and also an elu activation function. A Dropout layer with a rate selected from [0.7, 0.8] is applied preceding the final Dense output layer. This output layer consists of 3 units (corresponding to the three classes) and uses a softmax activation function to return the class probability vector.

The model is compiled using the Adam optimizer with a learning rate selected from [0.003, 0.0003], categorical cross-entropy as the loss function, and accuracy as the evaluation metric. StellarNet has a total of 52,869 parameters, of which 52,421 are trainable and 448 are not. Optimal values for dropouts, dense units, and learning rate of the architecture are determined by hyper-parameter tuning using Keras Tuner. The random search of hyperparameters was performed using both training set and validation set, with a search space of 5 due to each defined variable, the max trials parameters is set to 25, even if this value does not match the total parameters combination is a very good value to try parameter combinations without such a large processing time. The hyperparameter search which is performed for 30 training epochs is detailed in Table 2.

Table 2. Hyperparameters Settings

Hyperparameter	Best Value	Search Values
Dense Unit	1024	[256, 512, 1024, 2048]
FDense Unit	64	[32, 64, 128]
Dropout	0.25	[0.1, 0.2, 0.25]
FDropout	0.7	[0.7, 0.8]
lr	0.0003	[0.003, 0.0003]

Total Search Space: 144

The training process was performed over 250 epochs using both the training and validation sets with a batch size of 1024, which greatly accelerated the process. Techniques such as learning rate reduction and dropout layer were used in conjunction with real-time hyperparameter monitoring via Tensorboard to prevent overfitting of the proposed model. The process was conducted on an Intel(R) Core(TM) i7-12700 H computer with a 2.30 GHz CPU, an NVIDIA GeForce RTX 3060 8 GB GPU, and 16 GB RAM DDR5.

2.5   Real-Time Processing Pipeline

The final purpose of StellarNet is to facilitate real-time data labelling of incoming spectral characteristics and photometric filters captured by digital sky surveys and astronomical observatories. To achieve this, a real-time processing pipeline as depicted in Fig. 2 has been developed using Kafka and PySpark for streaming processing.

The captured data is sent to an input Kafka topic, where the core of the streaming processing pipeline is designed to listen to this input, perform preprocessing, inference, and, if used, streaming learning. The results, along with the classification using the proposed StellarNet architecture, are then returned to the output Kafka topic. Streaming processing is performed with a window time of 200 ms, ensuring timely and efficient data processing. Streaming learning, which is performed within the streaming processing pipeline that can be enabled or disabled, works in three main steps: first, the features obtained after applying preprocessing to the input stream are used to perform inference with the StellarNet model, which returns the predicted labels, Next, the features and the obtained labels are used to perform model training, thus obtaining a fine-tuned StellarNet, this approach is commonly known as streaming learning or online learning and is mainly used to perform self-maintenance of the deployed model [29].

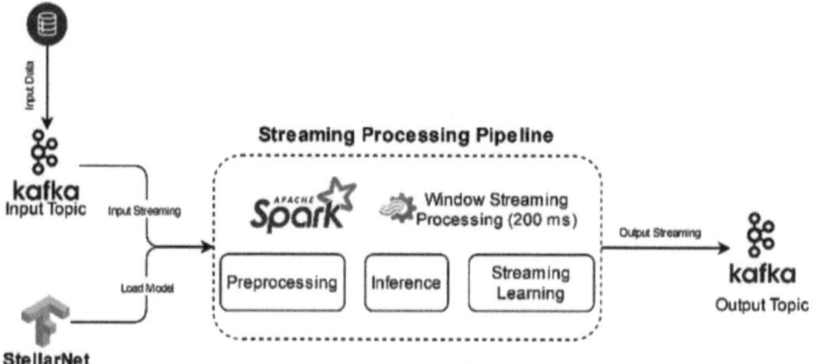

Fig. 2.   Streaming Processing Pipeline for Stellar Classification.

3   Results and Discussions

The early stop callback stopped the process at epoch 76 for each model after both models had been trained for 250 epochs. This occurred because the set patience value was exceeded without any improvement in the model based on the defined metrics. At this point, both models reported fairly similar accuracy values of approximately 0.97 for training and validation, with the Min Class approach slightly lower by 0.01. Both StellarNets models exhibit robust generalization capabilities, as evidenced by their consistent performance across the training and validation datasets.

The model using Min Class Balance is slightly less accurate, but given that the other approach, SMOTE Balance, is nearly twice as accurate and achieves slightly better results, it is considered superior between the two. This comparative analysis highlights the effectiveness of the SMOTE Balance approach in improving model accuracy and providing robust performance. After training is complete, the significant impact of the learning rate reduction callback on the model's performance on the validation data is evident. It also illustrates how the learning rate reduction stabilizes the model, keeping it close to the optimal metrics. Decreasing the learning rate also results in a smaller amplitude between the training and validation curve, since lower Adam learning rate enables gradual updates, ensuring stable convergence to the global minimum while avoiding overshooting or suboptimal areas [30]. The optimal values for each metric are reached at epoch 76, which is the model configuration saved by the checkpoint callback. This highlights the effectiveness of our approach, which combines advanced techniques such as learning rate reduction and early stopping to fine-tune the model and prevent overfitting. This ensures that StellarNets are not only accurate, but also robust and able to generalize well to unseen data.

The confusion matrices derived from both approaches show high-performance values. Both models show a remarkably low misclassification rate. However, both models have certain peculiarities, they are more sensitive to the correct classification of the star class. It seems that the spectral properties of stars differ more from galaxies and quasars than from each other, allowing the models to identify them more effectively.

Furthermore, an examination of the heatmaps of the confusion matrices reveals notable differences in the classification performance of the StellarNet model under the two strategies. The quantity of correctly predicted values for the QSO class is more discernible in the heatmap due to the slightly lighter shade of the corresponding square, indicating that the Minimum Class Balance strategy exhibits a lower classification performance for the QSO class. This is not the case for the SMOTE strategy, where all squares corresponding to correctly predicted classes exhibit a considerably darker shade, signifying near-maximum quantities.

The AUC score serves as a performance metric for the model per domain class, assessing the trade-off between true positives and false positives. The One vs. Rest (OvR) method is used to adapt the ROC curve and AUC score metrics, originally designed for binary classification, to multi class classification scenarios [31, 32].

StellarNet exhibits superior AUC values for the STAR class across the training, validation, and test sets, with an approximate value of 0.9980, approaching the maximum achievable value of 1. Overall, the model exhibits exceptional performance, with the lowest AUC values of 0.9908 and 0.9886 for the OvR in the test set for the SMOTE and Minimum Class Balance strategies, respectively. When examining the ROC curve and the AUC value, it was found that the results derived from the two strategies did not show significant differences. However, the STAR class performed slightly better in both cases, with the difference being slightly noticeable when comparing the AUC and ROC curves, as well as when examining the confusion matrix. Table 3 provides a detailed analysis and comparison of the performance of the StellarNet model using two different strategies. A cursory examination of the results reveals a slight superiority of the SMOTE approach in terms of performance. However, when considering the significant differences in data volume between the two strategies, this marginal superiority is amplified. This observation underscores the effectiveness of the SMOTE approach in handling unbalanced data sets, thereby improving the overall performance of the StellarNet model.

Table 3. Train, Test & Validation Metrics for Both Datasets

Min. Class Balance	Set	Accuracy	AUC	TP + TN	FP + FN
	Train	0.968	0.995	34242	1134
	Test	0.965	0.993	11376	417
	Validation	0.965	0.993	11373	419
SMOTE Balance	Set	Accuracy	AUC	TP + TN	FP + FN
	Train	**0.970**	0.995	104243	2758
	Test	**0.973**	**0.995**	34719	948
	Validation	**0.974**	**0.995**	34733	934

The values are highlighted in bold to emphasize superior performance

The proposed architecture of the 1D separable convolutional neural network, combined with its regularization techniques, allows StellarNet to achieve robustness in various class balance scenarios. This architecture, combined with an extensive hyperparameter search space of 144 and the strategic use of callbacks during the training phase, significantly increases the learning efficiency of the network, largely due to the ability to define, customize, adjust, and fine-tune the learning process to meet the specific requirements of the task at hand; such a level of specificity in the learning process is a key factor in optimizing the network's performance.

It is widely recognized that the primary limitation of artificial intelligence systems is the data itself, and StellarNet is not exempt from this challenge [33]. The most significant hurdle and limitation is the ability to establish communication with an institution that captures the spectral characteristics and photometric filters used to train our model, a critical step in validating the model on new observations and maximizing its potential.

Future research aims to evaluate the impact of incoming unbalanced data within the stream processing pipeline system with streaming learning. Since this approach has not undergone any balancing technique in the preprocessing step before training, this situation of training over uncontrolled unbalanced data could introduce bias into the model and affect its generalizability. In addition, is proposed to perform a thorough evaluation of the efficiency and effectiveness of the proposed model and streaming processing pipeline in a real-time acquisition and processing environment. For this, it will be necessary to establish contact with a center or institution equipped with the necessary tools to perform the task of capturing the spectral characteristics and photometric filters used in this study.

4   Conclusions

The application of StellarNet may contribute to the field of computational astrophysics by automating the classification of celestial objects as stars, galaxies, or quasars (QSOs) with an impressive accuracy of 97%. It uses spectral properties such as right ascension (alpha), declination (delta), photometric system filters (u, g, r, i, z), and redshift to perform classifications that can be used to integrate real-time automated data collection and labeling systems. By simplifying the identification and categorization of celestial objects, the proposed model allows researchers to focus more on data interpretation and hypothesis testing, thereby accelerating the pace of astronomical discovery. Its potential extends beyond research, demonstrating the power of artificial intelligence to transform space exploration. StellarNet is a testament to the synergy between astrophysics, astronomy, and artificial intelligence, providing a valuable resource for large sky surveys and researchers based on the income of automated labeling data without the need for manual sorting or annotations.

Disclosure of Interests. The authors have no competing interests to declare that are relevant to the content of this article.

References

1. Hebert, J.A.K.E.: Webb telescope continues to challenge big bang. Creation Science Update (2023)
2. Noble, F.W.: Surprising and unexpected discoveries the james Webb Space telescope will likely make: based upon our research. Appl. Phys. Res. **15**(1) 2023
3. Mann, A.: The James Webb Space Telescope prompts a rethink of how galaxies form. Proc. Natl. Acad. Sci. **120**(32), e2311963120 (2023)
4. Sutter, P.: AI is already helping astronomers make incredible discoveries. Here's how, Space (2023). https://www.space.com/astronomy-research-ai-future
5. Djorgovski, S.G., Mahabal, A.A., Graham, M.J., Polsterer, K., Krone-Martins, A.: Applications of AI in astronomy (2022). https://doi.org/10.48550/arXiv.2212.01493
6. En Kim, S.: The five big ways the james webb telescope will help astronomers understand the universe. Smithson. Mag. (2021)
7. Nasa Science: What is the james webb space telescope. Space Place. https://spaceplace.nasa.gov/james-webb-space-telescope
8. Hsieh, M.-L., et al.: Super planckian thermal radiation emitted from a nano-filament of photonic crystal: a direct imaging study. IEEE Photonics J. **11**, 1–8 (2019). https://doi.org/10.1109/jphot.2019.2948995
9. Sack, H.: Wilhelm Wien and the distribution law for blackbody radiation. SciHi Blog (2023). http://scihi.org/wilhelm-wien
10. Nolte, D.D.: The fall and rise of the Doppler effect. Phys. Today **73**(3), 30–35 (2020). https://doi.org/10.1063/PT.3.4429
11. Gray, R.O., Corbally, C.J.: Stellar spectral classification. Princeton University Press (2009)
12. Kaler, J.B.: Stars and their spectra: an introduction to the spectral sequence. Cambridge University Press (1989)
13. Bessell, M.S.: UBVRI passbands. Publ. Astron. Soc. Pac. **102**(656), 1181 (1990). https://doi.org/10.1086/132749
14. Hubble, E.: A relation between distance and radial velocity among extra-galactic nebulae. Proc. Natl. Acad. Sci. **15**(3), 168–173 (1929). https://doi.org/10.1073/pnas.15.3.168
15. Smart, W.M.: Text-book on spherical astronomy. Cambridge University Press (1931)
16. Swinburne: Harvard Spectral Classification. COSMOS. Harvard Spectral Classification | COSMOS (swin.edu.au)

17. Tonkin, S.: A guide to stellar spectral classifications. BBC Sky Night Mag. (2018). https://www.skyatnightmagazine.com/advice/a-guide-to-stellar-spectral-classifications
18. Rakshit, S., Stalin, C.S., Kotilainen, J.: Spectral properties of quasars from sloan digital sky survey data release 14: the catalog. Astrophys. J. Suppl. Ser. **249**(17), 24 (2020)
19. Vanden Berk, D.E., et al.: Composite quasar spectra from the sloan digital sky survey. Astron. J. **122**, 549–564 (2001)
20. Wang, L.-L.: Spectral classification of galaxies and identification of galactic HII regions based on LAMOST spectral line features. Publ. Astron. Soc. Pac. **131**(077001), 4 (2019)
21. Yang, P., Yang, G., Zhang, F., et al.: Spectral classification and particular spectra identification based on data mining. Arch. Comput. Methods Eng. **28**, 917–935 (2021). https://doi.org/10.1007/s11831-020-09401-93
22. Zhuang, Z., Jiyu, W., Bin, J.: Automated stellar spectra classification with ensemble convolutional neural network (2022). https://doi.org/10.1155/2022/4489359
23. Li, X., Lin, Y., Qiu, K.: Stellar spectral classification and feature evaluation based on a random forest. Res. Astron. Astrophys. **19**(8), 111 (2019). https://doi.org/10.1088/1674-4527/19/8/111
24. Tao, Y., Zhang, Y., Cui, C., Zhang, G.: Automated Spectral Classification of Galaxies using Machine Learning Approach on Alibaba Cloud AI platform (PAI) (2018). https://doi.org/10.48550/arXiv.1801.04839
25. Brito do Nascimento, F.J., Arantes Filho, L.R., Nogueira Frutuoso Guimarães, L.: Intelligent classification of supernovae using artificial neural networks. Inteligencia Artif. **22**(3), 39–60 (2019). https://doi.org/10.4114/intartif.vol22iss63pp39-60
26. Abdurro'Uf, et al.: The seventeenth data release of the sloan digital sky surveys: complete release of MaNGA, MaStar, and APOGEE-2 Data. Astrophys. J. Suppl. Ser. **259**, 35. https://doi.org/10.3847/1538-4365/ac4414
27. Soriano, P.F.: Stellar classification dataset-SDSS17 (2022). https://www.kaggle.com/fedesoriano/stellar-classification-dataset-sdss17
28. Chawla, N.V., Bowyer, K.W., Hall, L.O., Kegelmeyer, W.P.: SMOTE: synthetic minority over-sampling technique. J. Artif. Intell. Res. **16**, 321–357 (2002). https://doi.org/10.1613/jair.953
29. Benczúr, A.A., Kocsis, L., Pálovics, R.: Online machine learning in big data streams: overview. In: Encyclopedia of Big Data Technologies, Sakr, S., Zomaya, A.Y. (eds.) Springer, Cham (2019). https://doi.org/10.1007/978-3-319-77525-8_326
30. Martínez Pazos, J.F., Orellana García, A., Batard Lorenzo, D., Gulín González, J.: X-COVNet: externally validated model for computer-aided diagnosis of pneumonia-like lung diseases in chest X-Rays. In: Correia, L., Rosá, A., Garijo, F. (eds.). Advances in Artificial Intelligence – IBERAMIA 2024. IBERAMIA 2024. Lecture Notes in Computer Science, vol. 15277. Springer, Cham (2025). https://doi.org/10.1007/978-3-031-80366-6_14
31. Trevisan, V.: Multiclass classification evaluation with ROC curves and ROC AUC. Towards Data Science (2022). https://towardsdatascience.com/multiclass-classification-evaluation-with-roc-curves-and-roc-auc-294fd4617e3a
32. Scikit-Learn: Multiclass Receiver Operating Characteristic (ROC). https://scikit-learn.org/stable/auto_examples/model_selection/plot_roc.html. Last Accessed 15 July 2023
33. Zhang, K.: The data limitations of Artificial Intelligence algorithms and the political ethics problems caused by it. In: Big Data Analytics for Cyber-Physical System in Smart City, Atiquzzaman, M., Yen, N., Xu, Z. (eds.). Advances in Intelligent Systems and Computing, vol. 1303, Springer, Singapore (2021). https://doi.org/10.1007/978-981-33-4572-0_64

Description of the Closed Loop of an Object of Interest

Anatol Mitsiukhin[(✉)] and Nikolai Listopad

Belarusian State University of Informatics and Radioelectronics, P. Brovki Str. 6, Minsk 220013, Republic of Belarus
mityuhin@bsuir.by

Abstract. The abstract Solving problems related to digital representation of contour images is relevant for many applications, such as environmental monitoring using aerospace sensing technology for the Earth's surface. The method involves sequential application of three algorithms for 2-D processing of the initial data. Spatio-temporal representation of the initial data, coordinate transformation and dispersion filtering are used. At the first stage of processing, spatial data are transformed into a 2-D sequence. At the second stage of processing, the obtained data are represented by coordinate transformation coefficients. At the third stage of processing, transform filtering is implemented based on the dispersion criterion. The efficiency of describing the contour of the observed object is achieved by representing the contour as a functional series of expansion coefficients in terms of discrete eigenfunctions of the covariance matrix of spatial data. Application of the dispersion criterion to the coordinate transformation coefficients allows for virtually lossless data compression. The image restoration error in this case approaches zero. The article shows a solution to the problem of compact representation of an object contour based on statistical and transformation approaches. In this case, the efficiency is estimated from the point of view of virtually lossless data compression. The image restoration error after redundancy elimination in this case approaches zero.

Keywords: Contour · Coding · Compression

1 Introduction

When solving problems related to detection, search for specific objects in images, recognition and identification, the problem of effectively describing the shape of the object arises [1]. The same problem arises when identifying objects of interest in industrial control tasks. An always relevant task is the problem of environmental monitoring using aerospace sensing methods, for example, flooded areas, movement of catastrophic air flow areas [2, 3], etc. In these cases, a closed loop is a complete and compact representation of the external spatial parameters of the observation object. In many applications, such as topography, medical image analysis, etc., to reduce the amount of digital data describing the object of interest, it is possible to replace the set of pixels depicting the object with a description of its contour [4]. For example, a possible approach to solving

© The Author(s), under exclusive license to Springer Nature Switzerland AG 2026
Y. Hernádez Heredia et al. (Eds.): IWAIPR 2025, LNCS 16328, pp. 219–227, 2026.
https://doi.org/10.1007/978-3-032-11358-0_18

the problem of standardization of cytological diagnostics is based on the use of methods and techniques for recognizing patterns represented as contours of the nucleus and cell. Contour representation is suitable for cases where the focus is on the geometric characteristics of the object: border length, area of the region, bends, outlines, concavities [5]. External representation is usually chosen for applications that care about the shape characteristics of the region or the shape features of the observed object. After segmentation, as a rule, raw images are obtained, represented in the form of pixels located along the contour of the object. Efficient transmission or storage of segmentation data is based on their compact representation [6]. The article proposes effective mathematical approaches (foundations) for representing and descriptions of segmented closed loop data.

2   Problem Formulation

It is assumed that the observed image has been segmented [7]. The image details contained within objects or within the background are of no interest. The segmented image is represented as areas or objects of various shapes. The task of describing the shape of an object in an image arises when it is necessary to recognize or identify individual areas or objects in images, when the outlines of the objects present in the image are important. The solution to the problem of recognizing an object of interest is significantly complicated if the reference shapes are distorted by noise and are limited to a relatively small set. Accordingly, the task of classifying the shape of an object becomes more complicated, for example, using a neural network or applying optimal correlation algorithms for detection and recognition [8]. Describing the shape of an object is not widely used in practice if direct calculation of the shape parameters seems excessively expensive both from the computational and time points of view. For a number of applications, for example, remote multispectral observation and analysis of areas of the Earth's surface, it is desirable to use image processing methods that significantly reduce the time, frequency and energy costs of transmitting or storing high-dimensional data. For example, for Belarus, constant monitoring of territories from possible flooding in the southwestern regions of the country, from forest fires throughout the country is relevant. Storing information about constantly observed natural objects requires the use of significant hardware (server) resources. Energy consumption and heat output of server resources of neural networks is also currently becoming a serious problem.

2.1   Problem Solution

A distinctive feature of many images is the property of a significant level of correlation of the data that describe the images. The presence of this property allows for the implementation of effective representation and description of data. For the practice of effective data description, an approach is known in which the representation of data is reduced to transformational Fourier-like descriptors [9]. In the general case, this approach corresponds to the method of linear transformation coding of signals, for example, audio processes, 2-D signals. Signals by means of the appropriate linear orthogonal transform (Fourier, Hadamard, Hartley, Haar, wavelet transform) can be reduced to a form with partially eliminated redundancy. However, Fourier-like transforms are not optimal in terms of description efficiency and reliability. The feature of high correlation or, in other words, linear dependence is especially evident for images of objects in the form of contours. The presence of this property allows for a more effective representation and description of data, and high accuracy of restoration of the original image. A method for compactly describing linearly dependent values of contour pixels is proposed by representing them as random elements of a Cartesian product. In this case, it becomes possible to describe an object of interest based on a statistical approach [10], operate with such statistical characteristics as the mean, variance, and covariance. Since the covariance matrix is symmetric, there is an orthonormal basis for such a matrix in the form of eigenvectors. This basis can be used to decompose (encode) the original data. The result of encoding data with strong correlations between adjacent image elements is their complete decorrelation. The transition to a description in the basis of eigenvectors eliminates redundancy by redistributing the signal energy over the coordinates. The main share of the energy falls on the coefficients with small numbers (low spatial frequencies), and only a small part of it falls on others. Complete decorrelation of the data is obtained if the transposed matrix of eigenvectors of the covariance matrix of the image is used as the transformation kernel. Coefficients with small amplitude are omitted or quantized to a small number of levels, which allows using a smaller number of code bits for transmission over a communication channel or for storage. For effective transmission (storage) of the contour image, it is sufficient to use transformants that satisfy the dispersion criterion. Although the calculation of eigenvalues and eigenvectors is a comparatively labor-intensive computational task, at present its solution is quite feasible in real processing time.

3 Theoretical Principles

Let the original image consist $M \times N$ of pixels. The coordinate transformation of a set of correlated random variables $\mathbf{G}$ into uncorrelated variables $\hat{\mathbf{G}}$ in the generalized case and vector representation is determined by the expression

$$\hat{\mathbf{G}} = \mathbf{A}\mathbf{G}, \tag{1}$$

where $\mathbf{G}$ is the image matrix whose elements are numbers $g \in \mathbb{Z}^{+}$;

$\hat{\mathbf{G}}$ is the transform matrix whose elements are numbers $g \in \mathbb{R}$;

$\mathbf{A}$ is the transform matrix whose elements are numbers is the matrix of orthonormal functions of the transformation basis whose elements are numbers $a \in \mathbb{R}$. The order of the matrix $\mathbf{A}$ is M^2

$$c_m = M^2 N.$$

The computational complexity of expression (1) for the basic nonlinear operation multiplication (multiplicative complexity) in the field over real numbers is expressed as The computational quality of algorithm (1) can be significantly improved if we use the statistical nature of the observed object of interest. The image of any closed contour can be considered in the statistical relationship of changes in random variables. An estimate of the magnitude of this relationship is given by the covariance matrix Σ. It becomes possible to implement an optimal decorrelation process for the purpose of a compact representation of the coefficients (1) in the transformation domain. In addition, the statistical approach of implementation (1) allows for accurate efficiency estimates at the preliminary stage of data processing, which is important for some applications, in particular medicine, where lossy (distorted) data compression is unacceptable.

3.1 Efficient Representation and Description of the Contour

We represent the contour image as a discrete sequence $g(x, y)$, where $(x, y) \in \mathbb{Z}^2$. The elements of the sequence $g(x, y) = (g(x_1, y_1), g(x_2, y_2), ..., g(x_l, y_l))$ with length L define the energy characteristics of the image in the Cartesian coordinate system. The coordinates (x_i, y_j) and (x_{i+1}, y_{j+1}) are the nearest neighbors along the contour line. A digital contour image consisting L of pixels can be represented by a matrix

$$\mathbf{X} = \begin{pmatrix} \mathbf{x}_1 & \mathbf{x}_2 \end{pmatrix}, \tag{2}$$

where $\mathbf{x}_1 = (x_1, x_2, ..., x_L)$;

$$\mathbf{x}_2 = (x_1, x_2, ..., x_L).$$

The order of the matrix (2) displays only the contour line. In practical cases, the value of the matrix order is $X \ll (M \times N)$. Obviously, ordering the pixels as a matrix $\mathbf{X}$, i. e. without the set of pixels that make up the entire image $\mathbf{G}$, will reduce the computational complexity of processing. In addition, processing a significantly smaller array of data allows us to reduce the computational costs at the stage of calculating eigenvectors and eigenvalues. Each element $g(x_i, y_j)$ of the sequence $g(x, y)$ corresponds to a two-dimensional vector $\mathbf{x} \in \mathbb{R}^2$. Thus, the elements of the matrix $\mathbf{X}$ are considered as a set of realizations of a two-dimensional random process.

The second stage of the proposed solution to the problem under consideration is encoding by decomposing the matrix in the basis of the eigenvectors of its covariance matrix $\sum_X$. In this case, the matrix $\mathbf{X}$ is represented by a functional series in the basis of the eigenvectors of the matrix $\sum_X$. The encoding result is determined by the coefficient matrix

$$\hat{\mathbf{X}} = \mathbf{A}^T \mathbf{X}, \tag{3}$$

where $\mathbf{A}$ is the matrix of eigenvectors over the field of real numbers.

The transition from the coefficient domain to the spatial domain is written as

$$\mathbf{X} = \mathbf{A}\hat{\mathbf{X}}. \tag{4}$$

The computational complexity of the contour description can be reduced if operations (3) and (4) are performed taking into account the analysis of the values of the coefficients of the eigenvalue matrix $\hat{\Lambda}$ of the covariance matrix $\hat{\sum}$. The matrix $\hat{\Lambda}$ describes the distribution of the variances of the coefficients of the matrix $\hat{\mathbf{X}}$ (3). The variance distribution function in the matrix is defined by the expression

$$\hat{\Lambda} = \mathrm{diag}\big(\mathrm{eig}(\mathrm{cov}(\hat{\mathbf{X}}))\big) = \mathrm{diag}\big(\hat{\sigma}^2\big), \tag{5}$$

where $\hat{\Lambda}$ is the diagonal matrix of eigenvalues of the covariance matrix $\hat{\Sigma}$.

The result of (5) is a variance matrix whose main diagonal elements are positive numbers $\hat{\lambda}_{11}$, $\hat{\lambda}_{22}$. The remaining $\hat{\lambda}_{1j} = \hat{\lambda}_{2j} = 0$. Eigenvalues $\hat{\lambda}_{ij}$, $i = 1, 2; j = 1, 2,...,L$ in the transformation coefficient domain correspond to the variances of the coordinates of two-dimensional vectors $\hat{\mathbf{X}} = (\hat{\mathbf{x}}_1, \hat{\mathbf{x}}_2, ..., \hat{\mathbf{x}}_L)$.

For a compact description of contour information and transmission (storage), it is sufficient to use only the coefficients $\hat{x}_{ij} \in \hat{\mathbf{X}}$, which are characterized by the maximum values of the variances $\hat{\lambda}_{ij}$. After rearranging the variances in matrix (5) according to the rule $\hat{\lambda}_{ij} \leq \hat{\lambda}_{i(j+1)}$, a filtering matrix is formed, the structure of which allows the area of coefficients $\hat{x}_{ij}$ to be stored or transmitted over the channel to be selected. In this case, the efficiency of encoding the original contour image $\mathbf{G}$ is determined by the number of coefficients falling into this zone. In addition, rearranging the rows of the matrix $\hat{\Lambda}$ determines the type of truncated matrix for restoring the original data, which also increases the overall efficiency of contour image processing.

Illustration of the method of effective representation and description of the contour
A more practical hardware and software implementation of operation (2) is presented in another variant. To do this:

1. Form the mathematical expectation vector

$$\overline{\mathbf{x}} = E(\mathbf{X}),$$

where E is the averaging operator of the vectors of the matrix $\mathbf{X}$.
2. Form the mathematical expectation matrix $\overline{\mathbf{X}} = (\overline{\mathbf{x}}\ \overline{\mathbf{x}})$.
3. Form the matrix $\mathbf{X}' = (\mathbf{X} - \overline{\mathbf{X}})$. The matrix $\mathbf{X}'$ describes a random process without the constant component of the original matrix.
4. The decomposition coefficients of the matrix $\hat{\mathbf{X}}'$ in the basis of the eigenvectors of the covariance matrix Σ_X are defined as

$$\hat{\mathbf{X}}' = \mathbf{A}^T \mathbf{X}', \tag{6}$$

where $\mathbf{A}$ is the matrix of eigenvectors of the covariance matrix over the field of real numbers.

5. Multiplying the matrix $\mathbf{A}$ by expression (6), we obtain the reconstructed coefficients of the original matrix $\mathbf{X}$

$$\mathbf{X} = \mathbf{A}\hat{\mathbf{X}}' + \overline{\mathbf{X}}. \tag{7}$$

6. A preliminary assessment of the effectiveness of contour image compression is obtained based on an analysis of the distribution of the variances of the transformants (5).
7. Taking into account (5), the transformant filtering zone and the truncated matrix $\mathbf{A}_\varphi$ are formed. Instead of using all the eigenvectors of the covariance matrix $\hat{\Sigma}$, a truncated matrix $\mathbf{A}_\varphi$ is constructed that includes only the eigenvectors corresponding to the largest values of variances $\hat{\sigma}^2$ (4). When restoring the contour image at the

channel output using (7), the filtered coordinates of the matrix $\mathbf{A}$ are replaced by vectors $\bar{\mathbf{x}} = E(\mathbf{X})$..

8. The contour restoration error that occurs when discarding $\hat{x}_{ij}$ coordinates is defined as

$$\varepsilon = E\{|| \triangle \mathbf{X}||^2\},\tag{8}$$

where $\triangle \mathbf{X} = \mathbf{X} - \tilde{\mathbf{X}}$;

$\tilde{\mathbf{X}}$ is the restored contour image in matrix form.

9. The effectiveness of the description of the contour of the observed object is estimated as

$$C_R = \frac{X_{bit} - \tilde{X}_{bit}}{X_{bit}},$$

where X_{bit} is the cost of transmitting (storing) data without compressing the contour image;

$\tilde{X}_{bit}$ is the cost of transmitting (storing) data with compression.

Coding example

Figure 1 shows an image of a lake whose contour needs to be described. The starting and ending points (x_i, x_j) have coordinates $(0, 11)$ and $(1, 10)$ respectively.

Keywords:

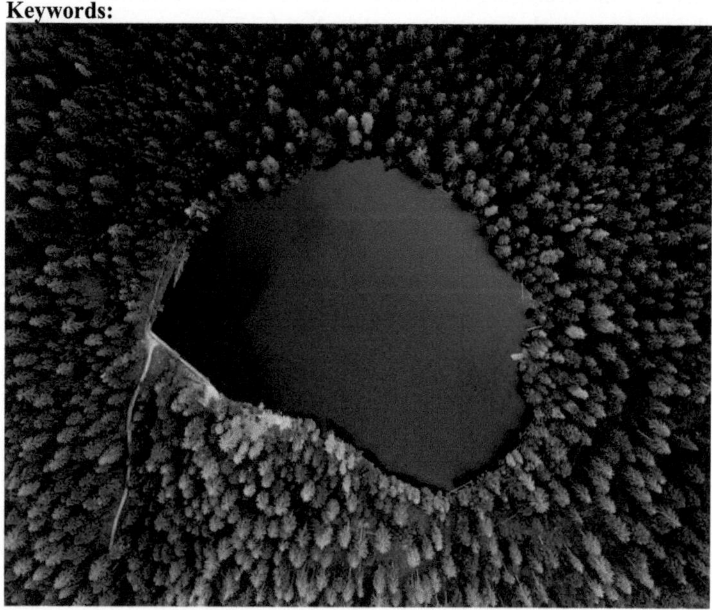

Fig. 1. Image of the object of interest

Below are digital representations of the lake contour image in the form of matrix vectors (2)

$$\mathbf{X} = \left(\mathbf{x}_1\ \mathbf{x}_2\right)^T = \begin{matrix} n \\ \mathbf{x}_1 \\ \mathbf{x}_2 \end{matrix} \begin{pmatrix} 1 & 2 & 3 & 4 & 5 & 6 & 7 & 8 & 9 & 10 & 11 & 12 \\ 0 & 1 & 2 & 3 & 4 & 5 & 6 & 7 & 8 & 9 & 10 & 11 \\ 11 & 13 & 15 & 16 & 17 & 18 & 18 & 18 & 18 & 18 & 19 & 20 \end{pmatrix} \rightarrow$$

$$\rightarrow \begin{matrix} n \\ \mathbf{x}_1 \\ \mathbf{x}_2 \end{matrix} \begin{pmatrix} 13 & 14 & 15 & 16 & 17 & 18 & 19 & 20 & 21 & 22 & 23 & 24 \\ 12 & 13 & 14 & 15 & 16 & 17 & 18 & 19 & 20 & 20 & 21 & 22 \\ 20 & 19 & 19 & 18 & 18 & 17 & 16 & 15 & 14 & 13 & 11 & 10 \end{pmatrix} \rightarrow$$

$$\rightarrow \begin{matrix} n \\ \mathbf{x}_1 \\ \mathbf{x}_2 \end{matrix} \begin{pmatrix} 25 & 26 & 27 & 28 & 29 & 30 & 31 & 32 & 33 & 34 & 35 & 36 \\ 22 & 21 & 20 & 20 & 20 & 21 & 20 & 19 & 18 & 17 & 16 & 14 \\ 9 & 8 & 7 & 6 & 5 & 4 & 3 & 2 & 1 & 0 & 0 & 0 \end{pmatrix} \rightarrow$$

$$\rightarrow \begin{matrix} n \\ \mathbf{x}_1 \\ \mathbf{x}_2 \end{matrix} \begin{pmatrix} 37 & 38 & 39 & 40 & 41 & 42 & 43 & 44 & 45 & 46 & 47 & 48 \\ 13 & 12 & 11 & 10 & 9 & 8 & 7 & 6 & 5 & 4 & 2 & 1 \\ 1 & 2 & 3 & 4 & 4 & 5 & 5 & 6 & 6 & 7 & 9 & 10 \end{pmatrix}.$$

To preliminarily assess the effectiveness of contour compression, the distribution of transformant variances (5) is calculated. Figure 2 shows a graph of the variance distribution $\hat{\sigma}^2$.

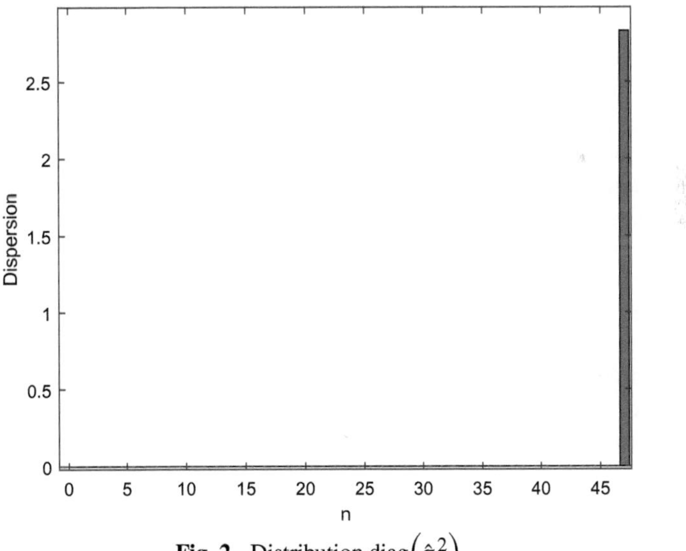

Fig. 2. Distribution $\mathrm{diag}\left(\hat{\sigma}^2\right)$

There are only two dominant values of transforms. All the signal energy in the coding region (4) is concentrated in two coefficients $\hat{\mathbf{x}}_{48} = \begin{pmatrix} -3,6165 \\ 3,6165 \end{pmatrix}$. In this case, the contour image is represented by two stored descriptors. The matrix $\mathbf{A}$ of size (48 $\times$

48) is transformed into a truncated matrix $\mathbf{A}_\varphi$ of order (48 × 1). In this case, the exact restoration of the original data is realized. The mean square error (8) is equal to $\varepsilon = 0$. The efficiency of the considered contour description method is equal to

$$C_R = \frac{X_{bit} - \tilde{X}_{bit}}{X_{bit}} = 0,956$$

or is $\simeq 95\%$.

4 Results and Their Discussion

1. The approach to reducing data redundancy was used, which took into account the statistical characteristics of the contour image. The presence of a high level of stochastic interrelation of the spatial coordinates of the contour image allows for a significant gain in compression compared to non-optimal Fourier-like, entropy or dictionary methods.
2. Since the original data were represented by the coefficients of the basis functions of the covariance matrix and the optimal algorithm for eliminating redundancy was used, it became possible to a priori estimate the efficiency of compression and the reliability of the obtained reconstructed data.
3 The considered approach to reducing data redundancy consisted in representing the pixels displaying the closed contour as random two-dimensional vectors. In this case, the description task is significantly simplified by reducing the dimensionality of the original processed data.
4. Instead of transmitting all the data describing the contour, it is sufficient to transmit (store) the coefficients characterized by the maximum values of variances.
5. The use of the dispersion criterion in describing the contour of the object of observation made it possible to perform data compression almost without losses.
6. Preliminary calculation of the dispersion distribution function Allows to speed up the process of transmission, processing and analysis of images, decipher its main characteristics and information features.
7. Simplifies the solution of problems, determination of boundaries or search for the definition of objects in images.
8. At present, the analytical method can be considered a practical computational procedure, since the calculation of the roots of the characteristic equations with the receipt of the kernel of the coding kernel for the original data sizes is not a computational problem.

4.1 Conclusion

1. An effective method for representing and describing an image in the form of data describing a closed contour of an object is proposed.
2. It was possible to obtain a significant gain in compression compared to non-optimal Fourier-like, entropy or dictionary methods.

3. In connection with the development of a modern high-speed electronic base for digital processing of signals and images, it is now possible to implement the processing of highly correlated signals in the current time mode using mathematically complex optimal algorithms in order to minimize the schemes of representation and description of such signals.
4. The use of the method in modern digital signal and image processing technology allows for effective transmission or storage of information about the shape of an object without distortion.
5. The Proposed Method is Feasible in Hardware and Software Implementation.
6. The subject area that the measurement method is aimed at includes such areas as object classification and pattern recognition, special electronic systems, industrial control, tomographic systems, dynamic medical diagnostics, image analysis, shape analysis, etc.

Disclosure of Interests. The authors have no competing interests to declare that are relevant to the content of this article.

References

1. Mitsiukhin, A.: Compressing the geospatial data of testing grounds. WSEAS Trans. Environ.Dev. **19**, 1386–1391 (2023). https://doi.org/10.37394/232015.2023.19.125
2. Zhu, X.: GIS for environmental applications a practical approach. Routledge, London (2016)
3. de Lange, N.: Geoinformatics in theory and practice: an integrated approach to geoinformation systems, remote sensing and digital image processing. Springer Spektrum, Berlin, Heidelberg (2020)
4. Longley, P.: Geographic information science & systems. Wiley, NJ (2015)
5. Gonzalez, R.C., Woods, R.E.: Digital image processing, 4th edn. Prentice Hall, New Jersey (2018)
6. Jahne, B.: Digital image processing. concepts. Algorithms, and Scientific Applications. Springer-Verlag, Heidelberg (2013)
7. Mitsiukhin, A.I., Konopelko, V.K.: Description of the binary image outline of the object of interest. Eighth Belarusian Space Congress. Proceedings of the Congress. Vol. 1, p. 250 253. OIPI NAS, Belarus, Minsk (2022)
8. Burger, W., Burge, M.J.: Digital image processing. Springer, London (2016)
9. Cover, T.M., Thomas, J.A.: Elements of information theory. John Wiley & Sons, Inc (2012)
10. Yan, L., Zhao, H., Lin, Y., Sun, Y.: Digital image compression. In: Math Physics Foundation of Advanced Remote Sensing Digital Image Processing. Springer, Singapore (2023)
11. Gray, R.M.: Entropy and information. Springer-Verlag, New York (2023)

A New Approach for Calculating the Collective Intensity of Circumstances of the Same Type in the M-LAMAC Model

Carlos Rafael Rodríguez-Rodríguez$^{(\boxtimes)}$, Yeleny Zulueta-Véliz,
Dainys Gainza Reyes, and Aylin Estrada Velazco

University of Informatics Sciences, Havana, Cuba
`{crodriguezr,yeleny,dgainza,avelazco}@uci.cu`

Abstract. Evaluating mitigating and aggravating circumstances in criminal liability poses significant challenges for judges, who must often make these assessments under uncertainty. While the M-LAMAC model assists judges in this task, its current framework lacks the ability to aggregate intensity values additively when circumstances of the same type must be combined—instead relying on minimum, maximum, or average values. This limitation restricts M-LAMAC's generality, particularly in cases requiring the application of Articles 81.1 and 81.2 of the Cuban Penal Code. To address this gap, we propose the 2-Tuple Linguistic Bounded Sum (2TLBS), a novel aggregation operator designed to compute the collective intensity of circumstances within the M-LAMAC model. We formally demonstrate its properties (commutativity, associativity, and non-decreasing monotonicity) and validate its practical utility through two criminal case studies. The results show that 2TLBS significantly improve the sanction intervals recommendation, highlighting its potential to enhance judicial decision-making.

Keywords: aggregation operator · judicial decision support · legal AI · 2-tuple
linguistic model · 2TLBS

1 Introduction

M-LAMAC [1] is a 2-tuple linguistic based model to support judges for assessing mitigating and aggravating circumstances in a criminal case. It provides structured decision support to determine appropriate punishment ranges, enhancing consistency and transparency in judicial deliberations. Figure 1 shows the structure of M-LAMAC.

In Step 4 of M-LAMAC, the collective intensity of all circumstances of the same type is calculated. At this point, the court may adopt one of the following attitudes:

1. The court may deem it sufficient, for sentencing purposes, to consider an overall impact equivalent to the one with the lowest intensity.
2. The court may consider it appropriate, for sentencing purposes, to take the total value as equivalent to the one with the highest intensity.
3. For sentencing purposes, all circumstances must be considered equally important, and the equilibrium point of their intensity must be sought.

Y. Hernádez Heredia et al. (Eds.): IWAIPR 2025, LNCS 16328, pp. 228–239, 2026.
https://doi.org/10.1007/978-3-032-11358-0_19

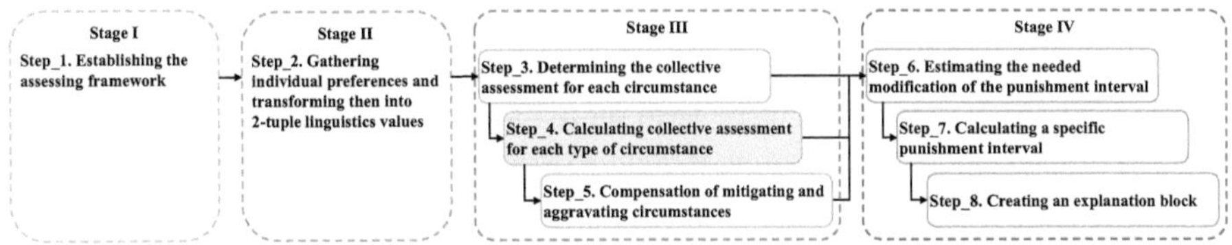

Fig. 1. Stages and steps of M-LAMAC [1].

4. Rather than selecting a single circumstance's intensity or averaging all of them, the overall intensity must be computed taken into account all available data.

To address attitudes 1–3, M-LAMAC includes three basic aggregation operators for the 2-tuple linguistic model [2]: *min*, *max*, and *average*.

However, the attitude 4 requires a handling that cannot be modeled with the conventional operators for the 2-tuple linguistic model [3]. See the following example:

Example 1. *Consider a case with two mitigating circumstances $C = \{c_1, c_2\}$ and intensity values $(s_2, 0.24)$ and $(s_3, -0.19)$. Given the specifics of this case, the judges will take into account both circumstances together to adjust the penal framework.*

In this context, according to Articles 81.1 and 81.2 of the Cuban Penal Code (CPC) [4], a punishment outside the initial interval's extremes may be forced, provided it is not less than half of the lower extreme nor greater than the upper extreme increased by half. In this case, the intensity of all circumstances of the same type must be aggregated to determine whether the sentence should fall within or outside the initial interval and to ascertain when the legally prescribed extremes should be applied.

This situation requires an upward reinforcement, such as that exhibited by *probabilistic sum* and *bounded sum* operators. Upon analyzing the behavior of these operators in [0, 1], we observe that the probabilistic sum attains the value of 1 only when at least one of the input arguments equals 1. This does not allow modeling the scenario where several circumstances of the same type require adjusting the interval to the extremes set by law. The bounded sum can model this behavior, but it is a numerical operator.

This paper introduces 2TLBS, a novel commutative, associative, and non-decreasing monotonic operator for 2-tuple linguistic model, specifically designed to address the additive aggregation requirement of circumstance intensities in judicial decision-making. The proposed operator extends the M-LAMAC capabilities to handle cases where existing aggregation methods (min/max/average) prove insufficient, particularly for legal scenarios requiring comprehensive assessment of cumulative circumstances.

The rest of the paper is organized as follows: Section 2 reviews the 2-tuple linguistic model; Section 3 introduces the 2TLBS operator; Section 4 details its integration into M-LAMAC; Section 5 resolves criminal case studies; conclusions are presented last.

2 Background on the 2-tuple Linguistic Model

The 2-tuple linguistic model [2, 3] is a computing with words model that represents the information with a pair of elements so-called 2-tuple linguistic, (s_i, α), where:

- $s_i \in S = \{s_0, \ldots, s_g\}$ is a linguistic term whose semantics are defined by a fuzzy membership function, and the syntax chosen according to the Fuzzy Linguistic Approach [5–7]. S is an linguistic term set (LTS) with cardinality $g + 1$.
- α, so-called symbolic translation, is a numerical value which indicate the translation of the fuzzy membership function that represents the closest term $s_i \in S$, if s_i does not match exactly the computerized linguistic information; see (1).

$$\alpha \in \begin{cases} [-0.5, 0.5) & \textit{if } s_i \in \{s_1, s_2, \ldots, s_{g-1}\} \\ [0, 0.5) & \textit{if } s_i = s_0 \\ [-0.5, 0) & \textit{if } s_i = s_g \end{cases} \tag{1}$$

A symbolic computation in $S = \{s_0, \ldots, s_g\}$ obtains a numerical value $\beta \in [0, g]$ that will be transformed into a 2-tuple linguistic value, (s_i, α), by means of the Δ_S function.

Definition 1. Let $S = \{s_0, \ldots, s_g\}$ be a LTS with cardinality $g + 1$, $\overline{S}$ the 2-tuple set associated with S defined as $\overline{S} = S \times [-0.5, 0.5)$, and $\beta \in [0, g]$ a value representing the result of a symbolic operation. The function $\Delta_S : [0, g] \to \overline{S}$ is given by (2)

$$\Delta_S(\beta) = (s_i, \alpha) \text{ with } \begin{cases} i = \textit{round}(\beta) \\ \alpha = \beta - i \end{cases} \tag{2}$$

where *round* is the rounding operator, $s_i \in S$ is the linguistic term with the index i i closest to β, and α is the value of the symbolic translation.

Thus, a 2-tuple linguistic value $(s_i, \alpha) \in \overline{S}$ is identified with a numerical value β in the interval of granularity of S $[0, g]$.

Proposition 1. Let $S = \{s_0, \ldots, s_g\}$ be a LTS with cardinality $g + 1$, and $(s_i, \alpha) \in \overline{S}$ a 2-tuple linguistic value. There is a function $\Delta_S^{-1} : \overline{S} \to [0, g]$ that returns a numerical value $\beta \in [0, g]$ equivalent to (s_i, α).

$$\Delta_S^{-1}(s_i, \alpha) = i + \alpha \tag{3}$$

The transformation of a linguistic term $s_i \in S$ into a 2-tuple linguistic value in $\overline{S}$ consists of adding a zero as a symbolic translation to the linguistic term:

$$s_i \in S \Rightarrow (s_i, 0) \in \overline{S} \tag{4}$$

The 2-tuple linguistic model remains widely used in decision-making (e.g., [8–11]. The main aggregation operators for this model are detailed in [3]. However, the additive aggregation scenario required by attitude 4 and CPC Articles 81.1-81.2 needs an upward-reinforcing, bounded operator not currently available in the literature.

3   The 2-tuple Linguistic Bounded Sum (2TLBS) Operator

The Lukasiewicz bounded sum (Λ), is an aggregation function whose lower bound is the sum of its arguments and bounded above by one. For all $x_i \in [0, 1]$, Λ is defined as:

$$\Lambda(x_i, \ldots, x_n) = \min\left(\sum_{i=1}^{n} x_i, 1\right) \tag{5}$$

Based on the Λ operator, the 2TLBS operator has been defined:

Definition 2. (Bounded sum for 2-tuples linguistic). Let X be the set of all 2-tuples linguistic values associated to S, where $S = \{s_0, s_1, \ldots, s_g\}$ is a LTS with cardinality $g + 1$. Let $\overline{S} = \{(s_1, \alpha_1), \ldots, (s_p, \alpha_p)\}$ be a subset of X with p element; the Bounded Sum operator for 2-tuples linguistic values, $2TLBS : \overline{S} \to (s_i, \alpha_i) \in X$, is defined as:

$$2TLBS\big((s_1, \alpha_1), \ldots, (s_p, \alpha_p)\big) = \Delta_S\left(\min\left\{\sum_{i=1}^{p}\left(\Delta_S^{-1}(s_i, \alpha_i)\right), \Delta_S^{-1}(s_g, 0)\right\}\right) \tag{6}$$

The 2TLBS operator is commutative, associative, monotonic not decreasing and the value $(s_0, 0)$ is its identity element. These properties are discussed below.

Theorem   1. (Commutativity).   Let φ be   the   2TLBS operator, $\overline{S} = \{(s_1, \alpha_1), \ldots, (s_p, \alpha_p)\}$ a set of p 2-tuples linguistic values associated with $S = \{s_0, s_1, \ldots, s_g\}$ and $\overline{S}^* = \{(s_1, \alpha_1)^*, \ldots, (s_p, \alpha_p)^*\}$ any combination of $\overline{S}$, then

$$\varphi\big((s_1, \alpha_1), \ldots, (s_p, \alpha_p)\big) = \varphi\big((s_1, \alpha_1)^*, \ldots, (s_p, \alpha_p)^*\big) \tag{7}$$

Proof. Let

$$\varphi\big((s_1, \alpha_1), \ldots, (s_p, \alpha_p)\big) = \Delta_s\left(\min\left\{\sum_{i=1}^{p} \Delta_s^{-1}(s_i, \alpha_i), \Delta_s^{-1}(s_g, 0)\right\}\right)$$

$$\varphi\big((s_1, \alpha_1)^*, \ldots, (s_p, \alpha_p)^*\big) = \Delta_s\left(\min\left\{\sum_{i=1}^{p} \Delta_s^{-1}(s_i, \alpha_i)^*, \Delta_s^{-1}(s_g, 0)\right\}\right) \tag{8}$$

Since $\overline{S}^*$ is any combination of $\overline{S}$, then

$$\sum_{i=1}^{p} \Delta_s^{-1}(s_i, \alpha_i) = \sum_{i=1}^{p} \Delta_s^{-1}(s_i, \alpha_i)^*$$

$$\min\left\{\sum_{i=1}^{p} \Delta_s^{-1}(s_i, \alpha_i)^*, \Delta_s^{-1}(s_g, 0)\right\} = \min\left\{\sum_{i=1}^{p} \Delta_s^{-1}(s_i, \alpha_i)^*, \Delta_s^{-1}(s_g, 0)\right\} \tag{9}$$

$$\therefore \varphi\big((s_1, \alpha_1), \ldots, (s_p, \alpha_p)\big) = \varphi\big((s_1, \alpha_1)^*, \ldots, (s_p, \alpha_p)^*\big)$$

232   C. R. Rodríguez-Rodríguez et al.

Theorem 2.2. (Associativity). Let φ be the 2TLBS operator and $\overline{S} = \left\{(s_1, \alpha_1), \ldots, (s_p, \alpha_p)\right\}$ a set of p 2-tuples linguistic values associated with $S = \left\{s_0, s_1, \ldots, s_g\right\}$, then

$$\varphi\big(\varphi\big((s_1, \alpha_1), \ldots, (s_{p-1}, \alpha_{p-1})\big), (s_p, \alpha_p)\big) = \varphi\big((s_1, \alpha_1), \varphi\big((s_2, \alpha_2), \ldots, (s_p, \alpha_p)\big)\big)$$
(10)

Proof. Let

$$(s, \alpha)_1^{\varphi} = \varphi\big((s_1, \alpha_1), \ldots, (s_{p-1}, \alpha_{p-1})\big) = \min\left\{\sum_{i=1}^{p-1} \Delta_s^{-1}(s_i, \alpha_i), \Delta_s^{-1}(s_g, 0)\right\}$$

$$(s, \alpha)_2^{\varphi} = \varphi\big((s_2, \alpha_2), \ldots, (s_p, \alpha_p)\big) = \min\left\{\sum_{i=2}^{p} \Delta_s^{-1}(s_i, \alpha_i), \Delta_s^{-1}(s_g, 0)\right\}$$
(11)

$$\varphi\big((s, \alpha)_1^{\varphi}, (s_p, \alpha_p)\big) = \Delta_s\left(\min\left\{\big(\Delta_s^{-1}(s, \alpha)_1^{\varphi} + \Delta_s^{-1}(s_p, \alpha_p)\big), \Delta_s^{-1}(s_g, 0)\right\}\right)$$

$$\varphi\big((s_1, \alpha_1), (s, \alpha)_2^{\varphi}\big) = \Delta_s\left(\min\left\{\big(\Delta_s^{-1}(s_1, \alpha_1) + \Delta_s^{-1}(s, \alpha)_2^{\varphi}\big), \Delta_s^{-1}(s_g, 0)\right\}\right)$$

Since

$$\Delta_s^{-1}(s, \alpha)_1^{\varphi} + \Delta_s^{-1}(s_p, \alpha_p) = \Delta_s^{-1}(s_1, \alpha_1) + \Delta_s^{-1}(s, \alpha)_2^{\varphi}$$
(12)

Then

$$\varphi\big((s, \alpha)_1^{\varphi}, (s_p, \alpha_p)\big) = \varphi\big((s_1, \alpha_1), (s, \alpha)_2^{\varphi}\big)$$

$$\therefore \varphi\big(\varphi\big((s_1, \alpha_1), \ldots, (s_{p-1}, \alpha_{p-1})\big), (s_p, \alpha_p)\big) = \varphi\big((s_1, \alpha_1), \varphi\big((s_2, \alpha_2), \ldots, (s_p, \alpha_p)\big)\big)$$
(13)

Theorem 2.3. (Monotonicity). Let φ be the 2TLBS operator and $\overline{S} = \left\{(s_1, \alpha_1), \ldots, (s_p, \alpha_p)\right\}$ a set of p 2-tuples linguistic values associated with $S = \left\{s_0, s_1, \ldots, s_g\right\}$, then

$$\varphi\big((s_1, \alpha_1), \ldots, (s_p, \alpha_p)\big) \geq \varphi\big((s_1, \alpha_1), \ldots, (s_{p-1}, \alpha_{p-1})\big)$$
(14)

Proof. Let

$$\varphi\big((s_1, \alpha_1), \ldots, (s_p, \alpha_p)\big) = \Delta_s\left(\min\left\{\sum_{i=1}^{p} \Delta_s^{-1}(s_i, \alpha_i), \Delta_s^{-1}(s_g, 0)\right\}\right)$$

$$\varphi\big((s_1, \alpha_1), \ldots, (s_{p-1}, \alpha_{p-1})\big) = \Delta_s\left(\min\left\{\sum_{i=1}^{p-1} \Delta_s^{-1}(s_i, \alpha_i), \Delta_s^{-1}(s_g, 0)\right\}\right)$$
(15)

Since $\Delta_s^{-1}(s_i, \alpha_i) = \beta_i \in [0, g]$, then

$$\sum_{i=1}^{p} \Delta_s^{-1}(s_i, \alpha_i) \geq \sum_{i=1}^{p-1} \Delta_s^{-1}(s_i, \alpha_i)$$

$$\min\left\{\sum_{i=1}^{p} \Delta_s^{-1}(s_i, \alpha_i), \Delta_s^{-1}(s_g, 0)\right\} \geq \min\left\{\sum_{i=1}^{p-1} \Delta_s^{-1}(s_i, \alpha_i), \Delta_s^{-1}(s_g, 0)\right\} \tag{16}$$

$$\therefore \varphi\big((s_1, \alpha_1), ..., (s_p, \alpha_p)\big) \geq \varphi\big((s_1, \alpha_1), ..., (s_{p-1}, \alpha_{p-1})\big)$$

Theorem 2.4. (Element identity). Let φ be the 2TLBS operator and $\overline{S} = \big\{(s_1, \alpha_1), \ldots, (s_p, \alpha_p)\big\}$ a set of p 2-tuples linguistic values associated with $S = \{s_0, s_1, \ldots, s_g\}$, then

$$\varphi\big((s_1, \alpha_1), ..., (s_p, \alpha_p), (s_0, 0)\big) = \varphi\big((s_1, \alpha_1), ..., (s_p, \alpha_p)\big) \tag{17}$$

where $(s_i, \alpha_i) \neq (s_0, 0) \forall i \in \{0, 1, \ldots p\}$

Proof. Let

$$\varphi\big((s_1, \alpha_1), ..., (s_p, \alpha_p), (s_0, 0)\big) = \Delta_s\left(\min\left\{\sum_{i=1}^{p} \Delta_s^{-1}(s_i, \alpha_i) + \Delta_s^{-1}(s_0, 0), \Delta_s^{-1}(s_g, 0)\right\}\right)$$

$$\varphi\big((s_1, \alpha_1), ..., (s_p, \alpha_p)\big) = \Delta_s\left(\min\left\{\sum_{i=1}^{p} \Delta_s^{-1}(s_i, \alpha_i), \Delta_s^{-1}(s_g, 0)\right\}\right) \tag{18}$$

Since $\Delta_s^{-1}(s_i, \alpha) = i + \alpha$, it follows that $\Delta_s^{-1}(s_0, 0) = 0 + 0 = 0$, then

$$\sum_{i=1}^{p} \Delta_s^{-1}(s_i, \alpha_i) + \Delta_s^{-1}(s_0, 0) = \sum_{i=1}^{p} \Delta_s^{-1}(s_i, \alpha_i)$$

$$\min\left\{\sum_{i=1}^{p} \Delta_s^{-1}(s_i, \alpha_i) + \Delta_s^{-1}(s_0, 0), \Delta_s^{-1}(s_g, 0)\right\} = \min\left\{\sum_{i=1}^{p} \Delta_s^{-1}(s_i, \alpha_i), \Delta_s^{-1}(s_g, 0)\right\}$$

$$\therefore \varphi\big((s_1, \alpha_1), ..., (s_p, \alpha_p), (s_0, 0)\big) = \varphi\big((s_1, \alpha_1), ..., (s_p, \alpha_p)\big) \tag{19}$$

The 2TLBS operator is useful when the court intends to aggregate the values of all circumstances of the same type. In the extreme case, the result may be $(s_g, 0)$, which means that one of the extremes of the interval should be reduced or increased by half.

Returning to Example 1, let us assume that the set S has a cardinality of $g + 1 = 7$. The resulting bounded sum of both circumstances is given as follows:

$$2TLBS((s_2, 0.24), (s_3, -0.19)) = \Delta_S\left(\min\left\{\left(\Delta_S^{-1}(s_2, 0.24) + \Delta_S^{-1}(s_3, -0.19)\right), \Delta_S^{-1}(s_6, 0)\right\}\right)$$

$$= \Delta_S(\min\{(2.24 + 2.81), 6\})$$

$$= \Delta_S(5.05) = (s_5, 0.05) = (vh, 0.05).$$

4   Integrating 2TLBS into M-LAMAC

We propose integrating the 2TLBS operator into Step 4 of M-LAMAC to addresses a key requirement in Cuban judicial practice where the collective intensity of all circumstances of the same type must be computed through comprehensive aggregation rather than selective approaches. Unlike existing operators that select individual circumstance intensities or compute averages, 2TLBS enables modeling of judicial reasoning that requires cumulative assessment and capturing the hybrid effect of all circumstances through additive aggregation. This extension significantly enhances M-LAMAC's capacity to mirror authentic judicial decision-making patterns. Namely, where current operators force judges to work with isolated values or averages, 2TLBS captures the essential practice of assessing the compounded effect of all circumstances of each type.

5   Solving Criminal Cases with M-LAMAC Involving 2TLBS

5.1   Description of a Real Case of Homicide and Its Modifications

We begin by examining a real-life homicide case judged by the Second Criminal Chamber of the Matanzas Provincial Court in Cuba: Case 139/2015. To rigorously assess the applicability of the 2TLBS operator, two more complex variants of this case were subsequently developed. A panel of 16 experts— including magistrates from the Supreme People's Court, judges, prosecutors, and professors, validated these modifications and the procedure described below. The cases will be referred to as case_1, case_2, and case_3, respectively. This approach allows us to test the operator's effectiveness across scenarios of varying intricacy while maintaining relevance to real judicial proceedings.

Case 1. Real facts. This case involved the death of a 17-year-old, MQI, due to electrocution. The landowner, LELS, sought to protect his agricultural products from theft by installing a high-voltage grid. On July 1, 2015, MQI entered the property and was fatally electrocuted. The defendant, LELS, had no prior criminal record and fully confessed to the crime while demonstrating genuine remorse. The Court classified the offense as homicide under Article 261, in conjunction with Article 9.2 of the CPC. The ruling recognized the mitigating circumstance outlined in Article 52 ch) of the same law, acknowledging the defendant's lack of criminal history and cooperative attitude.

Case 2. Modification 1: several mitigating circumstances - extraordinary mitigation. In addition to the previous facts, LELS was influenced by his wife, DRM. She repeatedly urged him to safeguard their agricultural products. Her motivation was tied to their wedding anniversary, as she expected him to purchase gifts from the earnings. Consequently, the defense argued that LELS acted under external pressure, invoking the mitigating circumstance outlined in Article 52 b) of the CPC.

Case 3. Modification 2: both types of circumstances - compensation. In addition to the facts described in the first two cases, after LELS had commented his intentions among his neighbors, the Chief of the Police Sector officially warned him of the illegitimacy and dangerousness of his pretensions and of their possible harmful consequences, and ordered him to desist from them. Therefore, the court appreciated the aggravating circumstance foreseen in Article 53 n) of the CPC.

5.2 Solving the Cases Following the M-LAMAC's Steps

Step 1. The primary elements involved in the problem resolution are the following:

- A single defendant is on trial in this case, $D = \{d_1\}$.
- The trial court is composed of 3 judges, $J = \{j_1, j_2, j_3\}$.
- The inclusion of the circumstances in each case is as follows: case_1 $= (c_1)$, case_2 $= (c_1, c_2)$, and case_3 $= (c_1, c_2, c_3)$.
- To express the intensity of circumstances, the predominance of one type of circumstance and the needed modification at one extreme of the punishment interval, the LTSs in Fig. 2 a) S^I, b) S^P and c) S^M are used, respectively.

$S^I = \{s_0^I$: not appreciated (NA), s_1^I: very low (VL), s_2^I: low (L), s_3^I: medium (M), s_4^I: high (H), s_5^I: very high (VH), s_6^I: full (F)$\}$.

$S^P = \{s_o^P$: are proportional (AP), s_1^P: very low (VL), s_2^P: low (M), s_3^P: moderate (M), s_4^P: high (H), s_5^P: very high (VH), s_6^P: almost full (AF)$\}$.

$S^M =:$ extreme decrease (ED), s_1^M: moderate decrease (MD), s_2^M: small decrease (SD), s_3^M: no change (NC), s_4^M: small increase (SI), s_5^M: moderate increase (MI), s_6^M: extreme increase (EI)$\}$.

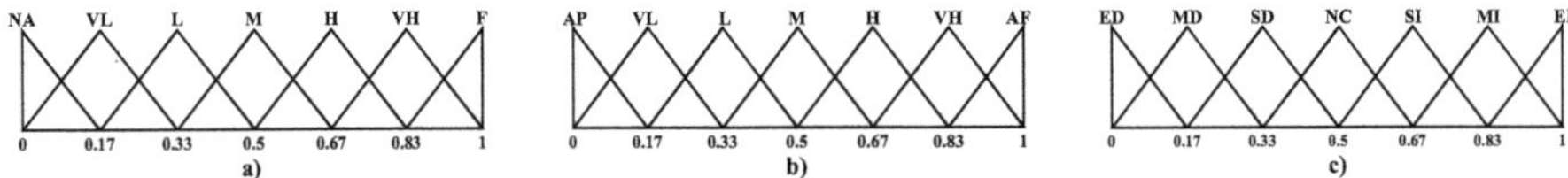

Fig. 2. Linguistic terms sets for expressing intensity (a), predominance (b) and modification (c).

Step 2. Using the LTS S^I (Fig. 2 a), the judges assessed the intensity of circumstance as shown in Table 1 a) and then, these preferences were transformed into 2-tuples linguistic values (Table 1 b).

Table 1. Judges' preferences and their transformation into 2-tuple linguistic values.

Circumstances	a)			b)		
	j_1	j_2	j_3	j_1	j_2	j_3
c_1 : 52 ch)	medium	medium	high	$(M, 0)$	$(M, 0)$	$(H, 0)$
c_2 : 52 b)	low	medium	low	$(L, 0)$	$(M, 0)$	$(L, 0)$
c_3 : 53 n)	medium	high	very high	$(M, 0)$	$(H, 0)$	$(VH, 0)$

Step 3. In each case, once the preferences were collected and transformed into 2-tuples linguistic values, the collective value of each circumstance was calculated using the 2TAM operator, resulting in: $c_1 = (M, 0.33), c_2 = (L, 0.33), c_3 = (H, 0)$; see Fig. 3.

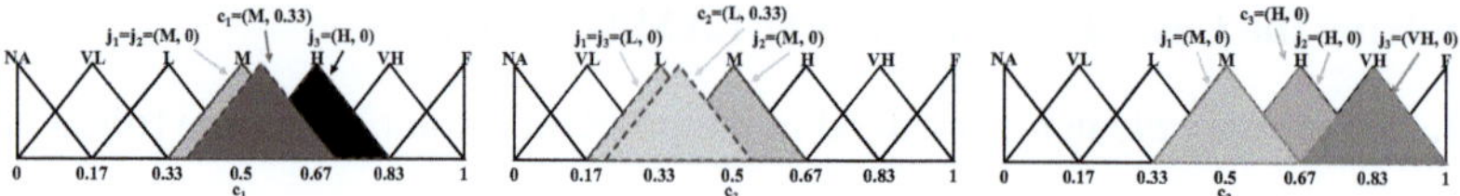

Fig. 3. Collective assessment of each circumstance.

Step 4. In case_1, there is only one mitigating circumstance, so this step is not required. But in case_2 and case_3 there are two mitigating circumstances, so their collective value was computed using the *min*, *max* and *average* operators included in M-LAMAC and the 2TLBS operator (20). Figure 4 shows the result obtained with the new operator.

$$\{2TLBS = (F, -0.34);\ min = (L, 0.33);\ 2TAM = (M, -0.17);\ max = (M, 0.33)\} \tag{20}$$

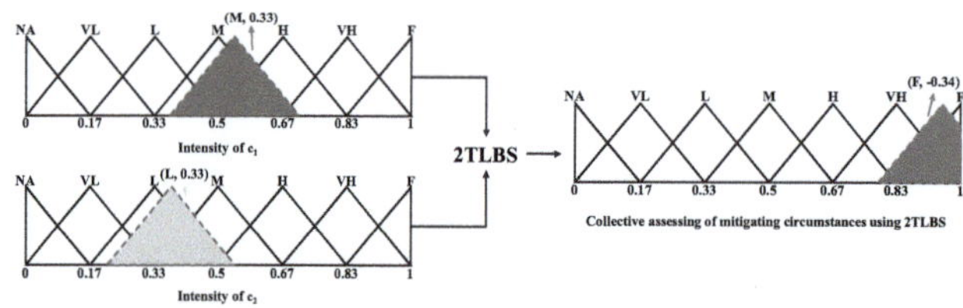

Fig. 4. Collective assessing of mitigating circumstances using 2TLBS.

Step 5. In case 3, there are both types of circumstances, thus their intensity values were compensated following step 5 of M-LAMAC, Eq. (9) in [1]. In (21) we present the compensation results considering the four possible intensity values of the mitigating circumstances reported in (20). For the first three cases (min, max, average) there were different degrees of predominance of the aggravating circumstance. Figure 5 Shows the compensation using the 2TLBS operator to aggregate the intensity of the mitigating circumstances; this resulted in a low predominance of mitigating circumstances.

$$\{2TLBS = (L, -0.38);\ min = (L, -0.33);\ 2TAM = (VL, 0.17);\ max = (VL, -0.33)\} \tag{21}$$

Step 6. For each case, the needed modification was estimated according to step 6 of M-LAMAC, Sect. 4.6, Eq. (10) in [1].

- For case_1 the value $(NC - 0.33)$ was obtained which, given its symbolic translation, $\alpha = -0.33$, to the left of the "not change" term, is interpreted as a very slight decrease in the lower extreme of the punishment interval, following the theoretical approach given in Sect. 4.6 in [1].
- In case_2 the estimation yielded different values of modification on the lower extreme of the punishment range for each value of intensity reported in (20); see (22).

$$\{2TLBS = (ED, 0.34);\ min = (SI, -0.33);\ 2TAM = (NM, 0.17);\ max = (NM, -0.33)\} \tag{22}$$

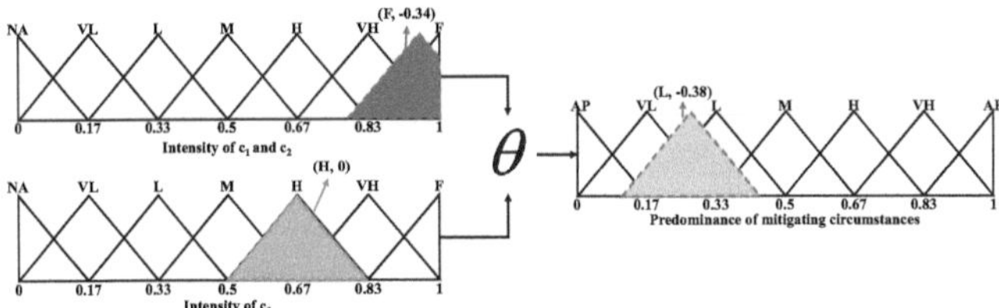

Fig. 5. Compensation of mitigating and aggravating circumstances. The mitigating circumstances c_1 and c_2 were aggregated using the 2TLBS operator.

- In case_3, the estimation yielded different modification values for each compensation value reported in (21); see (23). The predominance of the aggravating circumstance produced modification values on the upper extreme of the interval, while the predominance of the mitigating circumstances, aggregated with the 2TLBS operator, produced a modification on the lower extreme of the interval (Fig. 6).

$$\{2TLBS = (SI, 0.38); \ min = (SI, 0.33); \ 2TAM = (MI, -0.17); \ max = (MI, 0.33)\} \tag{23}$$

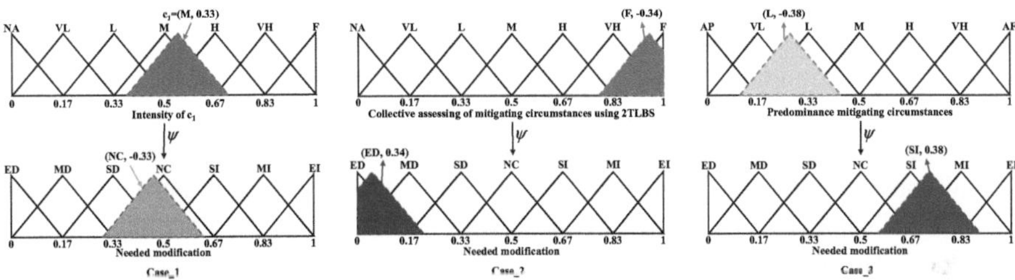

Fig. 6. Needed modifications in the punishment intervals for each case. Case_2 and case_3 show the modifications produced by using the 2TLBS operator in step 4.

Step 7. The analyzed crime carries a prison sentence ranging from 7 to 15 years. Taking into account the different values of needed modification obtained in the previous step, new intervals were calculated; see (24). In case_2 and case_3, each of the operators used to aggregate the mitigating circumstances were considered. Figure 7 shows the needed modification values and the calculated intervals for each case.

$$\begin{aligned}
case_1 &= [79, 132] \\
case_2 &= \{2TLBS = [47, 132]; \ min = [95, 132]; \ 2TAM = [87, 132]; \ max = [79, 132]\} \\
case_3 &= \{2TLBS = [106, 132]; \ min = [132, 143]; \ 2TAM = [132, 151]; \ max = [132, 159]\}
\end{aligned} \tag{24}$$

Step 8. Finally, for each case, an explanation including a logically ordered summary of the entire assessment process was generated. Its goal is to facilitate result interpretation and enhance their usefulness. Explanation are here.

Discussion. The 2TLBS operator introduces a new way for calculating the collective intensity of circumstances of the same type, so its outcomes influence subsequent steps.

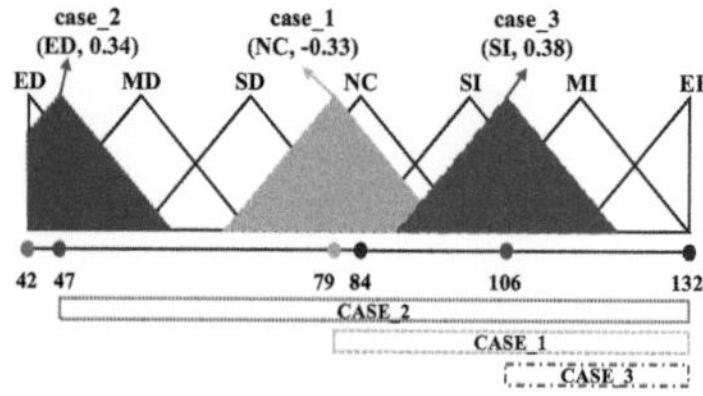

Fig. 7. Modifications and intervals for each case (using 2TLBS for cases 2 and 3).

In case_2, the inclusion of circumstance 52 b) with low intensity, aggregated to 52 ch) via the 2TLBS operator, produces an almost total intensity of the mitigating circumstances. This suggests a reduction of the lower extreme of the punishment interval by almost half, i.e., it enables the punishment extraordinary mitigation. The intervals induced by the different operators offer several options to the court. In all of them, the upper extreme is the mean of the original interval, because only mitigating circumstances occur. However, the lower extremes are very different. The value induced by 2TLBS (47) is lower than that of the original interval (84). The other three intervals allow the court to modify the lower extreme between 79 and 95 months.

In case_3, by including the circumstance 53 n) with high intensity and compensating it with the collective value of 52 ch) and 52 b) obtained with the 2TLBS operator, a low predominance of mitigating circumstances resulted. This also induces a modification of the lower extreme of the interval, but unlike the previous cases, it is a small increase because the predominance value of the mitigating ones is lower than the neutral term of the CTL S^P (Fig. 2 b). The proposed interval shares the same upper extreme of the previous cases, while the lower extreme is slightly higher than that of case_1 in which one mitigating circumstance with medium intensity was considered, but is noticeably higher than that of case_2 in which two mitigating circumstances with full intensity were considered. However, if the court had used any of the other three operators to aggregate the circumstances 52 ch) and 52 b), the result of the compensation would have induced a predominance (to varying degrees) of the circumstance 53 n) and thus modifications of the upper extreme of the punishment interval.

These tests confirm that using different operators to aggregate the intensity of all circumstances of the same type within M-LAMAC enables the generation of multiple decision intervals, thereby reinforcing judicial discretion. Ninety-three percent of the experts highlighted this strength of M-LAMAC, in which 2TLBS plays a key role.

6 Conclusions

The integration of the 2TLBS operator into M-LAMAC represents a meaningful advancement in computational legal decision-support systems, particularly within the Cuban judicial context. By introducing an aggregation method that aligns with the practical need to evaluate the cumulative intensity of circumstances, rather than relying on selective or averaged values, this work addresses a critical gap in existing models. The 2TLBS operator provides a mathematically sound framework for capturing the compounded effect of multiple mitigating or aggravating circumstances, a fundamental aspect of judicial reasoning often overlooked in traditional approaches.

This enhancement enables M-LAMAC to more accurately reflect real-world judicial decision-making, where the totality of circumstances—not just individual intensities—determines sentencing outcomes. Unlike conventional operators, which impose artificial constraints by isolating or averaging values, 2TLBS preserves the nuanced, additive logic employed by legal professionals. The operator's properties (commutativity, associativity, and monotonicity) ensure consistency with legal standards while accommodating the complexity of multi-factor assessment.

Ultimately, this work not only expands M-LAMAC functionality but also contributes to the broader field of AI-assisted legal systems by demonstrating how linguistic computational models can better adapt to jurisdiction-specific requirements.

Especially the associativity of the 2TLBS operator suggests as future work, to study its applicability in other problems such as dynamic linguistic decision-making and modeling consumer decision-making process, among others.

Disclosure of Interests.   The authors have no competing interests to declare that are relevant to the content of this article.

References

1. Rodríguez, C.R., Amoroso, Y., Zuev, D.S., Peña, M., Zulueta, Y.: M-LAMAC: a model for linguistic assessment of mitigating and aggravating circumstances of criminal responsibility using computing with words. Artif. Intell. Law **32**(3), 697–739 (2024)

2. Herrera, F., Martínez, L.: A 2-tuple fuzzy linguistic representation model for computing with words. IEEE Trans. Fuzzy Syst. **8**(6), 746–752 (2000)

3. Martínez, L., Rodriguez, R.M., Herrera, F.: The 2-tuple Linguistic Model: Computing with Words in Decision Making. Springer, Cham (2015)

4. ANPP, *Ley No. 151/2022 "Código Penal."* La Habana, Cuba: Gaceta Oficial de la República de Cuba (2022)

5. Zadeh, L.A.: The concept of a linguistic variable and its application to approximate reasoning—I. Inf. Sci. (Ny) **8**(3), 199–249 (1975)

6. Zadeh, L.A.: The concept of a linguistic variable and its application to approximate reasoning—II. Inf. Sci. (Ny) **8**(4), 301–357 (1975)

7. Zadeh, L.A.: The concept of a linguistic variable and its application to approximate reasoning—III. Inf. Sci. (Ny) **9**(1), 43–80 (1975)

8. Chang, K.H., Chen, Y.J., Liao, C.C.: A novel improved FMEA method using data envelopment analysis method and 2-tuple fuzzy linguistic model. Ann. Oper. Res. **341**(1), 485–507 (2024)

9. Shu, Z., Llorens-Marin, M., Carrasco, R.A., Romero, M.S.: Customer Electronic Word of Mouth Management Strategies Based on Computing with Words: The Case of Spanish Luxury Hotel Reviews on TripAdvisor. Electron. **14**(2), 325 (2025)

10. Ali, Z., Yang, M.S.: Industrialization in development countries based on the MABAC method and Hamacher power aggregation operators for circular spherical fuzzy 2-tuple linguistic information. Complex Intell. Syst. **11**(9), 1–30 (2025)

11. Qiyas, M., Naeem, M., Khan, N., Khan, F.: Group decision support system based on multi-granular fractional orthotriple fuzzy 2-tuple linguistic information model. Heliyon **10**(7) (2024)

A Straigforward Method for the Optimisation of the Electricity Operating Cost of a Water Desalination Plant Under a Variable Tariff

Deivis Avila[1]([✉]) , Yanelys Cuba Arana[2] , Ramón Quiza[2] , and Graciliano N. Marichal[1]

[1] Higher Polytechnic School of Engineering (EPSI), University of La Laguna, Apartado Postal 456, 38200 La Laguna, Santa Cruz de Tenerife, Spain
{davilapr,nicomar}@ull.edu.es
[2] Centre for Advanced and Sustainable Manufacturing Studies, University of Matanzas, Autopista a Varadero km 3.5, 44740 Matanzas, MT, Cuba

Abstract. The study presents a method for optimising the energy costs of a desalination plant by managing the working pressure according to variable electricity tariffs. A mathematical model was established that describes the relationship between desalinated water flow, brine pressure and pump power consumption, allowing the formulation of an optimisation strategy based on the allocation of loads in the periods of lowest energy cost. Based on these models, an algorithm was designed that adjusts the operation of the plant based on the hourly structure of the electricity tariffs, maximising the efficiency of the system. The results obtained show a significant reduction in operating costs, with a strong correlation between the lowest tariff times and the highest working pressure. It was verified that the algorithm was able to shift most of the energy consumption to the most economical hours, minimising activity in high-cost periods. Despite the variability in daily savings, the strategy proved to be effective in most cases, suggesting opportunities to improve the operational flexibility of the process.

Keywords: Desalination · Optimisation · Variable electric tariff

1   Introduction

In recent decades, the sustained growth in demand for drinking water, especially in arid regions and island areas, has driven the development and expansion of desalination technologies, with the reverse osmosis process standing out for its efficiency in producing water with low saline content [2]. However, one of the main challenges facing this technology is its high energy demand, which not only affects the operating costs of the plants, but also their environmental impact, particularly when the energy comes from fossil sources [3,10]. Against this backdrop, numerous research projects have focused their efforts on improving the

Y. Hernádez Heredia et al. (Eds.): IWAIPR 2025, LNCS 16328, pp. 240–254, 2026.
https://doi.org/10.1007/978-3-032-11358-0_20

energy efficiency of the desalination process, either through technological innovations in energy recovery systems or through operational management strategies that take into account the dynamic conditions of the environment [12,13].

In this context, variable electricity tariffs, also known as hourly tariffs or dynamic tariffs, are pricing schemes in which the cost of electricity fluctuates throughout the day depending on various factors, mainly the demand of the electricity system and the availability of generation [5]. Unlike flat or fixed tariffs, where the price per kilowatt-hour remains constant throughout the billing period, variable tariffs reflect hourly or daily changes in the cost of producing and distributing electricity [8].

The fundamental purpose of these tariffs is to encourage more efficient and balanced consumption of electricity. By setting lower prices during off-peak hours and higher prices during peak hours, they seek to shift part of the energy consumption to times of the day when the electricity system is less congested and generation is more efficient [4]. This contributes to better management of the energy infrastructure, reduces the risk of grid overloads and, in contexts with a high penetration of renewable energies, allows greater use to be made of intermittent sources such as solar or wind [6].

In the industrial sector, and particularly in energy-intensive processes such as desalination, the use of variable electricity tariffs represents an opportunity to optimise operating costs [1,14]. By adapting the operation of equipment to times of lower tariffs, it is possible to considerably reduce energy expenditure without affecting productivity, which makes these tariffs a key tool in energy efficiency and sustainability strategies [7,11].

The use of variable electricity tariffs in desalination processes represents an effective strategy to reduce energy costs, but brings with it significant challenges. One of the main challenges is the need to coordinate with predictive management of the operation under variable tariff conditions [9]. Effective implementation of this type of strategy requires mathematical models and optimisation algorithms that consider multiple factors, such as water demand, energy efficiency and electricity price forecasting [15].

The aim of this work is to develop a simple and efficient method to optimise the cost of the electricity consumed by a desalination plant, operating under a variable electricity tariff scheme. To this end, an algorithm is proposed that dynamically adjusts the operating pressure of the plant according to hourly electricity prices, guaranteeing the required daily production of desalinated water at the lowest possible cost.

This paper is organised as follows: After this introduction, the proposed approach is mathematically formalised. The third section portrays the optimisation algorithms. The fourth section describes the case study and explain how the data was collected and models were fitted. After that, the fifth section explains the optimisation process while the sixth one presents and analyses the obtained results. Finally, conclusions and future work are remarked.

2   Formalization

Let consider that the relationship between freshwater flowrate and brine pressure can be described by a linear equation, of the form:

$$Q_{\mathrm{F}} = \alpha p_{\mathrm{B}} + \beta; \tag{1}$$

where α y β are two constant terms. Let also consider that the same is true for the relationship between the electrical power consumed by the pumps and the pressure in the brine:

$$P_{\mathrm{p}} = \gamma p_{\mathrm{B}} + \delta; \tag{2}$$

where γ and δ are the constant terms of the equation.

Let consider, in addition, that the total running time, τ, is divided into two periods, τ' y τ'':

$$\tau' + \tau'' = \tau. \tag{3}$$

for each of which the electricity tariffs ξ' y ξ'', are set, respectively, such that:

$$\xi' \leq \xi''. \tag{4}$$

The problem, then, is to find the working pressures, p'_{P} and p''_{P}, that minimise the total cost of electricity consumed by the pumps, Z, while keeping the volume of desalinated water, V, constant.

This volume can be computed by the expression:

$$V = \tau' Q_{\mathrm{F}}(p'_{\mathrm{B}}) + \tau'' Q_{\mathrm{F}}(p''_{\mathrm{B}});$$

where, replacing the Eq. 1, we obtain:

$$V = \tau'(\alpha p'_{\mathrm{B}} + \beta) + \tau''(\alpha p''_{\mathrm{B}} + \beta);$$

which, in turn, can be transformed into:

$$V = \alpha(\tau' p'_{\mathrm{B}} + \tau'' p''_{\mathrm{B}}) + \beta(\tau' + \tau''). \tag{5}$$

From this expression, p''_{B} can be write as a function of p'_{B}:

$$p''_{\mathrm{B}} = \frac{V - \beta(\tau' + \tau'')}{\alpha \tau''} - \frac{\tau'}{\tau''} p'_{\mathrm{B}} \tag{6}$$

On the other hand, the total cost of electricity can be computed as:

$$Z = \tau' \xi' P_{\mathrm{p}}(p'_{\mathrm{B}}) + \tau'' \xi'' P_{\mathrm{p}}(p''_{\mathrm{B}});$$

where, replacing the Eq. 2, we obtain:

$$Z = \tau' \xi'(\gamma p'_{\mathrm{B}} + \delta) + \tau'' \xi''(\gamma p''_{\mathrm{B}} + \delta);$$

which can be finally written as:

$$Z = \gamma(\tau' \xi' p'_{\mathrm{B}} + \tau'' \xi'' p''_{\mathrm{B}}) + \delta(\tau' \xi' + \tau'' \xi''). \tag{7}$$

Replacing, now, p''_B from 6 in the previous equation, it is obtained:

$$Z = \gamma \left\{ \tau'\xi'p'_B + \tau''\xi'' \left[\frac{V - \beta(\tau' + \tau'')}{\alpha\tau''} - \frac{\tau'}{\tau''}p'_B \right] \right\} + \delta(\tau'\xi' + \tau''\xi'').$$

which can be rearranged into:

$$Z = \gamma\tau'(\xi' - \xi'')p'_B + \gamma\xi''\frac{V - \beta(\tau' + \tau'')}{\alpha} + \delta(\tau'\xi' + \tau''\xi''). \tag{8}$$

As the last two terms in this sum are just a constant, and $(\xi' - \xi'') \leq 0$, it can be noted that:

$$\min Z \implies \max p'_B. \tag{9}$$

It can therefore be concluded that: provided the conditions given in 1, 2 and 4 are met, electricity cost minimisation is achieved by maximising power in the time interval when the tariff is lowest.

3 Algorithm

Based on the conclusion of the previous section, an algorithm has been developed to optimise the cost of electrical energy, for a period of one day, $\tau = 24$ h, with a variable tariff with costs for each hour of the day, $\{\xi_1, \xi_2, ..., \xi_{24}\}$, and a volume to be achieved, $\hat{V}$. The input of these values is the first stage of the algorithm. Additionally, the lower value, p^L, and upper value, p^U, of the brine pressure working range, as well as the coefficients of the desalinated water flow equations, α and β, and of the electrical power of the pumps, γ and δ, must be entered.

After entering the data, the indexes of the tariff values are obtained, organised from lowest to highest. That is, if you have the following electricity tariff values:

$$\{\xi\} = [15.1, 14.8, 14.4, 14.2, 14.2, 14.8, 13.6, 15.6, \dots$$
$$\dots 19.5, 18.1, 21.8, 20.3, 19.9, 19.0, 13.9, 12.5, \dots$$
$$\dots 14.1, 15.8, 20.7, 21.7, 21.7, 21.4, 16.2, 15.0] \text{ EUR/kWh};$$

the corresponding indices would be:

$$\{id\} = [16, 7, 15, 17, 4, 5, 3, 2, 6, \dots$$
$$\dots 24, 1, 8, 18, 23, 10, 14, 9, \dots$$
$$\dots 13, 12, 19, 22, 20, 21, 11].$$

Based on these indices, a cycle is run through them, which allows the load from the periods with the lowest tariffs to be allocated to those with the highest tariffs. Within the cycle, several cases are analysed. Firstly, if there is still water volume to be desalinated, it is assigned, while otherwise, it is considered that the desalination plant will not work in that period and, consequently, both the

Algorithm 1. Electric cost optimisation algorithm

1: **procedure** ElectricCostOptimisation
2:     $\{\xi_1, \xi_2, ..., \xi_{24}\} \leftarrow$ **input** : values of electric tariff
3:     $\hat{V} \leftarrow$ **input** : target volume
4:     $p^{\mathrm{L}}, p^{\mathrm{U}} \leftarrow$ **input** : lower and upper values of brine pressure
5:     $\alpha, \beta \leftarrow$ **input** : coefficients of freshwater flowrate equation
6:     $\gamma, \delta \leftarrow$ **input** : coefficients of pumps electric power equation
7:     $id \leftarrow$ indexes of sorted $\{\xi_i\}$
8:     **for** $i \in \{id\}$ **do**
9:         **if** $\hat{V} > 0$ **then**
10:             **if** $(\alpha p^{\mathrm{U}} + \beta) < \hat{V}$ **then**
11:                 $p_i \leftarrow p^{\mathrm{U}}$
12:                 $\tau_i \leftarrow 1$
13:                 $V_i \leftarrow \tau_i(\alpha p_i + \beta)$ (Eq. 11c)
14:                 $Z_i \leftarrow \tau_i \xi_i(\gamma p_i + \delta)$ (Eq. 11d)
15:                 $\hat{V} \leftarrow \hat{V} - Q_i$
16:             **else**
17:                 **if** $\gamma\beta < \alpha\delta$ **then**
18:                     $p_i \leftarrow p^{\mathrm{U}}$
19:                 **else**
20:                     $p_i \leftarrow p^{\mathrm{L}}$
21:                 $\tau_i \leftarrow \hat{V}/(\alpha p_i + \beta)$ (from Eq. 11c)
22:                 $V_i \leftarrow \tau_i(\alpha p_i + \beta)$ (Eq. 11c)
23:                 $Z_i \leftarrow \tau_i \xi_i(\gamma p_i + \delta)$ (Eq. 11d)
24:                 $\hat{V} \leftarrow 0$
25:         **else**
26:             $p_i \leftarrow 0$
27:             $\tau_i \leftarrow 0$
28:             $V_i \leftarrow 0$
29:             $Z_i \leftarrow 0$
30:     $Z_{\mathrm{total}} \leftarrow \sum_i Z_i$
31:     **return** Z_{total}

---

working pressure, p_i, the working time, τ_i, the volume of water generated, V_i, and the cost of electricity, Z_i, for that period, take zero value:

$$p_i = 0; \tag{10a}$$

$$\tau_i = 0; \tag{10b}$$

$$V_i = 0; \tag{10c}$$

$$Z_i = 0. \tag{10d}$$

For the allocation, it is checked whether the volume that would be produced by the desalination plant working at the higher pressure is smaller than the remaining volume:

$$(\alpha p^{\mathrm{U}} + \beta) < \hat{V};$$

in which case, this pressure shall be used and the whole period shall be worked out. From these, the volume generated, V_i, and the cost, Z_i, will be calculated. Therefore, one will have that:

$$p_i = p^{\mathrm{U}};$$ (11a)

$$\tau_i = 1 \text{ h};$$ (11b)

$$V_i = \tau_i(\alpha p_i + \beta);$$ (11c)

$$Z_i = \tau_i \xi_i(\gamma p_i + \delta).$$ (11d)

In addition, the volume generated is subtracted from the volume to be generated:

$$\hat{V} = \hat{V} - V_i.$$ (12)

In case the volume to be generated is less than the volume generated if the brine pressure would be the maximum, then the pressure for which the minimum cost is obtained is assigned. To determine this pressure, the cost equation is written for a given volume, which is obtained by substituting into the cost equation:

$$Z_i = \xi_i \tau_i P_i = \xi_i \tau_i (\gamma p_i + \delta);$$

the value of the time, cleared from the volume Eq. (1):

$$\tau_i = \frac{V_i}{\alpha p_i + \beta};$$

resulting in the following:

$$Z_i = \xi_i V_i \frac{\gamma p_i + \delta}{\alpha p_i + \beta}.$$ (13)

Since the derivative of (13) with respect to brine pressure:

$$\frac{dZ_i}{dp_i} = \xi_i V_i \frac{\gamma \beta - \alpha \delta}{(\alpha p_i + \beta)^2};$$

cannot be zero (since the denominator of the expression is a constant), the function is monotonic and the maximum value will be one of the extremes:

$$p\,|_{Z=Z_{\max}} = \begin{cases} p^{\mathrm{U}} \iff \gamma\beta < \alpha\delta; \\ p^{\mathrm{L}} \iff \gamma\beta > \alpha\delta. \end{cases}$$

From this value, it follows that:

$$p_i = p\,|_{Z=Z_{\max}};$$ (14a)

$$\tau_i = \frac{V}{\alpha p_i + \beta};$$ (14b)

$$V_i = \hat{V};$$ (14c)

$$Z_i = \tau_i \xi_i(\gamma p_i + \delta);$$ (14d)

and a zero value is assigned to the remaining volume:

$$\hat{V} = 0.$$ (15)

Finally, the total cost is calculated by adding the costs of the twenty-four periods:

$$Z_{\mathrm{tot}} = \sum_{i=1}^{24} Z_i.$$ (16)

4 Case Study

4.1 Case Description

The case study used is a small-scale desalination plant based on the reverse osmosis process, located in the port facilities of Santa Cruz de Tenerife and operated by the University of La Laguna. This plant was acquired through the INTERREGMAC programme of the European Union and is conceived as a representative system of the real plants used in island environments, but with a reduced scale that allows its detailed study in experimental environments.

The main component of the system (see Fig. 1) is the reverse osmosis membrane module, which consists of three membrane tubes connected in series [A_1, ..., A_3]. These membranes are made of cross-coated aromatic polyamide, a type widely used in desalination applications due to its high salt rejection capacity.

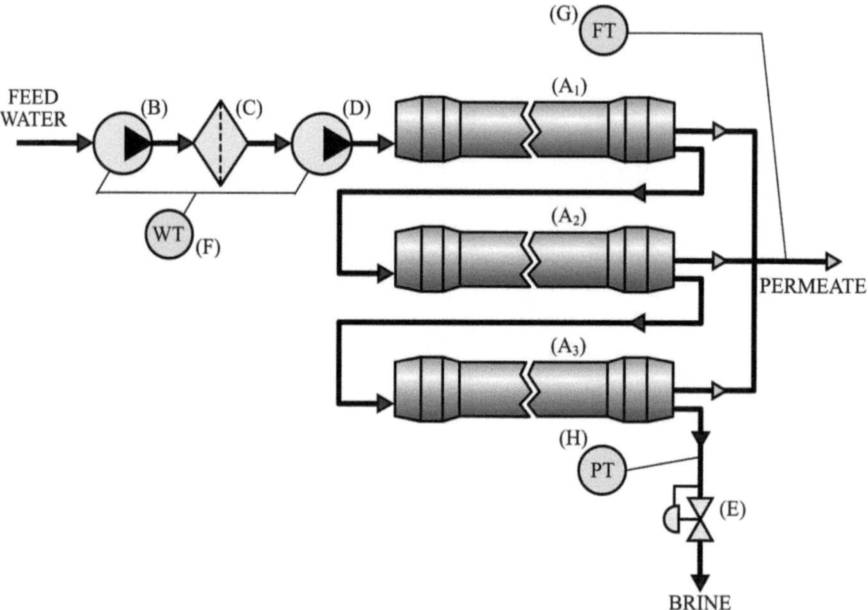

Fig. 1. Diagram of the system used as case study

The process begins with the capture of seawater by means of a low-pressure pump (between 0.25 and 0.30 MPa) [B], which drives the fluid towards a filtering system [C] where solid particles and coarse contaminants are removed. The pretreated water is then passed to a high-pressure pump [D] that raises the pressure to the values required to initiate the reverse osmosis process, reaching up to 0.70 MPa. At this stage, the saline water passes through membranes that allow water molecules to pass through, retaining the salts and producing two streams: permeate (desalinated water) and brine (concentrated reject).

The system is equipped with a pressure control valve [E] that regulates the internal pressure and, therefore, the resulting flow rates. It is also equipped with a set of industrial sensors to monitor the key operating parameters: electrical power consumed by the pumps [F], desalinated water flow rate [G], and brine pressure [H]. These sensors are integrated with a digital interface that allows data collection and storage in a database for further analysis.

4.2 Data Collecting

For data capture, an experimental protocol was established in which the system pressure (controlled process variable) was varied in a controlled manner within an experimental range from 0.389 to 0.694 MPa. This variation was performed in discrete steps, stopping at each pressure level for 10 min to allow the system variables to stabilise. During these periods, data sampling was carried out at a frequency of 1 sample per minute, which allowed the dynamics of the process to be adequately captured without generating unnecessary data overload.

The variables measured included brine pressure, p_B; desalinated water flow rate, Q_F; and the electrical power consumed by the pumps, P_P. These measurements were obtained using specific industrial sensors: an AHM1 sensor for electrical power (up to 6 kW, 0.5% accuracy), an SV8050 sensor for flow rate (range 9–150 L/min, 2% accuracy), and a PT5402 sensor for pressure (up to 10 MPa, 0.5% accuracy).

All captured data was transmitted via a digital interface to a centralised database, where it was stored for subsequent analysis and modelling. Figure 2 shows the captured values.

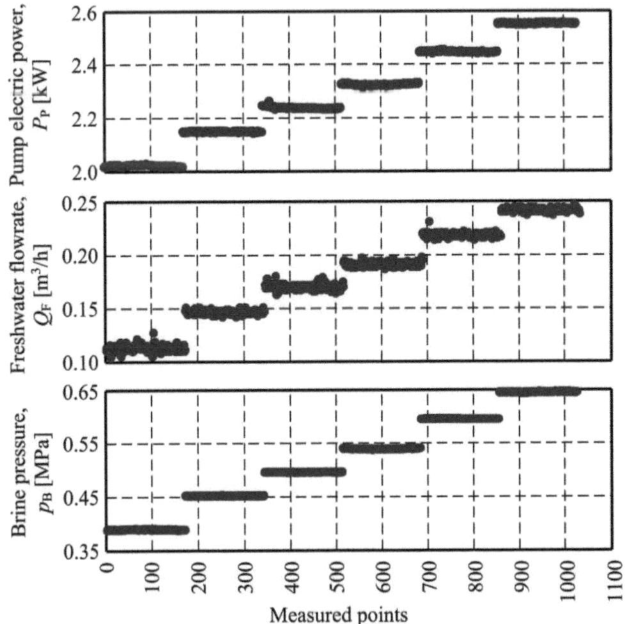

Fig. 2. Measured data

4.3   Model Fitting

The first model fitted was the one relating the electrical pumping power to the brine pressure. The coefficients of the model were obtained by the least squares method, giving the equation:

$$P_{\mathrm{P}} = 2.0667 p_{\mathrm{B}} + 1.2154; \tag{17}$$

which shows outstanding behaviour in terms of fit and significance. First, both the intercept and the slope of the model are highly significant, as evidenced by a p-value of less than 0.0001 in both cases. This implies that, at the 99.99% confidence level, there is a statistically robust relationship between the two variables, ruling out the null hypothesis of no relationship.

The analysis of variance (ANOVA) confirms this significance of the model, with an extremely high F-ratio (above two million), indicating that the variability explained by the model is much higher than the unexplained (residual) variability. The p-value associated with the full model is also virtually zero, strongly supporting the usefulness of the model as an explanatory tool.

In terms of fit, the coefficient of determination (R-squared) is 99.95%, indicating that almost all of the observed variation in the electric pump power can be explained by changes in the brine pressure. The correlation coefficient of 0.9998 indicates an almost perfect relationship between the two variables.

The model has a very low standard error of estimation (0.0038), which indicates that the dispersion of the residuals with respect to the fitted line is minimal. Also, the mean absolute error (MAE) of approximately 0.0030 reinforces the idea that the predictions are, on average, very close to the observed values, contributing to the high accuracy of the model. Figure 3-a shows the graphical representation of the fitted model of pump electric power vs. brine pressure.

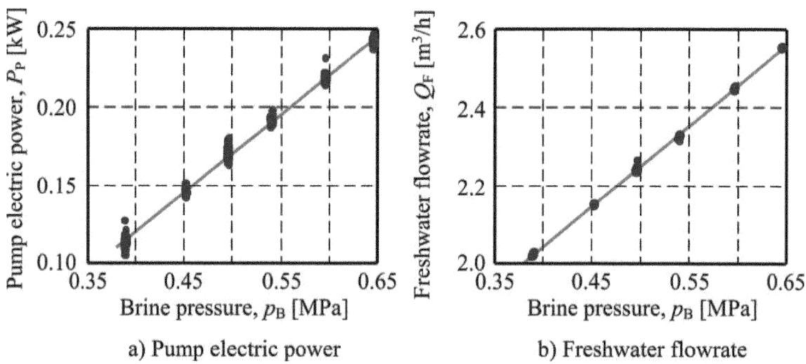

Fig. 3. Fitted models

Similarly, the linear regression model between desalinated water flow rate and brine pressure was obtained:

$$Q_{\mathrm{F}} = 0.5016 p_{\mathrm{B}} - 0.0806; \tag{18}$$

for which the analysis of the coefficients shows that both the intercept and slope are highly significant, with p-values less than 0.0001. This implies that pressure has a direct and measurable influence on the flow rate produced by the reverse osmosis system, which is consistent with the physical principle of operation of this type of plant.

From the point of view of statistical fit, the model gives a coefficient of determination of 99.65%, indicating that almost all of the observed variability in flow rate can be explained by variations in pressure. The correlation coefficient of 0.9983 confirms an extremely strong association between the two variables. Furthermore, the standard error of estimation is very low (0.0025), indicating that the model predictions are very close to the observed values, while the mean absolute error (MAE) of approximately 0.0019 reinforces this high accuracy.

The analysis of variance (ANOVA) supports these results, showing an F-value greater than 294 thousand and a p-value less than 0.01, confirming that the model is globally significant at 99% confidence. This allows us to strongly affirm that the fitted model is statistically valid and useful for predicting flow behaviour as a function of pressure. Figure 3-b shows the graphical representation of the fitted model of freshwater flowrate vs. brine pressure.

5   Optimisation Process

For the optimisation of the operation of the desalination plant, the method shown in Algorithm 1 was used. In this method, the coefficients obtained in the previous section are used as model parameters:

$$\alpha = 0.5016; \tag{19a}$$

$$\beta = -0.0806; \tag{19b}$$

$$\gamma = 2.0667; \tag{19c}$$

$$\delta = 1.2154. \tag{19d}$$

The working pressure limits from the experimental data were 5 and 8.

$$p^{\mathrm{L}} = 0.389 \text{ MPA}; \tag{20a}$$

$$p^{\mathrm{U}} = 0.694 \text{ MPA}; \tag{20b}$$

while the daily volume of water to be desalinated is:

$$V_0 = 4.0 \text{ m}^3. \tag{21}$$

The electricity tariffs used are for a period of 153 days from 1 April to 31 August 2024. Figure 4 shows graphically the hourly values of this tariff for the period considered.

6   Results and Analysis

As a result of the optimisation, the operating pressures (brine pressure) of the desalination plant were obtained for each hour of the period analysed (see Fig. 5).

The analysis of the working pressures over the period studied shows a clear correspondence between the times when the plant operates and the lowest tariff values. It is observed that the desalination plant operates predominantly during the periods when the cost of electricity is lowest, indicating that the optimisation algorithm has managed to minimise consumption at the most costly times and concentrate production at the most favourable times. This is especially evident during the early morning and some evening slots, where electricity tariff values are lower and working pressure is at its highest. On the contrary, in periods where the tariff rises, as in some night-time hours around 20:00, the plant tends to stop, which confirms the strategy of avoiding consumption at times of higher cost.

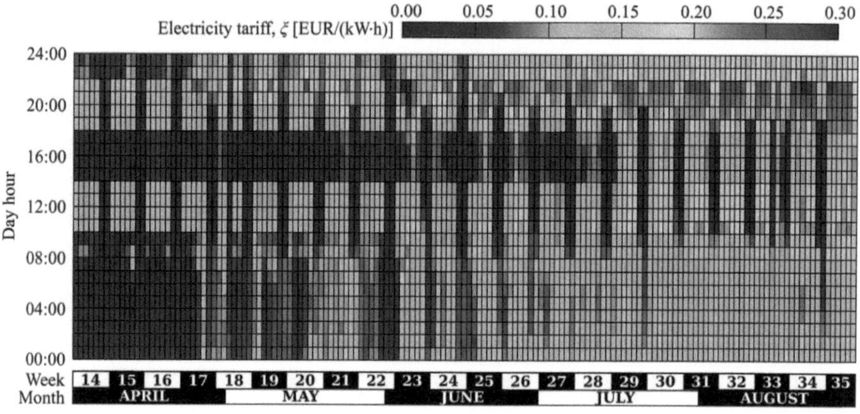

Fig. 4. Electricity tariff for the period considered

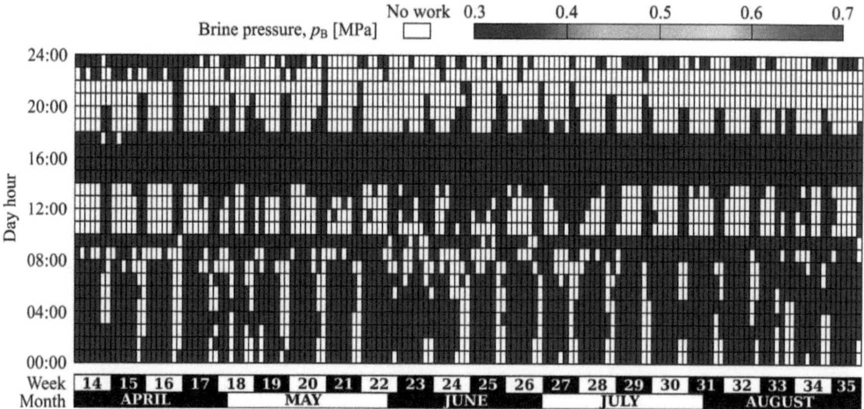

Fig. 5. Brine pressures for the optimized plant operation

Figure 6 shows the daily electricity costs for the optimised operating schemes previously shown. As can be seen, there is a marked correspondence with the electricity tariff, with higher costs on those days when the electricity tariff is higher.

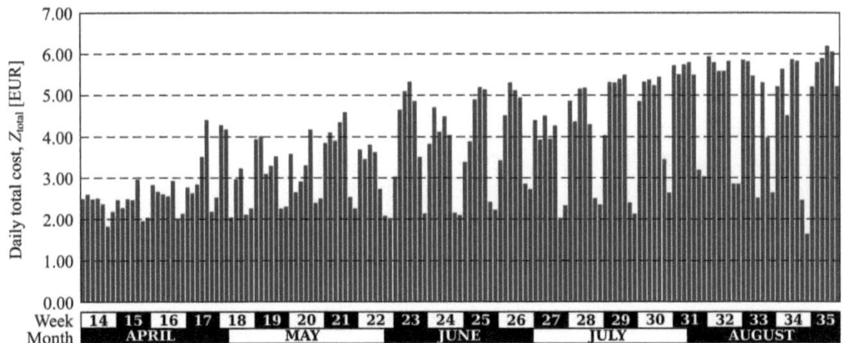

Fig. 6. Daily total costs for the optimized plant operation

Finally, in order to evaluate the savings achieved, the cost of the optimised operation was compared with that of an operation scheme at a fixed pressure, $p_\mathrm{B} = 0.493$ MPa, which guarantee the desired volume of desalinated water. Figure 7 shows the cost savings, both in absolute and relative terms.

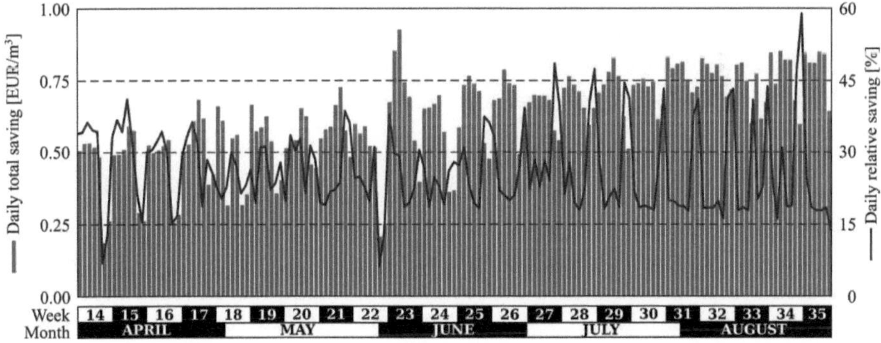

Fig. 7. Daily savings for the optimized plant operation

The analysis of daily savings shows an evolution with notable variations over the period studied. The absolute savings values in terms of EUR per cubic metre of desalinated water show an increasing trend over time, although with significant daily fluctuations. In the first days of the study, the savings remain at moderate values, but as the period progresses, an increase in the maximum values achieved is observed, especially in the months of June and July. This behaviour suggests that the optimisation strategy has managed to adapt progressively to changing electricity tariff conditions, maximising the benefits at key moments.

Relative savings, represented by the red line in the graph, show a more irregular evolution, with abrupt peaks and troughs reflecting the variability of electricity tariffs and the effectiveness of the optimisation strategy on each specific day. It is possible to identify times when the strategy achieved savings close to or above 50%, indicating a highly efficient operation on those days. However, there are also periods when the relative savings are significantly reduced, which could be related to less favourable tariff conditions or the need to ensure water production at times when energy was more expensive.

The overall behaviour of the graph suggests that optimisation has been effective in reducing operating costs without compromising water production. The presence of peaks in savings suggests that on certain days it was possible to take full advantage of the availability of low tariffs, while the fluctuations reflect the variability in the tariff structure and the need for adjustments in the operational strategy.

7   Concluding Remarks

The analysis of the images provided confirms that the optimisation of the desalination plant operation based on the electricity tariff has managed to significantly reduce energy costs without affecting water production. A clear correlation between work pressure and tariff variability has been demonstrated, with greater operational activity during periods of lower cost and strategic pauses at times of higher tariffs. This has allowed efficient control of energy expenditure to be maintained, avoiding abrupt increases in the total daily cost over the period studied. However, as the months progressed, a progressive increase in costs was observed, possibly due to changes in the base tariff or reduced availability of low-cost time slots.

Analysis of daily savings shows that the strategy has been effective in most cases, with absolute savings increasing over time. However, the relative savings fluctuate, suggesting that on certain days the optimisation was not fully efficient due to constraints on the availability of low tariffs or the need to guarantee production at specific times. Despite this, the presence of peak savings indicates that the system was able to take advantage of optimal times of operation. In conclusion, optimisation has proven to be an effective tool for cost reduction, although there are still opportunities for improvement, such as the incorporation of water storage strategies or greater operational flexibility to maximise energy efficiency.

For the future development of the proposed solution, it is recommended that complementary strategies be explored to increase operational flexibility and further improve energy efficiency. The implementation of a desalinated water storage system would allow partial decoupling of the plant's production from periods of higher energy costs, maximising the use of lower tariffs without compromising supply. Also, the integration of renewable energy sources, such as photovoltaic or wind systems, could reduce dependence on the grid and mitigate the impact of tariff fluctuations. From an operational approach, it would be beneficial to develop more advanced predictive models that incorporate tariff and water demand forecasts to optimise system scheduling in a more dynamic way. In addition, an analysis of the impact of the number of on/off cycles on the lifetime of key components, such as high-pressure pumps, is recommended to balance energy savings with the long-term sustainability of the equipment. Finally, it is suggested to evaluate the scalability of the solution in larger capacity plants, adjusting the optimisation parameters to different operating environments to validate its applicability in wider industrial contexts.

Acknowledgments. This work has been co-funded by INTERREG MAC 2021–2027 program, within the IDIWATER project (1/MAC/1/1.1/0022), which is integrated into the DESAL+ Living Lab Platform (https://www.desalinationlab.com).

Disclosure of Interests. The authors have no competing interests to declare that are relevant to the content of this article.

References

1. Abdelsalam, R.A., Farag, H., Zeineldin, H., El-saadany, E.: Optimal energy management system for green hydrogen production and seawater desalination plants with demand response integration. In: 2024 IEEE Industrial Electronics and Applications Conference (IEACon), pp. 136–140 (2024). https://doi.org/10.1109/IEACon61321.2024.10797401
2. Avila, D., Marichal, G., Hernández, A., San Luis, F.: Hybrid renewable energy systems for energy supply to autonomous desalination systems on isolated islands. In: Azar, A., Kamal, N. (eds.) Design, Analysis, and Applications of Renewable Energy Systems, pp. 23–51. Academic Press, Cambridge (2021)
3. Avila Prats, D., San Luis Gutiérrez, F., Hernández López, À., Marichal Plasencia, G.: Optimal arrangements of renewable energy systems for promoting the decarbonization of desalination plants. J. Marine Sci. Eng. **12**, 1193 (2024). https://doi.org/10.3390/jmse12071193
4. Förster, R., Harding, S., Buhl, H.U.: Unleashing the economic and ecological potential of energy flexibility: attractiveness of real-time electricity tariffs in energy crises. Energy Policy **185**, 113975 (2024). https://doi.org/10.1016/j.enpol.2023.113975
5. Hao, C.H., et al.: Dynamic pricing in consumer-centric electricity markets: a systematic review and thematic analysis. Energ. Strat. Rev. **52**, 101349 (2024). https://doi.org/10.1016/j.esr.2024.101349
6. Häseler, S., Wulf, A.J.: Promoting real-time electricity tariffs for more demand response from German households: a review of four policy options. Energy Sustain. Soc. **14**(1), 59 (2024)
7. Mekonnen, T., Bhandari, R., Ramayya, V.: Modeling, analysis and optimization of grid-integrated and islanded solar PV systems for the Ethiopian residential sector: Considering an emerging utility tariff plan for 2021 and beyond. Energies **14**(11), 3360 (2021). https://doi.org/10.3390/en14113360

8. Nakai, M., von Loessl, V., Wetzel, H.: Preferences for dynamic electricity tariffs: a comparison of households in Germany and Japan. Ecol. Econ. **223**, 108239 (2024). https://doi.org/10.1016/j.ecolecon.2024.108239

9. Okampo, E.J., Nwulu, N.I.: Optimal energy mix for a reverse osmosis desalination unit considering demand response. J. Eng. Design Technol. **18**(5), 1287–1303 (2020). https://doi.org/10.1108/JEDT-01-2020-0025

10. Padrón, I., García, M., Marichal, G., Avila, D.: Wave energy potential of the Coast of El Hierro Island for the exploitation of a wave energy converter (WEC). Sustainability **14**, 12139 (2022). https://doi.org/10.3390/su141912139

11. Rao, A.K., Atia, A.A., Knueven, B., Mauter, M.S.: Optimizing desalination operations for energy flexibility. ACS Sustain. Chem. Eng. **12**(42), 15696–15704 (2024). https://doi.org/10.1021/acssuschemeng.4c06353

12. Touati, K., Mulligan, C.N.: Energy consumption and energy efficiency of high-pressure reverse osmosis: effect of water recovery, number of stages, and energy recovery. Appl. Energy **382**, 125270 (2025). https://doi.org/10.1016/j.apenergy.2024.125270

13. Wang, C., et al.: Quantifying analysis and expanding application of desalination energy recovery technology. Desalin. Water Treat. **320**, 00807 (2024). https://doi.org/10.1016/j.dwt.2024.100807

14. Yujie, G., Hao, Y., Bowen, Z., Xinyi, C., Zhijun, H.: Optimal operation of new coastal power systems with seawater desalination based on grey wolf optimization. Energy Rep. **9**, 391–402 (2023). https://doi.org/10.1016/j.egyr.2023.04.299

15. Zaki, D.A., Hamdy, M.: A review of electricity tariffs and enabling solutions for optimal energy management. Energies **15**(22), 8527 (2022). https://doi.org/10.3390/en15228527

Detecting Economic Vulnerability via Multi-Agent LLM Architecture and Context-Aware Cluster Analysis

Vitali Herrera-Semenets[1]([✉]), Lázaro Bustio-Martínez[2], Jan van den Berg[3], and Miguel Ángel Álvarez-Carmona[4]

[1] Advanced Technologies Application Center (CENATAV), La Habana, Cuba
`vherrera@cenatav.co.cu`
[2] Iberoamerican University, México City, Mexico
`lazaro.bustio@ibero.mx`
[3] Intelligent Systems Department, Delft University of Technology, Delft, The Netherlands
`j.vandenberg@tudelft.nl`
[4] Centro de Investigación en Matemáticas, Monterrey, Mexico
`miguel.alvarez@cimat.mx`

Abstract. Social security programs aim to protect vulnerable populations; however, accurately identifying individuals with significantly lower incomes than their peers (accounting for age, occupation, and education level) remains an operational challenge. This article proposes an innovative method for detecting economic vulnerability by combining income data enrichment with large language models in a multi-agent architecture, unsupervised clustering techniques, and statistical heuristics. The developed algorithm analyzes demographic and labor-related variables to estimate expected annual income by profile, thereby identifying atypical discrepancies that suggest vulnerability. This approach not only optimizes the prioritization of beneficiaries for targeted assistance but also serves as a preventive mechanism against the inadvertent exclusion of eligible groups. Preliminary results demonstrate the method's effectiveness in detecting hidden vulnerability particularly among young adults aged 17–23, whose high underemployment rates ($\approx 40\%$) in recent national statistics closely align with the concentration of vulnerability detected. These findings underscore its potential as a complementary tool to enhance equity and efficiency in social policy implementation.

Keywords: multi-agent · large language models · clustering · economic vulnerability

1 Introduction

Social security programs serve as critical mechanisms for reducing inequality and protecting economically vulnerable populations. Yet, proactively identifying individuals whose incomes fall significantly below those of their peers due to underemployment, informal labor, or systemic barriers remains a persistent challenge. Conventional approaches, such as standardized poverty thresholds or self-reported income data, often fail to capture intragroup disparities. For instance, a Disability Insurance (DI) beneficiary with a college degree and part-time employment may face greater economic hardship than his profile suggests, but traditional systems rarely flag such cases.

The magnitude of economic insecurity in America underscores the urgency of this issue. About a quarter of Americans are economically insecure, defined as living in a household earning income below 200 percent of the federal poverty level amounting to roughly 29,000 annually for a single person or 60,000 for a family of four in 2023 [5]. This population includes not only those unable to meet basic needs but also those teetering on the brink of financial catastrophe due to unexpected expenses.

Critically, conventional eligibility criteria often fail to identify vulnerable individuals whose incomes are just above the poverty threshold. However, these incomes are still insufficient for their specific circumstances, which represents a systemic blind spot that results in false negatives. For instance, a credentialed teacher earning significantly less than peers with comparable education may face severe deprivation but remain ineligible for assistance due to rigid income cutoffs. These gaps are compounded by stark inequities: while the top 1 percent of earners captured over 20% of national income in 2018 [14], social assistance frameworks rely on outdated data systems where Internal Revenue Service reporting lags and self-reported income fails to capture contextual disparities. The result is a dual failure: those in acute need are overlooked, while arbitrary thresholds perpetuate cycles of deprivation among "near-poor" populations whose economic vulnerability is invisible to traditional metrics.

To address these limitations, we propose a novel method combining demographic similarity analysis and large language model (LLM)-based data enrichment to uncover hidden economic vulnerability. Our method leverages a LLM to estimate expected incomes using labor statistics, sectoral trends, and individual descriptors (e.g., occupation, education, work hours, and location). By clustering beneficiaries with comparable profiles, the system identifies atypical income discrepancies as potential markers of vulnerability.

This work makes two key contributions to the field. First, it introduces context-aware targeting, advancing beyond rigid poverty thresholds by incorporating contextual socioeconomic disparities for instance, differentiating between a college-educated part-time professional and a full-time unskilled laborer. Second, it reduces false negatives by identifying beneficiaries who technically qualify for assistance but whose incomes are inadequate relative to their demographic or occupational profiles, addressing a major limitation of conventional targeting systems. Together, these advances enhance equity by revealing hidden vulnerabilities where traditional poverty measures fail to capture contextually disadvantaged populations.

The remainder of this paper is organized as follows: Sect. 2 reviews related work on vulnerability metrics and AI applications in social policy; Sect. 3 details our methodology; in Sect. 4, the experimental results are presented and discussed; and finally in Sect. 5, the conclusions and future work are outlined.

2   Background

The identification of economic vulnerability through artificial intelligence techniques has been addressed from various perspectives in recent literature. A first group of studies has focused on approaches based on spatial data and remote sensing. Research such as [6] has demonstrated the potential of machine learning to estimate poverty levels at microgeographic scales using satellite data, including variables like nighttime luminosity and land cover. While methods like Random Forest achieve high predictive accuracy in this context, they present significant limitations, particularly in their inability to capture individual-level disparities and intrinsic socioeconomic dynamics such as educational attainment or occupation type. Comparative studies like that of Corral et al. [2] in Mexico have revealed that, contrary to expectations, traditional methods may outperform machine learning-based approaches in certain scenarios, highlighting the importance of adapting models to specific contexts.

A second approach in the literature has explored the integration of multi-modal data sources to improve the estimation of economic vulnerability. Some studies have combined spatial data with information from social networks, urban imagery, and telecommunications records. For instance, researchers have used geolocated Wikipedia articles [13], OpenStreetMaps points of interest [10], aerial photographs [12], street-level images [16], as well as mobile call records [9] and Facebook user data [7]. Although these approaches have shown promising results in terms of predictive accuracy, they continue to face fundamental challenges, particularly regarding data granularity, which remains predominantly geographic rather than individual, and limited capacity to contextualize dynamic socioeconomic factors like employment or income fluctuations.

A third group of studies has adopted approaches based on socioeconomic microdata. Works such as Nachev [11] have analyzed microdata databases (e.g., IPUMS USA) using machine learning techniques, identifying key variables like education and employment as significant predictors of economic vulnerability. However, these models tend to assume homogeneity within broad demographic groups, without considering critical variations such as hours worked or specific economic sector, which limits their ability to capture more subtle but equally significant vulnerabilities.

The analysis conducted on the works reviewed in this section revealed three main limitations commonly shared across current approaches. First, the lack of individual granularity, as most operate at geographic or group levels, without the ability to compare individuals with their demographic-labor peers. Second, the dependence on static characteristics, prioritizing physical environmental attributes over changing socioeconomic dynamics. Finally, a predominantly reactive approach, focused on measuring existing poverty rather than detecting emerging vulnerability, such as abrupt income drops within a reference group.

Our methodological proposal seeks to address these limitations through three key innovations. First, we incorporate data enrichment techniques using advanced language models (LLMs), which enable estimating expected income at the individual level even with incomplete data, leveraging sectoral and demographic patterns. Second, we implement a contextual clustering step that segments individuals by similarities in age, education, occupation, and hours worked. Third, we established a peer-comparison heuristic that identifies outlier cases where an individual's income deviates substantially from the expected range for their specific profile. Unlike existing approaches, our method is not only compatible with current social security systems but adds a layer of proactive prevention and overcomes the dependence on fixed thresholds through contextualized analysis of economic vulnerability.

3   Proposal

The proposed strategy is structured into three fundamental stages: (1) the estimation of annual incomes using large language models (LLMs), (2) data preprocessing, and (3) anomaly detection in the estimated incomes (see Fig. 1).

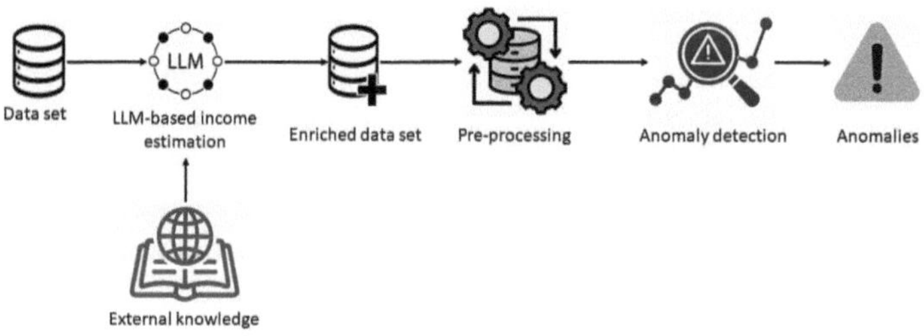

Fig. 1. General scheme workflow.

The estimation of annual incomes is based on socioeconomic statistics reported by official institutions responsible for collecting and analyzing labor data (e.g., the U.S. Bureau of Labor Statistics (BLS)[1]). These sources provide information on variables such as educational level, age, gender, and occupation, which serve as a basis for calculating regional or national salary averages.

To improve the accuracy of individual estimates, a large language model (LLM) is incorporated. This model enriches the dataset by processing demographic and occupational characteristics of each individual and combining them with relevant external knowledge. This process follows an unsupervised multi-agent architecture (*Conciliator Architecture*), where agents interact iteratively until reaching consensus. As shown in Fig. 2, the proposed architecture integrates three components:

---

[1] https://www.bls.gov/news.release/empsit.toc.htm.

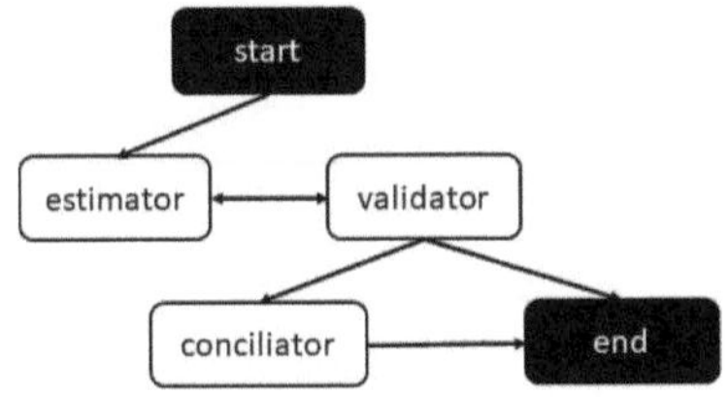

Fig. 2. Multi-agent architecture applied.

- **Estimator Agent**: Based on an LLM, this agent generates initial income estimates using both the available dataset information and additional statistical data obtained through *Retrieval-Augmented Generation* (RAG) [8].
- **Validator Agent**: This agent utilizes rules generated via machine learning techniques (e.g., decision trees). If an estimate is rejected, it requests a re-evaluation from the Estimator Agent and also provides the specific rule that triggered the rejection. This process is repeated up to a maximum of N iterations.
- **Conciliator Agent**: In the event that no agreement is reached after N attempts, the conciliator agent intervenes to resolve the conflict. This agent analyzes the history of estimates and responses generated, as well as the information used by the estimator agent, to make a final decision. Cases where the conciliator determines that the estimator agent's assessment was correct are used as labeled samples to generate new rules in the validator agent, thereby updating the rule base.

Once the annual income estimates for all individuals have been obtained, the dataset is preprocessed. This stage includes the identification of categorical and numerical features, encoding of categorical features using Label Encoding and normalization of numerical features to standardize their scale. These transformations are essential for preparing the data for subsequent analysis and ensuring that anomaly detection algorithms function correctly.

The final stage involves identifying potential cases of economic vulnerability within the dataset. For this purpose, the K-Prototypes clustering algorithm [4] is employed, which allows simultaneous handling of categorical and numerical features. The specific steps are as follows:

1. **Initial Clustering**: The K-Prototypes algorithm is applied to divide individuals into clusters, where each cluster C_j contains individuals with similar characteristics.
2. **Subset Selection**: Within each cluster, a subset $c_j \subset C_j$ of individuals closest to the cluster centroid is selected. This is achieved by defining a threshold $T_j = \mathrm{Percentile}_5(d_{i,j})$ based on the 5th percentile of distances to the centroid, where $d_{i,j}$ represents the distance between individual i and centroid j. An individual i belongs to c_j if the condition $d_{i,j} < T_j$ is satisfied.

3. **Anomaly Identification**: For each homogeneous subset c_j, we establish an income threshold $E(c_j)$ to detect statistically significant deviations below the cluster mean, as defined by Eq. 1:

$$E(c_j) = \mu_{c_j} - 2\sigma_{c_j}, \tag{1}$$

where μ_{c_j} and σ_{c_j} represent the mean income and standard deviation of subset c_j, respectively. An individual i is considered potentially vulnerable if their estimated income v_i satisfies the condition $v_i < E(c_j)$.

Individuals identified as vulnerable can be subject to further analysis or specific interventions, depending on the application context.

4 Experimental Results

This section details: (1) the dataset used and its preprocessing, (2) the experimental setup of the multi-agent system, and (3) a comprehensive analysis of the identified socioeconomic clusters and patterns of economic vulnerability detected through the proposed method.

4.1 Adult Income Dataset

The proposed method was evaluated using the Adult Income Dataset [1], a benchmark dataset containing socioeconomic information from individuals in the United States (1994 Census). The dataset comprises 48 842 entries, each described by 14 features (8 categorical and 6 numerical). The categorical feature with the highest cardinality is *native country* (42 unique values).

Originally, the dataset includes a binary label classifying annual income as $\leq \$50K$ (Class 0) or $> \$50K$ (Class 1). However, since actual income data is sensitive and subject to legal restrictions, we redefined the task: we removed the original label and trained an LLM model to estimate annual income, generating a new *"Estimated Income"* attribute. This approach allows assessing economic vulnerability without relying on confidential data.

4.2 Experimental Setup

For income estimation, we employed Llama 3.2 70B as the core model for the estimator agent. This choice was driven by its robust reasoning capabilities and scalability in handling complex demographic and labor-related variables. The validator agent leveraged a rule-based approach derived from a Decision Tree algorithm, trained on individual-level data indicating whether annual income exceeded \$50K. The decision rules extracted from the tree served as validation criteria for the estimator's outputs. The conciliator agent utilized Phi-4 model, tasked with resolving discrepancies between the estimator and validator. We set $N = 3$ as the maximum number of iterative refinements between the estimator and validator agents based on empirical observations during preliminary testing. This value provided a practical balance between computational efficiency and convergence reliability. In our experiments, the vast majority of disagreements between the estimator and validator were resolved within two iterations, with diminishing returns observed beyond the third refinement. Setting a higher value of N did not yield significant improvements in estimation quality but increased the overall runtime. Therefore, $N = 3$ was selected as a conservative yet efficient threshold that ensures sufficient opportunity for agent consensus while maintaining computational tractability.

Despite using two decade-old dataset where wage structures (e.g., hourly rates) have since evolved, the system demonstrated 92 % accuracy in income estimations when validated against the conciliator's decisions. This highlights two critical strengths: (1) the conciliator agent effectively bridges gaps between outdated classification rules (e.g., the \$50K threshold) and current economic realities, and (2) the multi-agent architecture mitigates data obsolescence by dynamically contextualizing historical patterns.

4.3   Cluster Analysis

After income estimation and preprocessing stage, a clustering step was applied to segment the population into five socioeconomically homogeneous groups. As shown in Fig. 3, the optimal number of clusters (k=5) was determined through application of the Elbow method [3], which identifies the point of diminishing returns in within-cluster variance reduction.

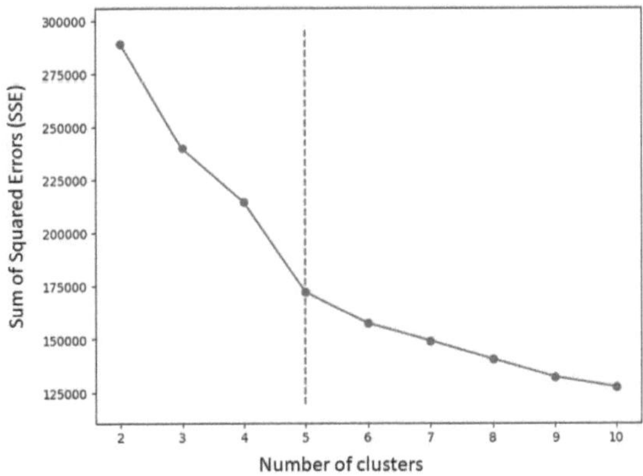

Fig. 3. Optimal number of cluster determination via Elbow method.

The clustering results revealed five distinct socioeconomic groups, summarized in Table 1 and detailed below.

Table 1. Cluster Comparison

Criterion	Cluster 0	Cluster 1	Cluster 2	Cluster 3	Cluster 4
Income	\$75K–\$150K	$\leq \$50K$	$> \$100K$	$> \$50K$ (maj.)	$\leq \$50K$ (maj.)
Education	Bachelor's+	HS/Some-college	Master's/Ph.D.	HS–Postgrad	HS-grad/Some-college
Occupations	Executives	Service	Exec-managerial	Mixed	Technical
Diversity	Low	High	Very low	Moderate	Minimal
Stability	High	Low	Very high	Medium	Low

Cluster 0: Highly Educated Professionals (Upper-Middle/High Class)
This cluster predominantly consists of middle-aged white males holding university degrees (Bachelor's or higher), particularly those with Ph.D. degrees achieving the highest income brackets (\$75K-\$150K). These individuals typically occupy executive positions, specialized professional roles, or sales occupations, working extended weeks of 40–60 hours. The cluster represents the established professional class, demonstrating a strong positive correlation between advanced education attainment and high-income levels, characteristic of the upper-middle and high socioeconomic strata.

Cluster 1: Working Class with Underemployment Characterized by demographic diversity in age and gender, this cluster comprises individuals with medium education levels (High School graduates or those with some college experience). They primarily work in service, manufacturing, or administrative roles, earning $\leq$\$50K annually. Notably, the cluster includes cases of educated individuals receiving low wages, indicating systemic underemployment. This group reflects the economic constraints of the lower-middle class, highlighting a distinct education-occupation mismatch prevalent in the labor market.

Cluster 2: Labor Elite The labor elite cluster is exclusively composed of married white males with advanced degrees (Master's/Ph.D.), working as executives (Exec-managerial) or highly specialized professionals. Their substantial incomes (>\$100K) are complemented by significant capital benefits, with work schedules typically exceeding 50 h weekly. This group represents the socioeconomic elite, distinguished by prevalent self-employment patterns and marked advantages in both professional status and compensation.

Cluster 3: Diverse Professionals This heterogeneous cluster contains married males across a broad age range with medium-to-high education (Bachelor's to postgraduate degrees). Their occupational distribution spans from executives to manual workers, with most members earning >\$50K (though some cases fall below this threshold). While showing relative economic stability compared to lower-tier clusters, this group displays less internal cohesion than other clusters, characterized by its occupational diversity and variable income levels.

Cluster 4: Manual Workers Primarily consisting of married white males with basic education (HS-grad or Some-college), this cluster engages in technical trades (craft-repair), machine operation, or transportation occupations. Most earn $\leq$\$50K annually, excepting specialized roles that occasionally exceed this threshold. Working standard 40–50 hour weeks, these individuals exhibit low economic mobility and minimal demographic diversity, typifying the characteristics of traditional manual labor sectors in the contemporary workforce.

The cluster analysis reveals significant socioeconomic stratification within the dataset, highlighting three key patterns. First, a pronounced disparity emerges between high-income clusters (0 and 2), characterized by advanced education and professional occupations, and lower-income clusters (1 and 4), which face persistent economic limitations despite varying educational backgrounds. Second, Cluster 1 presents a distinct case of underemployment, where mid-educated individuals remain confined to low-wage roles, suggesting inefficiencies in labor market allocation. Third, the demographic concentration of white males in high-earning clusters (0 and 2) contrasts with the greater diversity in lower-income groups, pointing to potential structural biases in occupational mobility and income distribution. Collectively, these findings validate the effectiveness of the proposed methodology in detecting nuanced economic vulnerability patterns while maintaining data privacy, as the approach successfully identifies critical socioeconomic divides without relying on sensitive income records. The results underscore not only the method's analytical robustness but also its applicability in policy-relevant assessments of labor market disparities.

4.4 Economic Vulnerability Analysis Findings Based on Anomaly Detection

Following the anomaly detection stage, 48 cases of potential economic vulnerability were identified in the sample, showing uneven distribution across predefined socioeconomic clusters (see Fig. 4). The analysis showed that 77 % of vulnerable cases (37 individuals) fell within Cluster 1, comprising young adults with secondary education (high school graduates or partial technical training) engaged in informal or unstable employment, indicating systemic barriers to formal labor market integration. Simultaneously, 8.3 % of cases (4 individuals) belonged to Cluster 4 of manual workers, predominantly older adults with basic education whose vulnerability stems from inadequate pension benefits and limited professional retraining opportunities. These findings highlight two critical socioeconomic challenges: persistent difficulties for educated youth in securing stable employment commensurate with their qualifications, and the economic fragility of aging workers transitioning out of the labor force.

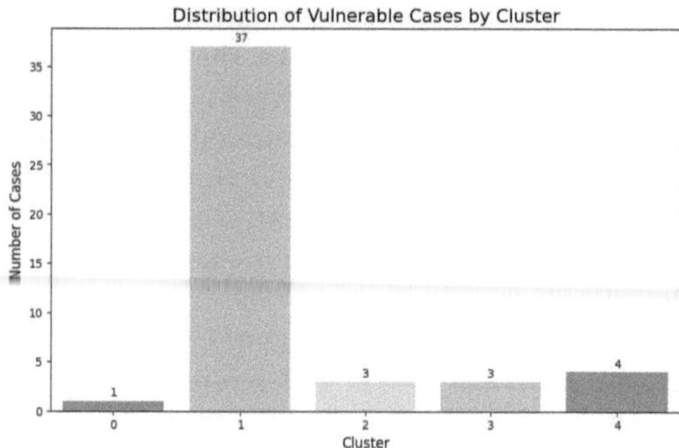

Fig. 4. Distribution of vulnerable cases by cluster.

A balanced gender distribution was observed, with 56.2% male representation compared to 43.8% female. However, the age distribution revealed significant disparities (see Fig. 5). The average age of the population was 35.5 years, with a notable concentration (39.5%) in the 17–23 age range. This observation becomes particularly relevant when contrasted with recent labor statistics: a study conducted in May 2024 reported that approximately 40% of newly graduated university students in the United States were underemployed, i.e., working in jobs that did not require a college degree [15]. This figure closely aligns with the 39.5% of individuals identified as economically vulnerable by our method, falling precisely within the typical age range of recent graduates.

Such an overrepresentation of young adults among the vulnerable cases suggests the existence of structural labor market challenges affecting this demographic. It supports the hypothesis that individuals at the early stages of their professional careers face heightened socioeconomic risks, likely linked to temporary or part-time employment, substandard wages, limited access to employment benefits, and high job turnover rates.

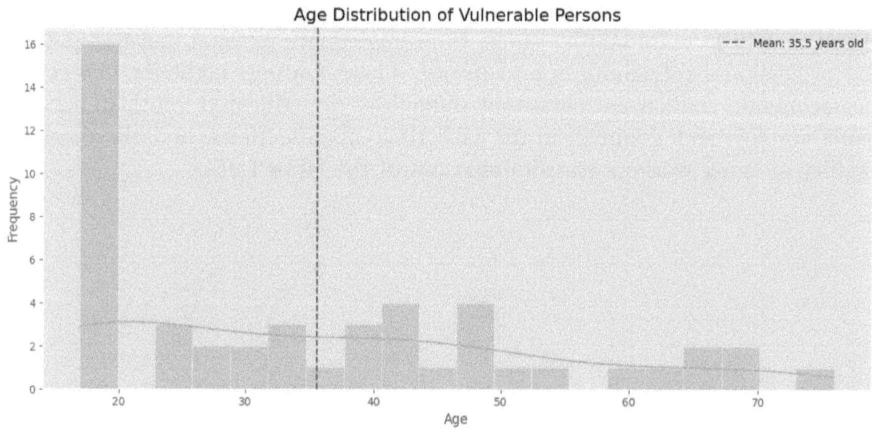

Fig. 5. Age distribution of vulnerable persons.

A determining factor was marital status (see Fig. 6), where more than half of the cases (54.2 %) corresponded to never-married individuals, followed by divorced (29.2 %) and widowed (8.3 %) persons. This pattern may indicate that lack of family support networks or post-separation financial instability increases the risk of insufficient income. Furthermore, educational attainment showed a clear correlation: most affected individuals had incomplete secondary education (11th grade) or only a high school diploma (HS-grad), while merely 4 cases held university degrees (Bachelors) (see Fig. 7).

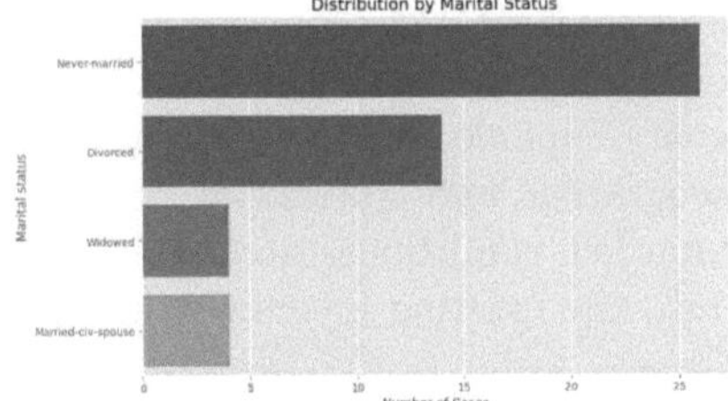

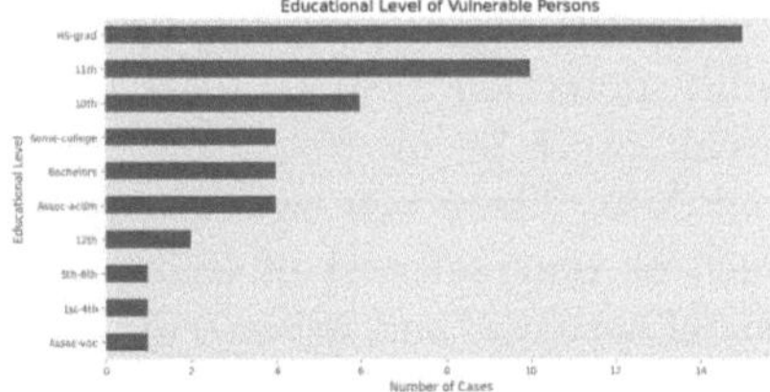

Fig. 7. Educational Level of Vulnerable Persons.

Fig. 6. Distribution by Marital Status.

This approach proves particularly valuable in policy applications, where outdated administrative data often necessitates compensatory logic to maintain operational relevance. The results demonstrate the necessity for differentiated policy interventions, including targeted vocational training programs to facilitate youth employment transitions, comprehensive pension system reforms coupled with flexible work arrangements for older workers, and enhanced wage protection measures in low-income sectors where vulnerable populations concentrate. This evidence-based assessment provides a foundation for developing tailored solutions to address distinct vulnerability patterns across different demographic groups in the labor market.

5   Conclusions

The proposed method represents a promising solution in identifying economic vulnerability by combining income data enrichment with LLMs in a multi-agent architecture, unsupervised clustering techniques, and statistical heuristics. This innovative approach detects atypical discrepancies in expected income based on demographic and labor profiles (occupation, education, age), uncovering hidden vulnerability patterns even in contexts with incomplete fiscal data. Preliminary results demonstrate its effectiveness by revealing critical socioeconomic stratifications, such as the concentration of vulnerability among young adults with secondary education trapped in informal employment (77 % of detected cases) and older adults with insufficient pensions, while also exposing structural biases in income distribution by gender and ethnicity. Also, these findings highlight a critical correspondence between the age distribution of detected vulnerable individuals and national underemployment statistics, reinforcing the potential of the proposed method to uncover hidden socioeconomic risks in demographically sensitive groups, such as recent graduates entering the labor market.

The proposal not only optimizes the prioritization of beneficiaries for targeted social assistance but also serves as a preventive tool against inadvertent exclusions, providing a robust analytical foundation for designing tailored policies such as youth vocational training programs or pension reforms thereby enhancing equity and efficiency in social policy implementation without compromising data privacy.

To further improve the precision and robustness of our economic vulnerability detection system, future work will focus on expanding the multi-agent architecture by incorporating specialized agents capable of processing geospatial data. These new agents will integrate geographic and contextual variables such as regional cost of living, local labor market conditions, accessibility to social services, and urban/rural disparities into the existing income estimation framework.

References

1. Becker, B., Kohavi, R.: Adult. UCI Machine Learning Repository (1996). https://doi.org/10.24432/C5XW20
2. Corral, P., Henderson, H., Segovia, S.: Poverty mapping in the age of machine learning. J. Dev. Econ. **172**, 103377 (2025)
3. Cui, M., et al.: Introduction to the k-means clustering algorithm based on the elbow method. Acc. Auditing Finance **1**(1), 5–8 (2020)
4. Huang, Z.: Extensions to the k-means algorithm for clustering large data sets with categorical values. Data Min. Knowl. Disc. **2**(3), 283–304 (1998)
5. Johnson, R.W., Smith, K.E., Furtado, K., Balu, R., Cosic, D.: Does the 2023 social security expansion act improve equity in key outcomes?: an equity scoring initiative demonstration analysis. Urban Institute (2024)
6. Lamichhane, B.R., Isnan, M., Horanont, T.: Exploring machine learning trends in poverty mapping: a review and meta-analysis. Sci. Remote Sens., 100200 (2025)
7. Ledesma, C., Garonita, O.L., Flores, L.J., Tingzon, I., Dalisay, D.: Interpretable poverty mapping using social media data, satellite images, and geospatial information. arXiv preprint arXiv:2011.13563 (2020)
8. Lewis, P., et al.: Retrieval-augmented generation for knowledge-intensive NLP tasks. Adv. Neural. Inf. Process. Syst. **33**, 9459–9474 (2020)
9. Moya-Gómez, B., Stępniak, M., García-Palomares, J.C., Frías-Martínez, E., Gutiérrez, J.: Exploring night and day socio-spatial segregation based on mobile phone data: the case of Medellin (Colombia). Comput. Environ. Urban Syst. **89**, 101675 (2021)
10. Muñetón-Santa, G., Manrique-Ruiz, L.C.: Predicting multidimensional poverty with machine learning algorithms: an open data source approach using spatial data. Soc. Sci. **12**(5), 296 (2023)
11. Nachev, A.: Exploring poverty factors through predictive modeling. In: Arabnia, H.R., Ferens, K., Deligiannidis, L. (eds.) Applied Cognitive Computing and Artificial Intelligence, pp. 329–342. Springer Nature Switzerland, Cham (2025)

12. Pokhriyal, N., Zambrano, O., Linares, J., Hernández, H.: Estimating and forecasting income poverty and inequality in Haiti using satellite imagery and mobile phone data (2020)
13. Sheehan, E., et al.: Predicting economic development using geolocated wikipedia articles. In: Proceedings of the 25th ACM SIGKDD international conference on knowledge discovery and data mining, pp. 2698–2706 (2019)
14. Smalligan, J., Boyens, C.: Encouraging work in the supplemental security income program. Soc. Secur. Adm. (2022)
15. Statista: Racién graduados universitarios en situación de infraempleo en ee.uu. 2017-2024. [online]. [cited april 11, 2025]. Available: https://es.statista.com/ estadisticas/1340423/porcentaje-de-recien-graduados-universitarios-de-ee-uu-subempleados/ (2024)
16. Suel, E., Bhatt, S., Brauer, M., Flaxman, S., Ezzati, M.: Multimodal deep learning from satellite and street-level imagery for measuring income, overcrowding, and environmental deprivation in urban areas. Remote Sens. Environ. **257**, 112339 (2021)

Feature Selection for Anomaly Detection in Banking Transactions Based on Deep Learning and Reconstruction Error

Alayn Lado Chaviano, Vladimir Milián Núñez[(✉)], and C. Orlando Grabiel Toledano López

Universidad de Las Ciencias Informáticas, 19370 La Habana, CP, Cuba
{alado,vmilian,ogtoledano}@uci.cu

Abstract. Since 2019 in Cuba, the need for more effective bank fraud detection systems has become apparent due to the increase in transactions and fraud. The problem is exacerbated by data imbalance, with the fraud class accounting for less than 1%. Banking data is inherently complex, making it difficult to separate effectively using traditional classification methods. Concept drift, where behavioural patterns change over time, further complicates accurate fraud detection and requires innovative solutions. Misclassification of data is due to the human factor, as some frauds go unreported to hide illegalities such as currency trafficking or tax evasion, while others are fabricated to obtain a refund from the bank. This study proposes an Autoencoder-based deep learning model for anomaly detection and feature selection. It is experimentally trained on normal transactions only, and the decision threshold is determined by the overall maximum value of the F-score. After identifying the best hyperparameters, feature selection is performed based on the sum of the individual reconstruction error of each feature with anomalies only, setting a new decision threshold for feature selection. Based on these results, a model with normal operations is trained with an F-score of 83.04% on the Kaggle credit card database. This approach provides an efficient solution to the problems.

Keywords: bank fraud detection · Concept Drift · data imbalance · deep learning · reconstruction error

1 Introduction

In an increasingly interconnected world thanks to the advances of the internet of things, 5G and social networks, more and more transactions are carried out at the reach of a mobile device. From paying for services and payments in official virtual stores, to evading taxes by buying directly from a reseller or accessing sites of dubious security and legality to make online payments. This leads to the user's bank details surfing the net without any kind of security and falling into the hands of unauthorized persons.

In the constantly evolving cybersecurity landscape, it is crucial to stay informed about the various cyberattacks that threaten individuals and organizations. The impact of these attacks is substantial, both in terms of financial and reputational losses. The

Y. Hernádez Heredia et al. (Eds.): IWAIPR 2025, LNCS 16328, pp. 268–278, 2026.
https://doi.org/10.1007/978-3-032-11358-0_22

Federal Bureau of Investigation's (FBI) Internet Crime Report for 2022 revealed that the public reported a total of 800,944 cybercrimes [1] of which credit card fraud alone accounted for 3%.

Electronic commerce in Cuba is a fact. Thousands of Cubans have benefited from the benefits of computerization. Even in times of pandemic, processes that some years ago were bogged down in long bureaucratic procedures, or as Cubans know, in long lines, have been simplified. Options for transportation and gastronomy were born and strengthened. The payment of electricity, gas, telephone, water and Internet services, among others, was facilitated. But in the era of online shopping and services, there are also shadows. Every day new methods to protect our data are unveiled, at the same time that new forms of fraud are unveiled. And Cuba is not exempt from that. Old forms of identity theft, what we know as phishing, computer viruses to steal information, tests and much more, also happen in our island. But something much simpler takes its toll on us, the lack of knowledge of information technologies [2].

Cuba is undergoing a process of bankarization that began with 14 million magnetic cards in the country. There are two payment gateways, EnZona with one million users and Transfermovil with five million, where the latter alone performs more than 110 million transactions monthly. In addition, there are 95,000 QR codes generated for online payment. In the state sector, in the agencies defined as those with the highest participation, i.e. Minag, Minal, Mintur, Mincin, a 96% deployment of electronic payment channels is being reported [3].

In Cuba there have been cases of bank fraud registered in Cubadebate, such as those that occurred in 2019 [4] and 2020 [2]. With the computerization of society and the increase of currency exchange in the informal market as of 2021, more cases occurred, in 2022 there were 200 people reported in the National Police (PNR) only in the municipality of Camagüey for fraud [5].

The challenge in detecting credit card fraud is that fraud does not have consistent patterns. The typical approach is to maintain a usage profile for each user and monitor them for any deviations. Given that there are billions of card users, this user profiling technique is not very scalable, this is where the nature of the problem allows it to be solved based on anomaly detection; this is able to detect attack patterns in real time based on anomalous behavior, which in the case of banking fraud could mean identity theft or credit card theft. The challenge associated with fraud detection is that in most cases it requires real-time detection and prevention [6].

2 Materials and Methods

2.1 Related Work

A description of the preprocessing is given for the research carried out on the database in question from 2018 to 2024. In addition to feature selection techniques and hyper plane models, based on probability, density, neural networks, trees or combination. The hyperparameter optimization techniques used by the authors are also described.

From the investigations in Fig. 1, [7] decides to work without the feature 'Time' and uses the NB and KNN models but without the preprocessed data, nor the automatic feature selection, nor treatment to the imbalance, nor automatic adjustment of the model parameters [8], unlike the previous author, does perform a treatment to the imbalance with using techniques such as random oversampling, SMOTE, ADASYN, generative models such as GAN, CGAN, WGAN, WCGAN. For anomaly detection he used the LR model [9] state to perform preprocessing, but does not describe it. The author uses information gain as a criterion to perform feature selection. He himself chooses not to deal with imbalance, but validates his models through cross-validation and averaging that result to show how the model behaves with different portions of the data. He uses a selection of hyperparameters based on Bayesian optimization, his models were Light-GBM, DT, RF, LR, SVMrbf, SVMLinear, KNN and NB [10] performs no preprocessing, no feature selection, no unbalance treatment, and no optimization of their models [11] performs a Standard Scaler in the preprocessing. It does not perform feature selection and treats the imbalance with undersampling. In hyperparameter selection it only tests with the Weights parameter. Its models were the SVM, LR and RF [12] performs a preprocessing to the data taking into account missing values, unique values and collinear features. It performs feature selection based on the zero importance and low importance function described in github by [13]. It also performs unbalance treatment with SMOTE or ADASYAN, does not perform automatic hyperparameter selection and its models were RF, LR, KNN, NB and MLP [14] does not perform preprocessing or feature selection. It uses techniques to deal with imbalance such as random oversampling, random undersampling, SMOTE, ADAYSAN, Sequense-aware UnderSamling. For model training he does not perform hyperparameter search. Its models were ANN, GRU, LSTM, LSTM-CRF [15] in the preprocessing performs a review and cleaning of null or duplicate values, and then normalize with the Min-Max. It does not perform feature selection and performs oversampling with SMOTE the training set. It performs the hyperparameter search with the "GridSearchCV" method. In this research the models were, DT, IF, RF, LR, SVM, GBM, KNN, NB, MLP [16] does not perform: preprocessing, feature selection, imbalance treatment and hyperparameter search. Their models were LR, KNN, NB, Staked generalization [17] does not perform preprocessing, but performs feature selection using the RF importance metric. It treats imbalance with SMOTE, but in the models it does not search for the best hyperparameters. I use LR, LDA, KNN, CART, NB, SVM, RF, XGB, LightGBM models [18] no preprocessing, feature selection, treatment to imbalance and hyperparameter search is performed. Their models were MLP, CNN, Simple RNN, LSTM, GRU, BiLSTM, BIGRU [19] does not perform preprocessing, feature selection, unbalance treatment and hyperparameter search. Their proposed model was Deep Q-network.

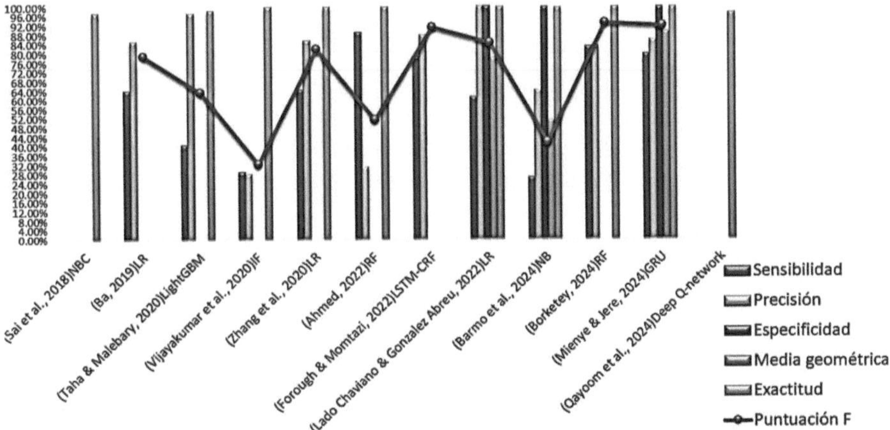

Fig. 1. Behavior of the performance measures according to each investigation.

2.2 A Subsection Sample

The database "cedit_card.csv" is located on the Kaggle site [20]. The selected dataset contains transactions performed in September 2013 during two days in Europe. It has 31 features, 284807 transactions, of these 473 fraudulent. The features from 'V1' to 'V28' are projected with Principal Component Analysis (PCA) 'Time' is the time in seconds, 'Amount' is the amount of money and 'Class' is the target variable describing as 1 the fraudulent transaction and as 0 the normal transaction. In the preprocessing, 1081 duplicate instances were detected and eliminated. There is no correlation between the data. The characteristics are type 'float' except for the characteristic 'class' which is type 'int'. It is decided to eliminate the feature 'Time' because of its behavior as an ascending counter. There is an imbalance in the data, where the anomalies represent 0.16% of the data. For the interests of the proposed solution in the training set there will only be operations of the majority class so the data will be divided into 80% and 20% with the head method, within the 20% will be included the 473 anomalies.

3 Proposed

For the selection of a model, the bibliography consulted showed aspects to be taken into account such as that the structure of banking data is complex, the viability and evolution of fraud (Concept Drift), the imbalance of classes and it is not viable to use fictitious data or to eliminate information. Within the neural network models, specifically those of generative adversarial networks, there is a model called Autoencoders that: molds complex structures, does not depend on time, useful when there are few examples of fraud, is less expensive in training with respect to the other models, depending on the architecture and has a high robustness to new frauds if the latent space is well trained.

An Autoencoder (AE) is a computational model based on neural networks, composed of an encoder and a decoder, used for unsupervised learning tasks [6]. It does not directly use its output as a way to detect anomalies, but uses the reconstruction error produced by reversing dimensionality reduction [21]. Dimensionality reduction methods allow the observations to be projected into a space of lower dimension than the original space, while trying to preserve as much information as possible. The way they manage to minimize the overall loss of information is by finding a new space in which the majority of observations can be well represented [21] (Fig. 2).

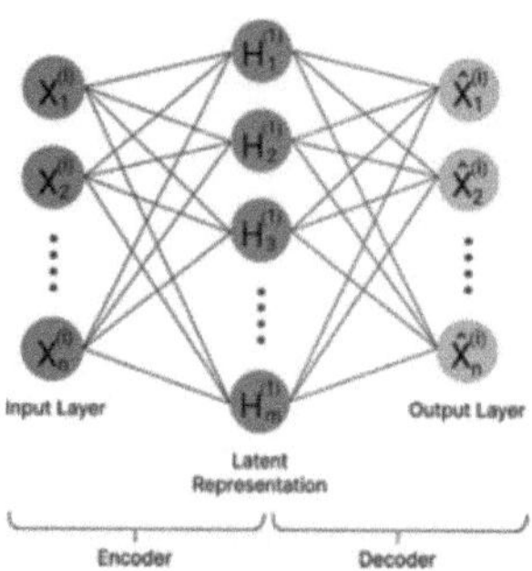

Fig. 2. Autoencoder example diagram [22]

The encoder transforms the input vector XXXX into a hidden representation $HHHH$ as follows: $H = \sigma(W_{xh}X + b_{xh})H = \sigma(W_{xh}X + b_{xh})H = \sigma(W_{xh}X + b_{xh})H = \sigma(W_{xh}X + b_{xh})$. Where $\sigma\sigma\sigma\sigma$ is an activation function such as a sigmoid function or a rectified linear unit (ReLU), $WWWW$ is a weight matrix and $bbbb$ is a polarization vector. The transformation operation is applied to the hidden representation $HHHH$ to reconstruct the initial input space using a decoder: $\hat{X} = \sigma(W_{h\hat{x}}h + b_{h\hat{x}})\hat{X} = \sigma(W_{h\hat{x}}h + b_{h\hat{x}})\hat{X} = \sigma(W_{h\hat{x}}h + b_{h\hat{x}})\hat{X} = \sigma(W_{h\hat{x}}h + b_{h\hat{x}})$. The difference between the reconstructed vector $\hat{X}\hat{X}\hat{X}\hat{X}$ and the original input vector XXXX yields the reconstruction error (RE), $rrrr$ as follows: $r = X - \hat{X}r = X - \hat{X}r = X - \hat{X}r = X - \hat{X}$. The AE is trained to minimize $rrrr$ with an unsupervised training approach [22].

El siguiente recuadro contiene los algoritmos desarrollados en esta investigación.

3.1 Configuration of the Experiments

Optimizer "Adam", batch size 32. Loss functions "msle". Input Layer $\in R^{29} \in R^{29} \in R^{29} \in R^{29}$ ReLU. Hidden Layer 1 $\in R^{24} \in R^{24} \in R^{24} \in R^{24}$, ReLU, Hidden Layer 2 $\in R^{16} \in R^{16} \in R^{16} \in R^{16}$, ReLU. Hidden Layer 3 $\in R^{8} \in R^{8} \in R^{8} \in R^{8}$, ReLU. Hidden Layer 4 $\in R^{16} \in R^{16} \in R^{16} \in R^{16}$, ReLU. Hidden Layer 5 $\in R^{24} \in R^{24} \in R^{24} \in R^{24}$, ReLU. Hidden Layer 6 $\in R^{29} \in R^{29} \in R^{29} \in R^{29}$, ReLU. Output Layer $\in R^{29} \in R^{29} \in R^{29} \in R^{29}$, sigmoid.

Twelve experiments are performed, four for each type of layer: Dense identified with 1, LSTM identified with 2 and BiLSTM identified with 3. Values of learning_rate, epoch will be modified and Dropout regularization layers will be added after each layer except the smallest and the last one.

3.2 Configuration of the Proposal Model

Input Layer $\in R^5 \in R^5 \in R^5 \in R^5$, ReLU, Dropout 10%. Hidden Layer 1 $\in R^4 \in R^4 \in R^4 \in R^4$, ReLU, Dropout 10%. Hidden Layer 2 $\in R^3 \in R^3 \in R^3 \in R^3$, ReLU, Dropout 10%. Hidden Layer 3 $\in R^2 \in R^2 \in R^2 \in R^2$, ReLU,. Hidden Layer 4 $\in R^3 \in R^3 \in R^3 \in R^3$, ReLU, Dropout 10%. Hidden Layer 5 $\in R^4 \in R^4 \in R^4 \in R^4$, ReLU, Dropout 10%. Hidden Layer 6 $\in R^5 \in R^5 \in R^5 \in R^5$, ReLU, Dropout 10%. Output Layer $\in R^5 \in R^5 \in R^5 \in R^5$, sigmoid.

3.3 Algorithms

This method seeks to separate the features that the model reconstructs with higher reconstruction error into anomalies and then train the model with normal operations on those features.

Selection of decision threshold:
1.   Initialize a data frame called '**Thresholds**': It contains characteristics that will be the performance measures and the threshold value.
2.   Loop for Various Thresholds: For each threshold value U_i in the range 0 to 1. Set $U_i = \frac{i}{1000}$, where i is the index of the iteration, where $i = 1,2,\ldots,1000$
3.   Model prediction: Generate predictions for data sets x_test_1_s (normal) and x_test_2_s (outlier) using the current threshold U_i.

$$pred\_1 = predict(model, x\_test\_1\_s, U_i) \begin{cases} if\ pred\_1 = 0\ is\ TN \\ if\ pred\_1 = 1\ is\ FP \end{cases}$$

$$pred\_2 = predict(model, x\_test\_2\_s, U_i) \begin{cases} if\ pred\_2 = 0\ is\ FN \\ if\ pred\_2 = 1\ is\ TP \end{cases}$$

4.   The metrics are calculated and stored in the data frame **Thresholds** together with the threshold.
The threshold where the **F-score** obtained its **global maximum** is selected.threshold where the **F-score** obtained its **global maximum** is selected.

Predict function
1.   Input data: model, x, threshold.
2.   Data reconstruction $\hat{x}_i = model(x_i)$
3.   Calculation of the RE: $RE = MAE(x_i, \hat{x}_i) = \frac{1}{n}\sum_{j=1}^{n}\left|\hat{x}_i^{(j)} - x_i^{(j)}\right|$

$\hat{x}_i^{(j)}$ are the values of the j features for instance i, and n is the total number of

4.   Comparison with the threshold:
$$prediction = \begin{cases} True\ (normal),\ if\ RE < threshold \\ False\ (outlier),\ if\ RE \geq threshold \end{cases}$$
Return: Boolean tensor where each value indicates whether the reconstruction for that instance is below the threshold

---

Feature selection
Let $X = \{x_1, x_2, \ldots, x_{473}\}$ be the test data set with 473 instances, and each instance x_i has 29 features, $V_1, V_2, \ldots, V_{28}, Amount$. $\hat{X} = \{\hat{x}_1, \hat{x}_2, \ldots, \hat{x}_{473}\}$ the set of predictions generated by the model for each instance in X. E vector of accumulated errors, a vector of 29 zeros, one for each feature.
$E_0 = [0, 0, \ldots, 0]$
For each instance i in $\{1, 2, \ldots, 473\}$:
         For each instance j in $\{1, 2, \ldots, 29\}$:
                  Calculate the absolute error: $a_i^{(j)} = \left|\hat{x}_i^{(j)} - x_i^{(j)}\right|$
                  Accumulate error: $E_i^{(j)} = E_{i-1}^{(j)} + a_i^{(j)}$
The decision threshold for the selection of characteristics is **selected as determined by the author**, for this research, 75% of the error of the variable with the highest error value in its last iteration.

4 Results and Discussion

The best combination of parameters was that of experiment 1 with F-score of 65.46% with dropout regularization layers after each layer minus the highest compression and the last at 10%, learning rate of 0.001 and 150 epoch. In this experiment as shown in

Fig. 3 both classes are separated, but there are still large amounts of both classes on the wrong side of the threshold selected by the global maximum F-score. With that better model performed the feature selection, 5 features were obtained that exceeded the threshold of 75% of the sum of the reconstruction error of the maximum value. Then, with the proposed architect of Fig. 4 and the best hyperparameters and only with the selected features, Fig. 5 shows the class separation achieved with this new feature selection approach, having a difference of + 18.15% F-score with respect to experiment 1 (Fig. 6).

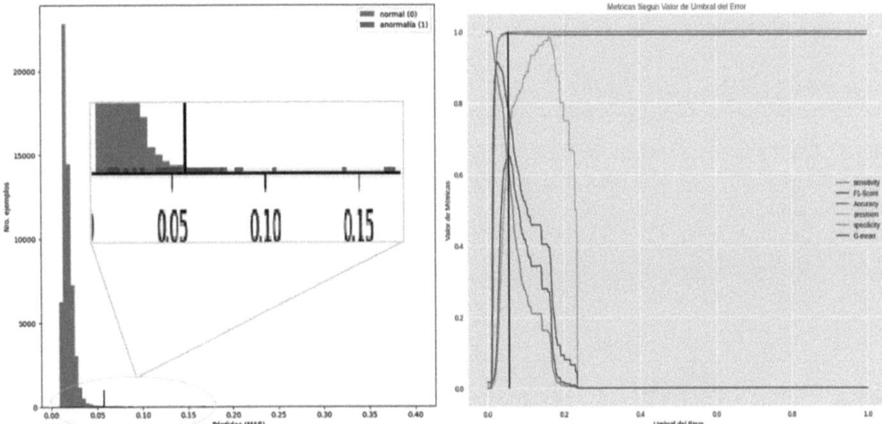

Fig. 3. On the left is a plot of number of normal operations in blue with respect to the error threshold and on the right is the value of each performance measure with respect to the error threshold of experiment 1.

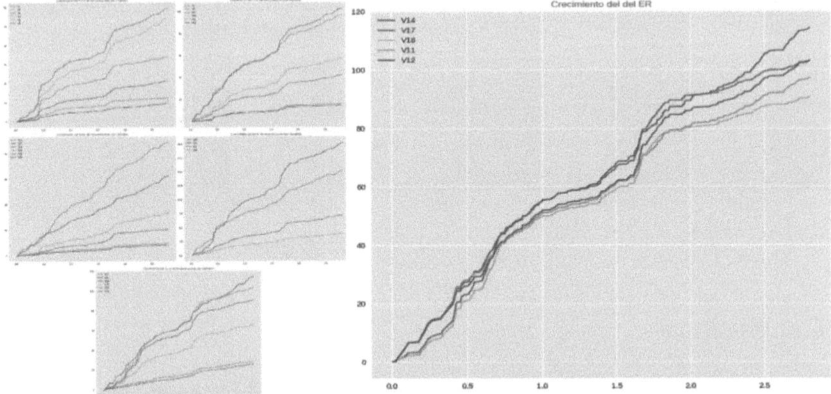

Fig. 4. On the left shows the behavior of the sum of the reconstruction error for each feature in the anomalies and on the right the features that passed the threshold of 75% of the highest sum of error

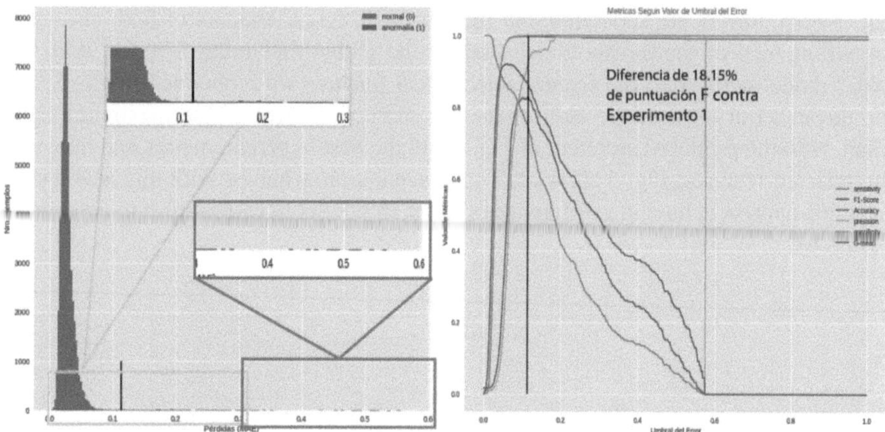

Fig. 5. On the left is a plot of the number of normal operations in blue with respect to the error threshold and on the right is the value of each performance measure with respect to the Proposal error threshold

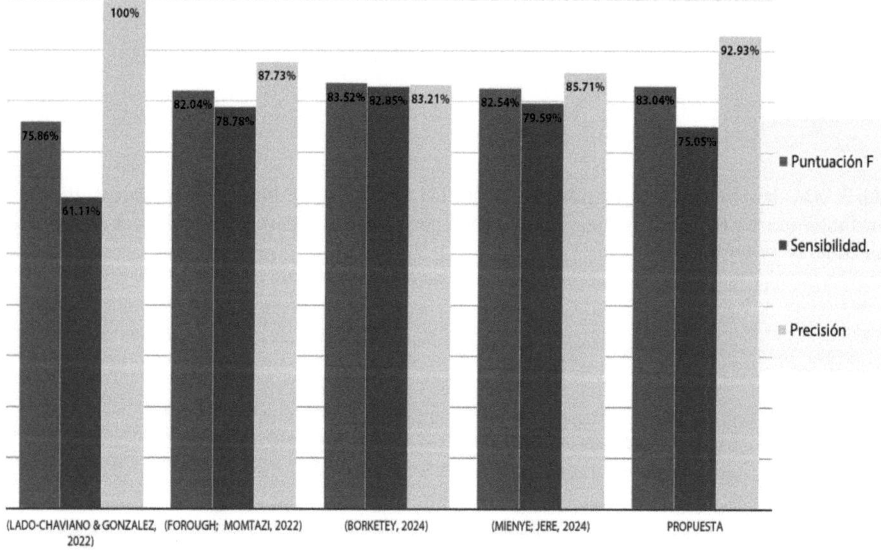

Fig. 6. Comparison against the highest F-scoring investigations in the literature.

5 Conclusions

With the development of the proposal, an F-score of 83.04% is obtained. Another point to take into account is that the Accuracy of the proposal of 92.93% is 9.72% higher than that reported in the literature, and the Sensitivity of 75.05% is 7.8% lower. Thus, false positives are reduced. The metrics behavior of the proposal allows when selecting the decision threshold to give up precision values and F-score to increase sensitivity values with numbers above 83% at the point where the three metrics intersect.

Initial experiments with different hyper-parameter configurations were outperformed by the results of the proposed new feature selection method. This method presents superior performance to previous approaches in the literature, due to its configurable threshold, which allows adjusting the metrics according to the specific problem. Furthermore, the method demonstrates an outstanding ability to separate classes, suggesting its applicability in other areas of anomaly detection. Since the feature selection threshold is adjustable, even better results can be obtained compared to current methods.

References

1. Kolesnikov, N.: 50 Estadísticas Clave de Ciberseguridad para Octubre de 2024. Techopedia. https://www.techopedia.com/es/estadisticas-ciberseguridad
2. Cubadebate: Alertan sobre posible estafa para hacerse con tu tarjeta electrónica. Cubadebate. http://www.cubadebate.cu/noticias/2020/11/24/alertan-sobre-posible-estafa-para-hacerse-con-tu-tarjeta-electronica/
3. Cubadebate: La bancarización precisa ser más activa. Cubadebate. http://www.cubadebate.cu/noticias/2024/07/06/la-bancarizacion-precisa-ser-mas-activa/
4. Cubadebate: Usuarios cubanos reportan suplantación de identidad de la web de ENZONA. Cubadebate. http://www.cubadebate.cu/noticias/2019/12/12/usuarios-cubanos-reportan-suplantacion-de-identidad-de-la-web-de-enzona/
5. Cubadebate: Estafas entre redes. Cubadebate. http://www.cubadebate.cu/especiales/2023/04/16/estafas-entre-redes/
6. González, H.R., Valdés, O., Ameijeiras, D.A.: Algoritmos de detección de anomalías con redes profundas. Revisión para detección de fraudes bancarios. RCCi **15**, 244–264 (2021). http://scielo.sld.cu/pdf/rcci/v15n4s1/2227-1899-rcci-15-04-s1-244.pdf
7. Sai, K., et al.: Credit card fraud detection using Naïve Bayes model based and KNN classifier. NTERNATIONAL J. Adv. Res. IDEAS Innov. Technol. **4**(3) (2018). https://www.ijariit.com/manuscript/credit-card-fraud-detection-using-naive-bayes-model-based-and-knn-classifier/
8. Ba, H.: Improving Detection of Credit Card Fraudulent Transactions using Generative Adversarial Networks (2019). http://arxiv.org/abs/1907.03355
9. Taha, A.A., Malebary, S.J.: An intelligent approach to credit card fraud detection using an optimized light gradient boosting machine. IEEE Access **8**, 25579–25587 (2020). https://doi.org/10.1109/ACCESS.2020.2971354
10. Vijayakumar, V., Divya, N.S., Sarojini, P., Sonika, K.: Isolation forest and local outlier factor for credit card fraud detection system. Int. J. Eng. Adv. Technol. **9**(4), 261–265 (2020). https://doi.org/10.35940/ijeat.d6815.049420
11. Zhang, D., Bhandari, B., Black, D.: Credit card fraud detection using weighted support vector machine. Appl. Math. **11**(12), 1275–1291 (2020). https://doi.org/10.4236/am.2020.1112087
12. Ahmed, M.H.: Credit Card Fraud Detection Techniques: A Survey (2022). https://doi.org/10.14293/S2199-1006.1.SOR-.PPFI7P0.v1
13. Koehrsen, W.: Feature selector is a tool for dimensionality reduction of machine learning datasets (2022). https://github.com/WillKoehrsen/feature-selector
14. Forough, J., Momtazi, S.: Sequential credit card fraud detection: a joint deep neural network and probabilistic graphical model approach. Expert Syst. **39**(1) (2022). https://doi.org/10.1111/exsy.12795
15. Lado-Chaviano, A., Gonzalez, L.: Método para la detección del fraude en transacciones bancarias con escenarios de Flujo de Datos (2022). https://repositorio.uci.cu/jspui/handle/123456789/10656

16. Barmo, A.U., Haruna, A., Wali, Y.U., Abid, K.: Analysis and Comparison of Fraud Detection on Credit Card Transactions Using Machine Learning Algorithms **7**(8), 293–299 (2024)
17. Borketey, B.: Real-time fraud detection using machine learning. J. Data Anal. Inf. Process. **12**(02), 189–209 (2024). https://doi.org/10.4236/jdaip.2024.122011
18. Mienye, I.D., Jere, N.: Deep learning for credit card fraud detection: a review of algorithms, challenges, and solutions. IEEE Access **12**, 96893–96910 (2024). https://doi.org/10.1109/ACCESS.2024.3426955
19. Qayoom, A., et al.. A Novel Approach for Credit Card Fraud Transaction Detection Using Deep Reinforcement Learning Scheme (2024). https://doi.org/10.21203/rs.3.rs-3092096/v1
20. kaggle: creditcard. https://www.kaggle.com/datasets/mlg-ulb/creditcardfraud/versions/1
21. Rodrigo, J.A.: Detección de anomalías: Autoencoders y Python. Mach. Learn. con R, 1–10 (2020). https://www.cienciadedatos.net/documentos/py32-deteccion-anomalias-autoencoder-python.html
22. Torabi, H., Mirtaheri, S.L., Greco, S.: Practical autoencoder based anomaly detection by using vector reconstruction error. Cybersecurity **6**(1), 1 (2023). https://doi.org/10.1186/s42400-022-00134-9

Machine Learning-Driven Hybrid Optimization Algorithm for PID Domain Constraints Identification in Servo Control Systems: Balancing Efficiency and Safety Through Neural Network Classifier

Zoulfikar Ahmad[1]([✉]) [iD] and Ali Mahmoud Mansour[2]([✉]) [iD]

[1] Department of Computer Control Systems, Moscow State Technological University (MSTU "Stankin"), 127055 Moscow, Russia
zoualfikarahmad@gmail.com

[2] Department of Computer Aided Design, Southern Federal University, 347900 Taganrog, Russia
mansur@sfedu.ro

Abstract. Automated optimization of proportional-integral-derivative (PID) parameters in servo control systems is crucial for ensuring stability, reducing noise, and minimizing mechanical wear, yet traditional evolutionary methods like genetic algorithms (GA) and particle swarm optimization (PSO) suffer from slow convergence and potential damage due to random parameter initialization. While offline simulations avoid physical damage, they fail to capture real-world nonlinearities. To overcome these challenges, in this work we propose a hybrid neural-evolutionary optimization algorithm with three key contributions: (1) a control system of servo motor enabling real-time interaction, (2) a neural classifier trained on a control system-generated data to constrain PID parameters to safe bounds, and (3) a genetic algorithm leveraging these constraints to halve the search space and accelerate convergence. Experimental results on SPSH-type servo motors demonstrate zero faults across 450 test runs while reducing mechanical vibrations and maintaining robust performance (0–1500 RPM). By unifying data-driven safety with evolutionary optimization, our framework addresses the triad of industrial requirements: computational efficiency, signal quality, and hardware safety.

Keywords: machine learning · PID tuning · servo motor · neural network · evolutionary algorithms · optimization

1 Introduction

Proportional-Integral-Derivative (PID) controllers remain the cornerstone of industrial motion control, with servo motors alone driving a \$12.8 billion global market. These precision actuators enable mission-critical applications from robotic assembly to renewable energy systems, where optimal PID tuning directly impacts operational efficiency and energy consumption. However, the industry-wide challenge of balancing tuning precision against computational cost persists, particularly as modern electromechanical systems demand both real-time responsiveness and operational safety [1, 2].

Traditional metaheuristic approaches like Genetic Algorithms (GA) and Particle Swarm Optimization (PSO) have advanced PID optimization by exploring complex parameter spaces. Implemented in industrial automation systems, these methods enhance precision in CNC machining, improve energy efficiency in conveyor systems, and stabilize robotic manipulators. Yet their stochastic nature introduces critical vulnerabilities: uncontrolled parameter exploration risks motor destabilization, while unguided searches waste 34–61% of computation on nonviable solutions according to recent benchmarks [3–6].

When using PSO or Genetic Algorithms (GA) for PID tuning, overly broad search ranges can lead to system instability or noise-like behavior during optimization. This occurs because these algorithms must test even unstable PID parameter combinations to evaluate their performance. The resulting temporary destabilization manifests in three key ways. First, the random exploration phase inherently tests problematic parameters—excessive proportional gain (K_p) may cause overshoot, high derivative gain (K_n) can amplify sensor noise, and unbounded integral gain (K_i) risks integral windup. Second, during objective function evaluation, each candidate parameter set is assessed on its actual performance, where unstable parameters generate high-cost metrics like overshoot before being discarded. Third, the impact differs significantly between simulation and real-world implementation: while simulations safely tolerate this exploratory instability, it slows convergence and face fundamental limitations: (1) not all motors can be accurately modeled mathematically, and (2) simulation cannot fully capture real-world dynamics and nonlinearities [7, 8].

Physical systems of optimization algorithms in other side face genuine risks of hardware damage or safety violations from testing unstable parameters. Randomly generated anomalous parameter values may physically damage the motor or cause dangerous operational noise, particularly when dealing with sensitive servo mechanisms. These risks emerge from three distinct PID tuning failure modes: (1) Excessive proportional gain (K_p) triggers aggressive overcorrection, forcing the motor to oscillate around the target speed through violent acceleration and braking cycles that stress mechanical components; (2) Oversized derivative gain (K_n) amplifies sensor noise instead of smoothing motion, producing erratic speed fluctuations and harmful vibrations; while (3) Integral gain (K_i) presents dual hazards - insufficient values cause steady-state error (never reaching target speed), whereas excessive values induce persistent low-frequency oscillations. These interrelated effects demonstrate why safety-constrained optimization frameworks are essential for practical servo control systems [9].

We present a specialized neural-evolutionary optimization control system designed for the servo motor type SPSH [10, 11], which addresses critical challenges in industrial servo motor control: safety constraints and optimization efficiency. Our solution combines:

1. A control system that enables safe interaction with the SPSH servo motor, allowing both real-time PID parameter adjustment and - crucially - comprehensive data collection through the software's built-in library functionality in our control system.

This control system enabled the systematic acquisition and analysis of experimental response patterns used for classifier training.

2. Neural Safety Filter: Through comprehensive benchmarking, we identified a Multilayer Perceptron (MLP) classifier [12, 13] as the most effective solution (outperforming SVM [14] and SGD [15] alternatives) for real-time parameter validation. Trained on 200 experimentally verified response patterns from SPSH servo motor, the classifier establishes safe operating boundaries, completely eliminating dangerous parameter combinations while preserving the full viable solution space.

3. Constrained Evolutionary Optimization: The genetic algorithm leverages these safety constraints to focus exclusively on high-probability solution regions, reducing the search space by 50%. This targeted approach accelerates convergence while maintaining the algorithm's ability to explore optimal solutions. The system dynamically adjusts optimization parameters based on real-time performance feedback from the MOTO-MASTER monitoring tools.

This integrated framework overcomes the SPSH control system's closed architecture limitations while resolving the fundamental tension between optimization thoroughness and operational safety. Experimental results demonstrate reliable operation across the servo motor's full RPM range (0–1500) with zero fault conditions in 450 test runs, validating both the safety and efficiency of our approach.

While the current implementation focuses on a specific servo motor type, the methodology is designed for scalability. Future work will expand the training dataset to enhance generalizability across servo motor classes and operating conditions – a logical next step given the framework's demonstrated effectiveness in targeted applications.

This paper is organized as follows. In the Materials section, a detailed description of the proposed control system with hybrid classification-enhanced genetic algorithm for PID optimization is provided. Subsequently, Sect. 4 provides implementation guidelines. The analysis of the results is shown in the Results section, followed by expectations and future plans in the Conclusions section.

2 Materials and Methods

This section describes the hardware configuration, including the proposed architecture of the suggested control platform, in addition to our hybrid genetic algorithm with neural classification, and the implementation methodology.

2.1 Control System Architecture and Hardware Configuration

The proposed control system employs an automated PID parameter tuning framework for servo motor speed regulation, integrating hardware and components to achieve real-time optimization. The hardware configuration consists of a Raspberry Pi 3 Model B microcomputer [16, 17] interfaced with an MCP2515 CAN bus controller module. The Raspberry Pi 3 microcomputer is a single-board computing module designed for embedded systems, automated applications, and educational purposes. It has compact dimensions, high energy efficiency, and support for various interfaces for connecting peripheral

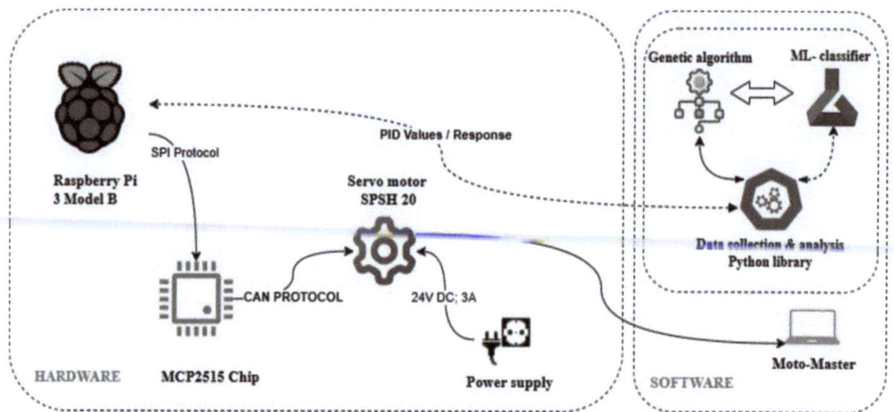

Fig. 1. The block diagram of the testbed and hardware configuration

devices. The MCP2515 processes data transmissions and receptions autonomously when interfaced with a Raspberry Pi 3 Model B (Fig. 1).

During transmission, the Raspberry Pi sends messages via SPI to the MCP2515's transmit buffers, where they undergo arbitration, bit stuffing, and error checking before being transmitted on the CAN bus. For reception, the MCP2515 filters incoming messages using acceptance filters, stores valid data in receive buffers, and triggers interrupts to notify the Raspberry Pi. The MCP2515 offloads CAN protocol tasks from the Raspberry Pi, enabling efficient data exchange in embedded systems.

The MCP2515 module facilitates communication with the SPSH 20 servo motor [10, 11] via a CAN protocol, forming a closed-loop control system architecture. The SPSH is an integrated servo drive based on a hybrid stepper motor, which uses stepless (vector) control based on an algorithm adapted specifically for stepper motors.

The SPSH servo motor is not an open control system for modification, but communication and manual parameter adjustment are possible using MOTO-MASTER. This software, developed by the manufacturer of the SPSH servo motor, enables users to modify specific parameters (e.g. PID, speed) values while also providing data monitoring capabilities for time and speed measurements. The software includes an integrated oscilloscope function that visually displays the motor's response characteristics during testing procedures.

The CAN protocol implementation serves the critical function of synchronizing multiple SPSH motors, allowing them to operate in coordination when connected to the same CAN network. We utilized this inherent CAN protocol functionality to create an external control system solution based on Raspberry Pi technology.

A CAN Bus-based control system has been developed that enables developers to: (1) read all servo motor parameters (speed, current, voltage, encoder position), and (2) modify PID coefficients with a single click - eliminating the need for individual parameter adjustments as required in MOTO-MASTER. This control system creates opportunities for other researchers to integrate more advanced algorithms (such as deep learning or fuzzy control). Key achievements include: being the first CAN Bus-based control system for automatic PID tuning with servo motor type SPSH; successfully merging classical

PID control with machine learning; and converting a proprietary closed control system into an open control system.

A separate USB connection links the servo motor to a laptop running Moto-Master software, which provides supplementary monitoring and configuration capabilities. The servo motor is powered by a 24 V DC, 3 A supply to ensure stable operation under dynamic load conditions.

Within this framework, the Raspberry Pi 3 serves as the computational core, performing dual functions: (1) real-time data acquisition of servo motor speed and temporal response characteristics, and (2) calculation of key control performance metrics, including overshoot, rise time, settling time, and steady-state error. These metrics are subsequently utilized as objective functions within an embedded genetic algorithm (GA) to iteratively optimize PID parameters. The GA systematically adjusts proportional, integral, and derivative gains to minimize transient oscillations and steady-state deviations, thereby enhancing the servo motor's dynamic response.

Notably, the integration of the MCP2515 CAN interface enables robust, low-latency communication between the microcomputer and servo motor, critical for maintaining synchronization in high-frequency control cycles. Experimental validation confirmed that the GA-driven PID tuning mechanism effectively reduced sensitivity to initial parameter selection, a common limitation in stochastic optimization methods. The Moto-Master software further validated system performance by providing independent verification of servo motor behavior under optimized PID settings.

To demonstrate the empirical significance of the proposed control platform, the following section describes its application in developing and implementing a genetic algorithm integrated with a machine learning classifier.

2.2 Genetic Algorithm-Based PID Optimization Enhanced with Classification

The proposed algorithm combines a genetic algorithm with a pre-trained neural network classifier to optimize PID (Proportional-Integral-Derivative) parameters for servo motor speed control. The approach uses the classifier to filter potentially good PID parameters during initialization and reproduction, while the genetic algorithm evolves solutions based on real motor performance metrics.

The algorithm implements a hardware-in-the-loop evaluation approach, performing real-world testing on physical servo motors to assess PID parameter performance. Built-in safety mechanisms enforce parameter boundaries, maintaining both P and I values within the operational range to prevent unsafe conditions. A pre-trained neural network serves as an intelligent filter, acting as a surrogate model to screen out poor parameter combinations before they reach hardware evaluation, significantly reducing unnecessary servo motor tests. Performance assessment occurs through direct measurement of servo motor response characteristics, capturing key metrics including overshoot (OS), rise time (RT), and settling time (ST) during operation. After iterating through multiple generations of the genetic algorithm, the algorithm outputs the optimal PID parameters demonstrating the best overall performance.

Algorithm 1– Genetic Algorithm for PID Optimization with Neural Network

---

inputs
- pop_size: Population size (default = 10)
- generations: Number of generations (default = 20)
- ML-classifier: Pre-trained classifier (default MLP)
- motor_interface: Connection to servo motor for real-time evaluation
- pi_bounds : [0,1.8]
- P: mutation probability (default = 0.2)

Output:
- Optimal PID parameters (P, I)

1: **Initialize population**:

    a. Generate random (P,I) pairs within bounds [0,1.8]
    b. Filter pairs using **ML-classifier (*neural network MLP*)**
    c. Repeat until population reaches pop_size

2: ***For each*** generation ***do***:

    2.1. Evaluate fitness for each individual:
    i. Set PID parameters on servo motor
    ii. Run motor at target speed S (S = 600 for example)
    iii. Collect speed readings
    iv. Calculate performance metrics: (OS, %), (RT, seconds), (ST, seconds)
    v. Combine metrics into fitness score (formula 4):

$$f = a \cdot OS + b \cdot RT + c \cdot ST$$

    vi. Reset motor
    2.2. Selection:

      i. Sort population by fitness (lower is better)
      ii. Select top 50% individuals

    2.3. Reproduction:

    i. While *offspring population not full **do***:

        - Select two parents randomly from top 50%
        - Perform average crossover to create child
        - Apply mutation with probability *P*
        - Filter child using neural network classifier
        - *If* rejected, generate new random individual

    End

    2.4. Form new population from selected parents + offspring

  End

3: *Return best individual from final population*

The proposed hybrid methodology effectively merges the global search capabilities of genetic algorithms with the pattern recognition strengths of machine learning, creating an efficient exploration of the PID parameter space that strategically minimizes computational resources by avoiding evaluation of unpromising configurations while still thoroughly searching for optimal solutions.

2.3　Experimental Research

Building upon our framework for monitoring dynamic response characteristics (overshoot, rise time, settling time), this section presents the experimental methodology for implementing the hybrid optimization system. We specifically detail the experimental setup for selecting and configuring the machine learning classifier and genetic algorithm components.

Classifier selection. We conducted a comparative evaluation of multiple classifiers, including a support vector machine (SVM) [14] implementing using different kernel type (Poly, rbf, linear), stochastic gradient descent classifier (SGD) [15], and multilayer perceptron (MLP) neural network [12, 13].

The classifiers were trained using a dataset generated by our proposed control system, which contains: PID parameters (P, I, D values), Corresponding servo motor speed response metrics (overshoot, rise time, settling time, steady-state error E), and Binary classification labels. The classifier's task is to determine whether a given (P, I) pair falls within safe operational bounds or not.

The F1 measure [18] was used to evaluate the accuracy of the classifier, which is the harmonic average between precision and recall:

$$Precision_{C_i} = \frac{TP_{C_i}}{TP_{C_i} + FP_{C_i}}, \tag{1}$$

$$Recall_{C_i} = \frac{TP_{C_i}}{TP_{C_i} + FN_{C_i}}, \tag{2}$$

$$F - score = \frac{(1 + \beta) \cdot Precision_{C_i} \cdot Recall_{C_i}}{\beta \cdot Precision_{C_i} + Recall_{C_i}}. \tag{3}$$

In our binary classification task, PID parameter are classified as either acceptable (class C) or unacceptable for genetic algorithm processing. True Positives (TP): Correctly identified acceptable (P,I) pairs. False Positives (FP): Unacceptable pairs incorrectly classified as acceptable. False Negatives (FN): Acceptable pairs incorrectly rejected. True Negatives (TN): Correctly rejected unacceptable pairs.

As seen from (Fig. 2) the MLP demonstrates superior classification performance against SVM and SGD. The selected neural network architecture features a two-neuron input layer (matching (P, I) dimensions) and two hidden layers for hierarchical feature extraction. Through systematic grid search across hyperparameters - testing first hidden layer sizes from 5 to 100 neurons (5-neuron increments) and second layer sizes from 5 to 30 neurons - we identified three top-performing configurations: (45, 10), (25, 5), and (50, 5), which achieved comparable test accuracy.

The (25, 5) architecture was selected for its optimal balance between model complexity and computational efficiency, maintaining robust classification performance while meeting the computational constraints of our Raspberry Pi deployment platform. Larger networks yielded diminishing returns while smaller ones underfit. In final testing, this configuration demonstrated reliable real-time filtering of PID parameters during genetic algorithm optimization, with quantitative results (presented in Sect. 4) confirming its operational effectiveness and stability.

The *Adam* optimizer was selected for training due to its adaptive learning capabilities and strong performance across diverse datasets. *ReLU* activation functions were used in hidden layers for their efficiency and effectiveness in preventing vanishing gradients.

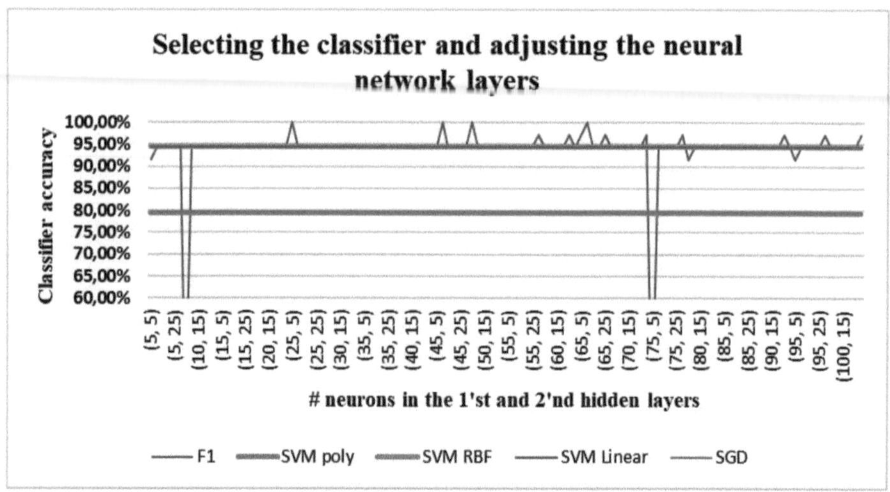

Fig. 2. Setting the parameters of the artificial neural network classifier

2. Genetic Algorithm Stage:

The first generation creates random (P, I) pairs within [0,1.8] bounds (Algorithm 1). Population size is 10, with a custom fitness defined as:

$$f = a \cdot OS + b \cdot RT + c \cdot ST + d \cdot E \tag{4}$$

where $a = b = c = d = 1$ in the current implementation. Future work may adjust these weights to prioritize specific performance metrics.

The algorithm terminates if either maximum generation are reached, or fitness improvement $\Delta f < 0.05\%$ for 5 consecutive generations, where:

$$\Delta f_{(t)} = \frac{f_{(t)} - f_{(t-1)}}{\left| f_{(t-1)} \right|} \cdot 100\% \tag{5}$$

This experimental design successfully validated the effectiveness of classification-enhanced genetic algorithms for PID optimization, demonstrating significant improvements in both computational efficiency and solution quality compared to conventional approaches.

3 Results and Discussion

The computational experiments evaluated the performance of the proposed hybrid algorithm (genetic algorithm integrated with a neural network classifier) against a standalone genetic algorithm without the neural network classifier. Specifically, we examined how each handles initialization noise in early generations.

Figure 3 reveals the consequences of unoptimized PID control through its oscillatory speed response (RPM vs microseconds). The servo motor, governed by unbalanced PID parameters selected without classifier guidance, exhibits sustained limit cycle oscillations between 367–1017 RPM around the 600 RPM setpoint (yellow line).

The green waveform demonstrates characteristic high-frequency, undamped oscillations with consistent amplitude - a direct result of three tuning flaws:

First, the disproportionately low proportional gain (P = 0.128) provides inadequate immediate error correction. Second, the excessive integral gain (I = 1.769, creating an unstable Ki/Kp ratio of 13.8) causes aggressive overcompensation for past errors. Third, the derivative gain (D = 0.6), while present, remains insufficient to counterbalance the excessive integral action. Though designed to predict errors through rate-of-change response, this derivative component fails to adequately dampen oscillations induced by the disproportionately high integral gain. This imbalance is further quantified by the extreme Ki/Kp ratio of 13.8 - far exceeding recommended stability thresholds.

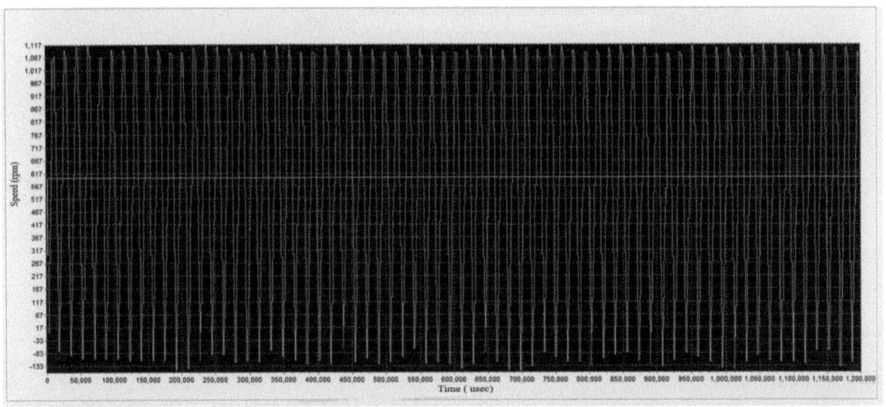

Fig. 3. Oscillatory Speed Response of a Servo Motor with Unsuitable PID Parameters (P = 0.128, I = 1.769, D = 0.6)

The resulting oscillations severely impact system performance: persistent speed fluctuations degrade positioning accuracy, while constant acceleration/deceleration cycles accelerate mechanical wear. Furthermore, the continuous corrective actions waste energy, and the oscillatory patterns risk exciting dangerous mechanical resonances if frequencies align with component natural frequencies.

An improperly tuned PID controller can amplify system noise, particularly when the derivative action is too aggressive, causing it to react to high-frequency noise and destabilize motor control. This noise manifests in two key ways: (1) Background noise from electrical interference or machinery disturbances, which an untuned PID fails to filter, resulting in erratic motor responses; and (2) Harmonic distortion (Fig. 4), where poor tuning introduces non-harmonic frequencies into the motor's speed response, creating disruptive vibrations and compounding noise issues.

After applying our hybrid architecture, the results demonstrate that the neural network classifier effectively mitigates instability caused by random initial PID values. Figures 4 and 5 present the motor speed response waveforms obtained during classifier-assisted PID optimization.

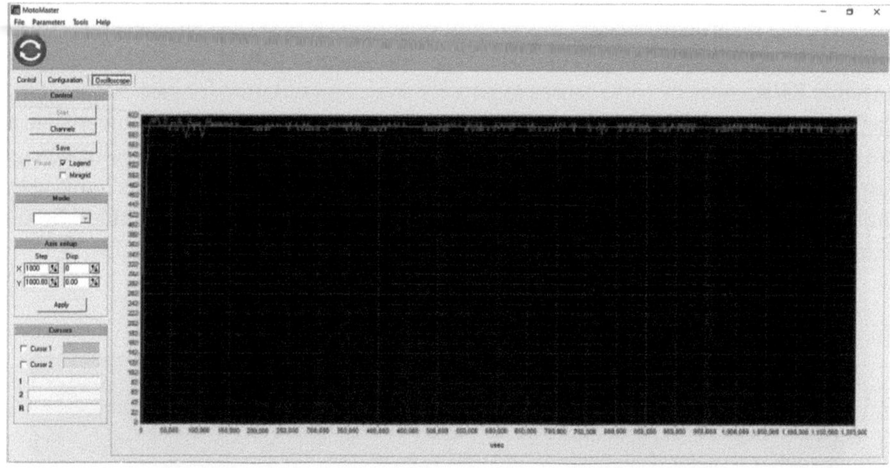

Fig. 4. Oscillatory Speed Response of a Servo Motor with suitable PID Parameters (P = 0.698, I = 0.188, D = 0.6)

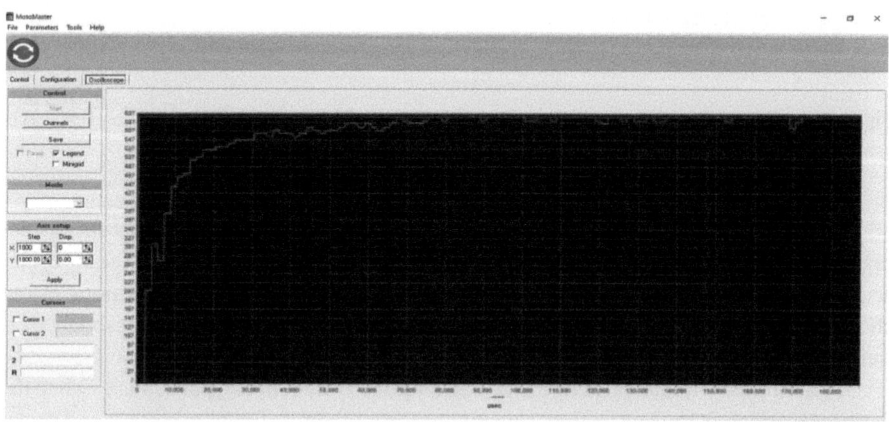

Fig. 5. Oscillatory Speed Response of a Servo Motor with suitable PID Parameters (P = 0.487, I = 0.05, D = 0.6)

The test results demonstrate noise-free operation across both trials. A minimal overshoot is visible in Fig. 4, while Fig. 5 shows complete elimination of overshoot during the PID parameter optimization process.

The results show our neural network classifier successfully prevents instability from random PID initialization, which typically causes transient noise. The hybrid architecture delivers two key advantages: (1) It eliminates dangerous operating conditions entirely, with zero motor faults observed across 450 test runs, thanks to effective parameter pre-screening; and (2) It enables ~ 50% faster convergence by restricting the genetic algorithm's search to high-probability regions (0–0.9 range versus the original 0–1.8), cutting the solution space in half. This constrained search space allows quicker identification of optimal PID values (see Table 1).

Table 1. The effect of varying P, I, and D parameters on the system output

PID values	Overshoot %	Rise Time (ms)	Settling Time (ms)	Error (rpm)
P = 0.487, I = 0.05, D = 0.06	0	22.5	82.5	2.25
P = 0.698, I = 0.188, D = 0.06	3.9	9	187	3

This distinction highlights the crucial role of the neural network (classifier) in stabilizing the optimization process during its initial phase by preventing the generation of abnormal determinant values. Each time potential solutions are explored, the classifier verifies whether the generated values fall within a safe range. The same principle applies throughout subsequent optimization steps until reaching the engine's optimal response. In future work, we plan to conduct broader comparisons with other PID tuning methodologies, as the current study primarily focused on addressing limitations related to inherent noise in random parameter initialization within genetic algorithms. This approach specifically aims to overcome these initialization challenges while maintaining optimization stability.

4 Conclusions

This work introduces a machine learning-driven hybrid optimization algorithm for pid domain constraints identification in servo control, showcasing its effectiveness through an enhanced genetic algorithm paired with a neural classifier. By training the classifier on control system-generated data, we have achieved two key advancements: (1) enforcing safe PID parameter bounds (0–0.9 vs. 0–1.8) to prevent motor faults (validated by zero failures in 450 runs), and (2) halving the search space to accelerate convergence by 50%. Future work will expand testing to diverse servo motors – particularly closed-circuit systems resistant to offline modeling – and explore adaptive tuning of fitness weights (a, b, c) to further optimize performance. Also, we will integrate reinforcement learning techniques to leverage historical optimization data, improving convergence speed and performance.

References

1. Saini, S., Hernandez, J., Nayak, S.: Auto-Tuning PID Controller on Electromechanical Actuators Using Machine Learning. SAE Technical Paper (2023)
2. Shi, G., Dai, C., Liu, S., Li, D., Ding, Y.: The Design of a Reference Model-Based Proportional-Integral-Derivative Controller with the Generalized Derivative. In: 2023 23rd International Conference on Control, Automation and Systems (ICCAS), pp. 547–552. IEEE (2023)
3. Majeed, D.A., et al.: Advanced optimization techniques for CNC machining: a comparative study of genetic algorithms, simulated annealing, and particle swarm optimization. In: 2024 International Congress on Human-Computer Interaction, Optimization and Robotic Applications (HORA), pp. 1–6. IEEE (2024)
4. Deng, E., Joykutty, L., Caulkins, J.: Comparison of Machine Learning Algorithms for DC Motor PID Control with Genetic Algorithm. J. Student Res. 12 (2023)
5. Ahmad, Z., Areg, R.: Intelligent Control System for Quadcopter Motor's (BLDC). In: 2023 Seminar on Electrical Engineering, Automation & Control Systems, Theory and Practical Applications (EEACS), pp. 7–10. IEEE (2023)
6. Ahmad, Z.: Sravneniye kolets PID-regulirovaniya i nechetkikh regulyatorov dlya regulirovaniya skorosti servodvigatelya [Comparison of PID control loops and fuzzy controllers for servo motor speed regulation]. In: Materialy KHV vserossiyskoy konferentsii s mezhdunarodnym uchastiyem Ma-shinostroyeniye: traditsii i innovatsii (MTI –2022) [Proceedings of the XV All-Russian Conference with International Participation Mechanical Engineering: Traditions and Innovations (MIT-2022)], pp. 141–148. Moskovskiy gosudarstvennyy tekhnologicheskiy universitet "STANKIN" [Moscow State Technological University "STANKIN" (2022)] (2022)
7. Wang, J.S., Wang, J.C., Wang, W.: Self-tuning of PID parameters based on particle swarm optimization. Control and Decision. **20**, 73–76 (2005)
8. Mishra, D.P., Raut, U., Gaur, A.P., Swain, S., Chauhan, S.: Particle swarm optimization and genetic algorithms for PID controller tuning. In: 2023 5th International Conference on Smart Systems and Inventive Technology (ICSSIT), pp. 189–194. IEEE (2023)
9. Bangera, A., Kinkar, B., Thombare, G., Bhusari, B., Trivedi, P.: Design and Verification of PID Controller for Unstable System with Hardware-in-Loop Simulation. In: 2021 6th International Conference for Convergence in Technology (I2CT), pp. 1–5. IEEE (2021)
10. Servoprivod SPŠ [Servo drive SPSh], https://www.servotechnica.ru/catalog/type/brand/index.pl?id=18. Last accessed 19 April 2025
11. Servotekhnika [Servo technology], http://servotechnica.ru/. Last accessed 18 April 2025
12. Dongare, A.D., Kharde, R.R., Kachare, A.D.: Introduction to artificial neural network. Int. J. Eng. Innov. Technol. (IJEIT). **2**, 189–194 (2012)
13. Wu, Y., Feng, J.: Development and application of artificial neural network. Wireless Pers. Commun. **102**, 1645–1656 (2018)
14. Xue, H., Yang, Q., Chen, S.: SVM: Support vector machines. The Top Ten Algorithms in Data Mining **6**, 37–60 (2009)
15. Amari, S.: Backpropagation and stochastic gradient descent method. Neurocomputing **5**, 185–196 (1993)
16. Raspberry Pi Documentation, https://www.raspberrypi.com/documentation/. Last accessed 18 April 2025
17. Pi, R.: Raspberry pi 3 model b. online]. https://www.raspberrypi.org (2015)
18. Sabbah, T., et al.: Modified frequency-based term weighting schemes for text classification. Appl. Soft Comput. **58**, 193–206 (2017)

Brief Review on the Application of Semi-Parametric Survival Analysis in Economics and Finance

Angel Alberto Vazquez Sánchez[1]([✉]) [ID], Carlos Cruz Corona[2] [ID], Dionisio Buendía Carrillo[3] [ID], and Lisset Salazar Gómez[4] [ID]

[1] Departamento de Inteligencia Computacional, Universidad de Las Ciencias Informáticas. Carretera a San Antonio de los Baños, Km 2 1/2, Reparto Torrens, Municipio Boyeros, La Habana, Cuba
aavazquez@uci.cu

[2] Departamento de Ciencias de La Computación E Inteligencia Artificial, E.T.S. de Ingenierías Informática y de Telecomunicación, Universidad de Granada. C/ Periodista Daniel, Saucedo Aranda S/N C.P. 18071, Granada, Spain

[3] Departamento de Economía Financiera y Contabilidad, Facultad de CC. EE. y Empresariales, Universidad de Granada, Campus Universitario de La Cartuja, S/N 18011, Granada, Spain

[4] Departamento de Informática, Facultad de Tecnologías Interactivas, Universidad de Las Ciencias Informáticas. Carretera a San Antonio de los Baños, Km 2 1/2, Reparto Torrens, Municipio Boyeros, La Habana, Cuba

Abstract. This study presents a narrative review of semi-parametric survival analysis applications in economics and finance from 2019 to 2024, analyzing trends and methodological implementations. Through a targeted search of Scopus and Web of Science databases, we identified and examined 73 relevant articles. The analysis reveals that the Cox proportional hazards model predominates (34 studies), particularly valued for its flexibility with censored data and effectiveness in modeling event risks like bankruptcies, firm survival, and credit defaults. The review uncovers consistent geographic and sectoral patterns, with economic conditions, innovation, and managerial factors emerging as critical determinants of business longevity. While demonstrating the method's robustness, we identify limitations in capturing nonlinear relationships and propose integrating advanced techniques to enhance future applications. These findings position semi-parametric survival analysis as a versatile analytical framework, while highlighting pathways for methodological innovation in economic and financial research.

Keywords: semi-parametric survival analysis · economics · finance · Cox model · narrative review

1 Introduction

Generally, Survival Analysis (SA) is a set of methods for longitudinal data where the main outcome of interest is the time until an event occurs. In this case, time corresponds to the time elapsed until the occurrence of a specific event (Emmert-Streib and Dehmer,

2019; Gao and He, 2020; Karim and Islam, 2019). The terminology has its origins in medical research where an event usually refers to death (Gao and He, 2020); and due to the wide use of this method in different fields, several synonyms are used such as: time-to-event analysis, time-to-failure analysis, duration analysis, mortality analysis, event risk analysis and Cox survival analysis. Alternative names are historical event analysis (social sciences), reliability theory (engineering) or duration analysis (economics). Survival analysis can be applied to many problems in different fields such as biology, medicine, engineering, marketing, social sciences or behavioral sciences (Emmert-Streib and Dehmer, 2019).

Survival time is a random variable that measures how long it takes a subject to reach an event of interest. The occurrence of the event is sometimes referred to as a failure (J. Li and Ma, 2013). Since this variable refers to *lifetime*, it is assumed that the values of the observations of these variables are non-negative. Formally, if we denote the lifetime by T then we have $T \geq 0$. Examples of failure times are: the lifetime of machine components in industrial reliability, the length of strikes or periods of unemployment in economics, the time it takes for subjects to complete specific tasks in psychological experimentation, the length of tracks on a photographic plate in particle physics, and patient survival times in a clinical trial (Cox and Oakes, 2018).

Observations of life times in a study can be incomplete and censored by a stopping criterion. These incomplete observations are called *censored observations*. Censored observations are classified into *right censoring*, *left censoring* and *interval censoring*. In *right censoring* we do not know the time when the event occurs for the observation and the best we can know is the minimum time that the unit has been observed as "alive". Therefore, in an incomplete observation of this type, the survival time is at least as long as the observed lifetime (Vaman and Tattar, 2022). Survival analysis methods include parametric, non-parametric, and semi-parametric approaches (Gao and He, 2020).

Traditionally, survival analysis has been used in fields such as biomedicine, but it has found significant applications in the economic field, especially in the investigation of the duration and behavior of companies. The objective of the present research is to present a brief analysis of the applications that semi-parametric survival analysis methods have had in the last 5 years in the economic and financial context.

2   Related Work

Previous studies on survival analysis methods provide valuable foundations. For example, (Wang, Li, et al., 2019) review statistical techniques and real-world applications, while (Flores, 2022) introduces advanced approaches like non-proportional effects and multi-state models. Key textbooks (David and Mitchel, 2012; E. T. Lee, 1994; J. Li and Ma, 2013; O'Quigley, 2021; Vaman and Tattar, 2022) offer general frameworks but lack economic applications. Although (Leclere, 2005) was a pioneer in applying survival analysis in this field and (Gao and He, 2020) provided a fundamental bridge with financial case studies, a critical review of the last five years is crucial. This period has seen an increase in economic complexity and data availability, leading to applications in emerging areas such as cryptocurrencies and platform economics (P2P lending). Our work differs by specifically analyzing how the Cox model and its extensions have performed in the face of these new phenomena, an area not covered in previous reviews.

3   Materials and Methods

For the development of this research, a narrative review (Traditional Review) was followed including articles from the Scopus database (124 articles) and the Web of Science (190 articles), all these between the years 2019 and 2024, resulting from applying the search term for Scopus:

TITLE-ABS-KEY("survival analysis") AND TITLE-ABS-KEY(economic* OR financ*)

For the Web of Science, the search term was:

TS=("survival analysis") AND TS=(economic* OR financ*)

We adopted (Alani, 2021)'s selection process. After screening all articles and excluding those unrelated to both survival analysis and our research goals, we retained 12 from Scopus and 61 from Web of Science for final analysis of which 34 were related to the use of semi-parametric survival analysis methods. The flowchart in Fig. 1 illustrates the process used to select the articles analyzed in this research.

4   Semi-Parametric Methods in Survival Analysis

Semi-parametric methods in survival analysis combine features of parametric and non-parametric approaches, allowing greater flexibility in data modeling. Unlike parametric models, which require strict assumptions about the shape of the hazard function, semi-parametric models, such as the Cox proportional hazards model, estimate the base hazard function from the data without imposing a specific shape. This makes them especially useful in situations where risk conditions are not constant over time, improving the accuracy of the analysis and the interpretation of the results (Guo and Zeng, 2014).

The Proportional Hazard Model (PHM) is a complement to the reliability analysis toolkit and offers some particular advantages. These types of models are of interest because of the possibility to process reliability data without specific assumptions about the functional form of the risk ratio (Kumar and Klefsjö, 1994). In PHMs the nature of the failure of an element can be modeled as the *risk ratio* $\lambda(t)$ from the following relationship $\lambda(t) = f(t)/S(t)$, given the density function $f(t)$ and the survival function $S(t)$, and where $\lambda(t)dt$ is approximately the probability of failure in the interval $(t, t + dt)$ given the survival time t. The survival ratio of an element is not only influenced by time, but also by the covariates under which it operates. PHMs are used to estimate their effect and to predict failure behaviour (Kumar and Klefsjö, 1994).

The core assumption of a Proportional Hazards Model (PHM) is that the *hazard ratio* (HR) $\lambda(t; x) = \lambda_0(t)\psi(x; \beta)$ can be separated into two parts. The first is a baseline hazard function $\lambda_0(t)$, , which depends only on time. The second is a function that incorporates the effect (β) of covariates (x) and is independent of time $\psi(x; \beta)$. . The base risk ratio is assumed to be identical and equal to the total HR when covariates have no influence on the failure pattern. Covariates may influence the hazard ratio given that the observed HR is higher or lower compared to the base hazard ratio (Fig. 2).

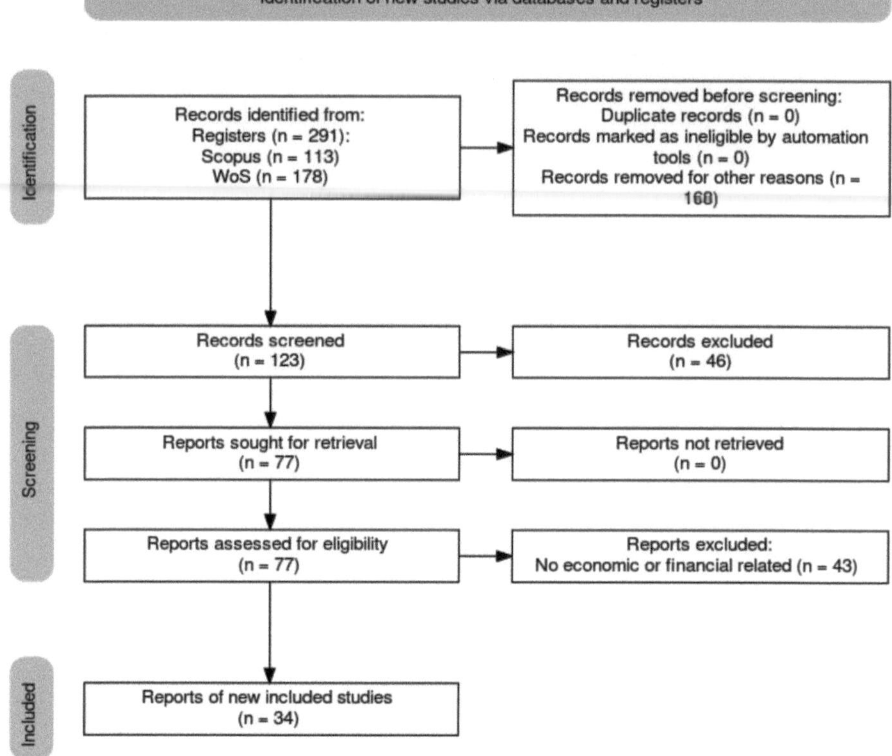

Fig. 1. PRISMA flowchart of the research.

The assumption of the multiplicative effect of the covariates on the base hazard ratio implies that the ratio of the hazard ratio of any two elements observed at any time associated with the covariates x_1 respectively will be a constant with respect to time and proportional to each other, for example, $\lambda(t; x_1) \propto \lambda(t; x_2)$ (Kumar and Klefsjö, 1994).

In general, it is assumed that the functional form of $\psi(x; \beta)$ is known, while $\lambda_0(t)$ it remains unspecified. Different functional forms of $\psi(x; \beta)$ can be used:Exponential $exp(x\beta)$, Logistics $log(1 + exp(x\beta))$, Inverse linear $1/(1 + x\beta)$ and Lineal $1 + x\beta$. Of these, the most commonly used form is the exponential form, and is known as the Cox Proportional Hazards model. The Cox proportional hazards model (Cox, 1972) is the most popular semi-parametric method for data fitting. This model is the cornerstone of modern survival analysis (Guo and Zeng, 2014).

This method does not assume a survival time distribution T. The model assumes that $S_i(t) = [S_0(t)]^{\psi}$ and that $\lambda_i(t) = \psi\lambda_0(t)$ for all t, where S_0 denotes the survival basis function and λ_0 the risk basis function. The hazard function is defined as: $\lambda_i(t) = \lambda_0(t)exp(\beta^T x_i)$, where β is the unknown regression data and λ_0 is a baseline hazard function. For two individuals, i and j, the *hazard ratio* (HR) is defined as the ratio of two

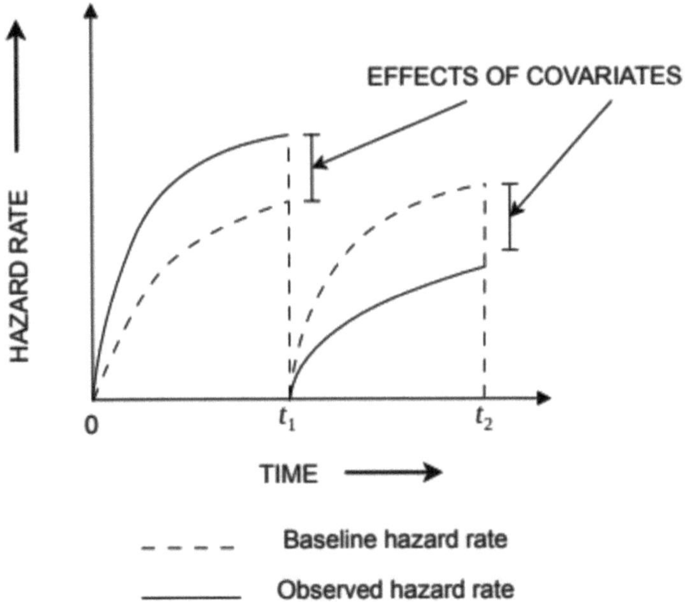

Fig. 2. Relationship between the total hazard ratio and the base hazard ratio in the presence of influential covariates. Source: (Kumar and Klefsjö, 1994).

hazard ratios,

$$\frac{\lambda_i(t)}{\lambda_j(t)} = \frac{\lambda_0(t)exp\left(\beta^T x_i\right)}{\lambda_0(t)exp\left(\beta^T x_j\right)} = exp\left[\beta^T\left(x_i - x_j\right)\right]$$

In the Cox proportional hazards model, HR was often used to measure the effect of an intervention on the occurrence of events (i.e., one group with a measure applied relative to another without such a measure applied). One of the major advantages of the Cox proportional hazard model is that there is no need to specify the baseline hazard function, since this function is canceled in the HR. Because $\beta^T x_i$ it is still used to estimate the regression parameters, the Cox proportional hazards model is a semi-parametric model.

The HR does not reflect a temporal unit of the study. Since the hazard rate (hazard function) is an instantaneous risk of an event occurring over time t, the HR can be interpreted simply as a ratio between the instantaneous risks of two groups over the entire study period.

The **partial likelihood estimation** in Cox's model processes independent individuals' data (observed time, event indicator, and covariates). The logarithmic partial likelihood function accounts for at-risk individuals at each survival time, enabling coefficient estimation via maximization without specifying the baseline hazard (Gao and He, 2020).

A key advantage of Cox's model is handling **time-dependent covariates** (e.g., yearly debt ratios), unlike static baseline variables. It maintains methodological robustness while modeling dynamic relationships, though requiring **counting process** data formatting (Gao and He, 2020).

Among Cox model extensions for complex analyses, the **Andersen-Gill (AG) model** stands out for handling recurrent events. It overcomes the single-event limitation by analyzing multiple occurrences per subject (Andersen and Gill, 1982). Assuming interval independence (while preserving event sequence dependence), the AG model uses a shared hazard function and partial likelihood via counting processes, yielding a unified global estimator (Sousa-Ferreira and Abreu, 2019).

The **Prentice, Williams, and Peterson (PWP) model** (Prentice et al., 1981), developed in 1981, extends the Cox model for analyzing multiple events. It operates by stratifying events based on their order of occurrence. This approach then assigns a specific hazard function to each stratum and ensures that only individuals who have experienced a prior event are included in the risk sets for subsequent events. It supports two time scales: time since study start (PWP-CP) or time since last event (PWP-GT). Estimation is performed via stratified partial likelihood, assuming within-subject independence while allowing global covariates to generate a unified maximum likelihood estimator (Sousa-Ferreira and Abreu, 2019).

5 Applications of Semi-Parametric Methods in the Economic and Financial Sector

Semi-parametric survival models are increasingly applied in economics and finance to analyze time-to-event data with censoring or dynamic covariates. This review examines twelve key applications: financial stability, corporate survival, trade dynamics, investor behavior, policy impacts, digital economy, labor markets, sectoral studies, innovation effects, corporate finance, behavioral economics, and regulatory analysis, showcasing their versatility in modeling economic uncertainties with censored data.

Financial Sector Stability and Risk Assessment: Banking sector studies have successfully utilized these methods to evaluate systemic risks and institutional resilience. Research in this area is diverse, for instance, some studies have predicted bank failures using CAMELS metrics in Czech and Japanese institutions (Kočenda and Iwasaki, 2022); while others have analyzed the distance-to-default in Italian banks (Coccorese and Santucci, 2019). Credit risk modeling plays a significant role, with applications in North African banking systems (Alkhawaldeh et al., 2019) and online retail credit markets (Rozo et al., 2023).

Corporate Longevity and Performance: The approach has proven particularly valuable for understanding firm survival determinants across industries. Manufacturing sector studies in China (Zhang and Mohnen, 2022) and India (Chawla, 2019) identify R&D investment and internationalization as critical factors, while service sector research in European emerging markets (Iwasaki et al., 2022) highlights institutional influences. Sector-specific analyses include Spanish maritime transport firms (Cordón-Lagares and García-Ordaz, 2020) and PropTech companies in the US (Kassner et al., 2023).

International Trade Dynamics: Export survival studies reveal how global value chain participation affects trade duration, with notable work on Chinese exports (Zhu et al., 2019) and Colombian manufacturing (Arguello et al., 2020). The methodology has been used to measure the impact of trade agreements, such as the effect of the AfCFTA on

Kenyan export resilience (Majune et al., 2024). In other studies, it has been applied to examine tariff effects in ASEAN + 6 nations (Lin, 2020).

Financial Markets and Investor Behavior: Capital market applications range from analyzing IPO performance in Pakistan (Mumtaz and Smith, 2021) to studying mutual fund investor psychology in China (Jiang et al., 2021). The approach has illuminated CEO turnover effects in Canada (Cziraki and Groen-Xu, 2020) and revealed speculative bubbles in Chinese markets (He et al., 2019).

Economic Policy Evaluation: Researchers have quantified stimulus package impacts during the 2008 crisis (Shiraishi and Yano, 2022) in China and assessed unemployment benefit systems (Lopes, 2022) in Spain. Tax policy studies examine compliance costs in South African SMEs (Matarirano et al., 2019) and fiscal risk in Chinese firms (Chen, 2021).

Emerging Digital Economies: Innovative applications include cryptocurrency market analysis and blockchain asset longevity studies (Gatabazi et al., 2022) in South Africa, and peer-to-peer lending platforms in the US (Basha et al., 2021).

Labor Market Dynamics: The methods have advanced understanding of unemployment duration in the Czech Republic (Malá and Čabla, 2022) and Portugal's labor contract mismatches (Menezes and Sciulli, 2022).

Sectoral Analyses: Semi-parametric methods have shown remarkable versatility across specialized sectors. Applications include analyzing the viability of nonprofits in the US, the survival of agricultural entrepreneurs in China, the duration of fisheries trade in Southeast Asia, and even prison recidivism in Brazil (Feng, 2020; Souza et al., 2024; Wang, Tran, et al., 2019; Yang et al., 2023). These applications demonstrate the methods' adaptability to diverse contexts with complex data structures. Their use in non-traditional sectors confirms their value for addressing specific problems with robust statistical approaches.

Innovation and R&D Impact: Research on innovation and R&D examines their impact on firm survival and export competitiveness. (Zhang and Mohnen, 2022) studied R&D's role in manufacturing firm survival in China, showing its protective effect against economic shocks. (Dai et al., 2020) found innovation extends export duration, particularly for direct export modes in China. (Z. Li et al., 2021) combined corporate governance with R&D indicators to predict financial distress, also in the Chinese context. These studies highlight innovation as a critical factor in firm survival analysis.

Behavioral and Psychological Economics: Semi-parametric methods have examined psychological factors across economic contexts. (Balloch et al., 2022) linked distress to net worth in NZ, (Jiang et al., 2021) studied loss aversion in Chinese funds, and (Haryanto et al., 2020) showed herding in Indonesian crypto traders.

Regulatory and Compliance Effects Analysis of policy/regulation impacts on economic agents: Studies demonstrate regulations' economic impacts. (Rhee and Jang, 2022) examined anti-dumping measure duration in South Korea. (Matarirano et al., 2019) measured tax compliance costs for South African SMEs. (Feng, 2020) assessed how compliance affects nonprofit audits in the US.

The Cox proportional hazards model emerges as the predominant approach (85% of studies) due to its effectiveness in handling censored data and analyzing the duration of critical events. Studies identify two categories of determining factors: external economic conditions (credit access, financial crises) and internal characteristics (innovation, strategic management), which interact to define business survival. Its cross-sectoral application in banking, e-commerce, and manufacturing demonstrates exceptional versatility in addressing industry-specific challenges.

While the model reveals clear patterns during disruptive events (e.g., zombie firms in China due to unsustainable credit), it shows limitations in capturing nonlinear dynamics between variables. The review highlights the need to complement it with advanced methods (Bayesian, machine learning) that integrate qualitative data and complex interactions. Although geographical diversity (China, Brazil, U.S., Japan) enriches the findings, it also exposes biases from overrepresentation in certain emerging markets.

6 Conclusions

This literature review (2019–2024) demonstrates the growing adoption of survival analysis in economics and finance, marking a clear transition of semi-parametric methods from their biomedical origins to business applications. The analysis reaffirms the central role of the Cox model, whose widespread use across 34 studies highlights its perceived value for handling censored data and linking covariates with event risks—from credit analysis to firm survival. The methodology's core value lies in its unique capacity to examine the temporal patterns of economic events while accommodating diverse data structures.

Three key strengths emerge from this body of work: methodological diversity, cross-sector applicability, and a unique capacity to model time-dependent shocks. Beyond academia, these applications have direct practical implications, offering robust tools for financial institutions to refine credit risk models, for policymakers to evaluate the long-term impact of unemployment benefits, and for managers to identify key drivers of corporate longevity. However, it is important to acknowledge the limitations revealed by this review. The literature shows a notable geographic bias, with a concentration of studies in certain emerging markets like China, which may limit the generalizability of some findings. Furthermore, while the methods prove robust, their underlying assumptions—such as proportional hazards—face challenges in capturing the highly nonlinear dynamics of volatile markets.

These limitations suggest promising avenues for future research. The integration of Bayesian methods or machine learning approaches could address the challenge of nonlinearity. Future work should prioritize the development of hybrid models that preserve the interpretability of traditional semi-parametric methods while incorporating the predictive power needed to model complex economic dynamics in real-time.

Acknowledgments. We gratefully acknowledge the support of the CADEMAS project: Study, Analysis and Evaluation of Cooperative Automated Decision Making Systems (PID2023-146575NB-I00), funded by the Spanish *Ministerio de Ciencia, Innovación y Universidades*. We also extend our thanks to the *Asociación Universitaria Iberoamericana de Postgrado* (AUIP) and the *Junta de Andalucía* for their institutional and financial support, which made this research possible.

References

Alani, M.M.: Big data in cybersecurity: a survey of applications and future trends. J. Reliab. Intel. Environ. **7**(2), 85–114 (2021)

Alkhawaldeh, A.A., Jaber, J.J., Boughaci, D.: A mortality approach for estimating the probability of default in credit risk. J. Adv. Res. Law and Econ. **10**(8), 2233–2243 (2019)

Andersen, P.K., Gill, R.D.: Cox's regression model for counting processes: a large sample study. The Annals of Statistics, 1100–1120 (1982)

Arguello, R., Garcia-Suaza, A., Valderrama, D.: Exporters' agglomeration and the survival of export flows: Empirical evidence from Colombia. Rev. World Econ. **156**, 703–729 (2020)

Balloch, A., Engels, C., Philip, D.: When it Rains it drains: Psychological distress and household net worth. J. Bank. Finance **143**, 106620 (2022). https://doi.org/10.2139/ssrn.3521323

Basha, S.A., Elgammal, M.M., Abuzayed, B.M.: Online peer-to-peer lending: a review of the literature. Electron. Commer. Res. Appl. **48**, 101069 (2021). https://doi.org/10.1016/j.elerap. 2021.101069

Chawla, I.: Determinants of firms' initial decision to invest abroad: an application of "survival" analysis to manufacturing firms in India. Emerg. Mark. Financ. Trade **55**(3), 562–583 (2019). https://doi.org/10.1080/1540496X.2018.1447461

Chen, W.: Too far east is west: Tax risk, tax reform and investment timing. Int. J. Manager. Fin. **17**(2), 303–326 (2021). https://doi.org/10.1111/acfi.12921

Coccorese, P., Santucci, L.: The role of downward assets volatility in assessing the book-value distance to default. J. Fin. Econ. Policy **11**(4), 485–504 (2019)

Cordón-Lagares, E., García-Ordaz, F.: Factors affecting the survival of maritime goods transport firms in Spain. Res. Transport. Bus. Manage. **37** (2020). https://doi.org/10.1016/j.rtbm.2020. 100520

Cox, D.R.: Regression models and life-tables. J. Roy. Stat. Soc.: Ser. B (Methodol.) **34**(2), 187–202 (1972)

Cox, D.R., Oakes, D.: The scope of survival analysis. En Analysis of Survival Data, pp. 1–12. Chapman and Hall/CRC (2018). https://doi.org/10.1201/9781315137438-1

Cziraki, P., Groen-Xu, M.: CEO turnover and volatility under long-term employment contracts. J. Fin. Quantit. Anal. **55**(6), 1757–1791 (2020)

Dai, M., Liu, H., Lin, L.: How innovation impacts firms' export survival: Does export mode matter? The World Economy **43**(1), 81–113 (2020)

David, G.K., Mitchel, K.: Survival analysis: A Self-Learning text: A Self-Learning Text. Spinger (2012). https://doi.org/10.1007/978-1-4419-6646-9

Emmert-Streib, F., Dehmer, M.: Introduction to Survival Analysis in Practice. En Machine Learning and Knowledge Extraction, Vol. 1, Número 3, pp. 1013–1038. MDPI (2019). https://doi. org/10.3390/make1030058

Feng, N.C.: The impact of noncompliance and internal control deficiencies on going concern audit opinions and viability of nonprofit charitable organizations. J. Acc. Audit. Financ. **35**(3), 637–664 (2020). https://doi.org/10.1177/0148558X18774904

Flores, A.Q.: Survival analysis. The SAGE Encyclopedia of Research Design (2022). https://doi. org/10.4135/9781412961288.n450

Gao, F., He, X.: Survival analysis: theory and application in finance. Handbook of Financial Econometrics, Mathematics, Statistics, and Machine Learning. (2020). https://doi.org/10.1142/ 9789811202391_0120

Gatabazi, P., Kabera, G., Mba, J.C., Pindza, E., Melesse, S.F.: Cryptocurrencies and tokens lifetime analysis from 2009 to 2021. Economies **10**(3), 60 (2022). https://doi.org/10.3390/economies 10030060

Guo, S., Zeng, D.: An overview of semiparametric models in survival analysis. J. Statist. Plann. Infer. **151–152**, 1–16 (2014). https://doi.org/10.1016/j.jspi.2013.10.008

Haryanto, S., Subroto, A., Ulpah, M.: Disposition effect and herding behavior in the cryptocurrency market. J. Indus. Bus. Econ. **47**, 115–132 (2020). https://doi.org/10.4108/eai.14-9-2020.2304467

He, Q., Qian, Z., Fei, Z., Chong, T.T.-L.: Do speculative bubbles migrate in the Chinese stock market? Empirical Economics **56**(2), 735–754 (2019). https://doi.org/10.51200/lbibf.v13i.346

Iwasaki, I., Kočenda, E., Shida, Y.: Institutions, financial development, and small business survival: Evidence from European emerging markets. Small Business Economics, 1–23 (2022)

Jiang, J., Shrider, D.G., Ting, H., Wu, Y.: Are mutual fund investors loss averse? Evidence from China. Financial Review **56**(2), 231–250 (2021)

Karim, Md. R., Islam, M.A.: Reliability and Survival Analysis. En Reliability and Survival Analysis. Springer Singapore (2019). https://doi.org/10.1007/978-981-13-9776-9

Kassner, A.J., Cajias, M., Zhu, B.: The PropTech investors' dilemma–What are the key success factors that secure survival? J. Property Invest. Fin. **41**(1), 76–91 (2023)

Kočenda, E., Iwasaki, I.: Bank survival around the World: A meta-analytic review. J. Econ. Surv. **36**(1), 108–156 (2022). https://doi.org/10.1007/s00181-023-02528-1

Kumar, D., Klefsjö, B.: Proportional hazards model: a review. Reliab. Eng. Syst. Saf. **44**(2), 177–188 (1994). https://doi.org/10.1016/0951-8320(94)90010-8

Leclere, M.J.: Modeling time to event: applications of survival analysis in accounting, economics and finance. Rev. Acc. Financ. **4**, 5–12 (2005). https://doi.org/10.1108/EB043434

Lee, C.F., Lee, J.C.: Handbook of financial econometrics, mathematics, statistics, and machine learning (in 4 volumes). World Scientific (2020)

Lee, E.T.: Statistical methods for survival data analysis. IEEE Trans. Reliab. **35**, 123 (1994). https://doi.org/10.2307/2533355

Li, J., Ma, S.: Survival analysis in medicine and genetics. Chapman and Hall/CRC (2013). https://doi.org/10.1201/b14978

Li, Z., Crook, J., Andreeva, G., Tang, Y.: Predicting the risk of financial distress using corporate governance measures. Pac. Basin Financ. J. **68**, 101334 (2021)

Lin, C.-H.: Impact of tariff rates on the probability of trade relationship survival: Evidence from ASEAN+ 6 manufactured goods. Pac. Econ. Rev. **25**(4), 457–474 (2020)

Lopes, M.C.: A review on the elasticity of unemployment duration to the potential duration of unemployment benefits. J. Econ. Sur. **36**(4), 1212–1224 (2022)

Majune, S.K., Türkcan, K., Moyi, E.: How the African continental free trade area impacts firms' export survival: Some lessons from Kenya. J. Int. Trade Econ. Dev. **33**(4), 574–597 (2024)

Malá, I., Čabla, A.: Modelling of the unemployment duration in the Czech Republic based on aggregated complete and individual censored data. Ekonomicky Casopis **70**(2), 171–187 (2022)

Matarirano, O., Makina, D., Chiloane-Tsoka, G.E.: Tax compliance costs and small business performance: Evidence from the South African construction industry. South African J. Bus. Manage. **50**(1), 1–9 (2019). https://doi.org/10.4102/sajbm.v50i1.336

Menezes, A., Sciulli, D.: The effects of contract-type mismatch and matching frictions on unemployment duration: Evidence for Portugal. J. Appl. Econ. **25**(1), 936–961 (2022). https://doi.org/10.1080/15140326.2022.2084687

Mumtaz, M.Z., Smith, Z.A.: Analyzing the duration of IPOs from offering to listing using the Cox proportional hazards model. Port. Econ. J. **20**, 5–43 (2021)

O'Quigley, J.: Survival Analysis: Proportional and Non-Proportional Hazards Regression. Proportional and Non-Proportional Hazards Regression. Springer International Publishing, En Survival Analysis (2021). https://doi.org/10.1007/978-3-030-33439-0

Prentice, R.L., Williams, B.J., Peterson, A.V.: On the regression analysis of multivariate failure time data. Biometrika **68**(2), 373–379 (1981)

Rhee, J.W., Jang, Y.J.: Determinants of Termination of Anti-dumping Measures: The Case of Korea. East Asian Economic Review **26**(2), 95–117 (2022)

Rozo, B.J.G., Crook, J., Andreeva, G.: The role of web browsing in credit risk prediction. Decision Support Systems 164 (2023). https://doi.org/10.1016/j.dss.2022.113879

Shiraishi, M., Yano, G.: The financial crisis in 2008, the Stimulus package, and distortion of financial intermediation in China: A survival analysis approach. Comp. Econ. Stud. **64**(2), 280–323 (2022). https://doi.org/10.2139/ssrn.4197204

Sousa-Ferreira, I., Abreu, A.M.: Hybrid Model for Recurrent Event Data. En Matrices, Statistics and Big Data, pp. 23–33. Springer International Publishing (2019). https://doi.org/10.1007/978-3-030-17519-1_2

Souza, R.G. de, Golgher, A.B., Silva, B.F.A. da.: Determinantes da reincidência prisional em Santa Catarina utilizando a análise de sobrevivência. Nova Economia **34**(3) (2024). https://doi.org/10.1590/0103-6351/8027

Vaman, H., Tattar, P.: Survival Analysis. CRC Press, En Survival Analysis (2022). https://doi.org/10.1201/9781003306979-9

Wang, P., Li, Y., Reddy, C.K.: Machine learning for survival analysis: a survey. ACM Comput. Surv. **51**(6), 1–36 (2019). https://doi.org/10.1145/3214306

Wang, P., Tran, N., Wilson, N.L., Chan, C.Y., Dao, D.: An analysis of seafood trade duration: The case of ASEAN. Mar. Resour. Econ. **34**(1), 59–76 (2019)

Yang, C., Yan, J., He, X., Tian, S.: What determines the survival of farmer entrepreneurship: Micro-evidence from China. Int. Rev. Econ. Financ. **86**, 334–348 (2023)

Zhang, M., Mohnen, P.: R&D, innovation and firm survival in Chinese manufacturing, 2000–2006. Eurasian Bus. Rev. **12**(1), 59–95 (2022)

Zhu, X., Liu, B., Wei, Q.: Does participation in global value chains extend export duration? Rev. Dev. Econ. **23**(3), 1282–1308 (2019)

Deep Learning for Space Situational Awareness: Addressing Kessler Syndrome with Efficient Spacecraft Detection a Preliminary Result

Jorge Felix Martínez Pazos[✉] and Jorge Gulín González

Centro de Estudios de Matemática Computacional, Universidad de Las Ciencias Informáticas,
La Habana, Cuba
jorgefmp.mle@gmail.com

Abstract. Accurate and efficient spacecraft detection is critical for mitigating collision risks in Earth's increasingly crowded orbital environment, where the proliferation of space debris threatens to escalate the Kessler Syndrome a cascading cycle of collisions that generate catastrophic debris fields. This study presents a YOLOv8n-based preliminary framework optimized for real-time spacecraft detection in synthetic images derived from NASA's Pose Bowl Challenge dataset. By performing rigorous preprocessing including bounding box area filtering (75th percentile, ≤ 2500 px2) and resolution reduction from HR to 256×256 pixels, we mitigate noise from structural outliers and maintain computational efficiency. Transfer learning on YOLOv8n achieved a validation mAP50–95 of 0.73 at 125 FPS, demonstrating near real-time capability critical for timely collision avoidance, even with limited hyperparameter tuning during 5 epochs and 10 iterations. Training stopped at epoch 356 for a patience value of 25, with peak performance at epoch 212 achieving 0.85 and 1.11 for mAP50 and box loss respectively. While domain gaps from synthetic data and suboptimal convergence highlight the need for deeper architectural refinement, this work underscores the potential of lightweight detection systems to enhance space situational awareness. By enabling rapid identification of spacecraft and debris, the proposed preliminary approach could reduce collision risks, mitigate debris generation, and contribute to long-term orbital sustainability.

Keywords: computer vision · Kesler Syndrome · object detection · space debris · spacecraft

1 Introduction

Kessler Syndrome, named after NASA scientist Donald J. Kessler, describes a scenario in which the density of objects in low Earth orbit (LEO) is high enough that collisions between objects could cause a cascade, leading to an exponential increase in space debris. This phenomenon poses a significant threat to satellite operations and, by extension, to the myriads of services that rely on satellite technology, including communication, navigation, and weather forecasting. The implications of Kessler Syndrome extend beyond technological disruptions; they could potentially impact global affairs, ecological systems, and human safety [1].

© The Author(s), under exclusive license to Springer Nature Switzerland AG 2026
Y. Hernádez Heredia et al. (Eds.): IWAIPR 2025, LNCS 16328, pp. 302–312, 2026.
https://doi.org/10.1007/978-3-032-11358-0_25

The potential outcomes of Kessler Syndrome are dire. The disruption of satellite operations could lead to crashes and the failure of essential utility services, which heavily depend on satellite communications. This could affect everything from global communications to weather prediction and disaster management, thereby endangering human lives and disrupting societal functions. The loss of satellite communications could also have cascading effects on global affairs, as many critical infrastructures and services are interlinked with satellite technology [1]. As humans are a dominant force on Earth, their endangerment would reverberate throughout the ecological system, potentially leading to the demise of other species [1].

NASA's LEGEND (LEO-to-GEO Environment Debris) simulation model [2] shows a continuous and significant increase in the number of cataloged objects larger than 10 cm in Low Earth Orbit (LEO) since 1957. This growth includes sharp rises following major fragmentation events and the rapid expansion of satellite launches. LEGEND's projections indicate that, without effective debris mitigation, the number of hazardous objects in LEO will continue to escalate, increasing the likelihood of collision cascades and exacerbating the potential for Kessler Syndrome [2].

The increasing accumulation of space debris and the associated risk of Kessler Syndrome has led to this study, which focuses on the development of a spacecraft detection system using monocular images and video from an on-board camera. The proposed system aims to identify nearby objects within the camera's field of view, with the long-term goal of enabling distance estimation between the host spacecraft and the detected objects.

The decision to separate detection and distance estimation stems from the inherent challenges of adapting terrestrial distance estimation algorithms to space. Terrestrial methods often rely on environmental features (e.g. atmospheric effects, calibrated reference objects) that are absent in space, where lighting conditions, lack of visual landmarks and dynamic relative motion impose unique constraints [3–6]. Dung et al. [7] proved that other computer vision tasks, such as semantic segmentation in space environments, present significant challenges for models designed for Earth-based scenarios, thereby highlighting the complexity of extrapolating computer vision capabilities from Earth to Space.

By prioritizing detection first, this work proposes an object detection model trained with synthetic spacecraft images to address immediate collision risks, while recognizing that distance estimation requires specialized solutions tailored to the orbital environment. Subsequent phases will explore these complexities to enhance navigational safety (Fig. 1).

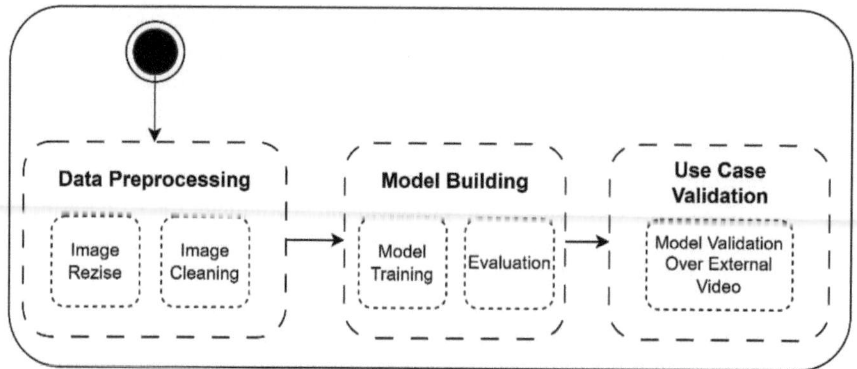

Fig. 1. Workflow of the proposed preliminary study

2   Related Works

Several research efforts have been directed toward understanding and mitigating the risks associated with Kessler Syndrome. Drmola, & Hubík [8] uses system dynamics methodology to model the interactions between satellites and debris over a 50-year period. It presents various scenarios, including business-as-usual, conflict-induced debris accumulation, and mitigation efforts through direct removal of inactive satellites. This study underscores the necessity for sustainable long-term solutions to manage orbital debris. Bernat [9] discusses the lack of a global legal system regulating the use of Earth's orbit, which exacerbates the threat of Kessler Syndrome. It highlights the need for international cooperation and legal frameworks to manage space debris effectively. The KESSYM model is a stochastic simulation that forecasts the evolution of the orbital environment and the potential occurrence of Kessler Syndrome. It evaluates various risks and mitigation measures, concluding that while Kessler Syndrome is almost inevitable within 200–250 years, proactive measures can delay or prevent it [10]. Active debris removal (ADR) has been identified as a crucial strategy to mitigate the risks of Kessler Syndrome. Research has focused on developing technologies for the active removal of debris, including rendezvous with non-cooperative, tumbling debris, and de-orbiting large objects. These efforts aim to reduce the number of debris objects in LEO and prevent further [11]. Roll et al. [12] introduce the CosmosDSR methodology, which leverages AI for the automated detection and tracking of orbital debris. This approach combines the YOLOv3 object detector with an Unscented Kalman Filter (UKF) to track satellites in sequential images. The methodology was tested using the SPARK dataset, achieving high precision in satellite detection and classification (Mean Average Precision = 97.18%, F1 = 0.95) with minimal errors (TP = 4163, FP = 209, FN = 237). The tracking accuracy was also impressive, with a mean squared error (MSE) and root mean squared error 2.83 and 1.66 respectively for UKF and; 2.84 and 1.66 for the Linear Kalman Filter (LKF) used for comparison. Although the study was limited to a space simulation environment, the CosmosDSR methodology shows great potential in mitigating the Kessler syndrome by effectively detecting and tracking space debris. Several Artificial Intelligence models have been assessed for their effectiveness in managing space debris, including Convolutional Neural Networks (CNNs), Kernel Principal

Component Analysis (KPCA), and Model-Agnostic Meta-Learning (MAML) [13–15]. These models have been evaluated with various data types to enhance the detection and tracking capabilities of space debris management systems.

3   Materials and Methods

3.1   Collected Data

The data used in this study were sourced from the challenge 'Pose Bowl: Spacecraft Detection and Pose Estimation Challenge' hosted on the Driven Data platform in collaboration with the NASA Tournament Lab. The dataset consists of simulated images of spacecraft, generated to replicate the perspective of a chaser spacecraft observing a host spacecraft from a nearby location in space. These images were created using the open-source 3D software Blender, which employed models of representative host spacecraft and simulated backgrounds. A limited set of models and backgrounds were utilized, with each model and background appearing across multiple images to ensure diversity within the dataset [16].

The images were enhanced with realism by applying post-processing techniques to simulate imperfections commonly encountered in real-world scenarios, including blur, hot pixels and random noise. This dataset provides a robust foundation for analyzing and developing computational methods to address challenges related to spacecraft imaging and recognition in dynamic and imperfect conditions [16].

The dataset contains a total of 22506 high-resolution images. In some cases, the bounding box labels include parts of the spacecraft that are barely visible to the human eye, such as large antennas or thin structural elements like booms and masts. These features, which often extend far from the main body of the spacecraft, are more frequently observed in images with larger bounding boxes, as identified by multiple stochastic iterations. Further within the dataset there is also a tendency of larger bounding box to be incorrect in a few cases as depicted in Fig. 2. The inclusion of such images can introduce noise and bias into any model trained on these data.

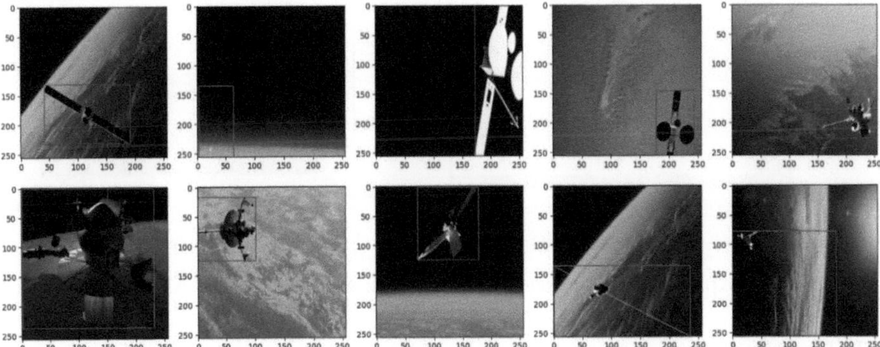

Fig. 2. A set of stochastic images from the spacecraft datasets, with its labeled bounding box.

3.2 Data Preprocessing

Since the images were in high resolution 1280 x 1024 was needed to resize both image and bounding boxes to a more reasonable resolution 256 x 256 was chosen mainly to improve efficiency of the model training and inference. The presence of these extended features in larger bounding boxes poses a challenge for object detection models, as they may misinterpret these structures as part of the main spacecraft body or fail to generalize effectively. To address this issue, we implemented a cleaning process focused on images with larger bounding box areas. This process aims to refine the dataset by ensuring that bounding boxes accurately represent the main spacecraft body while minimizing the inclusion of extraneous features that could compromise model performance.

The area of bounding boxes is computed to quantify the size of regions of interest within the images. The area A is defined as:

$$A = (x_{max} - x_{min}) \times (y_{max} - y_{min}) \tag{1}$$

where, xmax, xmin, ymax, and ymin represent the pixel coordinates of the bounding box boundaries.

The analysis of bounding box areas revealed that the 75th percentile corresponds to 2542 pixels2, with the maximum bounding box area reaching 65,536 pixels2 as depicted in Fig. 3. To ensure a robust and representative dataset without potential noise, we applied a filtering criterion to retain only those images with bounding box areas within the 75th percentile. For practical purposes, the 75th percentile value was rounded to 2500 pixels2. This filtering step helps mitigate the influence of excessively large bounding boxes given by the previously explained facts and behaviors. Out of a total of 22506 images, 15% were discarded during the filtering process, leaving a final set of 16821 images.

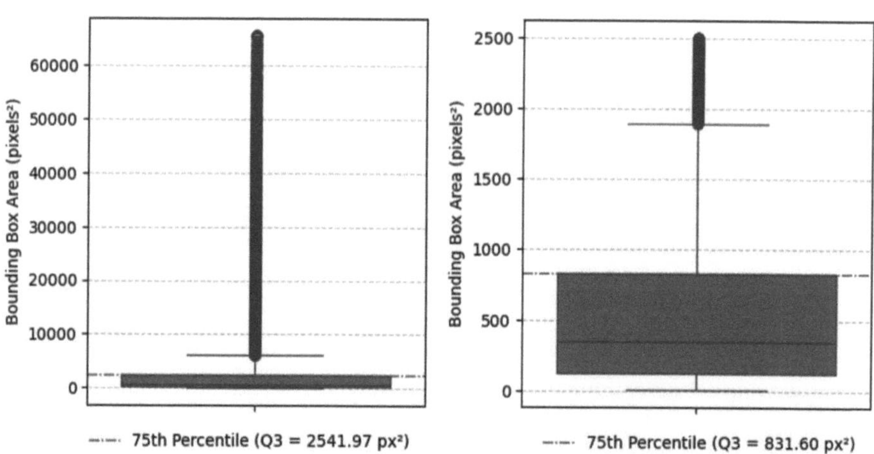

Fig. 3. Boxplots of the Calculated Bounding Box Areas Before and After Filtering.

3.3 Modeling

YOLO (You Only Look Once) is a state-of-the-art single-stage object detection framework renowned for its real-time inference capabilities and balance between speed and accuracy. Unlike traditional multi-stage detectors, YOLO processes images in a single forward pass through a convolutional neural network (CNN), simultaneously predicting bounding boxes and class probabilities. This architecture enables efficient deployment in time-sensitive applications, such as spacecraft detection or space debris monitoring, where rapid detection of high-velocity objects is critical to mitigating collision risks.

The YOLOv8n (nano) variant was chosen for this study due to its lightweight architecture, optimized for computational efficiency without compromising detection performance. YOLOv8n achieves inference speeds of 50–60 FPS on standard GPUs, critical for real-time space situational awareness.

These attributes align with the challenges of spacecraft detection, where targets often occupy $< 0.15\%$ of the image area in optical telescope data and exhibit low signal-to-noise ratios due to light interference and background clutter.

Therefore, this study aims to applied transfer learning and fine tuning over YOLOv8n the most efficient model of the YOLOv8 family, using the collected and preprocessed dataset of spacecrafts.

3.4 Environment

The experiments discussed in this study were carry out in a high-performance personal computer with NVIDEA CUDA and Torch as main tools, following is provide a brief description of the hardware and drivers used in the experiments (Table 1).

Table 1. Hardware and Drivers.

NVIDIA- SMI 560.94
CUDA Version 12.6
NVIDIA GeForce RTX 3060 80W 6144MiB
Intel(R) Core (TM) i7-12700H 2.30 GHz 16.0 GB RAM

3.5 Tunning and Training

For the training process the dataset was splitted into three sets train, test and validation representing 70%, 15% and 15% respectively. First, we perform a small hyperparameter tunning over the train set of 5 epochs and 10 iterations using an Adam optimizer which result in the first most optimal hyperparameters to start the training experiments. The model was trained during 500 epochs using batch of 64 and a patience value of 25, main hyperparameters of the training process are detailed in Table 2.

Table 2. Main Hyperparameters for training process.

Hyperparameter	Value
dropout	0.1
Iou	0.5
Conf	0.6
lr0	0.003
Lrf	0.003
Patience	25
Batch	64
momentum	0.9
weigth_decay	0.0005
warmup_epochs	2.96
warmup_momentum	0.8

4   Results and Discussions

The model starts from the first epoch with 0.7, 0.5, 1.7 and 2.0 for Mean Absolute Precision 50 (mAP50), Mean Absolute Precision 50 at 95% (mAP50–95), Box loss and Classification loss respectively. Those values are relatively high for the challenge task of spacecraft detection from synthetic images what reaffirm the potentials of YOLOv8 and its use as pretrained backbone.

The training process was stopped at epoch 356 by the early stop callback the model achieves the best results at epoch 212 with a Mean Absolute Precision 50 (mAP50) of 0.85 and a Mean Absolute Precision 50 at 95% (mAP50–95) of 0.73 both for validation set. At its best epoch the model reports a precision of 0.95 and a box loss and class loss of 1.11 and 0.74 respectively for validation as well. Even though this are preliminary results the obtained metrics form the first shallow training are promising. Figure 4 provides a sample of results during a validation batch where can be seen the correct classification and detection of the bounding box of the spacecraft during the validation process.

Fig. 4. Classification and detection of spacecraft during the validation process.

In terms of efficiency, the model achieves 0.1ms of preprocessing and 0.7ms of inference per image, processing a total of 5019 images in approximately 40 s, giving us an approximate ratio of approximately 125 frames per second (FPS).

To assess the model's performance in dynamic scenarios, we conducted an experimental evaluation on a video sequence from the internet depicting spacecraft traversing a space environment. Despite being trained on a limited hyperparameter configuration, as previously outlined, the preliminary model demonstrated functional capability in detecting moving spacecraft, with bounding boxes consistently localizing targets across frames as depicted in Fig. 5.

However, in several frames the model showed intermittent fluctuations in detection, and in some isolated cases even incorrect bounding box detections as details in supplementary materials Fig. 6, likely due to the shallow training regime and suboptimal hyperparameter calibration employed in this initial phase. These artefacts highlight the need for deeper architectural optimization and a more extensive hyperparameter search and tuning phase to achieve very smooth detection over video.

Future work will prioritize comprehensive hyperparameter search, extended training cycles, and fine-tuning of the model backbone to enhance detection robustness, reduce temporal instability, and improve accuracy metrics (e.g. exceeding the current validation mAP50–95 of 0.73). Such refinements aim to bridge performance gaps observed in dynamic environments while maintaining the model's computational efficiency (125 FPS).

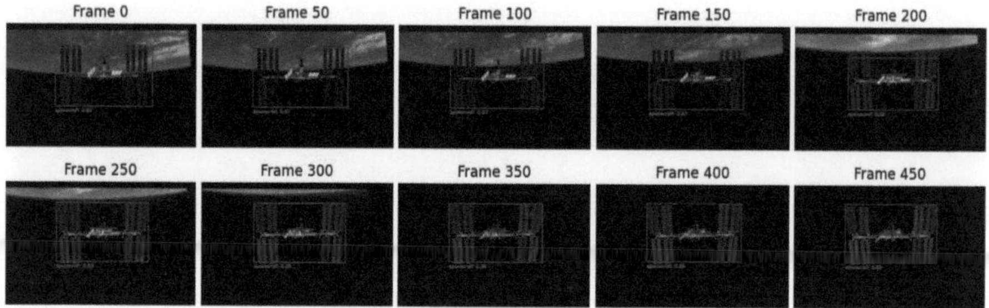

Fig. 5. Experimental spacecraft detection over video.

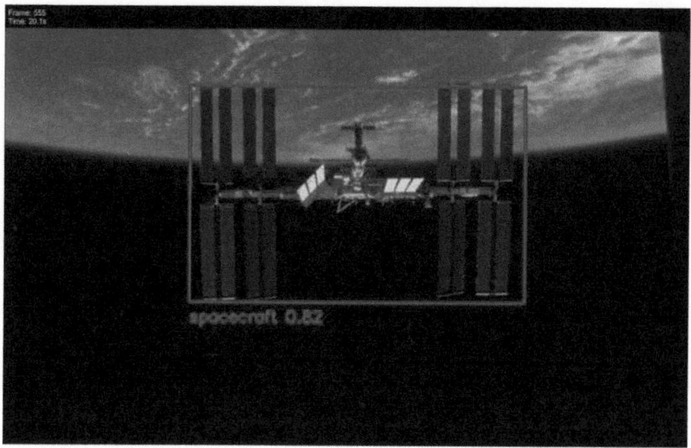

Fig. 6. Supplementary Material 1: Experimental spacecraft detection GIF.

The dataset used in this study was specifically curated to address the challenge of spacecraft detection from synthetic imagery, a task that requires robust preprocessing for model readiness. The images in the dataset were carefully pre-processed to meet the input requirements of state-of-the-art object detection models such as YOLOv8. This included steps such as resizing, normalization and filtering to ensure that the data was representative of the potential conditions the model would encounter in real-world scenarios. In addition, the bounding boxes around the spacecraft were normalized in the same way to the specified resolution to ensure consistency between the image and its bounding box.

Given the comprehensive nature of the dataset and its pre-processed state, it is well suited for further advances in spacecraft detection research. The dataset created by NASA and adapted in this study is designed for scalability, facilitating its use in future experiments with different object detection models and architectures. The high-quality annotations, combined with the carefully curated image set, provide a valuable resource for spacecraft detection research, enabling reproducible experiments, benchmark comparisons, and further model improvements.

The proposed YOLOv8 architecture demonstrates preliminary efficacy in spacecraft detection, achieving a validation mAP50–95 of 0.73 at 125 FPS, highlighting its suitability for near-real-time applications such as autonomous navigation or debris tracking. However, the model's performance remains constrained by its limited hyperparameter optimization and shallow training regimen (terminated at epoch 356), leading to suboptimal stability in bounding box predictions having a box loss of 1.11 during the validation scenario. Furthermore, reliance on synthetic data introduces domain adaptation challenges, while the absence of distance estimation limits operational utility in proximity-critical tasks.

Future efforts will prioritize rigorous hyperparameter tuning, extended training cycles, and integration of monocular depth estimation to infer relative distances between detected spacecraft. Additionally, domain adaptation techniques will be employed to bridge the sim-to-real gap, ensuring robustness in heterogeneous orbital environments. These enhancements aim to transition the proposal from a proof-of-concept to a deployable system for mission-critical space applications.

5 Conclusions

This study validates YOLOv8n as a computationally efficient backbone for real-time spacecraft detection, achieving high performance and efficiency on synthetic data preprocessed through bounding box area filtering and resolution reduction. While early stopping at epoch 356 and a box loss value of 1.11 reflect limitations due to shallow hyperparameter tuning and synthetic domain bias, the model's throughput demonstrates feasibility for collision avoidance systems critical to mitigating the risk of Kessler syndrome. Future work must prioritize depth-aware architectures for distance estimation, Bayesian hyperparameter optimization and domain adaptation to bridge the gap between simulation and reality. Advancing these elements will transform this prototype into an operational tool for protecting orbital environments from cascading debris collisions.

6 Disclosure of Interests

The authors have no competing interests to declare that are relevant to the content of this article.

References

1. Mariappan, A., Crassidis, J.: Kessler's syndrome: a challenge to humanity. Front. Space Technol. (2023). https://doi.org/10.3389/frspt.2023.1309940
2. NASA Orbital Debris Program Office. LEGEND: 3D/OD Evoluational Model. NASA. https://orbitaldebris.jsc.nasa.gov/modeling/legend.html. Retrieved July of 2025
3. Tian, J., Cui, W., Wu, S.: A novel method for parameter estimation of space moving targets. IEEE Geosci. Remote Sens. Lett. **11**, 389–393 (2014). https://doi.org/10.1109/LGRS.2013.2263332
4. Feng, J., Hejda, F., Carloni, S.: Relativistic location algorithm in curved spacetime. Physical Review D (2022). https://doi.org/10.1103/PhysRevD.106.044034

5. Rainjonneau, S., et al.: Quantum algorithms applied to satellite mission planning for earth observation. IEEE Journal of Selected Topics in Applied Earth Observations and Remote Sensing **16**, 7062–7075 (2023). https://doi.org/10.1109/JSTARS.2023.3287154

6. Andreis, E., Panicucci, P., Topputo, F.: Autonomous vision-based algorithm for interplanetary navigation. J. Guid. Control. Dyn. (2024). https://doi.org/10.2514/1.g007926

7. Dung, H.A., Chen, B., Chin, T.-J.: A spacecraft dataset for detection, segmentation and parts recognition. Computer Vision and Pattern Recognition, 2012–2019 (2021). https://doi.org/10.1109/CVPRW53098.2021.00229

8. Drmola, J., Hubík, T.: Kessler syndrome: system dynamics model. Space Policy (2018). https://doi.org/10.1016/J.SPACEPOL.2018.03.003

9. Bernat, P.: Orbital satellite constellations and the growing threat of Kessler syndrome in the lower earth orbit (2020). https://doi.org/10.37105/iboa.94

10. Hudson, J.: KESSYM: a stochastic orbital debris model for evaluation of Kessler Syndrome risks and mitigations. Journal of Student Research (2023). https://doi.org/10.47611/jsrhs.v12i1.4013

11. Bonnal, C., Ruault, J., Desjean, M.: Active debris removal: Recent progress and current trends. Acta Astronaut. **85**, 51–60 (2013). https://doi.org/10.1016/J.ACTAASTRO.2012.11.009

12. Roll, D., Kurt, Z., Woo, W.: CosmosDSR - a methodology for automated detection and tracking of orbital debris using the Unscented Kalman Filter (2023). ArXiv, abs/2310.17158. https://doi.org/10.48550/arXiv.2310.17158

13. Jharbade, P., Dixit, M.: Detecting space debris using deep learning algorithms: a survey. 2022 4th International Conference on Inventive Research in Computing Applications (ICIRCA), pp. 883–890 (2022). https://doi.org/10.1109/ICIRCA54612.2022.9985622

14. Caldas, F., Soares, C.: Machine Learning in Orbit Estimation: a Survey. ArXiv, abs/2207.08993 (2022). https://doi.org/10.48550/arXiv.2207.08993

15. Furfaro, R., Campbell, T., Linares, R., Reddy, V.: Space Debris Identification and Characterization via Deep Meta-Learning (2019)

16. NASA, DrivenData. Pose Bowl: Spacecraft Detection and Pose Estimation Challenge (2024). Retrieved September 24 of 2024

A Hybrid Deep Neural Network-Transformer Architecture for Consumer Price Index Forecasting: Integrating Non-Linear Feature Extraction with Multi-Head Attention Mechanisms

Reynaldo Rosado Roselló$^{(\boxtimes)}$![ORCID], Ana Marys Garcia Rodríguez ![ORCID], Héctor Raúl González Diez ![ORCID], and Yanio Hernández Heredia ![ORCID]

Universidad de Las Ciencias Informáticas, Carretera a San Antonio de los Baños, Km 2½, Torrens, Boyeros, La Habana, Cuba
rrosado@uci.cu

Abstract. Accurate forecasting of the Consumer Price Index is crucial for economic stability, enabling policymakers to design effective monetary strategies and mitigate inflationary risks. Traditional models like ARIMA struggle to capture complex non-linear patterns and long-term dependencies in Consumer Price Index data, often leading to suboptimal predictive performance. To address these limitations, this study proposes a hybrid deep learning model combining a Deep Neural Network and a Transformer architecture. The Deep Neural Network extracts non-linear features, while the Transformer's multi-head attention mechanism captures temporal dependencies, enhancing forecasting precision. The model incorporates advanced preprocessing techniques, including dynamic window normalization and outlier detection, ensuring robust data representation. Experimental results demonstrate superior performance, with a Mean Absolute Error (MAE) of 0.45, Root Mean Square Error (RMSE) of 0.62, and Mean Absolute Percentage Error (MAPE) of 1.8%, outperforming classical benchmarks. Interpretability tools such as SHAP and LIME provide actionable insights, enhancing the model's transparency and reliability for economic policy-making. This work bridges the gap between econometrics and cutting-edge Artificial Intelligence, offering a scalable solution for Consumer Price Index forecasting.

Keywords: Consumer Price Index · Deep Learning · Transformer · Attention Mechanism · Time Series Forecasting

1 Introduction

The Consumer Price Index (CPI) represents one of the most critical indicators of economic health, serving as the principal measure of inflation and the cost of living for millions of households. Its fluctuations are not merely statistical artifacts but they are deeply intertwined with a nation's economic fabric. Central banks, including the Federal

Y. Hernádez Heredia et al. (Eds.): IWAIPR 2025, LNCS 16328, pp. 313–322, 2026.
https://doi.org/10.1007/978-3-032-11358-0_26

Reserve and the European Central Bank, meticulously monitor the CPI data to inform monetary policy decisions, particularly interest rate adjustments to manage inflation and foster economic stability. Governments rely on CPI data for fiscal planning, adjusting social security benefits, pensions, and public sector wages to protect citizens´ purchasing power. In the private sector, the CPI server as a cornerstone for investment strategies, risk assessment, and crucial for labor negotiations, where it functions as a benchmark for cost-of-living adjustments. Given its profound and wide ranging impact, the ability to produce accurate and reliable CPI forecasts is not merely an academic challenge but an economic imperative. Precise predictions enable policymakers to act proactively rather than reactively, mitigating inflationary risks before they escalate, and enabling businesses and consumers to make informed financial decisions in an uncertain environment (Zamanzadeh Darban, 2024) (Praveen, 2025).

However, forecasting the CPI presents a notoriously complex challenge due to the intrinsic characteristics of the time series. The index exhibits a complex interplay of non-linearity, non-stationarity, and multi-scale seasonality, often compounded by structural breaks caused by major economic events. Its trajectory is perpetually influenced by a confluence of external factors, including volatile energy prices, global supply chain disruptions, geopolitical conflicts, and shifts in consumer behavior, as recently exemplified by the COVID-19 pandemic. These elements introduce a significant degree of noise and randomness, making the CPI signal difficult to model and predict using conventional methods (Muth, 2024). The inherent dynamism of the index means that historical patterns may not persist in the future, demanding forecasting models that are not only precise but also highly adaptive to new and unforeseen market conditions.

For decades, econometric forecasting has been dominated by classical statistical models, with the Autoregressive Integrated Moving Average (ARIMA) and Vector Autoregression (VAR) frameworks being the most prominent. These models, built upon principles of linear algebra and stochastic processes, have proven effective in capturing linear trends and simple seasonal patterns in relatively stable economic environments. However, their fundamental assumptions of linearity and stationarity, make them unsuitable for handling the complex dynamics of modern economic data such as the CPI. Their rigid, predefined lag structures struggle to capture long-term dependencies, and their linear nature fails to efficiently model sudden changes, such as inflation spikes or economic crises. While variants such as SARIMA can handle simple seasonality, they are often too inflexible to adapt to the changing and multi-layered cyclical patterns present in the CPI, leading to degraded predictive performance, especially over longer forecast horizons (Padariya, 2025) (Li, 2024).

The limitations of these traditional models have catalyzed research into more powerful and flexible alternatives, leading to the burgeoning field of Artificial Intelligence. The past decade has witnessed a paradigm shift, with machine learning and, more specifically, deep learning techniques demonstrating remarkable success in time series analysis. Early deep learning models such as Recurrent Neural Networks (RNNs) and their more advanced variants, Long Short-Term Memory (LSTM) and Gated Recurrent Units (GRU), offered a significant improvement by inherently modeling sequential data and capturing temporal dependencies (Kong, 2025). However, these architectures face challenges, most notably the vanishing gradient problem, which limits their ability to effectively learn and recall information over very long time sequences a critical requirement for modeling multi-year economic cycles (Thundiyil, 2025).

A revolutionary breakthrough emerged with the development of the Transformer architecture, first introduced in the context of natural language processing. At the heart of the Transformer lies the self-attention mechanism, a novel concept that allows the model to dynamically weigh the importance of different observations in the input sequence, regardless of their temporal distance. Unlike RNNs, which process data sequentially, the self-attention mechanism processes the entire time series simultaneously, creating a rich, contextualized representation of each data point by relating it to all other points. This capability is ideally suited for CPI forecasting, as it enables the model to identify and prioritize critical historical patterns—for instance, learning that an inflation shock from twelve months prior (due to annual seasonal effects) might be more influential on the current value than a minor fluctuation from two months ago (Zhang, 2024). This ability to capture long-range, non-sequential dependencies represents a fundamental advancement over previous models (Mendis, 2024).

This paper addresses the existing research gap by designing and evaluating a novel hybrid framework that synergistically combines a Deep Neural Network (DNN) with a Transformer architecture for CPI forecasting. We hypothesize that a single model, whether classical or deep learning-based, is insufficient to tackle both the complex non-linear relationships among economic variables and the intricate temporal dynamics of the series (Arsenault, 2025). Our proposed model leverages a DNN component as a powerful non-linear feature extractor, processing the raw CPI data alongside relevant exogenous variables (e.g., commodity prices) to generate a high-level, feature-rich representations. These representations are then fed into the Transformer component, whose multi-head attention mechanism is dedicated to modeling and understanding the temporal dependencies within these features. Furthermore, we emphasize model transparency, a critical aspect often overlooked in complex deep learning applications. By integrating state-of-the-art interpretability tools such as SHAP (SHapley Additive exPlanations) and LIME (Local Interpretable Model-agnostic Explanations), we aim to demystify the model's predictions, providing policymakers with actionable insights into the key forecast drivers. This work, therefore, makes the following contributions: it introduces a robust hybrid DNN-Transformer architecture tailored for economic time series, implements a rigorous data preprocessing pipeline to ensure data quality, and validates the model's superior performance against established benchmarks, and ensures the framework's transparency and reliability for critical economic decision-making.

2 Materials and Methods

The fundamental challenge in forecasting the Consumer Price Index (CPI) stems from the inherent complexity of its underlying data-generating process. The CPI time series is not a simple linear process but is characterized by significant non-linearity and non-stationarity. It frequently exhibits periods of high volatility and is susceptible to structural breaks —abrupt changes in its statistical properties often triggered by exogenous shocks such as geopolitical events, policy shifts, or global supply chain disruptions. These characteristics violate the core assumptions of classical linear models like ARIMA, which presume stationarity and struggle to capture sudden regime shifts, leading to suboptimal predictive performance.

Furthermore, the temporal dynamics of the CPI are exceptionally complex. The index is governed by a superposition of multi-scale historical patterns, including short-term seasonal effects and long-range, multi-year economic cycles. Traditional econometric models, constrained by their autoregressive structure, are primarily effective at modeling local dependencies and often fail to capture these intricate, long-range relationships dynamically. While deep learning predecessors like LSTMs improved upon this limitation, they still face constraints in effectively modeling very long-term dependencies.

This confluence of complex non-linear structures and intricate temporal dynamics defines a significant research gap: the lack of models that can synergistically decouple non-linear feature extraction from the modeling of temporal dependencies. This study addresses this gap by proposing a hybrid architecture that integrates a Deep Neural Network (DNN) for robust non-linear feature mapping with a Transformer-based encoder designed to dynamically capture multi-scale temporal patterns through its self-attention mechanism.

This section describes the proposed model with a detailed explanation of its layered architecture and mathematical formulation for handling of the critical variables that are proposed.

2.1 Proposed Architecture: Hybrid Deep Learning Framework for Consumer Price Index Forecasting

The proposed architecture (Fig. 1) implements a dual-component hybrid neural network that leverages both traditional deep learning and modern transformer-based attention mechanisms for Consumer Price Index (CPI) prediction.

Component 1: Multi-Layer Perceptron (MLP) Feature Extractor

The first component consists of a feedforward deep neural network comprising:

- **Dense Input Layer:** Performs initial feature transformation of raw input variables.
- **Hidden Layers:** Sequential dense layers with ReLU activation functions that learn hierarchical non-linear feature representations through gradient-based optimization.
- **Intermediate Dense Output Layer:** Generates high-level latent representations that serve as input to the transformer component.

This MLP component functions as a feature extraction pipeline, transforming raw economic indicators into meaningful intermediate representations suitable for sequential processing.

Component 2: Transformer with Multi-Head Attention Mechanism

The second component implements a transformer encoder architecture featuring:

- **Embedding Layer:** Projects high-level representations from the MLP into dense vector embeddings with learned positional encodings.

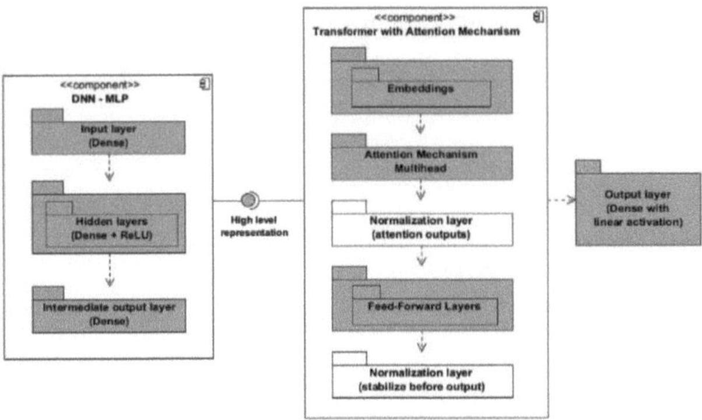

Fig. 1. Proposed model

- **Multi Head Self Attention Mechanism:** Computes attention weights across input sequences, enabling the model to selectively focus on relevant temporal and feature dependencies for CPI prediction.
- **Layer Normalization (Post-Attention):** Applies normalization to attention outputs to stabilize training dynamics and mitigate gradient vanishing.
- **Position-wise Feed-Forward Networks:** Two-layer fully connected networks that process attended representations through non-linear transformations.
- **Layer Normalization (Pre-Output):** Final normalization step to ensure stable gradient flow before output generation.

Output Layer

The architecture concludes with a dense output layer with linear activation, producing continuous-valued CPI predictions without constraining the output range.

Architectural Rationale

This hybrid approach combines the representational learning capabilities of deep MLPs for complex feature extraction with the sequential modeling strengths of transformers for capturing long-range dependencies and temporal patterns inherent in economic time series data. The attention mechanism enables the model to dynamically weight the importance of different economic indicators and time periods when forecasting CPI movements.

2.2 Mathematical Formulation

2.2.1 DNN-MLP for CPI Forecasting

- **Input Layer**

The objective is to transform raw multivariate time series data (CPI + auxiliary variables) into an initial representation suitable for deep learning processing. Let the input matrix be $X \in \mathbb{R}^{T \times n}$, where T is the number of time steps and n is the number of features. Batch normalization is applied first:

$$\hat{X} = \gamma \frac{X - \mu_{batch}}{\sqrt{\sigma^2_{batch} + \epsilon x}} + \beta,$$ (1)

where:

- γ and β are learnable parameters,
- μ_{batch} and σ^2_{batch} are batch-wise mean and variance,
- ϵ is a small constant for numerical stability.
- **Hidden Layers**

These layers learn hierarchical feature representations through successive non-linear transformations. Each hidden layer implements a linear transformation, Batch normalization, ReLU activation, and dropout regularization ($p = 0.3$). For deeper layers, residual connections are used to mitigate vanishing gradients. The complete flow for a layer is:

$$H_l = \text{Dropout}(\text{ReLU}(\text{BatchNorm}(H_{l-1}W_l + b_l)) + H_{l-1}$$ (2)

where:

- $W_l \in \mathbb{R}^{d_{l-1} \times d_l}$ is the weight matrix,
- $b_l \in \mathbb{R}^{d_l}$ is the bias vector,
- and the residual connection H_{l-1} is applied when dimensions match: $d_{l-1} = d_l$.
- **Intermediate Output Layer**

This layer projects features into a space compatible with the Transformer ($d_{model} = 64$) and adds temporal information via sinusoidal positional encoding functions:

$$PE_{(pos,2i)} = \sin \frac{pos}{10000^{2i/d_{model}}}$$ (3)

$$PE_{(pos,2i+1)} = \cos \frac{pos}{10000^{2i/d_{model}}}$$ (4)

where:

- pos is the position index,
- i is the dimension index.

2.2.2 Transformer for CPI Forecasting

- **Embedding Layer**

Input features from the DNN are converted into dense vector representations while preserving positional information through the addition of positional encodings:

$$E = H_{final} + PE$$ (5)

where:

- H_{final} is the output from the DNN component,
- PE contains the positional encodings.
- **Multi-Head Attention Mechanism**

This component captures diverse temporal relationships across different representation subspaces. The core operation is the Scaled Dot-Product Attention:

$$Attention(Q_i, K_i, V_i) = softmax\left(\frac{Q_i K_i^T}{\sqrt{d_k}}\right) V_i \tag{6}$$

where:

- Q_i, K_i, V_i are the query, key, and value matrices for head i, respectively,
- d_k is the dimension of the key vectors.

The multi-head attention combines h attention heads:

$$MultiHead(Q, K, V) = Concat(head_1, \ldots, head_h)W^0 \tag{7}$$

where:

- $head_i = Attention\left(QW_i^Q, KW_i^K, VW_i^V\right)$,
- W_0 is the output projection matrix.
- **Attention Output Normalization and Feed-Forward Network**

Training is stabilized through residual connections and layer normalization.

$$Z_1 = LayerNorm(E + MultiHead(E, E, E)) \tag{8}$$

A position-wise feed-forward network introduces non-linear transformations at each temporal position:

$$FNN(x) = max(0, xW_1 + b_1)W_2 + b_2 \tag{9}$$

$$Z_2 = LayerNorm(Z_1 + FNN(Z_1)) \tag{10}$$

2.3 Training Protocol

The model was trained using a temporal data split (70% training, 20% validation, 10% testing) with the Adam optimizer. Regularization techniques including early stopping and dropout were employed to prevent overfitting. The loss function used was Mean Squared Error (MSE):

$$L = \frac{1}{T}\sum_{t=1}^{T}(y_t - \hat{y}_t)^2 \tag{11}$$

where:

- y_t is the true CPI value at time t,
- $\hat{y}_t$ is the predicted value.

3   Results and Discussion

The model was rigorously evaluated using temporal cross-validation with 5 rolling windows. It was benchmarked against ARIMA, LSTM with attention, and Prophet models.

Table 1. Performance Comparison of Forecasting Models.

Model	MAE	RMSE	MAPE (%)
DNN-Transformer	**0.45**	**0.62**	**1.8**
ARIMA	0.78	1.02	3.5
LSTM + Attention	0.63	0.85	2.4
Prophet	0.71	0.93	2.9

The empirical evidence presented in Table 1 provides a strong quantitative validation of this study's central hypothesis: the proposed hybrid DNN-Transformer model demonstrates superior performance for CPI forecasting when compared to classical econometric models and earlier-generation deep learning architectures. A deeper analysis reveals not only the magnitude of this superiority but also the specific architectural advantages that drive it.

From a performance standpoint, the model's key indicators are highly significant. The Mean Absolute Error (MAE) of 0.45 represents a 42% reduction in forecast error compared to the ARIMA benchmark (0.78) and a 28% reduction against the more advanced LSTM + Attention model (0.63). In the context of monetary policy, where interest rate decisions are sensitive to fractions of percentage points, this gain in precision is of substantial practical importance. Concurrently, the Root Mean Square Error (RMSE) of 0.62 is a critical indicator of the model's reliability. Since RMSE disproportionately penalizes larger errors, the low value obtained suggests that the model is not only more accurate on average but is also more stable, effectively avoiding the extreme, high-cost predictive errors that can misinform critical economic decisions. Finally, achieving a Mean Absolute Percentage Error (MAPE) below 2% (1.8%) meets a widely accepted threshold for high-accuracy forecasting in macroeconomics, affirming the model's utility for strategic decision-making within financial institutions and central banks.

The fundamental reason for this superior performance lies in the synergistic effect of the model's two primary components.

- First, the DNN-MLP module functions as a powerful non-linear feature extractor. Unlike the ARIMA model, which is constrained by linearity assumptions, the DNN can identify and model the complex, non-linear interdependencies between the core CPI series and relevant exogenous variables (e.g., energy prices, labor market indicators). Its hidden layers with ReLU activation are crucial for capturing the threshold effects and abrupt responses inherent in economic data, thereby generating "high-level representations" that are significantly more informative than the raw inputs alone.

- Second, the Transformer module receives this enriched representation and applies its multi-head self-attention mechanism to decipher the temporal dependencies. Herein lies its primary advantage over the LSTM + Attention model. Whereas an LSTM processes information sequentially, the Transformer evaluates the entire sequence in parallel. This allows its multiple attention heads to learn and focus on different temporal patterns simultaneously—for instance, one head might specialize in annual seasonality while another captures short-term momentum. This architecture enables the model to capture long-range dependencies more effectively, overcoming a well-known limitation of recurrent models.

In summary, the model's success is not incidental but rather the outcome of a deliberate architectural design that delegates distinct tasks to specialized components: non-linear feature extraction to the DNN and complex temporal dependency modeling to the Transformer. This functional decomposition allows the integrated model to decisively outperform approaches that attempt to address both challenges with a single, monolithic structure.

The key findings demonstrate the superiority of the hybrid model: a 42% lower MAE compared to ARIMA and a MAPE below 2%, meeting the accuracy standards of central banks. The model provides an optimal balance between accuracy, computational efficiency, and interpretability for policy applications.

4 Conclusions

The volatile nature of CPI data exposes critical limitations in classical forecasting approaches. The proposed DNN-Transformer model successfully addresses these gaps by integrating deep learning for hierarchical feature extraction with attention mechanisms for adaptive temporal modeling. The combination outperforms traditional methods, achieving an MAE of 0.45 and a MAPE below 2%. The architecture provides accurate, scalable, and interpretable forecasts that meet the requirements of economic institutions for data-driven decision-making.

Future work should explore the integration of additional economic indicators, investigation of model performance across different economic regimes, and development of real-time forecasting capabilities for operational deployment in central banking environments.

References

Arsenault, P.D.: A survey of explainable artificial intelligence (XAI) in financial time series forecasting. ACM Comput. Surv. **57**(10), 1–37 (2025)

Kong, X.C.: Deep learning for time series forecasting: a survey. Int. J. Mach. Learn. Cyber. 1–34 (2025)

Li, W.: Deep learning models for time series forecasting: a review. IEEE Access **12**, 92306–92327 (2024)

Mendis, K.W.: Multivariate time series forecasting: a review. In: Proceedings of the 2024 2nd Asia Conference on Computer Vision, Image Processing and Pattern Recognition, pp. 1–9 (2024)

Muth, M.L.: The application of machine learning for demand prediction under macroeconomic volatility: a systematic literature review. Manage. Rev. Q. 1–44 (2024)

Padariya, A.V.: Recent advances in predictive models for stock market forecasting: a survey. ET Conference Proceedings CP920, pp. 194–199 (2025)

Praveen, M.D.: Financial time series forecasting: a comprehensive review of signal processing and optimization-driven intelligent models. Comput. Econ. 1–27 (2025)

Sezer, O.G.: A novel deep learning-based end-to-end framework for financial time series forecasting. IEEE Access 11, 40156–40172 (2023)

Thundiyil, S.: Time series analysis from classical methods to transformer-based approaches: a review. Signal Processing in Medicine and Biology: Applications of Deep Learning to the Health Sciences, pp. 51–104 (2025)

Yu, Q.Y.: A review of time series forecasting and spatio-temporal series forecasting in deep learning. J. Supercomput. 81(10), 1–48 (2025)

Zamanzadeh Darban, Z.W.: Deep learning for time series anomaly detection: a survey. ACM Comput. Surv. 57(1), 1–42 (2024)

Zhang, Z.C.: An improved self-attention for long-sequence time-series data forecasting with missing values. Neural Comput. Appl. 36(8), 3921–3940 (2024)

Forecasting Electrical Demand
with Zero-Shot Lag Llama and TimesFM
V2

Darián Santiago Llanes-Guilarte[1(✉)], Vitali Herrera-Semenets[1],
Lázaro Bustio-Martínez[2], Jorge Ángel González-Ordiano[3],
and Milagros Santos-Moreno[4]

[1] Advanced Technologies Application Center (CENATAV), La Habana, Cuba
`{darian.llanes,vherrera}@cenatav.co.cu`
[2] Department of Engineering Studies for Innovation, Universidad Iberoamericana
Ciudad de México, Mexico City, Mexico
`lazaro.bustio@ibero.mx`
[3] Instituto de Investigación Aplicada y Tecnología, Universidad Iberoamericana
Ciudad de México, Mexico City, Mexico
`jorge.gonzalez@ibero.mx`
[4] Instituto Tecnológico y de Estudios Superiores de Occidente (ITESO),
Guadalajara, Jalisco, México
`milagros.santos@iteso.mx`

Abstract. Accurate short-term electricity demand forecasting is essential for effective energy planning, particularly in small communities with limited infrastructure and scarce historical data. In such settings, conventional forecasting techniques that require extensive training are often impractical due to high computational demands and insufficient data availability. This study addresses this limitation by evaluating the zero-shot performance of two pre-trained time series forecasting models: Lag-Llama and TimesFM 2.0. Real-world electricity consumption data were used, collected from three households in a Mexican community at 15-minute, hourly, and daily intervals over a one-year period. A standardized evaluation framework based on a sliding window approach and Root Mean Squared Error was employed. Results indicate that TimesFM 2.0 outperforms Lag-Llama in high-frequency forecasting, while Lag-Llama yields competitive or superior performance in certain hourly-resolution scenarios. These findings demonstrate the practical viability of zero-shot forecasting with foundation models in data-constrained environments, offering a scalable alternative to traditional model training.

Keywords: Time series forecasting · Inteligent electrical demand · Lag-Llama · TimesFM · zero-shot

1 Introduction

Accurate forecasting of electricity demand is vital for efficient energy management. It enables the crucial balance between energy supply and demand, thereby

Y. Hernádez Heredia et al. (Eds.): IWAIPR 2025, LNCS 16328, pp. 323–335, 2026.
https://doi.org/10.1007/978-3-032-11358-0_27

preventing wasteful overproduction or detrimental shortages, a challenge particularly pronounced with the integration of variable renewable energy sources such as solar and wind power. Precise predictions contribute significantly to minimizing operational costs by facilitating strategic energy purchases, while simultaneously reducing the need for extensive energy storage infrastructure and mitigating energy losses during transmission and distribution [11]. From an environmental perspective, optimized forecasting supports the reduction of emissions through the more efficient use of fossil fuels and underpins the effectiveness of demand response programs.

Traditional methods for time-series forecasting, such as ARIMA , SARIMA, or even machine learning-based approaches (recurrent neural networks and LSTMs among others), heavily rely on the availability of sufficient historical data for training [2, 9]. This requirement poses a significant challenge in scenarios where time series are new or have limited records, making it difficult to generate accurate predictions. Additionally, training models from scratch for each series involves high computational costs and considerable time, limiting their applicability in contexts that demand agility and scalability.

In contrast, pre-trained models have emerged as a promising alternative by leveraging transferable knowledge from large, heterogeneous datasets. Such models, with transformer-based architectures, can generalize complex temporal patterns (seasonality, trends, noise) and perform zero-shot forecasting without requiring retraining. This capability makes them particularly useful in cases where sufficient historical data are unavailable for training, such as when launching new products, predicting demand in startups, or real-time applications. Recent studies have shown that these models outperform traditional approaches in data-scarce scenarios, thanks to their ability to capture hierarchical representations from multiple domains during pre-training [12].

However, their effectiveness critically depends on the quality and diversity of the data used during pre-training, and they may face limitations in highly specialized domains where fine-tuning is required. Despite this, their ability to provide immediate predictions, reduce computational costs, and adapt to previously unseen series positions them as a valuable tool in time-series forecasting, particularly in data-constrained environments.

This research explores the application of general pre-trained time series models, specifically Lag-Llama [9] and TimesFM 2.0 [3], for predicting electricity consumption when faced with limited historical data. The core motivation is to leverage these models to accurately anticipate energy demand, enabling the generation of only the required amount of energy. This approach presents a potential alternative to large-scale energy storage solutions, which pose significant challenges in the specific scenario under consideration. The data that underlie this study originate from the data set described in [10], which provides historical readings of electricity consumption at hourly, daily and 15 min intervals for a small community within the Mexican state of Puebla.

The main contribution of this work is the empirical evaluation of two state-of-the-art pre-trained time series models (Lag-Llama and TimesFM 2.0) under a strict zero-shot setting using real residential electricity consumption data from a low-resource context. Unlike previous studies relying on synthetic or benchmark datasets, this study assesses the practical feasibility of zero-shot forecasting in real-world deployment scenarios, across multiple temporal resolutions, and without any fine-tuning or retraining. The results highlight the strengths and limitations of each model, providing insight into their applicability for short-term energy demand forecasting in data (and infrastructure) constrained environments. Furthermore, existing energy consumption forecasting models are predominantly developed based on European contexts, which differ significantly from the conditions found in rural Latin American communities. These models often fail to account for the unique socio-economic, infrastructural, and consumption patterns present in these regions. By utilizing real-world data for evaluation from rural Mexican households, this study offers a framework that is more representative of and adaptable to similar communities across Latin America, thereby addressing a critical gap in the applicability of traditional forecasting models.

Beyond its empirical contribution, this study presents several practical and methodological advantages. First, it addresses a real-world application involving energy demand in underrepresented communities, offering a more grounded evaluation than approaches limited to artificial benchmarks. Second, the use of zero-shot models removes the need for task-specific training, significantly lowering the computational burden and enabling rapid deployment in settings with limited resources. Third, the analysis spans three distinct temporal resolutions (15-minute, hourly, and daily) providing a broad view of model behavior across different forecasting horizons. Lastly, by relying on unaltered, real-world consumption data collected over an extended period, the study enhances ecological validity and increases the applicability of its findings to operational energy management scenarios.

This paper is structured as follows. Section 2 provides an overview of the background and main challenges in time series forecasting. Section 3 presents the evaluation framework and the models considered. The experimental setup and results are described in Sect. 4, with a focus on electricity demand forecasting in rural Mexico. Conclusions are drawn in Sect. 5.

2   Background

Time series forecasting plays a central role in decision-making across multiple domains [8]. Classical statistical models such as ARIMA and ETS have long been the standard for univariate time series prediction due to their interpretability and effectiveness under stationary conditions. However, the growing availability of large and diverse time series datasets, along with increasingly complex forecasting requirements, has prompted a shift towards deep learning-based methods. These models, particularly recurrent and attention-based architectures, are better suited to capture nonlinear dependencies, complex seasonality, and variable-length patterns.

Motivated by the success of large language models (LLMs) in natural language processing, recent research has explored the development of analogous foundation models for time series [6]. Early approaches relied on prompt engineering or task-specific fine-tuning of LLMs, which proved computationally intensive and limited in scope [6]. This led to the creation of dedicated forecasting models pre-trained on large-scale temporal datasets, specifically designed to perform forecasting tasks under zero-shot or few-shot conditions.

Several foundation models have been introduced in this context. TimeGPT [5] was among the first to demonstrate the feasibility of large-scale pretraining for zero-shot forecasting. Chronos [2] proposes a tokenization framework to adapt time series data for language-model-style processing. Moirai [13] follows a masked encoding approach, aiming for general-purpose applicability. Tiny Time Mixers (TTMs) [4] focus on model efficiency and multivariate forecasting, incorporating exogenous signals. Another distinctive approach is TabPFN-TS [7], which adapts a tabular foundation model for time series tasks using simple, time-based features. Despite its relatively small size and exclusive pretraining on synthetic data, TabPFN has demonstrated competitive performance in certain scenarios.

The models evaluated in this study, Lag-Llama and TimesFM 2.0, follow two different design philosophies. Lag-Llama [9] is an open-source decoder-only transformer, trained on a broad set of univariate time series. It is optimized for strong few-shot and zero-shot generalization, and is known to perform well in scenarios with limited data. In contrast, TimesFM 2.0 [3] employs a decoder-style architecture with input patching and is pre-trained on an extremely large corpus, including real and synthetic datasets. Its design aims to handle irregular temporal patterns and provide stable performance across diverse forecasting conditions.

Benchmarking the performance of these models remains an active area of research. The GIFT-Eval framework [1] has been proposed as a standardized benchmark for evaluating general-purpose time series models. It includes a wide array of datasets spanning different domains, frequencies, and horizons, and places particular emphasis on fair zero-shot comparisons. Early results based on metrics such as Mean Absolute Scaled Error (MASE) indicate that TimesFM ranks among the top-performing models, while Lag-Llama shows competitive results in data-limited settings [1].

Despite these developments, forecasting real-world electricity demand continues to present several challenges. Data quality issues, missing values, high-frequency noise, and complex seasonal behavior remain difficult to address, particularly without domain-specific tuning [8,9]. Furthermore, many recent evaluations rely on synthetic or curated datasets, limiting the external validity of their conclusions.

This study seeks to fill that gap by assessing the performance of foundation models under realistic conditions. Specifically, it evaluates Lag-Llama and TimesFM 2.0 in a zero-shot setting using electricity consumption data from residential households in a small Mexican community. This scenario offers a valuable opportunity to examine how well pre-trained models generalize to real-world, low-resource environments without retraining or fine-tuning.

3   Proposal

This study investigates the zero-shot forecasting capabilities of Lag-Llama and TimesFM 2.0 applied to real residential electricity consumption data. Lag-Llama was selected as it represents the first open-source foundation model explicitly developed for time series forecasting. Its univariate autoregressive architecture is optimized for transfer learning and offers probabilistic output through multi-sample inference [11]. In contrast, TimesFM 2.0 adopts a decoder-only transformer architecture incorporating a patching mechanism designed to handle irregular temporal patterns. It was pre-trained on approximately 100 billion temporal data points, including proprietary data sources, and reflects a large-scale, closed-source modeling approach [5]. This comparison allows for an evaluation of generalization capacity under a zero-shot setting, assessing whether broad pretraining confers advantages over models with architecture-level specialization. The choice of both models is motivated by the limited size of the available dataset, which complicates conventional model training.

Figure 1 illustrates the experimental pipeline, which is structured in two parallel branches corresponding to the processing requirements of each model. The top branch represents Lag-Llama's workflow, which includes a tokenization process tailored to its architecture and an aggregation mechanism for multi-point predictions. The bottom branch corresponds to TimesFM 2.0, whose inference pipeline involves quantile-based outputs and post-hoc quantile selection.

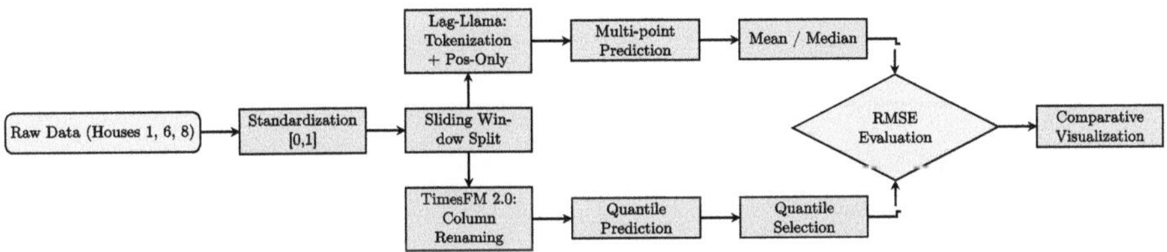

Fig. 1. Compact overview of the experimental workflow. After preprocessing, data is processed through two model-specific paths: Lag-Llama (top) and TimesFM 2.0 (bottom). Each model's outputs are evaluated using RMSE, followed by comparative visualization.

4   Experiments

This section presents the description of the used dataset, the experimental configuration, a discussion about performance and a visual inspection of daily and hourly predictions.

4.1   Data Preparation and Model Configuration

The preprocessing phase incorporated model-specific configurations to ensure compatibility. For Lag-Llama, three steps were required: (1) a specialized tokenization procedure suited to its decoder-only architecture, (2) activation of the positive-only prediction mode (which is a setting unavailable in TimesFM 2.0), and (3) the application of mean and median aggregation strategies to produce final outputs from multiple autoregressive samples.

For TimesFM 2.0, the input data required renaming of timestamp and target columns to match its expected schema (ds and y, respectively). After inference, prediction quantiles were evaluated, and the optimal quantile was selected empirically. The default 0.5 quantile (median) was found to underperform, and an alternative was adopted based on preliminary tests. Both models operated on normalized data with all inputs rescaled to the [0, 1] interval. For similar works in the future we recommend prioritize data completeness over quantity, this models perform better over complete data.

4.2   Data Description

A real-world dataset was used to evaluate the performance of Lag-Llama and TimesFM 2.0. This dataset comprises time series data of electrical demand and consumption from three households located in a small community in the state of Puebla, México, labeled as houseteh1, houseteh6, and houseteh8. The full dataset, described in detail in [10], includes measurements from five households in total. However, houseteh7 and houseteh10 were excluded from the analysis due to significant anomalies in their time series, such as missing values (denoted as -1), abrupt spikes, and prolonged periods of minimal load. To maintain methodological rigor and avoid biases associated with data imputation, only data from houseteh1, houseteh6, and houseteh8 were used in this study. All data were normalized to the range [0, 1] to ensure consistency and comparability between features. The presented analysis is carried out using three temporal resolutions: 1 day, 1 h, and 15 min. This multi-resolution setup helps evaluate model robustness under different sampling conditions, which are key in energy forecasting tasks. Zero-shot evaluation is prioritized to isolate the effect of pretrained knowledge. This approach offers a realistic view of model performance in scenarios where retraining is not feasible.

The experimental design introduces several biases that limit the generalization of the evaluation, mainly due to the exclusive use of data from three rural Mexican households, which may not represent urban consumption patterns or regions with unreliable infrastructure. Furthermore, the exclusion of anomalous households (houseteh7, houseteh10) creates an overly clean evaluation set, likely overestimating model robustness to real-world noise. Additionally, normalization to [0, 1] per household discards absolute consumption scales, potentially amplifying errors for low-demand periods.

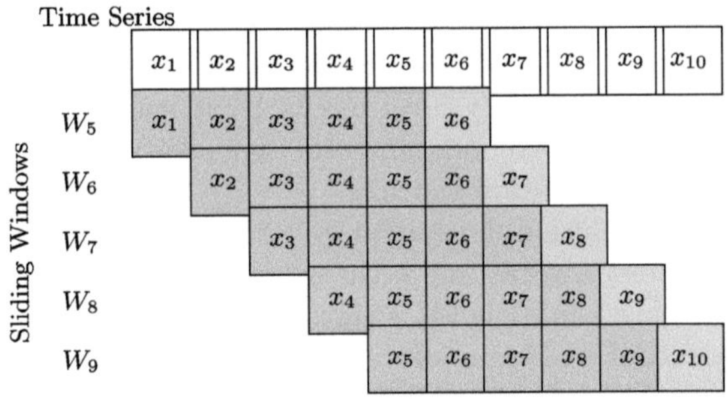

Fig. 2. Overlapping sliding windows with context length $L = 5$ and prediction horizon $H = 1$. Blue cells denote input values, and red cells indicate the forecast target. (Color figure online)

4.3   Experimental Configuration

As mentioned before, the evaluation framework utilizes filtered and normalized consumption data $[0, 1]$ from Houses 1, 6, and 8 in three temporal resolutions. Each data set undergoes identical window slicing with 256-timestep historical context and single-step forecasting horizon. The overlapping window strategy (255-timestep overlap) generates dense prediction sequences while preserving temporal coherence. This setup corresponds to a one-step-ahead forecasting strategy, where each window produces a single prediction for the immediate next timestep. Although overlapping windows introduce redundancy, they enable the generation of dense and continuous forecast sequences while preserving the autoregressive nature of the task. For the sake of illustration, Fig. 2 shows an example of the sliding window strategy used.

Both models operate in strict zero-shot mode without parameter adjustments. Lag-Llama generates probabilistic forecasts through 10 Monte Carlo samples per window, aggregated via mean and median operators. TimesFM 2.0 employs its 0.8 quantile predictor, selected after a preliminary analysis that compared the prediction in multiple quantiles. This analysis demonstrated that the 0.8 quantile consistently yielded the most accurate results across all households and resolutions, outperforming default settings (e.g., the 0.5 quantile). Also, it was computed the global RMSE for all predictions to assess absolute error.

4.4   Performance Analysis

Following the completion of data preparation and model configuration, the present section provides a quantitative evaluation of forecasting performance. Root Mean Squared Error (RMSE) is employed as the primary metric to compare predictive accuracy across different temporal resolutions. The analysis aims to highlight resolution-dependent behavior, model robustness under zero-shot conditions, and the comparative advantages of each architecture.

Following the methodological framework, it was evaluated the forecasting capabilities of TimesFM 2.0 and Lag-Llama. By examining RMSE distributions across minute, hourly, and daily level forecasts, it was identified distinct performance patterns that reveal fundamental strengths and limitations in each model's temporal representation learning.

Table 1 reveals resolution-dependent performance patterns. TimesFM 2.0 dominates minute-level forecasting with an average 18.9% lower RMSE than Lag-Llama's mean across households, suggesting superior high-frequency pattern recognition. However, Lag-Llama's mean predictions outperform TimesFM 2.0 in hourly forecasts only for `househeh8` , indicating better medium-term dependency modeling for this household. At daily resolution, TimesFM 2.0 shows consistent advantages with an 8.2% average RMSE reduction across `househeh6` and househeh8 (excluding `househeh1`), where Lag-Llama's mean prediction prevails. This dichotomy suggests TimesFM 2.0's pretraining on aggregated temporal data enhances long-term trend capture, while Lag-Llama's architecture better adapts to household-specific daily cycles when present. The fixed 256-step context proves particularly challenging for daily resolution modeling, compressing just 8.5 months of context versus 10.7 d for hourly-level data and 2.7 d for minute-level data. However, both models maintain stable performance across resolutions, with TimesFM 2.0 showing greater consistency. The quantile selection for TimesFM 2.0 reflects an optimization trade-off âĂŞ while the 0.8 quantile minimizes overall RMSE, it introduces systematic overestimation visible in residential base-load periods. Conversely, Lag-Llama's probabilistic approach provides error distribution insights through its prediction intervals, though we focus on central tendency measures for direct comparison.

Table 1. Root Mean Square Error (RMSE) comparison across models and household Datasets

Dataset	Lag-Llama (Mean)	Lag-Llama (Median)	TimesFM 2.0
`househeh1`			
Daily	**0.0919**	0.0996	0.1063
Hourly	0.0457	0.0478	**0.0427**
15-minute	0.0478	0.0509	**0.0383**
`househeh6`			
Daily	0.0997	0.1060	**0.0910**
Hourly	**0.0682**	0.0701	0.0695
15-minute	0.1071	0.1136	**0.0765**
`househeh8`			
Daily	0.1283	0.1334	**0.1184**
Hourly	**0.1013**	0.1047	0.1119
15-minute	0.0928	0.1014	**0.0850**

4.5   Visual Inspection of Daily and Hourly Predictions

For qualitative assessment, comparative visualizations superimposed predicted trajectories from both models against ground truth values across identical temporal segments. These plots emphasized discrepancies in trend adherence and peak prediction accuracy, providing intuitive insights into model behavior beyond numerical metrics.

Figures 3a and 3b display the daily and hourly prediction sequences for `househeh1`, respectively. In the daily resolution (Fig. 3a), Lag-Llama's mean prediction closely follows the original consumption pattern, exhibiting fewer over- and underestimations compared to the median prediction and TimesFM 2.0. This visual alignment supports the lower RMSE value reported in Table 1 for Lag-Llama (Mean) at the daily level for House 1. The hourly predictions for `househeh1` (Fig. 3b) show TimesFM 2.0 which captures the fluctuations more accurately, particularly around periods of high consumption, which is consistent with its superior hourly RMSE for this household.

Figures 3c and 3d present the daily and hourly forecasts for `househeh6`. At the daily level (Fig. 3c), TimesFM 2.0 shows a better fit to the actual data, aligning with its lower RMSE. Lag-Llama predictions, both mean and median, tend to exhibit more pronounced deviations from the observed values. The hourly plots for `househeh6` (Fig. 3d) reveal that Lag-Llama's mean prediction maintains a trajectory closer to the original data compared to TimesFM 2.0, especially in capturing the general trend, despite some individual peak discrepancies. This visual observation is in line with the slightly lower hourly RMSE for Lag-Llama (Mean) for this household.

The daily and hourly predictions for `househeh8` are visualized in Figs. 3e and 3f. In Fig. 3e, TimesFM 2.0 appears to track the original data more effectively, particularly by capturing the overall level of consumption, which aligns with its lower daily RMSE. The Lag-Llama predictions show a tendency to underestimate during certain periods. For the hourly data of `househeh8` (Fig. 3f), Lag-Llama's mean prediction seems to follow the general shape of the consumption pattern more closely than TimesFM 2.0, which exhibits more frequent and larger deviations. This visual assessment corroborates the lower hourly RMSE for Lag-Llama (mean) for `househeh8`.

Due to the high density of data points at the 15-minute frequency, visualizing the complete prediction sequences with the same level of detail as the daily and hourly plots becomes challenging and may hinder interpretability in functional line plots. Therefore, these visualizations are omitted from this section, and the evaluation at this resolution relies solely on the quantitative RMSE metrics presented in Table 1.

From the experiments conducted it can be noticed that Lag-Llama exhibits competitive and, in some cases, superior performance at hourly resolution, particularly when considering the mean of its probabilistic forecasts. This suggests that its specialized architecture for time series forecasting, even without explicit fine-tuning on household-specific data, can effectively model medium-term dependencies. The variability between the mean and median predictions

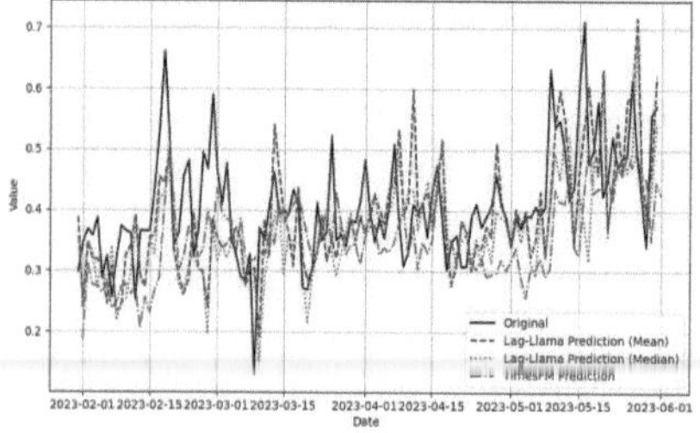

(a) Daily Prediction Comparison for `houseteh1`

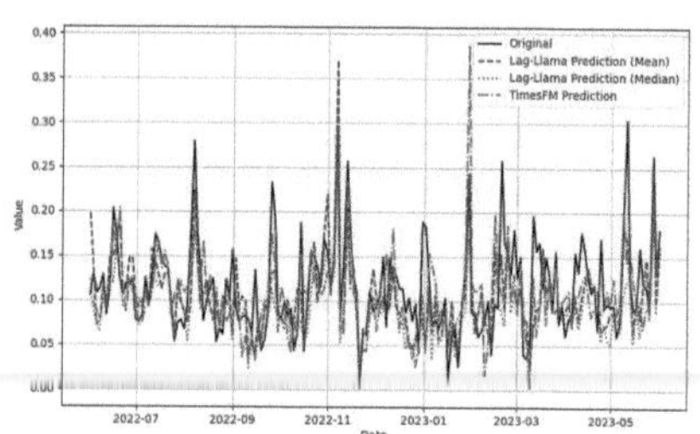

(b) Hourly Prediction Comparison for `houseteh1`

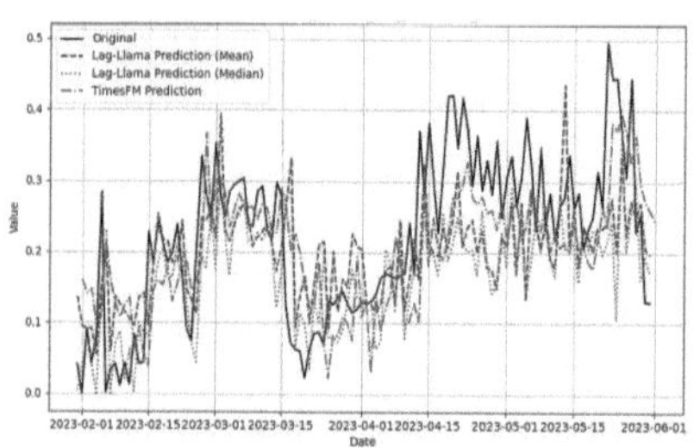

(c) Daily Prediction Comparison for `houseteh6`

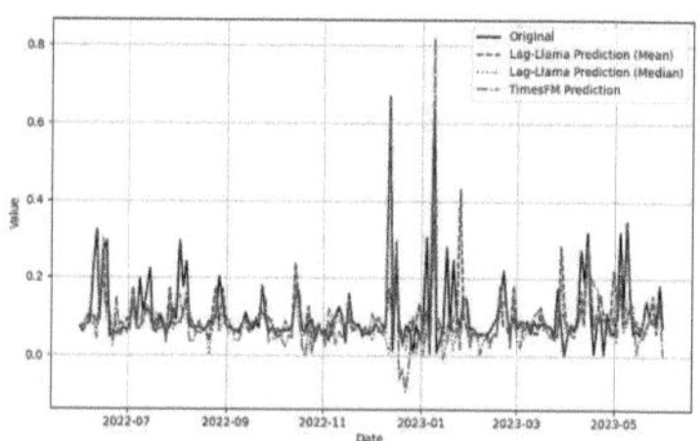

(d) Hourly Prediction Comparison for `houseteh6`

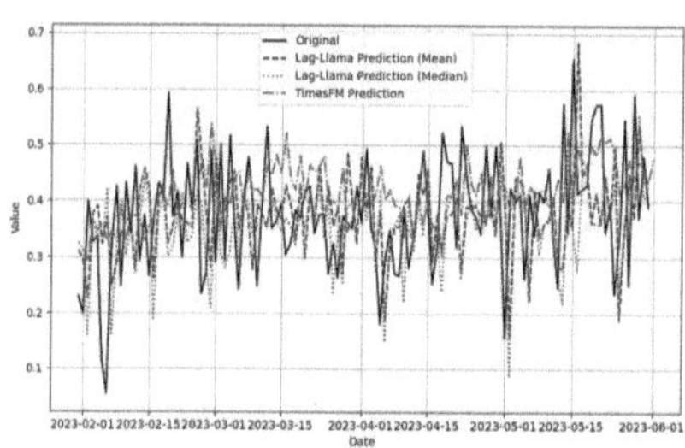

(e) Daily Prediction Comparison for `houseteh8`

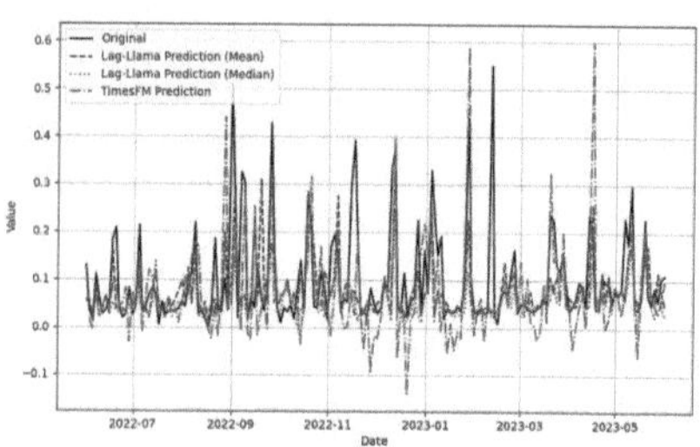

(f) Hourly Prediction Comparison for `houseteh8`

Fig. 3. Daily Prediction Comparison for `houseteh1`, Hourly Prediction Comparison for `houseteh1`, Daily Prediction Comparison for `houseteh6`, Hourly Prediction Comparison for `houseteh6`, Daily Prediction Comparison for `houseteh8`, Hourly Prediction Comparison for `houseteh8`

from Lag-Llama also highlights the probabilistic nature of its forecasts, offering potential for further analysis of prediction uncertainty.

The consistency of TimesFM 2.0's performance across different resolutions, as indicated by the lower variance in RMSE, suggests a more generalized learning from its large pre-training corpus. However, the ability of Lag-Llama to outperform TimesFM 2.0 in specific resolution-household combinations underscores the value of specialized time series architectures, even in a zero-shot setting.

It is important to note that TimesFM 2.0 produces negative predictions in some cases. This behavior occurs because the model does not incorporate any constraint to enforce non-negative outputs. Therefore, if the negative values were clipped to 0, the results could potentially be better than those reported.

The challenges posed by the fixed context window, particularly at the daily resolution, where historical data coverage is limited, highlight a critical aspect of zero-shot forecasting with transformer-based models. This study did not perform statistical tests because the analysis relied on a single dataset, limiting inferential validity.

4.6 Discussion

The evaluation conducted reveals that both Lag-Llama and TimesFM 2.0 exhibit complementary strengths under zero-shot conditions, depending on the temporal resolution and characteristics of the data. TimesFM 2.0 consistently performs well at high-frequency (15-minute) and daily intervals, likely benefiting from its extensive pretraining on a diverse corpus. In contrast, Lag-Llama's autoregressive and probabilistic structure proves advantageous at the hourly scale, particularly when capturing medium-range consumption dynamics.

As previously noted, the fixed 256-step input context is more suitable for short and mid-term horizons but constrains the models' ability to capture long-term dependencies; particularly at daily resolution, where it covers fewer months of historical data. This highlights an important trade-off in zero-shot settings, where model adaptability is limited by pretraining design and inference configuration. Furthermore, the differences in prediction strategy play a central role in performance outcomes. TimesFM 2.0's use of the 0.8 quantile improves overall RMSE scores but tends to overestimate during low-consumption periods. On the other hand, Lag-Llama's use of multiple Monte Carlo samples allows for probabilistic interpretation, although its aggregated predictions (mean or median) may obscure the full uncertainty range.

These results emphasize that zero-shot general-purpose forecasting models offer practical value in data-constrained scenarios, but their effectiveness is sensitive to architectural choices, context size, and output configuration. Therefore, selecting an appropriate model should take into account the forecasting resolution and specific deployment constraints, particularly in low-resource settings.

5 Conclusion

This work compared the zero-shot forecasting performance of Lag-Llama and TimesFM 2.0 using residential electricity consumption data at multiple temporal resolutions. The results show that TimesFM 2.0 performs better at high-frequency (15-minute) and daily intervals for most households, likely due to its large-scale pretraining. In contrast, Lag-Llama showed stronger results at the hourly level, highlighting the benefits of a dedicated time series architecture.

Overall, the choice between models depends on the temporal characteristics of the task. TimesFM offers robust generalization, while Lag-Llama provides more accurate results in specific scenarios. These findings suggest that zero-shot approaches are promising, but further investigation is needed to better understand how context size, external variables, and model design affect forecasting outcomes.

As future work, it is proposed to examine the effect of varying the input context length and to incorporate temporal features, such as the meteorological data available, to improve forecasting accuracy. Additionally, the impact of partial fine-tuning will be evaluated to determine whether it yields further improvements. A broader comparison with other foundation models is also encouraged to better understand their behavior in zero-shot forecasting scenarios.

References

1. Aksu, T., et al.: Gift-eval: a benchmark for general time series forecasting model evaluation (2024). https://arxiv.org/abs/2410.10393
2. Ansari, A.F., et al.: Chronos: learning the language of time series (2024). https://arxiv.org/abs/2403.07815
3. Das, A., et al.: A decoder-only foundation model for time-series forecasting (2024). https://arxiv.org/abs/2310.10688
4. Ekambaram, V., et al.: Tiny time mixers (TTMs): fast pre-trained models for enhanced zero/few-shot forecasting of multivariate time series (2024). https://arxiv.org/abs/2401.03955
5. Garza, A., Challu, C., Mergenthaler-Canseco, M.: Timegpt-1 (2024). https://arxiv.org/abs/2310.03589
6. Gruver, N., et al.: Large language models are zero-shot time series forecasters. In: Proceedings of the 37th International Conference on Neural Information Processing Systems. NIPS '23, Curran Associates Inc., Red Hook, NY, USA (2023)
7. Hoo, S.B., et al.: The tabular foundation model tabPFN outperforms specialized time series forecasting models based on simple features (2024). https://openreview.net/forum?id=H02X7RO3OC
8. Hyndman, R.J., Athanasopoulos, G.: Forecasting: principles and practice. OTexts, Melbourne, Australia, 3 edn. (2021). https://otexts.com/fpp3/
9. Rasul, K., et al.: Lag-llama: towards foundation models for probabilistic time series forecasting (2024). https://arxiv.org/abs/2310.08278
10. Santos-Moreno, M., Ángel González-Ordiano, J., Quiroz-Ibarra, J.E., et al.: Weather and electrical demand and consumption data of a small mexican community. Data Brief **52**, 109977 (2024)
11. Saravanan, H.K., Dwivedi, S., Arjunan, P.: Analyzing the performance of time series foundation models for short-term load forecasting. In: Proceedings of the 11th ACM International Conference on Systems for Energy-Efficient Buildings, Cities, and Transportation, pp. 237–238. BuildSys '24, Association for Computing Machinery, New York, NY, USA (2024). https://doi.org/10.1145/3671127.3698708

12. Schäfer, R., et al.: Overcoming data scarcity in biomedical imaging with a foundational multi-task model. Nature Comput. Sci. 4(7), 495–509 (2024)
13. Woo, G., et al.: Unified training of universal time series forecasting transformers. In: Proceedings of the 41st International Conference on Machine Learning. ICML'24, JMLR.org (2024)

51. Exposing Photoshop Demosaic with Zero-Shot Log Resolve and Smooth M-th ... 155

52. Smeulders, A.: On learning data search. In: Bayesian Reasoning with a variational international system. Computer Vision 477, 398–406 (2020)

53. Wang, Z.: On the fusion of classified neural network information for image translation for image caption in real-time neural network. International Conference on Computer Vision 30, 12 (2019)

AI Methods, Systems, and Biosignals

Threshold Estimation for CNNs in Multi-label Historical Press Classification via Metaheuristic Optimization

Orlando Grabiel Toledano-López[1], Yanio Hernández Heredia[1]([✉]), Kalliopi Vasilaki[2], Luis Augusto Aria Verdecia[1], Aurelio Antelo Collado[1], and Pedro Luis Basulto Ramírez[1]

[1] Universidad de las Ciencias Informáticas, La Habana, Cuba
`{ogtoledano,yhernandezh,ariasverde,aantelo,basulto}@uci.cu`
[2] Institute for Mediterranean Studies, Rethymno, Greece

Abstract. This work addresses the problem of automatic image classification, focusing on its application to historical press digitization. Specifically, it proposes a method for automatic image discrimination to detect issues such as skew, noise, curvature, and the combination of several previous problems. Empirically, we have observed that addressing some of these image problems increases the quality of optical character recognition and segmentation of newspaper columns. Therefore, it is necessary to predict the problem of a newspaper page and treat it appropriately within the workflow. For this purpose, the problem has been studied by evaluating different pre-trained Convolutional Neural Networks for computer vision problems, such as RestNet variants, AlexNet, VGG11, and EfficientNet. The main contribution of this work is the development of an algorithm for threshold estimation in deep neural networks using metaheuristic optimization, specifically designed for multi-label classification tasks. We employ Particle Swarm Optimization and Genetic Algorithm as representative metaheuristic approaches for optimizing decision thresholds. In addition, we introduce a novel dataset of historical press images, collaboratively annotated by human experts. As a baseline, we propose a Random Search strategy for threshold selection, which is compared against the metaheuristic-based methods. The paper outlines the full computational methodology, including problem formulation, neural architecture design, and dataset construction, and presents experimental results across various deep learning models. The proposed approach achieves consistent improvements in F1-score relative to both the naive thresholding strategy and the baseline method.

Keywords: Convolutional Neural Network · Multi-label classification · metaheuristic optimization · threshold estimation

© The Author(s), under exclusive license to Springer Nature Switzerland AG 2026
Y. Hernádez Heredia et al. (Eds.): IWAIPR 2025, LNCS 16328, pp. 339–350, 2026.
https://doi.org/10.1007/978-3-032-11358-0_28

1   Introduction

The problem of automatic image classification has been approached with special attention by the scientific community, where state-of-the-art contributions such as [6,9,23]. One of the direct applications of image classification is to allow automatic triage of images that can be labeled according to specific criteria, e.g., for image problem detection, identification of objects present, optical character recognition (OCR), disease detection [18], product inspection [10], and others.

One of the applications intended in this paper is its use in automatic image discrimination. This represents a key component of a larger workflow for digitizing scanned images of historical press. In this digitization process, we start with a newspaper page, from which we identify existing problems in the image that could potentially hinder the segmentation of the newspaper into parts and its further processing by OCR tools. If a newspaper page presents ink stains, any form of noise, such as transparency, illegible characters due to ink wear, paper folds, or even a bad alignment of the scanner, it can affect the digitization process of the material. It is therefore necessary to detect these problems beforehand to be able to apply automatic transformations to correct these defects.

To perform the final classification, it is necessary to adjust the thresholds of activation to detect the presence of one or more problems in the image [20,22], when the output neuron uses a threshold function, which is commonly used in these problems [16]. The threshold estimation process represents an optimization problem to be solved once the training of a neural network has been performed. The manual selection of these values is a time-consuming process that becomes more complex as the number of neurons in the output layer increases.

In this work, our main contribution is the development of an algorithm for threshold estimation in deep networks based on metaheuristic optimization in the multi-label image classification problem. As metaheuristic approaches, we use Particle Swarm Optimization (PSO) and Genetic Algorithm (GA). In addition, a dataset of historical press images is constructed from various sources of information, which were collaboratively labeled by humans.

We present the description of the proposal, the design of the neural architecture, the problem definition, and a detailed description of the database in the Computational Methodology section. An analysis of the experimental results on the database and different neural architectures is presented in the Results and Discussion section. Finally, conclusions and future work are presented.

2   Related Work on Multi-label Image Classification

Deep learning models, particularly Convolutional Neural Networks (CNNs), have been extensively used for multi-label image classification due to their ability to extract rich hierarchical features from images. Early approaches employed architectures like AlexNet for learning complex visual features [13]. In [14], document classification approaches are developed using EfficientNet [19] and ExtraTree in an ensemble combination. ResNet [9] addressed the issue of vanishing gradients in deep networks by incorporating residual connections, which are particularly advantageous for capturing intricate patterns and dependencies in multi-label data. VGGNet [17] uses small convolutional filters, but it has high computational requirements.

In [1], RestNet-50 and RestNet-101 models are trained with Binary Cross-Entropy and Logits Loss combined with Focal Loss to address multi-label classification for personality handwriting analysis. Both architectures are trained using SGD with momentum, Adam, and AdaBelief for pattern recognition in handwritten text. This study [11] builds on advancements in automated disease detection using deep learning, particularly in medical imaging for lung diseases. It evaluates state-of-the-art models, such as MobileNet, DenseNet, VGG-16, Efficient-Net, Xception, and InceptionV3 on the NIH Chest X-ray dataset, highlighting MobileNet's superior performance. To address dataset imbalance, a GAN model is used to generate synthetic X-ray images, resulting in a 5% improvement in the F1-score.

Several studies have tackled the challenges posed by imbalanced data in multi-label classification. A notable contribution is the Adaptive Decision Threshold-based Extreme Learning Machine (ADT-ELM) proposed by [7], which combines an Extreme Learning Machine with a dynamic thresholding mechanism optimized via PSO. Rather than relying on fixed decision thresholds, this approach learns optimal threshold combinations to maximize macro and micro F-measure scores. Addressing the often-overlooked aspect of cost sensitivity in multi-label classification, [2] introduces a general thresholding method that adapts existing classifiers to minimize the expected misclassification cost instead of conventional error metrics. Acknowledging that different misclassification types may incur varying, context-dependent costs, they explore both global and per-label thresholding strategies and propose cost curves and scatter plots as evaluation tools. Additionally, [21] presents two novel multi-label text classification methods—adaptive-threshold CNN (AT-CNN) and implicit-threshold CNN (IT-CNN)—designed to efficiently classify electronic health records by learning threshold functions that select relevant labels. The AT-CNN estimates thresholds by adjusting binary confidence scores per label, whereas the IT-CNN implicitly predicts the number of positive labels and selects the top-k scores. Both methods closely approximate the performance of binary CNNs while significantly improving runtime efficiency, particularly as the number of classes increases.

In general, approaches for solving the problem of multi-label image classification by adapting pre-trained models based on CNN have been observed in the literature. Some of the important challenges addressed are in the introduction of new building blocks in the architecture, such as attentional mechanisms and the treatment of imbalance in the database. In addition, the application of meta-heuristic algorithms or other optimization methods becomes relevant to solve specific problems that contribute to increasing the performance of deep neural networks in multi-label classification.

3   Computational Methodology

In the proposal, we applied a pre-trained deep neural network. For this, we used the encoder part of the pre-trained model and added a block of dense layers with a sigmoid activation function in both problems. The sigmoid function transforms any input value into a range between 0 and 1, which makes it useful in binary classification problems, where the output can be interpreted as a probability. This feature allows the neurons in the output layer to provide a measure of confidence in the prediction, facilitating threshold-based decision-making (Fig. 1).

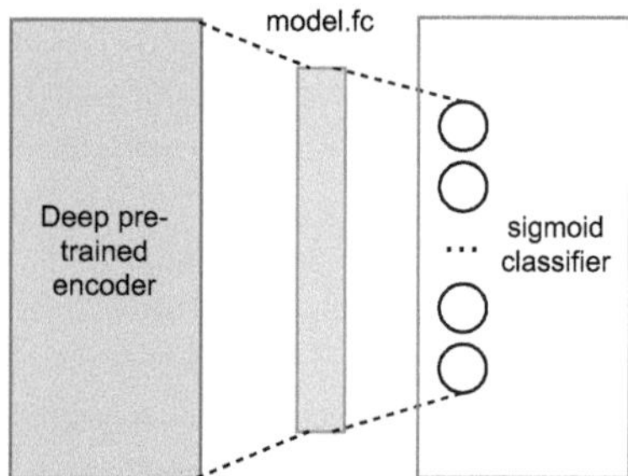

Fig. 1. Design of deep neural network for multi-label classification.

Although the problem is multi-class, it facilitates its usefulness to use each output neural unit as an independent binary classifier, since the same image can have more than one problem, such as curvature, skew, and noise.

3.1   Problem Definition for Image Discrimination

This paper addresses a fundamental problem in the digital processing of historical newspapers. The main task is to determine whether a page has skew, noise, curvature, no problem (keep it in its original format), or a combination of more than one of the problems (All). Figure 2 shows an example of each problem.

- Skew: An image is said to be skewed if it has an angular deviation from its expected orientation. In this case, the vertical axis of the image is not perpendicular to its base. This occurs because of a misalignment in the photo or the scanner.
- Noise: If the image has ink smudges that distort the characters, or its transparency causes the text behind it to be refracted.
- Curvature: The image shows folds in the paper that make the text look wavy; in general, the text and elements do not show a correct horizontal alignment.
- Original: The image does not present any problem.
- All: It presents more than one of the problems described above: Curvature, Noise, and Skew.

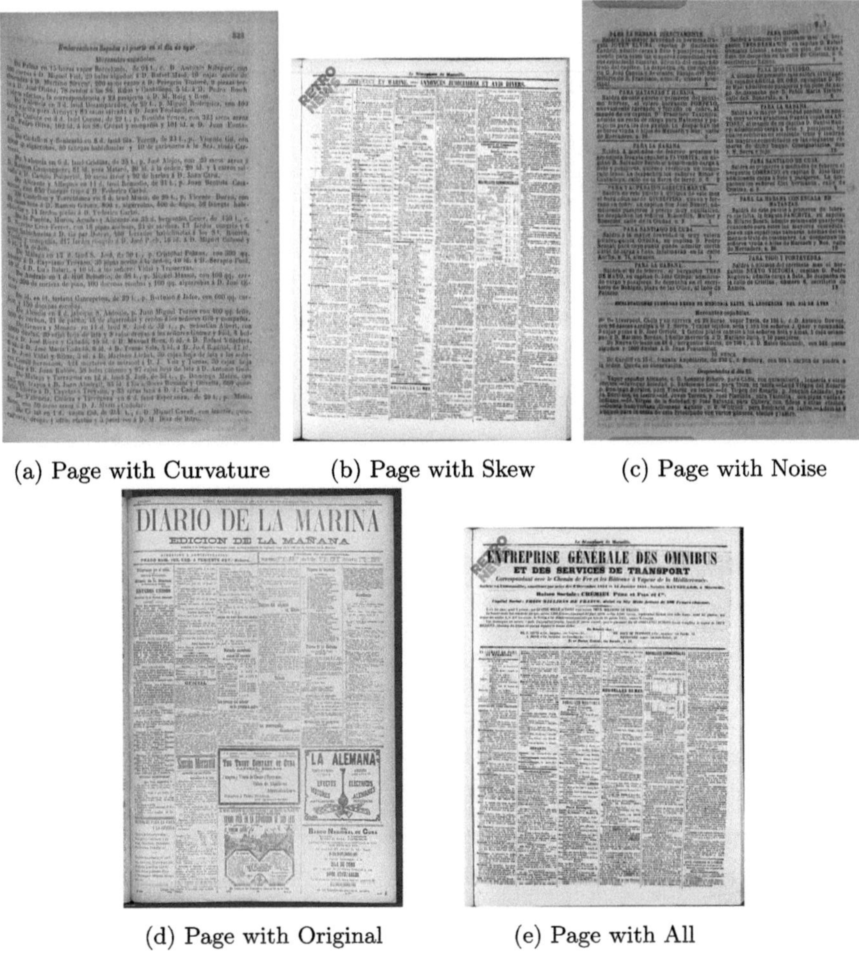

(a) Page with Curvature   (b) Page with Skew   (c) Page with Noise

(d) Page with Original   (e) Page with All

Fig. 2. Images examples for each defined problem in multi-label classification.

Let $\mathcal{X}$ be the input space of images and $\mathcal{Y} = \{C_1, C_2, C_3, C_4, C_5\}$ be the set of possible labels for Image Transformation Prediction Problem (ITPP), where C_1 corresponds to *Curvature*, C_2 corresponds to *Skew*, C_3 corresponds to *Noise*, C_4 corresponds to *Original*, and C_5 corresponds to *All* (indicating an image with multiple issues).

For ITPP, each image $x \in \mathcal{X}$ can be associated with one or more labels from $\mathcal{Y}$, leading to a multi-label classification problem. We define the dataset for the problem as N labeled images as: $\mathcal{D} = \{(x_i, \mathbf{y}_i)\}_{i=1}^{N}$, where $x_i \in \mathcal{X}$ is the i-th image, and $\mathbf{y}_i = (y_{i1}, y_{i2}, ..., y_{iC}) \in \{0, 1\}^C$ is a binary vector representing the presence (1) or absence (0) of each label in C labels.

The goal is to learn a function $f : \mathcal{X} \to [0,1]^C$ such that: $\hat{\mathbf{y}} = f(x)$, where $\hat{\mathbf{y}}$ is the predicted label vector for an image x. The model can be trained using a *binary cross-entropy loss* independently for each label:

$$\mathcal{L} = -\sum_{j=1}^{C}\sum_{i=1}^{N} [y_{ij} \log \hat{y}_{ij} + (1 - y_{ij}) \log(1 - \hat{y}_{ij})] \tag{1}$$

where $\hat{y}_{ij}$ is the predicted probability for label j on image i.

3.2 Threshold Estimation via Metaheuristic Approaches for 4-Class Classification

The goal of this computational problem is to optimize the estimation of decision thresholds for a 4-class classification task using metaheuristic optimization. The problem is limited to four classes because the C_5 class (All) represents a combination of any of the other four, making it more appropriate to focus threshold optimization on the distinct base classes. Moreover, the deep neural network design includes an output layer with four neurons, each representing the presence or absence of a specific problem in the image. Thus, each class is denoted as C_1, C_2, C_3, and C_4, and the classifier outputs probabilities for these classes, represented as $P(C_i)$, where $i = 1, 2, 3, 4$. The problem involves determining a set of thresholds $\mathbf{T} \in \mathbb{R}^4$ such that the classification performance is maximized while minimizing the misclassification rates.

The optimization problem is formulated as follows:

- **Input:** The described dataset $\mathcal{D}$ in Sect. 3.1.
- **Output:** Optimized thresholds $\mathbf{T}^* \in \mathbb{R}^4$.

The objective function is defined as:

$$\mathbf{T}^* \leftarrow \arg\max_{\mathbf{T}^{(i)} \in \mathcal{P}} f(\mathbf{T}^{(i)}) \tag{2}$$

where $f(.)$ is the measure of F1-score to maximize. The following Algorithm 1 describe the framework for threshold estimation problem:

Algorithm 1. General Metaheuristic Framework for Threshold Estimation

---

1: **Input:** Population size N
2: **Objective function** $f : \mathbb{R}^4 \to \mathbb{R}$, bounds $\mathbf{T}_{\min}, \mathbf{T}_{\max} \in \mathbb{R}^4$, algorithm-specific parameters
3: **Best solution found** $\mathbf{T}^* \in \mathbb{R}^4$
  Initialize a population $\mathcal{P} = \{\mathbf{T}^{(1)}, \ldots, \mathbf{T}^{(N)}\}$ with $\mathbf{T}^{(i)} \sim \mathcal{U}(\mathbf{T}_{\min}, \mathbf{T}_{\max})$
4: **for** $\mathbf{T}^{(i)} \in \mathcal{P}$ **do**
5:   Evaluate fitness $f(\mathbf{T}^{(i)})$
6: **end for**
7: Set $\mathbf{T}^* \leftarrow \arg\max_{\mathbf{T}^{(i)} \in \mathcal{P}} f(\mathbf{T}^{(i)})$
8: **while** stopping criterion is not met **do**
9:   Generate new candidate solutions $\mathcal{P}'$ using exploration/exploitation operators
10:   **for** $\mathbf{T}'^{(j)} \in \mathcal{P}'$ **do**
11:     Evaluate $f(\mathbf{T}'^{(j)})$
12:   **end for**
13:   Update the population: $\mathcal{P} \leftarrow \text{Update}(\mathcal{P}, \mathcal{P}')$
14:   Update best solution: $\mathbf{T}^* \leftarrow \arg\max_{\mathbf{T} \in \mathcal{P}} f(\mathbf{T})$
15: **end while**
16: **Output:** $\mathbf{T}^*$

The optimized thresholds should maximize classification performance, thereby improving the decision-making process for predicting whether images have Skew, Noise, Curvature, or no problem (Original label). The convergence criteria are to reach a maximum number of iterations.

3.3 Dataset Description

The dataset is compiled collaboratively from newspaper images from Diario de Barcelona (Spain) [3,5], Diario de la Marina (Cuba) [4,8], and Le Sémaphore de Marseille (France) [15]. The database is a set of raw pages of 614 images[1].

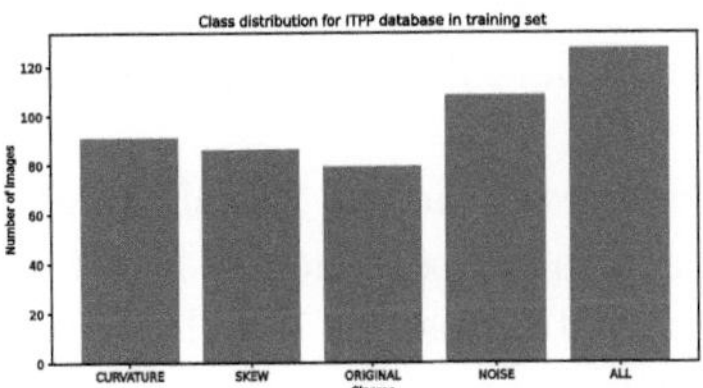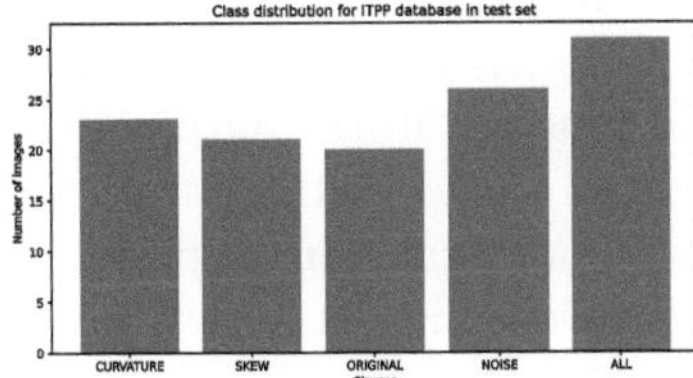

Fig. 3. Images distribution per classes.

Figure 3 shows the image distribution per class. The dataset was divided into 80% for training and 20% for testing.

---

[1] Dataset is available at: https://drive.google.com/file/d/1iNMXCorj6VnqtzwzOHm 98K2WSUiX2SvP/view.

4 Results and Discussion

We performed the experiments for both databases using Adam [12] as an optimizer, with a learning rate of $alpha = 5.5E - 5$, a batch size of 32, and a maximum of 30 training epochs. We implemented the proposal in Pytorch with pretrained image recognition models, such as VGG11, ResNet18, ResNet34, ResNet50, AlexNet, and EfficientNetB4[2].

In the preprocessing stage, we resize the images keeping the aspect ratio as much as possible, to a size of 1024×768 $(H \times W)$ for the ITPP problem. The normalization is applied as a transformation, taking as mean per channel the vector $\mathbf{t}_\mu = (0.485, 0.456, 0.406)$ and as standard deviation $\mathbf{t}_\sigma = (0.229, 0.224, 0.225)$.

Table 1. Evaluation metrics of the test set for deep learning models

Model	P	F1-score	R	ACC
VGG11	0.5054	0.4868	0.4808	0.4876
ResNet18	0.5674	0.5010	0.5224	0.5455
ResNet34	**0.6121**	**0.5500**	**0.5594**	**0.5537**
ResNet50	0.5895	0.5069	0.5143	0.5455
AlexNet	0.5677	0.5107	0.5192	0.5289
EfficientNetB4	0.5339	0.4825	0.5064	0.5207

Table 1 shows the evaluation metric among six deep learning models for multi-label image classification. The evaluation metrics reveal that ResNet34 outperforms other models across most measures, achieving the highest precision (P), F1-score, recall (R), and accuracy (ACC), indicating a strong balance between precision and recall. ResNet-based models consistently demonstrate competitive performance, with ResNet18 and ResNet50 performing moderately well, while VGG11 and EfficientNetB4 show lower scores across most metrics. This indicates that ResNet architectures are particularly well-suited for the ITPP problem. All evaluation metric was computed using a naive default threshold vector at the sigmoid function in the output $(0.5, 0.5, 0.5, 0.5)$.

Figure 4 shows distinct strengths and weaknesses across the six models. All models demonstrate strong performance in certain classes, such as Noise and All, with relatively high accuracy, particularly in distinguishing All. However, they also reveal challenges with specific labels. For instance, Skew consistently shows lower accuracy, with frequent misclassifications into other categories. Additionally, Curvature and Original exhibit moderate confusion in all models, often being mistaken for closely related classes. Overall, the models vary in their ability to handle inter-class ambiguities, indicating opportunities for optimization to improve classification balance and reduce specific errors.

---

[2] Colab   notebooks: https://github.com/portada-git/images_discriminators_ backend/tree/main/notebooks.

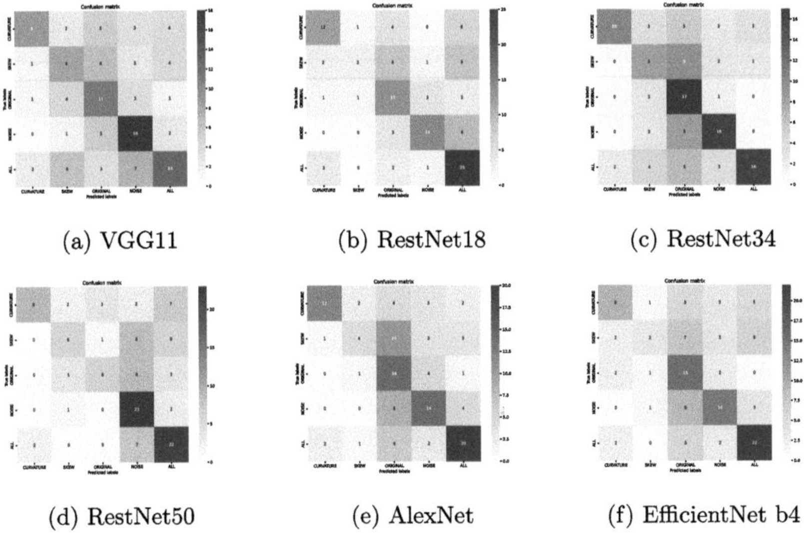

(a) VGG11   (b) RestNet18   (c) RestNet34

(d) RestNet50   (e) AlexNet   (f) EfficientNet b4

Fig. 4. Confusion matrix for six deep learning architectures.

Based on the best-performing neural architecture in terms of F1-score, namely the ResNet-based models, we proceed to optimize the decision thresholds using metaheuristic algorithms. As a baseline, we consider the average F1-score obtained through threshold estimation via Random Search (RS), with 100 iterations as maximum, on the same ResNet-based models.

We conduct metaheuristic optimization using a maximum of 20 generations and a population size of 20 individuals. For each algorithm, the hyperparameter configuration is selected manually based on commonly recommended values. Specifically, for PSO, we set the inertia weight to $\omega = 0.8$ and both acceleration coefficients to $c_1 = c_2 = 1.4$. For the GA, we use a mutation probability of $p_m = 0.1$ and a tournament selection size of $t = 5$.

Table 2. Evaluation metrics of the test set for deep learning models

Model	P	F1-score	R	ACC
ResNet18+RS	0.5955	0.5636	0.5573	0.5702
ResNet34+RS	0.6185	0.5833	0.5854	0.5950
ResNet50+RS	0.6321	0.5323	0.5374	0.5455
Baseline (AVG)	0.6153	0.5597	0.5600	0.5702
ResNet18+PSO	0.6403	0.6176	**0.6209**	**0.6198**
ResNet34+PSO	0.6441	0.5858	0.5886	0.5868
ResNet50+PSO	0.6173	0.5631	0.5648	0.5785
ResNet18+GA	**0.6621**	**0.6240**	0.6164	**0.6198**
ResNet34+GA	0.6350	0.5890	0.5873	0.5950
ResNet50+GA	0.6485	0.5818	0.5846	0.5868

Table 2 presents the evaluation metrics of three ResNet models (ResNet18, ResNet34, and ResNet50) with optimal threshold estimation via metaheuristic optimization for a multi-label classification problem. The metrics include Precision (P), F1-score, Recall (R), and Accuracy (ACC). Among the models, ResNet18 demonstrates the highest performance across all metrics. The best results are highlighted in bold type.

The evaluation results demonstrate that ResNet18, when optimized with GA, outperforms ResNet34 and ResNet50 in a multi-label classification problem. However, in general, estimating thresholds using metaheuristics proves to be more effective than a naive selection of thresholds or using RS, thereby exceeding the baseline. The confusion matrix, in Fig. 5 for ResNet18, reflects strong diagonal dominance, signifying fewer misclassifications. In contrast, ResNet34 and ResNet50 exhibit more off-diagonal misclassifications, leading to reduced overall performance. This suggests that shallower networks like ResNet18 are better suited for this dataset, likely due to their simplicity and reduced risk of overfitting compared to deeper models.

The diminishing performance of ResNet34 and ResNet50 may be attributed to optimization challenges or the complexity of deeper networks for this specific task. To further enhance performance, future work could focus on addressing overfitting in deeper models, exploring alternative optimization techniques, or improving dataset quality and size. For this task, ResNet18+GA offers the best trade-off between complexity and classification performance.

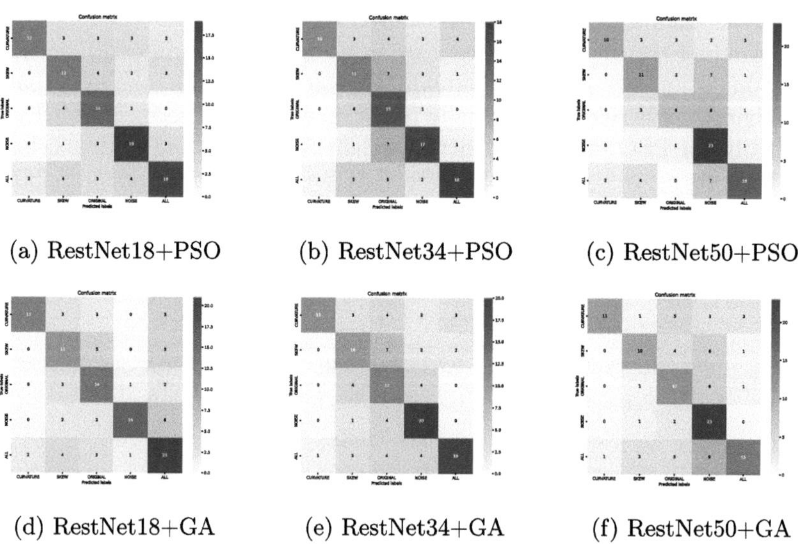

(a) RestNet18+PSO   (b) RestNet34+PSO   (c) RestNet50+PSO

(d) RestNet18+GA   (e) RestNet34+GA   (f) RestNet50+GA

Fig. 5. Confusion matrix for RestNet-based models with metaheuristic thresholds optimization.

5   Conclusions

In this paper, we present a metaheuristic algorithm for optimal threshold estimation in multi-label classification problems. The developed solution surpasses the naive selection of thresholds and the search strategy using RS, suggesting that the use of a metaheuristic approach explores the solution space in this problem more effectively. It can be noted that RestNet-based models achieve better results in identifying image problems such as curvature, skewness, and noise. However, neural models of higher complexity show worse results on the database used in the experiment. The optimal threshold estimation in the output neurons increases the generalization capability of the neural model, and this solution approach shows promise for application to multi-label classification problems, where the output requires the adjustment of thresholds. In future work, we will evaluate other metaheuristic optimization strategies, the incorporation of attentional mechanisms in the neural architecture, and the enrichment of the database by generating new instances.

Acknowledgments. We would like to acknowledge the partial funding of the PortADa project: Port Arrivals Data. A special acknowledgement to the researchers Jordi Ibarz, Nadia Pinedo, Mirian Galante Becerril, Apostolos Delis, Agustín Nieto, Maximiliano Camarda, and Brendan J. von Briesen.

References

1. Adeli Shamsabad, M., Suen, C.Y.: Deep Multi-label Classification of Personality with Handwriting Analysis, pp. 218–230 (2024)
2. Alotaibi, R., Flach, P.: Multi-label thresholding for cost-sensitive classification. Neurocomputing **136**, 232–247 (2021). https://doi.org/10.1016/j.neucom.2020.12.004
3. de Barcelona, A.: Diario de Barcelona 1885–1984 (2025). https://ahcbdigital.bcn.cat/hemeroteca/titol/diario+de+barcelona
4. del Caribe, B.D.: Diario de la Marina (2024). https://dloc.com/es/UF00001565/05637/citation
5. de Catalunya, G.: Diario de Barcelona 1792–1889 (2025). https://arca.bnc.cat/arcabib_pro/ca/publicaciones/numeros_por_mes.do?idPublicacion=384
6. Fei, X., Wu, S., Miao, J., Wang, G., Sun, L.: Lightweight-VGG: a fast deep learning architecture based on dimensionality reduction and nonlinear enhancement for hyperspectral image classification. Remote Sens. **16**(2) (2024)
7. Gao, S., Dong, W., Cheng, K., Yang, X., Zheng, S., Yu, H.: Adaptive decision threshold-based extreme learning machine for classifying imbalanced multi-label data. Neural Process. Lett. **52**(3), 2151–2173 (2020). https://doi.org/10.1007/s11063-020-10343-3
8. Gobierno de España: Diario de la Marina: periódico oficial del apostadero de La Habana (1844–1960) (2025). https://prensahistorica.mcu.es/es/consulta/registro.do?id=1029169
9. He, K., Zhang, X., Ren, S., Sun, J.: Deep residual learning for image recognition. In: Proceedings of the IEEE Computer Society Conference on Computer Vision and Pattern Recognition 2016-Decem, pp. 770–778 (2016)

10. Hridoy, M.W., Rahman, M.M., Sakib, S.: A framework for industrial inspection system using deep learning. Ann. Data Sci. **11**(2), 445–478 (2024)
11. Irtaza, M., Ali, A., Gulzar, M., Wali, A.: Multi-label classification of lung diseases using deep learning. IEEE Access **12**, 124062–124080 (2024)
12. Kingma, D.P., Ba, J.L.: Adam: a method for stochastic optimization. In: 3rd International Conference on Learning Representations, ICLR 2015 - Conference Track Proceedings, pp. 1–15 (2015)
13. Krishovsky, A., Sutskever, I., Hinton, G.E.. ImageNet classification with deep convolutional neural networks. In: Pereira, F., Burges, C.J., Bottou, L., Weinberger, K.Q. (eds.) Advances in Neural Information Processing Systems, vol. 25. Curran Associates, Inc. (2012)
14. Omurca, S.I., Ekinci, E., Sevim, S., Edinç, E.B., Eken, S., Sayar, A.: A document image classification system fusing deep and machine learning models. Appl. Intell. **53**(12), 15295–15310 (2023).https://doi.org/10.1007/s10489-022-04306-5
15. Retronews: Le Sémaphore de Marseille (2024). https://www.retronews.fr/journaux/semaphore-de-marseille
16. Saidabad, M.Y., Hassanzadeh, H., Seyed Ebrahimi, S.H., Khezri, E., Rahimi, M.R., Trik, M.: An efficient approach for multi-label classification based on advanced kernel-based learning system. Intell. Syst. Appl. **21**, 200332 (2024)
17. Simonyan, K., Zisserman, A.: Very deep convolutional networks for large-scale image recognition. In: Bengio, Y., LeCun, Y. (eds.) 3rd International Conference on Learning Representations, ICLR 2015, San Diego, CA, USA, 7–9 May 2015, Conference Track Proceedings (2015)
18. Talaat, F.M., El-Sappagh, S., Alnowaiser, K., Hassan, E.: Improved prostate cancer diagnosis using a modified ResNet50-based deep learning architecture. BMC Med. Inform. Decis. Mak. **24**(1), 23 (2024)
19. Tan, M., Le, Q.: EfficientNet: rethinking model scaling for convolutional neural networks. In: Chaudhuri, K., Salakhutdinov, R. (eds.) Proceedings of the 36th International Conference on Machine Learning. Proceedings of Machine Learning Research, vol. 97, pp. 6105–6114. PMLR (2019)
20. Yang, Y., Wei, J., Yu, Z., Zhang, R.: Multi-label neural architecture search for chest radiography image classification. Multimed. Syst. **30**(1), 8 (2024)
21. Yang, Z., Emmert-Streib, F.: Threshold-Learned CNN for Multi-Label Text Classification of Electronic Health Records (2023). https://doi.org/10.1109/ACCESS.2023.3309157
22. Yuan, Z., Zhang, K., Huang, T.: Positive label is all you need for multi-label classification. In: 2024 IEEE International Conference on Multimedia and Expo (ICME), vol. 1, pp. 1–6. IEEE (2024)
23. Zhang, X., Ding, T.: Style classification of media painting images by integrating ResNet and attention mechanism. Heliyon **10**(6), e27178 (2024)

Convolutional Neural Network for Burst Detection in Water Pipes

Christian Fernández Leal$^{(\boxtimes)}$, Jaime Chiang Cruz , Iliover Vega González ,
and Jorge Ramírez Beltrán

Center for Hydraulic Research, Technological University of Havana "José Antonio Echeverría",
Havana, Cuba
`chleal95@gmail.com`

Abstract. Water losses due to pipeline breakages are a global issue. Timely detection of these events would help mitigate the waste of this natural resource. Various approaches have been employed to address this problem, ranging from classical Machine Learning algorithms and Digital Signal Processing to Deep Learning architectures. This article presents a Convolutional Neural Network for classifying pressure signals identified as background noise or presence of a burst. The model's architecture comprises an initial normalization layer, four convolutional layers followed by max pooling layers with ReLU activation functions, a global pooling layer, and a final output neuron with a sigmoid activation function. With a lightweight design intended for implementation on low-power microcontrollers and an end-to-end architecture, it achieves 100% accuracy in identifying bursts over background noise in signals collected under controlled conditions.

Keywords: Convolutional Neural Network · burst detection · end-to-end model

1 Introduction

In urban areas, water is distributed through pipeline networks to cover the largest possible population. The Water Distribution Systems (WDS) deterioration can cause water leaks due to internal factors, such as pipe wear, and external factors, such as mechanical damage caused by excessive loading on the pipe [1]. Potable water losses from leaks in WDS pipes are estimated to be around 30% globally, which has made the study of detection methods an active research area.

When a break occurs in a water pipeline, a phenomenon known in the literature as a burst is generated. The leak that persists over time following the burst is referred to as a background leak. Although both the burst and the background leak stem from the same event, a clear distinction exists with regard to the detection method. One differentiating aspect is that once a background leak is generated, expensive methods must be used for its detection [2, 3]. In contrast, analyzing the burst enables the use of pressure sensors, which are less expensive and easier to install [4], besides offering the advantage of detecting the leak at the very moment the pipe ruptures.

Y. Hernádez Heredia et al. (Eds.): IWAIPR 2025, LNCS 16328, pp. 351–361, 2026.
https://doi.org/10.1007/978-3-032-11358-0_29

A burst in a water pipeline produces an abrupt drop in water pressure at the break point. This event occurs over a time interval ranging from milliseconds to seconds. From an analytical perspective, the occurrence of a burst produces a discontinuity in the pressure signal relative to its stable value [5]. Such discontinuity is a characteristic and defining feature for the identification of bursts. Various studies have focused on identifying these pressure patterns by using techniques such as statistical feature extraction, signal analysis in different domains, classical Machine Learning algorithms, and more advanced methods like Deep Learning.

Traditional pattern recognition models require a manually designed feature extractor to collect relevant input information and a classifier that categorizes the input based on the resulting features [6]. This approach is applied in [5, 7, 8] where the decomposition levels of the Wavelet Transform are used to extract the main features and reduce noise from pressure signals in water pipelines. Similarly, [9] presents an approach based on multiple pressure signal features applied to a decision tree for burst detection.

Manual feature extraction requires expert analysis of the problem domain. In classification tasks that use these features, scaling the solution or applying it to similar problems is challenging since the features are tailored to a specific case. Extracting defining features according to the nature and complexity of the signals requires transformations into various domains, which increases both algorithm complexity and development time. In contrast, Deep Learning models do not require manual feature extraction or pre-processing of the input signal. Deep Learning allows multi-layer computational models to learn data representations at various levels of abstraction and discover intricate structures in large datasets through the Backpropagation algorithm [10].

The use of Convolutional Neural Network (CNN) architectures is prominent in Deep Learning models due to their ability to extract and combine local features before performing spatial or temporal recognition [6]. CNNs for Time Serie Classification (TSC) can analyze signals in the time domain using a one-dimensional input when a single variable is analyzed, or two-dimensional inputs when several measurements from different variables are considered for classification.

The use of CNN-based algorithm for leak detection and localization in water pipelines is shown in [11–13]. These works focus on detecting pre-existing leaks, known as background leaks, rather than detecting bursts at the moment they occur. They also perform manual feature extraction and employ pre-trained models.

In [14], a leak localization and detection system is proposed that combines a one-dimensional Convolutional Neural Network (1D-CNN) with a Support Vector Machine (SVM) and a graph-based local search algorithm. In [15], the authors propose a model that integrates the detection results from six different statistical process control methods into a single input element for a CNN for final classification. In [16], a leak detection system is presented, consisting of a density-based clustering algorithm (DBSCAN) and a multi-scale module of a Fully Convolutional Network (FCN). In [17], a methodology for detecting and identifying bursts is proposed. Two neural networks based on 1D-CNN are presented, containing between 26808 and 81250 weights to be trained.

The state-of-the-art leak detection algorithms based on CNNs do not use the acquired signal in raw as input, instead, they perform feature extraction in a preceding step. The models are composed of several classifiers in order to improve performance or to both detect and localize leaks. A common characteristic in most studies utilizing Deep Learning models is that the datasets on which these proposals are evaluated are not made publicly available, making it difficult to adequately compare different architectures for a specific problem. Furthermore, insufficient details are provided regarding the parameters and hyperparameters used in model design and training, which hinders their implementation in other solutions or the verification of the results.

In this article, a Deep Learning model of the CNN type is proposed for bursts detection from a set of pressure measurements in water pipelines under controlled conditions. The model processes these pressure signals and provides a prediction based on features automatically extracted as the signal passes through the various layers of the network. The acquired signals are fed to the model without pre-processing, resulting in an end-to-end architecture. The inclusion of a normalization layer in the first stage of the model enables the analysis of pressure signals from different types of sensors. In addition to its evaluation performance, the presented architecture takes into account the number of parameters and floating-point operations performed, aiming to achieve a lightweight model with reduced inference times.

The main contribution of this article is the design of a lightweight CNN-based model with an end-to-end architecture for implementation on low-power microcontrollers and applications requiring real-time burst identification. The model achieves 100% accuracy in identifying pressure signals exhibiting bursts against background noise.

2 Data Preparation

The signals used for training and evaluating the model were acquired in the laboratory of the Hydraulic Research Center at Technological University of Havana José Antonio Echeverría (Cujae). The installation consists of a high-density polyethylene pipe with a diameter of 160 mm and a length of 65.2 m. The pipe is fed by a constant head tank that guarantees a pressure of 10 mwc (meters water column) at the pipe inlet. At the end of the pipe, a valve is regulated to ensure an average flow velocity of 2 m/s, this condition was established as the extreme scenario generating the highest noise, making leak detection more challenging. The pressure sensor is placed 7 m from the burst location [5].

The dataset is composed of 10-s files sampled at 400 Hz, so each file contains 4000 samples. It is divided into background noise signals and signals in which a burst is present. There are three groups of signals corresponding to bursts, defined by the leak flow: 0.8, 0.5, and 1.5 L/s. The data is separated into two classes: class 0 for signals classified as noise and class 1 for signals exhibiting a burst.

The files are in TSV (tab-separated values) format, where each row contains the samples of a 10-s measurement, with the first element holding the label corresponding to the signal's class, in this case, 0 or 1.

For measurements in which a burst is present, the pressure drop is centered; that is, within a 10-s window the burst starts between 4 and 6 s, and never at the very beginning or the end. This aspect could cause the model to learn undesired patterns and fail to correctly identify a burst occurring at the beginning or end of the time window. Therefore, generating synthetic data from the original signals would help improve the model's generalization. In Fig. 1, two signals are shown: one corresponding to measurements made in the laboratory and another generated from the first.

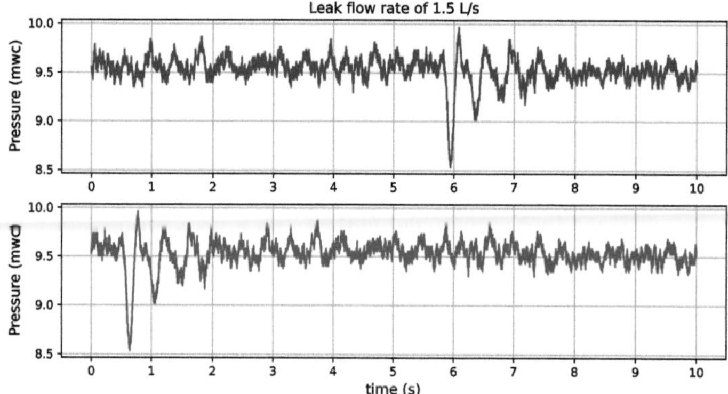

Fig. 1. Signal exhibiting a burst acquired in the laboratory (blue) and another generated synthetically (red).

In Deep Learning, a balanced dataset prevents the model from becoming biased towards the majority class, provides more reliable evaluation metrics, and aids in generalization. Each class should have the same number of samples or at least a proportional distribution that does not significantly favor one class over another.

The total dataset is split into two files: one for training and one for evaluation. The training set represents 40% of the dataset and is composed of 86 burst signals and 86 noise signals. For evaluation, the remaining 60% consists of 130 signals for each class. This split ratio was chosen to assess the model's ability to generalize in scenarios with limited training data, and it is consistent with the practices used in some datasets from the UCR Time Series Archive [18], which emphasize evaluation under few-shot learning conditions. Table 1 shows the distribution of the signals allocated to each dataset.

Table 1. Distribution of signals by dataset

Dataset	Signals class 1	Signals class 0	Total signals
Train	86	86	172
Test	130	130	260

With three different leak flow types for the burst signals, it is ensured that each distribution maintains a balance among all leak flow types even though they belong to the same class.

In addition to balancing the dataset and augmenting it with synthetic signals generated from the acquired signals, it is necessary to normalize the input data. Data normalization requires an additional step because it must be applied during both training and evaluation, yet its benefits justify its use. It helps models converge faster during training. When different features have distinct ranges, the resulting model may make fewer effective predictions. Without normalization, the model may pay too much attention to features with a wide range and not enough to those with a narrow one. Measuring the same variable with different sensors results in different value ranges, which would restrict a model to specific conditions. With normalization, the fundamental nature of the signal is not altered, only its numerical representation.

Figure 2 shows two representations of the same signal marked by a pressure drop corresponding to a leak with a flow rate of 0.8 L/s. The first graph shows the pressure signal in mwc units, and the second graph shows the signal after applying the Z-Score normalization technique.

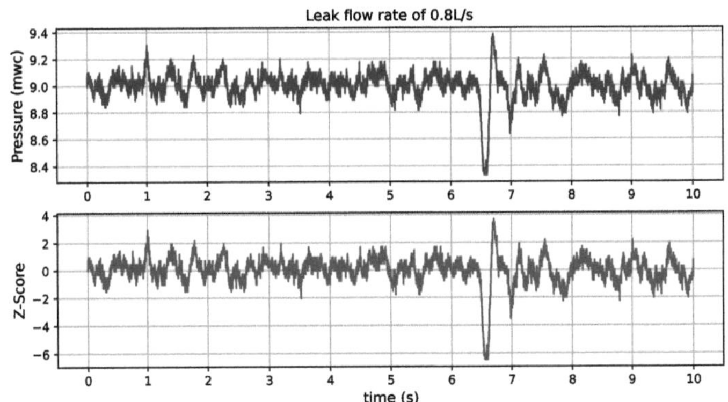

Fig. 2. Leak signal represented in mwc levels (blue) and after Z-Score normalization (red).

Data quality is critical in the development of Deep Learning models as it directly influences model performance. A poorly labeled dataset, incomplete information, or one with a clear imbalance can introduce bias and noise when the model is evaluated in real scenarios.

3 Performance Evaluation Metrics

During the training process, a loss function is calculated to adjust the model's weights. This loss can also be computed on a validation subset, which allows for a graphical representation of the model's behavior throughout training. Comparing the training and validation loss curves provides insights into whether the model is overfitting to the training data, underfitting, how well it is generalizing, and how many steps it takes to reach an optimal fit. Ideally, both curves should converge toward zero simultaneously as training progresses. Although training and validation loss curves are not metrics that evaluate the model's practical performance, they are diagnostic tools used to monitor the training process, which ultimately affects the final results.

Among the most commonly used metrics to evaluate the performance of binary classification models are:

- Accuracy: the proportion of correct predictions,
- Precision: the ability to avoid labeling a negative sample as positive,
- Recall: the ability to identify all positive samples.

These analyses are based on the confusion matrix resulting from the evaluation of the trained model. However, these metrics are not always sufficient, as it is possible for a model to show good performance according to these metrics while emphasizing non-defining features.

Deep Learning models are often referred to as black boxes due to their limited transparency and interpretability. Therefore, it is necessary to rely on tools that help explain the model's predictions and justify its outputs in a manner that is understandable to humans [19]. The tool that enables visualization of which part of an input signal is most influential in the final classification, specifically for CNNs, is the Class Activation Map (CAM).

The CAM is obtained by linearly combining the activation maps of the final convolutional layer with the weights of the linear layer associated with the target class. It is defined by:

$$L^c_{CAM} = \sum_n w^c_n A^n \tag{1}$$

where:

- w^c_n represents the weights associated with class c from the linear layer acting as the classifier, and
- A^n is the set of features from the final convolutional layer.

Thus, the performance evaluation of the model is based both on the resulting metrics and the visual confirmation that the features emphasized as most important for classification correspond with those identified by human experts.

4 Hyperparameters Selection

In the design of neural networks, there are generally two key concepts:

- Hyperparameters: These are external configurations that must be set before training. They include the number of layers in the network, the filter sizes in the case of CNNs, the learning rate, batch size, and the number of epochs.
- Parameters: These are the internal values of the network that are adjusted during training, the weights and biases.

The selection of some hyperparameters is an iterative process that is refined based on the results obtained during training and validation until a configuration meets the desired performance. Other hyperparameters are chosen based on the specific characteristics of the problem to be solved.

Since this is a binary classification problem, the use of a single output neuron and the application of the sigmoid activation function is sufficient. The sigmoid function converts the model's output into a probability of belonging to the positive class, which is typically labeled as class 1. Selecting a threshold within the range (0,1) is another hyperparameter that directly influences performance. For example, if a threshold of 0.5 is chosen, the model will classify signals as background noise when the sigmoid output is less than 0.5, and as signals with a burst when the output is equal to or greater than 0.5. The

Binary Cross-Entropy loss function is appropriate for this type of output. Additionally, the Gradient Descent optimization algorithm is selected, as it helps prevent overfitting and allows for better control over the learning rate.

To determine the values of the remaining hyperparameters, manual tuning is performed based on the performance observed for each tested architecture under the following conditions:

- Fifteen training and validation cycles are performed. In each cycle, the training set is randomly shuffled. The average of the metrics over 15 cycles is calculated. To enable reproducibility of the same data arrangement in each test, 15 seeds are defined for the random shuffling process.
- Training and validation are performed using the K-Fold Cross-Validation technique.
- Training is stopped when the validation loss does not improve over three consecutive epochs. This prevents the model from overfitting.

Figure 3 shows the block diagram of the architecture corresponding to the selected hyperparameters. The first layer is a normalization layer, responsible for applying Z-Score to the input signal. The model includes four convolutional layers with 8, 16, 16, and 32 filters of sizes 5, 7, 7, and 9 respectively.

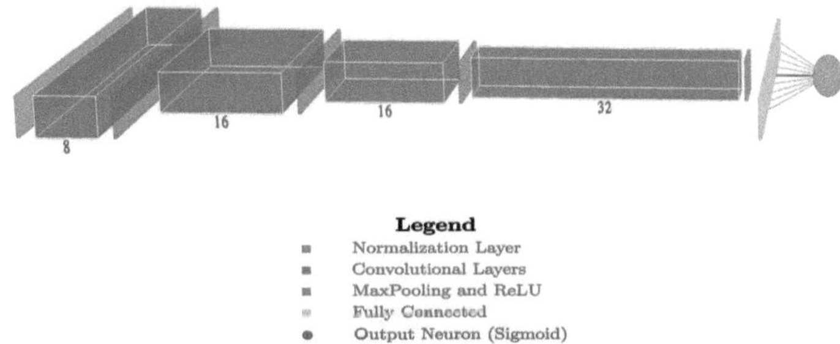

Fig. 3. Block diagram of the proposed CNN.

Each convolutional layer is followed by a Max Pooling layer and a ReLU activation function. The output neuron is connected to a linear layer, which receives the maximum value obtained from each of the 32 filters in the last convolutional layer. The selected architecture includes a total of 15441 parameters and performs approximately 12 million floating-point operations (FLOPs) for an input signal containing 4000 samples.

Figure 4 shows the average training and validation loss for each epoch. It can be observed that both the training and validation loss curves behave similarly, progressively approaching zero, which indicates the absence of overfitting. Additionally, the model ceases to improve after approximately 60 epochs, making further training cycles unnecessary.

The next step is to train the model using the entire training set, with a batch size of 16, 60 epochs, and a learning rate of 0.001. The model is then evaluated using the test dataset, whose signals have never been analyzed by the model during training or validation.

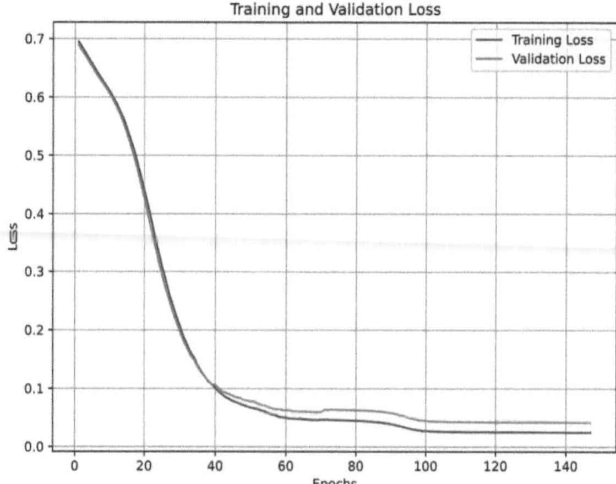

Fig. 4. Training and validation loss.

5   Model Performance Evaluation

As described in Sect. 2, class 1 consists of signals exhibiting bursts at three different leak flow rates, where a higher flow rate produces a more pronounced pressure drop. Figure 5 shows a signal belonging to class 1 along with the corresponding CAM generated by the model.

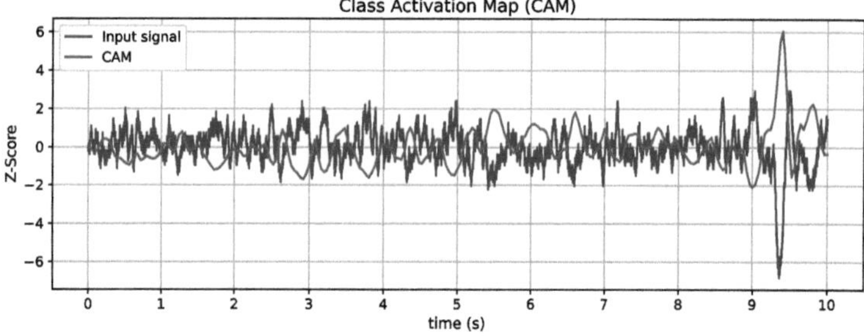

Fig. 5. Signal exhibiting a burst with a leak flow rate of 1.5 L/s and its corresponding CAM. Z-Score normalization is applied to both representations for improved visualization

Similarly, for signals with a leak flow rate of 0.8 L/s, the model is capable of distinguishing them from background noise with accuracies exceeding 98%. Figure 6 presents an example of such a signal along with its corresponding CAM.

In the case of bursts with a leak flow of 0.5 L/s, the model is able to highlight the pressure drop; however, the challenge lies in the fact that, given the noisy environment, background variations may prevent the model from detecting the singularity caused by the burst with the same level of accuracy achieved for higher flow rates. Figure 7 shows a signal exhibiting a burst at a flow rate of 0.5 L/s, for which the model outputs an 85.08%

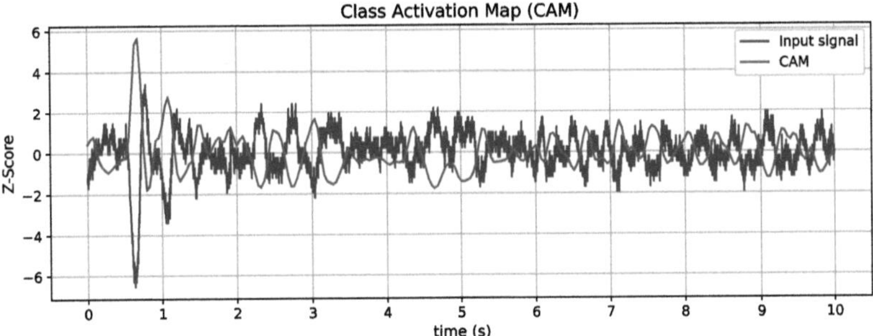

Fig. 6. Signal exhibiting a burst with a leak flow rate of 0.8 L/s and its corresponding CAM. Z-Score normalization is applied to both representations for improved visualization.

probability of belonging to class 1. It can be observed that the CAM representation for this signal reaches its peak intensity in the burst region, around the 5 s, but the variations throughout the rest of the signal impact negatively to the model's final decision.

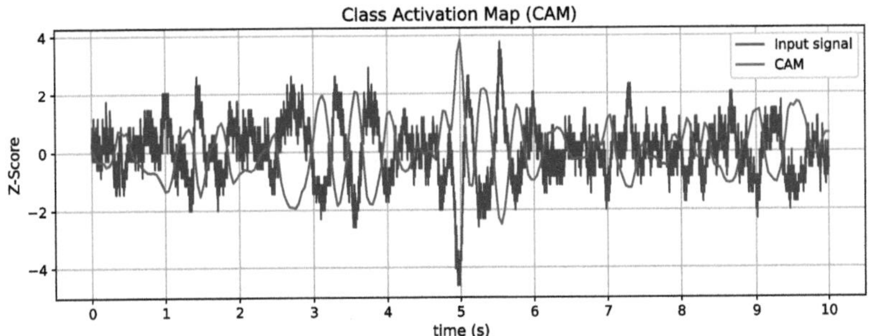

Fig. 7. Signal exhibiting a burst with a leak flow rate of 0.5 L/s and its corresponding CAM. Z-Score normalization is applied to both representations for improved visualization.

This behavior, observed in some signals with lower flow bursts, is expected. Since the pressure drop has lower amplitude, it can be masked by the natural fluctuations typical of a highly noisy environment such as water pipelines in distribution systems.

Figure 8 displays the True Positive Rate (TPR) and True Negative Rate (TNR) obtained from model evaluation across all possible thresholds. For a threshold range between 0.287 and 0.649, indicated by the red dashed lines in Fig. 8, the model is able to correctly identify 100% of the signals in the evaluation dataset.

The graph shows that both TPR and TNR remain stable and do not experience significant drops except at extreme threshold values, indicating that the model is highly effective at separating the two classes.

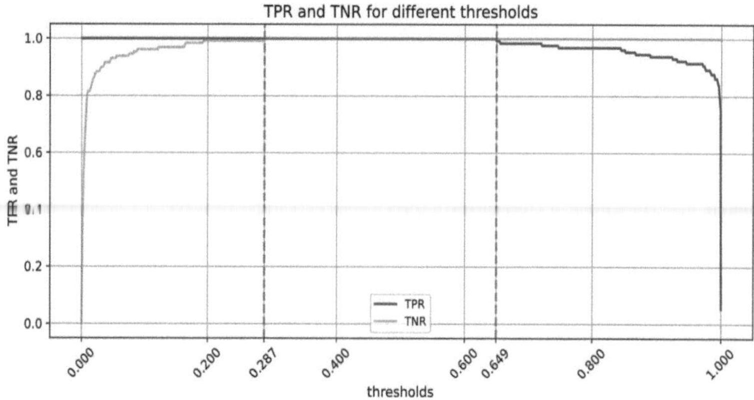

Fig. 8. TPR and TNR for different thresholds during model evaluation.

6 Conclusion

The choice of a Deep Learning based model eliminates the need for manual feature extraction in classification tasks. Expanding the dataset with signals generated from the acquired measurements is necessary for training, given the limited number of samples in the initial database.

Selecting a normalization layer as the first stage of the model enables an end-to-end architecture, where the signals are processed in raw form, without the need for any prior transformation.

The model consists of only approximately 15500 parameters, which correspond to roughly 60 kB of memory, making it feasible for implementation on low-power microcontrollers.

The model correctly classified 100% of the 260 evaluation signals for threshold values between 0.287 and 0.649.

As future work, it is proposed to expand the database through the use of additional pressure sensors and the acquisition of measurements in real-world environments. Additionally, implementation of the model on low-power, general purpose microcontrollers is planned, which would allow battery-powered devices to be installed in remote areas to detect burst events in real time.

Disclosure of Interests. The authors have no competing interests to declare that are relevant to the content of this article.

References

1. Chan, T.K., Chin, C.S., Zhong, X.: Review of current technologies and proposed intelligent methodologies for water distributed network leakage detection. IEEE Access. **6**, 78846–78867 (2018)

2. Yu, Y., Safari, A., Niu, X., Drinkwater, B., Horoshenkov, K.V.: Acoustic and ultrasonic techniques for defect detection and condition monitoring in water and sewerage pipes: a review. Appl. Acoust. **183**, 108282 (2021)

3. Mashhadi, N., Shahrour, I., Attoue, N., El Khattabi, J., Aljer, A.: Use of machine learning for leak detection and localization in water distribution systems. Smart Cities **4**(4), 1293–1315 (2021)

4. Romero-Ben, L., Alves, D., Blesa, J., Cembrano, G., Puig, V., Duviella, E.: Leak localization in water distribution networks using data-driven and model-based approaches. J. Water Resour. Plan. Manag. **148**(5), 04022016 (2022)

5. Vega-Gonzalez, I., Figueroa, O.P., Trutié-Carrero, E., Ramírez-Beltrán, J.: Algorithm to detect bursts in water pipes for implementation in low-power devices. Rev. Científica Ing. Electrónica Automática Comun. **43** (2022)

6. LeCun, Y., Bengio, Y.: Convolutional networks for images, speech, and time series. Handb Brain Theory Neural Netw. **3361**(10), 1995 (1995)

7. Srirangarajan, S., Iqbal, M., Lim, H.B., Allen, M., Preis, A., Whittle, A.J.: Water main burst event detection and localization. In: Water Distribution Systems Analysis 2010. Tucson, Arizona, United States: American Society of Civil Engineers, pp. 1324–35 (2011)

8. Trutié-Carrero, E., Valdés-Santiago, D., León-Mecías, Á., Ramírez-Beltrán, J.: Detección y Localización de Ruptura Súbita mediante Transformada Wavelet Discreta y Correlación Cruzada. Rev. Iberoam Automática E Informática Ind. **15**(2), 211 (2018)

9. Zhang, X., Long, Z., Yao, T., Zhou, H., Yu, T., Zhou, Y.: Real-time burst detection based on multiple features of pressure data. Water Supply. **22**(2), 1474–1491 (2022)

10. LeCun, Y., Bengio, Y., Hinton, G.: Deep learning. Nature **521**(7553), 436–444 (2015)

11. Shukla, H., Piratla, K.: Leakage detection in water pipelines using supervised classification of acceleration signals. Autom. Constr. **117**, 103256 (2020)

12. Tsai, Y.L., Chang, H.C., Lin, S.N., Chiou, A.H., Lee, T.L.: Using convolutional neural networks in the development of a water pipe leakage and location identification system. Appl. Sci. **12**(16), 8034 (2022)

13. Zhang, C., Alexander, B.J., Stephens, M.L., Lambert, M.F., Gong, J.: A convolutional neural network for pipe crack and leak detection in smart water network. Struct. Health Monit. **22**(1), 232–244 (2023)

14. Kang, J., Park, Y.J., Lee, J., Wang, S.H., Eom, D.S.: Novel leakage detection by ensemble CNN-SVM and graph-based localization in water distribution systems. IEEE Trans. Ind. Electron. **65**(5), 4279–4289 (2018)

15. Kim, S., Jun, S., Jung, D.: Ensemble CNN model for effective pipe burst detection in water distribution systems. Water Resour Manag. **36**(13), 5049–5061 (2022)

16. Hu, X., Han, Y., Yu, B., Geng, Z., Fan, J.: Novel leakage detection and water loss management of urban water supply network using multiscale neural networks. J. Clean. Prod. **278**, 123611 (2021)

17. Bohorquez, J., Simpson, A.R., Lambert, M.F., Alexander, B.: Merging fluid transient waves and artificial neural networks for burst detection and identification in pipelines. J. Water Resour. Plan. Manag. **147**(1), 04020097 (2021)

18. Dau, H.A., Bagnall, A., Kamgar, K., Yeh, C..CM., Zhu, Y., Gharghabi, S., et al.: The UCR time series archive. IEEECAA J. Autom Sin. (2019)

19. Anh, P.T.M.: Overview of class activation maps for visualization explainability (2023)

A Methodology for the Generation and Evaluation of Tabular Synthetic Data: A Case Study in Data Analysis in Intensive Care Units

Marcos Díaz Bastida[1]($\boxtimes$) , Ramiro APérez Vázquez[2] , and Rafael Bello Pérez[2]

[1] Hospital Provincial Arnaldo Milián Castro, Villa Clara, Santa Clara, Cuba
mdiazbastida@gmail.com
[2] Universidad Central "Marta Abreu" de Las Villas, Santa Clara, Cuba

Abstract. Limited availability and class imbalance in tabular data make it difficult the development of effective models using machine learning methods. Synthetic data generation is a promising solution, but requires rigorous methodologies and extensive evaluation. This work proposes a methodology for generating and evaluating synthetic tabular data, especially from imbalanced datasets, illustrated with a case study in Intensive Care Units. The methodology comprises: (1) class balancing by oversampling, selecting the best technique with a quality metric; (2) synthetic data generation from the optimal balanced dataset, using SMOTE RSB* Adapted with Gaussian Noise, CTGAN and TVAE; and (3) a novel quality metric, TabDSFidelity, that integrates distributional similarity, correlation preservation, and predictive utility to guide the selection at each stage. Applied to ten datasets, the methodology demonstrated that the use of synthetic data selected by a quality metric significantly improves the performance of classification models compared to using only the original data. SMOTE RSB* Adapted with Gaussian Noise consistently generated the highest quality data according to TabDSFidelity in this study. It is concluded that the proposed methodology offers an effective framework for mitigating data sparsity and imbalance, facilitating the creation of more accurate and robust models.

Keywords: Synthetic Data Quality · Synthetic Data Evaluation · Intensive Care Units

1 Introduction

Data quality and quantity are crucial for the success of machine learning (ML). However, data scarcity and class imbalance are common barriers in domains such as finance, manufacturing, and, especially, medicine [1, 2]. In the medical field, privacy regulations and the inherent complexity of health data exacerbate this limitation, hindering the development of robust ML models, particularly in critical areas such as Intensive Care Units (ICU) [3, 4]. Class imbalance, where important events are a minority, biases conventional models, leading to poor performance in predicting these classes [5, 6].

Y. Hernádez Heredia et al. (Eds.): IWAIPR 2025, LNCS 16328, pp. 362–373, 2026.
https://doi.org/10.1007/978-3-032-11358-0_30

Synthetic data (SD) generation is emerging as a key strategy to overcome these limitations [7]. SD can increase dataset size, mitigate imbalance, and protect privacy. However, ensuring the fidelity and quality of tabular SD is a significant challenge. Tabular data often combine variable types (continuous, discrete) with complex distributions and potential imbalances, making them difficult to model accurately [8]. Low-quality SD can propagate biases, resulting in poor ML models [9].

Therefore, a rigorous methodology is needed not only to generate DS, but also to thoroughly evaluate them, considering both their statistical similarity to real data and their practical utility for ML tasks. This work proposes a comprehensive methodology for this purpose, using a novel quality metric ("TabDSFidelity") that unifies these evaluation dimensions. The methodology is empirically validated through a detailed case study with real data from an ICU.

2 Related Works

The generation of tabular SD has received considerable attention. One prominent approach uses Generative Adversarial Networks (GANs). Conditional Tabular GAN (CTGAN) [8] was a key advance, designed to handle mixed data types and complex distributions. Subsequent work explored variants such as GANBLR [10] or causal approaches such as CAUSAL-TGAN [11]. Other methods include oversampling techniques such as SMOTE and its variants [12–14], and statistical methods focused on preserving correlations [15].

Assessing the quality of SD is equally crucial. It typically encompasses statistical fidelity (distribution similarity), utility for ML (performance on predictive tasks), and privacy (risk of re-identification). Given the multidimensionality, standardized evaluation frameworks have emerged. [16] propose a comprehensive framework, while [17] focus on the healthcare domain, covering similarity, utility, and privacy.

In the specific context of healthcare, the generation of SD is particularly relevant due to the sensitivity of the data. Tutorials [18], systematic reviews [9, 19, 20], automated platforms [21], and customizable methodologies [22] have been developed. Specific studies evaluate techniques [23] or investigate the usefulness of DS generated by GANs for class balancing in low-resource settings [24], a common scenario in ICUs.

While these works are valuable, few systematically integrate the assessment of statistical fidelity and ML utility into a single approach to guide a complete methodological process, from balancing to final generation. Many evaluate these dimensions separately. Our methodology addresses this gap through the TabDSFidelity metric, which combines both perspectives to select the most promising datasets at each stage, applied to a realistic ICU case study where both imbalance and sparsity are relevant issues.

The key contributions of this work are:

1. The design and validation of a comprehensive methodology that systematizes the synthetic data generation process in environments with scarce and imbalanced data. Unlike studies that evaluate techniques in isolation, our contribution lies in the unified workflow that integrates class balancing and data generation, using a quality metric to guide the selection of the optimal technique at each stage.

2. A comparative analysis of three different SD generation approaches: one based on domain-adapted SMOTE, one based on GANs (CTGAN), and one based on Variational Autoencoders (TVAE).
3. Empirical evidence, through an ICU case study, of the methodology's effectiveness in improving the performance of predictive models.

Note: Detailed tables, additional figures, and pseudocode are available on the article's companion website: https://mdiazbastida.github.io/codigomdb/investigaciones-det alles-metodologia-tds.html.

3 Methodology

We propose a general methodological framework for generating and evaluating high-fidelity tabular SD, particularly useful for unbalanced datasets. It consists of four sequential stages:

3.1 Preparation and Quality Assurance of the Original Dataset

The quality of the SD depends intrinsically on the quality of the original data. This stage focuses on obtaining a clean and well-understood dataset.

- **Acquisition and Characterization**: Identify the source, semantics, type, and restrictions of each attribute. In our case study (Sect. 4), the data comes from a specific web application [25] that allows generating ICU datasets with selected filters and variables.
- **Preprocessing and Proactive Quality**: We prioritize ensuring quality at the source or early stages. This stage includes input validation, format and terminology standardization, referential integrity maintenance, and a clear strategy for missing values (although we aim to minimize them during capture). In this case study, the source application already implements these measures (database normalization, client/server validations, standardized user interface controls, triggers), resulting in high-quality data initially that did not require extensive cleansing.

3.2 Managing Class Imbalance

Since class imbalance can compromise both the generation of representative synthetic data and the performance of subsequent models, this stage focuses on addressing this imbalance. The goal is to obtain a dataset with a more appropriate class composition for subsequent phases by assessing the imbalance, applying oversampling techniques, and selecting the best result through a comprehensive quality metric.

- **Detection**: Calculate the imbalance ratio. Thresholds (e.g., > 1.5 indicates some imbalance) can be used to decide whether to intervene [26].
- **Balancing Techniques (Emphasis on Oversampling)**: Since we work with potentially small data sets (such as those in ICUs), we prioritize oversampling to avoid losing information from the majority class. We explored several techniques, including Random Oversampling (simple duplication), SMOTE (synthetic interpolation), and variants such as Borderline SMOTE, ADASYN, and a domain-adapted version, SMOTE RSB* Adapted, based on [27], with clinical restrictions.

- **Selection of the Optimal Balanced Set**: Each selected upsampling technique is applied. The TabDSFidelity quality metric (described in 3.4) is then used to evaluate each resulting balanced ensemble against the original. The ensemble with the highest TabDSFidelity score is selected as input for the next generation stage.

3.3 Generation of Synthetic Data

Once the base dataset (either the original or the balanced dataset selected as optimal in step 3.2) has been prepared, the fundamental objective of this stage is to create additional data through synthetic generation. The goal is to significantly increase the size of the available dataset. To this end, we explore three representative approaches:

- **Focus 1** (SMOTE RSB* Adapted + Gaussian Noise): It extends the idea of SMOTE adapted to the domain used in balancing. It generates data by combining SMOTE-type interpolation, controlled addition of Gaussian noise to numerical variables within defined limits, and probabilistic variation of categorical variables, always applying domain restrictions to maintain clinical realism.
- **Focus 2** (CTGAN): It represents methods based on deep learning [8]. It uses a GAN architecture designed for tabular data, capable of modeling complex distributions and nonlinear relationships. It requires specific preprocessing (transformations, scaling) and postprocessing to obtain the final synthetic data.
- **Focus 3**: TVAE (Tabular Variational Autoencoder): As a representative of generative deep learning models alternative to GANs, TVAE [8] was included. This model uses a Variational Autoencoder to learn the data distribution and generate new samples. Its approach, based on likelihood maximization rather than an adversarial game, offers a different perspective for modeling data dependencies.

  The application of these methods produces one or more sets of candidate SDs.

3.4 Evaluation and Selection Using the TabDSFidelity Quality Metric

To guide the selection of the most suitable datasets both at the balancing stage (3.2) and at the final synthetic generation stage (3.3), a robust and unified evaluation criterion is essential. TabDSFidelity is applied for this purpose: to provide a single score that integrates multiple aspects of quality (statistical similarity and predictive utility) when comparing a generated set (balanced or synthetic) with its original reference.

- Calculation of Individual Metrics:
- Predictive Utility: A standard classifier (e.g., Random Forest) is trained on a training partition of the generated set and evaluated on the test partition of set same. Metrics: AUC-ROC, F1-score, Accuracy. Higher values are better.
- Distribution Similarity: For numerics attributes, Kolmogorov-Smirnov test (KS, p-value; higher is better) and Jensen-Shannon Divergence (JSD; lower is better) and for categorical attributes, Kullback-Leibler divergence (KL; lower is better).
- Similarity of Correlations: Pearson correlation (Mean of the absolute difference between correlation matrices. Lower is better).

- Aggregation and Normalization: Metrics are aggregated (e.g., KS summing p-values over numeric attributes, JSD/KL summing (1-Divergence), Correlation as 1-MeanAbsoluteDifference) and then normalized to [0, 1] (denoted by _norm).
- Calculating TabDSFidelity: Normalized metrics are combined using a weighted sum:

TabDSFidelity = w_auc * AUC_norm + w_f1 * F1_norm + w_acc * Acc_norm + w_ks * KS_norm + w_js * JS_norm + w_kl * KL_norm + w_c * C_norm

Where the terms X_norm represent normalized metrics [0, 1] (higher is better) and w_x their weights.

AUC_norm, F1_norm, Acc_norm: They measure Predictive Utility (based on AUC-ROC, F1-score and Accuracy of a stand-ard classifier).

KS_norm, JS_norm: They measure the similarity of numerical distribution (based on KS tests and JS divergence).

KL_norm: Measures Categorical Distribution Similarity (based on KL divergence).

C_norm: Measures the Similarity of Correlations between varia-bles.

In this study we used: w_auc = 2, w_acc = 2, w_f1 = 2 and w_ks = w_js = w_kl = w_c = 1.

Note: In this study, the following weights were assigned: w_auc = 2, w_f1 = 2, w_acc = 2, and the remaining weights equal to 1 (w_ks = w_js = w_kl = w_c = 1). This weighting was deliberately chosen to prioritize predictive utility, since the main objective in our clinical case study is to improve the performance of a final classification model. We recognize that the choice of weights can influence the selection of techniques. Therefore, a sensitivity analysis was performed to assess the robustness of our findings under different weighting schemes, the results of which are detailed and discussed in Section 5.

- **Final Selection**: The set (balanced or synthetic) with the highest TabDSFidelity score is selected as the "optimal" for the next stage or for final use.

4 Case Study: Application in ICU Data

We validated the methodology using 10 data sets (CD1-CD10) from the Arnaldo Milián Castro Provincial Hospital (from Santa Clara, Cuba), generated using the tool described in 3.1.1 [25]. Each CD corresponds to a specific medical condition in the ICU:

- **CD1**: Severe Community-Acquired Pneumonia, **CD2**: Chronic Obstructive Pulmonary Disease (COPD) Exacerbated by Respiratory Infection, **CD3**: Nosocomial Pneumonia, **CD4**: Diabetic Ketoacidosis, **CD5**: Brain Contusion, **CD6**: Posttraumatic Subarachnoid Hemorrhage (SAH), **CD7**: Urinary infection, **CD8**: Bacterial Meningoencephalitis, **CD9**: Weil's síndrome, and **CD10**: SPO for craniectomy and evacuation of subdural hematoma.

4.1 Case Study Data

Table 1 summarizes the characteristics of the original CDs. They vary in size (39 to 548 examples), number of attributes (20 to 46), and present different levels of imbalance in the binary target variable ('Deceased'), from minimal (e.g., CD1, Ratio = 2.36) to severe (e.g., CD4, Ratio = 6.80). They all share four numerical attributes (Age,

Stay, Ventilation Time, Apache Score), three common categorical attributes (Sex, Race, Ventilation Equipment), and specific binary variables.

Table 1. Summary of Characteristics of the Original Data Sets.

Dataset	No. Exs	No. Attr	No Cat. Attr	Positive Class Proportion ("Deceased" = 1)	Imbalance Ratio	Type of Imbalance
CD1	548	24	20	0.30	2.36	Minimum
CD2	216	26	22	0.17	4.68	Severe
CD3	548	21	17	0.30	2.36	Minimum
CD4	117	26	20	0.12	6.80	Severe
CD5	206	20	16	0.32	2.12	Minimum
CD6	206	39	35	0.32	2.12	Minimum
CD7	239	33	29	0.37	1.68	Minimum
CD8	39	24	20	0.25	2.90	Minimum
CD9	69	34	30	0.26	2.83	Minimum
CD10	206	46	42	0.32	2.12	Minimum
Approx. Average	239	29	25	0.27	2.99	Minimum

4.2 Application of the Methodology

- **Preparation**: The high initial quality of the data (see 3.1) obviated the need for further cleaning.
- **Imbalance Management**: Five oversampling techniques (Random Oversampling, SMOTE, Borderline SMOTE, ADASYN, SMOTE RSB* Adapted) were applied to each CD. TabDSFidelity was calculated for the resulting 50 sets. The highest-scoring technique was selected for each original CD. Across the ten datasets, the techniques with the best fidelity were SMOTE RSB Adapted and ADASYN (selected three times each), followed by Random Oversampling (twice), and finally SMOTE and Borderline SMOTE (once each). This suggests that for some data sets, simple replication was sufficient or even preferable to more complex synthetic methods at this stage. All 10 selected balanced sets achieved an imbalance ratio close to 1.
- **Generation and Selection of Synthetic Data**: The three generative methods (SMOTE RSB* Adaptive + Gaussian Noise, CTGAN, and TVAE) were applied to each of the 10 selected balanced ensembles, generating an additional 10,000 synthetic samples in each case. The resulting 30 synthetic ensembles (3 for each original CD) were evaluated using TabDSFidelity, comparing each pair to its respective original reference set. The SMOTE RSB* Adapted with Gaussian Noise method was selected as the optimal generator on 9 of the 10 datasets, consistently obtaining the highest

TabDSFidelity score. Notably, for the CD9 dataset, TVAE obtained the best score, proving to be a competitive alternative. CTGAN was not the preferred method in any of the cases evaluated in this study. This suggests that while the domain-adapted approach with noise addition outperformed deep learning approaches in this case study, VAE-based models can excel in certain scenarios.

4.3 Impact Assessment on the Classification Model

To validate the ultimate benefit of the methodology and ensure a rigorous evaluation free from data leakage, a strict separation protocol was implemented.

Step 1: Primary Data Partition. For each of the 10 datasets, the original dataset was divided into a training partition (75%) and a test partition (25%). The test partition was kept completely isolated and used only in the final evaluation of the predictive model, without participating in any prior data selection or generation stages.

Step 2: Technique Selection within the Training Partition. The entire methodology described in Sect. 3 was applied exclusively to the training partition (75% of the original data). To select the most appropriate technique (both balancing and generation), each candidate dataset was evaluated using the TabDSFidelity metric.

- To calculate the Predictive Utility components (AUC, F1, Accuracy) of the TabDS-Fidelity metric, each candidate set (either balanced or synthetic) was partitioned into training (75%) and test (25%) subsets.
- A standard classifier (Random Forest) was trained using the training subset (75% of the generated set) and evaluated on its corresponding test subset (25% of the generated set).
- The results guided the selection of the best technique, without ever using the final test partition (25% of the original real data).

Step 3: Training and Final Evaluation. Finally, three Neural Network models (Multi-layer Perceptron with two hidden layers of 50 and 25 neurons, respectively. The activation function for the hidden layers was ReLU, and the Adam optimizer was used for training) were trained and evaluated only on the previously unseen (real) test partition:

- **Original Model**: Trained on the original training partition (75%).
- **Balanced Model**: Trained on the training partition (75%) after applying the best balancing technique selected by TabDSFidelity.
- **Synthetic Model**: Trained on an augmented version of the training partition, consisting of the original training data (75%) plus the 10,000 samples from the selected best synthetic set.

Table 2 summarizes the average comparative performance of these three models on the isolated test partition.

Table 2. Average Performance of the Neural Network Model on the 10 CDs.

Dataset	AUC-ROC	F1-score	Accuracy
Original	0.557	0.593	0.646
Balanced (selected as the Best)	0.560	0.588	0.597
Synthetic (selected as the Best)	0.660	0.653	0.645
% Improvement (Synthetic vs Original)	+22.35%	+12.62%	+2.25%

The results, averaged across the ten datasets, show a clear benefit from applying the full methodology. Training with the synthetic sets selected by TabDSFidelity produced an average increase in AUC-ROC of 22.35% and F1-score of 12.62% compared to using the original data. While the improvement was not uniform across all datasets, these averages indicate a robust positive trend and validate the overall effectiveness of the approach in overcoming the limitations of sparse and imbalanced data.

4.4 Fidelity Analysis of Synthetic Data

In addition to quantitative metrics such as TabDSFidelity and model performance, we performed visual analyses comparing the distributions of key variables between the original data and synthetic data generated by the optimal method (SMOTE RSB* Adapted with Gaussian Noise). For example, for CD1, the distribution of 'Apache Score' (numeric) in the synthetic data maintained a similar shape to the original, while the distribution of 'Deceased' (target) reflected the intentionally introduced class balancing. These visualizations suggest that the synthetic data capture important features of the original data, contributing to realism.

5 Discussion

The results of this study provide several key insights into the generation and evaluation of tabular synthetic data in a real-life medical context.

First, in the class balancing stage, a key finding is the diversity of techniques selected as optimal by the TabDSFidelity metric. Across the ten datasets, the techniques with the best fidelity were SMOTE RSB* Adapted and ADASYN (selected 3 times each), followed by Random Oversampling (2 times), and finally SMOTE and Borderline SMOTE (1 time each). This variety underscores that there is no single universal solution to class imbalance. This heterogeneity in selection validates the sensitivity of the TabDSFidelity metric, demonstrating its ability to guide a data-driven decision toward the most appropriate balancing approach for each particular scenario.

Second, at the large-scale synthetic data generation stage, the SMOTE RSB* Adapted with Gaussian Noise technique demonstrated overall superiority over the evaluated deep learning approaches (CTGAN and TVAE). Several reasons could explain this: (a) Explicit domain adaptation and constraint enforcement in the modified SMOTE method may have been crucial to generate realistic and useful data in the specific medical context. (b) The combination of local interpolation (SMOTE) with controlled noise addition could offer a good balance between preserving local structure and generating diversity. (c) The datasets, although augmented by balancing, might not have been large or complex enough for the deep learning models to fully learn the underlying distribution. Notably, for the CD9 dataset, TVAE scored the best, proving to be a competitive alternative. CTGAN did not turn out to be the preferred method in any of the cases evaluated in this study.

Central to our methodology is the role of the TabDSFidelity quality function. By integrating distribution similarity, correlation preservation, and predictive utility metrics, it provided a unified and objective criterion for selection at each stage. To address the influence of weights on the metric, a sensitivity analysis was performed comparing three weighting schemes: (1) the one used in this study, which prioritizes predictive utility (weights of 2 for AUC, F1, and Accuracy), (2) a balanced weighting (all weights equal to 1), and (3) one that prioritizes statistical fidelity (weights of 2 for both distribution and correlation metrics). The results revealed two key findings. First, SMOTE RSB* Adapted with Gaussian Noise was selected as the superior method in 28 of the 30 evaluated scenarios. Second, the selection of the optimal balancing technique proved to be sensitive to the weights, validating the flexibility of the TabDSFidelity metric. For example, by prioritizing predictive utility, more complex techniques such as ADASYN (which focuses on hard-to-learn samples) and the adapted SMOTE RSB* variant were favored. Conversely, by giving more weight to statistical fidelity, the selection leaned toward methods that better preserve the original structure, such as simple Random Oversampling or the constrained version SMOTE RSB* Adapted. This sensitivity confirms that TabDSFidelity functions as an effective guidance tool, capable of adapting to different research objectives. Therefore, our initial choice of weights is justified by the explicit objective of this work: to maximize the performance of the final classification model.

Finally, the analysis of the impact on the classification model reveals the practical effectiveness and nuances of the methodology. The key finding is the substantial, average improvement in performance: a 22.35% increase in AUC-ROC improves the classifier from near-chance performance to providing predictions with useful and clinically applicable predictive power. However, a deeper analysis of the results by dataset is revealing. While the methodology produced dramatic improvements in most cases, a decrease in performance is observed in two of the ten datasets (CD2 and CD8). Interestingly, these two datasets start from relatively high original AUC-ROC values (0.659 and 0.714).

In contrast, on sets with weaker signals (e.g., CD1, AUC = 0.429), synthetic data generation had a transformative impact. This underscores that the proposed methodology is a tool whose greatest benefit is obtained in scenarios with greater data sparsity and weak predictive signals, which are precisely the most challenging in medical research. The stability of the Accuracy metric, along with the increase in the F1 score, confirms that the improvement is due to better identification of the minority class and not simple bias.

6 Conclusion and Future Work

This work presents a methodology for the generation and evaluation of tabular synthetic data, designed to address the common challenges of data sparsity and class imbalance, with empirical validation in the challenging context of Intensive Care Units. The proposed methodology integrates stages of data preparation, class balancing through oversampling, and synthetic data generation using approaches based on both adapted variants of SMOTE (SMOTE RSB* with Gaussian Noise) and deep learning (including CTGAN and TVAE), and a thorough evaluation guided by a unified quality metric.

The results of the case study on 10 ICU datasets demonstrate the overall effectiveness of the methodology. Applying the proposed approach resulted in significant average improvements, with increases of over 22% in AUC-ROC and 12% in F1-score compared to training using only the original data. Although effectiveness may vary depending on the characteristics of the initial dataset, the strong positive trend demonstrates that the methodology is a robust framework for mitigating the limitations imposed by data scarsity and imbalance, facilitating the development of more accurate and reliable machine learning models in critical domains.

Future Work. A promising avenue for future work is the more formal integration of domain knowledge. Exploring the use of ontologies or knowledge graphs to actively guide generation could further improve the robustness and reliability of generated synthetic data, especially in high risk applications such as medicine.

Acknowledgements. This work was made possible thanks to the support of the "Platform for Decision Support Services in Critical Care Units" and "Theoretical contributions to AI in handling problems with complex data" under the National Program of Science, Technology and Innovation in Automation, Robotics, and Artificial Intelligence, CUBA projects.

References

1. Velasco-López, J.-E., Carrasco, R.-A., Cobo, M.J., Fernández-Avilés, G.: Data-driven scientific research based on public statistics: a bibliometric perspective (2023)
2. Yang, S., Berdine, G.: 'Small' sample size. Southwest Respiratory and Critical Care Chronicles **11**, 52–55 (2023). https://doi.org/10.12746/swrccc.v11i49.1251
3. Ibrahim, H., Liu, X., Zariffa, N., Morris, A.D., Denniston, A.K.: Health data poverty: an assailable barrier to equitable digital health care. Lancet Digital Health **3**(4), e260–e265 (2021). https://doi.org/10.1016/S2589-7500(20)30317-4
4. Sufi, F.: Addressing data scarcity in the medical domain: a GPT-Based approach for synthetic data generation and feature extraction. Accessed: 22 Mar 2025. https://www.mdpi.com/2078-2489/15/5/264
5. Buda, M., Maki, A., Mazurowski, M.A.: A systematic study of the class imbalance problem in convolutional neural networks. Neural Netw. **106**, 249–259 (2018). https://doi.org/10.1016/j.neunet.2018.07.011
6. Wang, Y., Gan, W., Yang, J., Wu, W., Yan, J.: Dynamic curriculum learning for imbalanced data classification. 15 Aug 2019. arXiv: arXiv:1901.06783. https://doi.org/10.48550/arXiv.1901.06783
7. James, S., Harbron, C., Branson, J., Sundler, M.: Synthetic data use: exploring use cases to optimise data utility. Discover Artificial Intelligence **1** (2021). https://doi.org/10.1007/s44163-021-00016-y
8. Xu, L., Skoularidou, M., Cuesta-Infante, A., Veeramachaneni, K.: Modeling tabular data using conditional GAN. arXiv:1907.00503 [cs, stat], Accessed: 19 Feb 2025 (2019). http://arxiv.org/abs/1907.00503

9. Guo, X., Chen, Y.: Generative AI for synthetic data generation: methods, challenges and the future. 07 Mar 2024. arXiv: arXiv:2403.04190. https://doi.org/10.48550/arXiv.2403.04190
10. Zhang, Y., Zaidi, N.: (PDF) GANBLR: a tabular data generation model. Accessed: 02 Apr 2025. https://www.researchgate.net/publication/356159733_GANBLR_A_Tabular_Data_G eneration_Model
11. Wen, B., Colon, L.O., Subbalakshmi, K.P., Chandramouli, R.: Causal-TGAN: generating tabular data using causal generative adversarial networks. 21 Apr 2021. arXiv: arXiv:2104.10680. https://doi.org/10.48550/arXiv.2104.10680
12. Fernández, A., García, S., Galar, M., Prati, R.C., Krawczyk, B., Herrera, F.: Learning from Imbalanced Data Sets. Springer (2018)
13. Haibo, H., Yang, B., Garcia, E.A., Shutao, L.: ADASYN: adaptive synthetic sampling approach for imbalanced learning. In: 2008 IEEE International Joint Conference on Neural Networks (IEEE World Congress on Computational Intelligence), Hong Kong, China: IEEE, pp. 1322–1328 (2008). https://doi.org/10.1109/IJCNN.2008.4633969
14. Han, H., Wang, W.-Y., Mao, B.-H.: Borderline-SMOTE: a new over-sampling method in imbalanced data sets learning. In: Advances in Intelligent Computing, vol. 3644, Huang, D.-S., Zhang, X.-P., Huang, G.-B. (eds.). Lecture Notes in Computer Science, vol. 3644. , Berlin, Heidelberg: Springer Berlin Heidelberg, pp. 878–887 (2005). https://doi.org/10.1007/11538059_91
15. Jävergård, N., Lyons, R., Muntean, A., Forsman, J.: Preserving correlations: a statistical method for generating synthetic data. 11 Nov 2024. arXiv: arXiv:2403.01471. https://doi.org/10.48550/arXiv.2403.01471
16. Hansen, L., Seedat, N.: Reimagining synthetic tabular data generation through data-centric AI: a comprehensive benchmark.
17. Hernandez, M., Epelde, G., Alberdi, A., Cilla, R., Rankin, D.: Synthetic tabular data evaluation in the health domain covering resemblance, utility, and privacy dimensions. Methods of Information in Medicine 62 (2023). https://doi.org/10.1055/s-0042-1760247
18. Yan, C., Zhang, Z., Nyemba, S., Li, Z.: Generating synthetic electronic health record data using generative adversarial networks: a tutorial (Preprint). JMIR AI 3 (2023). https://doi.org/10.2196/52615
19. Hernandez, M., Epelde, G., Alberdi, A., Cilla, R., Rankin, D.: Synthetic data generation for tabular health records: a systematic review. Neurocomputing 493, 28–45 (2022). https://doi.org/10.1016/j.neucom.2022.04.053
20. Pezoulas, V.C., et al.: Synthetic data generation methods in healthcare: a review on open-source tools and methods. Comput. Struct. Biotechnol. J. 23, 2892–2910 (2024). https://doi.org/10.1016/j.csbj.2024.07.005
21. Rashidi, H.H., Albahra, S., Rubin, B.P., Hu, B.: A novel and fully automated platform for synthetic tabular data generation and validation. Scientific Reports. Accessed: 22 Mar 2025. https://www.nature.com/articles/s41598-024-73608-0
22. Vero, M., Balunović, M., Vechev, M.: CuTS: customizable tabular synthetic data generation. 02 Jun 2024. arXiv: arXiv:2307.03577. https://doi.org/10.48550/arXiv.2307.03577
23. Miura, T., Kimura, E., Ichikawa, A., Kii, M., Yamamoto, J.: Evaluating synthetic data generation techniques for medical dataset. In: Proceedings of the 17th International Joint Conference on Biomedical Engineering Systems and Technologies, Rome, Italy: SCITEPRESS - Science and Technology Publications, pp. 315–322 (2024). https://doi.org/10.5220/0012314500003657
24. Chereddy, N.V., Bolla, B.K.: Evaluating the utility of GAN generated synthetic tabular data for class balancing and low resource settings. In: Multi-disciplinary Trends in Artificial Intelligence, vol. 14078, Morusupalli, R., Dandibhotla, T.S., Atluri, V.V., Windridge, D., Lingras, P., Komati, V.R. (eds.). in Lecture Notes in Computer Science, vol. 14078, Cham: Springer Nature Switzerland, pp. 48–59 (2023). https://doi.org/10.1007/978-3-031-36402-0_4

25. Bastida, M.D., López, A.C., Font, A.C.: Software para el análisis de datos en el Servicio de Cuidados Intensivos. Acta Médica del Centro **18**(1), 1 (2024)
26. Ali, H., Salleh, M., Saedudin, R., Talpur, K., Mushtaq, M.: Imbalance class problems in data mining: a review. Indonesian J. Electr. Eng. Comput. Sci. **14** (2019). https://doi.org/10.11591/ijeecs.v14.i3.pp1552-1563
27. Ramentol, E., Caballero, Y., Bello, R., Herrera, F.: SMOTE-RSB *: a hybrid preprocessing approach based on oversampling and undersampling for high imbalanced data-sets using SMOTE and rough sets theory. Knowl. Inf. Syst. **33**(2), 245–265 (2012). https://doi.org/10.1007/s10115-011-0465-6

Fast Continuous Wavelet Transform (fCWT) at the Edge: Enabling the fCWT Computation in ARM Cortex Cores

Alejandro Perdomo-Campos[1]([⊠])[ID], Alejandro Iglesias Gutiérrez[2][ID], Jaime E. Chiang Cruz[3][ID], and Jorge Ramírez-Beltrán[3][ID]

[1] Center for Microelectronics Research, Technological University of Havana "José Antonio Echeverría", 114 e/Ciclovía & Rotonda, Marianao, Havana, Cuba
`aperdomoc@tele.cujae.edu.cu`
[2] Faculty of Telecommunication and Electronic Engineering, Technological University of Havana "José Antonio Echeverría", 114 e/Ciclovía & Rotonda, Marianao, Havana, Cuba
[3] Center for Hydraulic Research, Technological University of Havana "José Antonio Echeverría", 114 e/Ciclovía & Rotonda, Marianao, Havana, Cuba

Abstract. In this paper a new embedded software package for efficiently computing the Continuous Wavelet Transform (CWT) in ARM Cortex cores, based on the original fast Continuous Transform (fCWT) algorithmic implementation is introduced. To execute the operations in ARM Cortex cores efficiently, the generic C++ implementation of the fCWT was adapted to a CMSIS-DSP based implementation in order to exploit the capabilities of the floating point unit (FPU) and the DSP instructions set with SIMD capabilities of ARM Cortex-M and Cortex-A cores. The package can be used for Continuous Wavelet Transform based feature extraction in edge computing signal processing applications that involve ARM based microcontroller families. A functional verification and a specific application oriented performance measurement approach in terms of real-time analysis ratio (RAR) for embedded processors is provided.

Keywords: Continuous Wavelet Transform · edge computing · ARM

1 Introduction

The wavelet transform has become a powerful mathematical tool in modern signal analysis. As it employs localized, finite-duration waveforms as the basis for signal decomposition, it enables simultaneous time-frequency analysis, offering high versatility in addressing the limitations of traditional Fourier-based methods. This unique capability has proven indispensable for analyzing non-stationary signals where transient features, abrupt changes, or multi-scale phenomena demand adaptive analytical techniques. Over recent decades, wavelet

Y. Hernádez Heredia et al. (Eds.): IWAIPR 2025, LNCS 16328, pp. 374–385, 2026.
https://doi.org/10.1007/978-3-032-11358-0_31

theory has catalyzed advancements in diverse applications, from image compression and noise reduction to real-time sensor data processing [4].

According to the way in which the dilation and translation parameters of the wavelet transform are discretized to achieve the wavelet domain representation of a signal, wavelet transforms are defined using two main approaches: the Discrete Wavelet Transform (DWT) and the Continuous Wavelet Transform (CWT) [1]. The DWT, grounded in dyadic scaling, decompose signals into approximation and detail coefficients using a discretization approach that allows to describe a function by the minimal possible number of coefficients, resulting in a lower computational complexity. Its computational efficiency and non-redundant representation make it ideal for applications like signal denoising. Other approaches like the Wavelet Packet Transform (WPT) extend the DWT by recursively decomposing both approximation and detail coefficients, offering adaptive frequency band partitioning for enhanced feature extraction in classification tasks, such as fault diagnosis in mechanical systems. However, a more detailed representation of the signal is often needed in several applications to achieve proper resolution in signal analysis. In these cases, it is possible to define a wavelet transform with arbitrary discretization, in which case it is called a Continuous Wavelet Transform (CWT). This provides a more redundant but richly detailed time-frequency representation suited for detecting transient phenomena in signals [7].

The computational implementation of wavelet transforms has diversified into several approaches in the last decades since the evolution of wavelet theory. As algorithms for computing wavelet transforms are computationally expensive, their implementation in resource-constrained edge devices like microcontrollers has always been a challenge. Despite this, wavelet transforms have been implemented in microcontroller-based platforms in several applications with the DWT as the predominant approach, due to its lower computational load [9].

Among the most widely adopted microcontroller core architectures for signal processing in edge computing applications are the ARM Cortex-M series, Texas Instruments' MSP430, Microchip's PIC, and Atmel's AVR architectures. Traditional 8/16-bit architectures like AVR or PIC, while energy-efficient, often lack the arithmetic throughput required for real-time multi-resolution analysis, relegating them to simpler tasks. In the case of MSP430, despite having powerful hardware resources for signal processing like the Low Energy Accelerator (LEA), exploited in wavelet transform implementations like the one developed in [9], may be limited for some applications due to its 16-bit architecture, which affects the resolution of data and makes floating point operations difficult. On the other hand, ARM Cortex-M cores, particularly the Cortex-M4 and M7 variants, have gained prominence due to their 32-bit architectures, powerful hardware resources for accelerating operations and enhanced clock speeds, which enable the efficient execution of computationally intensive algorithms [6].

In 2010 ARM introduced CMSIS-DSP, an open-source software library that implements common compute processing functions optimized for use on ARM Cortex-M and Cortex-A processors. The library is freely available as part of the CMSIS release from ARM and includes basic and complex math functions, filters and transforms, exploiting the specific features of the ARM Cortex architectures to accelerate operations. The routines have been optimized to take advantage of the digital signal processing (DSP) extensions, single instruction multiple data (SIMD) capabilities and floating point units (FPU) found in the Cortex-M and Cortex-A processors, including support for the Helium M-Profile Vector Extension (MVE) and Neon advanced single instruction multiple data (SIMD) architecture extension [6].

Some recent works found in literature where computationally expensive signal processing algorithms like the Short-Time Fourier Transform (STFT) and the Discrete Wavelet Transform (DWT) are implemented in ARM Cortex-M cores are [3,8]. However, few works can be found where the Continuous Wavelet Transform (CWT) is implemented. The ones found, provide little detail about their implementation. For instance, Hasanpoor et al. implement a CWT for feature extraction in an ARM Cortex-M based microcontroller for real-time stress detection, but provide no insights about their implementation of the CWT [5].

The most efficient implementation of the CWT that can be found in literature was proposed by Arts and van den Broek in [2], named the fast Continuous Wavelet Transform (fCWT), which is open-source and available for execution in high-level C++ and Python environments. The main contribution of this paper is the adaptation of this fCWT algorithmic implementation to enable the efficient computation of the Continuous Wavelet Transform in ARM Cortex cores, proposing a new open-source and hardware-specific oriented software package. The embedded software package uses the CMSIS-DSP kernels for efficiently computing the operations defined in the original fCWT implementation in generic C++, oriented to be executed on high-performance operating systems. In addition to this, some dependent steps in the fCWT computing pipeline were separated in order to facilitate the reuse of non-varying data and shorten the number of operations in continuous real time embedded signal processing loops.

2 Overview on the Fast Continuous Wavelet Transform (fCWT)

2.1 Mathematical Overview on the Continuous Wavelet Transform

The Continuous Wavelet Transform (CWT) of a signal is defined as:

$$W_\psi(a, b) = w(a) \int_{-\infty}^{\infty} x(t)\psi^* \left(\frac{t - b}{a} \right) dt \tag{1}$$

where a is the dilation parameter and b is the translation parameter. These allow to perform the two basic manipulations that make wavelets more flexible for time-frequency analysis. On the other hand, $w(a)$ is a weighting function, typically set to $1/\sqrt{a}$ for reasons of energy conservation as it ensures that the wavelets at every scale all have the same energy. However, $w(a) = 1/a$ or $w(a) = 1/|a|$ are sometimes used. The $*$ indicates that the complex conjugate of the wavelet function is used in the transform [1].

Using the weighting function $w(a) = |a|^{-1}$ Eq. 1 may be rewritten as:

$$W_\psi(a, b) = |a|^{-1} \int_{-\infty}^{\infty} x(t)\psi^* \left(\frac{t - b}{a}\right) dt \tag{2}$$

For discrete time signals, Eq. 2 adopts the form:

$$W_\psi[a, b] = |a|^{-1} \sum_{n=0}^{N-1} x[n]\psi^* \left[\frac{n - b}{a}\right] \tag{3}$$

Computing wavelet transforms in digital systems using Eq. 3 results highly computational expensive [2]. A considerable reduction in computational complexity can be achieved by using Parseval's theorem. A Fourier-based wavelet transform equation can be written by applying Parseval's theorem to Eq. 2.

$$W_\psi[a, b] = \frac{1}{2\pi} \int_{-\infty}^{\infty} X(f)\Psi^*(f)df \tag{4}$$

Then, $\Psi^{(}f)$ may be defined in terms of the Fourier Transform of the mother wavelet function $\psi(t)$ using its time-shifting and time-scaling properties as:

$$\Psi^{(}f) = \frac{1}{a}\psi(f)e^{-ibf} = \psi(af)e^{-ibf} \tag{5}$$

Substituting in Eq. 4 it is obtained:

$$W_\psi[a, b] = \frac{1}{2\pi} \int_{-\infty}^{\infty} X(f)\psi^*(af)e^{ibf}df \tag{6}$$

This representation can be seen to have the form of an inverse Fourier Transform. In discrete time this may be written as:

$$W_\psi[a, b] = \frac{1}{K} \sum_{k=0}^{K-1} X(k)\psi^*(ak)e^{i2\pi bk/K} \tag{7}$$

This equation describes the CWT $W[a, b]$ as the inverse Discrete Fourier Transform (DFT) of $X(k)\psi^*(ak)$, which can be computed in digital systems efficiently using the inverse FFT algorithm. Moreover, this way the Wavelet Transform computational complexity no longer depends on the translation parameter b.

Based on Eq. 7, the DFT of the signal $X(k)$ can be calculated beforehand, and the computation of the CWT reduces to 3 distinct steps per scale [2]:

1. Generate $\psi^*(ak)$
2. Calculate $X(k)\psi^*(ak)$
3. Compute the inverse DFT and obtain $W_\psi[a, b]$.

2.2   The Fast Continuous Wavelet Transform (fCWT) Implementation

The fCWT algorithm separates scale-independent and scale-dependent operations, which have to be performed separately for each wavelet's scale. A detailed schematic of this algorithmic implementation for a given number of M scales is provided in Fig. 1, taken from the original work presenting the fCWT implementation [2].

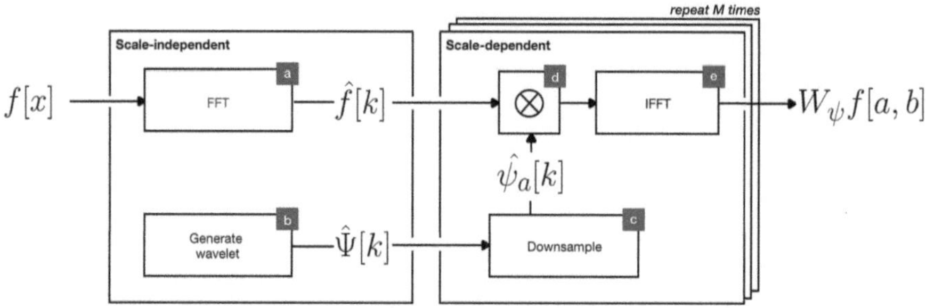

Fig. 1. Block diagram of the algorithmic implementation of the fCWT [2].

As depicted in Fig. 1, the algorithmic implementation behind fCWT can be divided into: i) scale-independent and ii) scale-dependent operations.

The scale-independent operations are performed first as their result forms the input for the scale-dependent steps. Two functions are pre-calculated: the input signal's FFT and the FFT of the mother wavelet function at scale $a_0 = 2$. Both functions are independent of the scale factor a, so they can be pre-calculated and used as look-up tables in the processing pipeline.

The scale-dependent operations each calculate the wavelet coefficients of a single scale-factor in the final time–frequency matrix. By repeating the scale-dependent part $m = |a|$ times, the time–frequency matrix is build up one row at a time. The fCWT implementation focuses on the optimization of this scale-dependent stage by exploiting its repeated nature and high parallelizability.

A pseudocode describing the fCWT implementation in a more detailed manner is provided in Algorithm 1.

The optimization strategies used by the fCWT algorithmic implementation highlighted in [2] include: writing the complex-valued FT to memory in an interleaving format to exploit the CPU's predictive caching behavior and hence reduce memory access in the next steps; generating the mother wavelet function at scale $a_0 = 2$ from start to save memory as scales must be at least $a_{min} = 2$; using the mother wavelet as a look-up table to generate the daughter wavelets; using the float- and AVX2-enabled Fastest Fourier Transform in the West (FFTW) library to accelerate the FFT computations; using the single instruction, multiple data (SIMD) model to execute eight multiplications at once during the

---

Algorithm 1 Compute fast Continuous Wavelet Transform (fCWT)

Require: Signal x, number of samples N, sampling rate f_s, initial frequency f_0, final frequency f_{end}, number of scales M and wavelet Morlet bandwidth BW.

Ensure: Wavelet coefficients matrix W

    Pre-computing stage

    Compute set of scales $\{s_1, s_2, \ldots, s_M\}$

    Scale independent stage

    Pad the signal x to length L corresponding to the next power of 2 to obtain x_{pad}

    Compute the FFT of the padded signal: $X \leftarrow \text{FFT}(x_{\text{pad}})$

    Generate mother wavelet Ψ in the frequency domain of the same length as X

    Scale dependent stage

    for each scale $s \in \{s_1, s_2, \ldots, s_M\}$ **do**

        Generate the Fourier transform ψ_a of the wavelet ψ at scale s

        Compute element-wise product: $W_s \leftarrow X \odot \psi_a^*$ $\{\psi_a^*$ is the complex conjugate$\}$

        Compute inverse FFT: $w_s \leftarrow \text{IFFT}(W_s)$

        Store w_s in W as coefficients for scale s

    end for

    return W {Matrix of wavelet coefficients (M × N)}

---

elemental-wise multiplication between ψ_a^* and $f[k]$; merging the generation of the daughter wavelet and the multiplication with $f[k]$ in one loop to eliminate memory access and using a pre-calculated optimization based on the input signal's zero-padded length in the computation of the inverse FFT.

In order to provide a complete brief description of the fCWT original implementation, it is important to point out that it does not include any of the boundary-handling strategies commonly used to mitigate the boundary effects of the CWT, leaving boundary strategy selection to the user. This approach maintains algorithmic independence from implicit assumptions.

3 Description of the Embedded Software Package for Computing the fCWT Algorithm in ARM Cortex Cores

In order to enable the fCWT computation in ARM Cortex cores, the original fCWT implementation introduced in [2] was adapted by translating all the vectorial operations and signal processing routines in the processing pipeline to a CMSIS-DSP based implementation. The new library was designed following an embedded C style, transforming the high-level object oriented approach used in the original C++ implementation of the fCWT. The use of the kernels available in the CMSIS DSP driver for the fCWT computation allowed to execute the operations on vectors with high computational efficiency.

3.1 Package Organization

The library is made up by three components: the independent *wavelet* and *scales* packages and the *cwt* package which depends on the former two. Each of them provides a set of functions implementing the different operations needed for the computation of the fCWT using a modular approach.

The *wavelet* package defines a set of structures to handle wavelets and complex values, and the functions to initialize these structures and generate a mother wavelet in the frequency domain. Following the original implementation of the fCWT, the Morlet wavelet is used, so the package provides a special structure and functions to handle Morlet wavelets in addition to the general Wavelet structure. For the Morlet case, the library includes a function dedicated to initialize the values to use as a look-up table in the fCWT processing pipeline. The values are generated according to the definition of the wavelet Morlet in the frequency domain given in [1]. Equation 8 shows this definition of the Fourier Transform of the Morlet wavelet, where f_0 is the central frequency.

$$\Psi(f) = \pi^{-1/4}\sqrt{2}e^{-\frac{1}{2}(2\pi f - 2\pi f_0)^2} \tag{8}$$

The routine that performs the Morlet wavelet generation is implemented in a computationally efficient way using the signal processing routines available in the CMSIS-DSP driver to operate on vectors.

Despite no other wavelets are included, these may be easily defined to satisfy other specific applications needs by using the general Wavelet structure. In this case the user would have to define the way to initialize the values for the wavelet vector in the frequency domain.

The *scales* package defines a structure to handle the scales to use in the computation of the fCWT and a set of functions to compute the scales. As in the original fCWT implementation, support for defining scales with linear and log steps is provided. This operations are independent from the mother wavelet initialization routines, allowing to use any mother wavelet defined with the defined set of scales.

The *cwt* package contains the set of functions that actually compute the CWT, using a pre-defined mother wavelet and set of scales. In the following subsection, the processing pipeline implemented and its use are explained.

3.2   The Embedded fCWT Computing Pipeline

The fCWT computing pipeline used in the *cwt* package is very similar to the original fCWT presented in Algorithm 1. However, adaptations were made to accelerate the computing process in ARM Cortex cores in real time signal processing applications. The pseudocode presented in Algorithm 2 shows the details of the adapted pipeline for the fCWT computation.

In the original fCWT implementation, every time a new CWT is computed, the Morlet mother wavelet is generated as part of the computing pipeline. In signal processing embedded applications where the delays and the number of operations are critical to ensure real time behavior, and signals are generally from the same nature and are processed in regular window sizes, this step becomes unnecessary. In this sense, in the proposed library, the mother wavelet generation is pulled out of the CWT processing pipeline, and is designed to be executed as

---

Algorithm 2 Compute fast Continuous Wavelet Transform (fCWT) in adapted pipeline oriented to execution in ARM Cortex cores

---

Require: Signal x, number of samples N, sampling rate f_s, initial frequency f_0, final frequency f_{end}, number of scales M and wavelet Morlet bandwidth BW.

Ensure: Wavelet coefficients matrix W

  Pre-computing stage

  Generate mother wavelet Ψ in the frequency domain of length equal to the next power of 2 of signal length N.

  Generate the set of scales $\{s_1, s_2, \ldots, s_M\}$

  Scale independent stage

  Pad the signal x to length L corresponding to the next power of 2 to obtain x_{pad}.

  Allocate memory for temporary buffers to store the intermediate results of the FFT and initialize with zero values.

  Compute the real FFT of the padded signal: $X \leftarrow \text{FFT}(x_{\text{pad}})$ using CMSIS-DSP optimized FFT kernel.

  Scale dependent stage

  for each scale $s \in \{s_1, s_2, \ldots, s_M\}$ **do**

    Generate the Fourier transform ψ_a of the daughter wavelet at scale s downsampling the mother wavelet by the corresponding scale factor.

    Compute element-wise product: $W_s \leftarrow X \odot \psi_a^*$ $\{\psi_a^*$ is the complex conjugate$\}$ using CMSIS-DSP optimized complex multiplication kernels.

    Compute and normalize complex inverse FFT: $w_s \leftarrow \text{IFFT}(W_s)$ using CMSIS-DSP optimized FFT kernel.

    Store w_s in W as coefficients for scale s

  end for

  return W $\{$Matrix of wavelet coefficients (M $\times$ N)$\}$

---

a "one-time" step during the pre-computing stage. This allows to reuse the same mother wavelet in real time signal processing loops that are present in most embedded applications, shortening the number of operations to execute every time a new signal window is processed.

Also, due to edge devices limitations of memory, in the adapted CWT computing pipeline, dynamic memory allocations made for temporary buffers to store intermediate results were replaced by static memory allocations inside the functions. This way, memory faults are avoided during execution time and the efficient use of memory is kept as the allocated memory taken from the stack is released every time the program finishes the corresponding subroutine.

The pseudocode in Algorithm 3 illustrates the steps to carry out in order to use the software package in a C based development framework for a typical real time signal processing application in which signal windows are constantly received and processed in real time. An example of use will be provided in the package repository.

Algorithm 3 Using the introduced package for CWT feature extraction in real time signal processing embedded applications

---

Require: Input signal stream x; constants defining number of samples N, sampling rate f_s, initial frequency f_0, final frequency f_{end}, number of scales M and wavelet Morlet bandwidth BW.

Ensure: Including the *cwt.h* header in the program file where CWT computation is performed.

    1. Allocate memory for the CWT output matrix and initialize with zero values.

    2. Define a wavelet Morlet object using the structure defined in *wavelet.h*.

    3. Initialize the wavelet Morlet object with values according to the number of samples N of the signals to analyze.

    4. Generate array containing the mother wavelet's Discrete Fourier Transform.

    5. Define a scales object using the structure defined in *scales.h*.

    6. Initialize the scales object generating the array with the values for the scales to use.

while new signal window is available to process **do**

    7. Perform CWT computation using the *cwt()* function in the *cwt.h* package.

    8. Compute the magnitude squares for the complex values in the CWT matrix obtained using the *arm_cmplx_mag_squared_f32()* optimized function.

    9. Use CWT energy values as feature matrix for further processing.

end while

    10. Release dynamically allocated memory.

return

---

4   Validation and Results

A series of experiments were conducted in order to validate the results obtained by using the fCWT embedded software package. The experiments consisted on computing the CWT for the same signal in a high-performance computer using the original fCWT package and in an ARM Cortex-M based microcontroller using the embedded software package in order to compare the results.

The fCWT Python wrapper was used to generate a Python script that takes an artificially generated signal, computes its CWT and plots the resulting CWT energy matrix. On the other hand, the embedded fCWT software package was evaluated in a STM32L432KC microcontroller, which is a 32-bit microcontroller from the low-power L4 series of STMicroelectronics based on the ARM Cortex-M4 core. As the ARM Cortex-M4, based on the Armv7E-M architecture is the lowest performance ARM Cortex core that includes a DSP extension and a floating-point unit (FPU), this was selected as the critical use case to test the fCWT embedded software package. Moreover, the STM32L432KC is a very resource-limited microcontroller able to run at a maximum clock frequency of 80 MHz, and containing just 256 kB of Flash memory and 64 kB of SRAM. This way, it becomes a restricted platform in terms of processing speed and memory availability compared to many ARM Cortex based platforms.

In order to compare the results obtained by the embedded fCWT software package and the original package, the same artificial signal used in the Python script for the fCWT computation was stored in the microcontroller's memory as a constant values array. A testing firmware was designed for the microcontroller in which the CWT of this signal is computed and the resulting energy matrix is sent by UART to the computer to be processed by a Python program that receives the computed matrix and plots the results.

Figure 2 shows an artificially generated signal, which is a sinusoidal chirp that increases its frequency over time between 50 Hz and 300 Hz. The signal was computed for a length of 256 samples, in order to fit the memory restrictions of the STM32L432KC microcontroller.

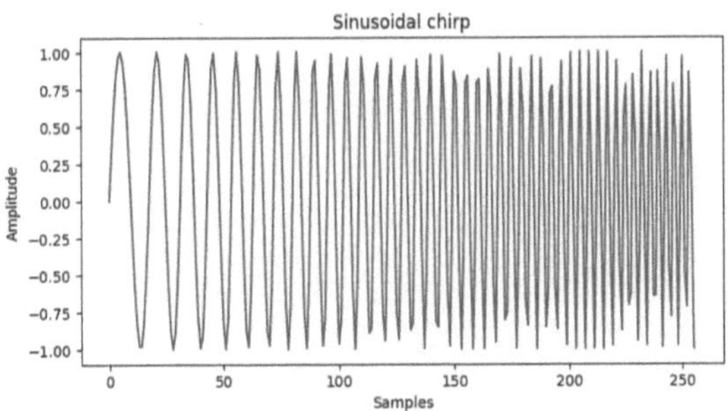

Fig. 2. Sinusoidal chirp signal used to evaluate the fCWT embedded software package.

Figure 3 shows the results for the experiment conducted on the sinusoidal chirp. It shows from top to bottom: the CWT matrix computed in the STM32L432KC microcontroller using the embedded software package introduced in this paper and the CWT matrix computed using the original fCWT package in a computer. The CWT in the images was computed for 25 scales using log steps between 50 Hz and 300 Hz.

It can be seen that the results are very similar, with small differences in the numerical values due to the differences in the way in which both platforms handle data alignment and bit-reversal, and the differences that may exist between the FFT implementation in CMSIS-DSP kernels and in the FFTW library used in the original fCWT.

Some measurements were carried out to evaluate the performance of the fCWT implementation on the STM32L432KC. By accessing the CYCCNT core register in the Data Watchpoint Trigger (DWT) module of the processors architecture it was measured the number of cycles it took the microcontroller to perform the CWT computation, which includes executing the *cwt()* routine and computing the magnitude squares for the CWT matrix.

The real-time analysis ratio (RAR) defined in [2] for embedded processors can be computed as:

$$RAR = \frac{\Delta t_{computation}}{\Delta t_{signal}} = \frac{Number\ of\ cycles\ to\ compute\ CWT \times 1/f_{CLK}}{Number\ of\ signal\ window\ samples \times 1/f_s} \quad (9)$$

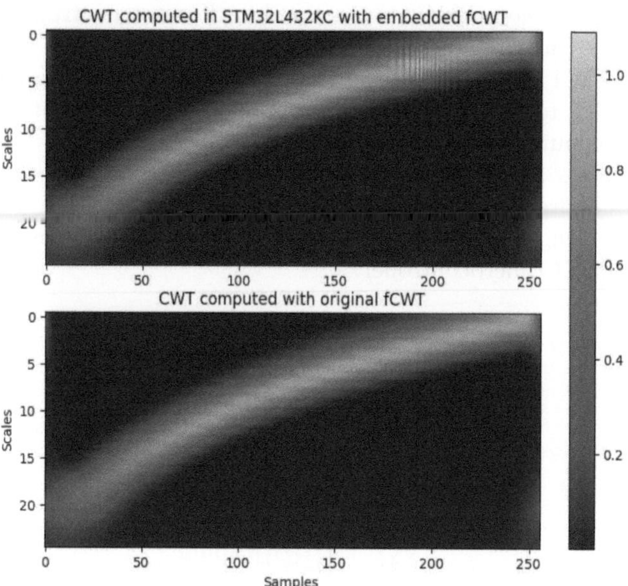

Fig. 3. CWT of sinusoidal chirp computed using the original fCWT library and the introduced embedded package for a signal length N=256 and a number of scales M=25.

where f_{CLK} is the processors operating clock frequency and f_s is the sample rate of the signals that are acquired by the embedded system in real time for processing.

As may be seen from this definition, the RAR analysis is completely platform and application dependent, as it depends on the number of scales and window sizes needed for the CWT computation and the processing and speed capabilities of the embedded system to use. For the experiment results shown in Fig. 3, according to the measured number of cycles, the RAR is:

$$RAR = \frac{1077696 \times 1/80\,MHz}{256 \times 1/f_s} \tag{10}$$

Which is below 1 for sampling frequencies below 19 kHz, indicating real time computation capability in a wide range of possible applications. This approach may be used as a reference to evaluate the embedded software package performance in specific applications where the parameters of the CWT computation and the hardware platform to use are well defined.

5   Conclusions

In this paper, a new embedded software package to compute the CWT in ARM Cortex cores using the fCWT algorithm was presented. Its implementation uses the routines available in the CMSIS-DSP kernel to execute the operations with computational efficiency and efficient use of memory. The results show that real time computation may be achieved in resource-constrained microcontrollers for sampling frequencies suitable for a broad range of applications.

The software package source code and the source files to reproduce the experiments will be put and maintained at the community's disposal under Apache License Version 2.0 in a public GitHub repository available at https://github.com/iesi-research/fCWT-for-ARM-Cortex.

Disclosure of Interests. The authors have no competing interests to declare that are relevant to the content of this article.

References

1. Addison, P.S.: The Illustrated Wavelet Transform Handbook: Introductory Theory and Applications in Science, Engineering, Medicine and Finance. CRC Press, Taylor and Francis Group, Boca Raton, FL, (2nd edn) (2017)
2. Arts, L.P.A., van den Broek, E.L.: The fast continuous wavelet transformation (fCWT) for real-time, high-quality, noise-resistant time-frequency analysis. Nat. Comput. Sci. **2**(1), 47–58 (2022). https://doi.org/10.1038/s43588-021-00183-z
3. Gragnaniello, M.: Real-Time myocardial infarction detection approaches with a microcontroller-based edge-AI device. Sensors **24**(3), 828 (2024). https://doi.org/10.3390/s24030828
4. Guo, T.: A Review of wavelet analysis and its applications: challenges and opportunities. IEEE Access **10**, 58869–58903 (2022). https://doi.org/10.1109/ACCESS.2022.3179517
5. Hasanpoor, Y., Rostami, A., Tarvirdizadeh, B., Alipour, K., Ghamari, M.: Real-Time stress detection via Photoplethysmogram signals: implementation of a combined Continuous wavelet transform and convolutional neural network on resource-constrained microcontrollers. In: 2024 32nd International Conference on Electrical Engineering (ICEE), pp. 1–5 (2024). https://doi.org/10.1109/ICEE63041.2024.10668302
6. Lorenser, T.: The DSP capabilities of ARM® Cortex®-M4 and Cortex-M7 Processors. Technical report, ARM (2016)
7. Łuczak, D.: Machine fault diagnosis through vibration analysis: continuous wavelet transform with complex Morlet wavelet and time-frequency RGB image recognition via convolutional neural network. Electronics **13**(2), 452 (2024). https://doi.org/10.3390/electronics13020452
8. Rodriguez, V.H., Medrano, C., Plaza, I.: A Real-Time QRS complex detector based on discrete wavelet transform and adaptive threshold as standalone application on ARM microcontrollers. In: 2018 International Conference on Biomedical Engineering and Applications (ICBEA), pp. 1–6 (2018). https://doi.org/10.1109/ICBEA.2018.8471741
9. Vega-Gonzalez, I., Ramírez-Beltrán, J.: Energy-Efficient wavelet transform implementation for fault diagnosis. In: Llanes-Santiago, O. (ed.) Proceedings of 19th Latin American Control Congress (LACC 2022), pp. 109–118. Springer International Publishing, Cham (2023). https://doi.org/10.1007/978-3-031-26361-3_10

Brain Mapping Through Entropic Analysis

Ania Mesa Rodríguez[1,2]($\boxtimes$) , Ernesto Estévez Rams[3] , Holger Kantz[1] ,
and Andy Abrahantes Acevedo[3]

[1] Max Planck Institute for the Physics of Complex Systems,
Noethnitzer Str. 38, 01187 Dresden, Germany
[2] Facultad de Matemática, Universidad de la Habana,
San Lázaro y L, 10400 Habana, Cuba
`ania@pks.mpg.de`
[3] Facultad de Física, Universidad de la Habana, San Lázaro y L, 10400 Habana, Cuba

Abstract. Understanding how information flows between different brain regions during cognitive processes is fundamental to neuroscience. In this work, we apply Information Theory to analyze brain activity under Motor task and Resting State using task-based fMRI data from the Human Connectome Project. Specifically, we employ a range of entropic tools—including Entropy Density, Effective Measure Complexity, and Informational Distance—to capture both linear and non-linear dynamics in brain connectivity. Unlike conventional methods that rely on predefined models or assumptions, our entropic approach does not assume specific underlying dynamics; instead, it captures the intrinsic complexity of the signals by quantifying randomness, structure, and the potential for creating novel patterns.

Keywords: entropy · complexity · fMRI · brain connectivity

1 Introduction

The brain's complexity spans microscopic to macroscopic scales, encompassing individual neurons, cortical columns, and large-scale networks. Mapping structural and functional connections—the connectome—helps us understand cognition, perception, emotion, and memory, as well as identify disruptions in clinical conditions. Traditional methods such as causal models and graph-theoretic approaches often rely on linear assumptions or specific prior knowledge. By contrast, entropy-based methods can reveal hidden or unexpected non-linear dynamics across different brain regions, making them well-suited for exploratory research.

In fMRI data analysis, numerous strategies have been applied to estimate direct interactions between brain regions. These include causal modeling [6,21], which relies on strong model assumptions and is generally unsuitable for exploratory work; Granger causality and the WAGS framework [5,21], both assuming linearity and stationarity and unable to detect instantaneous

Y. Hernádez Heredia et al. (Eds.): IWAIPR 2025, LNCS 16328, pp. 386–394, 2026.
https://doi.org/10.1007/978-3-032-11358-0_32

or nonlinear effects; spectral methods [16]; correlation and covariance analyses, which capture only linear relationships and are influenced by indirect links [20]; partial directed coherence [2], which also assumes linearity and is sensitive to model order and parameter estimates; graph-theoretical approaches [7], which are highly dependent on threshold choices; and community detection techniques [1], whose results vary with the selected algorithm and which may overlook overlapping or hierarchical structures, among others.

We propose a new method to analyze brain dynamics from an entropic perspective that does not rely on prior assumptions about the data, making it highly suited for exploratory studies and enabling the detection of previously unknown links or patterns in brain activity. Its ability to capture non-linear dynamics is particularly valuable for investigating brain connectivity, given the brain's pronounced non-linear interactions across various functional scales [13]. We tested our method on fMRI data from the Human Connectome Project, confirming its robustness and adaptability. By analyzing a motor task, we explore how entropy-based measures reflect the complexity of brain activity and the emergence of patterns in this cognitive state.

2   Materials Y Methods

Functional MRI data were taken from the Human Connectome Project [22] of subjects during the motor task. This task consists of showing visual cues to the participants, instructing them to either tap their left or right fingers, squeeze their left or right toes, or move their tongue, with the objective of analyzing the brain during these basic movements. Each movement block was preceded by a 3-s visual cue and lasted 12 s (consisting of 10 movements). In this study, we compare the level of brain activity during the motor task using the resting-state fMRI (rfMRI) scans as a baseline of activation. In this scan, the participants leave their minds in a blank with their eyes open, maintaining a relaxed fixation on a bright cross-hair projected onto a dark background in a dark room.

The data was preprocessed with the Human Connectome Project standard pre-processing pipeline to reduce movement distortions, remove noise and artifacts, spatial smoothing, and alignment to a standard brain template, among others, with the goal of making the data suitable for the analysis. The brain was parcellated into 360 regions of interest using the atlas of Glasser [14]; the first 180 regions correspond to the left hemisphere, while the remaining 180 represent the right hemisphere's homologous region.

The fMRI signals from each region were binarized about their mean value, creating discrete time series as shown in Fig. 1. For the posterior analysis of the time series three entropic measures were computed, the entropy density (h) which gauges the rate of new pattern creation, reflecting unpredictability [8,9], the effective measure complexity (E) which estimates the system's memory or redundancy by capturing persistent patterns in the data [12], and the information distance (d), which quantifies how similar or different two signals are in terms of their algorithmic or information-theoretic descriptions [11,24].

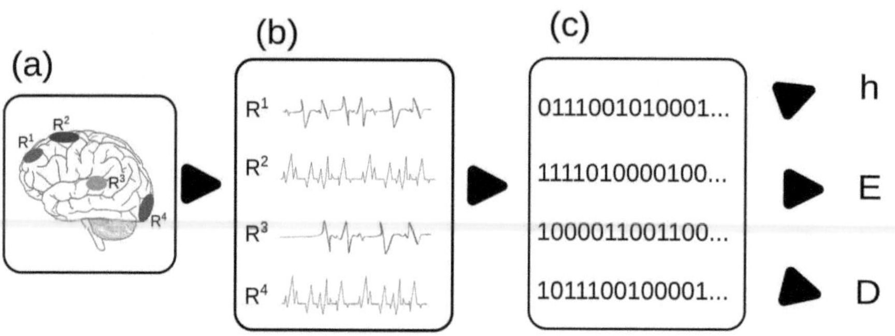

Fig. 1. **Analysis pipeline** (a) The brain was divided into Regions of Interest (ROIs), and (b) the time series from the fMRI measurements of each region (360 brain areas by the Glasser parcellation) were (c) discretized and further analyzed using entropic measures h: entropy density, E: Effective Measure Complexity and D: Lempel Ziv distance.

The Entropy density or Entropy rate, measures the amount of randomness or unpredictability when observing an infinitely long time series [8], calculated as:

$$h_\mu = \lim_{L \to \infty} \frac{H(L)}{L},$$ (1)

where $H(L) = -\sum p(s^L) \log p(s^L)$ is the block entropy over the probabilities $p(s^L)$ of a given subsequence s^L of length L in the time series. Summation is made over all possible sequences of length L [8].

On the other hand, as a complementary measure in many circumstances, the effective measure complexity is the mutual information between the two halves of an infinite time series [15], usually interpreted as the amount of information that one half has on the other half and therefore, measures the "apparent" memory or structuring of the system at all length scales. To estimate the effective measure complexity, we employ a related magnitude [9] which is based on the random shuffling of the data [10,18] usually referred to as Total Redundancy and expressed as follows:

$$E_r(S) = \sum_{k=1}^{\infty} [h_\mu^k(S_r) - h_\mu(S)]$$ (2)

Here, $h_\mu^k(S_r)$ represents the Entropy Density obtained by taking the chain S, partitioning it into units of size k, and randomizing it by blocks, the subscript r indicates the randomization of units of size k in S; while $h_\mu(S)$ denotes the Density Entropy of the original sequence S.

To avoid big computational cost, having to estimate the probability of appearance of each character in the sequence and avoid inaccuracy given that in practice, an infinite-length time series cannot be analyzed, we employ the Lempel Ziv complexity to estimate the entropy density. This has been proven to be a robust estimate even for short sequences [17]. The estimated entropy density will be denoted by h_{LZ} and the effective measure complexity by E_{LZ}.

The Lempel-Ziv Complexity is based on a specific factorization of a sequence, adding a new factor whenever a new pattern appears. A factorization of a sequence S of length N is defined as its partition into disjoint blocks:

$$F(S) = S(1, l_1), S(l_1 + 1, l_2), S(l_2 + 1, l_3), ..., S(l_{m-1} + 1, N)$$

The factorization $F(S)$ is called the Lempel-Ziv factorization or exhaustive history if each factor $S(l_{k-1} + 1, l_k)$ is not a substring of the string $S(1, l_k - 1)$, while $S(l_{k-1} + 1, l_k - 1)$ is a substring of $S(1, l_k - 2)$

As the exhaustive history for each sequence is unique [11], the Lempel-Ziv complexity of the sequence S can be defined as the number of factors in its exhaustive history and denoted as $C_{LZ}(S)$.

For example, given the sequence $S = 11011101000011$, its exhaustive history is $F(S) = 1.10.111.010.0001.1$, where each factor is delimited by a dot. This factorization contains 6 elements, so $C_{LZ}(S) = 6$.

Jacob Ziv demonstrated that if S is the output of an ergodic process with Entropy Density $h_\mu(S)$, then the following holds [24]:

$$\overline{\lim_{N \to \infty}} \frac{C_{LZ}(S)}{N / \log N} = h_\mu(S) \tag{3}$$

Equation (3) is valid in the infinite limit; however, in practice, it is used as an estimate of the Entropy Density.

As the Lempel-Ziv complexity is algorithmically computable, it is advantageous to use C_{LZ} to estimate the Entropy Density when $N \gg 1$ from a computational point of view.

These measures form "complexityâĂŞentropy maps" for identifying activated regions, and distance matrices for evaluating how regions cluster hierarchically. These distance matrices are calculated with the Lempel Ziv distance, which is a metric in terms of information coming from the Kolmogorov distance, which more than measuring how the two sequences differ point by point, it quantifies their informational similarity, determining the degree of correlation between them from an algorithmic perspective [11]:

$$d_{LZ}(S, Q) = \frac{C_{LZ}(SQ) - \min\{C_{LZ}(S), C_{LZ}(Q)\}}{\max\{C_{LZ}(S), C_{LZ}(Q)\}} \tag{4}$$

3   Results and Discussion

If we plot the relationship between entropy density and effective measure complexity for all brain regions involved in the experiment, we obtain the complexity-entropy map, which describes the level of unpredictability and creativity of the time series vs the level of structure at all length scales. In this sense, regions with strong activity present more patterns and structure given the increase of electric potential in response to the repeated stimuli, and hence, present lower entropy density and higher effective measure complexity in comparison to the rest of the areas.

The entropy map presented in Fig. 2 illustrates how different brain regions respond to motor tasks compared to the resting state by calculating the difference of h and E in both tasks. By using the resting state as a baseline, we highlight which areas increase or maintain activation, revealing functional patterns across Motor tasks.

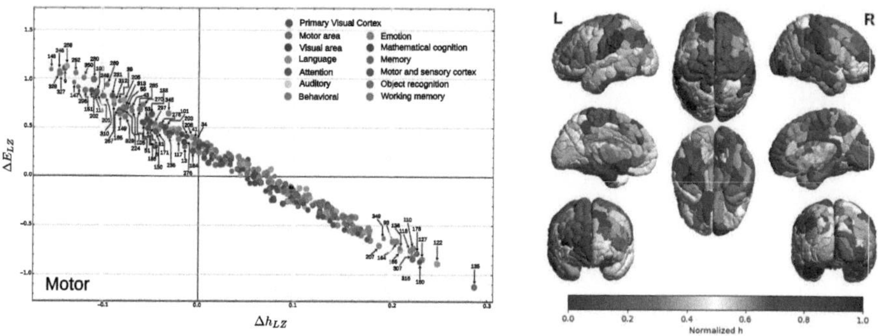

Fig. 2. **Activation of regions in Motor task with the resting state as the baseline** Left: Entropic map showing the difference of the h_{LZ} and E_{LZ} of all the brain regions during the Motor stimuli and resting state. Right: Level of activation by the difference of the normalized entropy density during Motor task and resting state. At lower h (red color) the regions are more active than at higher h (blue color). Observe the strong activation of the motor cortex in the posterior precentral gyrus, immediately anterior to the central sulcus. Notice how the visual regions in the occipital area are strongly activated during motor task where the subjects receive a visual cue.

During Motor stimuli, regions that maintain their activation when using the resting state as baseline, include the Primary Motor Cortex ROIs **8** and **188**, Primary Sensory Cortex ROIs **9** and **189**, and Primary Sensory Areas ROIs **51, 231, 52, 232, 53** and **233**, which are mainly involved in the movement engaged activity. Other regions with strong activity are regions associated with attentional processing and motor response like PF Complex (ROIs **148** and **328**), which is primarily activated during motor cue and social Theory of Mind (ToM) tasks, PFm Complex (ROIs **149** and **329**) which plays a key role in attentional processing, decision-making, language syntax, and is activated in working memory, motor cues, and gambling tasks, area PF opercular (ROIs **147** and **327**) and Area PFt (ROIs **116** and **296**) both usually active during motor planning and action-related [4, 23].

As the motor task includes a visual cue, regions involved in visual and attentional processing tasks appear active, like ROIs **150** and **151**, and visual areas

ROIs **181, 184, 185, 186** and **249**. Notably, other visual and attentional areas, such as ROIs **1, 4, 5, 69, 325** and **330** are also active during the resting state; their exclusion from activation on this map should not be interpreted as inactivity, since the brain remains functionally engaged even in the resting state. [3,14]

Figure 2 right, shows the level of activity during the Motor task with respect to the Resting state in the brain, for lower h (red color) regions are more active than for higher h (blue color).

The Lempel-Ziv distance -which is a distance in terms of information- was calculated between all brain regions to analyze the functional connections between them. The two strongest connections, which are the lowest distance for each region, were displayed after applying a threshold. This revealed the emergence of hubs and connections between regions specialized in similar activities for the Motor tasks, as can be appreciated in Fig. 3. This pattern contrasts with the resting-state graph of connections in Fig. 4, where no hubs are observed, maybe

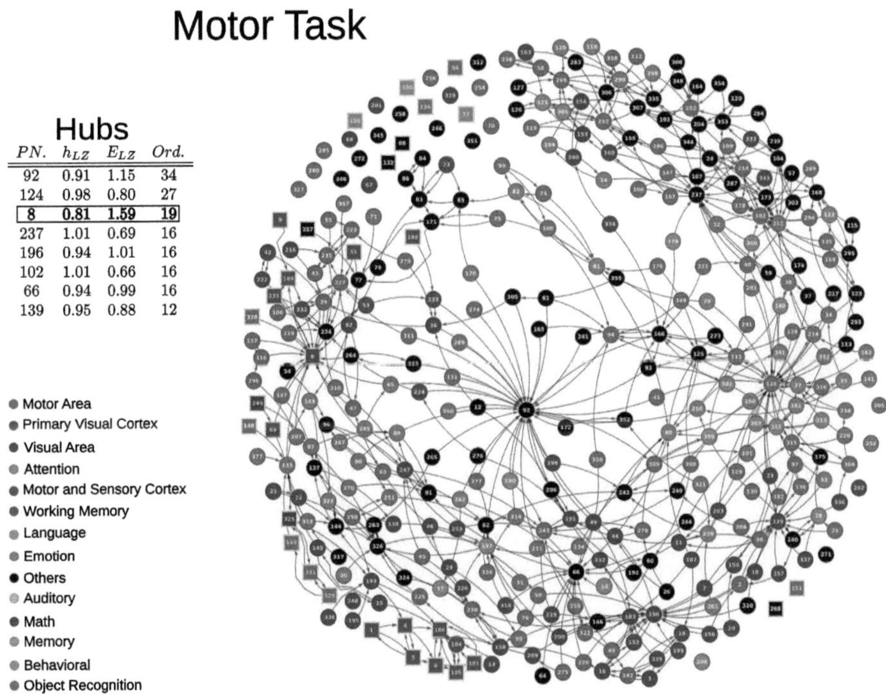

PN.	h_{LZ}	E_{LZ}	Ord.
92	0.91	1.15	34
124	0.98	0.80	27
8	0.81	1.59	19
237	1.01	0.69	16
196	0.94	1.01	16
102	1.01	0.66	16
66	0.94	0.99	16
139	0.95	0.88	12

Fig. 3. Brain connectivity analysis in Motor task. The Lempel Ziv distance was calculated between all brain regions, and the two strongest connections for each region after applying a threshold were displayed, revealing the emergence of hubs and connections between regions specialized in similar activities, very different from Resting State, where no hubs were observed.

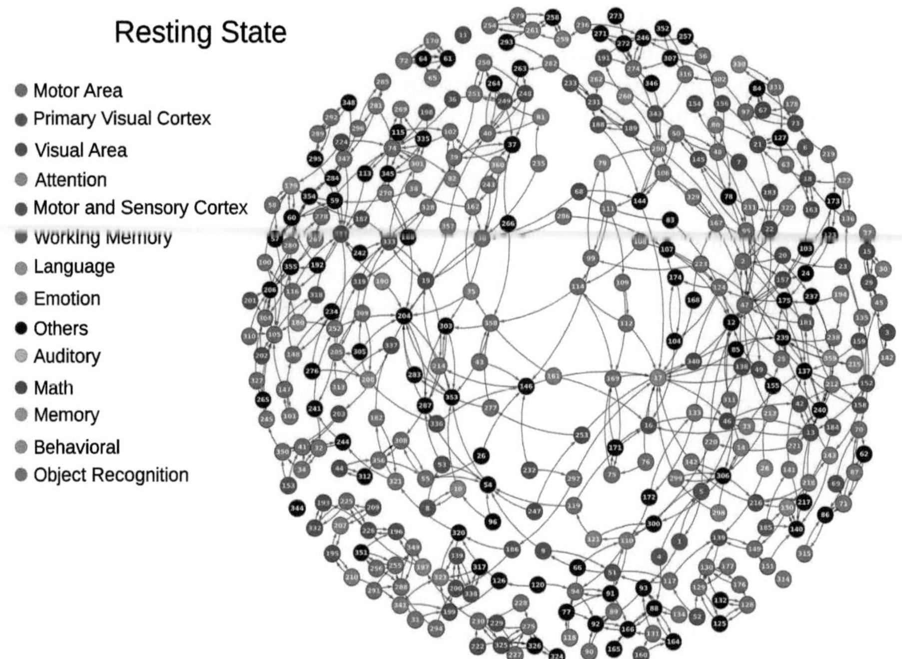

Fig. 4. Brain connectivity analysis in Resting State. The Lempel Ziv distance was calculated between all brain regions, and the two strongest connections for each region after applying a threshold were displayed, revealing a graph with no hubs; this pattern contrasts with motor task data.

due to the lack of synchronization or coordination of brain regions during the Resting State, consistently with previous studies [19].

4   Conclusions

Using information-theoretic measures to analyze task-based fMRI data is an approach that detects linear and non-linear dynamics in brain activity and connectivity. The method does not require prior models or assumptions, making it valuable for exploratory studies that could uncover previously unrecognized interactions. Since the brain reveals pronounced non-linear interactions at different scales, the ability of the framework proposed in this paper to detect such dynamics is highly relevant. Entropy-derived metrics offer a robust lens through which to understand how different tasks modulate regional activity, paving the way for deeper insights into the functional architecture of the human brain.

Disclosure of Interests. The authors have no competing interests to declare that are relevant to the content of this article.

References

1. Akiki, T.J., Abdallah, C.G.: Determining the hierarchical architecture of the human brain using subject-level clustering of functional. Networks **9**(1), 19290 (2019). https://doi.org/10.1038/s41598-019-55738-y
2. Baccalá, L.A., Sameshima, K.: Partial directed coherence: a new concept in neural structure determination **84**(6), 463–474 (2001). https://doi.org/10.1007/PL00007990
3. Baker, C.M., et al.: A connectomic atlas of the human cerebrum—chapter 1: introduction, methods, and significance **15**, S1–S9 (2018). https://doi.org/10.1093/ons/opy253
4. Baker, C.M., et al.: A connectomic atlas of the human cerebrum—chapter 7: the lateral parietal lobe **15**, S295–S349 (2018). https://doi.org/10.1093/ons/opy261
5. Barnett, L., Seth, A.K.: Granger causality for state space models **91**(4), 040101 (2015). https://doi.org/10.1103/PhysRevE.91.040101
6. Bielczyk, N.Z., et al.: Thresholding functional connectomes by means of mixture modeling **171**, 402–414 (2018). https://doi.org/10.1016/j.neuroimage.2018.01.003
7. Bullmore, E., Sporns, O.: Complex brain networks: graph theoretical analysis of structural and functional systems **10**(3), 186–198 (2009). https://doi.org/10.1038/nrn2575
8. Cover, T.M., Thomas, J.A.: Elements of Information Theory. John Wiley & Sons, Hoboken (1999)
9. Crutchfield, J.P., Feldman, D.P.: Regularities unseen, randomness observed: levels of entropy convergence **13**(1), 25–54 (2003). https://doi.org/10.1063/1.1530990
10. Estevez-Rams, E., Estevez-Moya, D., Garcia-Medina, K., Lora-Serrano, R.: Computational capabilities at the edge of chaos for one dimensional systems undergoing continuous transitions. Chaos **29**, 043105 (2019)
11. Estevez-Rams, E., Lora-Serrano, R., Nunes, C.A.J., Aragón-Fernández, B.: Lempel-Ziv complexity analysis of one dimensional cellular automata **25**(12), 123106 (2015). https://doi.org/10.1063/1.4936876
12. Feldman, D.P., Crutchfield, J.P.: Structural information in two-dimensional patterns: entropy convergence and excess entropy **67**(5), 051104. https://doi.org/10.1103/PhysRevE.67.051104
13. Gautama, T., Mandic, D.P., Van Hulle, M.M.: Indications of nonlinear structures in brain electrical activity **67**(4), 046204 (2003). https://doi.org/10.1103/PhysRevE.67.046204
14. Glasser, M.F., et al.: A multi-modal parcellation of human cerebral cortex **536**(7615), 171–178 (2016). https://doi.org/10.1038/nature18933
15. Grassberger, P.: Towards a quantitative theory of self-generated complexity. Int. J. Theo. Phys. **25**, 907–938 (1986)
16. Kaminski, M.J., Blinowska, K.J.: A new method of the description of the information flow in the brain structures **65**(3), 203–210 (1991). https://doi.org/10.1007/BF00198091
17. Lesne, A., Blanc, J.L., Pezard, L.: Entropy estimation of very short symbolic sequences. Phys. Rev. E **79**, 046208–046217 (2009)
18. Melchert, O., Hartmann, A.K.: Analysis of the phase transition in the two-dimensional ising ferromagnet using a lempel-ziv string-parsing scheme and black-box data-compression utilities. Phys. Rev. E **91**, 023306–023317 (2015)
19. Raemaekers, M., Schellekens, W., Petridou, N., Ramsey, N.F.: Knowing left from right: asymmetric functional connectivity during resting state. Brain Struct. Funct. **223**(4), 1909–1922 (2018). https://doi.org/10.1007/s00429-017-1604-y

20. Schiefer, J., et al.: From correlation to causation: estimating effective connectivity from zero-lag covariances of brain signals. PLoS Comput. Biol. **14**(3), e1006056 (2018)
21. Valdes-Sosa, P.A., Roebroeck, A., Daunizeau, J., Friston, K.: Effective connectivity: influence, causality and biophysical modeling **58**(2), 339–361 (2011). https://doi.org/10.1016/j.neuroimage.2011.03.058
22. Van Essen, D., et al.: The human connectome project: a data acquisition perspective **62**(4), 2222–2231 (2012). https://doi.org/10.1016/j.neuroimage.2012.02.018
23. Wu, S.S., Chang, T.T., Majid, A., Caspers, S., Eickhoff, S.B., Menon, V.: Functional heterogeneity of inferior parietal cortex during mathematical cognition assessed with cytoarchitectonic probability maps **19**(12), 2930–2945 (2009). https://doi.org/10.1093/cercor/bhp063
24. Ziv, J.: Coding theorems for individual sequences **24**(4), 405–412 (1978). https://doi.org/10.1109/TIT.1978.1055911

Exploring the Correlation Between the Type of Music and the Emotions Evoked: A Study Using Subjective Questionnaires and EEG

Jelizaveta Jankowska[1]([✉]), Bożena Kostek[1], Fernando Alonso-Fernandez[2], and Prayag Tiwari[2]

[1] Audio Acoustics Lab, Faculty of Electronics, Telecommunications and Informatics, Gdańsk University of Technology (GUT), Gdańsk, Poland
jelkur23@student.hh.se, bozena.kostek@pg.edu.pl
[2] School of Information Technology, Halmstad University, Halmstad, Sweden
feralo@hh.se, prayag.tiwari@hh.se

Abstract. The subject of this work is to check how different types of music affect human emotions. While listening to music, a subjective survey and brain activity measurements were carried out using an EEG helmet. The aim is to demonstrate the impact of different music genres on emotions. The research involved a diverse group of participants of different gender and musical preferences. This had the effect of capturing a wide range of emotional responses to music. After the experiment, a relationship analysis of the respondents' questionnaires with EEG signals was performed. The analysis revealed connections between emotions and observed brain activity.

Keywords: Music and Emotion · EEG-Based Emotion Recognition · Brain-Computer Interface (BCI)

1 Introduction

Music, as an art form based on sounds, has been an integral part of human existence, transforming and evolving over time. Neurological studies revealed that music has the ability to release dopamine, the happiness hormone, and can evoke diverse emotions, influencing the perception of time [6]. Advancements in brain activity research allowed for a scientific approach to understanding how music affects the human psyche and physiology [7].

Different types of music can affect human emotions, as observed through EEG recordings. Studies have shown that music across genres, including Indian classical music (ICM) and melodies played with different instruments, can evoke a variety of emotions [13,22]. EEG experiments have been conducted to assess the neural responses of both musicians and non-musicians to different emotional stimuli in music, revealing that musicians tend to exhibit higher complexity and coherence in their brain responses compared to non-musicians [11]. Furthermore, EEG-based emotion recognition has shown promising results in accurately identifying and classifying different emotions using music audio signals. Additionally, the impact of music stimuli on the brain and its physiological function system has been studied, providing insights into the role of music in clinical treatment and neurological interventions [8].

But despite advancements in technology and insights from previous studies, significant gaps remain in the understanding of how music affects individuals. While AI and brainwave technology offer potential paths for recognising people's emotions, there has been limited exploration into how various music styles relate to emotional states and physiological responses [10,12,18]. Accordingly, this research aims to find answers to questions regarding the impact of music on human emotions. It involves investigating the correlation between different types of music and the emotions they evoke, employing questionnaires and EEG signal recordings. The objective is to establish a relationship between participants' subjective responses in questionnaires regarding their emotional experiences and the objective EEG signal data during music listening, determining whether there is a visible connection between subjective emotional perceptions and physiological responses measured through EEG signals.

2 Background

2.1 Study of Emotions

Emotional states encompass various phenomena such as feelings, affects, motivations, moods, passions, and sentiments, which, though theoretically distinct, are closely interrelated in practice [20]. Emotions are defined as complex processes involving arousal, subjective experience, physiological changes, expressions, and behavioural tendencies [21]. Two dominant theories explain emotional emergence: Ekman's theory of six universal emotions (happiness, sadness, anger, fear, disgust, and surprise) [5], identifiable through facial and body expressions and from which all other emotions derive; and Barrett's constructivist approach [4], which views emotions as culturally shaped and individually variable experiences. A widely adopted framework in affective science is Russell's circumplex model [17] (Fig. 1, left), which maps emotions along valence (pleasure vs. displeasure) and arousal (activation or alertness vs. deactivation) axes. Additional variables like intensity (the extent to which the process influences behaviour, thought processes, etc.) and content (meaning of the stimulus and predisposition to specific behaviours such as fear leading to escape, or anger leading to aggressiveness) can be used to characterize emotional states further [15].

Emotion recognition methods can be based on physiological or non-physiological signals [12]. Non-physiological approaches include analysis of written or spoken language, speech, and body behaviour, often using self-report tools like questionnaires or structured interviews. Physiological methods, on the other hand, rely on objective signals such as EEG, ECG, facial muscle activity, eye movement, and skin conductance. In principle, these are not susceptible to subjective factors or interpretation, offering more reliable and accurate assessments of emotional states. To elicit and study emotions, researchers use diverse stimuli: static images, auditory inputs (music, speech), videos, and immersive Virtual Reality (VR) environments, each one enabling observation of emotional responses through both self-reports and physiological monitoring.

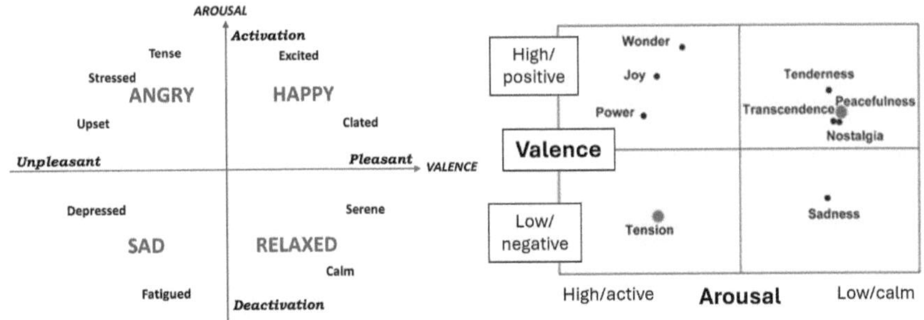

Fig. 1. Left: Russel's model of emotions based on valence-arousal scale [17]. Right: Geneva Emotional Music Scale (GEMS) [3] and mapping to the V-A scale.

2.2   Electroencephalography (EEG)

Electroencephalography (EEG) is a non-invasive technique for measuring spontaneous brain electrical activity, with amplitudes typically between 1âĂŞ100 μV and frequencies from 0 to 100 Hz. Unlike MRI or PET, EEG offers millisecond-level temporal resolution. EEG is primarily used for diagnosing and monitoring neurological conditions. In scientific research, it is utilised in neuroscience, cognitive psychology, neurolinguistics, and psychophysiological studies. It is also increasingly applied to emotion research [12,23], due to the relation between activated frequency bands and brain states:

- Delta (0.5–3 Hz): deep sleep; linked to neurological disorders and depression.
- Theta (4–7 Hz): light sleep, meditation, cognitive processing, daydreaming.
- Alpha (8–12 Hz): relaxed wakefulness, calmness, positive mood; decreases with attention or mental effort.
- Beta (13–28 Hz): active thinking, learning, and emotional arousal, both pleasant or unpleasant (e.g. anger or agitation).
- Gamma (>30 Hz, up to 100 Hz, with the relevant information below 50 Hz): high-level cognition, positive meditative states, gratitude, love, and joy.

EEG offers portability and high resolution, operating quietly, and it is relatively affordable compared with other neuroimaging techniques. Despite advantages, it has limitations too. It is sensitive to movement and muscle artefacts such as blinking, requiring signal filtering. In addition, the preparation process can be lengthy and uncomfortable. Conductive gel may be needed, which can be inconvenient, with dry EEG methods offering less accuracy.

3   Methodology and Results

The methodology includes several key components, which are addressed in the following subsections: **i)** the creation of a music database aimed at evoking various emotional responses; **ii)** the analysis of musical parameters of the selected music samples; **iii)** the development of a structured subjective survey to capture participants' emotional reactions; **iv)** the execution of EEG experiments using EEG device to gather brain activity data; **v)** the processing of this EEG data to extract meaningful insights, exploring the relationship between subjective emotional experiences and objective EEG-based measures.

Table 1. Left: total counts per emotion/music genre of Emotify. Centre/right: the calmest tracks of classical music/the most tense tracks of electronic music.

Emotion (GEMS)	Classical	Rock	Electronic	Pop	Classical track ID	Average calmness	Electronic track ID	Average tension
Wonder	423	253	224	219	93	88%	260	82%
Transcendence	694	288	425	265	99	88%	262	82%
Tenderness	558	385	132	476	82	81%	229	73%
Nostalgia	676	**630**	238	**627**	4	76%	245	73%
Calmness	**919**	518	509	615	2	74%	254	73%
Power	388	458	459	226				
Joy	748	484	516	397				
Tension	464	400	**693**	333				
Sadness	464	437	109	434				

3.1   Database Creation

For this study, a customised dataset of music fragments was created based on open-source data collections. We use a valence-arousal scale classification method [17]. For such purpose, we employed the Emotify dataset [3] as base, which comprises 400 music fragments, each lasting one minute, categorised into four genres: rock, classical, pop, and electronic. Each genre contains 100 music fragments, and the emotional annotations were collected using the GEMS scale [19]. The Geneva Emotional Music Scale (GEMS) is a model designed specially to measure musical emotions, identifying nine fundamental emotions experienced by humans while listening to music, which can be mapped onto the valence-arousal (V-A) scale (Fig. 1, right). When listening, participants of Emotify were asked to select up to 3 emotions of the GEMS scale that they felt were evoked by the music fragments. To analyze the dataset, we calculated the total counts per emotion for every music genre (Table 1, left). The results reveal that classical music predominantly elicits positive emotions, with high counts for emotions such as

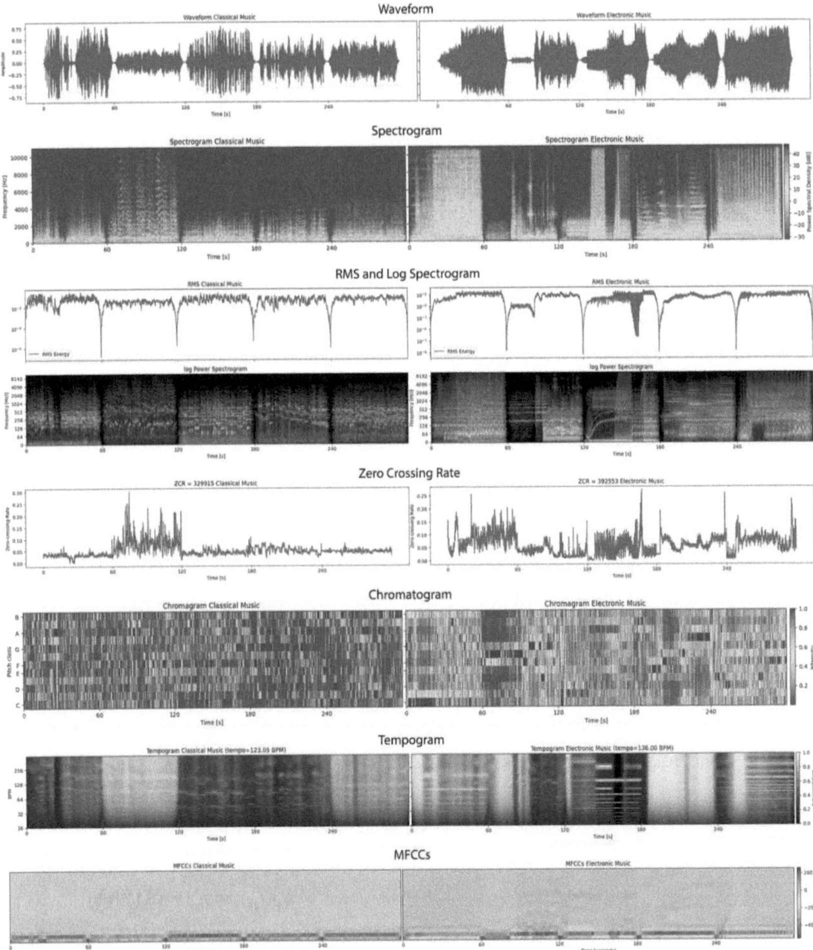

Fig. 2. Musical parameters of classical (left column) and electronic music (right).

calmness (peacefulness), indicating its calming and uplifting effects. Conversely, electronic music most commonly induces tension, with the highest count for this emotion among all genres. Rock and pop music both strongly evoke nostalgia, as reflected in their high scores for this emotion. Tension and calmness are opposing emotions on the V-A scale (red dots in Fig. 1, right). The prevalence of calmness in classical music and tension in electronic music suggests that these genres have significantly different emotional impacts.

Based on the above, we decided to compare classical and electronic music. Since the dataset comprises one-minute fragments, we created longer recordings by concatenating several fragments with similar emotional qualities. To do so, we identified the five most calming classical and the most tension-inducing electronic tracks (Table 1, center, right). The selected tracks were arranged sequentially, with fade-in and fade-out between them to avoid abrupt changes, resulting in two 5-minute files, one classical and one electronic.

3.2   Musical Parameters

Music is composed of various elements that interact to create a wide variety of sounds, including melody, harmony, rhythm, texture, timbre, dynamics, form, and tempo [9]. We analyzed various audio parameters of the created 5-minute tracks to understand the impact of musical elements on listener emotions. Figure 2 presents their waveform, spectrogram, RMS, zero crossing rate (ZCR), chromatogram, tempogram and Mel-frequency cepstral coefficients (MFCCs).

The waveforms reveal characteristic patterns. Classical music displays repetitive, cyclical structures with prominent peaks corresponding to the first beat of each measure. In contrast, electronic music has more irregular/unpredictable high peaks. Notably, the second classical track (seconds 60–120), featuring a solo piano, exhibited lower amplitude compared to other tracks.

The spectrogram is a heat map representation of frequencies' intensity over time. In classical music, lower frequencies dominate, with high frequencies having lower power spectral density. Electronic music shows sharper and more unpredictable changes, as observed in the waveform previously, and reflected here by higher frequency energy at individual times.

Root-mean-square (RMS) measures the total magnitude of the signal, often interpreted as the loudness or energy. Classical music has lower RMS ($\sim 10^{-2}$) compared to electronic music ($\sim 10^{-1}$), consistent with their respective loudness and energy levels seen in the spectrogram. The RMS graphs, aligned with logarithmic spectrograms, highlight these differences further.

Zero crossing rate (ZCR) measures the change rate of the signal from positive to negative or vice-versa. Higher ZCR values are common in percussive sounds. ZCR for classical music is relatively stable (0.05-0.1), except for the second piano track (0.2-0.3). Electronic music exhibits more variability (0.02-0.25), confirming its percussive and dynamic nature.

The chromatogram shows the dominance of pitches (e.g., C, D, E, etc.) in the audio. Classical music exhibits harmonic blends of tones, while electronic music displays more inconsistent tonal shifts.

The tempogram visualises the tempo, or speed, of the audio piece, measured in beats per minute (bpm). Upbeat genres tend to have higher tempos. A relatively similar average tempo for both genres is observed (123 vs. 136 bpm). However, classical music shows smoother patterns across time, while electronic music has distinct, sharp lines reflective of sudden changes in tempo.

Finally, Mel-frequency cepstral coefficients (MFCCs) represent the short-term power spectrum of a sound on a Mel scale, useful for distinguishing different sounds, especially speech. MFCC show negligible differences between classical and electronic music, as both recordings lack significant vocal components.

Table 2. STOMP analysis for every participant. Bold indicates the highest count per ID.

ID	Reflective & Complex	Intense & Rebellious	Upbeat & Conventional	Energetic & Rhythmic
1	**22**	15	21	10
2	**24**	20	23	17
3	17	15	**18**	16
4	**23**	19	22	10
5	**23**	21	22	19
6	13	9	**20**	18
7	13	14	15	**17**
8	18	**20**	19	13
9	17	**18**	17	15
10	18	12	**20**	17

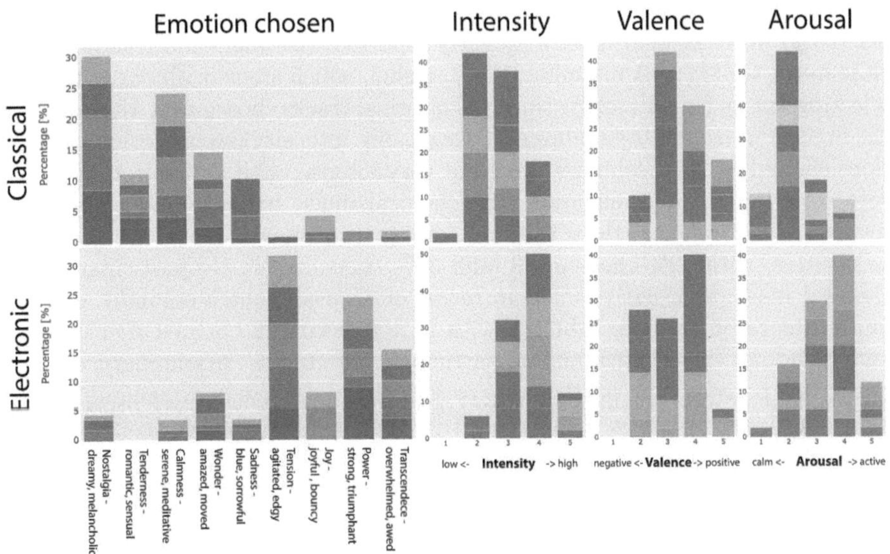

Fig. 3. Questionnaire results.

3.3 Survey Development and Results

A structured subjective survey (available at [2]) was formulated to elicit participants' emotional responses to music stimuli. We created a Google Form with embedded YouTube video links containing the audio tracks. An introductory section collects participant information (gender, age), music preferences and music background. Two sections with four questions each followed to rate emotional responses to classical and electronic music, respectively, after listening to the tracks. We engaged 7 male and 3 female participants aged 20–29 from (**hidden for double blind**). Users were asked to select up to 3 GEMS emotions that felt while listening to each track, how intense they were (1–5), the valence level (1–5, from negative to positive), and arousal level (1–5, from calm to active).

Nine out of ten participants reported enjoying music, with one being ambivalent. Only one participant had musical training. No formal musical training was preferred to avoid professional bias in both EEG and survey results. Musical preferences were assessed with the STOMP (Short Test of Musical Preferences) questionnaire [16], which involves rating 14 music genres on a scale from 1 to 7. Then, they are grouped into 4 types (Table 2, with the highest value per participant in bold). The results show a wide variety of participants, with 4 belonging to the Reflective & Complex category, 2 to Intense & Rebellious, 3 to Upbeat & Conventional, and 1 to Energetic & Rhythmic. Interestingly, participants in the Reflective & Complex category also showed high scores in the Upbeat & Conventional (1–2 points difference only).

Figure 3 shows the results of the emotional responses answers. Regarding the selected emotion (first column), nostalgia was the most dominant response to classical tracks, reported by 30% of respondents. Tranquility (25%) and wonder (15%) were the next most frequently reported. Nostalgia and tranquility are close in the GEMS V-A mapping (Fig. 1, right), which aligns with our criteria for selecting tracks from Emotify, since the classical tracks chosen were those scoring the highest in tranquility (calmness). Regarding intensity (second column), emotions elicited by classical music were not very intense, with 42% selecting '2' and 38% selecting '3'. This suggests that classical music induces milder emotional responses. For valence (third column), classical music was perceived as neutral to positive, with 42% choosing '3' and 30% choosing '4'. No participant rated classical music as negative ('1'). In terms of arousal (fourth column), classical music was rated as more calming, with 55% selecting '2'. Scores of '1', '3', '4', and '5' did not exceed 20%, and no participant selected '5'. In summary, classical music was perceived by participants as inducing calmness and tranquility, with mild emotional intensity, a more positive than neutral valence, and decidedly low arousal, indicating a calming effect.

Electronic music, on the other hand, elicited different emotional responses. Tension was the predominant emotion (31%), in line with our track selection criteria, followed by power (25%) and transcendence (15%). The contradiction between tension and power (they have opposite valence, Fig. 1, right) suggests that electronic music can be perceived both positively and negatively, depending on the listener. For valence, opinions were more varied, reflecting these oppositions. While 40% rated it as '4' (positive), 28% rated it as '2' (negative), and 25% rated it as '3' (neutral). In terms of arousal, electronic music was perceived as more stimulating, with 40% selecting '4' and 30% selecting '3'. This contrasts with classical music, where '2' was dominant. Regarding the intensity of emotions, electronic music induced more intense emotions, with 50% selecting '4' and 32% selecting '3'. Despite listening to the recordings for the first time, electronic music elicited more intense emotional responses.

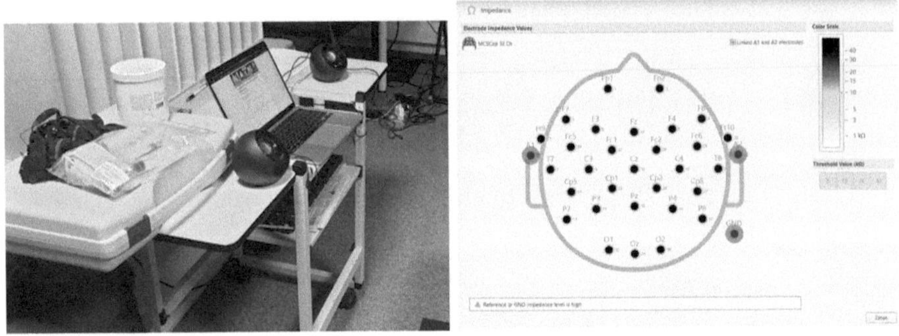

Fig. 4. EEG experimentation. Left: equipment. Right: Electrodes conductivity (yellow-white colour preferable). (Color figure online)

3.4 EEG Experiments and Analysis

For the EEG studies, we employed the MITSAR medical measurement device [1], with 32 electrodes. To ensure no disturbances, the experiment was conducted in a sound-isolated room at **hidden for double blind** (Fig. 4, left). Comfortable seating and high-quality speakers were set up to ensure comfortable music listening. The EEG cap was fitted by applying gel to the electrodes to achieve a low resistance level below 5kOhm (Fig. 4, right). Participants first completed the general section of the questionnaire. EEG recording started a few seconds before playing classical music to capture the participant's baseline state, followed by 5 min of classical music playback, and a few seconds of resting state. Then, participants filled out the section to rate emotional responses to classical music. Afterwards, the recording restarted to play the electronic music section, concluding with another short period of rest.

To process EEG data, we applied filtering to remove frequencies below 0.1 Hz and above 45 Hz. We then applied Independent Component Analysis (ICA) to remove artefacts due to eye movements, blinking, etc. Figure 5 shows the average topographic maps of the users with the EEG activity across the scalp for the first and last 20 s of classical and electronic music listening. Recall that theta and alpha waves are associated with relaxation and meditation. In contrast, beta and gamma are associated with intense thinking and action, and delta is associated with tensional states or disorders. Examining the topomaps, we see that before listening to classical music (first row), there was tension in the frontal delta region (forehead and eyes), which dissipated at the end (second row, observe the different scales). Then, theta and alpha power increased (relaxation), beta slightly increased, and gamma decreased. Before listening to electronic music (third row), frontal dental tension increased again, and it was further amplified to very high levels in the lateral regions after the session, maybe indicating jaw clenching. Theta and alpha (relaxation) remained medium-low and even decreased during the electronic session. In contrast, beta and gamma (action) increased significantly.

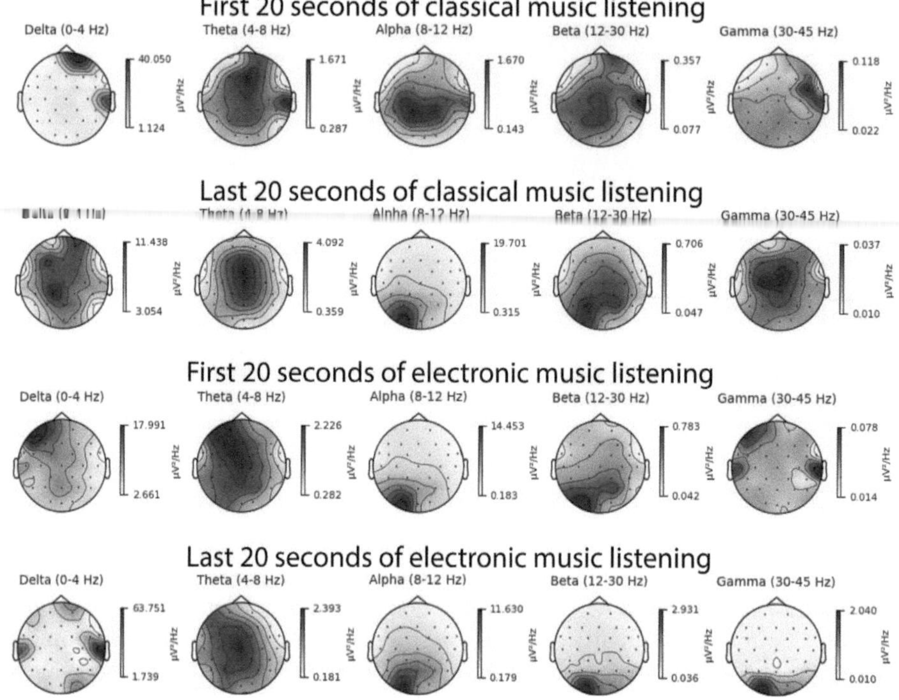

Fig. 5. Topomap of EEG data at the beginning and end of classical and electronic music listening.

4   Conclusions

This study aims to explore how different music genres impact human emotions. During the experiments, subjective surveys and EEG measurements were conducted using music fragments identified to be calm-inducing (classical music) and tension-inducing (electronic music).

The analysis revealed correlations between music genres and emotional responses. The research involves participants of various backgrounds, providing a range of emotional reactions to music. The survey results indicated that classical music is associated with calm and tranquil emotions, lower emotional intensity, positive valence, and low arousal. In contrast, electronic music elicits a wider range of emotions, including tension and power, higher arousal, and more intense emotional responses. This diversity in emotional reactions highlights the subjective nature of music perception.

Regarding EEG analysis, it showed that classical music promotes relaxation, increasing theta and alpha wave activity while decreasing frontal tension. In contrast, electronic music increases delta tension and beta and gamma activity, suggesting a more stimulating and arousing effect. The combination of subjective survey responses and objective EEG data provided a comprehensive understanding of the emotional and neural impact of different music genres on individuals.

Future work will involve the study of machine learning algorithms to characterize emotions automatically by EEG [14] and assess if they match with the self-reported answers. We are also working on including more participants across a wider age range to better generalize our findings, as well as providing more granularity in music genres by incorporating tracks with other styles.

Acknowledgements. This work has been carried out by J. Jankowska in the context of her Master degree in Biomedical/Medical Engineering at Gdańsk University of Technology. The work was partly done while J. Jankowska was an exchange student at Halmstad University (Computer Science and Engineering program). F. A.-F. thanks the Swedish Research Council (VR) for funding his research.

References

1. Mitsar eeg device. https://mitsar-eeg.com/
2. Questionnaire complementing the EEG experiments. https://docs.google.com/forms/d/e/1FAIpQLSdnvVFjj-l96xf1GqHmrLn1t39-tDoxuUL9jLc4D7w-NFhf6w/viewform
3. Aljanaki, A., Wiering, F., Veltkamp, R.C.: Studying emotion induced by music through a crowdsourcing game. Inf. Process. Manag. **51**(5), 682–693 (2015). https://doi.org/10.1016/j.ipm.2015.03.003
4. Barrett, L.F.: How Emotions Are Made: The Secret Life of the Brain. Houghton Mifflin Harcourt, New York (2017)
5. Ekman, P.: Emotions Revealed: Recognizing Faces and Feelings to Improve Communication and Emotional Life. Times Books, New York (2003)
6. Ferreri, L., et al.: Dopamine modulates the reward experiences elicited by music. Proc. Natl. Acad. Sci. U.S.A. **116**(9), 3793–3798 (2019). https://doi.org/10.1073/pnas.1811878116
7. González, A., Santapau, M., González, J.J.: Eeg analysis during music perception. In: IntechOpen (2021). https://doi.org/10.1016/B978-0-323-90585-5.00009-6
8. Hua, T., et al.: EEG emotion recognition applied to the effect analysis of music on emotion changes in psychological healthcare. Int. J. Environ. Res. Public Health (2022). https://doi.org/10.3390/ijerph20010378
9. Jooya, J.: What are the 8 elements of music? (2020). https://juliajooya.com/2020/10/11/what-are-the-8-elements-of-music/
10. Li, X., et al.: EEG based emotion recognition: A tutorial and review. ACM Comput. Surv. **55**(4), Article 79, 57 pages (2022). https://doi.org/10.1145/3524499
11. Lin, Y.: Emotional evoked analysis of classical music. In: Proceedings of the SSEHR-17 Conference (2018). https://doi.org/10.2991/SSEHR-17.2018.66
12. Liu, H., Zhang, Y., Li, Y., Kong, X.: Review on emotion recognition based on electroencephalography. Front. Comput. Neurosci. **15**, 758212 (2021). https://doi.org/10.3389/fncom.2021.758212
13. Medha, B., Sanyal, S., Banerjee, A., Banerjee, K., Ghosh, D.: Does musical training affect neuro-cognition of emotions? An EEG study with instrumental Indian classical music. Berkeley Prog. Law Econ. (2022). https://doi.org/10.1121/10.0010655

14. Menezes, M.L.R., et al.: Towards emotion recognition for virtual environments: an evaluation of EEG features on benchmark dataset. Pers. Ubiquit. Comput. **21**(6), 1003–1013 (2017). https://doi.org/10.1007/s00779-017-1048-x
15. Plutchik, R.: A general psychoevolutionary theory of emotion. In: Plutchik, R., Kellerman, H. (eds.) Emotion: Theory, Research and Experience, Theories of Emotion, vol. 1, pp. 3–33. Academic Press, New York (1980)
16. Rentfrow, P.J., Gosling, S.D.: The do re mi's of everyday life: the structure and personality correlates of music preferences. J. Pers. Soc. Psychol. **84**(6), 1236–1256 (2003). https://doi.org/10.1037/0022-3514.84.6.1236
17. Russell, J.A.: A circumplex model of affect. J. Pers. Soc. Psychol. **39**(6), 1161–1178 (1980). https://doi.org/10.1037/h0077714
18. Suhaimi, N.S., Mountstephens, J., Teo, J.: Eeg-based emotion recognition: a state-of-the-art review of current trends and opportunities. Comput. Intell. Neurosci. **2020**, 8875426 (2020). https://doi.org/10.1155/2020/8875426
19. Trost, W., Ethofer, T., Zentner, M., Vuilleumier, P.: Mapping aesthetic musical emotions in the brain. Cerebral Cortex **22** (2011). https://doi.org/10.1093/cercor/bhr353
20. Walat, W., Warchoł, T.: Analysis of the concept and classification of emotions from the point of view of learning processes. Edukacja – Technika – Informatyka **3**(29), 80–85 (2019), https://repozytorium.ur.edu.pl/items/13c1f463-0600-4469-867a-7ae08bb2891a
21. Więch, M.: What are emotions? (2020). https://www.dobra-przestrzen.pl/artykuly/czym-sa-emocje/. Accessed: 2025-04-13
22. Wu, X., Sun, G.: Music-induced emotions and musical regulation and emotion improvement based on eeg technology. Neuroquantology (2018). https://doi.org/10.14704/NQ.2018.16.6.1593
23. Yu, C., Wang, M.: Survey of emotion recognition methods using EEG information. Cogn. Rob. **2**, 132–146 (2022). https://doi.org/10.1016/j.cogr.2022.06.001

Lightweight Neural Networks for Multi-modal and Cross-Modal Biometric Matching: Experimental Evaluation on Audio-Visual Data

Yoanna Martínez-Díaz[1], Heydi Méndez-Vázquez[1(✉)],
Gabriel Hernández-Sierra[1], and Anthony Larcher[2]

[1] Advanced Technology Application Center (CENATAV), Havana, Cuba
`{ymartinez,hmendez,gsierra}@cenatav.co.cu`
[2] Université du Mans - LIUM, Le Mans, France
`anthony.larcher@univ-lemans.fr`

Abstract. Fusing audio and visual data on multi-modal approaches has become a powerful solution to improve the accuracy and robustness of biometric recognition systems, particularly in real-word scenarios where single-modality systems face limitations. Additionally, cross-modal matching has emerged as a valuable approach in scenarios where direct comparisons between voice and face are impractical. While deep learning has significantly advanced biometric recognition, the computational complexity of state-of-the-art models hinders their deployment in resource-constrained environments. Recently, efficient architectures offer a promising solution, but their effectiveness in multi-modal and cross-modal scenarios has not been fully exploited. In this paper, we assess the performance lightweight neural networks across a comprehensive experimental evaluation on the standardized VoxCeleb dataset. The obtained results demonstrate that lightweight models can achieve competitive verification rates while drastically reducing computational overhead, making them viable for deploying in edge devices and real-word applications.

Keywords: multi-modal fusion · cross-modal association · lightweight neural networks

1 Introduction

Biometric recognition systems play a critical role in modern security and identity authentication, offering robust solutions across various applications. Traditional unimodal biometric systems rely on a single physiological and behavioral characteristic including face, voice, fingerprint, iris scans, signatures and others [15]. Among these biometric traits, face and voice are two of the most practical and widely adopted modalities in both academia and industry since their convenience, accessibility and versatility.

Recently, multi-modal biometric systems are increasingly combining audio and visual modalities by leveraging the complementary relationships across them to enhance accuracy and reliability on previously considered single-modality tasks or to tackle new complex problems. Traditional approaches include score-level and early feature-level fusion [16], while newer approaches explore attention mechanisms to effectively capture the rich inter-modal relationships [14].

Additionally, cross-modal biometric association, where one modality (e.g., voice) is matched against another (e.g., face), has emerged as a valuable approach in scenarios where direct comparisons are impractical, such as forensic investigations or surveillance [22]. Existing techniques [29] emphasize the correlation between face and voice modalities rather than their integration, by learning of a common yet discriminative embedding space.

Most of existing multi-modal and cross-modal matching approaches involve using separate models previously to extract feature embeddings for each modality. With the advancement of deep learning technologies in the last decades, both face and voice systems have individually shown significant performance improvements using different network architectures and effective loss functions [3,13]. However, these models often demand high computational resources which outweighs benefits in practical scenarios. While prior research has explored lightweight models in unimodal face and speaker recognition, their effectiveness in multi-modal and cross-modal scenarios remains understudied. Using lightweight alternatives can offer a better trade-off for deploying on real-word applications and edge devices [4].

In this paper, we present a systematic experimental evaluation of lightweight neural networks for multi-modal and cross-modal biometric matching using audio-visual data. Specifically, we select three lightweight models for face modality: MobileFaceNet [6], ShuffleFaceNet [19] and EdgeFace [11], and three voice models: EfficientTDNN [35], UtteranceLevel [36] and ECAPA-TDNN [10]. Our findings aim to guide the development of efficient multi-modal and cross-modal biometric systems, that meet the demands of real-world applications without compromising recognition performance.

The main contributions of this work are as follows: (a) we investigate the effectiveness of using multi-modal and cross-modal approaches based on lightweight neural networks, and (b) we provide an extensive experimental evaluation on the VoxCeleb dataset and comparison with state-of-the art methods on both cross-modal and multi-modal biometric matching tasks.

This paper is organized as follows. Section 2 takes an overview of existing multi-modal and cross-modal approaches, as well as lightweight deep neural networks for voice and face recognition. Section 3 introduces our experimental setup and Sect. 4, presents the obtained results and exposes some discussion about this study. Finally, Sect. 5 summarizes the conclusions of this work.

2   Related Work

In this section, we review the recent approaches for multi-modal biometric fusion and cross-modal biometric association using audio-visual data. Additionally, we cover existing lightweight deep neural networks for face and speaker recognition.

2.1   Multi-modal Fusion

Multi-modal fusion of face and voice features has emerged as a powerful solution to enhance the accuracy and robustness of biometric systems under challenging conditions, such as pose variations or low resolution (for face), or speaking style differences or noise of the channel (for voice). Traditional fusion approaches include early feature-level fusion and score-level fusion [16]. Early feature-level fusion integrates raw or extracted audio-visual embeddings through simple operations such as concatenation or averaging [26,34], while score-level fusion combines the matching scores obtained from separate speaker and face recognition algorithms [28]. Although these methods have enhanced fusion performance compared to unimodal systems, they still do not fully exploit the rich complementary relationships between audio and visual information.

Recent advances in deep learning have introduced the attention-based mechanism [14]. These methods outperform traditional fusion by preserving modality-specific information while learning joint representations. Most of the existing attention-based models treat intra-modal and inter-modal relationships as separate learning tasks instead of unified phenomena [18]. Another research direction focuses on enhancing robustness against noisy modalities by exploiting the complementary relationships between face and voice samples [32]. Chen et al. [8] advanced this paradigm by optimizing embedding-level fusion strategies, demonstrating that gating-based fusion outperforms alternatives under noisy conditions. In [31] a multi-view model is introduced that uses a shared classifier to map audio and video into a unified space.

The above methods do not fully exploit the interdependencies between modalities, limiting their ability to model cross-modal interactions. Recent advances address this gap by employing self- and cross-attention mechanisms to explicitly capture complementary audio-visual cues, thereby enhancing verification accuracy [27]. In [25] a recursive joint cross-attention (RJCA) framework is adopted for iteratively refines audio-visual feature fusion by aggregating temporal features into utterance-level embeddings. Recent work also highlights multimodal foundation models, which natively process multiple data types (text, audio, images) through unified architectures, achieving state-of-the-art results in biometric matching [1]. Despite significant advancements, critical challenges remain, including handling missing modalities, mitigating bias, ensuring privacy, and improving computational efficiency.

2.2   Cross-Modal Association

Associating faces and voices involves cross-modal techniques that in most of the cases are based on the same strategies used for multi-modal fusion. Earlier approaches explore the feasibility of linking face and voice features extracted with separate models by learning shared embedding spaces via triplet or contrastive loss, minimizing distances between face-voice pairs of the same identity while maximizing separability across identities [21,22]. In order to replace contrastive/triplet loss with identity centroids to eliminate the need for paired or triplet samples, a single-stream network to extract audio-visual features into a shared latent space was proposed in [23]. Aiming at emphasizing enriched feature representations and supervised alignment for discriminative joint spaces, the Fusion and Orthogonal Projection (FOP) method was later introduced [29].

Most of subsequent works integrate cross-modal contrastive learning and self-supervised strategies: Chen et al. [7] combined StyleGAN-based face generation with prototype contrastive learning to align voice-face pairs, while Zhang et al. [37] exploited audio-visual concurrency via curriculum learning for latent supervision. Stevenage et al. [33] further highlighted the role of familiarity in strengthening cross-modal associations, suggesting neural cross-talk strengthens robust recognition. Innovations like multilingual chaining-cluster frameworks [24] and single-branch networks [30] challenges in real-world deployments.

2.3 Lightweight Models for Face and Speaker Recognition

Developing lightweight network architectures that prioritize computational efficiency over the complexity of traditional CNNs has emerged as a key strategy to optimize the trade-off between inference speed and model accuracy.

For face recognition, the dominant approach involves adapting lightweight architectures, originally developed for general computer vision tasks, and optimizing them to address the unique challenges of biometric identification. This is the case of MobileFaceNet [6], ShuffleFaceNet [19], GhostFaceNets [2] and Edge-Face [11] among others. These methods are a good choice for edge devices with strict latency and memory constraints, since they are based on already optimized end-to-end models with some architectural innovations for the particular case of face recognition. Other works aim at improving those lightweight face recognition models such as SeesawFaceNets [38]. Another approach is to automatically design efficient models specifically designed for face recognition [5].

In a similar way, recent studies for speaker verification have focus on designing efficient models while maintaining high accuracy. The utterance-level aggregation [36] was one of the first lightweight model designed for speaker recognition, based on a *thin* ResNet trunk architecture. Afterwards, several architectures have been designed trying to reduce the model complexity [10,17]. Recently, the neural architecture search (NAS) technique was applied to design an efficient model which obtained a high accuracy with very low computational complexity [35]. In general, three main strategies have been used to gain on efficiency: (1) designing computationally efficient convolutional operations [36], (2) distilling knowledge into compact student models [17], and (3) optimizing architectures via manual or neural architecture search [35].

3   Experimental Setup

In this section, we introduce the lightweight deep models used for obtaining face and voice embeddings, the multi-modal and cross-modal approaches used for the benchmark evaluations and the datasets employed for testing. Also, some implementation details of selected methods are described.

3.1   Voice and Face Lightweight Deep Models

In order to obtain the feature embeddings, we used three lightweight architectures such as MobileFaceNet [6], ShuffleFaceNet [19] and EdgeFace [11] for face modality, while voice models include EfficientTDNN [35], UtteranceLevel [36] and ECAPA-TDNN [10].

MobileFaceNet: is an extremely efficient CNN model tailored for high-accuracy real-time face verification on mobile and embedded devices. It uses residual bottlenecks as their main building blocks with small expansion factors. To achieve a more discriminative face representation, the authors replace the Global Average Pooling layer for a Global Depth-wise Convolution layer (GDC), and use the Parametric Rectified Linear Unit (PReLU) as non-linear activation function due to its accuracy improvement over the Rectified Linear Unit (ReLU) function for face recognition.

ShuffleFaceNet: is an efficient and lightweight architecture built upon ShuffleNetv2 for the face recognition domain. It introduces several modifications for improving accuracy demonstrating its feasibility in real-time applications or computationally limited platforms. Similar to MobileFaceNet, ShuffleFaceNet adopts PReLU activation function as non-linearity and uses a linear 1×1 convolution layer following a GDC layer as the feature output.

EdgeFace: is a lightweight and highly accurate face recognition model inspired by the hybrid architecture of EdgeNeXt. It effectively combines the strengths of CNN and Transformer models, and introduces Low Rank Linear (LoRaLin) module to further reduce the computation in linear layers while providing a minimal compromise to the network performance. Thus, EdgeFace not only maintains low computational costs and compact storage, but also achieves high face recognition performance, making it suitable for deployment on edge devices.

EfficientTDNN: is an efficient architecture search framework consisting of a TDNN-based supernet and a TDNN-NAS algorithm. The proposed supernet is capable of emulating various TDNN architectures, which improves the diversity of locality to boost the capabilities of discriminating speakers. On top of it, the TDNN-NAS quickly search for the desired TDNN architecture without retraining via weight-sharing subnets, which significantly reduces computation. Three subnets of EfficientTDNN are considered from different training stages of the supernet: EfficientTDNN-Small, EfficientTDNN-Mobile and EfficientTDNN-Base, respectively, which present different storage, computation and performance.

UtteranceLevel: is a powerful speaker recognition deep network, that uses a modified ResNet in a fully convolutional way to encode input 2D spectrograms, followed by a dictionary-based NetVLAD or GhostVLAD layer in order to aggregate features across time, that produces a fixed-length output descriptor. To allow efficient verification like low memory and fast similarity computation, a fully connected layer is further added for dimensionality reduction. The entire network can be trained end-to-end for speaker identification.

ECAPA-TDNN: is a novel speaker embedding extractor based on architectural enhancements to the TDNN network. It introduces Squeeze-and-Excitation blocks in 1-dimensional Res2Net modules to explicitly model channel interdependencies and uses additional skip connections to propagate and aggregate features of different hierarchical levels throughout the system. In addition, channel attention that uses a global context is incorporated in the frame layers and statistics pooling layer to improve the results even further.

Computational Complexity: In Table 1 we present the number of parameters and the model size of the selected lightweight face and voice models that will be used for obtaining the feature embeddings on multi-modal and cross-modal matching tasks. As we can see, face models are generally smaller in both parameters and model size compared to voice models. Among face models, MobileFace is the most lightweight and EdgeFace is the largest one, while in the case of voice models, ETDNN-Mobile has the fewest parameters, but its model size is similar to ETDNN-Base, being ECAPA-TDNN the heavy voice model. We would like to highlight that, although ECAPA-TDNN is not a very lightweight model, its inclusion in our experimental evaluation will be very useful since ECAPA-based models are currently the state-of-the-art on speaker recognition.

Table 1. Computational complexity of the selected lightweight face and voice models.

Modality	System	#Params (M).	Model size (MB)
Face	MobileFaceNet	2.0	8.2
	ShuffleFaceNet	2.6	10.5
	EdgeFace	3.7	14.7
Voice	EfficientTDNN-Mobile	2.4	35.1
	EfficientTDNN-Base	5.8	35.1
	UtteranceLevel	7.7	31.1
	ECAPA-TDNN	15.4	66.7

3.2   Multi-modal and Cross-Modal Fusion

For multi-modal matching, we have implemented a simple score-level fusion, where scores are obtained from individual modalities and then fused to verify the identity of a person. In the case of cross-modal scenario, we used the Fusion and Orthogonal Projection (FOP) [29], a lightweight, plug-and-play mechanism that exploits the complementary cues in both voice and face modalities to form enriched fused embeddings and clusters them based on their identity labels via orthogonality constraints.

3.3 Dataset and Implementation Details

In the case of face recognition models, we use pretrained models on the cleaned MS1M dataset [12] that includes 5.1 million photos from 93K face identities. The faces are cropped and resized to 112×112, and each pixel (ranged between [0; 255]) in RGB images is normalised by subtracting 127:5 then divided by 128. All experiments in this paper are implemented on PyTorch.

For the voice, we used pretrained models on VoxCeleb2 [9], a significantly large dataset with 1,092,009 utterances from 6,112 speakers. For the ECAPA-TDNN architecture, we used 1024 channels in the convolutional frame layers, and in the case of the EfficientTDNN model, we test Mobile and Base variants.

Our test set is the VoxCeleb1 [20], an audio-visual dataset derived from YouTube interviews. It contains 153,516 utterances from 1,251 celebrities captured "in the wild" conditions, with background noise and varying lighting.

4 Results and Discussion

In this section, we present and discuss the performance achieved by the selected methods on multi-modal and cross-modal matching tasks and compare them with state-of-the-art methods.

4.1 Multi-modal Matching Results

The presented results in Table 2 comprehensively evaluate the verification performance across unimodal (face, voice) and multi-modal (fusion) systems on the VoxCeleb1 database, measured in terms of Equal Error Rate (EER) and the minimum Detection Cost Function (minDCF). As we can see, face models consistently outperform voice-only approaches, with EdgeFace achieving the lowest EERs across all test sets Vox1-O, Vox1-E and Vox1-H. In contrast, voice systems exhibit significantly higher error rates, particularly in challenging scenarios like Vox1-H, where even the best voice model (ECAPA) reaches 2.99 of EER, nearly $20\times$ higher than EdgeFace (0.1583). This gap underscores the inherent advantage of facial recognition in controlled verification tasks.

On the other hand, it can be appreciated that multi-modal fusion substantially enhances verification accuracy over unimodal systems on VoxCeleb1. We can observed that, for each test set, the best results are obtained by fusing a face model with the Utterance voice model. For instance, ShuffleFace+Utterance achieves the lowest EER (0.0053 on Vox1-O), demonstrating a $16\times$ reduction compared to ShuffleFace and a $572\times$ with respect to Utterance alone, which highlight the synergy between face and voice modalities. Notably, the fusion benefits are most pronounced on Vox1-O, reaching near-perfect metrics. Although the more challenging Vox1-H set retains higher errors, fusion still provides significant gains. For example, MobileFace+Utterance reduces the EER gap (0.1209 vs. 5.0671 for voice-only and 0.1209 vs. 0.1695 for face-only).

Table 2. Verification performance in terms of **EER** and minDCF on VoxCeleb1 database.

Modality	System	Vox1-O		Vox1-E		Vox1-H	
		EER	minDCF	EER	minDCF	EER	minDCF
Face	MobileFace	0.0904	0.0075	0.1307	0.0061	0.1695	0.0079
	ShuffleFace	0.0851	0.0033	0.1483	0.0078	0.2026	0.0102
	EdgeFace	0.0638	0.0043	0.1104	0.0070	0.1583	0.0089
Voice	Utterance	3.0316	0.2240	3.1440	0.2121	5.0671	0.2962
	ETDNN-Mobile	1.6115	0.1026	1.6608	0.1059	2.9683	0.1766
	ETDNN-Base	1.1382	0.0733	1.3187	0.0850	2.4143	0.1474
	ECAPA	0.9839	0.0700	1.2056	0.0811	2.9888	0.1436
Fusion	MobileFace+Utterance	0.0213	0.0003	0.0818	**0.0037**	**0.1209**	**0.0057**
	MobileFace+ETDNN-Mobile	0.0425	0.0020	0.1059	0.0061	0.1903	0.0109
	MobileFace+ETDNN-Base	0.0160	0.0012	0.0883	0.0050	0.1644	0.0084
	MobileFace+ECAPA	0.0159	0.0011	0.0966	0.0054	0.1761	0.0095
	ShuffleFace+Utterance	**0.0053**	0.0004	0.0883	0.0040	0.1325	0.0062
	ShuffleFace+ETDNN-Mobile	0.0213	0.0007	0.0986	0.0061	0.1895	0.0108
	ShuffleFace+ETDNN-Base	0.0266	0.0003	0.0855	0.0051	0.1590	0.0087
	ShuffleFace+ECAPA	0.0106	**0.0002**	0.0928	0.0052	0.1721	0.0093
	EdgeFace+Utterance	0.0160	0.0003	**0.0728**	**0.0037**	0.1212	0.0060
	EdgeFace+ETDNN-Mobile	0.0372	0.0016	0.0918	0.0057	0.1794	0.0108
	EdgeFace+ETDNN-Base	0.0213	0.0007	0.0804	0.0045	0.1500	0.0082
	EdgeFace+ECAPA	0.0213	0.0007	0.0862	0.0049	0.1674	0.0089

From Table 2 we select three fusion methods with a balanced performance, which means not just best on Vox1-O, but also competitive on Vox1-E and Vox1-H test sets, and compare them with state-of-the-art multi-modal methods. Specifically, we selected EdgeFace+Utterance, ShuffleFace+Utterance and ShuffleFace+ECAPA. The performance comparison is shown in Table 3. As it can be seen, the proposed lightweight multi-modal systems outperform most of the included state-of-the-art methods and achieve remarkably competitive results compared to heaviest method ResNet50+ECAPA. Notably, Shuffle-Face+Utterance matches ResNet50+ECAPA on Vox1-O (0.01) and Vox1-H (0.13), while EdgeFace+Utterance remains close on Vox1-O (0.02), equal in Vox1-E (0.07) and better in Vox1-H (0.12), suggesting that efficient models can achieve state-of-the-art performance similar to deeper networks without

Table 3. Performance comparison of our three best multi-modal methods with state-of-the-art results in terms of EER on VoxCeleb1 database.

System	Vox1-O	Vox1-E	Vox1-H
Sari et al. [31]	0.90	–	–
Qian et.al. [26]	0.71	0.48	0.85
Chen et al. [8]	0.59	0.43	0.74
ResNet18+ECAPA [34]	0.16	0.23	0.42
ResNet50+ECAPA [34]	0.01	0.07	0.13
EdgeFace+Utterance	0.02	0.07	0.12
ShuffleFace+Utterance	0.01	0.09	0.13
ShuffleFace+ECAPA	0.01	0.09	0.17

sacrificing accuracy. This balance between efficiency and accuracy makes such approaches particularly promising for real-world applications where computational resources are constrained.

4.2   Cross-Modal Matching Results

Table 4 presents the cross-modal verification performance of FOP method with different face and voice embeddings using both linear and gated fusion mechanisms under unseen-unheard configurations of VoxCeleb1 database. The evaluation metrics used are the EER and the Area Under the Curve (AUC) (higher is better). As it can be seen, for linear fusion, FOP (MobileFaceNet, ETDNN-Base) achieves the lowest EER (24.9%) and highest AUC (82.5%), while FOP (MobileFaceNet, ECAPA) is the best performing one for the gated mechanism (EER: 25.0%, AUC: 82.7%). We can appreciate that, the face embedding choice significantly impacts performance, with MobileFaceNet consistently outperforming ShuffleFace and EdgeFace-S across nearly all speaker encoder pairings. In the case of speaker models, ETDNN-Base and ECAPA embeddings generally yield superior results compared to ETDNN-Mobile and Utterance embeddings, likely due to their more sophisticated modeling capabilities. Furthermore, the performance gap between linear and gated fusion is minimal, suggesting that the added complexity of gated mechanisms does not universally guarantee better results.

In Table 5 we compare the two best results obtained from Table 4 with state-of-the-art methods on the VoxCeleb1 dataset under unseen-unheard configurations. We can observed that our proposals achieves competitive EER and AUC values, performing similarly to the original FOP method [29], which uses VGGFace and UtteranceLevel as face and voice embedding, respectively.

5   Conclusion

In this paper, we presented a comprehensive evaluation of multi-modal and cross-modal biometric matching systems based on lightweight deep learning repre-

Table 4. Cross-modal verification on VoxCeleb1 under unseen-unheard configurations.

Method	Linear		Gated	
	EER	AUC	EER	AUC
FOP (MobileFaceNet, Utterance)	29.5	78.0	29.4	78.0
FOP (MobileFaceNet, ETDNN-Mobile)	26.0	82.0	25.6	82.3
FOP (MobileFaceNet, ETDNN-Base)	24.9	82.5	25.7	81.8
FOP (MobileFaceNet, ECAPA)	25.1	82.2	**25.0**	**82.7**
FOP (ShuffleFace, Utterance)	28.6	78.3	29.3	77.6
FOP (ShuffleFace, ETDNN-Mobile)	26.4	80.6	26.3	81.0
FOP (ShuffleFace, ETDNN-Base)	26.1	81.0	25.9	81.6
FOP (ShuffleFace, ECAPA)	25.8	81.1	26.4	81.0
FOP (EdgeFace, Utterance)	31.4	74.6	32.3	74.4
FOP (EdgeFace, ETDNN-Mobile)	29.0	77.3	29.3	77.5
FOP (EdgeFace, ETDNN-Base)	28.5	78.0	29.2	77.6
FOP (EdgeFace, ECAPA)	29.0	77.5	28.6	78.1

Table 5. Performance of our two best proposed approaches in comparison to state-of-the-art on VoxCeleb1 under unseen-unheard configurations.

Method	EER	AUC
Learnable Pins [21]	29.6	78.5
MAV-Celeb [21]	29.0	78.9
Single Stream Network [23]	29.5	78.8
Single-branch [30]	25.7	82.5
FOP [29]	**24.9**	**83.5**
FOP (MobileFaceNet, ECAPA) - Ours	**24.9**	82.5
FOP (MobileFaceNet, ETDNN-Base) - Ours	25.0	82.7

sentation with face and voice data. Our study demonstrates that lightweight neural networks offer a compelling balance between accuracy and efficiency for these tasks. The extensive experimental evaluation on the VoxCeleb dataset, show that lightweight architectures achieve competitive verification performance while drastically reducing computational costs, enabling deployment in resource-constrained environments like edge devices. Future work should focus on including cross-attention mechanisms and distillation strategies to further enhance lightweight frameworks without sacrificing discriminative power.

Acknowledgements. This project has received funding from the European Union's Horizon 2020 research and innovation program under the Marie Skłodowska-Curie grant agreement No 101007666.

References

1. Abdrakhmanova, M., Yermekova, A., Barko, Y., Ryspayev, V., Jumadildayev, M., Varol, H.A.: One model to rule them all: a universal transformer for biometric matching. IEEE Access (2024)
2. Alansari, M., Hay, O.A., Javed, S., Shoufan, A., Zweiri, Y., Werghi, N.: Ghost-FaceNets: lightweight face recognition model from cheap operations. IEEE Access **11**, 35429–35446 (2023)
3. Amirgaliyev, B., Mussabek, M., Rakhimzhanova, T., Zhumadillayeva, A.: A review of machine learning and deep learning methods for person detection, tracking and identification, and face recognition with applications. Sensors **25**(5), 1410 (2025)
4. Awad, A.I., Babu, A., Barka, E., Shuaib, K.: Ai-powered biometrics for internet of things security: a review and future vision. J. Inf. Secur. Appl. **82**, 103748 (2024)
5. Boutros, F., Siebke, P., Klemt, M., Damer, N., Kirchbuchner, F., Kuijper, A.: Pocketnet: extreme lightweight face recognition network using neural architecture search and multistep knowledge distillation. IEEE access **10**, 46823–46833 (2022)
6. Chen, S., Liu, Y., Gao, X., Han, Z.: MobileFaceNets: efficient CNNs for accurate real-time face verification on mobile devices. In: Biometric Recognition, pp. 428–438 (2018)
7. Chen, W., Zhu, B., Xu, K., Dou, Y., Feng, D.: VoiceStyle: voice-based face generation via cross-modal prototype contrastive learning. ACM Trans. Multimed. Comput. Commun. Appl. **20**(9), 1–23 (2024)
8. Chen, Z., Wang, S., Qian, Y.: Multi-modality matters: a performance leap on VoxCeleb. In: Interspeech, pp. 2252–2256 (2020)
9. Chung, J.S., Nagrani, A., Zisserman, A.: VoxCeleb2: deep speaker recognition. In: INTERSPEECH (2018)
10. Desplanques, B., Thienpondt, J., Demuynck, K.: ECAPA-TDNN: emphasized channel attention, propagation and aggregation in TDNN based speaker verification. arXiv preprint arXiv:2005.07143 (2020)
11. George, A., Ecabert, C., Shahreza, H.O., Kotwal, K., Marcel, S.: EdgeFace: efficient face recognition model for edge devices. IEEE Trans. Biomet. Behav. Identity Sci. **6**(2), 158–168 (2024)
12. Guo, Y., Zhang, L., Hu, Y., He, X., Gao, J.: MS-Celeb-1M: a dataset and benchmark for large-scale face recognition. In: Leibe, B., Matas, J., Sebe, N., Welling, M. (eds.) ECCV 2016. LNCS, vol. 9907, pp. 87–102. Springer, Cham (2016). https://doi.org/10.1007/978-3-319-46487-9_6
13. Hassanzadeh, H., Qadir, J.A., Omer, S.M., Ahmed, M.H., Khezri, E.: Deep learning for speaker recognition: a comparative analysis of 1D-CNN and LSTM models using diverse datasets. In: 2024 4th Interdisciplinary conference on electrics and computer (INTCEC), pp. 1–8. IEEE (2024)
14. Hörmann, S., Moiz, A., Knoche, M., Rigoll, G.: Attention fusion for audio-visual person verification using multi-scale features. In: 2020 15th IEEE International Conference on Automatic Face and Gesture Recognition (FG 2020), pp. 281–285. IEEE (2020)
15. Jain, A.K., Flynn, P., Ross, A.A.: Handbook of Biometrics. Springer, Heidelberg (2007)
16. Jiao, T., Guo, C., Feng, X., Chen, Y., Song, J.: A comprehensive survey on deep learning multi-modal fusion: methods, technologies and applications. Comput. Mater. Continua **80**(1) (2024)

17. Liu, B., Wang, H., Chen, Z., Wang, S., Qian, Y.: Self-knowledge distillation via feature enhancement for speaker verification. In: ICASSP 2022-2022 IEEE International Conference on Acoustics, Speech and Signal Processing (ICASSP), pp. 7542–7546. IEEE (2022)
18. Liu, M., Lee, K.A., Wang, L., Zhang, H., Zeng, C., Dang, J.: Cross-modal audio-visual co-learning for text-independent speaker verification. In: ICASSP 2023-2023 IEEE International Conference on Acoustics, Speech and Signal Processing (ICASSP), pp. 1–5. IEEE (2023)
19. Martinez-Diaz, Y., Luevano, L.S., Mendez-Vazquez, H., Nicolas-Diaz, M., Chang, L., Gonzalez-Mendoza, M.: ShuffleFaceNet: a lightweight face architecture for efficient and highly-accurate face recognition. In: IEEE International Conference on Computer Vision Workshops (2019)
20. Nagrani, A., Chung, J.S., Zisserman, A.: VoxCeleb: a large-scale speaker identification dataset. In: INTERSPEECH (2017)
21. Nagrani, A., Albanie, S., Zisserman, A.: Learnable pins: cross-modal embeddings for person identity. In: Proceedings of the European Conference on Computer Vision (ECCV), pp. 71–88 (2018)
22. Nagrani, A., Albanie, S., Zisserman, A.: Seeing voices and hearing faces: cross-modal biometric matching. In: Proceedings of the IEEE Conference on Computer Vision and Pattern Recognition, pp. 8427–8436 (2018)
23. Nawaz, S., Janjua, M.K., Gallo, I., Mahmood, A., Calefati, A.: Deep latent space learning for cross-modal mapping of audio and visual signals. In: 2019 Digital Image Computing: Techniques and Applications (DICTA), pp. 1–7. IEEE (2019)
24. Nawaz, S., et al.: Cross-modal speaker verification and recognition: a multilingual perspective. In: Proceedings of the IEEE/CVF Conference on Computer Vision and Pattern Recognition, pp. 1682–1691 (2021)
25. Praveen, R.G., Alam, J.: Audio-visual person verification based on recursive fusion of joint cross-attention. In: 2024 IEEE 18th International Conference on Automatic Face and Gesture Recognition (FG), pp. 1–5. IEEE (2024)
26. Qian, Y., Chen, Z., Wang, S.: Audio-visual deep neural network for robust person verification. IEEE/ACM Trans. Audio Speech Lang. Process. **29**, 1079–1092 (2021)
27. Rajasekhar, G.P., Alam, J.: Audio-visual speaker verification via joint cross-attention. In: Karpov, A., Samudravijaya, K., Deepak, K.T., Hegde, R.M., Agrawal, S.S., Prasanna, S.R.M. (eds.) SPECOM 2023. LNCS, vol. 14339, pp. 18–31. Springer, Cham (2023). https://doi.org/10.1007/978-3-031-48312-7_2
28. Sadjadi, S.O., et al.: The 2019 NIST audio-visual speaker recognition evaluation. In: Odyssey, pp. 259–265 (2020)
29. Saeed, M.S., Khan, M.H., Nawaz, S., Yousaf, M.H., Del Bue, A.: Fusion and orthogonal projection for improved face-voice association. In: ICASSP 2022-2022 IEEE International Conference on Acoustics, Speech and Signal Processing (ICASSP), pp. 7057–7061. IEEE (2022)
30. Saeed, M.S., et al.: Single-branch network for multimodal training. In: ICASSP 2023-2023 IEEE International Conference on Acoustics, Speech and Signal Processing (ICASSP), pp. 1–5. IEEE (2023)
31. Sarı, L., Singh, K., Zhou, J., Torresani, L., Singhal, N., Saraf, Y.: A multi-view approach to audio-visual speaker verification. In: ICASSP 2021-2021 IEEE International Conference on Acoustics, Speech and Signal Processing (ICASSP), pp. 6194–6198. IEEE (2021)
32. Shon, S., Oh, T.H., Glass, J.: Noise-tolerant audio-visual online person verification using an attention-based neural network fusion. In: ICASSP 2019-2019 IEEE

International Conference on Acoustics, Speech and Signal Processing (ICASSP), pp. 3995–3999. IEEE (2019)

33. Stevenage, S.V., Edey, R., Keay, R., Morrison, R., Robertson, D.J.: Familiarity is key: exploring the effect of familiarity on the face-voice correlation. Brain Sci. **14**(2), 112 (2024)

34. Tao, R., Lee, K.A., Shi, Z., Li, H.: Speaker recognition with two-step multi-modal deep cleansing. In: ICASSP 2023-2023 IEEE International Conference on Acoustics, Speech and Signal Processing (ICASSP), pp. 1–5. IEEE (2023)

35. Wang, R., Wei, Z., Duan, H., Ji, S., Long, Y., Hong, Z.: EfficientTDNN: efficient architecture search for speaker recognition. IEEE/ACM Trans. Audio Speech Lang. Process. **30**, 2267–2279 (2022)

36. Xie, W., Nagrani, A., Chung, J.S., Zisserman, A.: Utterance-level aggregation for speaker recognition in the wild. In: ICASSP 2019-2019 IEEE International Conference on Acoustics, Speech and Signal Processing (ICASSP), pp. 5791–5795. IEEE (2019)

37. Zhang, J., Xu, X., Shen, F., Lu, H., Liu, X., Shen, H.T.: Enhancing audio-visual association with self-supervised curriculum learning. In: Proceedings of the AAAI Conference on Artificial Intelligence, vol. 35, pp. 3351–3359 (2021)

38. Zhang, J.: SeesawFaceNets: sparse and robust face verification model for mobile platform. arXiv preprint arXiv:1908.09124 (2019)

Proactive Frequency Forest: A Forest Construction Scheme Based on Proactive Forest

Javier García Hernández [ID], Nayma Cepero Pérez [ID],
and Daniel Pardo Echevarría[(✉)] [ID]

Universidad Tecnológica de La Habana José Antonio Echeverría,
CUJAE. 114 No.11901, e/Ciclovía y Rotonda, Marianao, La Habana, Cuba
{jgarciah,ncepero,dpardo}@ceis.cujae.edu.cu

Abstract. Increasing diversity in decision forests without compromising efficiency represents a challenge in machine learning. In this sense, the Proactive Forest algorithm has been proposed as an improvement of Random Forest, by introducing an adaptive scheme for attribute selection based on probabilities. However, the proactive scheme that uses this algorithm depends on the importance of the attributes to build new trees has a disadvantage. At a certain point, the probability of training trees with attributes of low predictive power can increase considerably, affecting the efficiency of the model. As a solution to this possible problem, a new variant is presented, called Proactive Frequency Forest, which incorporates two main components. These components focus on: (1) an initial weighted assignment of attribute selection probabilities, calculated using four statistical techniques, and (2) a dynamic updating strategy based on the frequency of occurrence of attributes during forest construction. Experimental validation, performed on multiple data sets, shows that the proposal significantly increases model diversity without negatively affecting predictive performance.

Keywords: machine learning · decision forest · Proactive Forest · feature importance

1 Introduction

Data mining enables the generation of useful knowledge from large volumes of information [1]. To achieve this goal, machine learning algorithms are employed to obtain models that represent hidden patterns within the data [2]. Within machine learning, supervised approaches stand out for their ability to generate predictive models. In particular, these approaches focus on using labeled examples to train models that can infer the class value of new instances [1, 2].

Among the most widely used supervised techniques are decision tree-based algorithms, which are known for their interpretability [3]. However, the resulting models tend to overfit when faced with complex data distributions. To overcome this limitation, decision forest algorithms have gained prominence [3]. These are based on ensemble models, which combine multiple predictive models in this case, a series of decision trees [4]. Decision forest algorithms are characterized by two main elements: the high

Y. Hernádez Heredia et al. (Eds.): IWAIPR 2025, LNCS 16328, pp. 420–431, 2026.
https://doi.org/10.1007/978-3-032-11358-0_35

predictive power of each individual classifier and the diversity within the model, where each new classifier must be as different as possible from the others [5].

One of the most successful approaches in this regard is Random Forest (RF), which builds a set of trees trained on random subsets of features, ensuring model diversity [6, 7]. However, the random feature selection proposed by RF can lead to unbalanced exploration of the feature space. As a result, redundancies may arise among trees, leading to uncontrolled diversity, which negatively impacts the model [3, 8].

As a way to address the issues presented by RF, Proactive Forest (PF) was introduced. PF proposes a "proactive" construction scheme based on adjustable probabilities for feature selection [3, 8]. Unlike the random approach, PF initializes the attribute selection probabilities uniformly and updates them dynamically. The update process uses feature importance and follows an inverse principle: less important attributes receive a higher increase in their selection probability to encourage their inclusion in future trees [8].

This approach, aimed at broadening the coverage of the feature space, seeks greater control over the diversity generated within the forest [8]. However, as construction progresses, this scheme may lead to excessive selection of originally less relevant attributes. This could result in a decline in diversity that ultimately harms the predictive performance of trees generated in later stages, and of the forest as a whole [3].

In this context, the present work proposes an alternative approach that aims to better balance exploration and exploitation during forest construction. The proposal, named Proactive Frequency Forest (PFF), is based on two components: (1) a weighted initialization of attribute selection probabilities based on statistical measures of attribute importance, and (2) a dynamic update strategy guided by the frequency of attribute usage instead of their estimated importance. In this way, PFF seeks to counteract bias toward initially dominant features and promote broader exploration of the feature space.

2 Related Works

The Random Forest (RF) algorithm, introduced by [6], has been one of the most influential techniques in supervised machine learning. This algorithm employs a fully random scheme for decision forest construction. Its effectiveness has been validated in numerous recent studies and across various domains, including cybersecurity [9], medicine [10], and education [11], among others.

However, due to the disadvantages posed by RF random scheme, many studies in the literature have focused on developing alternative construction approaches [3, 8]. One such example is found in [12], where the authors propose a method that uses subspacing techniques and bootstrap sampling to explore a greater variety of data while maintaining complementary trees. Another variation, developed by [13], introduces a weighting scheme called Markowitz RF, which uses the covariance matrix to regulate the risk of increasing diversity at the cost of effectiveness. Furthermore, the approach developed in [14] suggests using a new strategy called iSat to classify new instances with previously unseen classes.

Along this line, Proactive Forest (PF) was introduced in [8] and [3] as an approach designed to correct the random selection of features through a proactive construction scheme. The PF algorithm introduces a probability distribution over the features to regulate their participation in the construction of each tree. These probabilities are initialized uniformly and updated based on feature importance measures observed during training [3]. In this way, features that have been less considered throughout the forest construction are selected [3].

The update mechanism in PF uses a classic importance metric proposed by [6], which evaluates a feature's influence based on its impact on impurity reduction or information gain. Additionally, works such as [7, 15] highlight feature importance as a simple metric that quantifies each variable's predictive power in a supervised classification problem. Nevertheless, several alternative statistical methods exist for quantifying feature importance, including:

- **Chi-squared:** A statistical measure proposed by [16] and used in [17] to evaluate the independence between a feature and the target variable.
- **Mutual Information:** Captures the amount of shared information between two variables, as proposed in [18].
- **Analysis of Variance (ANOVA):** Used in [19] to quantify the discriminative power of a feature by evaluating the ratio between inter-class and intra-class variance.
- **Goodness Metric:** Proposed by [20] and used in [21], it evaluates the relevance of a feature with respect to the class, while considering redundancy among features.

These metrics have been applied in recent works such as [15] and [21]. Their usage is mainly within feature selection tasks in supervised contexts. These studies highlight the effectiveness of each metric in improving the predictive quality of models and reducing data dimensionality in an informed manner.

Despite advances in feature selection and weighting strategies, there is still a limited number of studies that use feature importance as a construction approach [3, 7, 15]. In this context, the PF algorithm stands out as one of the few effective algorithms that employ this metric during forest construction. The results obtained in [3] support this claim through an experimental study comparing the PF and RF algorithms, in which PF achieved superior results in most scenarios. Additionally, recent studies such as [9] reaffirm these findings by applying the PF algorithm in a cybersecurity context, where PF produced results comparable to or even better than those of RF.

3 Proposed Method

This work proposes a new construction variant of the PF algorithm. Based on the results obtained by PF in comparison with RF as a construction approach that incorporates feature importance and considering the limitations it presents, a new method named Proactive Frequency Forest (PFF) is introduced. This approach integrates two key components or phases aimed at increasing the structural diversity within PF: (1) an initial weighted assignment of feature selection probabilities based on statistical importance metrics, and (2) a dynamic update strategy guided by the frequency of feature usage throughout the forest construction process.

These two phases are integrated into the execution flow of the PF algorithm training process, as shown in Fig. 1, and are highlighted in green. The second proposed component is located directly within the forest construction phase. The following sections describe each of these aspects in detail, supplemented with flowcharts that illustrate the logic of the process.

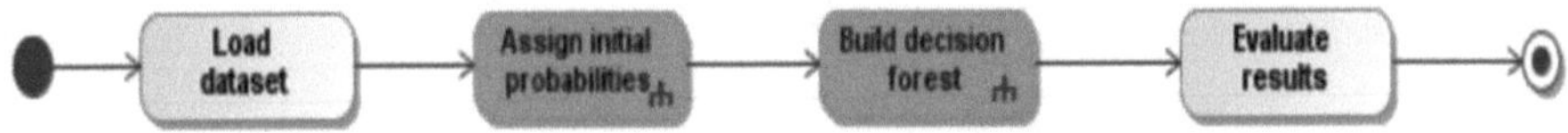

Fig. 1. PFF basic flow

3.1 Weighted Initialization of Feature Selection Probabilities

As part of the proposed solution, this work introduces an approach to assign an initial feature selection probability within the Proactive Forest (PF) construction scheme. To achieve this, an initialization component is proposed, based on four importance metrics selected for their adaptability to different types of data. These metrics evaluate the relevance of features by considering both statistical relationships and structural aspects of the data. The employed variants are [17–19, 21]:

- **Chi-squared**: Assesses the statistical independence between each feature and the target variable. It is especially useful for categorical variables, determining whether the distribution of a feature significantly differs across classes.
- **Mutual Information**: Quantifies the amount of shared information between the feature and the class, capturing non-linear dependencies. It offers robustness in domains with complex relationships and mixed variable types.
- **F-Classif (Analysis of Variance)**: Measures the ratio between inter-class variance and intra-class variance. This is particularly useful when features are continuous and the target variable is discrete.
- **Goodness Metric**: Combines relevance to the target class with redundancy among features, aiming to balance the selection of informative attributes while avoiding redundant ones.

The selection of these approaches is based on obtaining an initial statistical measure of the importance of the variables, without considering other effective alternatives that could complicate the process. Each metric produces a set of importance scores that are normalized to form a probability distribution used during the feature selection process. This step requires prior preprocessing to ensure consistency in the calculations. Figure 2 illustrates the execution flow corresponding to this stage, highlighting that for each new dataset to be analyzed, preprocessing is performed whenever conversion to numerical values is required.

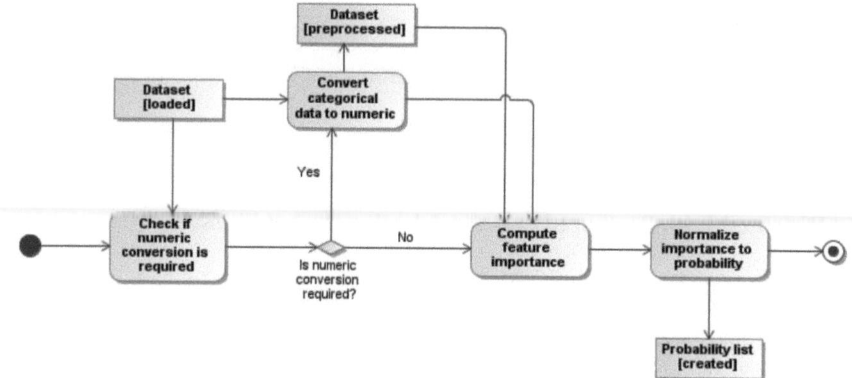

Fig. 2. Execution flow of the probability initialization component

3.2 Frequency-Based Dynamic Update

In the proposed solution, once the initial attribute selection probabilities have been set and after the construction of each tree, these probabilities are dynamically updated. Unlike the original approach in Proactive Forest, in [8], which favors features with higher importance, this work adopts an alternative strategy based on the frequency of attribute usage. The Fig. 3 illustrates the execution flow of the update process as an integral part of the forest construction iterative cycle. Activities associated with the proposed method are highlighted in green within the forest construction workflow.

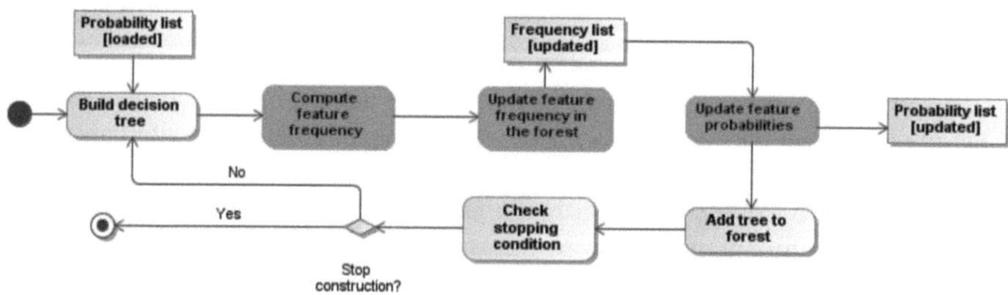

Fig. 3. Dynamic probability update flow based on feature usage frequency

As shown in Fig. 3, after each tree is built, the frequency with which each attribute has been selected is recorded. Attributes with lower frequency have their selection probability increased, promoting their inclusion in subsequent trees. Frequency is defined as the total number of times an attribute has been selected in the splits of a tree. This process is repeated iteratively until the stopping condition defined by the algorithm is met. This stop condition is set when a predefined number of trees to be constructed is reached, as defined by the authors of [8], in the original version of PF. The strategy aims to encourage broader exploration of the feature space, which may lead to increased ensemble diversity without compromising predictive performance.

4 Solution Validation

This section describes the experimental strategy defined to validate the proposed solution. A series of experiments were designed to separately analyze the effect of the probability initialization and the frequency-based dynamic update. Both approaches are evaluated on a diverse collection of datasets with the aim of observing their impact on both predictive performance and model diversity.

4.1 Experimental Setup

To carry out the validation, 32 datasets were selected from the UCI Machine Learning Repository. These datasets vary in terms of the number of instances, number of features, variable types, and class distribution. This diversity allows the representation of common scenarios in classification tasks and enables the evaluation of the model's behavior under heterogeneous conditions. The Table 1 presents the selected datasets.

Table 1. Selected datasets

Datasets	Id	Ins	Atr	Clss	Datasets	Id	Ins	Atr	Clss
balance scale	BS	625	4	3	molecular	MC	106	58	2
car	CA	1728	6	4	nursery	NS	12960	8	5
cmc	CC	1473	9	3	optdigits	OP	5620	64	10
credit-g	CG	1000	20	2	page blocks	PB	5473	10	5
diabetes	DB	768	8	2	pendigits	PD	10992	16	10
ecoli	EC	336	7	8	segment	SG	2310	19	7
flags religion	FR	194	29	8	solar flare 1	S1	323	12	6
glass	GS	214	9	6	solar flare 2	S2	1066	12	6
haberman	HB	306	3	2	sonar	SN	208	60	2
heart-statlog	HS	270	13	2	spambase	SB	4601	57	2
ionosphere	IS	351	34	2	splice	SP	3190	61	3
iris	II	150	4	3	tae	TA	151	5	3
kr-vs-kp	KK	3196	36	2	vehicle	VH	846	18	4
letter	LT	20000	16	26	vowel	VW	990	13	11
liver	LV	345	6	2	wdbc	WB	569	30	2
lymph	LY	148	18	4	wine	WN	178	13	3

The experimental study to evaluate PFF arises from an analysis of the two proposed components. These experiments were organized into two main blocks:

1. **Evaluation of probability initialization**: The FP algorithm without initialization and with the four attribute probability initialization variants, corresponding to the four metrics described in Sect. 3.1, are compared. The objective is to take the best performing initialization variant for each data set analyzed.

2. **Evaluation of dynamic update**: We compare the behavior of PF with and without the frequency-based update component, on the same data configuration. Only the initialization variant change, as indicated in the previous experimentation.

The performance of each approach was measured using two complementary metrics, each corresponding to key characteristics of forests: predictive power and diversity. The selected metrics are:

- **Accuracy**: Used to measure the effectiveness of the forest. It represents the proportion of correctly classified instances over the total, reflecting the model's predictive performance.
- **Proportion of Correctly Distinguished instances (PCD)**: Used to measure the forest's diversity. It represents the proportion of instances classified by trees built using different sets of features, reflecting the internal structural diversity of the ensemble.

To ensure a reliable evaluation, stratified 10-fold cross-validation was used. In each iteration, one subset was held out as a test set, while the remaining data was used for training. Metrics were averaged after completing all 10 repetitions.

4.2 Discussion of the Results for Probability Initialization

As part of the experimentation performed, the results obtained when initializing the FP attributes probabilities with each of the variants proposed in Sect. 3.1 should be evaluated. The five variants were evaluated, with the following nomenclature: Chi-square (CHI2), mutual information (MI), F-Classif (F), goodness metric (BON) and original FP initialization (PF). The results are shown in Table 2, where the accuracy performance obtained for each data set is indicated. An additional column indicates which metric produced the best performance on each set, for better identification of the most effective scheme used in the experiment in the next section, to evaluate the proposal as a whole.

Table 2. Results for initialization probabilities variants

Datasets	CHI2	MI	F	BON	PF	Best	Datasets	CHI2	MI	F	BON	PF	Best
BS	0,815	0,818	**0,822**	0,818	0,818	F	MC	0,866	**1**	0,861	0,891	0,886	MI
CA	**0,954**	0,95	0,851	0,935	**0,978**	PF	NS	0,934	0,91	0,793	0,921	**0,999**	PF
CC	0,532	**0,525**	0,524	0,52	0,523	CHI2	OP	0,968	0,971	0,968	0,976	**0,977**	PF
CG	0,759	0,746	0,762	0,758	**0,765**	PF	PB	0,956	0,974	0,973	0,973	**0,975**	PF
DB	0,735	0,752	**0,767**	0,762	0,757	F	PD	0,988	0,99	0,99	0,99	**0,991**	PF
EC	0,786	0,855	0,85	**0,859**	0,853	BON	SG	0,976	0,979	0,968	0,951	**0,98**	PF
FR	**0,685**	0,655	0,679	0,683	0,674	CHI2	S1	0,609	0,713	0,719	0,714	**0,721**	PF
GS	0,735	**0,774**	0,749	0,742	0,768	MI	S2	0,72	0,727	0,717	**0,759**	0,734	BON
HB	0,728	0,719	**0,753**	0,728	0,692	F	SN	0,823	0,826	**0,83**	0,792	0,806	F
HS	0,799	0,813	0,803	0,818	**0,827**	PF	SB	0,943	**0,956**	0,953	0,952	0,952	MI
IS	0,937	0,938	0,938	0,937	**0,94**	PF	SP	0,949	**0,999**	0,95	0,957	0,959	MI
II	**0,956**	0,939	0,949	0,943	0,94	CHI2	TA	0,613	**0,684**	0,591	0,577	0,671	MI
KK	0,964	0,972	0,969	0,979	**0,996**	PF	VH	0,725	**0,749**	0,745	0,741	**0,746**	MI

(continued)

Table 2. (*continued*)

Datasets	CHI2	MI	F	BON	PF	Best	Datasets	CHI2	MI	F	BON	PF	Best
LT	0,951	0,952	0,951	0,949	**0,959**	PF	VW	0,911	0,92	0,924	0,929	0,961	PF
LV	0,664	0,728	0,671	0,724	**0,742**	PF	WB	0,947	0,959	0,962	0,961	0,968	PF
LY	0,83	0,822	0,821	0,835	**0,837**	PF	WN	0,944	0,962	0,97	0,961	0,975	PF

As can be seen in Table 2, the best results are obtained when using the default initialization of the PF algorithm, with a total of 17 times, followed by using the MI variant with 6 and F with 4. However, it is necessary to perform a statistical analysis to verify if the behavior of the results is statistically correct. In this case a Friedman statistical test is used, which allows the values of more than two data samples to be compared on the basis of their median. This test is performed because each method was compared on the same data sets [22]. To perform the test, a significance value $\alpha = 0.05$ and the following hypotheses were defined:

H0: There are no significant differences in the median values of the results of each variant.
H1: There are significant differences in the median values of the results of each variant.

As a result of the test, a p-value $= 0.000$ was obtained, lower than the declared significance level. For this reason, there is sufficient evidence to reject the null hypothesis, so there are significant differences in the results of each variant evaluated. To corroborate that this difference may favor PF, Fig. 4 shows a diagram of individual values, where similar results are observed for PF, BON and MI over the rest of the variants. However, a slight superiority for MI is discernible. Nevertheless, for the next experiment, the attributes will be initialized according to the variant indicated in the last column of Table 2.

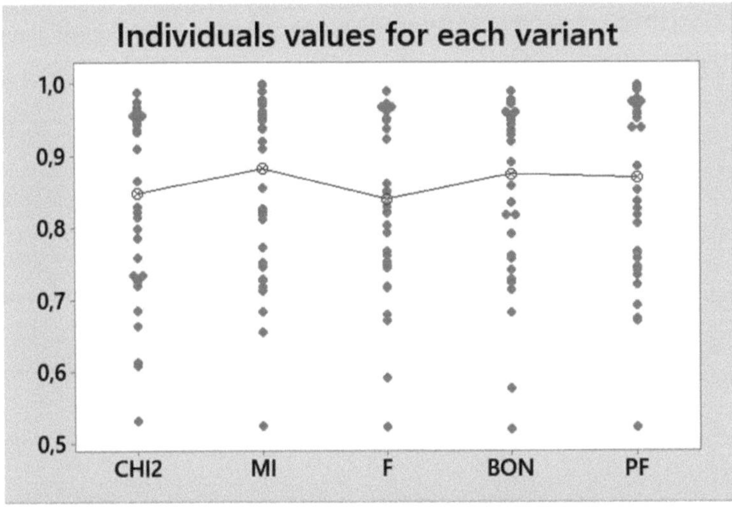

Fig. 4. Individual values for initialization variants results

4.3   Discussion of the Results for Probability Update

This section analyzes the results obtained for the probability update strategy proposed by PFF. Table 3 presents the accuracy and PCD results for the 32 datasets. These results are compared with those of the original PF algorithm, with bold highlighting used to indicate cases where PFF outperforms the original version. For easier identification, the following notation was used for each metric: PFF Accuracy (AccPFF), PF Accuracy (AccPF), PFF PCD (PCDPFF), PF PCD (PCDPF).

Table 3. Com Comparison between the original Proactive Forest approach and the attribute frequency-based approach.

Datasets	AccPFF	AccPF	PCDPFF	PCDPF	Datasets	AccPFF	AccPF	PCDPFF	PCDPF
BS	0,816	**0,818**	0,382	0,382	MC	**0,907**	0,886	**0,964**	0,806
CA	0,973	**0,978**	**0,258**	0,169	NS	0,976	**0,999**	**0,233**	0,199
CC	**0,528**	0,523	**0,84**	0,824	OP	0,976	**0,977**	**0,776**	0,335
CG	0,758	**0,765**	**0,776**	0,754	PB	**0,975**	0,974	**0,081**	0,078
DB	**0,76**	0,757	**0,717**	0,704	PD	0,991	0,991	**0,144**	0,142
EC	0,824	**0,853**	**0,57**	0,418	SG	0,968	**0,98**	**0,998**	0,129
FR	**0,676**	0,674	**0,809**	0,753	S1	**0,726**	0,721	**0,584**	0,521
GS	**0,784**	0,768	0,729	**0,74**	S2	0,706	**0,734**	**0,776**	0,332
HB	0,691	0,691	**0,623**	0,622	SN	**0,818**	0,806	**0,82**	0,786
HS	0,819	**0,827**	0,65	**0,659**	SB	**0,956**	0,952	**0,244**	0,228
IS	0,935	**0,94**	**0,345**	0,309	SP	**0,959**	0,958	**0,298**	0,184
II	**0,948**	0,94	0,101	**0,156**	TA	0,617	**0,671**	**0,892**	0,857
KK	0,993	**0,996**	**0,101**	0,028	VH	**0,747**	0,746	0,648	0,652
LT	0,953	**0,958**	0,365	**0,373**	VW	**0,97**	0,961	**0,831**	0,787
LV	0,731	**0,742**	0,911	**0,923**	WB	0,963	**0,968**	**0,187**	0,182
LY	**0,848**	0,837	**0,654**	0,611	WN	**0,977**	0,975	**0,334**	0,317

When analyzing the results shown in Table 3, it can be observed that both Proactive Forest and Proactive Frequency Forest achieve the best accuracy performance in 15 cases each and two results with equal performance. To determine whether there are significant differences between the results, a non-parametric statistical test was applied. The selected test was the Wilcoxon Signed-Rank Test, which compares the results of both construction schemes based on their median values [23]. The significance level used was $\alpha = 0.05$, and the hypotheses were defined as follows:

H_0: There are no significant differences in the median values of the results from each scheme.

H_1: There are significant differences in the median values of the results from each scheme.

The test produced a p-value $= 0.494$, which is greater than the stated significance level. Therefore, there is not enough evidence to reject the null hypothesis. It can thus be concluded that the accuracy results from both schemes are not significantly different. Regarding PCD results, Proactive Frequency Forest achieves the best diversity performance in 25 out of 32 datasets, representing approximately 78% of the cases. In the remaining 7 cases, Proactive Forest yields the best diversity. This indicates that the proposed approach achieves better diversity results. However, it is necessary to perform the appropriate statistical tests to validate this claim.

As in the previous comparison regarding accuracy, the Wilcoxon Signed-Rank Test was used to compare diversity (PCD) results, with the same hypotheses and significance level $\alpha = 0.05$. The results of the test indicate a statistically significant difference between the two approaches in terms of PCD. The p-value = 0.0001709 suggests that the null hypothesis can be rejected, as it is lower than the declared significance level. Therefore, the increase in diversity provided by PFF (Frequency-based Approach) over PF (original version) is statistically significant. This conclusion can be verified with the analysis of Fig. 5, where through a diagram of individual values, it can be observed how the median value of PFF is higher than that of PF.

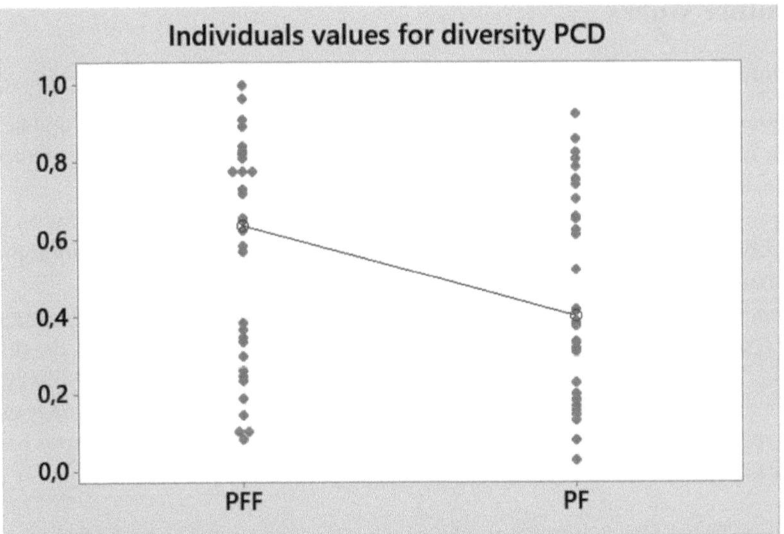

Fig. 5. Individual values for update probability approach PCD diversity

Although there are no notable improvements in terms of accuracy for PFF, the results are statistically similar. However, the PCD diversity measure shows better performance for PFF in most databases; in addition, the results are statistically favorable to the proposed approach, as shown in Fig. 5. This evidence supports the fact that the proposed approach outperforms the previous approach in terms of diversity, which is particularly relevant considering the properties of forest-based algorithms. In this type of method, both diversity and predictive power must be considered together. Therefore, the proposed solution is presented as an effective approach for forest construction.

5 Conclusions

From the results obtained in the present work, it can be concluded that:

1. Although algorithms such as Proactive Forest propose an effective solution to the random construction scheme proposed by Random Forest, it has limitations that affect the diversity generated, based on the way of selecting the attributes to train each tree.
2. Proactive Frequency Forest approach, which combines a weighted probability initialization based on statistical metrics with a dynamic update strategy guided by the frequency of attribute usage, significantly improves the structural diversity of decision forests without compromising model accuracy.
3. The proposed weighted initialization allows a more efficient exploitation of the relevant attributes from the beginning of the forest construction process.
4. Frequency-based updating favors a more equitable exploration of the feature space, reducing redundancy and promoting the inclusion of new attributes.

6 Future Works

As future lines of work, we propose:

1. Incorporate adaptive learning rate mechanisms during probability update, with the objective of adjusting the rate of attribute space exploration throughout the construction process.
2. Develop a component to select the best variant of probability initialization for the attributes, taking into account the nature of the data and the classification problem at hand.
3. Conduct a comparative study with similar solutions and contemporary approaches to forest construction, in order to evaluate the relative performance of the proposal in terms of diversity and predictive capacity.
4. Conduct a study of the proposal's, performance considering additional metrics, such as recall, to evaluate the handling of class imbalance, as well as an analysis based on the confusion matrix focused on the false positive rate.

References

1. Saxena, G., Kumar, R., Dash, Y.: A review of pattern mining approaches: insights and comparisons. SSRN 5222067 (2025). https://doi.org/10.2139/ssrn.5222067
2. Mahesh, B.: Machine learning algorithms-a review. Int. J. Sci. Res. (IJSR). **9**(1), 381–386 (2020). https://doi.org/10.21275/ART20203995
3. Cepero-Pérez, N., Moreno-Espino, M., Morales, E.F., López-González, A., Yáñez-Márquez, C., Pavón, J.: A proactive approach for random forest. Appl. Intell. **55**(6), 432 (2025). https://doi.org/10.1007/s10489-025-06339-y
4. Dietterich, T.G.: Ensemble methods in machine learning. In: Multiple Classifier Systems Springer, pp. 1–15 (2000)
5. Rokach, L.: Decision forest: twenty years of research. Inf. Fusion 111–125 (2017). https://doi.org/10.1016/j.inffus.2015.06.005

6. Breiman, L.: Random forests. Mach. Learn. **45**, 32 (2001). https://doi.org/10.1023/A:101093 3404324

7. Rehill, P.: How do applied researchers use the causal forest? A methodological review. Int. Stat. Rev. (2025). https://doi.org/10.1111/insr.12610

8. Cepero-Pérez, N., Denis-Miranda, L.A., Hernández-Palacio, R., Moreno-Espino, M., García-Borroto, M.: Proactive forest for supervised classification. International Workshop on Artificial Intelligence and Pattern Recognition, pp. 255–262 (2018). https://doi.org/10.1007/978-3-030-01132-1_29

9. Pardo Echevarría, D., Cepero-Perez, N., Moreno-Espino, M., Chissingui, H.J., Díaz-Pando, H.: Detection of malicious bots using a proactive supervised classification approach. In: International Workshop on Artificial Intelligence and Pattern Recognition, pp. 297–309 (2023). Springer. https://doi.org/10.1007/978-3-031-49552-6_26

10. Khoirunnisa, A., Adytia, D., Deris, M.M.: Comprehensive review of hybrid feature selection methods for microarray-based cancer detection. IEEE Access (2025). https://doi.org/10.1109/ACCESS.2025.3564706

11. Lopez, S.: The switch: determinants of family school modality choices during the COVID-19 pandemic (2025)

12. Adnan, M.N., Ip, R.H., Bewong, M., Islam, M.Z.: BDF: a new decision forest algorithm. Inf. Sci. **569**, 687–705 (2021). https://doi.org/10.1016/j.ins.2021.05.017

13. Kouloumpris, E., Vlahavas, I.: Markowitz random forest: weighting classification and regression trees with modern portfolio theory. Neurocomputing **620**, 129191 (2025). https://doi.org/10.1016/j.neucom.2024.129191

14. Rahman, M.G., Islam, M.Z.: Adaptive decision forest: an incremental machine learning framework. Pattern Recogn. **122**, 108345 (2022). https://doi.org/10.1016/j.patcog.2021.108345

15. Liu, Y.W., Dou, H., Zhang, Y., Zheng, H.X.: Variable importance-weighted random forest for classification. Knowl.-Based Syst. **118** (2017). https://doi.org/10.1007/s40484-017-0121-6

16. Divgi, D.: A minimum chi-square method for developing a common metric in item response theory. Appl. Psychol. Meas. **9**(4), 413–415 (1985). https://doi.org/10.1177/014662168500900410

17. Huang, Y.: Application of an improved CHI feature selection algorithm. J. Appl. Math. **2021**, 9963382 (2021). https://doi.org/10.1155/2021/9963382

18. Guyon, I.E.A.: An introduction to variable and feature selection. J. Mach. Learn. Res. **3**, 1157–1182 (2003)

19. James, D.W.G., Hastie, T., Tibshirani, R.: An introduction to statistical learning: with applications in R. Springer, New York (2013)

20. Peng, H.L., Ding, F.C.: Feature selection based on mutual information: criteria of max-dependency, max-relevance, and min-redundancy. IEEE Trans. Pattern Anal. Mach. Intell. **27**(8), 1226–1238 (2005). https://doi.org/10.1109/TPAMI.2005.159

21. Souza, F.P., Araújo, C.R.: High-order conditional mutual information maximization for dealing with high-order dependencies in feature selection (2022). arXiv preprint. https://doi.org/10.1016/j.patcog.2022.108895

22. Liu, J., Xu, Y.: T-Friedman test: a new statistical test for multiple comparison with an adjustable conservativeness measure. Int. J. Comput. Intell. Syst. **15**(1), 29 (2022). https://doi.org/10.1007/s44196-022-00083-8

23. Chechile, R.A.: A Bayesian analysis for the Wilcoxon signed-rank statistic. Commun. Stat.-Theory Methods **47**(21), 5241–5254 (2018). https://doi.org/10.1080/03610926.2017.1388402

Implementation of a Neural Network in an Embedded System for Burst Detection in Water Pipelines

Jaime E. Chiang Cruz[1]($\boxtimes$) , Christian Alejandro Fernández Leal[1] ,
Alejandro Perdomo-Campos[2] , and Jorge Ramírez-Beltrán[1]

[1] Center for Hydraulic Research, Technological University of Havana "José Antonio Echeverría", Havana, Cuba
jchiangjr@gmail.com
[2] Center for Microelectronics Research, Technological University of Havana "José Antonio Echeverría", Havana, Cuba
aperdomoc@tele.cujae.edu.cu

Abstract. This paper presents a novel implementation of a Neural Network model in a low-power embedded system for burst detection in pipelines. It combines a quantized model with the LEA (Low-Energy Accelerator) and FRAM memory to perform signal processing and inference operations, optimizing the balance between accuracy and energy efficiency. The model was trained on a dataset of 187 signals (80 noise, 107 ruptures). Accuracy, precision, and recall metrics were used for model evaluation. After implementation in the microcontroller, a validation protocol was executed to assess the impact of quantization on the method's accuracy.

Keywords: Embebbed Sistems · Machine Learning · Digital Signal Processing

1 Introduction

The risk of depleting hydraulic resources has increased significantly in recent years due to growing pollution and climate change, both of which are considered imminent threats. The greatest contributors to water losses in hydraulic systems are burst and background leaks. The former are large-scale water leaks occurring within a short time frame, caused by abrupt failures in pipelines and their assembly components. Background leaks, on the other hand, have a low flow rate and mainly originate in tanks and pipes. Although both contribute to water loss, bursts account for a substantially greater volume.

The occurrence of a burst generates abrupt pressure changes that propagate through the pipeline. The detection of these transient pressure variations is a field of study that has evolved significantly over the years. The need to understand and mitigate these effects has led to the development of mathematical models and analytical methods for their detection [11].

Y. Hernádez Heredia et al. (Eds.): IWAIPR 2025, LNCS 16328, pp. 432–443, 2026.
https://doi.org/10.1007/978-3-032-11358-0_36

Within the scientific community, two paradigms have been established, each comprising techniques that detect and locate these phenomena. The first relies on data acquired through Supervisory Control and Data Acquisition (SCADA) systems, which enable an accurate representation of fluid dynamics within the network. Despite the advancements achieved with this approach, its main limitation is its inability to detect the event at the moment of its occurrence [9].

The second paradigm is the data-driven approach, which uses a much smaller sampling period to achieve a more precise appreciation of the moment when the event occurs, enabling real-time infrastructure monitoring [10]. In this approach, events are detected through statistical analysis and signal processing of acquired data. This method is particularly promising for water distribution systems with a large number of sensors, as it eliminates the need for complex hydraulic model construction. These technologies are designed to identify anomalous values in the data that may indicate abnormal events based on the usual patterns recorded in the pipeline system [2].

The data-driven approach typically involves two steps: data acquisition, pre-processing, and transformation, followed by the event detection strategy. The primary objective of data preprocessing is to eliminate erroneous or missing data from time series records to facilitate subsequent analysis. Although challenges related to variability and uncertainty may arise during the processing of measurement data, these can be mitigated to some extent through preprocessing and transformation techniques [13]. The main event detection strategies using transient pressure signals rely on feature set classification methods.

Traditional fixed-feature extraction methods depend on the quality of predefined feature extraction and require significant signal preprocessing, parameter tuning, and training phases [4]. The application of innovative machine learning algorithms has yielded promising results; for instance, Convolutional Neural Networks (CNNs) have proven to be more effective in classifying time-series signals [5]. The literature highlights the use of artificial neural networks [12], support vector machines [1], and naive Bayes classifiers [6].

These event detection methods need to be implemented in low-power edge devices, as the data-driven paradigm requires their deployment at various points in the water distribution system, often in locations that are difficult to access and lack electrical networks. In recent years, significant strides have been made in the implementation of complex algorithms for signal processing and pattern recognition in microcontrollers, with the introduction of concepts such as embedded intelligence and TinyML [12].

In this context, microcontroller families such as STM32 from STMicroelectronics and nRF from Nordic Semiconductor stand out. However, many of their solutions depend on GPUs or complex processing units that typically require high power consumption and significant memory capacity. This is not the case with the MSP430 family from Texas Instruments, which includes a Low-Energy Accelerator (LEA) module—a low-power coprocessor capable of performing signal processing, matrix multiplication, and other operations such as FIR, IIR, and FFT [7].

Although numerous machine learning-based proposals exist, as previously discussed, their implementation in edge devices with stringent power and memory constraints remains a largely unexplored area in specialized literature. This gap is particularly evident in hydraulic applications, where real-world implementations of pressure transient detection algorithms in low-power embedded systems are scarce.

This paper presents an innovative implementation of a burst detection system in hydraulic pipelines using a low-power embedded system such as the MSP430 microcontroller series. It integrates the LEA module for efficient signal processing, Q15 quantization for optimization, and FRAM memory for ultra-low-power operation, enabling the execution of an efficient machine learning model in this environment.

2   Data Acquisition and Preprocessing

The data used in this study were obtained experimentally from the test bench at the Hydraulic Research Center of the Technological University of Havana. The experimental system consists of a high-density polyethylene (HDPE) pipe with a nominal diameter of 160 mm and a total length of 65.2 m, supplied by a constant-head tank that maintains a static pressure of 10 m of water column (mwc) at the inlet. A controllable valve at the downstream end allows for the establishment of a flow with an average velocity of 2 m/s, a condition that generates the highest level of hydraulic noise and represents the most challenging scenario for fault detection. The pressure sensor is positioned 7 m upstream from the simulated burst point, enabling the capture of transient pressure variations [3].

The signals were originally acquired at a sampling frequency of 400 Hz, following the recommendations outlined in [10] for the detection of transient phenomena in water distribution systems. Three signal groups corresponding to the burst event were defined based on the leakage flow rate: 0.8, 0.5, and 1.5 L/s. These signals are stored in 5-second files with a sampling frequency of 400 Hz, resulting in each file containing 2000 samples. The data are divided into two classes: class 0 for signals classified as noise and class 1 for signals exhibiting a burst. A total of 80 files are classified as class 0, while 107 files are classified as class 1.

To optimize processing in the embedded system, the signals were resampled to 100 Hz using a linear-phase anti-aliasing filter. In [13], it is demonstrated that sampling frequencies between 80–100 Hz are suitable for most hydraulic monitoring applications when combined with optimized processing algorithms.

2.1   Anti-aliasing Filter Implementation

The process of reducing the sampling frequency (downsampling) from 400 Hz to 100 Hz is based on well-established mathematical principles of digital signal processing. As demonstrated by the discrete-time Fourier transform (DTFT) expressed in (1), when a signal ($x(t)$) is sampled at intervals of (T), its frequency representation consists of periodic repetitions of the original spectrum (X(f)), spaced every (1/T) Hz.

$$\sum_{n=-\infty}^{\infty} x(nT)e^{-i2\pi f nT} = \frac{1}{T} \sum_{k=-\infty}^{\infty} X\left(f - \frac{k}{T}\right) \tag{1}$$

When applying downsampling by a factor of (M = 4) (from 400 Hz to 100 Hz), the new sampling frequency becomes (1/(MT)), which reduces the spectral spacing to (1/(MT)) Hz, as expressed in (2).

$$\sum_{n=-\infty}^{\infty} x(nMT)e^{-i2\pi f nMT} = \frac{1}{MT} \sum_{k=-\infty}^{\infty} X\left(f - \frac{k}{MT}\right) \tag{2}$$

To prevent spectral overlap (aliasing), a low-pass FIR filter was implemented with the following characteristics:

- Cutoff frequency: 100 Hz ($\frac{1}{4}$ of the original frequency),
- Order: 50 coefficients (optimal compromise between selectivity and computational load),
- Passband ripple: <0.1 dB,
- Stopband attenuation: >60 dB,

This filtering ensures that the useful spectral content (0–100 Hz) necessary for event detection is preserved, as most of the signal's energy remains within the target bandwidth. In Fig. 1, the effect of the filter on one of the acquired signals can be observed. The processed files now contain 500 samples each, representing 5 s of a signal sampled at 100 Hz.

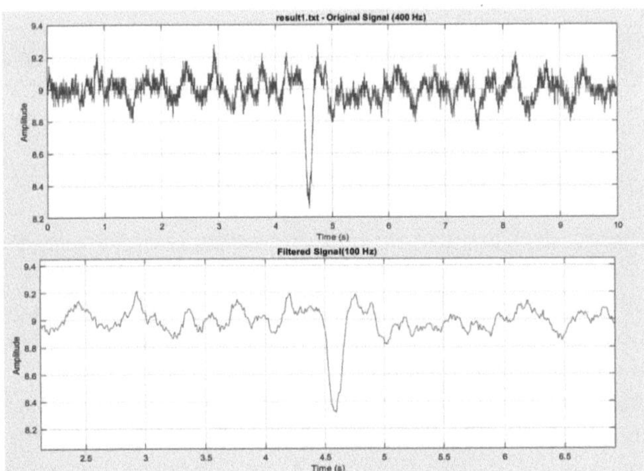

Fig. 1. Top: Original signal input to the FIR filter. Bottom: Filtered signal output from the FIR filter.

2.2   Q15 Format Conversion

The Q15 format (also known as fractional fixed-point representation), unlike floating-point numbers which consume more resources, allows decimal values to be represented within a range of -1 to nearly +1 using only 16 bits (1 bit for the sign and 15 for the fractional part). This encoding is ideal for applications where processing speed is a priority, such as hydraulic sensors, motor control, or digital signal filtering.

One of the key reasons for using the Q15 format in MSP microcontrollers is its compatibility with the Low-Energy Accelerator (LEA) module, a coprocessor designed to accelerate mathematical operations. While a floating-point multiplication may take dozens of clock cycles, the LEA executes the same operation in Q15 format within a single cycle, drastically reducing energy consumption and increasing processing speed (Algorithm 1).

Algorithm 1. Integer-Only Implementation (MSP430 Optimized)

```
 1: FUNCTION: float_to_Q15_saturated
 2: INPUT: (float_value: float, max_range: float)
 3: OUTPUT: (int16_t)
 4: SCALE = 32767.0
 5: normalized_value = float_value / max_range
 6: if normalized_value >1.0: then
 7:     return 32767 // Upper limit
 8:     if normalized_value <-1.0: then
 9:         return -32768 // Lower limit
10:     else
11:         Return (int16_t)(normalized_value * SCALE)
12:     end if
13: end if
```

2.3   Preprocessing with LEA and Feature Extraction

The data obtained after acquisition and processing (100 samples per file in Q15 format) contains excessive redundant information, making direct processing in a resource-limited microcontroller inefficient. Extracting essential features from this data helps reduce dimensionality, preserve discriminative patterns, and simplify the required classification model.

The selection of implemented features is based on an extensive review of specialized literature [5,8] and experimental tests conducted with the dataset. These features capture distinguishing patterns between bursts and hydraulic noise. A set of 10 key features is extracted using LEA vector operations, as presented in Table 1.

Table 1. Table of features with mathematical expressions

Feature	Description
RMS Value	Detects global energy variations $RMS = \sqrt{\frac{1}{N} \sum_{i=1}^{N} x_i^2}$
Crest Factor	Identifies characteristic peaks in transients $CF = \frac{\max|x_i|}{RMS}$
Standard Deviation	Quantifies signal dispersion
Spectral Coefficients (5 values) (FFT with LEA)	Captures energy redistribution in critical bands $E_{\text{band}} = \sum_{k=f_1}^{f_2} |X[k]|^2$
Estimated Signal-to-Noise Ratio	Differentiates burst patterns from hydraulic noise
Max/Min	Signal maximum and minimum values

Using the microcontroller's LEA module, subroutines for calculating each feature were implemented. The pseudocode for its configuration is shown in Algorithm 2.

Algorithm 2. Pseudocode for LEA Module Configuration

1:		▷ Configure LEA clock source (SMCLK @ 16MHz
2:	**LEACTL0** = 0x0000	▷ Clear control register 0
3:	**LEACTL0** ‖= LEACLKSEL_4	▷ Select SMCLK
4:	**LEACTL0** ‖= LEAPMD_1	▷ Low-power mode when idle
5:	**LEACTL1** = 0x0000	▷ Clear control register
6:	**LEACTL1** =LEADATAT_1	▷ Q15 data format 1
7:		▷ Set LEA RAM segment (128-word blocks)
8:	**LEASAP** = 0x2400	▷ Start address
9:	**LEASAP** = 0x27FF	▷ End address (1KB total)
10:	**LEAIE** ‖=LEAIFG0	▷ Enable completion interrupt
11:		▷ LEA Configuration Registers
12:	**LEAPMS** ‖=&signal_buffer	▷ Input buffer address
13:	**LEAPDS** ‖=&feature_vec	▷ Output feature vector

Table 2 shows the execution time required by the microcontroller and the dedicated RAM consumption of the LEA module for each of the subroutines created to obtain the features. These values demonstrate the impact on processing speed, considering that a single floating-point multiplication (32-bit IEEE 754) on the MSP430FR5994 at 16 MHz using only the CPU (#__mspabi_mpyf function) takes 84 clock cycles. Figure 2 illustrates the extracted features behavior for one of the sampled signals.

Table 2. LEA commands and their respective specifications

Feature	LEA Command	Time (µs)	LEA RAM (Bytes)
RMS Value	LEA_CMPYR2 + LEA_SQRTQ15	150	64 (input buffer)
Std Deviation	LEA_VECSUM + LEA_VARQ15 + LEA_SQRTQ15	300	128 (temp storage)
Max Value	LEA_MAXV	50	32
Min Value	LEA_MINV	50	32
Crest Factor	LEA_DIVQ15	25	16
FFT Bands (6-10)	LEA_RFFT_Q15 + LEA_BANDENERGY (x5)	750	512 (FFT buffers)

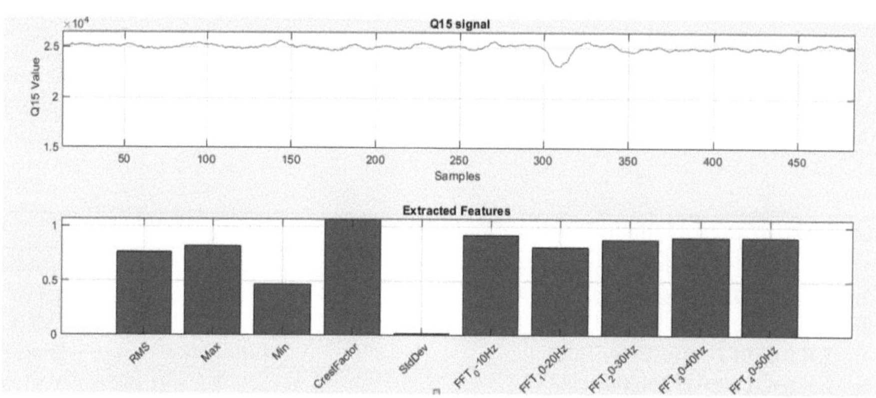

Fig. 2. Feature representation for one of the obtained signals.

3   Neural Network Creation, Quantization and Implementation

3.1   Model Design, Training and Quantization

The selected neural network model is a sequential architecture with two hidden layers (64 and 32 neurons, respectively) and an output layer with a sigmoid activation function for binary classification (see Table 3). This structure was chosen for its balance between learning capacity and computational efficiency, making it ideal for signal classification problems with features extracted in the time and frequency domains. The hidden layers use ReLU (Rectified Linear Unit) to introduce nonlinearities and enhance discrimination capability, while Dropout (30% in the first layer and 20% in the second) was included to reduce overfitting, a technique supported by previous studies on hydraulic anomaly detection.

Table 3. Model Architecture

Layer (type)	Output Shape	Param #
dense_12 (Dense)	(None, 64)	704
dropout_6 (Dropout)	(None, 64)	0
dense_13 (Dense)	(None, 32)	2,080
dropout_7 (Dropout)	(None, 32)	0
dense_14 (Dense)	(None, 1)	33
Total params:		2,817 (11.00 KB)
Trainable params:		2,817 (11.00 KB)
Non-trainable params:		0 (0.00 B)

The dataset, whose initial portion is presented in Tables 4 and 5, was divided into 80% for training and 20% for testing, with stratification to maintain the class proportion. Normalization (StandardScaler) ensured all features had zero mean and unit variance, improving model convergence.

Table 4. First Part of the Data Table

Label	RMS	Max	Min	CrestFactor	StdDev
1	0.762	0.817	0.469	1.071	0.016
1	0.761	0.840	0.473	1.103	0.017
1	0.762	0.834	0.477	1.094	0.017
⋮	⋮	⋮	⋮	⋮	⋮

Table 5. Second Part of the Data Table

Label	FFT_0-10 Hz	FFT_10-20 Hz	FFT_20-30 Hz	FFT_30-40 Hz	FFT_40-50 Hz
1	0.924	0.810	0.878	0.898	0.900
1	0.937	0.798	0.910	0.907	0.903
1	0.921	0.796	0.896	0.892	0.931
⋮	⋮	⋮	⋮	⋮	⋮

Training was optimized with the Adam algorithm (learning rate = 0.001), which dynamically adapts the learning rate during training, and was monitored with Early Stopping (patience = 10 epochs) to halt the process if validation loss stopped improving. Binary cross-entropy was used as the loss function, suitable for binary problems, and additional metrics such as precision and recall were evaluated to ensure a balance between false positives and false negatives.

To implement the designed model on the microcontroller, it was quantized to TensorFlow Lite (TFLite) with default optimizations, reducing its size and accelerating inference. Quantization converts 32-bit weights into 8-bit integers.

3.2   Model Implementation on the Microcontroller

To deploy the neural network model (Fig. 3) on the MSP430FR5994 microcontroller, an optimized workflow is followed that leverages the Low-Energy Accelerator (LEA) for vector operations and FRAM memory for efficient storage. The process consists of two main stages:

- Quantized Model Loading: The trained and converted TensorFlow Lite model (with INT8 quantization) is stored in FRAM memory as a constant array. Weights and biases are organized in pre-adjusted matrices to facilitate access during inference.
- Accelerated Inference: Each layer of the neural network is executed using LEA matrix operations,
  - Hidden Layer 1 (64 neurons): Matrix multiplication (Q15) with LEA_MatrixMultiply, followed by the ReLU activation function (implemented as max(0, x) in Q15),
  - Hidden Layer 2 (32 neurons): Same process, with dimensionality reduction,
  - Output Layer: Dot product computation using LEA_DotProduct and sigmoid approximation implemented through a 256-value LUT (Look-Up Table) in Q15.

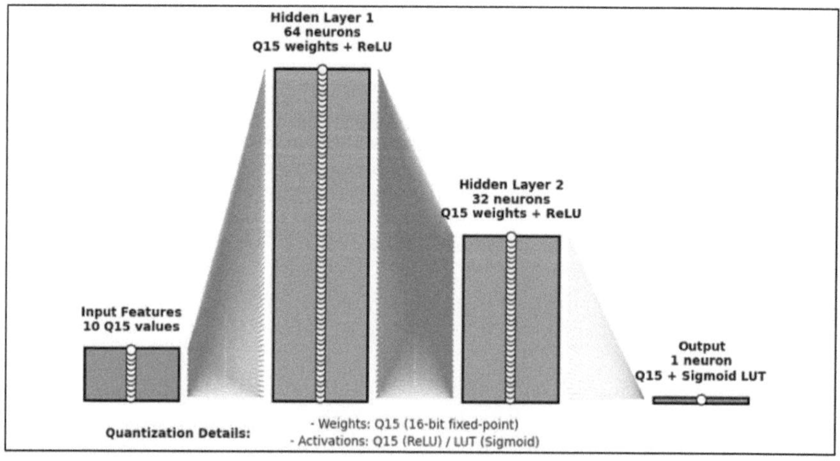

Fig. 3. Quantized model architecture.

4 Validation and Results

The neural network model trained outside the microcontroller demonstrated exceptional performance during the evaluation phase. The learning curves showed stable convergence in both accuracy and loss function, confirming that the training process was effective and that the model generalizes well to unseen data (Fig. 4). The metrics obtained in the independent test set—100% accuracy, 100% precision, and 100% recall—indicate that the model was able to classify all samples correctly, distinguishing without errors between noise signals and pipe rupture events. This performance was also reflected in the confusion matrix, where no false positives or false negatives were observed among the 44 samples evaluated.

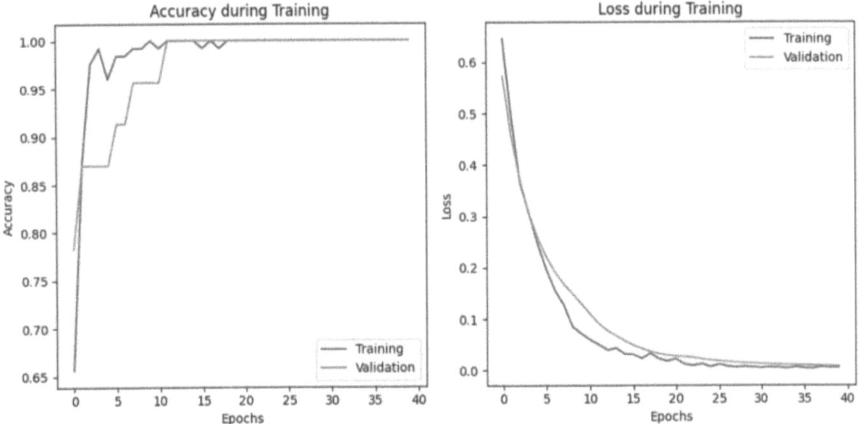

Fig. 4. Learning curves during training.

A validation protocol was implemented to measure accuracy on the microcontroller, consisting of loading the same test signals used in the original evaluation, processing them through the implemented model, and comparing predictions with known labels. Upon implementing the quantized model on the MSP430FR5994 microcontroller, a slight performance reduction was observed. The model's accuracy decreased from 100% to 93.2%, representing a 6.8% loss in classification capability (41 out of the 44 evaluated signals were correctly classified). This reduction is primarily due to factors such as weight quantization from 32-bit to Q15 (16-bit), which introduces small approximation errors in calculations, and the implementation of approximated activation functions (such as sigmoid via LUT) instead of the exact mathematical versions used during training (Table 6).

The detailed comparison between both versions of the model reveals that, despite the loss of accuracy and inference speed, the quantized model maintains

Table 6. Comparison Between the Original Model and the Microcontroller Model

Parameter	Original Model (Float32)	Microcontroller Model (Q15)	Difference
Accuracy	100%	93.2%	6.8%
Model Size	11KB	7.45KB	32.3%
Inference time (avg.)	~56 ms	~173 ms	209%
RAM Usage	8.4 KB	3.7 KB	56%
Numerical precision	Float32 (23-bits mantissa)	Q15 (15-bits fractional)	8 bits
Activation Functions	Exact (math.h)	Approximated (LUT)	-

excellent performance for practical applications. Notably, this 6.8% accuracy reduction is offset by advantages in embedded implementation: a 32% reduction in model size (from 11 KB to 7.45 KB), which is crucial for memory-constrained devices. These results demonstrate that the trade-off between precision and computational efficiency is favorable, allowing practical deployment in resource-limited devices without significantly sacrificing detection capabilities.

5   Conclusions

The integration of the LEA accelerator module and quantization enables Machine Learning models to run efficiently, maintaining over 93% accuracy for rupture detection. The use of FRAM and vector operations with LEA reduces resource consumption compared to Cortex-M implementations, which is key for remote nodes. The precision loss (6.8%) is compensated by gains in model size and memory consumption, effectively addressing limitations in traditional SCADA systems. The proposed architecture is replicable across other MSP430 microcontrollers with LEA, providing a framework for deploying complex algorithms in resource-constrained environments.

Disclosure of Interests. The authors have no competing interests to declare that are relevant to the content of this article.

References

1. Cody, R.A., Dey, P., Narasimhan, S.: Linear prediction for leak detection in water distribution networks. J. Pipeline Syst. Eng. Pract. **11**(1), 04019043 (2020). https://doi.org/10.1061/(ASCE)PS.1949-1204.0000415
2. Geelen, C.V.C., Yntema, D.R., Molenaar, J., Keesman, K.J.: Monitoring support for water distribution systems based on pressure sensor data. Water Resour. Manage. **33**(10), 3339–3353 (2019). https://doi.org/10.1007/s11269-019-02245-4
3. Gonzalez, I.V., et al.: Algorithm to detect bursts in water pipes for implementation in low-power devices. Revista Científica de Ingeniería Electrónica, Automática y Comunicaciones **43**(1), 4 (2022)

4. Harmouche, J., Narasimhan, S.: Long-term monitoring for leaks in water distribution networks using association rules mining. IEEE Trans. Ind. Inform. **16**(1), 258–266 (2020). https://doi.org/10.1109/TII.2019.2911064
5. Kang, J., et al.: Novel leakage detection by ensemble CNN-SVM and graph-based localization in water distribution systems. IEEE Trans. Ind. Electron. **65**(5), 4279–4289 (2018). https://doi.org/10.1109/TIE.2017.2764861
6. Kumar, D., et al.: In-line acoustic device inspection of leakage in water distribution pipes based on wavelet and neural network. J. Sens. **2017**, 5789510 (2017). https://doi.org/10.1155/2017/5789510
7. Lin, C.-C., et al.: Intermittent-Aware Neural Network Pruning, pp. 1–6 (2023). https://doi.org/10.1109/DAC56929.2023.10247825
8. Manzi, D., et al.: Pattern recognition and clustering of transient pressure signals for burst location. Water **11**(11) (2019). https://doi.org/10.3390/w11112279
9. Mounce, S.R., Mounce, R.B., Boxall, J.B.: Identifying sampling interval for event detection in water distribution networks. J. Water Resour. Plann. Manage. **138**(2), 187–191 (2012). https://doi.org/10.1061/(ASCE)WR.1943-5452.0000170
10. Srirangarajan, S., et al.: Wavelet-based burst event detection and localization in water distribution systems. J. Sign Process. Syst. **72**(1), 1–16 (2013). https://doi.org/10.1007/s11265-012-0690-6
11. Trutié-Carrero, E.E., et al.: Detección y Localización de Ruptura Súbita mediante Transformada Wavelet Discreta y Correlación Cruzada. Revista Iberoamericana de Automática e Informática industrial **15**(2) (2018). https://doi.org/10.4995/riai.2017.8738
12. El-Zahab, S., Mohammed Abdelkader, E., Zayed, T.: An accelerometer-based leak detection system. Mech. Syst. Signal Process. **108**, 276–291 (2018). https://doi.org/10.1016/j.ymssp.2018.02.030
13. Zaman, D., et al.: A review of leakage detection strategies for pressurised pipeline in steady-state. Eng. Failure Anal. **109**, 104264 (2020). https://doi.org/10.1016/j.engfailanal.2019.104264

Author Index

A

Acevedo, Andy Abrahantes 386
Ahmad, Zoulfikar 279
Almeida-Cruz, Yudivian 125
Alonso-Fernandez, Fernando 26, 39, 395
Álvarez-Carmona, Miguel Á. 15, 152
Álvarez-Carmona, Miguel Ángel 255
Arana, Yanelys Cuba 240
Aranda, Ramón 15, 152
Arencibia-Lago, Maylen 3
Aria Verdecia, Luis Augusto 339
Avila, Deivis 240

B

Bastida, Marcos Díaz 362
Basulto Ramírez, Pedro Luis 339
Batard Lorenzo, David 207
Beltrán Varela, Alejandro 125
Beltrán, Jorge Ramírez 351
Berg, Jan van den 255
Bigun, Josef 26
Buades Rubio, Jose Maria 26
Bustio-Martínez, Lázaro 255, 323

C

Carrillo, Dionisio Buendía 291
Cedeño, Roberto Marti 125
Chaviano, Alayn Lado 268
Chen, Yunwei 207
Chiang Cruz, Jaime E. 374
Collado, Aurelio Antelo 339
Consuegra Ayala, Juan Pablo 125
Corona, Carlos Cruz 291
Cruz, Jaime Chiang 351
Cruz, Jaime E. Chiang 432

D

Díaz-Pacheco, Ángel 15
Diez, Héctor Raúl González 313

E

Echevarría, Daniel Pardo 420
Elejalde-Larrinaga, Ángel René 3
Estevanell-Valladares, Ernesto Luis 125
Estevez-Velarde, Suilan 125

F

Färm, Gabriel 39
Fernández Leal, Christian Alejandro 432
Font, Armando David Caballero 178

G

Garcia Rodriguez, Roberto 125
García, Neili Machado 91
García-Borroto, Milton 52, 166
Garea-Llano, Eduardo 3
Gómez, Lisset Salazar 291
González Ferrales, Niley 125
González, Iliover Vega 351
Gonzalez-Dalmau, Evelio 3
González-Ordiano, Jorge Ángel 323
Gulín-Gonzalez, Jorge 207
Gulín-González, Jorge 302
Gutiérrez, Yoan 125

H

Heredia, Yanio Hernández 313, 339
Hernández Rodríguez, Gabriel 125
Hernández, Javier García 420
Hernandez-Diaz, Kevin 26, 39
Hernández-Sierra, Gabriel 407
Herrera-Semenets, Vitali 152, 255, 323

I

Iglesias-Gutiérrez, Alejandro 374

J

Jankowska, Jelizaveta 395

K

Kantz, Holger 386
Kostek, Bożena 395
Kravchenko, Yury Alekseevich 139

L

Larcher, Anthony 407
Lastre Figueroa, Leonardo 192
Leal, Christian Fernández 351
Leguen-de-Varona, Ireimis 192
Listopad, Nikolai 219
Llanes-Guilarte, Darián Santiago 323
López, Armando Caballero 178
López, C. Orlando Grabiel Toledano 268
Lorenzo, Maria Matilde Garcia 178

M

Machado, Claudia Farrada 91
Madera, Julio 192
Mansour, Ali Mahmoud 139, 279
Marichal, Graciliano N. 240
Martínez Pazos, Jorge Felix 207, 302
Martínez, Yadier Betancourt 178
Martínez-Díaz, Yoanna 407
Martínez-López, Yoan 192
Mateo, Gabriela Espinosa 80
Mederos, Amed Leiva 178
Méndez-Vázquez, Heydi 166, 407
Mitsiukhin, Anatol 219
Mohammad, Juman Hussein 139
Montoyo, Andrés 125
Morales-González, Annette 52, 166
Muñoz Guillena, Rafael 125

N

Norrby, Hugo 39
Núñez, Vladimir Milián 80, 268

O

Olivas, José A. 67

P

Pagola, José Eladio Medina 80
Palomar, Manuel 125

Peña, Ray Maestre 67
Perdomo-Campos, Alejandro 374, 432
Pérez Valera, Carla Sunami 125
Pérez, Nayma Cepero 420
Pérez, Rafael Bello 178, 362
Piad-Morffis, Alejandro 125

Q

Quiza, Ramón 240

R

Ramirez Alvarez, Ariel 207
Ramírez-Beltrán, Jorge 374, 432
Rams, Ernesto Estévez 386
Reverón, Erick Taylor 102
Reyes, Dainys Gaínza 113
Reyes, Dainys Gainza 228
Rocha, Gabriel A. 15
Rodríguez Horta, Elena 125
Rodríguez Rodríguez, Carlos Rafael 113
Rodríguez, Ana Marys Garcia 313
Rodríguez, Ania Mesa 386
Rodríguez, Deborah Famadas 125
Rodríguez-Rodríguez, Carlos Rafael 228
Romero, Francisco P. 67
Roselló, Reynaldo Rosado 313

S

Sánchez, Angel Alberto Vazquez 291
Santos-Moreno, Milagros 323
Sepúlveda-Torres, Robiert 125
Siliceo Guzmán, Isaias 152
Simón-Cuevas, Alfredo 102
Simon-Cuevas, Alfredo 192
Simón-Cuevas, Alfredo 67, 91

T

Tiwari, Prayag 395
Toledano-López, Orlando Grabiel 339
Toledo, Raciel Yera 102

V

Valdés Pérez, Daniel Alejandro 125
Vasilaki, Kalliopi 339
Vázquez, Ramiro APérez 362
Velazco, Aylin Estrada 113, 228

Z

Zulueta-Veliz, Yeleny 113
Zulueta-Véliz, Yeleny 228